This book is to be returned on
or before the date stamped below

CANCELLED

1 5 MAR 2001

- 4 JUN 2001

- 2 APR 2002

13.

10. MAR 1999

1 2 NOV 2002

27 MAR 2003

CANCELLED

CANCELLED

1 8 FEB 2004

2 4 MAR 2004

3 1 MAR 2004

2 8 MAY 2004

UNIVERSITY OF PLYMOUTH

PLYMOUTH LIBRARY

Tel: (0752) 232323
This book is subject to recall if required by another reader
Books may be renewed by phone
CHARGES WILL BE MADE FOR OVERDUE BOOKS

TIKHOOKEANSKII NAUCHNO-ISSLEDOVATEL'SKII INSTITUT
RYBNOGO KHOZYAISTVA I OKEANOGRAFII

Pacific Scientific Research Institute of Fisheries and Oceanography

A.A. Berzin

THE SPERM WHALE

(Kashalot)

Edited by A. V. Yablokov

Izdatel'stvo "Pishchevaya Promyshlennost'"
Moskva 1971

Translated from Russian

Israel Program for Scientific Translations
Jerusalem 1972

Copyright © 1972
Israel Program for Scientific Translations, Ltd.
IPST Cat. No. 60070 7

ISBN 0 7065 1262 6

Translated by E. Hoz and Z. Blake
Edited by H. Mills

Printed in Jerusalem by Keter Press
Binding: Wiener Bindery Ltd., Jerusalem

Contents

Section III. DISTRIBUTION

Section IV. MAIN FEATURES OF BIOLOGY

" . . . The great Leviathan is that one creature in the
world which must remain unpainted to the last . . .
The living whale, in his full majesty and significance,
is only to be seen at sea in unfathomable waters . . ."

Herman Melville. "Moby Dick"

INTRODUCTION

Whales, the most amazing mammals, are important commercial items, sources of raw material for food and industry.

The sperm whale (Figure 1*) is the largest (length up to 21 m) of the toothed whales (Odontoceti) and one of the most peculiar and intriguing representatives of the entire order Cetacea.

The great cachalot, as it was called by scientists and writers at the end of the 19th and beginning of the 20th century, was scientifically de-scribed in 1758 by Linné under the name Physeter macrocephalus. The name cachalot derives from the Latin quichal or from the Spanish quixal (teeth and jaw) (Beddard, 1900).

The sperm whale, like all the Cetacea and in particular the toothed whales, is an animal with a strong schooling instinct; the females and their young stay together in families. The sperm whale occurs in practically all the seas and oceans, performing seasonal migrations. Large solitary males venture into higher latitudes of the northern and southern hemispheres than the females and the young, and approach the edge of drift ice.

Sexual dimorphism is more sharply expressed in the sperm whale than in any other species of Cetacea (the males are twice as large as the females).

The structure of all the systems of organs and the morphological peculiarities of these whales are fitted to their aquatic mode of life and testify to their excellent adaptation to submersion and prolonged stay at great depths (to 2,000 m).

The species is the main catch item in most commercial whaling areas of the northern and southern seas. In recent years, owing to the depletion of baleen whale reserves, the sperm whale has begun to constitute a greater share in Antarctic catches. The annual landings have lately reached 30,000 specimens and more, half of this number being taken in the northern part of the Pacific (USSR and Japan).

Information on the sperm whale goes back to ancient times. The story of Perseus and Andromeda is supposed to be connected with the existence of a cruel sperm whale and tells how Perseus saved Andromeda by harpooning the monster. There is a legend concerning the battle that took place between the guard headed by the Emperor Claudius and a gigantic sperm whale in the port of Ostia (Melville, 1851; Beddard, 1900). The first, very general descriptions by Olaus Magnus (1567) and Gesner (1567) (Figure 2) date back to the 16th century. They were based on observations of the animals swimming in the sea or stranded on the shore.

---

* Unless otherwise indicated, all figures are original.

1

FIGURE 1. Sperm whale swimming (photo by Veinger)

By the beginning of the 19th century the literature contained sometimes detailed descriptions of this interesting animal (Ray, 1713; Artedi, 1738; Despellette, 1744; Daubenton, 1751; Brisson, 1756; Sibbald, 1773; Hunter, 1787; Colnett, 1798). Many works of this period were devoted to the precious ambergris, a product of the vital activity of sperm whale (Boylsten, 1724; Dudley, 1725; Schwediawer, 1783; and others).

In the first half and the middle of the 19th century, comprehensive studies were published on the order Cetacea as a whole (Lacépède, 1804; Sonnini, 1804; Camper, 1820; Dewhurst, 1834; Cuvier, 1835—1836; Rapp, 1837; Reichenbach, 1846; etc.), alongside with faunistic reviews, notes from diaries presenting information on all cetaceans including sperm whale (Lepekhin, 1805; Dvigubskii, 1829; Simashko, 1851; and others), descriptions of observations by seafarers and travelers (Scoresby, 1820; Gray, 1846), and individual scientific communications on the morphology of this animal (Bennett, 1836; Jackson, 1845). In these works the sperm whale figured importantly. But studies also appeared with sperm whale as the exclusive subject (Desmoulins, 1822; Hunter, 1829; Thompson, 1829; Charlesworth, 1845), in particular, the monographs by Beale (1835—1839) and Bennett (1840).

In 1851, H. Melville, seaman, whaler, and writer, published his novel "Moby Dick, or the White Whale." In this book, that later won world renown, many accurate biological observations are given side by side with fascinating descriptions of the sea and sperm whale hunting.

The second half of the 19th century saw the appearance of numerous surveys (Hamilton, 1852; Brem, 1866; Murray, 1866; Scammon, 1869—1874; Blanford, 1888—1891; Beneden, 1888; Cope, 1890; Murie, 1892; Bolau, 1895; and others). Thorough studies on morphology, in particular on osteology, were also published at that time (Gill, 1871; Sanctis, 1881; Pouchet and Beauregard, 1889; and others); of these the monograph by W. Flower (1867), the atlas by P. Beneden (1868—1879) and the legends to it by Beneden and Gervais (1868—1880) deserve special attention. At the

dawn of the 20th century Beddard's very detailed work "A Book of Whales"
(8) (1900) was published. Of the works which followed, the anatomical studies
by Lillie (1910) and Beddard (1915—1919), the systematic works by Thomas
(1911) and Oliver (1922), the historical surveys by Harmer (1928), and,
finally, the monograph of Howell (1930) on marine mammals are of considerable scientific value.

7

FIGURE 2. Drawings of sperm whale by various authors illustrating different stages of
study of the animal (from 1554 to 1836, after Boschma, 1958)

8   The development of Soviet commercial whaling in the Far East and Soviet
investigations of large Cetacea began in the thirties (Zenkovich, 1933—1936;
Tomilin, 1935—1937). Several studies by Soviet authors (Klumova and
Arsen'ev) on small cetaceans and a series of papers on dolphins by Kleinenberg and Sleptsov were published during these years. These investigations,
their methods and their conclusions greatly contributed to the development
of Soviet research into large whales in general and sperm whale in particular.

Of the works published outside the USSR at that time, those by Townsend
(1931, 1935) on the distribution of whales, the substantial work by Slijper
(1936), and also the studies by Kellog (1938), Boschma (1938), and Matsuura
(1935) are of great interest.

The scientific committee "Discovery" organized marine investigations of
whales on a large scale and this led to the publication of several monographs
on individual whale species including one on sperm whale by Matthews (1938),
in which the results of investigations on this species were summarized.

In these years original data concerning the morphology and functions of
various organs of sperm whale were published by Raven and Gregory (1933),
Haynes and Laurie (1937), and Ries and Langworthy (1937).

In the early forties, war conditions naturally resulted in there being very
few specialized studies on whales (Raven, 1942; Zenkovich, 1945; Vadivasov,
1946; and others).

In 1946 the first Soviet Antarctic whaling fleet "Slava" operated in the
Antarctic, and as a result, papers on baleen and toothed whales including the
sperm whale were published (Kirpichnikov, 1949). Of the same period are the
the works by Norman and Fraser (1948), Scheffer and Slipp (1948), Bolognari
(1949), Sleptsov (1950), Kirpichnikov (1950), Zenkovich (1950), Omura (1950),
and Pike (1950).

In 1948 in the USSR the third whaling fleet was commissioned; it was
based on the Kurile Islands and contributed to the development of Soviet
investigations of whales. In 1951—1956 an expedition was organized by IOAN*
and TINRO for studying Cetacea. Following this expedition, works were published on sperm whale among others (Sleptsov, 1952, 1955; 1958, 1961;
Ivanova, 1955, 1961; Akimushkin, 1954, 1955, 1963; Klumov, 1955, 1956,
1958; Chuzhakina, 1955, 1961, 1965; Betesheva, 1960, 1961; and others).

Despite the great advances achieved during the last decade in the organization, management and results of the investigations carried out on marine
mammals (the setting up or expansion of laboratories at VNIRO and the
Institute of Morphology of Animals of AN SSSR, similar laboratories of
TINRO in Vladivostok, in the institutes of Odessa and Kaliningrad, scientific
groups of the Antarctic and North Pacific fleets, the coordination of their
9 work by VNIRO, the annual seminars of workers of the scientific groups
of the whaling fleets, regular All-Union conferences on the study of marine
mammals, as well as the fruitful activity of the Ichthyological Commission
of the Ministry of Fisheries of the USSR), the level of research conducted,
the technical equipment, the degree of coordination, as well as the number
of specialists engaged in investigations of whales do not yet satisfactorily
meet the high requirements of current science and technology.

In 1946 in Tokyo a special research institute was set up for the study of
whales. Works, mostly dealing with the sperm whale, were published by
Nemoto, Nishiwaki, Ohsumi-Kimura, Omura, Uda, and many other specialists
in 1948.

* [For all abbreviations occurring in the text, see list at the end of the book.]

4

of Postnatal Ontogenesis of the Institute of the Biology Development of AN SSSR) under the guidance of Doctor of Biological Sciences, the late Prof. S. E. Kleinenberg.

I am grateful to Doctor of Biological Sciences Prof. A. G. Tomilin for his consultations on problems of reproduction and age determinations, to Candidate of Biological Sciences A. S. Sokolov (ZIN AN SSSR) for his critical analysis of morphological data, and to Candidate of Histological Sciences A. V. Abuladze (IBR AN SSSR) for his examination and analysis of histological material; appreciation is also expressed to the leaders and teams of the whaling fleets, whale-processing combines and explorator, vessels who were of great help to me and my associates in their research.

The head of the anatomy department of the Maritime Territory Agricultural Institute, Candidate of Biological Sciences V. M. Malyshev, participated in writing the chapter "Musculature." Other contributors were the head of the Zoology Department of the Crimean Pedagogical Institute, Doctor of Biological Sciences S. L. Delyamure and Candidate of Biological Sciences A. S. Skrjabin, who described the helminths in the chapter "Enemies, Diseases and Parasites."

SYSTEMATICS

Chapter 1

POSITION AMONG THE CETACEA

The sperm whale belongs to the order Cetacea of toothed whales (Odontoceti), to the family Physeteridae, which comprises two genera: P h y s e t e r (sperm whale) and K o g i a (pygmy sperm whale).

FAMILY PHYSETERIDAE

This family is characterized by a strongly developed corpus adiposum which forms a frontal protuberance of the head resting on the bony bed of the trough-shaped, expanded rostrum. The skull is markedly asymmetrical, particularly in the rostral part, with its powerfully developed frontal-occipital crest. Lower jaw narrow, much narrower than the contour of the head, with a long symphysis. Teeth of lower jaw conical, arranged in a groove of the mandibular symphysis (up to 30 pairs). In the upper jaw the teeth (up to 18 pairs) are reduced and have lost their function; frequently they do not erupt at all. The petrous temporal bone grows in together with the skull while the lacrimal and zygomatic bones become fused.

There are 49—54 vertebrae; the atlas is free; the sternum consists of three bones and is articulated with 3—5 pairs of ribs.

The members of this family are squid eaters, and their morphological-physiological characteristics are determined by the deep-sea mode of life of the majority of food items that make up their diet.

Genus Physeter Linnaeus, 1758

1758   P h y s e t e r Linnaeus, C. Systema Naturae, edit. 10.
1761   C a t o d o n Linnaeus, C. Fauna Suecica, edit. 2.
1804   P h y s a l u s Lacépède, Historie Naturelle des Cetaces, XV.
1806   P h y s a l u s Dumeril, Zool. Anal.
1806   P h y s e t e r u s Dumeril, Zool. Anal.
1816   C e t u s Oken, Lehrb. Nat. 111 (2).
1822   T u r s i o Fleming, Philos. Zool., II.
1839   M u l a r Leiblein, Grundz. meth. Uebers. Thierr., I.
1839   C a c h a l o t Smith, H., Mammalia. Jardine's Naturalist's library, Vol. IX.
1865   M e g a n e u r o n Gray, J. E., Proceedings of Zoologica Soc. of London.

The largest toothed whales show a marked sexual dimorphism in their dimensions (males attain a length of 18—21 m, females are about 12 m long). The body of a toothed whale is dark, with a light pattern on the belly. The enormous, anteriorly almost perpendicularly truncated head constitutes $1/4 - 1/3$ of the total length. The left nasal passage opens by the slit of the blowhole, which is S-shaped, drawn out along the body axis and shifted forward into the left corner of the head. The right nasal passage has no direct outlet but communicates with the blowhole by a narrow slit.

There are not less than 18 pairs of simple, peglike, slightly recurved teeth on the lower jaw; the teeth of adults are without enamel. The upper jaw has up to 11 pairs of small rudimentary teeth which are concealed in the gums in the young.

The skull of an adult male reaches 5—5.5 m in length and is distinguished by its thick, massive bones, a developed frontal-occipital crest, and by a sharp asymmetry, particularly in the intermaxillary and nasal bones. On a trough-shaped bed formed by the greatly widened rostrum of the maxillary bones that have grown out upwards lies the gigantic spermaceti organ, the anterior part of which forms a frontal protuberance that overlaps far beyond the very narrow and long lower jaw. The length of the symphysis constitutes about half that of the lower jaw.

The dorsal fin is thick and low and merges into the back. Some additional humps frequently follow the fin.

Formula of vertebral column: C 7, D 11, L 8—9, Ca 20—25. Ribs 11 pairs. Atlas free. Sternum consisting of 3—4 bones and articulating with 3—5 pairs of ribs.

Scapula high, with a large coracoid process. The wide pectoral fins are five-fingered, with the following number of phalanges: I_{0-1}, II_{5-6}, III_{5-6}, IV_{4-5}, V_{2-3}.

At sea the sperm whale is readily distinguishable from other whales by its vaporous, low spouting, directed forward and to the left at an angle of about 45°.

Genus monotypic, only one species (P. macrocephalus).

Physeter macrocephalus L., 1758

1758   Physeter catodon Linné., Syst. Nat., ed. 10.
1758   Physeter macrocephalus Linné, Syst. Nat., ed. 10.
1758   Physeter microps Linné, Syst. Nat., ed. 10.
1758   Physeter tursio Linné, Syst. Nat., ed. 10.
1761   Catodon macrocephalus Linné, Fauna Svec., ed. 2.
1773   Physeter katodon Müller, Linné vollst. Natursyst., I.
1781   Physeter novae angliae Borowski, Gem. Nat. Thierr., II.
1781   Physeter andersonii Borowski, Gem. Nat. Thierr., II.
1789   Physeter macrocephalus Bonnaterre, Tabl. Enc. Meth., Cetol.
1789   Physeter catodon Bonnaterre, Tabl. Enc. Méth., Cétol.
1789   Physeter trumpo Bonnaterre, Tabl. Enc. Méth., Cétol.
1789   Physeter cylindricus Bonnaterre, Tabl., Enc. Méth., Cétol.
1789   Physeter microps Bonnaterre, Tabl. Enc. Méth., Cétol.
1789   Physeter mular Bonnaterre, Tabl. Enc. Méth., Cétol.

13	1792	Physeter macrocephalus niger Kerr, Anim. Kingd.
	1792	Physeter macrocephalus cinereus Kerr, Anim. Kingd.
	1792	Physeter microps falcidentatus Kerr, Anim. Kingd.
	1792	Physeter microps rectidentatus Kerr, Anim. Kingd.
	1792	Physeter gibbosus von Schreber. Säugthiere.
	1798	Physeter maximus Cuvier, Tabl. Elém. Hist. Nat. Anim.
	1802	Catodon trumpo de Lacépède, Tabl. Mamm.
	1802	Physalus cylindricus de Lacépède, Tabl. Mamm.
	1802	Physeter orthodon de Lacépède, Tabl. Mamm.
	1802	Physeter mular de Lacépède, Tabl. Mamm.
	1803	Physeter trumpo Virey, Nouv. Dict. Hist. Nat., IV.
	1803	Physeter cylindricus Virey, Nouv. Dict. Hist. Nat., IV.
	1806	Phylasus (genus) Duméril, Zool. Anal.
	1806	Physeterus (genus) Duméril, Zool. Anal.
	1816	Cetus microps Oken, Lehrb. Nat., III(2).
	1816	Cetus. microps Oken, Lehrb. Nat., III (2).
	1816	Cetus tursio Oken, Lehrb. Nat., III (2).
	1816	Cetus orthodon Oken, Lehrb. Nat. III (2).
	1817	Physeter microps Gérardin, Dict. Sc. Nat., VI.
	1817	Physeter orthodon Gérardin, Dict. Sc. Nat., VI.
	1818	Physeterus sulcatus de Lacépède, Mém. Mus. Hist. Nat., Paris., IV.
	1822	Physeter australasianus Desmoulins, Dict. class. Hist. Nat., II.
	1822	Tursio vulgaris Fleming, Philos. Zool., II.
	1822	Tursio microps Fleming, Philos. Zool., II.
	1824	Physeter polycyphus Quoy and Gaimard, Voyage l'Uranie et la Physicienne, Zool.
	1827	Cetus cylindricus G. J. Billberg, Syn. Faunae Scand., I(1).
	1827	Catodon polycyphus Lesson, Man. Mamm.
	1827	Physeter sulcatus Lesson, Man. Mamm.
	1828	Catodon sibbaldi Fleming, Hist. Brit. Anim.
	1834	Physeter cetadon Dewhurst, Nat. Hist. Order. Cetac.
	1834	Physeter gibbosa Dewhurst. Nat. Hist. Order. Cetac.
	1839	Mular tursio Leiblein, Grundz. meth. Uebers. Thierr., I.
	1839	Mular microps Leiblein, Grundz. meth. Uebers. Thierr., I.
	1842	Physeter pterodon R. P. Lesson, Echo Monde Savant. IX, 18 Aug.
	1844—1845.	Physeter australis Gray, Zool. Erebus and Terror.
	1851	Catodon australis Wall, Skeleton new Sperm Whale.
	1887	Physeter tursio Knauer, Handw. Zool.

The names* kashalot, kashelot, spermatsetovyi kit, bol'shoi plavun, bol'shoi plevun [great spouter] are Russian; all except the first one are at present considered bookish.

Spermaceti whale, sperm whale	(English)
Cachelot, cachalot	(French)
Pottfisch, Pottwal	(German)
Rod-kammen, burhvalur	(Icelandic)

* After M. Lacépède (1804), A. G. Tomilin (1957), and others.

Potfisk, pottfisk, kaskelot, spermhval,
  trold-hual, huns-hval, sue-hval,
    buur-hval, bardhvalir   (Norwegian)
Potvisch, potvis, kaizilot   (Dutch)
Capidoglio, capodoglio   (Italian)
Spermacethval, kaskelot   (Danish)
Kaskelot   (Swedish)
Makko-kuzira   (Japanese)
Cachalote   (Spanish)
Olbrotowick   (Polish)
Vorvan tuponocý   (Czech)

14   Local names: agidagikh, agdagig, ach-tkha-gikkh, aggadakhgik (Aleutian), koyapchak (Koryakian); chigat (old Kamchadal name for it); kigutulik, kigutilik (Eskimos of Greenland).

Nomenclature notes. From the time it was established that the genus is monotypic, all the animals described under the name "cachalot" have been referred to one species. However, in different publications the animal has continued to be named either P h y s e t e r   c a t a d o n or P h y s e t e r   m a c r o c e p h a l u s. All other names have been reduced to synonyms.

Up to the end of the 19th and during the first decade of the 20th century the name P h y s e t e r   m a c r o c e p h a l u s had been more widely used both in Russia and in other countries.

Later on, particularly, after O. Thomas published his systematic notes (1911), a considerable number of authors: Matthews (1938), Rode (1939), Harmer (1927) adopted the name P. c a t o d o n for the sperm whale.

No fewer authors, however, continue to adhere to the species name P. m a c r o c e p h a l u s (Beddard, 1915, 1919; Oliver, 1922; Neuville, 1929; Peters, 1930; Slijper, 1936; Boschma, 1938; and others).

Nevertheless, in recent years the name P. m a c r o c e p h a l u s is hardly ever encountered in research studies on Cetacea, while the name P. c a t o d o n is being more and more widely adopted, also by Soviet authors.

After a careful and thorough study of the chronology of descriptions of the species in the available substantial works on systematics, particularly the latest data and especially those on the structure of shoals and the geographical distribution of herds of different-aged animals, I became convinced that Boschma was justified (1938) in believing that O. Thomas (1911) had made a mistake in his species determination of a herd of 105 animals that were stranded on the Orkney Islands in 1693. It was this error that induced researchers to give the species name of P. c a t o d o n to the sperm whale.

Before Linné, the diagnostic descriptions of various species of sperm whale were based on diagnoses by Sibbald. Ray and others (after Boschma) copied Sibbald. Ray (1713) describes four species of sperm whale: B a l a e n a   m i n o r, B a l a e n a   m a j o r, B a l a e n a   m a j o r,* B a l a e n a   m a c r o c e p h a l a. Allen (1881) considers the first species (after Ray)

---

* The diagnostic characters of the second and third species are different.

identical to Beluga catodon (Delphinapterus leucas), the
second species identical to Physeter macrocephalus, and the
third and fourth species identical to Physeter tursio.

Artedi (1838) includes in his lists four species according to Sibbald
and Ray: the third and fourth species are placed in the genus Physeter,
and the first and second species in the genus Catodon.

Still before Linné, Brisson (1956) described seven species of sperm
whale. One of them, Cetus albicans, had been known earlier under
the name Beluga catodon. This may have been the white whale;
at that time this animal was mentioned under two names: Cetus
albicans and Cetus minor. It is also possible that the "small
whale" (Cetus minor) was a pilot whale, Globicephalus melas
(Boschma, 1938). Lacépède (1804) considers it to be a synonym of
Catodon svineval (whereas this is the Norwegian name for white
whale, given to it by Bonnaterre). The other species, judging from the
dimensions of the body, are closely related to the sperm whale.

In the tenth edition of "Systema Naturae" (1758) Linné described four
species of the genus Physeter. The synonymic series of each of these
15 is cited after Ray, and moreover all four species are presented in the
same order as in Ray. Linné gave them the names catodon, macrocephalus, microps and tursio.

It is of interest to note that the entire systematics went over without
any alteration into the twelfth edition of "Systema Naturae" (1789): the
four species of sperm whale are again described in the same order, while
the synonyms of the first species, P. catodon, are the first species
after Ray, Balaena minor, and Cetus minor (after Brisson, 1756),
i. e. either white whale, or, according to Boschma (1938), pilot whale.

The synonyms given by Linné for the second species, macrocephalus,
were the following: Le Cachalot-Cetus (after Brisson), Balaena major
(after Ray), Cachalot blanc-cetus albicans (after Brisson),
Le Cachalot de le Nouvelle Angleterre-Cetus Novae Angliae (after Brisson).
The third species microps and the fourth one tursio did not arouse
any controversy.

Kerr (1792), who established a trinominal nomenclature for sperm
whales, nevertheless named only two species: Physeter macrocephalus and P. microps.

Lacépède (1804) presented eight species of sperm whale belonging to
three genera. The species macrocephalus, trumpo, svineval,
and "blanchâtre" (albicans) are included in the first genus Cachalot
(Catodon). The first two are sperm whales (according to Lacépède, the
synonym is P. macrocephalus, while according to Linné it is
Catodon macrocephalus). According to Lacépède, Cachalot
svineval had the synonym of Physeter catodon after Linné,
Catodon fistula after Artedi, petit cachalot after Bonnaterre and
Cetus minor fistula in rostro after Brisson, i. e. these names,
which passed over from one edition to the next, were meant to designate
whales not longer than 7.3 m (24 feet). The very name of the last species
speaks for itself and suggests that it is the white whale (Boschma, 1938).
The second genus, Physalus, includes the species cylindricus;
the third genus includes three species: microps, orthodon and
mular. Orthodon is a new name.

11

Six genera and 19 species of different forms of sperm whale were described. Some of them are synonyms of the earlier described species (Boschma, 1938).

Having critically examined the main peculiarities of the forms of sperm whale described earlier, Cuvier (1812, 1823) came to the conclusion that only one species exists. In 1836 he defined this as P. macro-cephalus. E. Blyth (1863) gave the sperm whale the name Catodon macrocephalus, regarding P. catodon as one of synonyms of these names. Here, the interrelationship of the specific names is note-worthy, while the priority of the generic name Physeter given by Linné in 1758 is no longer questioned by anyone.

Murray (1866) and Trouessart (1898—1899) gave the sperm whale the name P. macrocephalus considering P. catodon together with microps and tursio after Linné and other names as synonyms. Flower (1867) also pointed to the existence of only one species of sperm whale — P. macrocephalus — despite the error in the diagnostic expression "fistula in rostro," while in both his and many other authors' opinion, P. catodon was a relatively small animal, possibly the white whale. Later on, Sclater (1901, in Boschma, 1938) and T. Palmer (1904) indicated that macrocephalus is the type species of the genus Physeter.

Thus, P. catodon is considered a synonym of P. macrocephalus. Despite the considerable confusion in the nomenclature during those years, none of the specialists had any doubts as to the species name of the sperm whale, but in 1911 Thomas, confirming that the genus is mono-typic, writes that its true representative should be the first species described by Linné in 1758, basing himself on Artedi who, in his turn, had cited from Sibbald's and Ray's "Catodon fistula in rostro." According to Ray, this is the first species — Balaena minor — and it was described after the 105 animals that were beached on the Orkney Islands. According to Thomas, the absence of teeth in the upper jaw of these animals is a distinct character of great importance. The small size of the whales (maximum 24 feet, or 7.3 m) was attributed by the author to the fact that they might have been females, and the large number—105 — implied to him that sperm whales may form herds. From these data Thomas drew the conclusion that the species name of the sperm should be P. catodon, and all other names are synonyms.

16

As already mentioned, after the publication of Thomas' paper various authors again began to give the sperm whale one of the two species names, preference being given to P. catodon.

Oliver (1922), refuting the identity of P. catodon with the sperm whale, claimed that it had become fashionable to use the name catodon for this species, whereas their identity was doubtful; on the other hand, the identity of Physeter macrocephalus with the sperm whale was quite evident. This author rightly pointed out that this name had been used for the sperm whale alone since the moment of its first publication.

In 1938 Boschma, having thoroughly examined numerous systematic works of scientists from many countries, analyzed them in detail in his large and interesting work "On the Teeth and Some Other Particulars of the Sperm Whale (Physeter macrocephalus L.)." Unfortunately, this book did not receive the distribution and recognition it deserved among specialists. The author traces objectively the history of description of the species and demonstrated again that c a t o d o n was not and could not be sperm whale because of the small size of even the largest among those that had been cast up on the shore. Moreover, Boschma points out, firstly, that Murray (1866) had already made c a t o d o n one of the synonyms of P h y s e t e r   m a c r o c e p h a l u s. Secondly, and no less important, according to the principles of zoological systematics, m a c r o c e p h a l u s is a true name because it has never been used for any other animal but the sperm whale; this cannot be said of c a t o d o n; according to Linné, the identity of this species is extremely vaguely determined.

Without pausing to dwell on the controversial problems of systematics, but agreeing with the objections put forward by Oliver (1922) and Boschma (1938), let us examine the ecological-morphological aspect of the topic that has provoked arguments down the years, i.e. could the herd of animals that were stranded on the Orkney Islands have been one of sperm whales?

Data on the structure of sperm whale herds, including small shoals of the animals, show that there are not and cannot be such shoals of sperm whales of the dimensions indicated for the whales stranded on the Orkney Islands (maximum length 7.3 m). The large majority of females are not yet sexually mature at these dimensions (even saying they were maximal for dried-up animals); the average size of a sperm whale in this kind of herd would be at least 9—10 m. Moreover, the number of simultaneously stranded animals (105) is more than three times that ever known for sperm whales (see Chapter 15).

17   Finally, the animals stranded on the Orkney Islands had teeth (and large teeth at that) only in the lower jaw, but no specimens of the type were preserved, and the description was obviously made according to an external examination of the animals. But in any case, in sperm whales of such dimensions and, all the more so, of a smaller size, teeth are absent not only in the upper but also in the lower jaw.

As regards the species of these cetaceans from the Orkney Islands, it is our belief that they could hardly have been white whales [D e l p h i n - a p t e r u s   l e u c a s] because 1) no cases of such mass stranding of these animals has been recorded and 2) in that case the white color of the animals would have been mentioned in the diagnostic descriptions. They were most probably pilot whales (as many authors have repeatedly pointed out), typical inhabitants of these waters; moreover, these animals stay together in large shoals and are subject to beaching on a huge scale. Finally, these whales are about the same size as those from the Orkneys. The mention of the absence of teeth in the upper jaw of the animals stranded on the Orkneys may testify to inaccuracy of description, but not to their affiliation to sperm whales.

The reference to "fistula in rostro" as a characteristic sign of a sperm whale is not conclusive for us. For example, in his description of one of the species of baleen whales (B a l a e n a) Linné indicated "fistula duplici in rostro," which, if one adheres strictly to the character "fistula in rostro," is known not to exist in any of the species of the baleen whales; the word "rostro" obviously meant the wide area of the head.

Subspecies

As already mentioned, the various researchers accumulated considerable morphometric material, but the results of the investigations by Matthews (1938), Arsen'ev and Zenkevich (1955), Clarke (1956), and Fujino (1956) are largely contradictory. More convincing data were presented by E. I. Ivanova (1955, 1961), who demonstrated differences in the arrangement of the dorsal fin in sperm whales of the northern and southern hemispheres. This character, together with some other comparative characters, were utilized by Tomilin (1957) for the purpose of showing that the sperm whale from the southern hemisphere, described once as a species of sperm whale from the coastal waters of Australia, is a southern subspecies of sperm whale distinguished from the northern subspecies.

In addition to the conclusions drawn by Ivanova, Tomilin (1957) utilized other characters as proof of the existence of systematic differences between the animals of the northern and southern regions, e. g. the difference in the length of the body at which, according to available information, the onset of sexual maturity occurs in the males and the differences in their average dimensions.

Recent investigations have shown that the first of these differences does not even exist. Without denying the possibility of differences in the average sizes of specimens, we consider that so far there is not enough material to substantiate such a difference (males of the northern hemisphere proved to be 130 cm shorter than males of the southern hemisphere); moreover, the important thing is not the number of specimens measured but the various size-age structure of the herds of these animals in various parts of their range. In particular, animals from shoal-type herds inhabiting Japanese waters (less in the waters of Kamchatka) were mainly compared with the herds of animals inhabiting antarctic waters. The increased catches of sperm whales in low latitudes of the southern hemisphere in recent years 18 introduced a correction in the average length of the southern animals, which in our opinion, taking into consideration the sharp differentiation of the herds of sperm whales, is indicative only when animals from the same regions are compared.

In 1963, Nishiwaki, Ohsumi, and Maeda added another difference, that in the distance from the bifurcation of the tail to the umbilicus in animals of the southern and northern hemispheres, to the difference, discovered by Ivanova, in the arrangement of the dorsal fin (difference in the distance from the bifurcation of the tail to the posterior margin of the dorsal fin).

The existence of differences in the dimensions of the caudal parts of the body of sperm whales of the northern and southern hemispheres has been confirmed and substantiated by us (Chapter 2) on the basis of a comparison of morphometric data of recent years processed by various statistical methods that made it possible to verify the reliability of the characters.

This precise morphological distinction validates the existence of two subspecies of sperm whale: the northern Physeter macrocephalus

macrocephalus L. (1785) and the southern Physeter macro-cephalus australis Wall* (1785).

Morphological differences among the populations of sperm whales of other areas of the World Ocean have not been revealed so far.

---

* Boschma (1938) proved that despite the references of Beneden (1888) and of others, MacLeay was wrongly considered to be the author of the primary description of the southern sperm whale; Flower (1867) supported the same view.

MORPHOLOGY

> "Whales epitomize the adaptation of a higher vertebrate
> to life in water."
>
> I. I. Shmal'gauzen

Chapter 2

EXTERIOR, SIZE, PROPORTIONS

FORM OF THE BODY

The body of the sperm whale is streamlined (Figure 1), more massive (especially in the male) than in other representatives of the order Cetacea.

The species is characterized first and foremost by its gigantic and very distinctive head,* which constitutes up to $\frac{1}{4}-\frac{1}{3}$ of the length of the body (generally accepted data) but in some cases up to 38% of the entire length (from measurements of a male of 17.4 m) (Hentschel, 1910). The head is high, thick, barrel-shaped, blunt, truncated anteriorly, with a vertical forehead. The greatest width of this surface, perpendicular to the body axis, was noted by Hentschel (1910) to be 90 cm in a sperm whale 17.4 m long. The head narrows somewhat anteriorly for better streamlining, especially below the blowhole, forming the semblance of a keel at the base in the anterior part.

A section through the middle of the head is quite a regular oval; it becomes narrower downward, so that the closer the section is to the base of the head, the more circular it becomes.

M. M. Sleptsov's remark (1952) that the sperm whale has a completely streamlined body is certainly correct, but on the dressing platform, when inflated with air,** the whale becomes disfigured and has a somewhat unnatural appearance (compare Figures 1 and 3).

The animal's distinctive outward appearance is caused by the disproportionately narrow, loglike lower jaw with rounded end; part (about half) of the jaw fits snugly into the corresponding recess of the upper jaw (see Figure 43). The proximal part of the lower jaw widens, since the branches of the jaw diverge, articulating with the skull. The end of the head protrudes far (1 m in large males) beyond the end of the upper and lower jaw.

The character distinguishing the sperm whale from other whales is the asymmetrical arrangement of the nostrils on the left distal end of the head. The longitudinal slit of the blowhole resembles an S (see Figure 64). The size of the slit varies according to the size of the animal: in prenatal embryos, according to our measurements, and in newborn whales (Bolognari, 1957) the slit is 8—10 cm long; in large males of 14—16 m it is up to 48 cm long (our measurements). According to Hentschel (1910) and Boschma (1938), in males 17.4 and 18.5 m long it is 50 cm, according to Sleptsova (1952), 57 cm long.

In most sperm whales, as in other whales, there is no cervical sinus. In large embryos the boundary is seen as a groove which separates the head from the main body.

---

* In whales the head is bounded by a line passing through the aural opening.
** Air is pumped into the carcass of a killed whale to give it buoyancy.

FIGURE 3. Sperm whale on the dressing deck of the whaling base "Sovetskaya Rossiya" (photo by Veinger)

The diameter of the body is greatest around the thoracic fins, where the body is nearly circular. In the direction of the tail the corpus becomes gradually thinner and is laterally compressed, passing into a caudal peduncle with clearly defined keel-like processes (the dorsal relatively short and low, the ventral longer and higher). The shape of the body corresponds to the hydrodynamic requirements of rapid vertical submergence. In particular, the greater height, and also the somewhat more convex upper profile (in contrast to the profile of baleen whales), which causes the rotary momentum instrumental in lowering the anterior end of the body, facilitates vertical turns (Chepurnov, 1965).

These investigations indicate that in the sperm whale (and in the right whale B a l a e n a) the maximum height of the body exceeds its maximum width, so that the body does not act as a supporting surface and does not increase the lifting force of the whale as it moves, as must be the case in Balaenopteridae and dolphins. The body ends in a strong, horizontal caudal fin with a deep notch dividing it into right and left flukes. The margin of one fluke at the caudal peduncle (at the notch) may lie on the margin of the other fluke.

21   The caudal fins begin to be formed in embryos 3—5 cm long. The shape of the fins changes rapidly with age, and when the embryo is about 350 cm long they assume a form resembling that in the adult (Figures 4 and 5).

Naturally, the size of the caudal fins largely depends on the age of the animal. The span of the flukes in prenatal embryos and in the newborn is 80—100 cm, which averages about 20—22% of the length of the body. As the body increases in length with age, so do both the absolute and relative dimensions of the tail; in large adult males the flukes occupy up to $\frac{1}{3}$ of the body length (according to Chepurnov, 1965, 27.4%), measuring 5—6 m (according to Sleptsov, 1952). The flukes of sperm whales are stronger than those of many Cetacea. " ... in the tail the confluent measureless force of the whole whale seems concentrated to a point.

Could annihilation occur to matter, this were the thing to do it. Nor does this — its amazing strength, at all tend to cripple the graceful flexion of its motions; where infantileness of ease undulates through a Titanism of power. On the contrary, those motions derive their most appalling beauty from it .... its flexions are invariably marked by exceeding grace. Therein no fairy's arm can transcend it" ("Moby Dick"). Only the humpback whale (Megaptera) and the right whales equal the sperm whale in development of the tail (Chepurnov, 1965).

The flukes and caudal peduncle constitute an organ of forward movement in the sperm whale as in other whales. Basically, tail movement in the sperm whale is no different from that in dolphins (Shuleikin, 1941; Slijper, 1962; etc.). The caudal peduncle, moving in the vertical plane, bends very steeply, almost vertically in relation to the trunk in the region of the anus (Slijper, 1962). Recent investigations have revealed that as the tail moves downward, it deviates from the midline to the right, on the midline of the body approaches the center, then passes very slightly to the left downward, at the lowest point shifts back again to the right, proceeds upward to the center, intersects this and continues to the left, i.e. it describes a sort of figure 8, only flatter (Bel'kovich, Kleinenberg, and Yablokov, 1967). The slight screwlike movement of the tail from side to side was also mentioned by Bennett (1932) and Aschley (1942). Apart from acting as a propeller, the flukes act as depth controls. The working area of the sperm whale's fluke is more than twice as great as that of any other whale, and this, in conjunction with the very slight degree of emargination of the caudal fin, probably promotes appreciable acceleration during sudden jerking. These hydrodynamic features of the flukes ensure effective submersion.

22

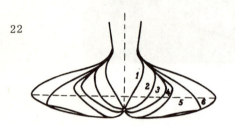

FIGURE 4. Changes in the caudal fin with age:

1 — in an embryo 9 cm long; 2 — same, 11 cm;
3 — same, 16 cm; 4 — same, 30 cm;
5 — same, 130 cm; 6 — in an adult 15 m long.

The thoracic fins are short and wide, with blunt and irregularly rounded ends (Figure 6), set low, approximately at the level of the angle of the mouth in the widest part of the body (see Figure 13).

According to our data, in prenatal embryos the length of the thoracic fins is more than twice their maximum width (one measurement 42 × 20 cm, another 40 × 18 cm). With age the fins become relatively wider (according to our own index of the thoracic fin); in newborn sperm whales (Wheeler, 1933) the relative width of the fins already increases somewhat, and in large specimens the length of the fin is only 1.6 times its width — 115 × 70 cm (Boschma, 1938). Such a ratio occurs in other toothed whales (e.g. white whale).

23   Asymmetry in the dimensions of the thoracic fins was observed by Hentschel (1910) in one large male and by Beddard (1919) in two small embryos.

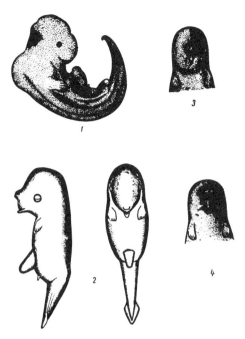

FIGURE 5. External appearance and some developmental features of sperm whales in the early embryonic stages:

1 — embryo 8 mm long (length from sinciput to tip of tail); 2 — same, 7.3 cm (female, ventral and lateral); 3 — head of embryo (male 12.5 cm long); 4 — head of embryo (male 20 cm long).

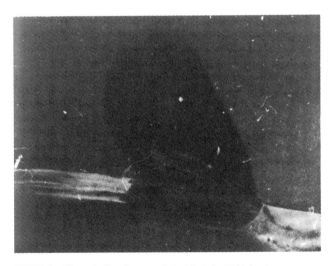

FIGURE 6. Thoracic fin of sperm whale (photo by Yablokov)

The line of insertion of the fins is directed obliquely forward, upward and back; the point of insertion of the anterior margin lies below that of its posterior margin. The anterior-lower margin of the fins is straight in comparison with the curved posterior-upper margin. In their usual position the thoracic fins can be tightly pressed to the body.

The distance between the thoracic fins on the ventral side is approximately a third of this distance on the dorsal side (Tomilin, 1957). In all embryos and young sperm whales, and also in some adults, the surface of the fins has a certain radial bumpiness corresponding to the phalanges of the digits of the limb (Matthews, 1938; our observations).

Observation of the movements of sperm whales when a wounded animal is being pulled to the side of a whaling boat gives the impression that the thoracic fins are less mobile than, for example, in the white whale (according to Kleinenberg et al., 1964) and that their functional importance is not very great. Nevertheless, since they can be deflected at 90° to the body surface, as is observed quite often, they can be said to act as brakes. The same conclusion was reached by Nishiwaki, Ohsumi, and Maeda (1963) on the basis of changes in fin shape in late embryonic development. At present, a difference is noted in the position of the line of insertion of the fins and therefore also of the plane of the thoracic fin surface in sperm whales and in most other species of whales. Due to this direction of line of insertion in sperm whales (obliquely forward, upward, and back), in forward motion the plane of the fin has a negative angle of attack, which means that as the animal moves forward without expenditure of energy, certain lowering forces must arise. In most other whales, in which the lines of insertion of the fins are differently arranged and the plane is differently oriented during forward motion, a lifting force is generally created, according to Aleev (1965).

Thus, in contrast to many other whales, in sperms both the body and the thoracic fins during forward motion automatically create forces which promote submersion. This can be explained as follows. The body of a sperm whale has positive buoyancy, since its density is 0.95 g/cm^3 (Sleptsov, 1952), i.e. less than the density of water, unlike that of the bodies of most other whales. It may be assumed that the permanently acting corpus momentum in sperm whales and the positive buoyancy of the body (see above) neutralize one another as it were, thus causing movement to be horizontal. At this time the fins can be pressed to the body. When these are withdrawn to the side, additional lowering forces are created, which in conjunction with the force created by the powerful and effective depth control — the caudal fin — ensure abrupt and steep diving.

The dorsal fin is situated approximately at the level of the anal-genital fold, very slightly anteriorly, at the boundary between the dorsal and caudal sections of the body; it is often regularly triangular with a rounded, sometimes pointed tip, with smoothly sloping margins and a wide base which is almost fused with the back (this makes it difficult to select a fixed point for measurement, see Figure 13). Evidently, for this reason Boschma (1938) considers that the dorsal fin of the sperm whale hardly deserves such a name, since it is merely a small rise on the dorsal part of the body, and he recalls that in the past whalers used to call it a hump. At its base the dorsal fin is up to 160—175 cm long (Sleptsov, 1952; Tomilin, 1957) or

24

even 225 cm (Hentschel, 1910). The height of the fin also varies (individual and sex-age variations), reaching 55—57 cm (according to the same authors).

Around the apex or at the base of the dorsal fin of immature males and adult females caught in the coastal waters of Japan, Kasuya and Ohsumi (1966) noted the frequent presence of excrescences — round or oval calluses — with a rough surface and a thick epidermis (up to 17 mm thick, i.e. 3 times as thick as on other parts of the back), and also with more strongly developed dermal papillae, the color of these excrescences being lighter than that of adjacent parts of the body. The authors assume that this is not connected with a skin disease but has to do with the activity of the sex glands.

In the large majority of sperm whales (according to our data, in approximately 90% of them) there are immediately behind the dorsal fin four, sometimes three, dermal protuberances (Figure 13). Their number may be from one to six (Howell, 1930; Sleptsov, 1952; Clarke, 1956; Tomilin, 1957; etc.) or eight (Bennett, 1840). Our material included only one specimen with five dorsal protuberances.

The protuberances are of various size and shape; mostly they are smooth but sometimes pointed. According to Ivanova (1961), in some cases the protuberances are as large as the dorsal fin. She noted a correlation between the fin and the protuberances: in the absence of protuberances the dorsal fin is very low and short.

Fraser (1937) gives a figure in which three or four dorsal protuberances with the dorsal fin seem to constitute a unified series of mounds which gradually decrease in size toward the tail. According to our observations the dorsal protuberances following the dorsal fin, if expressed at all, are approximately equal in size and always smaller than the fin. In the illustration of Quoy and Gaimard (1824, in Boschma, 1938), apart from the four distinct, small protuberances on the caudal peduncle, several small eminences are visible between the head and the dorsal fin (see Figure 2, fifth drawing from the top on the right), which have never been mentioned before by anyone.

Development of the dorsal fin and protuberances during the embryonic period indicates strong individual variation. Thus, in an embryo 50.8 cm long Beddard (1915) did not even find signs of a dorsal fin or dorsal protuberances, but in 1919, in two embryos measuring 11.4 and 24.1 cm, he observed clearly expressed dorsal fins. In the larger embryo the fin took the form of a well defined sharp crest 22 cm long. In the smaller embryo, apart from the distinctly expressed dorsal fin, a peculiar dorsal crest was visible extending to the very end of the tail and intersected by narrow furrows that formed a series of segments. According to Beddard (1915), the presence of such a crest is proof of the existence of a more strongly expressed dorsal fin in the evolution of the species. The author furnishes additional evidence in the fact that the white whale, which as an adult has no dorsal fin, has a clearly defined 25 crest in the embryonic state. According to our observations, in the embryo 1.3 m long the dorsal fin was not yet expressed. In large embryos (more than 2.5 m long) both the dorsal fin and the dorsal protuberances were already well developed. In sperm whale embryos of such a size the dorsal fin, evidently for convenience while in the uterus, bends abruptly — with a break at the base — aside and lies adjacent to the back, as in dolphins.

In accordance with the degree of development of the dorsal fin, the sperm whale must be referred to whales with a small dorsal fin. Sleptsov (1952) places them among the whales with a greatly reduced dorsal fin, and yet according to his same data of numerous measurements, the height of the fin in the sperm whale is up to 3.2% of the body length, which exceeds the corresponding proportions (according to Tomilin, 1957) in all Balaenopteridae referred by Sleptsov (1952) to the group of whales with small dorsal fins.

The length of the base of the fin in sperms can reach 14% of the length of the body (Tomilin, 1957), which is 2—3 times the corresponding ratio in baleen whales.

A survey of the views of various authors on the function of the dorsal fins and caudal keels in whales (Kleinenberg et al., 1964) led to the conclusion that the dorsal fin is important as a stabilizer. This is certainly true regarding the killer whale. It is unlikely, however, that small or even medium-sized dorsal fins which, moreover, do not have the necessary rigidity, somehow limited the maneuverability of whales, especially of large ones. According to this viewpoint maneuverability would be preserved only in "finless" whales. Our observations from a helicopter of the movement of large Balaenopteridae in the Antarctic in 1962 indicated that when feeding, these whales rotate about their axis without losing speed. A final solution to this problem obviously requires additional observations and experiments.

It seems, however, that the sperm whale shows a perfect union between the dorsal fin, which has a relatively large area and a higher degree of rigidity than in other whales and can act to some extent as a stabilizer, and the powerful caudal fin (which is larger than those of most other whales). This union evidently enables the sperm whale to perform sharp forward spurts and does not greatly limit its maneuverability.

The eyes are placed higher than and somewhat beyond the corners of the mouth. In large specimens the length of the eye slit is up to 9—12 cm (Hentschel, 1910; Sleptsov, 1952; our measurements).

The aural opening is located 50—60 cm from the eyes and very slightly below them. In adults it is faintly marked, and in some whales it is completely indiscernible (mostly sickle-shaped). The opening lies in a longitudinal fold and is 3—7 cm long (Hentschel, 1910; our measurements).

The lateral surface of the body, the surface of the back, and often the abdomen in the large majority of adult sperms are uneven, covered with parallel horizontal, sloping folds 15 cm apart (Matthews, 1938). The folds sometimes branch out (see Figure 18). This folding is found already in the late stages of embryonic development, when it is often even more clearly defined than in the adults.

At the late stages of embryonic development folds are formed between 26 the corners of the mouth and on the throat; these have a different nature, origin and significance than the protuberances on the body surface. These throat folds are for the most part longitudinal, resembling deep wrinkles; their number, size, and arrangement vary in different whales (Figures 7, 8, and 9). Their number is from 10 to 40, their depth up to 1 cm, and their length from 3 to 75 cm (Sleptsov, 1952; Tomilin, 1957).

Hentschel (1910) presents a scheme of the arrangement and size of the throat folds of sperm whales: three pairs of folds of equal size are arranged in perfect symmetry to the right and left of the midline of the abdomen, and one short fold lies in the middle. Boschma (1938) mentions two clearly defined furrows of the same nature, arranged symmetrically. Not one of the adult sperms which we examined had such a well-constructed system of throat folds. Embryos studied by Kükenthal (1914) had no such folds. In almost all the large embryos which we investigated the throat folds were very distinct, and were even relatively deeper and longer than those of adult whales. In individual cases symmetry was observed in their arrangement (Figure 8).

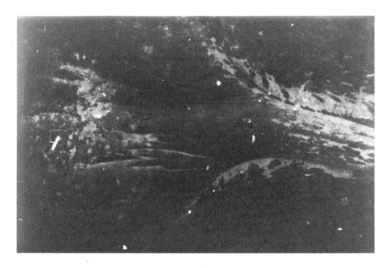

FIGURE 7. Arrangement of folds on the throat of a male sperm whale (16.6 m long). Scars and spots are visible

Sanctis (1881) suggested that the folds, which are observed in several other whales, particularly in the Ziphiidae and in pygmy sperm whales, may act to stretch the skin when the jaw is moved. Beddard (1900) and Stead (1930) believed that the folds facilitate widening of the pharynx when a large item of prey is swallowed. The great difference in the number of folds in individual whales with the same ecology and physiology, and also the development of the folds as early as in uterine life (as already mentioned, during embryogenesis they are relatively long and deep), raise doubts as to whether this is their purpose.

28   Apart from the longitudinal folding, we observed several cases and clearly expressed transverse folding in embryos, consisting of smaller and denser furrows on the throat and the upper jaw. One embryo 245 cm long showed fine longitudinal and transverse folding on the occiput. Fine transverse folding has not been observed on the body of adult whales.

FIGURE 8. Folds on the throat and abdomen of a sperm whale embryo of prenatal size

FIGURE 9. Large embryo of female sperm whale. The typical position of folded flukes, appressed thoracic fin, and folds on the throat and abdomen can be seen.
Conditions of exposure of the photograph fail to reveal details of coloration (whaling base "Dal'nii Vostok," 1965)

COLORATION

The coloration of sperm whales is more or less uniform. As a rule it is from gray or dark bluish gray to grayish brown and blackish brown with a light spottiness of varying intensity, configuration, and arrangement. The black color noted by Sleptsov (1952) is in our opinion due to the delay in delivery to whale-processing plants. An indication that the color of killed sperm whales gradually turns darker can be found in Hentschel's work (1910). According to other data and our observations, distinct darkening is observed 40—50 minutes after death, and after 3—4 hours the color can become almost black.

Matthews (1938) and Omura (1950) separate several main types of general coloration. In particular, Omura divides all the examined sperm whales caught in the waters of Japan into the following four color groups:

1) entire body dark gray;
2) lighter color on underside of head and lower jaw;
3) entire head slightly whitish.
4) entire body slightly whitish.

We did not consider this division to be the most accurate in describing the coloration of sperm whales obtained in the North Pacific, and for comparison we tried to classify them as far as possible according to the same principle. Information for a similar classification was selected also from the material of Matthews (1938), and the results are given in Table 1.

TABLE 1. Percentage of sperm whales with various body coloration

Type of coloration	Antarctica (Matthews, 1938)	Waters of the Sea of Japan (Omura, 1950)		Northeastern Pacific (our data)	
		males	females	males	females
Dark or dark gray	70	67.6	73.1	78.3	68
Lighter color of underside of head and lower jaw	25.7	12.8	17.3	15	21.5
Entire head slightly whitish	—	1.7	1.9	1.7	—
Entire body slightly whitish	—	17.9	7.7	5	10.5
Lighter color on abdomen	4.3	—	—	—	—

Basically, the ratio between these color groups is more or less constant for the different regions of the World Ocean (particularly if one allows for a certain subjectivity in the assessments of different investigators and for color discrepancies due to age differences in whales obtained in different regions).

The dark-colored group is the most widespread in all the oceans (from 68 to 78% of all sperm whales examined in the three main regions of habitat).

Ivanova (1961) and Gudkov (1963) separate different types of sperm whale coloration in the same area of the Kurile Islands; however, Ivanova's data also show a predominance here of animals with a dark body and a more or less dense marbled pattern on the abdomen.

Most sperm whales of both sexes have light spots in the umbilical region (Figure 10). Two types of such spots can be distinguished (though rather arbitrarily): 1) light gray spots consisting of dots and speckles without distinct boundaries, resembling triangles with their apexes toward the umbilicus, extending in a horizontal light pattern onto the flanks; 2) bright white spots with distinct but irregular boundaries, in the form of triangles with the apexes toward the head and as it were, abutting against the umbilicus (Table 2; Figure 10).

FIGURE 10. Typical pattern on the abdomen of sperm whale (female, North Pacific, 1965)

Hentschel (1910) reports that in a male sperm whale caught in Newfoundland waters the angle formed by the white stripes was approximately 80°.

30 TABLE 2. Percentage of sperm whales with various coloration inhabiting different regions of the World Ocean (Matthews, 1938; Omura, 1950; data of the author)

Habitat	Spottiness on abdomen	Spots		Stripes and streaks on flanks
		first type	second type	
Northern hemisphere				71
Sea of Japan area		87	75	
Northeastern Pacific	96	47.4	23.5	
Southern hemisphere				24.3
Antarctica	91	64–67		

According to Matthews (1938), in 64% of southern hemisphere sperm whales having a light pattern, a so-called umbilical ring is formed, beginning in the umbilical region and diverging to surround the genital opening. The umbilical spot may extend onto the flanks with bright stripes or streaks, which sometimes cover a considerable area.

The thoracic and dorsal fins are colored like the flanks and back (respectively), but in 7% of sperm whales a light pattern is observed on the inner surface of the fins and behind the anus (Matthews, 1938).

Tomilin (1957) mentions the possible occurrence of light spots and a certain difference in coloration between the upper and lower surfaces of the flukes and the thoracic fins. In addition we noticed a certain spottiness on the dorsal fin and in certain cases quite intensive spottiness of the underside of the thoracic fins.

In the anterior part of the head, on the forehead in 25.6% of sperm whales inhabiting southern (antarctic and subantarctic) waters there are light streaks forming a spiral pattern converging on its central light part

31 (Matthews, 1938). Matthews does not agree with Beale (1839) that such a pattern is peculiar to old males, called gray-headed, because in the region of Durban he found males 13.6 and 13.9 m long and two females 10.1 and 10.6 m long with such patterns on the forehead. Our data confirm the presence of such a pattern in young animals; Beale's view apparently stemmed from the fact that at the time of his observations very few females and young sperm whales were caught.

There are cases of complete albinism among sperm whales. Melville's (1851) legendary "Moby Dick" was a white whale. Zenkovich (1952) reports catching off the Komandorskie Islands two unusually light albino sperm whales with pinkish-white eyes. A male albino sperm whale 10.7 m long caught in 1957 in the waters of Japan (Ohsumi, 1958) had eyes with no pink or red. The same author reports having caught a large female (15.2 m) with a white head and gray back in the Antarctic in 1950.

(30)

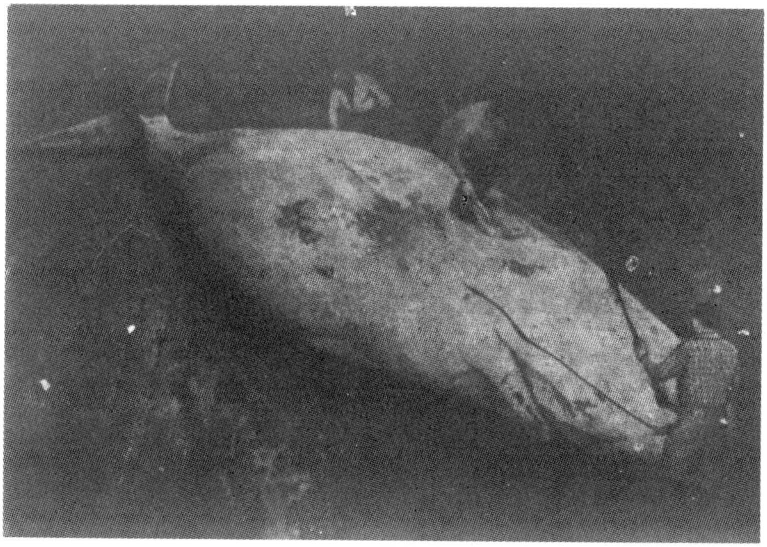

FIGURE 11. Albino sperm whale (female, northern Pacific Ocean, 1966; photograph by Khabibrakhmanov)

27

In recent years two albino sperm whales have been caught by Soviet fleets. In one of them (a female caught in 1966 in the southern part of the Gulf of Alaska) on a pure white background there were very small, very slightly grayish areas under the thoracic fins and around the genital cleft (Figure 11). Its embryo, 419 cm long, was normally pigmented.

Scars and abrasions often change the natural pigmentation of the skin of sperm whales. They are caused by skin injuries inflicted in the course of life by parasites, food items (particularly cephalopods), wounds, etc.

Signs of injury in the form of light, depigmented spots of various shape are observed mainly in the anterior part of the body, especially on the head; toward the tail their number decreases. The traces left by cephalopods take the form of paired rows of incisions — rings up to 3.7 cm in diameter (Lillie, 1910) depending on the size of the mollusks — left by the horny rings of the tentacle suckers, or else bands with ragged edges, sometimes of considerable length and width, left by the horny hooks of the tentacles (Tomilin, 1957) and possibly of the beaklike jaws (Figure 12). Parallel bands may be left by the teeth of other sperm whales, since the distance between the bands (scars) is approximately equal to the spaces between the teeth of these animals, and the width of the scars roughly equals the thickness of the apex of the mandibular teeth (Shaler, 1873; Bennett, 1932; Boschma, 1938; Rosenblum, 1962; Slijper, 1962; Gudkov, 1963).

Boschma (1938) suggests that when one whale bites another, the body of the latter slides along the row of teeth.

On the body of nearly every sperm whale there are light spots of varying shape, type, and origin. Naturally the number of lesions is greater in large (adult) whales, in which different types of depigmented traces can significantly change the coloration, especially that of the head, which becomes lighter.

The general tone of coloration can also be affected by the body's becoming strongly overgrown with certain yellow or cinnamon-colored diatoms (see Chapter 16). The lips and jaws are most often subject to this. The density and area of overgrowth depend on the season, being greatest in the fall. The head of one sperm whale was found to be covered with a coating of pink algae.

According to available data, sexual dimorphism in regard to color is not observed at all. The lips of the upper jaw and the dorsal (inner) half of the lower jaw, i.e. that part of the jaw which occupies the recess of the upper jaw, are generally white. According to Matthews (1938), pigmentation of the upper lips and of the alveolar part of the lower jaw is observed in 20% of sperm whales.

31)

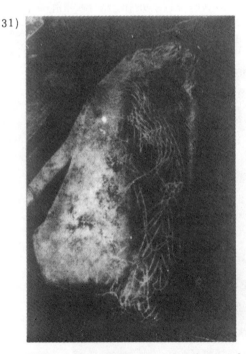

FIGURE 12. Large male sperm whale with traces of scars and abrasions

In some sperm whales (17%, according to Matthews) the entire lower jaw or its distal part may be completely white. According to our data, a white distal part of the lower jaw is found mainly in old specimens. The lips and lower jaw are generally overgrown with diatoms, which give them a yellow color.

Development of coloration. Pigmentation in the embryo begins to appear at a length of about 50 cm. According to Matthews (1938), unpigmented parts (paler than the general tone) extend along the flanks and under the head, from the dorsal tubercles to the fin bifurcation and from the genital fold to the anal opening.

Pigmentation begins on the back and gradually spreads to the flanks. When the body is 1.5 m long, the pigment on the back becomes a dark shade of cinnamon, while the ventral surface, lateral surfaces of the head, and lower jaw become creamy yellow or flesh-colored. Light zones can be seen on the tail behind the anus and on the underside of the fins. The flukes are darker above than below. On the abdomen there is a dark area from the umbilicus to the level of the thoracic fins.

When the embryo is about 2.5 m long, the pigment becomes dark gray, but occupies only a small area. At a length of about 3 m, dark blue pigment occupies a greater part of the body, while the underside, the lower jaw, and the region of the anal-genital slit remain pale pink. Matthews (1938) indicates that in embryos of this size the ventral surface between the anus and the thoracic fins is of a pale or light gray color, while the remainder of the ventral surface is darker. When the body is about 3.5 m long, the pink color becomes a pale blue.

In an embryo of about 4 m nearly the entire trunk is dark gray; only the surfaces of the lower part of the head and of the lower jaw are light gray, almost white. An embryo of this size shows on the general grayish back-
33 ground of the abdomen an already clearly distinguishable spottiness around the umbilicus similar to that of a pregnant female. Our material confirms the data of Matthews (1938), which indicate that the light coloration of individual parts of the body characteristic of most adult animals may not only be acquired with age but may also be inborn. Moreover, Matthews (1938) analyzed the coloration of a newborn sperm whale 4.04 m long, described by Wheeler (1933), which had more light areas on the body — in particular, on the abdomen — than adult animals; Matthews expressed the opinion that the dark pigment may develop after the whale is born. In his view, the difference in intensity of pigmentation between the upper and lower parts of the body in embryos and the presence of light spots in adult whales indicate that the ancestors of sperm whales had more variegated coloration, as is characteristic, for example, of recent dolphins.

According to the types of coloration distinguished by Yablokov (1963), sperm whales should belong to the group with uniform body coloration (first type). This is perhaps explained by the fact that the sperm whale feeds at great depths, where vision ceases to be an important source of information, and consequently color loses the significance which it had on the surface both for the attacker and for the victim.

SIZE*

The largest known male sperm whale, according to reliable measurements at our disposal (and subjected to biological analysis), was 17.3 m
long (caught off the Northern Kuriles in 1959). Males of record size —
20.7 m — were found in the Atlantic, 20.4 m in the Far East, and 19.5 m
in the Antarctic (Tomilin, 1962). The largest male sperms from southern
waters caught in the last century were as a rule 18.3 m long (Bennett, 1836).
Reports of males reaching a length of 25.6 m (Bennett, 1840) are doubtful.
A length of 23.1 m (Bennett, 1840) and similar sizes may have been obtained
by measuring the whale along the curves of the body.

At present, sperm whales longer than 17.5 m are very seldom caught,
although recently quite a few exceeding 18.5 m were caught in the North
Pacific. Among 902 males caught in the waters of Japan in the years
1929—1933, only 43 were longer than 18.5 m (Matsuura, 1935).

The average commercial length of sperm whales is constantly changing
(mainly decreasing). On the whole, whales from the northern hemisphere
are perhaps a little smaller than those from the Antarctic (Tomilin, 1957;
Ivanova, 1961a; etc.). According to statistical data, in the 1930s and 1940s
this difference was 130 cm (average length of 25,000 sperm whales caught
in the northern hemisphere was 14.6 m; average length of 15,500 obtained
in Antarctica was 15.9 m). Tomilin (1957) believes that this difference may
be due not only to a population (subspecies) difference but also to the penetration of older and larger males into the cold antarctic waters.

Female sperms are much shorter than the males. Sleptsov (1952) re-
34 ports that in 1948 he examined a female 14.3 m long. One of the females
which we examined at the Whaling base "Aleut" in 1958 was 11.7 m long,
but it had no middle pair of teeth and the pulp cavity of the neighboring
teeth was exposed; the teeth showed more than 60 layers of dentine with
a closed pulp cavity and worn-down tip. All this indicates that a size of
about 12 m is close to the limit for females.

It is doubtful whether there are females 15.86 m long (according to
data of the 1946 International Whaling Statistics). These data may be
faulty due to wrong determination of sex at whale-processing plants. It
is significant that reports of such dimensions in females appeared after
intensification of whaling with the yield of a large number of females. For
example, more than 100 years ago Bennett (1836) indicated that the average
length of female sperm whales in southern waters is 8.5 m, while the length
of 10.6 m is rare for females. Thus, sexual dimorphism in size is much
more clearly expressed in this species than in other whales.

PROPORTIONS

Works specifically on this subject have been published by Ivanova
(1955, 1961), Fujino (1956), and Nishiwaki, Ohsumi, and Maeda (1963).
Matthews (1938), Sleptsov (1952), Arsen'ev and Zenkovich (1955),
Tomilin (1957), and other authors have also presented material on the

---

* The growth rate of male and female sperm whales is dealt with separately in Chapter 14.

proportions of the body of sperm whales. Most such investigations are based on the data of measurements according to the scheme of the "Discovery" (Figure 13).

Sex- and age-determined differences in the proportions. The greatest difference between males and females is in the distance from the genital opening to the center of the anal opening, which is much greater in males (Matthews, 1938; Fujino, 1956). In pregnancy this distance at first gradually increases, but in the later stages it decreases (Nishiwaki, Ohsumi, and Maeda, 1963).

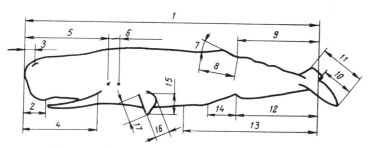

FIGURE 13. Diagram of measurements in the sperm whale:

1 — zoological line (distance from end of snout to bifurcation of tail); 2 — distance from end of snout to end of lower jaw; 3 — distance from end of snout to blowhole; 4 — distance from end of snout to angle of mouth; 5 — distance from end of snout to center of eye; 6 — distance from center of eye to center of ear; 7 — height of dorsal fin; 8 — base length of dorsal fin; 9 — distance from bifurcation of tail to posterior margin of dorsal fin; 10 — length of caudal fin from bifurcation to end; 11 — span (width) of caudal fin; 12 — distance from bifurcation of tail to center of anus; 13 — distance from bifurcation of tail to umbilicus; 14 — distance from center of anus to center of genital opening; 15 — distance from axilla to tip of fin; 16 — maximum width of thoracic fin; 17 — distance from outer point of insertion of fin to center of fin along a straight line.

35   Measurements in the anterior part of the trunk (from end of head to angle of mouth, from end of head to center of eye, length of head separated from trunk, etc.) are relatively greater in males; on the other hand, measurements in the posterior part of the trunk (from notch of flukes to center of anus, from notch of flukes to center of umbilicus, etc.) are smaller in males, i.e. the head part is larger in males and the posterior part of the trunk is larger (Fujino, 1956) in females. Stating this conclusion more precisely, Nishiwaki et al. (1963) write that growth of the head as compared with growth of the skull proceeds more rapidly in males.

According to Matthews (1938), the width of the flukes (at the point of their insertion) is much greater in males, while according to other investigators such a difference between the sexes is not fixed (Fujino, 1956). As regards other measurements, sex-determined differences have not been mentioned.

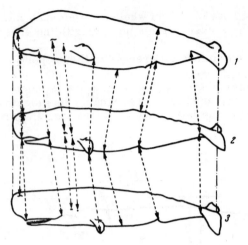

FIGURE 14. Sex- and age-determined changes in the proportions and shape of body of the sperm whale:

1 — male embryo 0.3 m long; 2 — female, 5.0 m long; 3 — male, 15.0 m long (Nishiwaki, Ohsumi, and Maeda, 1963).

As the overall length increases, the relative rate of growth of the anterior part of the body also increases, while the growth rate of the posterior part decreases, which leads to considerable enlargement of the head. Morphologically this is due to the fact that ossification of the posterior end of the vertebral column is completed more rapidly than that of its anterior end (Nishiwaki et al., 1963). These authors note that in males the distance from the penis to the center of the anus increases gradually from birth to the onset of sexual maturity and then decreases. Some of the changes in the body proportions occurring at sexual maturity are shown in Figure 14. Most of the proportions change insignificantly with age.

Population differences in the proportions. The determination of any stable differences between animals, with consideration of sharply expressed sexual dimorphism and individual variation, on the scales of different populations is of prime importance both for systematics and for determining, for example, the local character of herds, etc.

Morphometric findings are still the basis for establishing objective differences of any kind. Regarding sperm whale osteology, not enough material has been accumulated for a morphometric comparison of animals inhabiting different regions of the World Ocean.

Although quite numerous data have been collected on the morphometry of sperm whales, there are considerable contradictions in the conclusions of various investigators.

Matthews (1938) presents morphometric data of sperms from the southern hemisphere (81 caught off South Africa and South Georgia Island). 36 Ivanova (1955) carried out similar investigations in the North Pacific (area of the Kuriles); comparing her results with similar data of Matthews, she

concluded that in whales of the northern hemisphere the distance from
the bifurcation of the tail to the posterior margin of the dorsal fin is
somewhat shorter than in animals from the southern hemisphere (she
attributed this only to the difference in the position of the dorsal fin in
northern and southern hemisphere animals); she also noted that the flukes
of northern hemisphere whales are much wider. Moreover, according to
Ivanova, in the northern sperm whale the snout protrudes above the jaws
somewhat less than in the southern animal. Tomilin (1957) uses these
differences to confirm the existence of two subspecies — a northern and a
southern — in the World Ocean. Arsen'ev and Zenkovich (1955) and Fujino
(1956), who made similar comparisons (they used only the means of the
variations in percentage of the overall body length), observed no differences.

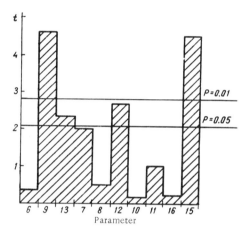

FIGURE 15. Degree of differences in characters between
male sperm whales of the northern and southern hemispheres

In a later work (1961) Ivanova indicated that there are some differences
between northern and southern hemisphere sperm whales in the position of
the dorsal fin and in the size of the snout protuberance in young animals.

Sleptsov (1952), without presenting any factual evidence, denies in principle the possibility of any morphological differences between herds of
southern and northern sperm whales, since he speaks in general of the unity
of herds of whales. Clarke (1956) found no population differences between
sperm whales from the North Atlantic and from the North Pacific.

Nishiwaki et al. (1963), supplementing Fujino's material with new data
on measurements of North Pacific sperm whales and comparing them with
Matthews' material (1938), indicated a difference between animals caught
in various oceanic regions, expressed in the fact that the caudal part of the
body of North Pacific whales is somewhat shorter than that of whales in the
southern part of the ocean (measurements from notch of caudal fin to base
of dorsal fin and from notch to umbilicus).

TABLE 3. Comparative characteristics of the proportions of male sperm whales of the northern and southern hemispheres

No. of measurements according to the scheme	Measurement	Northern hemisphere (Pacific Ocean)				Southern hemisphere (Antarctica)				
		n	$M_1 \pm m_1$	δ	CV, %	n	$M_1 \pm m_1$	δ	CV, %	t
6	From center of eye to center of ear	16	3.29 ± 0.07	0.27	8.34	88	3.32 ± 0.04	0.40	11.99	−0.3
7	Height of dorsal fin	30	1.94 ± 0.05	0.27	14.06	86	2.07 ± 0.04	0.38	18.3	−2.02
8	Length of dorsal fin base	30	7.95 ± 0.18	0.97	12.15	85	9.78 ± 3.63	3.35	5.41	−0.50
9	From bifurcation of tail to posterior margin of dorsal fin	29	32.19 ± 0.34	1.86	5.76	87	34.23 ± 0.27	2.54	7.41	−4.6
10	Length of caudal fin from bifurcation to tip	16	14.30 ± 0.58	2.32	16.23	10	14.28 ± 0.34	1.07	7.49	+0.20
11	Span (width) of caudal fin	13	26.35 ± 0.91	3.29	12.48	8	25.38 ± 0.58	1.64	6.44	+0.89
12	From bifurcation of tail to center of anus	29	28.75 ± 0.38	2.05	7.12	88	29.98 ± 0.26	2.46	8.18	−2.66
13	From bifurcation of tail to center of umbilicus	28	46.81 ± 0.46	2.42	5.16	88	48.17 ± 0.33	3.05	6.34	−2.43
15	Length of thoracic fin	29	8.42 ± 0.24	1.32	15.65	85	7.10 ± 0.16	1.54	21.3	+4.48
16	Maximum width of thoracic fin	27	4.85 ± 0.07	0.47	9.6	88	4.73 ± 0.51	0.27	5.63	+0.23

In the morphometric investigations and comparisons presented above, diametrically opposite conclusions are frequent, and unfortunately the degree of mathematical treatment of the material is not indicated, which detracts from the reliability of the findings; or else only arithmetic mean data are used, which at the given level of knowledge render the results insufficiently conclusive.

In order to obtain comparative material we mathematically processed 37 the data of 118 measurements of large (more than 13 m long) male sperm whales caught by Soviet whaling fleets in antarctic waters and in the North Pacific. The "Discovery" scheme was also used in the measurements.

Unfortunately, due to the difficulty of taking certain measurements owing to the intensity of current whale processing, it was possible to compare northern and southern hemisphere sperm whales [only] according to 10 measurements: Nos. 6, 7, 8, 9, 10, 11, 12, 13, 15, 16 (Table 3; Figure 15).

The material was processed by the standard statistical methods, with calculation of the arithmetic mean (M), its error (m), the standard deviation (σ), and the coefficient of variation. The reliability of the differences was determined by the formula

$$t = \frac{M_1 - M_2}{\sqrt{m_1^2 + m_2^2}}$$

It is seen from Table 3 and Figure 15 that the differences between adult male sperms of the northern and southern hemispheres are reliable (with accuracy of 0.01) in two measurements: from bifurcation of tail to posterior margin of dorsal fin (9th measurement), which distance is greater in southern animals, and the length of the thoracic fin (15th), which is greater in northern animals. Attention is drawn to the difference (with $P > 0.05$), also with a high degree of reliability, in the measurement from the bifurcation of the tail to the center of the anus (12th measurement) and from the bifurcation of the tail to the center of the umbilicus (13th): these distances are greater in antarctic sperm whales.

Continuing the analysis of the measurement data, let us examine (Figure 16) the coefficient of variation of the body proportions of northern and southern animals. The position of the curves on the graph and the figures given in Table 3 indicate that the differences in measurements — 38 (9th) from bifurcation of tail to posterior margin of dorsal fin, (13th) from bifurcation of tail to center of umbilicus, and (12th) from bifurcation of tail to center of anus — are all stable characters with a low coefficient of variation.

All three parameters characterize the caudal part of the whale body and complement and confirm one another. It should be stressed that all the large measurements of the caudal part of the trunk used according to the accepted scheme of measurements indicate that differences do exist between northern and southern sperm whales.

The proportion of the thoracic fin length (15th measurement) is an unstable parameter with a high coefficient of variation (CV = 15.65%, Table 3, see Figure 16) since, despite the high degree of its reliability, reservations should be maintained regarding the existence of differences between northern and southern whales according to this character.

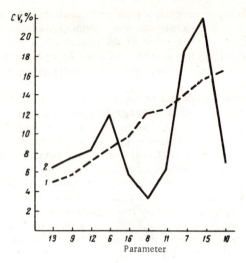

FIGURE 16. Coefficients of variation CV (in %) of
several measurements of northern (1) and southern (2)
sperm whales

Comparison of our conclusions with the material of previous morphometric investigations by other authors confirms that the differences noted
between sperm whale populations from different areas of the World Ocean
have already been reflected, with greater or lesser clarity and according
to a greater or lesser number of characters, in the results of most studies.
In a few cases the differences can be regarded as having been recorded
irrespective of the author's conclusions. For example, Fujino (1956)
discovered a difference in proportions but denied its existence in the conclusions of his work, attributing this to a possible confusion in the measurements.

Ivanova (1955) already noted several morphometric differences in the
proportions of northern and southern sperm whales, particularly in the
size of the protruding part of the snout; these differences not only could
but had to exist when there was a difference in the contingent of animals
measured: length of main part of sperm whales, according to Ivanova,
10—12 m, but according to Matthews, 14—16 m, the difference obtained
undoubtedly being due to age. In making population diagnostics using such
characters one must be very careful to work only with material of the
same age.

Thus, morphometric studies with the use of diverse mathematical processing indicate a distinct morphological difference between males from
39 the northern and southern hemispheres in that the caudal part of the body
is relatively large in the southern whales.

Chapter 3

SKIN COVER

The morphological and histological structure of the sperm whale's skin has been described relatively thoroughly by Sleptsov (1952), Levasheva (1954), and Sokolov (1955, 1962, 1963). The present description is based on the data of these authors and also on material presented by Tomilin (1951) and Bel'kovich (1961).

The skin of the sperm whale, like that of other whales, is clearly distinguished from the skin of other mammals mainly by being thicker and also by being smoother and devoid of sebaceous and sweat glands. Moreover, in contrast to the skin of baleen whales and many dolphins, on which there are short hairs or vibrissae on the head, the skin of the sperm whale (adult and embryo) is hairless.

The skin of sperm whales is both relatively and absolutely one of the thickest among whales; the thickness of the skin of four sperms is given in Table 4.

TABLE 4. Thickness of skin in various parts of the sperm whale body (Sokolov, 1955), cm

Sex	Date of capture	Length of body, m	Abdomen			Back		Flank at thoracic fin	Lateral part of head
			under thoracic fins	at umbilicus	in front of vulva	above thoracic fins	in front of dorsal fin		
Female . . .	7 August	10.2	15	10	—	21	—	6.5	6
" . . .	7 August	9.8	18	14.3	22	20	25	9.5	8.5
" . . .	7 August	9.3	16	11.5	15.5	12	16	10	7.5
Male	13 Sept.	14.8	31	30	—	38	33	22	8

The skin of the sperm whale, as of other whales, consists of three layers: epidermis, dermis, and hypodermic tissue (fatty layer or hypodermis) (Figure 17).

The very thick epidermis consists of three layers (unlike that of land mammals, in which it has four layers): an outer horny layer, a spiny layer, and a base layer.

The thickness of the epidermis and of the horny layer varies considerably in different parts of the body, as is seen from the data in Table 5.

In the sperm whale (just as in Berardius) the horny layer is not as thick as in many other whale species. The sperm whale's horny layer consists of long, parallel, transparent cells forming a thin membrane; nuclei are retained in many cells. The layer consists of several hundred (more than 200) rows of cells.

On the inside of the epidermis are numerous cells, into which, rising toward the surface of the skin, outgrowths of the dermis — dermal papillae — penetrate as far as the horny layer. In the sperm whale these cells are not arranged in such regular rows as in the epidermis of other whales but are distributed at random. The cells are more rounded in the sperm whale than in the rorqual, due to the need to counteract the counterflow during rapid submersion (Sokolov, 1955).

All the epidermal cells surrounding the dermal papillae and forming the epidermal septa are arranged in regular rows.

In the middle of the epidermal septa the rows of epidermal cells pass along the dermal papillae, bending round the tips of the papillae. As the cells of the epidermis approach the outer surface of the skin, they become flattened parallel to the skin surface.

The epidermis has minute pigment granules, which are distributed in the cell plasm and impart a dark color to the layer and thus to the entire animal. The cells in the lower parts of the epidermal septa are particularly strongly pigmented.

On the back and flanks the skin surface is bumpy (Figure 18). In depressions between the protuberances the epidermis forms excrescences into the dermis (Sokolov, 1955).

The dermis consists of two layers:* a subpapillary (reticulate) and a papillary layer, the papillae of which enter the cells of the epidermis. The total length of the papillae, according to Levashova (1954), is 2.3—2.4 mm, but according to Sokolov (1955) it is from 4—7 mm, i.e. their length is in fact almost equal to the thickness of the epidermal layer. The papillae consist of thin fibrils of connective tissue which lie parallel to the long axis of the papillae and have a rich network of blood vessels.

The subpapillary layer consists of a dense plexus of thick bundles of collagenous and elastic fibers which intersect in various directions (Table 6).

(41)

40

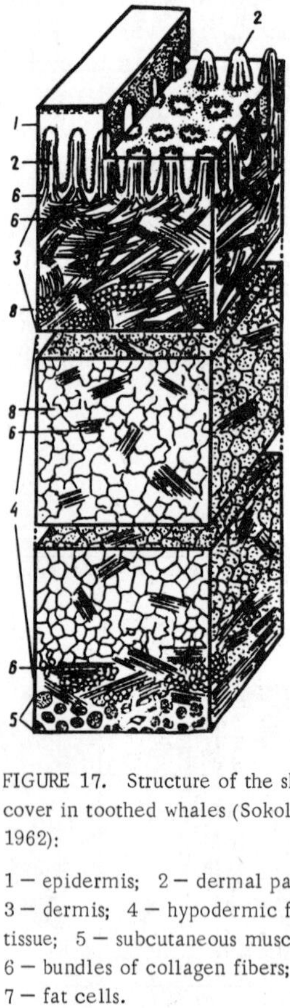

41

FIGURE 17. Structure of the skin cover in toothed whales (Sokolov, 1962):

1 — epidermis; 2 — dermal papillae; 3 — dermis; 4 — hypodermic fatty tissue; 5 — subcutaneous musculature; 6 — bundles of collagen fibers; 7 — fat cells.

* Sokolov (1955) does not subdivide the dermis into layers.

38

(40) TABLE 5. Thickness of the skin and its layers in sperm whale (female 11.5 m long; Sokolov, 1955)

Place of sampling	Thickness			Greatest height of dermal papillae, mm	Thickness			
	skin, cm	epidermis, mm	horny layer, μ		nonfatty part of subpapillary layer of dermis, mm	subpapillary layer of dermis, mm		hypodermic tissue, cm
Head								
anteriorly	5.9	6.3	45	5.4	11.2	3.0		2.2
dorsally	3.6	3.8	36	2.7	8.0	3.2		Absent
laterally	6.5	4.8	36	3.8	6.5	1.9		4.0
Back	10.1	5.8	24	4.4	5.0	1.5		8.1
Flank	11.6	4.8	45	3.9	4.5	1.5		9.5
Abdomen	13.6		Torn off		4.5	1.6		11.9
Lateral part of caudal peduncle	6.5	4.8	36	3.8	6.5	1.9		4.0
Thoracic fin								
anterior margin	2.1	3.3	Torn off	2.8	11.3	1.8		Absent
dorsal surface	1.2	3.2	36	2.7	6.7	0.8		"
Caudal fin								
anterior margin	1.7	4.3	36	3.3	13.1	1.3		"
dorsal surface	1.1	3.1	18	2.2	5.4	0.8		"

FIGURE 18. Bumpiness of sperm whale skin (to show the scale: knife and exposure meter 7 x 9 cm. Photo by Veinger)

TABLE 6. Dimensions of bundles of collagen fibers and fat cells in sperm whale skin (Sokolov, 1955)

Index	Place of sampling							thoracic fin		caudal fin	
	head			back	flank	abdomen	lateral part of caudal peduncle	anterior margin	dorsal surface	anterior margin	dorsal surface
	anteriorly	dorsally	laterally								
Greatest thickness of bundles of collagen fibers											
dermis · · ·	360	450	225	126	99	90	198	294	144	405	190
hypodermic tissue · · ·	360	—	360	630	455	1,135	450	—	—	—	—
Greatest size of fat cells											
dermis · · ·	189× ×360	63× ×135	81× ×144	81× ×117	54× ×72	42× ×63	153× ×189	102× ×130	36× ×63	Ab- sent	36× ×63
hypodermic tissue · · ·	420× ×588	—	270× ×450	210× ×270	270× ×333	315× ×450	234× ×297	—	—	—	—

40

This layer forms the densest part of the skin, and from it most valuable material can be obtained for the production of sole leather.

In the subpapillary layer the intermediate spaces are minimal, and so in this layer of the dermis there is very little fatty tissue. The thickness of the densest parts of the subpapillary layer of the derma varies from 12 to 17 mm.

Away from the skin surface (from the epidermis) the number of fat cells constantly increases and the dermis imperceptibly passes into the hypodermic tissue. It is therefore impossible to draw a sharp boundary between the two. Sleptsov also separates a boundary layer 15—22 mm thick, which comprises the lower layer of the dermis and the upper layer of hypodermic tissue, in which the thickness of the bundles of collagen fibers is still considerable.

42   Levasheva (1954) proposes to distinguish a third (lowest) layer of dermis, a dermal-fatty layer up to 125 mm thick (on the back), formed by strong, rarely interlaced, ramified bundles of collagen fibers, the space between which is filled with fat cells.

In the hypodermic tissue the bundles of collagen fibers lie far apart, and the entire space between them is filled with masses of polygonal fat cells, unlike those of the skin cover of land animals, which are drop-shaped. The density of the ligature of the bundles of collagen fibers decreases with depth, while their thickness increases. The number and size of the fat cells increase with depth. The bundles are differently oriented in the upper and middle layers, and as the subcutaneous musculature is approached their direction becomes more and more nearly horizontal, while the density of the ligature again increases. Around the subcutaneous musculature the bundles of collagen fibers run parallel to the surface of the skin. The network of elastic fibers is less well developed in the hypodermic tissue than in the dermis. The thickness of the hypodermic tissue depends on its situation on the body (from 2.2 to 11.9 cm, see Table 5).

Large blood vessels are rare in this layer, but a network of capillaries is well developed. The lowest layer of the hypodermic tissue is connected with the fasciae of the trunk musculature.

The loss of many properties of the skin structure of land mammals and the acquisition of new features in the structure as a whole are due to adaptation to permanent dwelling in water. In particular this explains the disappearance of the hair cover and the sebaceous and sweat glands, which cannot fulfill their functions in water; with loss of its function the organ becomes reduced.

As indicated by the measurements made by Sokolov (1955), the epidermis and the horny layer are thicker in those places in the skin lying in the parts
43 of the body subjected to greatest water resistance, i.e. the anterior part of the head, the anterior margins of the fins, etc. This can also explain the somewhat thinner horny layer in the sperm whale and Berardius as relatively slow-moving whales as compared with the thickness of this layer in faster moving cetaceans — rorquals and dolphins. However, it is not merely a matter of speed, since in the white whale — one of the slow movers — the epidermis with a network of tonofibrils forming a springy supporting system is much more strongly developed than in the more rapidly swimming whales (Kleinenberg et al., 1964). The increase in thickness of the epidermis in the arctic Delphinapterus (and apparently in all Cetacea) is linked with thermoregulation.

41

Due to the need for a tough skin cover, in some parts of the body the dermis has become thicker both in absolute units and as a percentage of the overall thickness of the skin. Thus, according to Sokolov (1955), on the anterior part of the head and the anterior margin of the caudal fin the dermis constitutes 51 and 75% of the skin thickness, respectively, but on the back, abdomen, and flank 13.6—14.7% (Table 7). It is also evident that the sperm whale needs this strengthening of the skin cover more than other whales if one is to judge by the relative thickness of the dermis in all parts of the body in the sperm whale and in other cetaceans. Moreover, on those areas of the sperm whale body surface where this is necessary, the density of the ligature of the collagen fiber bundles has increased while the number of fat cells has decreased (Table 6).

TABLE 7. Thickness of the dermis in various parts of the body in certain Cetacea (Sokolov, 1955; Kleinenberg et al., 1964), % of skin thickness

Species	Part of body				
	back	abdomen	flank	caudal fin	anterior part of head
Sperm whale	14.7	13.6	13.6	75.2	51.3
Striped dolphin (Lagenorhynchus obliquidens)	10.1	2.7	10.4	27.7	—
White whale (Delphinapterus leucas)	5.45	6.9	8.53	56.5	15.42
Minke whale (Balaenoptera acutirostrata)	3.00	1.8	—	50.3	—

The adaptive thickening and unusual reinforcement of the dermis in the anterior part of the head and lower jaw of sperm whales are determined also by the skirmishes occurring between these animals, struggles with squid, and the need to catch food on the bottom; the strengthened dermis on the caudal fin lends rigidity to the main locomotory organ.

The hypodermic tissue contributes less than the dermis to the strengthening of the skin; on the flanks it constitutes 81—82% of the skin thickness, on the back 79—80%; in the frontal part the thickness of the hypodermic tissue decreases to approximately 38% of the thickness of the skin (Table 8), while on the thoracic and caudal fins there is no hypodermic tissue. The cellular structure of the epidermis increases the productive surface of its horny layer, which may be compensation for the rapid desquamation of cells during movement in a dense aquatic medium.

The orientation of the epidermal cells in the skin of the caudal fin has a clearly expressed adaptive nature in all whales: "On the dorsal and ventral sides of the fin the cells are directed narrow side forward, against the current. Toward the anterior margin of the fin their direction changes. They bend in an arch in the direction of the caudal peduncle and just at the anterior edge of the fin lobe they pass along it" (Sokolov, 1955). Such a topography of the epidermal cells coincides with the direction of the counterflows as the whale moves.

44

TABLE 8. Thickness of the hypodermic tissue in various parts of the body in certain Cetacea (Sokolov, 1955)

Species	back, %		flank, %		abdomen, %	
	of body length	of skin thickness	of body length	of skin thickness	of body length	of skin thickness
Sperm whale	0.72	80.1	0.85	81.03	1.06	87.5
Berardius bairdii	2.01	98.5	1.26	94.2	1.32	97.2
Orcinus orca. . . .	—	—	0.48	79.1	0.45	80.0
Striped dolphin	—	79.2	—	73.3	—	89.0
Minke whale	0.33	89.6	—	—	0.53	97.6
Finback whale (Balaenoptera physalus)	0.28	91.6	0.26	91.1	0.26	93.3

Sokolov (1955, 1958) believes that the skin of the sperm whale with its structural features to a certain degree acts as a resistant to the enormous external pressure of the water (although he denies that the skin has any important protective function). The authors of "Belukha" exclude such a function, since it was shown (Dyuma and Kusto, 1958; Yablokov, 1961, 1962) that the water pressure affects both the skin and all the internal organs to an equal degree.

Kleinenberg et al. (1964) believe that there are better grounds for linking the great thickness of the fat layer in good divers with thermoregulation. However, if the thickening of the dermal-fatty layer in diving whales is associated with thermoregulation, how are we to explain 1) that it is not the hypodermic tissue which is thickened (see Table 8), as would be expected, but the supporting layer — the dermis, with a relatively low fat content; 2) the denser ligature; 3) the thickening of the bundles of collagen fibers as compared with the skin of other Cetacea?

Investigations of recent years have considerably widened our knowledge concerning the role of the dermal-fatty cover of whales. However, a description of its complex structure already made it possible to confirm that such a structure is conditioned by the need to fulfill a variety of functions.

It was established that the main purpose of the thick epidermis — permeated by dermal papillae, the rows of which impart to the epidermis compactness in the complex with the dermis, the hypodermis and the adjoining musculature — is to facilitate rapid movement in the water (Sokolov, 1962; Tomilin, 1962; and others). The whale's skin, a perfect and inimitable structure, tames and transforms the turbulent eddies into a laminar flow, ensuring a greatly increased speed with the same expenditure of muscular energy. This does not preclude the skin's acting as an organ of mechanical protection and thermoregulation. The latter function of the skin has been the subject of numerous investigations by many authors (Tomilin, 1951; Sleptsov, 1952; Scholander and Schevill, 1955; Sokolov, 1958; Utrecht, 1958; and others).

The whale's skin acts as an organ of thermoregulation owing to the following structural features. Permeating the hypodermis is a ramified capillary network, and at the provisional boundary with the dermis a not very dense plexus of vessels is formed. In the dermis the number of these diminishes, while at the boundary with the epidermis they again form a strong vascular plexus, from which there pass into each dermal papilla arterioles which ascend to its very end, almost to the horny layer (Bel'kovich, 1961).

It was established (Scholander, 1955; Irving and Hart, 1957) that the temperature of the skin cover of Cetacea is always lower than that of water, and the body temperature of arctic and antarctic whales can be 4—20 times higher than that of their outer coverings (Bel'kovich, 1961). Naturally, a constant and intensive supply of blood to the surface tissues (which is possible in principle) would lead to supercooling of the organism as a whole. It was demonstrated, however (Irving, 1939; Scholander, 1940), that when respiration is impeded there is a considerable reduction or even cessation of the supply of blood to the muscles and to the entire periphery of the organism. Thus intensive heat emission is possible, at first, only at the water surface, and owing to the above-described feature of a "stage-by-stage" blood supply to the skin (Bel'kovich, 1961). Depending on the intensity of the load, the blood can remain at various levels from the body surface, which enables effective regulation of heat transfer. In the dermis of the fins there are, in addition, so-called complex vessels (Tomilin, 1951; Scholander and Schevill, 1955; and others), consisting of an artery surrounded by 9—20 veins. When the lumen of the vessels is changed, these veins can very sharply alter heat transfer, for which there exist all the conditions in the fins, washed by water from all sides.

Skin development in the sperm whale occurs mainly in the postembryonic period (involving the subepidermal layers), and its thickness in the adult animal, especially on the back, is 43 times greater than in the most developed embryo (Sokolov, 1963). In the finback whale the skin of the back is three times as thick as that of the embryo. The development of the epidermis and of the horny layer proceed mainly during embryogenesis (Sokolov, 1963). On this basis Sokolov concluded that most of the characters, especially the cellular structure of the epidermis peculiar to Cetacea, appear fairly early in embryos, which may indicate the substantial and phylogenetically ancient changes which have taken place in the structure of the skin cover, and the difference in the histogenesis of the skin of embryos of toothed (e.g. sperm) whales and baleen whales indicates considerable differences between them.

Thus, the skin cover of sperm whales is much stronger than that of many Cetacea both absolutely and relatively. The skin of the sperm whale is distinguished by bumpiness on the back and flanks, the absence of vibrissae at all stages of development, a considerably thicker dermis (relative to skin thickness) over all parts of the body than in other Cetacea, and the dense ligature of the collagen fibers. Its structure reflects adaptivity to a specific ecology and the fulfillment of a number of functions, many of which are probably still unknown to us.

THE SKELETON

A description of the skeleton of the sperm whale or of different parts of it can be found both in works of fiction (Melville, 1851) and in the scientific literature (Lacépède, 1804; Beneden, 1868—1879; Beneden and Gervais, 1880; Beddard, 1900; Turner, 1912; Howell, 1930; Slijper, 1936; Smirnov, 1936; Boschma, 1938; Zenkovich, 1952; Sleptsov, 1952; Tomilin, 1957, 1962; and others).

The most complete description was given by Flower (1867). A later work, dealing with the osteology of this whale and containing numerous careful measurements and illustrations without anatomical descriptions, was the article by Omura, Nishiwaki, Ishihara, and Kasuya (1962).

Much has been written about the teeth of the sperm whale. The most detailed description of the sperm whale's upper and lower jaw teeth was given by Boschma (1938) (see Chapter 6).

We have utilized data from the sources mentioned and also the results of work on the skeleton of a male sperm whale from antarctic waters, caught by the AKF "Slava" and preserved in the ZM AN SSSR. Several sections of skeleton and bones from the collections of the TINRO Museum were measured and described; lower jaws preserved in various Soviet museums were examined, as were several dozen fragments of skeletons obtained during the dressing of sperm whales at whale-processing plants in the North Pacific and in the Antarctic. Also used was osteological material (especially of the skull) obtained from more than 30 embryos of various age.

HEAD

Skull

The skull of the sperm whale (Figure 19) has been compared to a trough (Kleinenberg et al., 1964), a chariot (Melville, 1851; Beneden and Gervais, 1868—1880), and even "a pointed shoe with a high counter and a worn-down toecap" (Flower, 1867), owing to the cup-shaped recess which forms a gigantic, almost spherical cavity bounded posteriorly by a single, strongly developed occipital bone. The crest of the occipital adjoins the maxillaries, forming a remarkably strong vertical wall. At the sides the cavity is formed by the edges of the maxillaries, highly elevated in the form of a frontal-maxillary crest.

Flower (1867) correctly writes that in no other mammal does the skull differ so greatly from the usual structure. The widenings, elongations, flattenings, and twistings of the many cranial and facial bones, which occur to a certain degree in all Cetacea, are so pronounced in the sperm whale (at least in the adult) that it is difficult to homologize them. Whereas the skull of any other marine mammal has a distinct division into cranium viscerale and cranium cerebrale, in the sperm whale the cerebral part of the skull is relatively negligible and is concealed under the expanded trough-shaped bed of the cranium visceral. In general configuration the skull of the sperm whale resembles that of Mesoplodon and other beaked whales (Ziphiidae).

47   The maxillaries form a triangular rostrum, the shape of the triangle (and also the form and external appearance of the skull) depending on age and sex.

A characteristic feature of the skull is asymmetry in size, shape, and position of bones and openings. Such asymmetry is inherent in all toothed whales but is particularly pronounced in the sperm whale, in which there is complete reduction of several of the paired bones. For example, there is only one nasal bone. In none of the six skulls examined by Flower (1867) nor in the skull of a sperm whale from ZM AN SSSR, nor in 20 skulls of variously aged embryos were there even traces of a left nasal. The left bony nasal passage in the skull is well developed, the right one much less so.

The nasal apertures open at the bottom of the cup-shaped recess of the skull. The surface of the skull in front of the nasal apertures is relatively flat (slightly raised at the sides), formed by the premaxillaries, which take the form of long, narrow bands. The flat upper surface of the premaxillaries consists of very thin, strong but brittle lamellar bony tissue, while the internal structure of the bones is coarse and cellular "as in honeycombs" (Flower, 1867). Between the premaxillaries is the vomer.

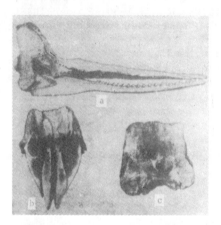

FIGURE 19. Skull of large male sperm whale:

a — lateral; b — anterodorsal; c — posterior.

On the lateral surface of the skull there is a small oval orbit, which passes posteriorly into a very small temporal notch lying between the squamosal bone posteriorly and the orbital process of the frontal bone dorsally. The greater part of the base of the skull is formed by the surfaces of the maxillaries, by the massive pterotic bones, and by the clearly visible vomer, which is situated entirely in front of the palatines. There is a conspicuous groove on the underside of the maxillaries. Flower (1867) regards this as a remnant of the dental groove of the maxillary teeth, but Boschma (1938) rejects this.

The ontogenetic development of the sperm whale skull is of interest, in that it does not proceed as in other mammals and most Cetacea, and in particular not as in the dolphin (Sleptsov, 1939). Sleptsov indicates irregular compression of the interparietal bone in the ontogeny of toothed whales.

On the basis of an examination of 20 skulls of variously aged embryos a preliminary conclusion can be drawn that in the sperm whale the inter-parietal bones are more or less distinctly expressed only at an early age — up to a body length of 30—40 cm (about three months of age). In some embryos measuring 50—60 cm (about four months) the interparietals fuse with the parietals without their symmetry of arrangement being disturbed 48 (indicated by Sleptsov), even without traces of sutures. The boundary of the interparietal bones is indiscernible in all embryos of an even earlier age. The frontals, which are gradually displaced aborally, press on the parietals, and by the end of pregnancy it is already difficult to discern them from the surface. The occipital bone, unlike that of other mammals, straightens out, and by the end of pregnancy it forms merely the posterior wall of the skull (in old males the wall is almost straight and vertical, see Figures 19 and 20). In the skull of an embryo about 20 cm long there is only a small, smoothed-down recess on the frontal part of the still well-expressed cranium and short maxillaries and premaxillaries. In the skull of an embryo 70—80 cm long the rostral recess is small in relation to the size of the skull itself, but is already distinctly expressed, with sharp borders formed by the widening crests of the maxillaries. As the embryo continues to grow, the recess becomes larger and larger (until it becomes cup-shaped), and the cerebral part of the skull correspondingly continues to decrease in size, the maxillaries are drawn out, and the bed formed by them is deepened (see Figure 20). The relative length of the rostrum increases in accordance with the age of the animal. Thus, in skulls of embryos about 20 cm long it constitutes about 43% of the condylobasal length, in embryos 80—90 cm long about 59%, in embryos of prenatal size up to 63%; in a 14-meter male measured by Omura et al. (1962) it was 69.9%, and in still larger animals measured by Flower (1867) and by us in the exhibition of the ZM AN SSSR it was 72.3—73% of the condylobasal length (Table 9).

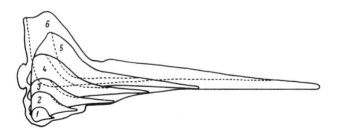

FIGURE 20. Changes in the shape of the sperm whale skull with age:

1 — embryo 20 cm long (female); 2 — same, 63 cm (female); 3 — same, 130 cm (male); 4 — same, 260 cm (female); 5 — same, 365 cm (male); 6 — adult male (length of skull 510 cm).

Asymmetry of the skull is observed in all toothed whales by the early embryonic stages (Sleptsov, 1939), but it is especially marked in the sperm whale. Thus, for example, according to our data, in the skull of an embryo

TABLE 9. Skull measurements in the sperm whale

Measurement	Tasmania (Flower, 1867) cm	%	Japan (Omura et al., 1962) cm	%	Antarctica (ZM AN SSSR) cm	%	Embryo 20 (female) mm	%	Embryo 87 (female) mm	%	Embryo 365 (male) mm	%
Condylobasal length	510.0	100.0	359.0	100.0	473.0	100.0	39.0	100.0	175.0	100.0	730.0	100.0
Length of rostrum	371.0	73.0	251.0	69.9	342.0	72.3	17.0	43.6	103.0	58.8	460.0	63.0
Width of rostrum:												
at its base	155.0	30.5	12.3	34.3	153.0	32.3	17.0	43.6	72.0	41.1	255.0	34.9
at middle length	119.5	23.5	83.0	23.1	115.0	22.6	10.0	25.6	37.0	21.1	173.0	237.4
Transverse width of bone at 3/4 of its length from tip of rostrum:												
right maxillary	58.4	11.5	—	—	67.0	14.1	5.0	12.8	23.0	13.1	88.0	12.1
left maxillary	61.0	12.0	—	—	69.5	14.6	5.0	12.8	23.0	13.1	99.0	13.6
right premaxillary	12.7	2.5	—	—	12.0	2.5	3.0	7.7	5.0	2.8	18.0	2.5
left premaxillary	15.2	3.0	—	—	20.0	4.2	3.0	7.7	5.0	2.8	20.0	2.7
Transverse width of bone at midlength:												
right maxillary	33.0	6.5	37.0	10.3	63.3	13.3	3.0	7.7	10.0	5.7	53.0	7.3
left maxillary	33.0	6.5	37.0	10.3	60.0	12.7	3.0	7.7	12.0	6.8	63.0	8.6
right premaxillary	22.9	4.5	—	—	10.0	2.1	3.0	7.7	6.0	3.4	21.0	2.9
left premaxillary	22.9	4.5	—	—	10.0	2.1	2.0	5.1	5.0	2.8	19.0	2.6
Shortest distance between posterior edges of maxillary apertures	—	—	8.9	24.8	128.0	27.0	9.0	23.1	52.0	29.7	235.0	32.2
Greatest width of nasal passage	—	—	33.0	9.2	45.0	9.5	—	—	17.0	9.7	43.0	5.8
Shortest distance between maxillary apertures	—	—	L. 37.0	10.3	52.0	10.9	—	—	16.0	9.1	—	—
	—	—	R. 25.0	6.96	32.0	6.7	—	—	13.0	7.4	43.0	58.0
Distance between anterior ends:												
of premaxillary (rostrum) and vomer	109.2	21.5	52.0	14.5	47.0	9.9	5.0	12.8	23.0	13.1	63.0	9.3
of premaxillary and maxillary	55.9	11.0	—	—	42.0	8.8	4.0	10.2	21.0	12.0	49.0	6.7
Height of occipital condyles	36.8	7.25	—	—	39.0	8.2	—	—	5.0	2.8	29.0	3.9

TABLE 9 (continued)

Measurement	Specimen from waters of Tasmania (Flower, 1867) cm	%	Specimen from waters of Japan (Omura et al., 1962) cm	%	Specimen from waters of Antarctica (ZM AN SSSR) cm	%	Embryos (length in cm) 20 (female) mm	%	87 (female) mm	%	365 (male) mm	%
Width of occipital aperture	20.3	4.0	18.0	5.01	20.0	4.2	—	—	16.0	9.1	72.0	9.8
Distance from upper edge of occipital aperture to occipital crest	88.9	17.5	—	—	94.0	19.6	13.0	33.3	32.0	18.3	153.0	20.9
Condylar width	59.7	11.7	51.0	14.2	59.0	12.5	9.0	23.1	41.0	23.4	158.0	21.6
Length of zygomatic bones	73.3	14.5	54.0	15.0	—	—	—	—	—	—	—	—
Diameter of orbits	—	—	L. 16.0 / R. 16.0	4.5 / 4.5	33.0 / 28.0	6.9 / 5.9	7.0	17.9	22.0	12.6	—	—
Depth of orbits	—	—	30.5	8.5	38.0	8.1	—	—	—	—	—	—
Length: of lower jaw	454.0	89.1	300.0	83.6	426.0	90.0	32.0	82.0	140.0	80.0	576.0	78.9
of branch of lower jaw	—	—	L. 301.0 / R. 305.0	83.8 / 84.9	443.0 / 450.0	93.5 / 95.1	—	—	—	—	—	—
of symphysis of lower jaw	—	—	L. 171.0 / R. 161.0	47.6 / 44.8	190.0 / 200.0	40.2 / 42.3	10.0	25.6	48.0	27.4	230.0	31.5
Distance between anterior end of lower jaw and posterior end of alveolar row	—	—	L. 185.0 / R. 189.0	51.5 / 50.4	175.0 / 177.0	36.9 / 37.4	15.0	38.4	71.0	40.6	320.0	43.8
Width of mandibular condyles	—	—	13.0	3.6	12.6	2.6	—	—	—	—	—	—
Greatest height of lower jaw with coronoid process	—	—	L. 55.0 / R. 56.0	15.3 / 15.6	58.5 / 58.6	12.4 / 12.2	8.0 / 8.0	20.5	31.0	17.7	118.0	16.2
Distance between mandibular condyles	—	—	148.0	41.2	189.0	37.8	22.0	56.4	83.0	47.4	365.0	50.0

about 20 cm long (condylobasal length 39 mm) it is quite clearly seen that the nasal bone is single and that the size of the premaxillaries and frontal bones is unequal. This indirectly indicates an asymmetrical skull structure already in the ancestors of toothed whales, particularly in those of sperm whale. Paleontological finds confirm the asymmetry of the skull of ancient toothed whales in the Eocene, Oligocene, and particularly in the Miocene (Valen, 1967). The many theories (Abel, Kükenthal, Lillie, etc.) regarding asymmetry in the skull structure of toothed whales were thoroughly examined by Sleptsov (1939), who regards the reduction of the olfactory nerves and displacement of the nasal bones and nasal apertures way back in the forerunners of toothed whales to be primary.

51

Sexual dimorphism in the development of the skull bones during embryogenesis is of interest. For example, in a male embryo 365 cm long the occipital bone formed a much more conspicuous crest than in a larger female embryo (376 cm).

The petrous temporal bone (os petrosum) is relatively small.

The bulla tympani of the sperm whale (Figure 21) has a more compact and rounded form than in baleen whales; it is smaller not only than that in baleen whales but is even smaller than in the relatively small Bagridae (Flower, 1867; our data). Its size, according to Tomilin (1962), is 56 mm, but according to our data 70 — 74 mm. The large relative and absolute dimensions of the tympanic bullae in sperm whale embryos (as in baleen whales), are striking. For example, in an embryo 73 cm long the tympanic bulla measured 27 mm, while in a prenatal embryo (365 cm) it had already attained the size of the tympanic bulla of an adult (72 mm); this is apparently because of the equal functional load on the organ of hearing in newborn and adult animals.

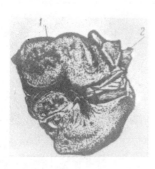

FIGURE 21. Bulla tympani of a sperm whale from antarctic waters:

1 — bulla; 2 — mastoid process.

The lower jaw (mandibula), which in large males is up to 5 m long (Flower, 1867), is V-shaped and shows an original structure (Figure 22) in that the symphysis of the right and left bones is very highly developed. Its relative size increases with age to 48—54% of the overall length (Table 9: Tomilin, 1957). The length of the symphysis is smaller in the embryo, but this also increases with age, reaching 32% of the length of the jaw in the prenatal embryos (Table 9); with the increase in absolute size of the lower jaw the index of the width between the condyles decreases from 78.7 to 34.8% of its length (Tomilin, 1957; our data).

In the cranial part each half of the lower jaw has a more or less regular round shape in cross section; in the middle part it is oval, and toward the caudal end it is gradually drawn out in height. The maxillary canal, which passes inside each branch of the jaw, is of irregular form close to the proximal end, and then gradually becomes rounded and drawn out in height, repeating in general the shape of the section of the jaw.

The bony tissue of the lower jaw is denser than that of the other large bones of the skeleton and is apparently the densest tissue in the skeleton

of any of the Cetacea. According to A. P. Astananin (1958), its increased
density and also its strength are due to the great mechanical load on the
jaw, particularly in the caudal part.

The literature contains many descriptions and illustrations of lower
jaws which to a greater or lesser degree are curved or even broken (see
Figure 125). Beale (1939), Thompson (1867), and Sleptsov (1952) believe
that the sperm whale receives jaw injuries during fights. In the opinion
of Murie (1865), a curvature of the lower jaw is the result of inflammation
52 of the periosteum during the growth period (periostosis). Beneden
(1868—1879) attributes curvature of the jaws to irregular occlusion.

In recent years in Soviet whale-processing plants scientific workers
have noted more than 15 curved and shortened (perhaps broken off) lower
jaws of sperm whales, mostly belonging to males. However, curvature of
the jaw is observed in females as well. For example, out of four sperm
whales with curved jaws described by Nasu (1958) one belonged to a female
10.9 m long. The possible existence of sperm whales with such jaws is
examined from the functional aspect in Chapter 6.

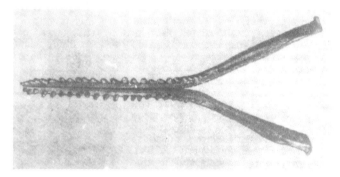

FIGURE 22. Lower jaw of male sperm whale (dorsal, ZM AN SSSR)

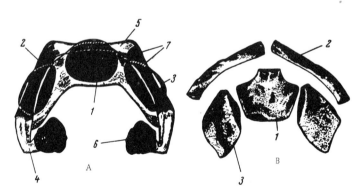

FIGURE 23. Hyoid bones of the sperm whale:

A — embryo of prenatal size (schematic, our data); B — adult male (Omura,
Nishiwaki, Ishihara, and Kasuya, 1962).
1 — body of hyoid bone — basihyoid; 2 — middle segment — stylohyoid;
3 — sternohyoid; 4 — proximal segment — tympanohyoid; 5 — keratohyoid;
6 — bulla tympani; 7 — centers of ossification (our designations).

On the dorsal side along the entire symphyseal part of each lower jaw and somewhat farther toward the condyles runs the groove of the dental row, the length of which reaches 275 cm (our measurements) or more. The dental groove is divided by transverse septa, which are much lower than the mandible surface, into small cavities (alveoli). The dental alveoli 53 are up to 16—20 cm long and up to 6—8 cm wide (Turner, 1903, Boschma, 1938). The dental rows do not correspond among themselves: in each half of the jaw the two anterior alveoli are at one level, while the subsequent teeth of the left side protrude forward and the seventh tooth on the left side corresponds to the sixth tooth on the right (Boschma, 1938). In the sperm whales from antarctic waters which we examined, either there was no symmetry at all in the arrangement of teeth on the right and left sides of the jaws or else symmetry was observed in a certain part of the dental row, but it was never complete. The shape, number, structure, and development of the lower and upper jaw teeth of sperm whales are described in Chapter 6.

The hyoid bones (os hyoideum) are large and consist of many parts (segments) (Figure 23). In their structure they in no way resemble the hyoid bones of land mammals and other Cetacea, including certain toothed whales, in particular the white whale (according to Kleinenberg et al., 1964), but they do resemble those of the pygmy sperm whale and the bottlenose whale Hyperoodon (Flower, 1867; Schulte and Smith, 1918).

The hyoid bones of the sperm whale consist of an unpaired, almost flat bone, which may be called the body of the hyoid (Flower calls it the lingual bone), which, according to Omura et al. (1962), measures 43 × 35 cm, and then pairs of elongate, almost cylindrical, slightly curved bones each 60—62 cm long and 11—12 cm thick (Flower, 1867; Omura et al., 1962), which by analogy with such bones in other toothed whales and land mammals can be called middle segments. The third pair of thickened bones, which are close to rhomboid and measure 45—52 × 27—32 cm (Flower, 1867; Omura et al., 1962), can be called (by analogy with such bones in white whale) the posterior cornua of the hyoid bone. Finally, the cartilaginous proximal segments and parts linking the middle segments (see Figure 23, A, 5), which never ossify and therefore were evidently not noted earlier in the sperm whale, are apparently homologous with the small cornua and the distal segment.

TRUNK

Vertebral column

The vertebral column of the sperm whale, consisting of 47—51 vertebrae (Table 10) as in other Cetacea, has four sections. The first, cervical, section constitutes 4.5%, the thoracic section 25%, the lumbar section 30%, and the caudal section 40.5% of the length of the vertebral column (Tomilin, 1957). There is no sacral section in sperm whales, nor in other Cetacea (Figure 24).

General descriptions of the vertebral column in the sperm whale and its basic characteristics can be found in various keys. Slijper (1936) establishes types of articulation of ribs and gives a schematic arrangement of the bones of the sperm whale truncal skeleton (Figure 25). Osteological descriptions of this whale in the work by Flower (1867) are more or less exhaustive. In cases where its formulations and descriptions are most exact, they are used with necessary abridgments.

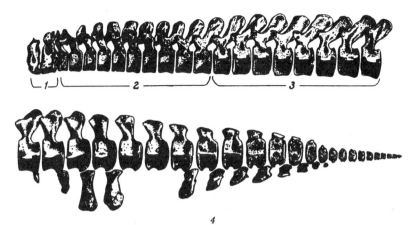

FIGURE 24. Vertebral column of the sperm whale:

1 — cervical section; 2 — thoracic section; 3 — lumbar section; 4 — caudal section (Flower, 1867).

FIGURE 25. Skeletal structure of the sperm whale (Slijper, 1936)

TABLE 10. Components of the vertebral column in the sperm whale

Section				Total	Reference and notes
cervical	pectoral	lumbar	caudal		
7	11	8	24	50	Flower (1867)
7	11	8	23	49	Flower (1867)
7	11	8	23	49	Flower (1867)
7	11	32		50	Beneden and Gervais (1880)
7	11	9	20	47	Slijper (1936)
7	11	8	25	51	Boschma (1938)
7	11	8	22*	48	Boschma (1938)
7	11	8	24	50	Omura et al. (1962)
7	11	8	24	50	Our material: ZM AN SSSR
7	11	8	21	47**	Embryo 23 cm long
7	11	8	21	47	Embryo 32 cm long
7	11	8	21	47	Embryo 54 cm long
7	11	8	21	47	Embryo 73 cm long
7	11	8	21	47	Embryo 135 cm long

* According to Boschma, the two vertebrae are fused.

** Quantitatively the vertebral column is fully formed.

By comparison with the bones of the vertebral column in baleen whales, those of the sperm whale are characterized by a coarse, rough surface and porous tissue. On their surface there are conspicuous convexities and excrescences, which develop at the sites of attachment of muscles.

54 Of interest is the waveform curvature of the entire vertebral column of the embryo in the early stages of development (determined by preparations and from X-ray photographs of embryos about 20, 30, 50 and 70 cm long without posthumous changes in the form of the body and vertebral column). It is reminiscent of the curvature of the vertebral column in 55 quadrupeds and also in the ancient zeuglodon (according to an illustration in Howell, 1930, p. 175). This curvature disappears in larger embryos and is absent in adult whales, in which there is only one sloping bend, which passes mainly into the thoracic section and enables the animal, while preserving a regular and streamlined form, to increase the volume of the thorax. In an initial approximation it can be said that a similar S-shaped curvature was retained in embryogenesis from the quadruped ancestors of whales and evidently took place at somewhat later stages of evolution already after loss of the hind limbs in the forerunners of Cetacea.

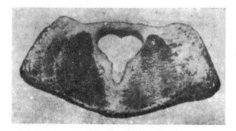

FIGURE 26. Atlas of cervical section of the vertebral column in the sperm whale (anterior, ZM AN SSSR)

The postcranial skeleton of the sperm whale most closely resembles that of the bottlenose whale (Flower, 1867). This similarity, manifested in the structure not only of the postcranial skeleton but also of the skull, can be caused on the one hand by identity of ecological factors and on the other by deep phylogenetic affinity.

Our own material and available data are still insufficient for categorical conclusions to be reached, but nonetheless it is of interest to note the difference in the number of vertebrae between sperm whales of the northern and southern hemispheres (in southern animals their number is greater). This feature clearly accords with the existence of similar differences in the length of the caudal parts in sperm whales of these stocks.

Cervical section. The cervical section in the sperm whale, as in most mammals, consists of seven vertebrae. In all sperm whale skeletons examined the first cervical vertebra is separate from the other six, which are fused. This combination of cervical vertebrae is observed only in the sperm whale (Flower, 1867; Tomilin, 1957). Sleptsov (1952) moreover indicates that the cervical vertebrae of the sperm whale may unite into two blocks consisting of different numbers of vertebrae.

The total length of the cervical section is relatively smaller than in other mammals (Flower, 1867). The atlas, examined anteriorly, has a more or less regular rectangular form (Figure 26) similar to that of the first cervical vertebra of other Cetacea. It is strongly compressed in the anterior-posterior direction, although to a lesser degree than the other cervical vertebrae. Its length is 10—15.2 cm and width 90—125 cm (Flower, 1867; Omura et al., 1962; our data). The anterior surface has wide, shallow notches up to 11 cm deep without sharp boundaries which are approximated at the base for the occipital condyles; this gives a certain mobility to the skull relative to the atlas.

The form of the vertebral foramen in the sperm whale specimen described by Flower resembles an isosceles triangle, one angle of which is directed downward, the upper side nearly straight, and the angles rounded. Judging from the photograph (Omura et al., 1962), the vertebral foramen
56 of the atlas has such a shape in a sperm whale from the waters of Japan. That of a sperm whale from the collections of ZM AN SSSR is not as wide and more T-shaped, with almost equal width and height (about 25 cm).

On the basis of the form of the vertebral canal of the atlas and of the entire cervical section, Gray distinguished a separate species of sperm whale from a single specimen caught off the shores of Australia. Beneden (1868—1879) was certainly right in considering that the form of the vertebral canal, like that of the atlas itself, changes considerably with age.

On the lower part of the posterior surface of the atlas there is a triangular protuberance (without an articular facet), which enters the corresponding recess in the second cervical vertebra. This protuberance on the atlas of sperm whales is shorter and more massive than that on the atlas of other Cetacea, in which the cervical vertebra is separated from the epistropheus Flower, 1867).

The six subsequent vertebrae of the cervical section are usually united not only by their bodies but also by spinous processes, and only at the base of the neural arches are they separated one from another (Figure 27), forming passages for the cerebrospinal cervical nerves. The union is so complete that even on a section made along the midline through the fused vertebrae the boundaries of the vertebrae are not visible, and the bone tissue of the entire block is uniform and cancellous (Beneden, 1868—1879). The boundaries of the individual vertebrae can be determined from the lateral surfaces: on the fused spinous processes of the cervical vertebrae there are shallow grooves and rows of openings for blood vessels. Fusion of the seventh cervical vertebra with the bodies of the other vertebrae is more complete in the sperm whale than in most other whales.

One of the notable features of the second to seventh cervical vertebrae of the sperm whale is their strong anterior-posterior compression, particularly in the fourth middle vertebrae (Flower, 1867; Omura et al., 1962). Moreover, the bodies of the united vertebrae are slightly squeezed downward. The vertebral foramen in this block of cervical vertebrae has a transversely elongate rhomboid shape with rounded corners. The odontoid process of the second cervical vertebra is a crestlike protuberance.

The neural arches attain their greatest width at the second and seventh vertebrae. As in most other Cetacea, in the sperm whale there are no facets for attachment of the first rib, but on the last cervical vertebra there are two rough crests, one of which is united with the first rib. Transverse processes are well developed on this vertebra. The posterior articulated surface of the last cervical vertebra is strongly concave and articulates with the convex articulation surface of the first thoracic vertebra. However, no true mobile articulation is formed here either, since with the central part of its body the seventh cervical vertebra grows together (ankylosis) with the central part of the body of the first thoracic vertebra (in all specimens described).

FIGURE 27. Second to seventh vertebrae of the cervical section of the vertebral column in the sperm whale (lateral, ZM AN SSSR)

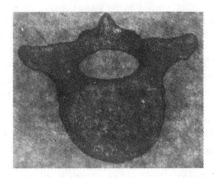

FIGURE 28. Vertebra in thoracic section of vertebral column in the sperm whale (anterior, 'ZM AN SSSR)

57   The shortening (and strengthening) of the cervical section, noted as a secondary phenomenon in all Cetacea, may be elicited by the need for a streamlined form, but the main point lies in the strong and little-mobile connection between head and trunk. This strengthening of the entire anterior section of the body is designed for the attachment of the strong body muscles, which effect intensive movement of the caudal peduncle toward the occipital region of the skull. Having a mobile neck, the whale beats not only with its tail but also, as it were, with its head (Sokolov, in litt.). The example of the sperm whale tends to confirm the reverse correlation between size of head and length of neck: the heavier and larger the head, the shorter and less mobile the neck.

Thoracic section of the vertebral column. This section of the truncal skeleton usually consists of 11 vertebrae, 11 pairs of ribs, and the sternum, which together form the thorax.

Thoracic vertebrae (Figure 28). Of the 11 thoracic vertebrae, 10 are distinctly united by lateral processes with 10 ribs. The eleventh is very similar in shape to the lumbar vertebra, but it belongs to the thoracic section, inasmuch as it articulates with the last pair of ribs.

The length of the vertebrae in the thoracic section gradually increases (Figure 29); there is also an increase in the height of the spinous processes and their inclination backward; they are narrowed at the base. The spinous process of the first thoracic vertebra is the smallest and often has an irregular form. The spinous processes of the sperm whale vertebral column are distinguished from those of many other toothed whales in that due to their strong backward inclination with considerable length, each process passes beyond the boundary of the posterior surface of the body of its vertebra, while a considerable part of the process (usually the greater part) overhangs the following vertebra.

The articular processes for articulation with ribs from the 1st to the 10th vertebrae inclusive gradually decrease in size, forming a small thickening on the last, 11th vertebra of the thoracic section. On the lateral surfaces of the bodies of the thoracic vertebrae there are articular facets for the capitula of the ribs. They gradually become more and more distinct, and on the 9th vertebra the process is already well marked, having a facet for the capitulum of the 9th rib. On the 10th vertebra the process is already long and massive, with a large, concave facet for the 10th rib. The 11th vertebra has an even longer transverse process. This vertebra could be referred to the lumbar section if at its end there were not a small, rough articular facet for union with the 11th rib. The vertebral canal of the first five or six vertebrae (in cross section) is first triangular, then oval (see Figure 28).

Certain differences are observed in the structure of the thoracic vertebrae in the skeleton of different sperm whales, particularly in the degree of development of the transverse processes. For example, in the 9th
58 thoracic vertebra of a skeleton from Yorkshire (Flower, 1867) the lower transverse process was so well developed that it met the upper process and formed a complete ring on both sides of the vertebra. This indicates the presence of considerable individual and age-determined variation in the structure of the vertebral column.

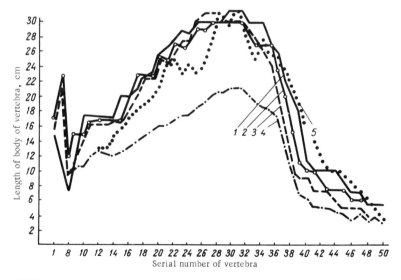

FIGURE 29. Length changes in bodies of vertebrae in various sections of the vertebral column of five sperm whales:

1, 2, 3 — after Flower (1867); 4 — after Omura, Nishiwaki, Ishihara, and Kasuya (1962); 5 — from our measurements of a skeleton from ZM AN SSSR.

57

In the thoracic section of the sperm whale's vertebral column the upper transverse processes gradually decrease in size and disappear on the 11th vertebra, but in place of it from the facet on the body of the 10th thoracic vertebra there develops the main transverse process, which attains considerable development on the lumbar vertebrae (see Figure 24).

Ribs. Eleven pairs of ribs articulate with the vertebrae of the thoracic section (according to Sleptsov, 1952, there are ten pairs of ribs). The ribs of the sperm whale are long (except the 11th); they are formed from dense bony tissue, yet are extremely brittle and relatively light. Flower (1867) gives weight data on the ribs of the bowhead whale (B a l a e n a m y s t i c e t u s) and the sperm whale, which show that the 11 pairs of ribs of even a somewhat larger sperm whale weighed half or less than half as much as the 12 pairs of ribs of the bowhead whale. The first rib is the shortest (not counting the 11th) but more massive and wider. Moreover, it is very steeply curved and has no distinctly expressed capitulum, which distinguishes it from the ribs of other toothed whales. The second rib resembles the first in shape but is much longer and the curve is gentler. The third and several subsequent ribs are similar to one another.

Each of these ribs articulates by tubercles with the transverse process of the corresponding thoracic vertebra, and by the capitulum with the facet on the posterior edge of the body of the preceding vertebra. The longest are the 3rd—5th pairs of ribs, whose curved length reaches 223 cm in the skeleton of a sperm whale from the waters of Japan, and 240 cm, according to our measurements, in one from the Antarctic. The 10th rib is much smaller than the preceding ribs. The 11th, 28—34 cm, as mentioned above, is underdeveloped and nearly straight.

It is believed (Slijper, 1936; Sleptsov, 1952; Tomilin, 1957; and others) that the sperm whale has only three pairs of true sternal ribs. However, Flower (1867) noted the presence of four pairs of such ribs, and according to Japanese investigators (Omura et al., 1962), there are five pairs. In our material (Antarctica and the North Pacific) different numbers of such ribs were observed. The number of sternal ribs in the sperm whale is thus apparently a matter of considerable individual variation. However, it is to be noted that there are fewer in the sperm whale than in other cetaceans. This feature is usually regarded (Sleptsov, 1952, and others) as proof of the high degree of mobility of the thorax.

Ewell (after Flower, 1867) noted that the ribs of the left side are larger than those of the right side. Flower, in weighing the ribs, also observed that the left ribs were much heavier. However, he indicated considerable individual variations in the length of the corresponding ribs. Judging from the measurements of Omura et al. (1962), the opposite conclusion could be reached: nearly all the right ribs are longer than the left ones. All in all, it is probably correct to conclude that there is asymmetry in the structure of this part of the thorax.

The sternum is large and massive but markedly shortened; in shape it resembles a triangle with the apex directed downward (Figure 30), but there are individual differences. The sperm whale sternum can consist of differ- ent numbers of segments — from one to six (Flower, 1867; Turner, 1912; Boschma, 1938; Omura, et al., 1962), separate or united to varying degrees; this is also connected with individual variation, but perhaps also with age.

The width of the sternum along the anterior edge is 80—115 cm and the
length about 1 m (Flower, 1867; Omura et al., 1962). The total length
of the sternum equals or very slightly exceeds the width. The upper
60 lateral corners form protuberances with rough oval surfaces for articulation with the first pair of ribs. Along the sides of the sternum there
are articulation surfaces for union with the cartilage of the sternal ribs.

(59)

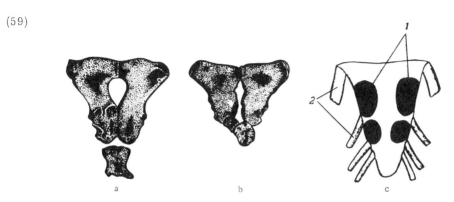

FIGURE 30. Sterna of sperm whales:

a, b — adults (Flower, 1867; Omura, Nishiwaki, Ishihara, and Kasuya, 1962);
c — prenatal embryo (our material): 1 — centers of ossification; 2 — ribs.

In general structure the sternum of sperm whales is reminiscent of
that of the bottlenose whale (Hyperoodon) and the beaked whale
(Ziphius).

In embryogenesis ossification of the sternum, which is almost regularly
triangular (according to our material, Figure 30), begins at the four centers
situated between the points of attachment of the first and second and third
and fourth pairs of sternal ribs. The centers of ossification, particularly
the first two, are usually well expressed in embryos about 70 cm long.

FIGURE 31. Separate chevron bones of the sperm whale vertebral column (ZM AN SSSR)

59

The thoracic section of the sperm whale skeleton thus shows a number of distinctive features as compared with that of other Cetacea, in particular the smaller number of comparatively weak sternal ribs and the shortened sternum, which leads to the formation of an extremely short and light thorax. This shortening and general weakening of the thorax in conjunction with its considerable mobility can be explained by the great change in volume of the thoracic cavity as a result of compression of the lungs by hydrostatic pressure at great depths (Tomilin, 1951; Kleinenberg, 1956; Yablokov, 1961; see also Chapter 14).

Lumbar section of vertebral column. This consists of eight vertebrae, which resemble each other in form and size (see Figure 24). The section is characterized by the highest spinous and largest transverse processes (the size of the latter increases slightly toward the fifth vertebra and then gradually decreases). The transverse processes are flat, somewhat inclined downward, and with rounded ends. The processes, which arise from the neural arches, are well developed, directed forward and upward, and half-encompassing the spinous process of the preceding vertebra.

Caudal section of vertebral column. In the skeletons examined this consists of 21—25 vertebrae (see Table 10). The boundary between the lumbar and caudal sections is determined by the appearance of chevron (hemal) bones and by the presence of articulation areas on the lower surface of the vertebrae, with which they are articulated. The first 11—14 vertebrae of the section have such bones at their base. Within this large section the shape and size of the vertebrae change sharply. On the lower surface of the first caudal vertebra two articular facets for the chevron bone are clearly seen. The body of the first caudal vertebra is somewhat larger than that of the last lumbar vertebra. The first vertebrae of the caudal section are the largest in the vertebral column of the sperm whale (see Figures 24 and 29). Up to the fifth vertebra there is a continuous increase in the length of the body of the vertebrae. The body of the fifth vertebra is the largest, and then there is a gradual decrease in the size of the vertebrae from the fifth to the last. From the first caudal vertebra there begins a gradual decrease in height of the spinous processes, and at the 14th or 15th vertebra the spinous processes disappear. Even more abrupt is the shortening of the transverse process, which disappears completely with the ninth or tenth caudal vertebra.

The number of chevron bones varies, according to available data, from 11 to 14 (Flower, 1867; Slijper, 1936; Omura et al., 1962). In a skeleton from ZM AN SSSR the chevron bones were not fully represented, there being only eight (Figure 31). The first chevron bones are small, columnar bones (Flower, 1867). The subsequent bones are archlike; the third and fourth are the largest, after which the bones gradually decrease in size (Figure 24).

LIMBS

The scapula in the sperm whale is very high, the height exceeding the width much more than in other Cetacea (Figure 32) (Flower, 1867). The maximum height of the scapula is 72—100 cm, at a width of 58—86 cm. The acromion is large and wide, attaining a length of 40 cm. The coracoid process, which rises directly above the articular notch, is narrow, slightly

FIGURE 32. Skeleton of forelimb in the sperm whale (male 11.9 m long, North Pacific)

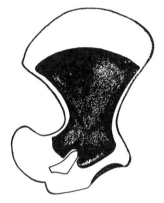

FIGURE 33. Scapula of prenatal sperm whale embryo (male from the North Pacific), X-ray photograph: dark area — bone, light area — cartilage.

(63) TABLE 11. Number of phalanges in digits of the sperm whale

Number of phalanges in the digits					Reference and notes
I	II	III	IV	V	
1	5	5	4	3	Flower (1867)
1	5	5	4	3	Beddard (1900)
1	5	5	4	3	Omura et al. (1962)
2	6	5	4	2 }	Data of A. V. Yablokov
1	6	6	5	3 }	(northwestern Pacific)
1	5	4	4	3*)	
1	5	5	4	2 }	Our data (northeastern Pacific)
0	5	5	4	2 }	

* Prenatal embryo.

61

wider at the end, and varies greatly in length (from 17 to 30 cm). The socket is large (about 20 cm), oval or ovoid, with protruding margins. Ossification proceeds by a single bony formation (Figure 33; see Figure 35).

Humerus and antibrachium. The bony elements of the limb proper in the sperm whale, as in other toothed whales, grow together into a single strong formation. The only true functional joint (and accordingly the only mobility) is preserved between the scapula and the humerus.

According to available material, considerable differences are observed in the structure of the bones of the humerus and antebrachium, mainly in the degree of their concrescence. In skeletons described by Flower (1867), in photographs presented by Omura et al. (1962), and in our material (see Figure 32) three bones, constituting part of the forelimbs, are united by means of articular surfaces. In a skeleton from the collection of ZM AN SSSR the humerus is concrescent with the ulna and radius, while a scarcely discernible boundary is preserved as a groove at the point of their former union. The ulna and radius have also grown together in the proximal part, without a noticeable boundary (Figure 34). This concrescence was noted earlier by van Deinse (1916) and later by Boschma (1938) in one or two specimens which he examined. This may also be an individual peculiarity, since there is no special reason for assuming that these animals were older than the other animals described; it is more likely that the growing together of the ulna and radius is due to age-dependent changes.

The large capitulum humeri is separated from the body of the bone by a 62 neck. The distinguishing feature of this bone in the sperm whale is a tubercle which is directed distally from the middle of the bone and is evidently a greatly changed analogue of the crest of the large tubercle, with deltoid tuberosity, of the humerus of ungulates. A similar formation, but incomparably more weakly expressed, is present only on the humerus of the bottlenose whale. In the humeral bones articulating with the ulna and radius of sperm whales there are two almost equal rough, irregularly shaped facets. The humerus is 40—57 cm long (according to eight measurements by various authors and our measurements in large males).

The ulna is lighter, thinner, and in general somewhat shorter (26—35 cm) than the radius (30—39 cm). Both bones widen at the distal and proximal ends. From the proximal end of the ulna departs a well-developed olecranon.

The hand is strong, short, and wide (see Figure 32). Flower (1867) notes that the carpal bones flare out strongly to the sides and create the impression that they lie in one row. Their total number is five or six (Flower, 1867; Omura et al., 1962; our material); apart from one outermost bone, which as it were protrudes outside the general contour of the hand, all these bones have an almost identical shape and size, which virtually excludes their homologization with the analogous bones in other mammals. In the opinion of Flower (1867), the sperm whale wrist has the simplest type of structure among the Cetacea. It seems, however, that such a conclusion was premature. As has been shown (Yablokov, 1959; Kleinenberg et al., 1964), the white whale is characterized by a large number of variants in wrist structure from 63 extremely simple (even simpler than in the sperm whale, according to the present description) to differentiated. Further detailed investigations will evidently show the presence of individual differences in the wrist and hand structure of sperm whales. They promise, in particular, to establish to which family particular animals belong and intragroup differentiation.

The hand of the sperm whale has five digits; these are set very wide apart, this explaining the great overall width of the hand. The first digit is the shortest and the second the longest; the third, fourth, and fifth are progressively shorter. The phalanges are elongate; those of them in the middle are somewhat narrower than those at the ends. This feature is more characteristic for the proximal phalanges. It is difficult to determine exactly the total number of phalanges since as a rule they are partly lost in preparations (Table 11).

The ontogeny of the forelimb skeleton is seen in Figure 35 from X-ray photographs. In embryos about 40 cm long, two metacarpal bone nuclei and the bone nucleus of one phalanx of the second digit appear. In embryos about 70 cm long, ossification proceeds in the four metacarpal bones, and three digits (II, III, IV) have two bone nuclei. There are as yet no bony elements in the wrist of embryos of this size. In embryos about 3 m long, all the metacarpal bones have become ossified, and in the phalanges of four digits the wrist bones begin to ossify. Figure 35:3 shows the additional foci of ossification in the wrist bones which form around the main nucleus, as described by Flower in 1867.

Pelvic bones. The sperm whale, as other Cetacea, has no true pelvic girdle; all that have remained of it are relatively small pelvic bones that are not connected with the vertebral column. In most cases these are solitary, elongate bones situated horizontally, almost parallel to the vertebral column opposite the first caudal vertebra. In the TINRO collections pelvic bones were examined from six male and female sperm whales (Figure 36). Their length varies, reaching 42 cm according to our material, and the width up to 8.5 cm.

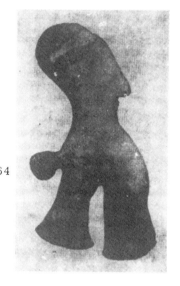

64

FIGURE 34. Humerus and antibrachium of the sperm whale (ZM AN SSSR)

Despite the large individual variation, noted already by Flower (1867), these formations are relatively more massive and rougher than their counterparts in baleen whales, with a large number of small and large, variously shaped but mainly irregular protuberances. The bones of males are almost twice as large as those of females, which are smoother and have fewer protuberances and a more regular shape than those of males. In two males (V. M. Latyshev's collections) from the North Pacific, on each side of the body there were two more bones left over from the pelvis. The second bones are small (up to 8 cm long), close to ovoid or round, very porous, set perpendicular to the main bone. According to all the characters these bones are the remains of femurs. Such was also the opinion of A. V. Yablokov (1966), whose 1959 collections (Northern Kuriles) included one male with an additional bony element in the pelvic bones. Yablokov (1963a) examined the functional value of these formations and concluded that one of the names used for the remains of the pelvis in the sperm whale — "rudiment of pelvic bones" — is inexact and that another name — "rudiment of the hind limbs" — is incorrect. In water the role of

65

supporting the body above the substrate is lost, and the function of the pelvic bones, which is connected with the urogenital system, becomes more important. In the process of evolution the pelvic bones became modified in accordance with the change in functions, and their present-day functions are also vitally important for the organism (for mating, birth of both the relatively and absolutely very large young suckling).

(64)

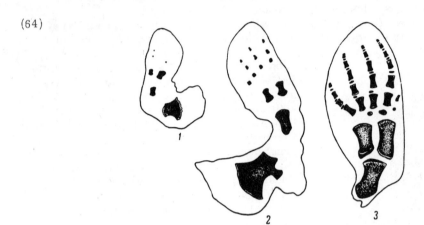

FIGURE 35. Development of ossification of the forelimb in sperm whale embryos (North Pacific, 1965—1966; from X-ray photographs):

1 — male, 40 cm long; 2 — male, 70 cm long; 3 — female of prenatal size.

(64)

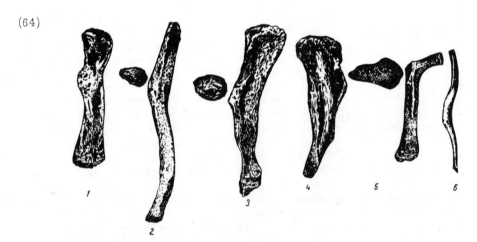

FIGURE 36. Pelvic bones of sexually mature sperm whales (North Pacific):

1, 2, 3, 4 — males; 5, 6 — females.

It is known that in the ancient toothed whales from the Eocene the hind limbs had already completely disappeared (Kellogg, 1928). On the other hand, the hind limbs in whales are always laid down at the early stages of embryonic development. All this indicates that reduction of the hind limbs took place way back in their phylogeny. Of interest is an analysis of the data accumulated on the manifestation of atavism, expressed in the formation of modified hind limbs, since there are very few paleontological data from which to judge the organizational features of the remote transitional forms of Cetacea (survey carried out by Valen, 1967).

The first description of atavistic hind limbs of baleen whales (one femur and a femur with tibia) were given in the late 1880s by Flower, Struther, Eschricht, and Reinhardt and Beneden et al. (Sleptsov, 1939). The first description of atavistic hind limbs in toothed whales, in particular in the sperm whale, was given by Abel (1907).

(66)

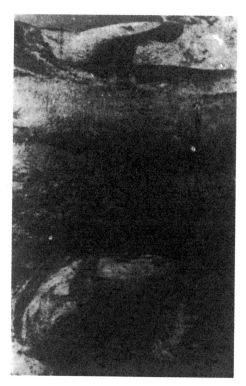

FIGURE 37. Atavistic hind limbs in the sperm whale
(North Pacific)

Ogawa and Kamiya (1957) describe the hind limbs of a female sperm 10.6 m long, caught in November 1956 off Japan. The limbs were set deep in the musculature, and only bulges with a base diameter of up to 15 cm and a height of 5.3 and 6.6 cm protruded onto the surface. The skeleton of each limb consisted of two elements, evidently corresponding to femur and tibia.

In 1958 we examined a male sperm 11.6 m long caught in the Bering Sea, with unusual excrescences in the pelvic region and along the sides of the genital fold (Figure 37) with a total length (height) of 28 and 34 cm, pigmented like the rest of the body. The distal section of the left excrescence had the appearance of the rounded blade of a propeller, while the right one looked like a fin with finger-shaped processes. The bones were enclosed in dense connective tissue. Judging from an X-ray photograph (Figure 38) of the skeleton of the excrescences in this specimen, the proximal section of the excrescences corresponds to the femur, and the middle section to the tibia and the fibula. The distal section corresponds to the step of the hind limb, and the elements composing it are probably phalanges of the digits. Accord-ing to the number of phalanges visible in the X-ray photograph, these are the 66 fifth and fourth digits. The skeleton of these limbs is distinguished from the typical structure of the skeleton of the pentadactyl limb of mammals by the absence of tarsal elements. It may be, however, that they were simply not found due to their small size, weak ossification, and the abundance of connec-tive tissue (Zemskii and Berzin, 1961).

In 1961 and 1962 V. I. Borisov discovered examples of atavistic hind limbs in two sperm whales caught off the Kurile Islands.

T. Nemoto (1963) mentions two more finds of rudimentary hind limbs in sexually mature male sperm whales from the Bering Sea and Aleutian waters of the North Pacific, caught by Japanese whalers.

(67)

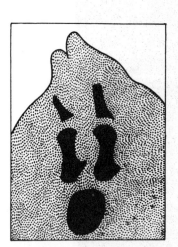 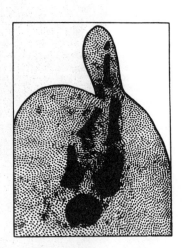

FIGURE 38. X-ray photograph of atavistic hind limbs of a sperm whale from the North Pacific (Zemskii and Berzin, 1961)

There is one known case of a catch in the Gulf of Alaska area by Soviet whalers in 1964; this was a sperm whale with rudiments not covered with skin, i.e., similar to those described by Andrews (1921). Unfortunately, no detailed description and no illustrations are available.

According to Nemoto (1963), the proportion of sperm whales with such formations is 0.02%, i.e., they occur in one sperm in five thousand. He considers that this percentage might be higher if the animals caught were more thoroughly examined.

Thus, according to available material, each whale has one pair of modified pelvic bones, and in a large proportion of specimens there is in addition a small bone homologous with the femur. It may be that it is present in all (or nearly all) sperm whales but is never found because it is situated deep in the cartilaginous and connective tissue. Whales with one or two atavistic bones of the tibia are found in ever-decreasing numbers, and finally, there are isolated cases of animals with a fairly well-developed skeleton of the limbs protruding along the flanks in the inguinal region.

A. V. Yablokov (1966), who examined the bones of the pelvic girdle, considers it possible to distinguish several types of structure of the sperm whale pelvic girdle; these are shown in Figure 39. He writes that finds of such diverse types of limbs in the sperm whale "are obvious proof that the process of evolution of this organ is far from complete and that, figuratively speaking, we are observing only a certain moment in this process. These finds indicate that in the mobilization reserve of variability of sperm whales, in its evolutionary specific "memory" possibilities of development have been preserved along a path different from the present paths. Under particular conditions these paths of development, characteristic for the distant forerunners of the forms and apparently rejected long ago in the course of adaptive evolution, can again be realized" (p. 279).

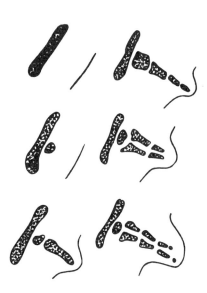

FIGURE 39. Certain structural variants of elements of the pelvic girdle ("rudiments of hind limbs") after various authors (A. V. Yablokov, 1966)

68

Hind limbs have not been found in sperm whales examined from the northern hemisphere, although the number of antarctic animals examined was no smaller. It is noteworthy that the frequency of occurrence of these limbs in sperm whales (in one in 5,000—10,000 animals) closely matches the frequency of manifestation of many mutations (Lobashov, 1967), which suggests genetic determination of the given character.

In such a case analysis of the incidence of sperm whales with this character may prove to be an additional argument revealing the intragroup and intergroup relationships between sperm whales of different herds or populations (just as cleavage of the fifth or fourth digit on the forelimb of white whales characterizes the genetic unity of the northern and Far Eastern populations of this species).

The sperm whale skeleton, especially the cranial skeleton, has a quite specific structure characterized by the strongly expanded trough-shaped bed of the facial part, the curved, elongate, and widened bones of which, together with the single, strongly developed occipital bone, form an almost spherical cavity.

The main distinguishing features of the postcranial skeleton of the sperm whale are the complete fusion of six (second to seventh) cervical vertebrae, which are strongly flattened, and the firm union of the bodies of the seventh cervical and first thoracic vertebrae, which ensures a considerable decrease in mobility and strengthening of the cervical section. The thoracic section of the sperm whale skeleton, which is distinguished by high mobility and a lightened thorax, indicates good adaptation to changed hydrostatic pressure at great depths.

While it may be considered that the structure of the sperm whale skeleton has been better studied than that of most other systems of organs, this knowledge is now already insufficient; what is required is a comparative analysis of as much material as possible, both from a single and from several different regions for a study of the variability of the skeletal elements. This would contribute to both study of the systematics of the species and understanding of functional morphology.

Chapter 5

MUSCULATURE*

The literature gives no descriptions of the muscular system of the
sperm whale, nor of that of other large Cetacea.   However, the muscular
structure of large whales, particularly that of the sperm whale and small
cetaceans, which has been described in several works, shows much in
common (more than the structure of other organs).   The musculature of
the pygmy sperm whale is well described in the work by Schulte and Smith
(1918) and that of the dolphin and narwhal (M o n o d o n m o n o c e r o s) in
the works by Howell (1927, 1930a).   In writing this chapter we also drew
on the investigations of Druzhinin (1924) and Narkhov (1937).

We used fresh material and large embryos (from 1.5 m long to prenatal
embryos) fixed in formalin.   The main characteristics of the muscles were
examined in detail in adults during their processing at the whaling base
"Dal'nii Vostok."

69 THE VERTEBRAL COLUMN

M. **splenius** begins with a strong, triangular, anteriorly widened sheet
at the spinous-transverse fascia in the limits of the first nine or ten
thoracic vertebrae (Figures 40: 2 and 42: 8).   It terminates on the crest
of the occipital bone and the wing of the atlas, bending around the atlanto-
occipital joint.

M. **longissimus dorsi** begins with separate tendon bundles on the
spinous processes of the caudal, the lumbar, and the last thoracic vertebrae
(Figure 40: 4).   The lateral teeth of the bundles terminate on the transverse-
costal processes of the lumbar vertebrae.   On the outer surface of the
vertebral ends of the ribs in the region of the lumbar-caudal section the
muscle is strongly developed; in the cranial direction the mass of the
muscle is diminished.

In the region of the caudal peduncle from m. longissimus dorsi six
tendinous strands depart toward m. spinalis dorsi.   In this section
m. longissimus dorsi acquires a conical form, circular in cross section,
and, not reaching the caudal fluke, passes caudally into the tendon.   The
latter divides and joins with another, earlier formed tendon of this muscle.

* This chapter was written jointly with the Director of the Department of Anatomy at the Agricultural
  Institute of the Maritime Territory, Candidate of Biological Sciences V. M. Malyshev.

In the thoracic section m. longissimus dorsi is forced back from the spinous processes of m. spinalis dorsi, to which it is tightly connected. It participates in bending the body and together with m. iliocostalis raises the caudal peduncle.

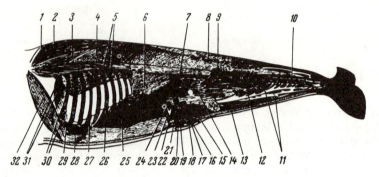

FIGURE 40. Trunk musculature of the sperm whale:

1 — occipital crest; 2 — m. splenius; 3 — m. longissimus; 4 — m. longissimus dorsi; 5 — m. iliocostalis; 6 — m. lumbocostalis; 7 — bundle of m. psoas major; 8 — m. spinalis dorsi; 9 — tendinous end of m. rectus abdominis; 10 — caudal vertebrae; 11 — tendons of m. psoas major; 12 — lateral elevator of tail; 13 — long depressor muscle of tail; 14 — belly of m. psoas major; 15 — mammary gland; 16 — muscular bundle of constrictor of vulva to mammary gland; 17 — anal-genital slit; 18 — external aperture of nipple of mammary gland; 19 — clitoris; 20 — pelvic bones; 21 — sphincter vaginae; 22 — urethra; 23 — vagina; 24 — rectum; 25 — m. transversus abdominis; 26 — m. intercostalis internus; 27 — m. intercostalis externus; 28 — beginning of m. rectus abdominis; 29 — m. rectus thoracis; 30 — m. serratus ventralis; 31 — m. scalenus; 32 — sterno-cephalic muscle.

M. longissimus is arranged in a triangle formed by m. splenius above, m. iliocostalis below, and m. longissimus dorsi posteriorly, the latter covering its caudal section externally. It begins at the mamillary processes of the first four or five thoracic vertebrae and terminates at the temporal and occipital bones (Figures 40: 3 and 42: 9).

70   M. iliocostalis is a paired longitudinal muscle in the form of a long muscular band extending from the temporal bone to the caudal third of the caudal peduncle (Figures 40:5 and 42:9). In the region of the head it begins as a large fleshy tooth and is more developed.

The upper margin of this muscle fuses with m. longissimus in the region of the head. In the thoracic section the muscle is distributed in the form of fleshy teeth along the vertebral column on the surface of the vertebral ends of the ribs, laterally adjoining the lower margin of m. longissimus dorsi. In the thoracic section m. iliocostalis lies along the free ends of the transverse-costal processes, and in the region of the caudal peduncle it passes onto the dorsal surface of the vertebrae. It participates in raising the tail and, in the case of a unilateral contraction, in raising the tail and at the same time moving it to the side.

M. spinalis dorsi is set mediodorsally with respect to m. longissimus dorsi, passing along the vertebral column as far as the caudal fluke (Figure 40: 8). Its bundles begin at the mamillary processes of the

vertebrae, pass upward and forward, and beyond the third or fourth
segment are attached to the lateral surface of the spinous processes.
The outer portion of the cranial end of the muscle (in the region of the
first 5–10 thoracic segments) is connected with m. longissimus dorsi,
while its inner portion is concrescent with m. splenius. The muscle
is particularly strongly developed in the section between the tenth thoracic
vertebra and the beginning of the caudal peduncle; here its outer margin
is closely connected with m. longissimus dorsi and does not divide.
Retreating some way from the region indicated m. spinalis dorsi forms
a round, muscular-tendinous band, rather closely connected with the tendinous band lying on the other side. By spinous processes this muscle is
divided into two symmetrical right and left portions. From the dorsal
margin of m. longissimus to the outer surface of this band six or seven
relatively strong tendons are directed dorsocaudally and strengthen
m. spinalis dorsi. Thus, m. spinalis dorsi and m. longissimus dorsi
are synergists; they participate in straightening the vertebral column as
a whole and in raising the caudal peduncle.

The tendons of the dorsal muscles of the vertebral column (m. longissimus dorsi and m. spinalis dorsi) widen and branch out in the caudal
fluke into a large number of tendon bundles that extend to the caudal vertebrae, and they are inserted mainly along their margins. Some of the tendon
bundles, which lie more superficially, form wide, thin, tendinous sheets that
diverge fanwise and enter the deep layers of the skin, becoming intertwined
in its powerful layer of connective tissue.

M. m. interspinales lie between the spinous processes of the vertabrae.
They occur in all sections of the vertebral column. Their function consists
in bringing the upper ends of the spinous processes close together, which
permits straightening of the vertebral column as a whole and elevation of
the caudal peduncle.

M. m. intertransversarii are situated between the transverse and
transverse-costal processes of the vertebrae. They are well developed.
These short muscles indicated are present also on all vertebrae of the
caudal peduncle. They attain their highest degree of development in the
anterior section of the fluke.

71   In the case of bilateral contraction they fix the vertebrae, while upon
unilateral contraction they participate in the execution of turns.

M. iliocostalis lumborum seu m. Hypaxialis is the largest, strongest,
and most complex muscle in the posterior half of the body, filling its lower
lateral part. It begins with fleshy bundles at the vertebral ends of the tenth
to eleventh ribs and at the body of the last two thoracic and transverse-
costal processes of the lumbar vertebrae. The fully formed flagellate,
thick, laterally compressed belly of the muscle medially adjoins the belly
of the corresponding muscle on the other side of the body. The caudal-
iliolumbar muscle, gradually narrowing, passes into a thick tendon, which
follows along the lower lateral surface of the caudal peduncle and, passing
posteriorly onto the ventral surface of the fluke, becomes gradually thinner.
From the ventral margin of this muscle depart a large number of tendon
bundles. Some of the bundles fuse, forming the above-described thick
tendon extending into the fluke. The other bundles, situated more superficially, are dorsocaudally directed and are attached either to the fascia
covering this muscle or else to the last caudal vertebra. In addition, two
or three thin tendons unite with the tendon of the lower-lying muscle,
which originates at the pelvic bone.

The dorsal-iliolumbar muscle borders on m. longissimus dorsi and is covered here by the iliocostal muscles, and in the caudal section also by m. ischiococcygous, the small, flat belly of which passes into the wide, ribbonlike tendon, which terminates fanlike at the last caudal vertebra.

At the level of the sixth to seventh lumbar vertebra the belly of the iliolumbar muscle divides in its lower half into a superficial and a deep part. The superficial part of m. psoas major is a thinner muscle layer. It originates on the ventral surface of the transverse-costal processes of the first seven lumbar vertebrae and, gradually narrowing, passes into the thick main tendon, to which the tendons from the deep part of the muscle are also united.

From the ventral margin of the superficial portion of m. psoas major, at about the level of the tenth lumbar segment, a large number of thick tendon bundles depart which at the level of the 20th–21st lumbar-caudal segment unite with its thick main tendon.

The deep portion of m. psoas major is approximately twice as thick as its superficial portion. Externally it directly adjoins the chevron bones and their ligaments, from which several of their muscle bundles originate. From the lateral surface of the deep portion of the iliolumbar muscle arise more than ten quite wide, ribbonlike tendons which unite with the tendinous margin of the superficial portion of this muscle. Approximately at the level of the 15th lumbar-caudal segment the two portions of the iliolumbar muscle begin to concresce firmly, and in the region of the 18th–19th segment they form one very thick tendon. Set ventrally on the caudal fluke, the tendon of the iliolumbar muscle, gradually becoming thinner, gives off a large number of tendon bundles caudally and to the sides, laterally and medially. The outer ones of these pass into the skin of the fluke, while the inner ones are attached to the chevron (hemal) bones of the caudal vertebrae. The inner tendon bundles include short muscle bundles, which ensure still greater
72 mobility of the caudal fluke.

Contraction of the iliolumbar muscle contributes to flexion of the caudal half of the body and lowering of the tail fluke. When m. longissimus dorsi, m. m. iliocostales, m. spinalis dorsi, and the iliolumbar muscles contract bilaterally, the caudal peduncle moves up and down, causing the animal to move progressively forward.

M. ischio-coccygous forms the most ventral contour of the caudal section posterior to the anal-genital slit. It originates at the pelvic bone, the posterior margin of the intraabdominal fascia, and the aponeurosis of m. rectus abdominis. Some of its muscle bundles begin at the fascia covering the iliolumbar muscle. In addition, m. ischio-coccygous obtains here from the iliolumbar muscle a thick muscle bundle and two or three tendons (in the end section). At its point of origin, approximately at the level of the 11th lumbar-caudal segment, this muscle, together with the corresponding muscle of the other side, embraces from the sides the posterior half of the anal-genital slit. Behind the slit the two muscles come close together and, concrescing firmly, extend along the free ends of the chevron bones, to which they are attached by individual teeth.

At the level of the 17th–18th lumbar-caudal vertebra this muscle passed into the tendon which extends along the chevron bones, and is gradually reduced to nothing at the caudal fluke.

M. **obliquus abdominis externus** begins with fleshy teeth on the outer surface of the thoracic ends of the ribs, the strongest teeth being those on the first six or seven ribs. The anterior tooth of this muscle begins at the posterior edge of the thoracic end of the first rib; the line of insertion of the last teeth lies almost midway along the ribs. The posterior section of m. obliquus abdominis externus also originates with a thin tendinous plate at the lumbar-dorsal fascia. The bundles of muscle fibers of m. obliquus abdominis are directed ventrocaudally and gradually become thinner posteriorly. The caudal part of the muscle becomes tendinous in its lower half, then fleshy again, and finally passes into the aponeurosis, participating in the formation of the white line of the stomach.

M. **obliquus abdominis internus** originates at the fascia covering the musculature of the dorsal part of the caudal peduncle at a level from the 4th to the 12th lumbar-caudal segment. The layers of its muscle fibers run obliquely ultraventrally, the deepest layers being directed more steeply. By its anterior margin the muscle is attached externally to the thoracic ends of the ribs parallel to the costal-cartilaginous line. The posterior margin of the muscle is set obliquely, parallel to the termination of m. transversus abdominis.

M. **transversus abdominis** begins with wide, segmented sheets at the thoracic ends of the last ribs on the inside of them and at the transverse processes of the lumbar and anterior caudal vertebrae. Running toward the white line of the stomach, the muscle gradually passes into the thin aponeurosis, uniting with the aponeurosis of m. obliquus abdominis internus.

M. **rectus abdominis** lies in the ventral abdominal wall and partly on the
73 thorax along the white line of the stomach, bordering on the corresponding muscle of the other side of the body. It begins with isolated teeth at the outer surface of the thoracic end of the first and subsequent ribs and at the sternum. Externally it is covered by tendons of m. obliquus abdominis externus and internus, and on the median side by the aponeurosis of m. transversus abdominis (in the region of the 4th—5th rib it is surrounded also by the medial tendinous plate of m. obliquus abdominis internus). The anterior end of m. rectus abdominis in the region of the 1st—5th costal cartilage covers m. rectus thoracis.

From the anal-genital slit m. rectus abdominis runs upward and to the side. Bending round the anterior-upper edge of the mammary gland, it gives off several muscle bundles which are attached to the pelvic bone and, narrowing abruptly, it passes into a long, thin tendon which, extending obliquely dorsocaudally, becomes gradually thinner and ends in a thick fascia covering the muscles of the base of the caudal peduncle.

These muscles of the abdominal wall, which in mammals constitute an abdominal press, exert an effect on the act of respiration, reducing the cavity of the thorax, and when the muscle walls contract simultaneously with the diaphragm they work to support the genital organs in the pelvic cavity.

The **diaphragm** is a thick, lamellar, cupola-shaped muscle with an indistinctly expressed tendinous center represented by three strong, triangular tendinous bands. The cupola of the diaphragm cranially reaches the third intercostal space.

The lumbar part of the diaphragm consists of two crura. The stronger right crus originates in three tendon bundles at the ventral surface of the bodies of the first four lumbar vertebrae. The left crus begins at the same place but with one tendon bundle. Between the crura lies the opening for the aorta. To the right of and somewhat below the center of the diaphragm there is an aperture for the caudal vena cava; to the left of and above the latter in the right crus of the diaphragm an aperture is formed for the esophagus. The diaphragm participates in the act of respiration, enlarging the thoracic cavity.

THORACIC WALL OF THE TRUNK

Inspiratory muscles

M. scalenus supracostalis is triangular. It originates at the outer surface of the first and the anterior margin of the second rib and ends on the transverse processes of the complex vertebra.

M. scalenus medius begins on the outer surface of the first and second rib and it ends on the cervical vertebra. It lies ventrally on the right. Both scalene muscles are dilators of the thorax.

M. rectus thoracis is thick and short. The first bundle begins at the posterior edge of the manubrium. Running ventro-caudally, it inserts on the anterior margin of the thoracic end of the second rib and at the anterior outer surface of its costal cartilage. The second bundle begins at the posterior edge of the lower section of the manubrium and the adjacent part of the sternum body; it ends at the anterior edge and outer surface of the third, fourth, and fifth costal cartilages, being attached to the last two by narrow lamellar tendons. On contraction it assists in drawing out the costal cartilages forward and laterally, thereby causing widening of the thorax.

M. m. intercostales externi lie in the intercostal spaces (Figure 40: 27). The muscle bundles begin at the caudal margin of one rib and, descending obliquely down and back, end at the cranial margin of the following rib. At the level of the upper half of the ribs the muscle bundles of m. intercostalis externus are very thick, but toward the sternum they become much thinner. Each of the first three intercostal muscles has in the upper half one or two longitudinally situated tendinous interlayers, owing to which this section has a plumose structure, which imparts great strength to the muscle during contraction.

M. serratus inspiratorius was not found by us in the sperm whale.

Expiratory muscles

M. m. intercostales interni lie under m. m. intercostales externi (Figure 40: 26). They begin at the cranial margin of one rib and, passing down and forward, are attached to the caudal margin of the rib which lies in front. The thickness of m. intercostalis externus increases by 5—6 times in the part which is situated in the lower half of the intercostal spaces.

The thickness of the intercostal muscles (internal and external) increases caudally, reaching a maximum in the third intercostal space, after which it gradually decreases.

M. **lumbocostalis** begins with a wide lamellar tendon at the transverse-costal processes of the 1st—3rd (4th) lumbar vertebrae. It inserts on the posterior margin of the last rib and the outer surface of the costal carti-lages (to the fifth costal cartilage) along the costal-cartilaginous line. It covers the origin of m. transversus abdominis. M. lumbocostalis is covered externally by m. obliquus abdominis externus. When it contracts, it draws out the ribs caudally and medially.

M. **transversus thoracis** has a segmented structure. It lies in the section from the 1st to the 4th rib. It begins with isolated bundles at the dorsal surface of the sternum in the area of its union with the costal cartilages. Each muscle bundle ends at the medial surface of the upper end of the same costal cartilage.

This whole group of muscles, especially the first two sets, help to decrease the volume of the thorax.

M. **serratus dorsalis expiratorius** was not found by us in the sperm whale.

PECTORAL GIRDLE

M. **rhomboideus.** The cephalic part of the muscle arises from the occipital crest of the occipital bone and inserts on the anterior margin of the upper third of the scapula. The muscle takes the form of a narrow ribbon which widens downward (Figure 41: 2, 3).

(75)

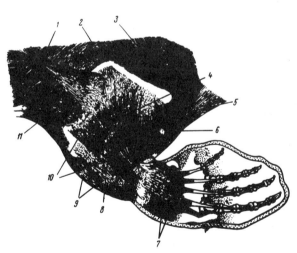

FIGURE 41. Musculature of the pectoral girdle and forelimb of the sperm whale:

1 — omocervical muscle; 2 — anterior (deep) and 3 — posterior (superficial) portion of m. rhomboideus; 4 — infraspinatus muscle; 5 — tricipital muscle; 6 — m. latissimus dorsi; 7 — extensor digi-torum communis; 8 — m. supraspinatus; 9 — biceps; 10 — deltoid muscle; 11 — m. cleido-mastoideus.

75

The dorsal part of m. rhomboideus is a short but wide muscular plate, which originates with a lamellar tendon at the supraspinous ligament and fascia of the relevant muscles and ends at the dorsal margin of the posterior half of the scapula. It lies within the 1st—3rd thoracic segments.

When contracting simultaneously, both parts of m. rhomboideus pull the 75 dorsal edge of the scapula forward and upward. In sperm whales this muscle is less developed than in land mammals.

M. pectoralis superficialis begins as a wide sheet at the sternum and inserts with its narrowed end on the crest of the large protuberance of the humerus. The anterior edge of this muscle grows together with the cervical-cephalic part of the cutaneous (or subcutaneous) muscle — m. panniculus carnosus.

M. pectoralis profundus originates at the thoracic ends of the 3rd—5th bony ribs and ends at the medial surface of the antebrachium. The upper margin of this muscle is tightly joined to m. latissimus dorsi.

The superficial and deep pectoral muscles work to move the thoracic fins.

M. latissimus dorsi is a small, narrow, triangular muscle. It begins with a thin lamellar tendon at the fascia of m. iliocostalis (Figure 41: 6).

Its fleshy belly lies within the 3rd—5th ribs. Narrowing abruptly, the muscle forms a thin, short tendon that unites with the posterior margin of m. teres maior, together with which it is attached to the crest of the small protuberance of the shoulder joint.

When it contracts, m. latissimus dorsi draws the shoulder back and in. This muscle is less developed in the sperm whale than in land mammals.

M. cleido-mastoideus begins with a narrow belly at the posterior edge of the petrous temporal bone, somewhat above the level of the orbit (Figure 41: 11). Its muscular-tendinous end inserts on the medial surface of the humerus, together with its capitulum. On contraction, it brings the 76 shoulder joint forward and up, and, like the same muscle in small Cetacea (Kleinenberg et al., 1964), may participate in altering the volume of the thorax.

M. sterno-mastoideus begins at the anterior edge of the sternum and ends at the petrous temporal bone together with m. cleido-mastoideus. On unilateral contraction it turns the head sideways, and on bilateral contraction it raises the head.

M. serratus ventralis is represented by two narrow but fairly thick muscle bundles. The anterior bundle lies on the medial side of the lower third of the scapula. It begins at the thoracic end of the first bony rib and ends on a special process of the anterior edge of the scapula.

The posterior bundle is less developed than the anterior and is situated at a considerable distance from it. It begins at the outer surface of the second bony rib close to its sternal end and inserts medially on the caudal corner of the scapula.

The anterior muscle bundle helps to shift the shoulder backward; the posterior bundle, on the other hand, works to bring it forward, since it lowers the posterior corner of the scapula. When they move simultaneously, the scapula is lowered and with it the entire fin.

M. trapezius was not found by us in the sperm whale, nor in dolphins (Druzhinin, 1924).

FREE FORELIMB

Extensors

M. **supraspinatus** arises from the anterior margin of the acromion and at the prespinous fossa in its lower third. Obliquely encompassing the shoulder joint, it ends at the crest of the humerus. This muscle is short but wide and well developed. It extends the shoulder joint and diverts it toward the shoulder.

M. **coracobrachialis** begins at the coracoid process of the scapula, proceeds with a short belly along the medial surface of the shoulder joint, and inserts on the medial protuberance of the humerus. It helps turn the fin inward.

Flexors

M. **deltoideus** begins at the spina scapulae and covers the infraspinatus muscle, growing together with it (Figure 41:10). Its triangular belly ends at the crest of the large tubercle. When it contracts, it raises the fin and maintains it perpendicular to the body. The deltoid muscle is much better developed in the sperm whale than in land mammals.

M. **teres minor** arises from the posterior margin of the lower half of the scapula and is attached just below the capitulum of the humerus and on the medial tubercle of the latter.

M. **teres maior** begins with a wide, thick sheet at the posterior edge of the scapula and ends, together with m. latissimus dorsi, on the crest of the small tubercle. These two muscles participate in lowering and turning the fin.

M. **infraspinatus** is narrow and long, originates on the whole surface of
77 the prespinous fossa of the dorsal edge of the scapula (see Figure 41:4), and ends at the deltoid tuberosity of the humerus together with the tendon of the deltoid muscle. On contraction it raises the limb (abductor).

M. **biceps brachii** begins with a fleshy belly at the anterior margin of the acromion (Figure 41:9). The terminal section of the muscle is attached to the tuberosity of the proximal end of the radius, growing closely together at this point with the anterior edge of the thoracic surface of the muscle. It contributes to straightening of the shoulder joint and flexion of the elbow joint, and thereby helps to carry the thoracic fin forward.

M. **triceps brachii** begins at the posterior edge of the scapula, the prespinous fossa, and the spina scapulae. The powerful fleshy bellies of this muscle insert on the large, reflexed bony protuberance (analogue of the olecranon), which lies at the proximal end of the ulna. On contraction the muscle straightens the elbow joint and flexes the shoulder joint.

In contrast to the pilot whale (Murie, 1874), the embryo of Delphinus delphis (Druzhinin, 1924) and the white whale (Kleinenberg et al., 1964), an extensor digitorum communis was found among the wrist muscles in a large sperm whale embryo.

As the sperm whale moves in the water, if the thoracic fin is drawn aside, especially to a position perpendicular to the body, the counterflow tends to bend and press it to the body. In the proximal part of the fin its

flexion in the region of the shoulder joint may be counteracted by the
extensors of the shoulder joint, and in the carpal region (the very surface
of the fin) by ext. digitorum communis. Thus, its function of lending
maneuverability to the animal can be very important.

FACE AND JAW

   M. **levator labi superioris proprius** (Figure 42: 6) begins with a triangular sheet on the frontal and maxillary bones. Initially the two muscles
of the right and left sides are tightly joined. In each muscle two bundles,
a superficial and a deep one, can be discerned. The superficial bundle of
m. levator labi superioris proprius begins at the upper anterior margin
of the orbit. On the left side of the body it is directed forward in the form
of a narrow wedge-shaped plate, while on the right side it takes the form of
a wide layer which is widened anteriorly. The two muscles converge and
unite to the right and rear of the left naris. The thin narrow, tendon bundle
of the left muscle runs into the wide lamellar tendon of the right muscle.
The common tendon radiates anteriorly into the hypodermic layer.
   The tendinous termination of the deep bundle of m. levator labi superioris proprius in the form of a thin but wide sheet runs forward and down in
the region of the upper lip and the angle of the mouth. This muscle is less
developed asymmetrically, being less developed on the left side.
78   The so-called longitudinal muscle of the sperm whale's head is an extremely well developed m. levator nasolabialis (Figure 42: 5). It originates
on the upper jaw (the posterior boundary of the muscle proceeds along a
transverse line linking the middle of the right and left orbits), and also at
the anterior upper surface of the orbit and the outer edge of the cheekbone.
The origin of m. levator nasolabialis is covered externally by m. levator
labi superioris proprius (Figure 42: 6). The massive belly of the muscle
occupies the entire anterior and upper half of the lateral part of the facial
region; it closely adjoins, and over a large area grows together with the
belly of the corresponding muscle on the other side of the body.
   In the posterior corner of the left naris the left m. levator nasolabialis
is divided into two bundles: a narrow medial bundle encompassing the inner
edge of the naris, and a wide lateral bundle which bends round the outer edge
of the naris. The medial bundle of the muscle gradually passes into a
tendon which terminates deep in the skin of this region. The lateral bundle,
having given to the medial bundle part of its fibers, at the anterior corner
of the left naris abruptly narrows and passes into a short, thin, lamellar
tendon. Most of the fibers of this tendon are attached to the anterior upper
edge of the nasal diverticulum. The other (superficially lying) tendinous
fibers unite on the anterior wall of the diverticulum with the tendinous fibers
of the right m. levator nasolabialis. On contraction of these bundles of the
right and left muscles the diverticulum is compressed, its outer wall is
pressed to the inlet of the right subdermal naris and overlaps the canal
through which the left naris communicates with the right naris.
79   Anteriorly the lower margin of m. levator nasolabialis adjoins the
nasal end of the spermaceti sac. From the outer surface of this muscle
(its anterior third) emerges a wide, thin sheet of muscle fibers which

become embedded in the spermaceti cushion and in the skin of the apical section of the head.

(78)

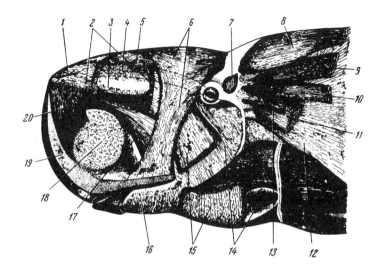

FIGURE 42. Musculature of the face and jaw in the sperm whale (embryo 135 cm long):

1 — blowhole; 2 — left longitudinal muscle of head (m. levator nasolabialis, part of muscle removed); 3 — outer wall of left nasal passage; 4 — transverse muscle of nose; 5 — right longitudinal muscle of head; 6 — m. levator labi superioris proprius; 7 — temporal muscle; 8 — m. splenius; 9 — m. longissimus; 10 — m. iliocostalis; 11 — brachiocephalic muscle; 12 — sterno-cephalic muscle; 13 — omocervical muscle; 14 — deep and 15 — superficial portion of large masseter; 16 — intermaxillary muscle; 17 — m. caninus; 18 — part of spermaceti organ; 19 — skin-fat layer; 20 — lateral dilator of blowhole. The cartilaginous nasal septum is indicated by a dotted line.

The beginning of m. levator nasolabialis is closely connected with m. retractor nasi situated at its lower margin (see below).

Deep in m. levator nasolabialis there is a strong, wide tendinous layer which, extending almost the entire length of the muscle, divides it into a thicker outer and a thinner inner layer. The ends of each of the tendinous fibrils which constitute the tendinous layer pass into the muscle endings.

M. levator nasolabialis encompasses the nasal passage above and laterally with a wide band and sends to its dorsomedial, dorsal, lateral, and lateroventral walls a large number of its inner muscle bundles. Particularly strong bundles approach the ventral wall of the nasal passage.

The dorsal margin of the deep layer of m. levator nasolabialis covers the spermaceti sac, attached to it by some of its bundles. In addition, some bundles form fairly strong tendinous layers which cut across the spermaceti sac. Enveloping the dorsal semicircumference of the sac, they pass into the tendon bundles of the right m. levator nasolabialis.

Contraction of this part of the muscle results in compression of the dorsal wall of the spermaceti sac. In addition to this function, m. levator nasolabialis works, during unilateral action, to move the "soft" nose to the side and somewhat upward. Simultaneous contraction of the right and left muscles results in retraction of the nasal part backward and its elevation, which goes along with compression of the spermaceti sac. The deep bundles of m. levator nasolabialis contribute to enlargement of the lumen of the right nasal passage. The isolated effect of the other muscle bundles of m. levator nasolabialis causes widening (opening) of the nares.

M. retractor nasi at its very origin is covered above and externally by m. levator nasolabialis, with which it is closely connected at this point. Its triangular belly begins at the middle of the outer edge of the maxillary bone. Running forward and upward, the muscle narrows abruptly and passes into a tendinous band, most of whose fibers concresce with the lower margin of the anterior end of m. levator nasolabialis. Some of the tendinous fibers of this muscle, extending downward and forward, become embedded in the labial margin of the mouth. Contraction of m. retractor nasi causes compression of the spermaceti sac.

M. dilatator nasi ventralis takes the form of a very thick, long, semi-circular muscular band below m. levator nasolabialis.

This muscle extends from the orbit to the end of the nose (more exactly, to the left naris) obliquely upward and forward, enveloping the spermaceti sac laterally. Along its dorsomedial margin passes the left nasal passage, on the lateral wall of which the muscle inserts. The lower margin of the muscle gradually passes into a thick layer of connective tissue which extends ventrally into the spermaceti cushion. Some of the muscle bundles of m. dilatator nasi ventralis originate in the deep layer of m. levator nasolabialis, with which the muscle is closely connected in its lower part. It causes dilatation of the entrance to the nasal passage.

80   **M. masseter** begins at the lateral edge of the maxillary and cheek bones with a thick, wide muscular layer (Figure 42: 14, 15), the outer surface of which is covered by m. panniculus and is concrescent with it.

The muscle bundles of m. masseter, which lie in a deep and a superficial layer, run ventrocaudally (in the deep layer the bundles pass more steeply) and are attached to the dentary in the region of the masseferic fossa.

M. temporalis is weakly developed. Its small, flat and thin belly lies in the temporal fossa (Figure 42: 7). The bundles of this muscle converge and terminate at the coronoid process of the lower jaw.

M. masseter and m. temporalis participate in moving the lower jaw, and when they contract simultaneously they cause the jaws to close very powerfully.

We have not shown in the illustrations the dermal musculature that covers the entire body — m. panniculus carnosus. We did not receive the impression, at least from our investigations, that in whales this muscle reaches its highest degree of development, as was earlier reported (Druzhinin, 1924).

A description of the muscles of individual organs is given in addition in the appropriate chapters of the book.

The main groups of muscles in the sperm whale are similar in structure to those of other species of Cetacea as regards the common character of the functions they fulfill. Basic and considerable differences between the structure of sperm whale muscles and those of many other whales, especially baleen whales, are expressed in the characteristic strong development of the cephalic muscles, which probably control the air streams in the communicating nasal ducts and cavities and change the shape of the complexly constructed and perfected spermaceti organ.

Chapter 6

DIGESTIVE SYSTEM

A description of the external structure of the digestive system of a young sperm whale was given by Jackson (1845). E.I.Betesheva and N.I.Sergienko (1964) examined the anatomy and histology of the sperm whale stomach and intestine. The literature contains many descriptions of the type of dentition, the best of which is definitely that by Boschma (1938).

At the early stages of embryonic development (length 8.5 mm) the digestive system is a tube which opens at the cranial end with the oral inlet which passes directly into the pharynx. The stomach is seen as a widening of the alimentary canal, the dorsal wall of which is gathered into rather deep folds (Golub, Leontyuk, and Novikov, 1968).

ORAL CAVITY

The lower jaw enters the upper jaw. It is covered laterally by its lips, and is tightly pressed to the rough, plicate palate which, like the entire
81 cavity, is covered with flat, multilayered epithelium that is keratinized at the surface. The palate is usually white or grayish white, rarely very slightly pinkish in places. Occasionally patches of dark pigment appear. The oral cavity is very small (Figure 43).

The **tongue** of the sperm whale is mobile and relatively short but wide, thick, and muscular, with a pointed tip. The outer surface is light, the inner surface pink, sometimes very bright. The tongue is about 80 cm long (in young animals). Its lower surface has longitudinal and transverse folds. The middle part of the dorsal surface (dorsum) is covered with deep (up to 3 cm), strongly twisting, thick (up to 1.5 cm), closely adjacent folds. (Figure 44). The tip of the tongue is covered with smooth, flat, multilayered epithelium. The horny layer is very thin. In the sperm whale, as in other toothed whales, the glands which are characteristic for the tongue of land mammals are absent.

The base of the tongue is covered with flat, multilayered epithelium with a distinctly expressed, thick layer of horny epithelium.

In places where the connective-tissue papillae, passing through the layer of multilayered epithelium (which is a characteristic feature of the base of the sperm whale tongue), rise together with blood vessels (and nerves?) to the very surface, we found spherical groups — not observed in other parts of the beginning sections of the alimentary canal — of nonkeratinized epithelial cells resembling the taste buds of the tongue of other mammals and apparently acting as chemoreceptors (see Figure 89, Chapter 9).

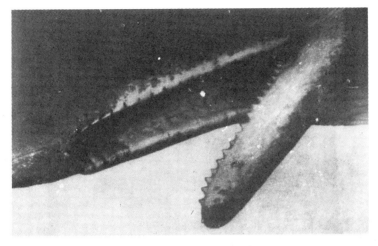

FIGURE 43. Oral cavity of the sperm whale (large male)

(82)

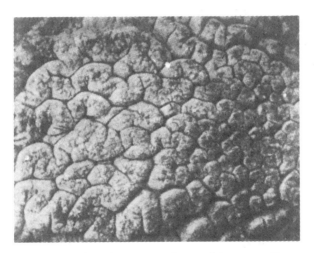

FIGURE 44. Surface of middle part of sperm whale tongue. The folds are visible

    The bottom of the oral cavity is also covered with flat, multilayered epithelium, but here this is quite smooth and with weaker keratinization.

    The functions of the tongue in the sperm whale, as in any other toothed whale, are as follows: orientation of the captured prey in the oral cavity (this function is apparently less important in sperm whales than in other whales, due to the great difference between the length of the oral cavity and the length of the tongue), thrusting of the catch into the pharynx with simultaneous expulsion of water from the oral cavity (Yablokov, 1958), and finally, the function of taste analyzer.

82

Dentition. The upper and lower jaws of sperm whales contain different numbers of teeth, which also differ in shape, size, and functional significance (Figure 45).

Naturally, the teeth of the largest toothed animal in the earth's history have awakened the interest of naturalists, and the literature contains a great number of diverse, often contradictory descriptions, reports, and mentions of sperm whale dentition.

Boschma (1938), for example, listed about 70 authors who contended that sperm whales have teeth only in the lower jaw. In addition, several investigators (Beneden and Gervais, 1868—1880; Abel, 1919; Wing, 1918, 1921, 1924; and others) believed that maxillary teeth are present only in young animals and that with age they become completely atrophied and disappear. Meanwhile Bennett (1836, 1840) gave a fairly clear and accurate characterization of sperm whale dentition.

We studied the structure and development of the teeth of this whale comparatively thoroughly (Berzin, 1961, 1963), while working out methods for age determination during 1957—1960.

The lower jaw teeth lie mainly in the region of the mandibular symphysis, but several pairs of the last teeth are outside its limits.

The large teeth of the lower jaw are made up of a strong dentine core, its surface covered with a layer of cement. The teeth of the adult animal are without enamel. The teeth are all of similar form and function without change throughout life. The sperm whale tooth has no root as such (although this term is nearly always used in the literature), since the tooth does not have a narrowed base or any noticeable constriction marking the boundary between root and crown (Figure 45). On the contrary, nearly all sperm whale teeth have wide open bases (see Figure 107), which receive the dental papillae of the pulp nerves and vessels which supply the teeth; this is characteristic for the teeth of many mammals with long growth periods and subject to intensive wear (Shmal'gauzen, 1947).

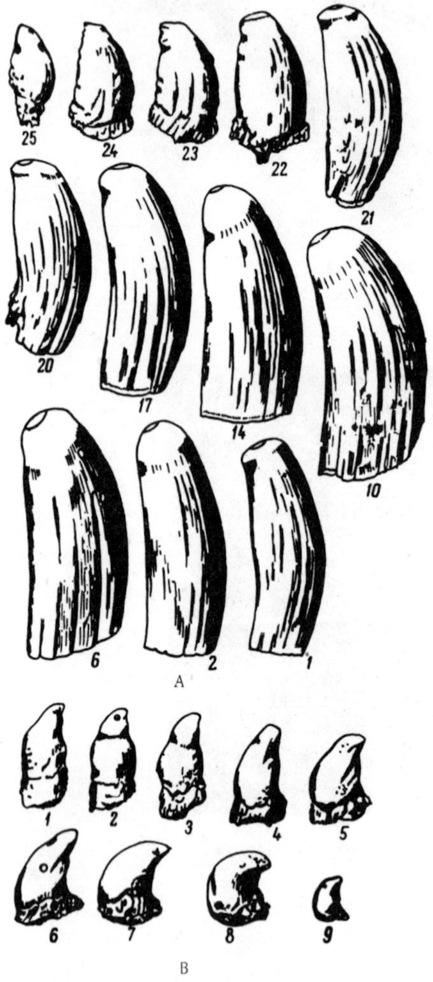

(83)

FIGURE 45. Teeth of the sperm whale (male):

A — lower jaw; B — upper jaw (Boschma, 1938); 1, 2, etc. — serial number of tooth in the jaw.

The mandibular teeth of large sperm whales attain a length of 20 cm according to Freund (1932) and Tomilin (1957), 23 cm according to our data, and 27 cm according to A. V. Yablokov (1958). Yablokov indicates that, according to information from workers at whaling plants, the teeth can be as long as 50 cm. But this is doubtful. According to Beale (1835), the maximum weight of one tooth is 1,600 g.

Above the gum only $\frac{1}{4} - \frac{1}{3}$ of the tooth is usually visible, depending on its position in the row and on the age of the animal. The number of teeth on the left side of the lower jaw may differ by one or two teeth from the number on the right side. In sexually mature male sperms living in the North Pacific there are generally 23 mandibular teeth, in females 22–23 (Table 12). The maximum number of teeth on one side of the lower jaw is 28–29 (Omura, 1950; Ivanova, 1955) to 30 (Tomilin, 1957).

(84) TABLE 12. Frequency of occurrence of teeth in the lower jaw of North Pacific sperm whales (Omura, 1950; our material*), %

Number of teeth	Males		Females		Number of teeth	Males		Females	
	right side	left side	right side	left side		right side	left side	right side	left side
17	1.0	1.3	0	0	24	17.8	19.1	15.8	19.5
18	1.8	0.8	1.4	1.4	25	11.3	8.4	7.6	7.6
19	2.3	3.3	2.8	4.2	26	4.2	4.8	3.5	3.5
20	7.0	6.9	9	7.6	27	2.6	2.8	0.7	0.7
21	13.4	13.7	11.6	14.5	28	1.0	1.3	0.7	0.7
22	16.0	14.3	22.1	21.5	29	0	0.2	0	0
23	21.6	23.2	24.8	18.8					

* A total of about 400 counts of teeth in specimens of both sexes were made by Omura, and more than 1,000 in our materials.

The interval between the teeth in the middle part of the lower jaw depends on the size of the animal; in large males it reaches 15 or even 20 cm (Boschma, 1938; Tomilin, 1957; our data).

In the upper jaw of male and female sperm whales the teeth are usually of irregular form or are strongly curved, small, but sometimes of medium 84 size (Figure 45:B). The maximum size of the maxillary teeth is 8–11 cm (Pouchet and Beauregard, 1891; Rhithie and Edwards, 1931). The maximum height of these teeth was reported by Boschma (1938) as 13.8 cm.

The maximum number of maxillary teeth noted by Boschma (1938), i. e., 30 (15 on each side), was in a male around 18 m long. However, some authors without carrying out tooth counts of their own, report that the upper jaw of the sperm whale contains as many teeth as the lower jaw (Pouchet and Beauregard, 1889a; Neuville, 1932).

In our material the maximum number of maxillary teeth in males was 19; in two animals 15.1 and 16.4 m long there were 9 teeth on one side and 10 on the other, while in a third animal 15.1 m long there were 8 on one side and 11 on the other side of the upper jaw.

The frequency of occurrence of erupted teeth in the upper jaw is shown in Table 13.

TABLE 13. Frequency of occurrence of erupted teeth in the upper jaw of North Pacific sperm whales (Omura, 1950; our material*), %

Number of teeth	Males		Females		Number of teeth	Males		Females	
	right side	left side	right side	left side		right side	left side	right side	left side
0	75.3	78.1	75.4	73.4	6	0.3	0	2.7	2.7
1	7.1	6.5	4.1	3.4	7	1.6	1.2	1.4	1.4
2	6.5	4.6	2.0	6.1	8	0.6	0.6	1.4	1.4
3	3.4	0.9	4.1	4.8	9	0.6	0.6	0.7	0.7
4	2.8	4.4	4.1	2.7	10	0.3	0	0.7	1.4
5	1.2	1.9	3.4	2.0	11	0.3	1.2	0	0

* See note to Table 12.

85   It is interesting that the proportion of sperm whales with teeth visible in the upper jaw varies from one region to another. Omura (1950) reported that in the Sea of Japan the percentage of sperm whales without maxillary teeth was nearly 80%, but in antarctic waters only 50%. A similar picture is observed (according to our data) in different areas of the North Pacific. In the region of the Komandorski and Aleutian Islands during 1958—1959 teeth were found in the upper jaw of 45% of the sperm whales caught; in animals taken in the region of the Kurile Islands teeth were found in only 19%. Apparently, however, this is due not to any morphological differences (although in principle this is also possible) but to incomparability of the material due to a different latitudinal distribution of animals of different age groups (see Chapter 10). If we calculate the number of sperm whales more than 13 m long from the Kuriles area in which teeth are seen in the upper jaw, this comes to about 30% (Berzin, 1963).

Thus it is quite clear that if we are debating whether teeth are present in the upper jaw in a particular specimen (and if present, their number), we mean here only teeth which have erupted. Analysis of the material indicates that generally the number of teeth (or, more precisely, the number of erupted teeth) depends on the size (age) of the animal. It is difficult to decide whether maxillary teeth are always present in the animal if they are not visible upon external examination; however, the absence of maxillary teeth in very young animals, their increased number with age, and also the data of Boschma (1938) — who in a processed carcass of a large male counted all the teeth, of which some were not visible from the surface of the palate — lead us to believe that maxillary teeth are present in all animals without exception, as was already suggested by Bennett (1836). If they are not visible on the surface, we may take it that they have not yet erupted, or else due to reduction they will never erupt. We have no doubt that in most of our counts of upper teeth their true number was greater. In view of this, it was Boschma (1938) who indicated the true maximum number of teeth. In the animals we examined we found no cases of teeth having fallen out from the upper jaw, as reported by Neuville (1932).

The maxillary teeth are as a rule situated in the alveoli of the gum of the upper jaw which correspond to the mandibular teeth but are often between them (Figure 46). Sometimes some teeth are set directly on the palate between the rows of teeth and alveoli and even on the lips, protruding beyond the limits of the oral cavity. All these typical and atypical positions of maxillary teeth can be observed in a single animal. Mostly the maxillary teeth do not rise at all above the gum surface and only their apexes are visible. Sometimes, however, eruption proceeds quite intensively, and then these teeth protrude several centimeters (up to 5 cm) above the gum. In this case, when they are located in the alveoli from the teeth of the lower jaw, from contact with the latter they become either worn down or else curved, generally with the apex backward (but they may curve in any direction).

Growth and development of the teeth. As our material showed, the first bony elements of the lower jaw teeth are laid down when the embryo is about 50 cm long (Berzin, 1963). When the body is about 80 cm long, the spindle-shaped papillae of the pulp of the second to sixth teeth have dentin cases or caps which in form already resemble teeth. The bony cap sits firmly on the pulpar papilla, which is more than twice the size of the cap itself. The caps of the third and fourth teeth are highest
86 (about 1.5 mm). The papilla together with the cap sits freely in the gum tissue. On the surface of the gum there are up to 22 inconspicuous ridges above the dental alveoli.

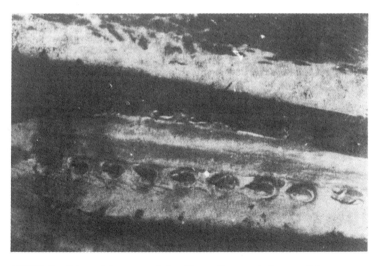

FIGURE 46. Palate of the sperm whale with maxillary teeth (large male)

In an embryo about 1.3 m long the first six pairs of teeth are laid down. The dental caps are slightly laterally compressed. The caps of the third and fourth teeth are highest (about 2 mm). The ridges on the surface of the gums are more conspicuous.

The teeth of embryos in the later stages of development, shortly before birth, are of great interest. We examined the teeth of three embryos: two males 400 and 412 cm long and one female 398 cm long. A total of 22—24 pairs of teeth are set deep in the gum tissue. Soft tubercles, abundantly permeated by blood vessels, protrude above the surface. The size of the tubercles increases gradually from the first to the last. The tooth together with the papilla of the pulp is set rather mobilely in dense tissue on connective-tissue bands which emerge from the tissue above the tooth, cling firmly to the tip of the tooth and, enveloping the tooth itself in a thin film, are attached to its papilla (Figure 47).

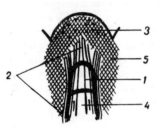

FIGURE 47. Position of teeth in jaw of prenatal sperm whale embryo:

1 — tooth; 2 — bands of connective tissue; 3 — blood vessels; 4 — dental papilla; 5 — dense connective tissue.

87

At this stage of development the teeth are hollow cones, differing somewhat mainly in the size and shape of their tips. The teeth of the 13th to 16th pairs are highest (10.3—10.8 mm). The first tooth has a thin spire-shaped tip; the 6th to 12th teeth have wide spear-shaped tips with conspicuous cusps; the 12th—24th pairs of teeth have a more or less distinctly expressed tricuspid serrate structure (Figure 48), the middle cusp being the highest. The serrate tip is particularly well expressed in the last teeth (Figure 49). According to Nishiwaki, Ohsumi and Hibuya (1958), all the teeth of large embryos except the first four and last four pairs have a tricuspid tip. Our data conform much better to the biogenetic rule that it is the middle and last teeth of embryos which must have the most complicated structure, if the sperm whales are descendants of terrestrial carnivores (Berzin, 1963).

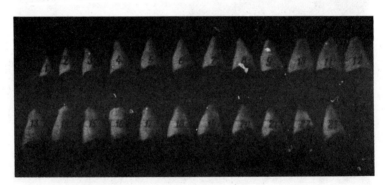

FIGURE 48. Teeth of sperm whale embryo (female, 398 cm long)

In the process of phylogenesis of the sperm whale, with the transition to feeding mainly on cephalopods the usual functions of the teeth (tearing, chewing, etc.) were gradually lost. Thus the teeth gradually became modified and took on their present form, keeping only the function of retaining the prey.

Until the eruption of the lower jaw teeth the cement completely covers the tooth in the sperm whale, but it splits off immediately after eruption of the tooth, exposing the dentin, which immediately begins to wear off from contact with the surface of the palate of the upper jaw and with food. Ohsumi, Kasuya and Nishiwaki (1963) noted in a sperm whale that the tip of a still unerupted tooth had a thin layer of enamel which was formed during embryonic development and was later covered with cement. The presence of enamel on the teeth of embryos indicates that an enamel crown was present on the teeth in the ancestors of the sperm whales (Slijper, 1962).

The first teeth to erupt are the seventh to ninth pairs, this evidently being due to the relatively greater functional significance of the middle teeth. According to the material of Nishiwaki et al. (1958), the teeth erupt
88 when the length of male and female sperm whales is about 9—10 m at the age of 4—5 years*; according to these authors, this coincides with the onset of sexual maturity.

According to our material, such a coincidence occurs only in males, whereas in females the teeth erupt slightly after the onset of sexual maturity (at the age of 5—6 years), when, moreover, the body length can vary greatly. Thus in a pregnant female 9 m long (5 ½ years old) and in a female 8.9 m long (4 ½ years old) which had given birth once, no teeth had yet erupted. On the other hand, in a female 8.3 m long which had given birth a number of times (7 ½ years old) all except the first and last pairs of teeth had erupted.

(87)

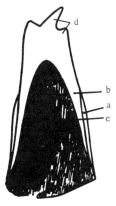

FIGURE 49. Longitudinal section of the last tooth of a male sperm whale embryo 400 cm long:

a — cement; b — dentin; c — pulp cavity; d — cusps of tooth.

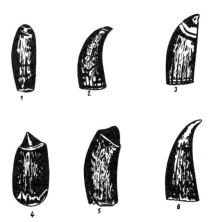

FIGURE 50. Several forms of wearing of sperm whale teeth:

1 — first pairs (animal 15.8 m long);
2—5 — middle pairs (animals 12.3, 13.5, 15.5, and 16.0 m long, respectively);
6 — last pairs (animal 13.5 m long).

After eruption of the middle teeth, teeth begin to appear in a row on each side, but eruption proceeds more intensively in the direction of the back of the jaw.

* Here and elsewhere, age is determined according to the dentin layers of the teeth, reckoning the formation of two wide, light layers of dentin per year.

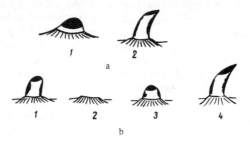

a

b

FIGURE 51. Form and wearing of mandibular teeth
of sperm whales:

a — male 14.7 m long (17 years old): 1 — 8th tooth;
2 — 13th tooth;
b — female 11.7 m long (more than 30 years old):
1 — 1st tooth; 2 — alveolus from lost 7th tooth;
3 — 12th tooth; 4 — 19th tooth.

At the age of 8—9 years in males the first pair of teeth and one or two pairs at the end of the tooth row remain in the gums. At an average body length of 13 m at the age of 10—12 years, the first pair and the last pairs of teeth have erupted in most sperm whales. In individual animals eruption of teeth (the first and last pairs, only the first, or only the last pairs) can be delayed. The middle pairs erupt first and are first to wear; they also wear down more intensively than the other teeth, since they bear a greater mechanical load. As already mentioned, wearing begins with splitting off of cement and exposure of dentin. The shape of worn teeth depends on the age of the animal and on the position of the teeth in the row (Figures 50, 51; also Figure 45).

89

FIGURE 52. Exposure of the pulp
cavity of a middle tooth with age
(11th tooth of a male sperm whale
16.2 m long; the dotted line denotes the pulp cavity)

However, general patterns can be discerned in the type of wearing of the lower jaw teeth. The first one or two pairs never become sharp, or at any rate not as sharp as the middle and last pairs. The middle pairs are sharp in young animals, peglike in medium-aged animals, and blunt in old specimens. In very old sperm whales the teeth wear down to the gum and the pulp cavity of the middle teeth is eventually exposed (Figure 52). Finally, the teeth may fall out. For example, in a female 11.7 m long and more than 30 years old the seventh pair of teeth had fallen out and the adjacent teeth had an open pulp cavity (see Figure 51, b). In our extensive material we did not observe loss of teeth, as described by Sleptsov (1952). This may be due to the absence of old males as a result of whaling. According to Sleptsov (1952), at the sites where teeth have fallen out hardened epithelial protuberances are formed which perform the functions of the lost teeth. In view of the considerable diminishment of functions of the teeth themselves, in our opinion it is unlikely that such a change is determined by functional necessity.

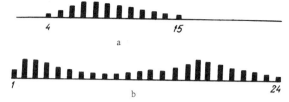

FIGURE 53. Change with age in the relationship between lower jaw teeth of male sperm whales protruding above the gum (1—24 are serial numbers of teeth):

a — at the age of about 7 years; b — at 15—17 years.

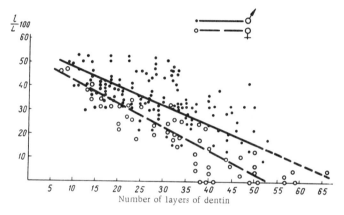

FIGURE 54. Graph showing the filling of the pulp cavity of mandibular teeth in sperm whales, with age:

L — length (height) of tooth; l — length (height) of pulp cavity.

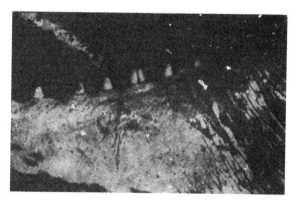

FIGURE 55. Closely approximated mandibular teeth (male sperm whale, North Pacific)

The last pairs of teeth remain more or less sharp almost throughout life, due to the different densities of the cement and dentin. The cement is always worn down more intensively than the dentin, which is why more or less sharp tips are preserved in most teeth. Wearing of the dentin of the first and the last teeth proceeds more slowly than its renewal, so that the tooth becomes continually larger. The dentin of the middle teeth wears more rapidly than it is deposited, resulting in exposure of the pulp cavity, which with age gradually grows to a considerable size.

The differences in the degree of wearing of the dentin in the tooth row are seen in the following example: in a male 13.1 m long 15 layers were counted in a middle tooth, while in the first and last teeth only the cement was split off and 20 layers of dentin were counted in each tooth. In a male sperm whale 14.7 m long the last tooth had 47 layers (approximately two layers were worn down), and a middle tooth only 27 layers. With age the difference in number of dentin layers between the first, last, and middle teeth becomes even greater. Thus, as a result of irregular eruption and wearing down of teeth in the process of growth the ratio of the heights to which the teeth protrude above the gum constantly changes (Figure 53).

Closure of the pulp cavity also proceeds irregularly. As a rule the pulp cavities of the middle teeth remain wide and large throughout life until the teeth are completely worn down and fall out; in an old tooth the pulp cavity in fact occupies the whole tooth.

The pulp cavity of the first teeth of male sperm whales is filled at the average age of 30—35 years. The pulp cavity of the anterior teeth of 90 females, like that of the last teeth in both sexes, is filled earlier, at the age of 20—25 years (Figure 54). The pulp cavity of the upper jaw teeth (according to which Japanese investigators recommend determining age) is filled earlier (Nishiwaki et al., 1958), at an age above ten years. The early filling of the pulp cavity of the maxillary teeth apparently misled Sleptsov (1952) to report on the characteristic absence of a pulp cavity in these teeth. Sometimes teeth are crowded very close in the jaw (Figure 55), and sometimes two are even joined in a pair (Figure 56) to a greater or lesser degree. Boschma (1938a) described in great detail a case in which "double" teeth were found.

In two sperm whales caught in Aleutian waters we found an intersymphyseal position of a mandibular tooth at the anterior end of the jaw (thus the first three teeth were obtained), the middle tooth being slightly smaller than those normally arranged at the sides of it.

A large number of the teeth (in old sperm whales most teeth), both mandibular and maxillary, have a certain amount of so-called osteodentin in the form of isolated small oval fragments, which may merge into masses of various size, sometimes filling the pulp cavity completely.
92 Osteodentin initially occurs as individual isolated formations in the tissue of the pulp papilla; it then comes in contact with the last layer of the growing dentin and gradually becomes implanted in the dentin layer of the tooth, there sometimes being such a large amount of it that the dentin layers can be discerned only with difficulty, if at all. Descriptions and reports on the existence of osteodentin can be found in Beneden and Gervais (1868—1880), Boschma (1938), and others. Boschma considers that formation of the usual dentin and osteodentin takes place regularly (like winter rings on scales), and he suggests that osteodentin is laid down when the animal lives under unfavorable conditions.

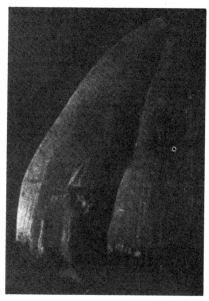

FIGURE 56. Paired mandibular teeth (male sperm whale, North Pacific)

FIGURE 57. Curved lower jaw of a sperm whale (male, Northern Pacific. Photo by Doroshenko)

The functional value of the teeth of large toothed whales has been disputed repeatedly (Raven, 1942; Sleptsov, 1952; Tomilin, 1954; Kleinenberg
et al., 1964). All authors who studied this question reached the conclusion
that there is a diminishment of the importance of the teeth in squid-eaters,
particularly in those in which all or nearly all the teeth are outside the oral
cavity (family Ziphiidae). Kleinenberg et al. (1964) believe that in these
animals the teeth have lost completely their "digestive" function, and in
sperm whales the role of the teeth as graspers of the food is far less important than is usually claimed.

Our own numerous direct observations and available published reports
(Caldwell et al., 1966; after a description by Ries) indicate that apart from
the very rare exception, even on large food items found in sperm whale
stomachs (squid and sharks measuring up to 3 m) no traces of teeth are
visible. It is pertinent to recall here that in general, teeth erupt only in
sexually mature sperm whales. Moreover, our material included up to
93 ten sperms with well filled or at least normally filled stomachs in which
the entire jaw was either turned aside already at the very base, or turned
inside out with the tooth row outward, or else rolled up in a ring, arch, etc.
(Figures 57, 126). Beale (1839) and Bullen (1899) mentioned finds of similar
sperm whales. In such animals not a single tooth nor even the jaw could
take any part in gripping the prey. Analysis of all these data leads one to
a conclusion which at first glance appears preposterous: there is reduction
not only of the function of the teeth but also of that of the entire lower jaw
in the digestive process of the sperm whale. Only thus can the facts, which
contradict what is generally accepted, be explained.

PHARYNX

In the sperm whale, as in other toothed whales (Jackson, 1845; Weber,
1928; Kleinenberg, 1956a; Kleinenberg and Yablokov, 1958; and others),
the esophageal and respiratory tracts intersect in the pharynx, being completely and permanently separated due to the peculiar structure of the
larynx (see Chapter 7), which rises as an elongate tube (the arytenoid cartilages and epiglottis) from the bottom of the pharynx somewhat obliquely
forward, crosses the lumen of the pharynx, and passes into the choana.
Here the widened head of the laryngeal tube is tightly closed by a strong
laryngo-pharyngeal (palatopharyngeal) sphincter (Figure 58).

The laryngeal tube, like the entire surface of the pharynx, is covered
with a thick layer of flat multilayered epithelium, which in places is keratinized and permeated by dermal papillae which apparently increase its
strength. There is a particularly large number of such papillae on the
side of the larynx directed toward the food which is being squeezed through
(Kleinenberg et al., 1964). The pharyngeal walls of toothed whales may
stretch at the laryngeal tube under the influence of the passing food.

The mucoprotein glands, situated in the anterior part of the pharynx,
from the root of the tongue to the base of the laryngeal tube, and forming
94 together with the glands on the surface of the root of the tongue, the aboral
part of the palate and the cheeks, coat the food and the wall of the alimentary
canal with a secretion that permits the food to advance along the pharynx.

The laryngeal tube contains a maximum number of gland ducts (Kleinenberg et al., 1964).

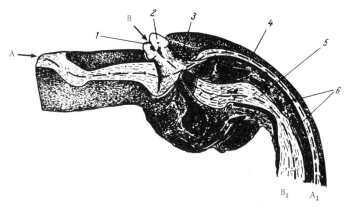

FIGURE 58. Cross section of the pharynx in the sperm whale (embryo of prenatal size):

1 — upper part of epiglottis; 2 — upper part of arytenoid cartilages; 3 — palatopharyngeal sphincter; 4 — esophagus; 5 — trachea; 6 — cartilages of trachea wall.
A—A₁ — path taken by food; B—B₁ — path taken by air.

It was reported for dolphins (Kleinenberg, 1956a) that the esophageal tract, and together with it the food bolus, divide at the laryngeal tube. For the sperm whale, which consumes food that is by no means always soft (squid, including big ones), such an organization of the alimentary canal would be unsuitable, and, as has been shown (Pouchet and Beauregard, 1892; Lillie, 1910; Malyshev, 1966), in these whales the alimentary canal is left-sided only owing to the asymmetrical arrangement of the laryngeal tube.

ESOPHAGUS

In the sperm whale, as in other animals, the esophagus is a thick-walled tube, but it is shorter and wider than in other whales. The size of the esophagus, and especially its diameter, depends on the size of the animal. In a young specimen (about 5 m long) the esophagus is about 50 cm long, in a large male (16 m long), 170 cm. The diameter varies from 25—30 to 45—50 cm (in large males).

The surface of the epithelium in this section is smoother in the region of the stomach and more plicate (width and height of folds 3—4 cm) in the direction of the pharynx.

The mucosa of the esophagus is characterized by a total absence of glands (this distinguishes it from the esophageal mucosa of land mammals) and by a rich supply of blood vessels. The multitipped connective-tissue papillae pass into an epithelium which is flat with weak keratinization.

Keratinization is intensified toward the end of the esophagus (Yablokov, 1958). The walls of the esophagus characteristically have a thick muscular layer.

The thoracic part of the esophagus is very short, and just beyond the diaphragm the esophagus enters the stomach.

STOMACH

This all-important organ consists of three compartments in the sperm whale (Jackson, 1845; Sleptsov, 1952; Yablokov, 1958; and others) (Figures 59, 60).

(95)

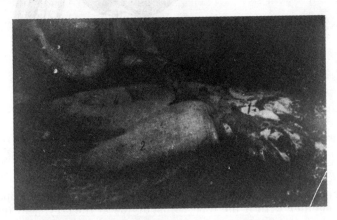

FIGURE 59. Stomach of sperm whale (female):

1 — first compartment (opened, remains of squid visible); 2 — second compartment; 3 — third compartment; 4 — ampulla of duodenum.

TABLE 14. Size of compartments of the sperm whale stomach

Length of animal, m	Sex	Compartment						Reference
		first		second		third		
		length, cm	width, cm	length, cm	width, cm	length, cm	width, cm	
9.0	Female	50	47	60	40	115	14	Our measurements
11.8	Male	100	40	140	72–80	150	15–40	Betesheva and Sergienko (1964)
15.0	"	95	49	169	57	136	34	Our measurements
16.0	"	175	85	210	65	165	55	Sleptsov (1952)

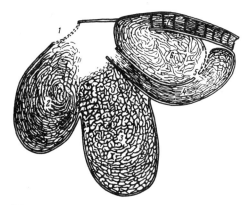

FIGURE 60. Structure of sperm whale stomach:

1 — passage of esophagus into stomach; 2 — first compartment; 3 — second compartment; 4 — third compartment; 5 — sphincter; 6 — ampulla of duodenum; 7 — beginning of duodenum.

The first two stomach compartments are of approximately equal volume (sometimes the second has a somewhat greater volume but it is more drawn out). Betesheva and Sergienko (1964) report and illustrate that the esophagus opens directly at the border of the first and second stomach compartments. Our examinations and sketches of the stomachs of variously aged sperm whales and embryos indicate that the opening of the esophagus lies in the first compartment and reaches the border between the two compartments only with one margin, as in the white whale (Kleinenberg et al., 1964).

The first compartment of the stomach, which has a more regular round shape than the other two compartments, can be regarded as a widened section of the esophagus (Jackson, 1845; Weber, 1888; Sergienko, 1965).

The dimensions of the various compartments of sperm whale stomach are given in Table 14.

The very dense surface of the mucosa of the first stomach compartment has a yellowish white tone and is gathered into thick, densely compressed folds of various size; there is no distinct boundary between the esophagus and the stomach.

According to the data of Sergienko (1965), the mucosa of the first compartment consists of multilayered epithelium up to 1.55 mm thick. The upper layer of epithelium, which is up to 0.55 mm thick and consists of keratinized cells, is nearly twice as thick in the sperm whale as in baleen whales. Under the epithelium, entering it by papillae, lies loose connective tissue with complexly interwoven fibers and a dense network of blood vessels. Below this lies a layer of longitudinal muscle fibers interlaced with vessels, below this remains of adipose tissue, and finally a layer of longitudinal, transverse, and oblique muscle fibers. It is known that the muscles of the walls of the first stomach compartment are strongly developed (Jackson, 1845). This is because not only does the first compartment store the swallowed food until it enters the other compartments, but it also grinds and macerates it in view of the fact that the teeth have lost their chewing function.

The discovery of gastroliths in the stomachs of marine mammals led to the view that they contribute to grinding of the food (Beddard, 1900; Sleptsov, 1952) or even, working like a millstone, promote the destruction of helminths (Howell, 1930). Stones are also sometimes found in sperm whale stomachs, 96 but such finds being very rare, they are noted only for those marine mammals which feed or are able to feed on the seabed; thus one can agree with the well-founded opinion of V. S. Yablokov and A. V. Yablokov (1961) concerning the chance occurrence of gastroliths in the first compartment of Cetacea. The fact that the sperm whale can swallow completely inedible objects is confirmed by our data obtained from analyses of stomach contents (see Chapter 12 and Figure 101).

The source of the digestive secretions is the second stomach compartment, but despite this, A. V. Yablokov (1958) was right in not limiting the functional significance of the first compartment to mechanical softening of the food bolus, the treatment of which would not be so effective if this process was not aided by the secretion of the glands of the second stomach compartment, which communicates with the first compartment by a wide opening. It is clear that digestion takes place also in the first compartment, otherwise it would be difficult to explain the frequent presence in it of several rostrums of squid and fishbones. In fact, the action of the muscle walls and the plicate keratinized epithelium in conjunction with the action of the gastric juices of the second compartment apparently make the first compartment the main digestive center. The first compartment communicates broadly, with no signs of any sphincter, with the second compartment. The border between the two compartments is distinct: the whitish-gray keratinized epithelium of the first compartment borders without transitions on the brown-reddish mucosa of the second compartment (Figure 61).

(97)

FIGURE 61. Surface of epithelium and border between first and second compartments of the sperm whale stomach (size of knife 27 cm; rostra of squid are visible in the first compartment)

The second compartment of the stomach is glandular, somewhat larger than the first, and takes the form of a sac. The folds of the mucosa are mainly high, strongly coiled, and soft. At the tip of this compartment (from the level of the lower boundary of the union of the first and second compartments, to the fornix) there is a section of mucosa which does not form folds but is fairly smooth; there are still few digestive glands in this section.

The mucosa of the second stomach compartment has a strong glandular layer up to 2.1—2.7 mm thick (Betesheva and Sergienko, 1964), consisting of numerous, simple, tubular, scarcely branching fundus glands, which are of very great significance in the digestive process. The walls of the glands consist of so-called main oxyntic and accessory cells. The most intensive secretory activity and, as a result, the most intensive action on the food bolus among all Cetacea occurs in the sperm whale, as can be ascertained by counting the number of glands in the second stomach compartment per 97 unit area. This number in the Balaenopteridae varies on the average from 20.9 in the great blue whale (in our opinion the minimal number of glands in the stomach of this whale is due to the fact that the species does not feed on fish, and its diet is made up mainly of the more delicate plankton) to 28.6 in the finback whale. In the sperm whale the number of glands in the same area averages 38.5, i.e. one third more (Sergienko, 1965).

In the upper sections of the glands (one third of the gland's length) there are accessory cells; in the second quarter appear oxyntic cells, which in certain sections of the middle parts of the glands replace the accessory cells. The main cells appear here. Finally, in the bottom sections of the glands the number of oxyntic cells is far smaller and the main cells predominate. At the beginning of the second compartment, at its border with the first, there are simple tubular glands which branch out at the ends (Sergienko, 1965).

The submucosal layer of the second compartment consists of loose connective tissue with a large number of collagenous and elastic fibers, and also plexuses of vessels.

The musculature of the second compartment consists of several rows of longitudinal and transverse bundles of smooth fibers which ensure greater mobility of the mucosa (Sergienko, 1965).

The third compartment of the stomach begins in the upper third of the second compartment with an entrance which has tough walls. This compartment, which is gutlike, long, narrow and a little widened only at the end, little resembles a stomach compartment. The third compartment lies in common membranes with the ampulla of the duodenum and its tubelike beginning, and externally seems to constitute a single unit with it. The third compartment is united with the ampulla of the duodenum by a power-98 ful, narrow sphincter 1.5—1.7 cm in diameter (in young animals). The mucosa of this compartment contains simple tubular glands and corresponds to the pyloric part of the stomachs of other mammals (Sergienko, 1965). According to our histological data, the nature of the mucosa of the middle part of this compartment corresponds to that of the bottom of the second stomach compartment.

INTESTINE

The intestine of the adult sperm whale exceeds the length of the body (from the tip of snout to fork of tail) as follows: according to Slijper (1962) (Figure 62) it is 9—10 times longer, according to Betesheva and Sergienko (1964) 12.3—14.6 times, according to Jackson (1845) and Sleptsov (1952) 15—16 times, and according to A. V. Yablokov (1958) 17.5 times. Large embryos have approximately the same or a slightly smaller ratio between length of intestine and body length.

A. V. Yablokov (1958) indicates that these usual figures for the relative length of the cetacean intestine cannot be compared with figures for the relative length of the intestine of other mammals, since the length of a whale's intestine should be referred not to the overall body length but to the distance from tip of snout to anal opening.

In absolute figures the length of the intestine in a sperm whale suckling is approximately 80 m (Jackson, 1845), in a young sexually mature animal

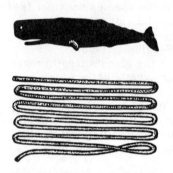

FIGURE 62. Length ratio between body of adult sperm whale and its intestine (Slijper, 1962)

138—163 m (Betesheva and Sergienko, 1964), and in a large male from 150 m (Slijper, 1962)* to 250 m (Sleptsov, 1952). The diameter of the intestine changes from 40 to 65 cm over its length (the smallest diameter is at a distance of 80 m from the stomach), and the thickness of its walls varies from 6 to 16 mm (Betesheva and Sergienko, 1964).

The intestine begins with the ampulla of the duodenum (Figure 60), which, as noted by many authors, resembles in shape and is just as large as the stomach compartments (Sleptsov, 1952; Betesheva and Sergienko, 1964) and forms (with the surface) a single whole with the third stomach compartment; this is clearly seen in Figure 59.

In adults the mucosa of the ampulla is light yellow, gathered into straightened and low folds.

The histology of the mucosa of the intestinal ampulla shows a certain resemblance to the pyloric part of the stomach, but at the surface of the mucosa solitary, small lymph follicles appear (in one row with the glands) which have an external outlet; this is a character of the beginning of the intestine.

The ampulla passes abruptly into the intestine, which initially has a diameter of about 10 cm (in a young animal).

99   The section of mucosa at the point where the expanded saclike ampulla passes into the tube of the duodenum is characterized by resilient annular folds or constrictions about 4—5 cm high; these evidently prevent stretching of the intestine and the passage from the ampulla of a large amount of food which is being digested. They may also slow down the movement of food so that it should ferment better.

---

* The author indicates that after dissection the length of the intestine is greatly increased; in particular, in large specimens it becomes twice as long. This apparently explains the smaller absolute and relative sizes of the intestine mentioned by Slijper.

The duodenum describes five short loops and with no change in thickness passes into the small intestine, which in a large male may reach a length of 16 m (Sleptsov, 1952).

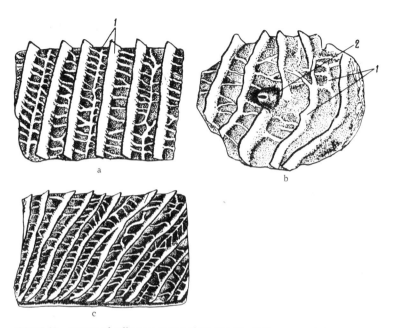

FIGURE 63. Mucosa of different sections of the intestine in the sperm whale:

a — duodenum not far from its beginning; b — duodenum at the point where the hepato-pancreatic duct ends: 1 — folds of mucosa; 2 — papilla of hepato-pancreatic duct; c — middle of small intestine.

The area of mucosa at the point where the duodenum leaves the formation common with the stomach is represented by a developed network of circular folds (softer than at the beginning of the intestine) which are mainly high, and sometimes divide into two and follow one another for a distance of 1.5—2 cm. In addition, between these folds there are well developed transverse and longitudinal low folds which unite with the main circular folds (Figure 63, a).

At a point approximately 3 m (in a young animal) from the beginning of the duodenum the common bile-pancreatic duct empties. Its length is about 70 cm, about 20 cm of which run within the intestinal wall. The diameter of the duct is 2.5 cm. The duct has a slitlike opening 8 × 3 mm at the tip of a papilla about 4 cm high (4.5—5.0 cm, according to Betesheva and Sergienko, 1964) (Figure 63, b).

The mucosa of the duodenum in this section forms high (up to 0.9 cm) circular folds 1.7—2.cm apart. The folds often split in two.

The jejunum of the sperm whale's digestive tract forms 69 loops, 15 of which are shorter than the others. The total length of this section can exceed 200 m (Sleptsov, 1952).

100

101

The circular folds of the mucosa of the small intestine are denser than those of the duodenum (up to 1 cm apart) and are lower (up to 0.4 cm), inclining gradually toward the long axis of the intestine. In this section the folds bifurcate more often, decrease in height, and are interrupted. Between certain of the large folds arise lower folds which are also circular. In addition, there is a well-developed network of longitudinal branching folds linking the low and high transverse folds (Figure 63, c).

The height of the circular folds gradually decreases to the height of the longitudinal folds; they are interrupted, end in branchings, and cease to be circular. The slant of these folds continues to increase and they mingle with the longitudinal folds, forming a single, slanted network; the number of short longitudinal folds (or transverse folds linking the circular ones) then decreases. The circular folds become essentially longitudinal, their height decreases, and finally they disappear.

The mucosa of the large intestine, which in large animals is about 26 m long (Sleptsov, 1952), does not form folds. In adults the thickness of the large intestine is about four times that of the small intestine.

LIVER

Only the most general descriptions of whale livers are available; in particular, in the case of the sperm whale, most of the data on this largest gland of the digestive system and of the organism as a whole consist of size and weight characteristics (Jackson, 1845; Sleptsov, 1952; and others). D. M. Golub et al. (1968) mention that in an embryo 8.5 mm long (length from sinciput to coccyx) there is already the anlage of the liver in the form of a large accumulation of cells gathered in loose strands reminiscent of a sponge.

The dimensions of this bilobate gland in the sperm whale are in general proportionate to those of the animal (Table 15), but it is noteworthy that in embryos the relative dimensions of the liver (as of several other internal organs) are greater than in adults; this may explain the great importance of the liver for the processes of growth.

TABLE 15. Size of the liver in the sperm whale, cm

Length of whale, m	Sex	Size of lobe, cm		Weight, kg	Reference
		first	second		
3.5 (embryo)	Female	36 × 56	35 × 49	18	Our data
4.86 (newborn)	"	62	85* 60	—	Jackson (1845)
15.0	Male	207 × 159**			Our data
16.0	"	210 × 170	188 × 150	519	Sleptsov (1952)

* Width of whole liver.
** Size of whole liver.

101   Jackson (1845) noted in a newborn sperm whale that the left lobe is distinctly larger than the right lobe. The liver as a whole resembles a butterfly's wing, the approximately uniform lobes being connected as it were by an isthmus.

The liver is situated behind the diaphragm,* on which it borders anteriorly; posteriorly it adjoins the stomach. It is divided by a round ligament (in fetuses by the umbilical vein) into left and right lobes; the lateral edges of the lobes are recurved, so that a bed is formed for the stomach. The pointed caudal end of the liver forms a shallow cleft, which envelops the tip (lower end) of the second compartment of the stomach. Thus the second stomach compartment is surrounded by the liver on three sides. In the region of attachment of the round ligament the posterior margin of the liver has a relatively deep cleft separating the left from the right lobe. The anterior margin of the liver adjoining the diaphragm is the thickest and is blunt. The upper posterior margin is somewhat sharper than the anterior margin, and the posterior lower margin is sharp. The left lobe has the form of a triangle, the wide, rounded base of which is directed toward the cupola of the diaphragm. The narrowed end of this lobe is directed toward the tail. The posterior two thirds of the left lobe adjoin the lateral part of the abdominal wall, while the anterior third adjoins the part of the diaphragm near the wall. Along the lower edge of this lobe, not far from the posterior corner, there is a cleft. The dorso-caudal edge of the left lobe is blunt and medially covers the small intestine. Approximately midway along, this edge of the left lobe touches the left kidney, but there is no renal depression.

The anterior lower half of the left lobe is adjoined medially by the first and second stomach compartments and the spleen, while the posterior upper third medially adjoins the intestine. The bluntly rounded anterior upper edge lies adjacent to the diaphragm, from which a wide fold of serous membrane descends to the liver, forming a strong wide triangular ligament at the upper corner. This ligament covers the spleen. On the posterior surface of the left lobe there is quite a deep stomachal depression, the long axis of which proceeds vertically.

The right lobe of the liver (lateral dissection on the right side) takes the form of an equilateral triangle, its apex directed upward. Its blunt, semicircular dorsocranial edge follows the contours of the diaphragm. The lateral surface is convex, the medial surface concave, covering the third stomach compartment and the ampulla of the duodenum. The ventro-caudal corner of the right lobe is pointed; it is adjoined by the tip of the urinary bladder, and in females, in addition, by part of the uterus and by the ovary, while the tip of the right lobe abuts against the uterus. The greater part of the posterior margin of the liver adjoins the anterior lower surface of the kidney, but there is no renal depression. Here one or two loops of the small intestine reach between the kidney and the posterior edge of the right lobe. The upper corner of the right lobe is externally and dorsally connected with the diaphragm by a wide triangular ligament, which anteriorly passes into a sickle-shaped ligament that passes along the outer surface of the liver and diaphragm. The sickle-shaped

---

* The detailed description of the gross morphology and topography of the liver is given mainly according to the prenatal embryo, but also according to young animals.

ligament proceeds forward and converges with the corresponding ligament of the other side of the liver. Along the upper margin of the liver from right to left passes a coronary ligament, which is a continuation of the triangular ligaments. The upper edge of the right lobe medially covers the duodenum.

102

The right and left parts of the coronary ligament, which run along the upper anterior edge of the corresponding lobe of the liver and the diaphragm, diverge and pass into the sickle-shaped ligament which, proceeding vertically in the sagittal plane, extends down and back to terminate in the region of the deep cleft dividing the left and right lobes of the liver, where it then passes into the round ligament of the liver. This ligament unites the liver with the umbilical aperture in the abdominal wall.

Deep in the upper anterior margin on the medial side of the right lobe runs the wide vena cava superior, passing obliquely forward and upward. It receives more than 20 hepatic veins from both the right and the left lobe, five or six of these veins being larger than the others.

The bile duct emerges in the region of the porta hepatis (from its visceral surface), some way above the point of attachment of the round ligament of the liver (in one line with it), proceeds backward, upward and to the right, and enters deep inside the pancreas, where about ten of its smaller-diametered ducts open into it.

The common bile-pancreatic duct protrudes into the duodenum approximately 1 m from its beginning on the side of the mesenteric margin. In all whales the liver fulfills the function of the absent gallbladder, which indicates that the liver of the sperm whale is less important for the digestive process as compared with the liver of other animals and more important for metabolic and growth processes due to its high content of vitamin A.

The entire digestive system is constructed in conformity with the fact that the sperm whale feeds mainly on cephalopods at great depths. The oral cavity and dentition are adapted to seizing, holding, and guiding the mobile prey. The strong muscular-glandular stomach of the sperm whale probably exerts a stronger muscular and secretory action on food bolus than in the case of other whales, while the long intestine and the digestive apparatus as a whole ensure intensive digestion of food.

Chapter 7

RESPIRATORY SYSTEM

"The sperm whale breathes only about one seventh
or Sunday of its time."

Moby Dick

The respiratory organs of whales, particularly of toothed whales, have
attracted the attention of many investigators, since in these animals the
adaptability of the respiratory organs to life in the water, with the maintenance of a terrestrial pulmonary type of respiration, has necessarily
become manifested particularly strongly. This applies first and foremost
to the deep-diving sperm whale, which is the perfect example of complete
adaptation to the aquatic mode of life.

It will be recalled that:

1) the amount of time spent by toothed whales on the surface is very
brief: 30—60 times less than underwater;

103   2) the duration of submergence by a large toothed whale reaches
1—1.5 hours;

3) no mammal under normal conditions is subjected during its life
to a pressure reaching 100 atm at depths of up to 1,000 m, but according
to the latest data the sperm whale dives even deeper than this. Moreover,
this is not an exceptional, chance occurrence, when the animal is obliged
to "fight for its life," as might be thought (Slijper, 1962), but a natural,
normal circumstance, an element of its customary medium of its habitat.

This is the angle from which we should consider the adaptations that
have evolved in deep-diving mammals.

In this chapter we deal also with the spermaceti organ, which is an
exceptional phenomenon in the animal world and which reaches its highest
degree of development in the sperm whale. The functions and performance
of the spermaceti organ are apparently more diverse than human knowledge
can yet fathom — certainly they go beyond what anyone has established so far.

EPICRANIAL RESPIRATORY PASSAGES

In the sperm whale and the other toothed whales (as distinct from baleen
whales) the respiratory tract begins with an unpaired respiratory opening,
the distinctively shaped blowhole (Figure 64). In the sperm whale the blowhole is situated in the front left corner of the head, whereas in other toothed
whales and baleen whales it lies in the upper middle part of the head, above

105

the bony nasal apertures. As in all whales, in the sperm whale the blowhole is at the highest point of the head; it is thus the first thing to emerge from the water when the animal surfaces. Unlike the blowhole of other toothed 104 whales, that of the sperm whale lies parallel to the body axis. Its size depends mainly on that of the body (see Chapter 2).

The epicranial respiratory passages have become of more and more interest to scientists, especially in recent years due to broader concepts of their functions. At present they are considered to act as sound-generating organs. The most thorough description of the nasal passages and spermaceti sacs was given by Pouchet and Beauregard (1885), Raven and Gregory (1933), and Sleptsov (1952). With regard to the illustrations in Sleptsov's work (1952), particularly Figure 22, serious inaccuracies have been allowed to creep in, especially in the position of the left nasal passage (which, incidentally, does not correspond to the position of the nasal passage shown in our Figure 20). The descriptions and illustrations of a cross section of the sperm whale head given by Pouchet and Beauregard (1885) are more accurate and in general match our descriptions, which resulted from an analysis of the structure of the spermaceti organ and nasal passages. For a thorough analysis, segmental and sagittal sections of the heads of several prenatal embryos, photographs, and accompanying sketches were provided; the correctness of the descriptions was confirmed for adult animals when these were processed commercially.

(103)

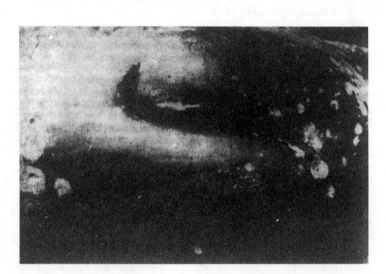

FIGURE 64. Blowhole of the sperm whale

The system and arrangement of the sperm whale's nasal passages differ sharply from those of small toothed whales. The sperm whale's nasal passages are drawn out along the long axis of the skull, from the naris to the bony nasal apertures, and they have a fairly complex configuration.

The left and right nasal passages differ in both structure and function. The solitary naris, which is a deep dermal-muscular fold, opens by means of special muscles (Figure 66: 2) (lateral dilator of the blowhole), i.e., as in dolphins (Lawrence and Schewill, 1956), into the narrow, almost cylindrical nasal passage (Raven and Gregory, 1933). According to our data, its shape changes: it is relatively round at first and at the end but in the middle of the head crescent-shaped, with the convex side downward. The left nasal passage initially passes under a layer of covering fat and powerful tendons into dense connective tissue, and then departs obliquely into the wide left bony nasal passage (Figures 65:2, 66:1).

In its distal part the left nasal passage (in the anterior lower corner of the slit of the nostril) is joined by a narrow passage to the large but strongly flattened oval cavity which from the side has the appearance of a lumen. It is called the distal cavity (distal sac according to Raven and Gregory, 1933) and extends far onto the right side of the distal part of the head (Figure 65:3). A small pouchlike cavity communicates by a passage with the distal cavity and lies below it in the same plane (Figure 65:4). The distal cavity is connected along the entire lower side on the right with the wide but strongly dorsoventrally compressed (to virtually slit-shaped) right nasal passage (Figure 66:5). The latter is situated almost in the middle of the head, somewhat below the left nasal passage (according to Sleptsov's data (1952), 80—90 cm below). The greater part (from the beginning) of the right nasal passage is set obliquely to the medial plane of the head at an angle of about 50°.

(105)

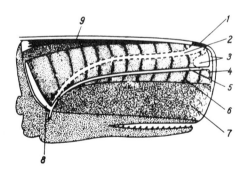

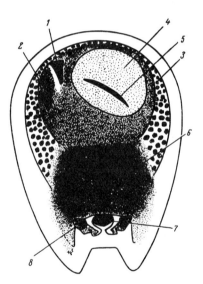

FIGURE 65. Structure of spermaceti organ and system of epicranial nasal passages of the sperm whale:

1 — blowhole; 2 — left nasal passage; 3 — distal cavity; 4 — pouchlike evagination of distal cavity; 5 — right nasal passage; 6 — upper spermaceti sac; 7 — lower spermaceti sac; 8 — frontal cavity; 9 — muscular-tendinous layer.

FIGURE 66. Cross section of sperm whale head (prenatal embryo, from a photograph and illustrations from nature; posterior view):

1 — left nasal passage; 2 — lateral dilator of blowhole; 3 — muscular-tendinous layer; 4 — upper spermaceti organ; 5 — right nasal passage; 6 — lower spermaceti sac; 7 — vomer; 8 — maxillaries.

107

The length of the right nasal passage reaches 2.5—3 m at a width of 80 cm (Sleptsov, 1952). The right nasal passage reaches the considerably 105 smaller right cranial nasal opening and passes (in the posterior left part) into a rounded duct separated from the left epicranial nasal duct by a sheet of dense cartilage.

Above the right bony nasal passage, at the level of the terminal rounded part of the epicranial passage and above it, the large and voluminous, spherically curved (exactly following the shape of the occipital part of the skull) frontal cavity is formed, called the frontal sac by Pouchet and Beauregard (1885) (Figure 65:8). Its diameter reaches 130 cm (Sleptsov, 1952). The posterior wall of this sac is covered with mucous epithelium which is usually dark, less often light or of variegated coloration, forming blisterlike opaque or semitransparent swellings of various diameter (Figure 67). The largest of them reach a diameter of 4—5 cm. They are filled with a fluid which causes irritation of the mucous membrane of the eyes; however, the color of red or blue litmus paper does not change when it is placed in this fluid (Sleptsov, 1952). The purpose of these formations is not clear.

The epithelium lining all the epicranial nasal passages and cavities is of the dermal type and intensely dark, almost black. Sometimes, however, a light, almost white, or gray epithelium lines the frontal sac.

Pouchet and Beauregard (1885) report on glands of the sebaceous type in some areas of the epithelium lining the distal and frontal cavities, i. e., the system of the right nasal passage. According to their description, some of these glands are visible to the naked eye. These authors note that there are no glands in the system of the left nasal passage.

The distal and frontal cavities serve to delimit the upper spermaceti sac at the distal and proximal ends (Figure 65:6). Despite the differences in structure between the epicranial passages of the sperm whale and those 106 of other toothed whales, investigators have suggested a genetic affinity between them and homologize the various parts of the upper nasal passages of toothed Cetacea and, in particular, the distal cavity of the sperm whale, with the dorsal sac of the white whale, harbor porpoise (P h o c a e n a   p h o c a e n a), and pygmy sperm whale, as well as with the vestibular sacs of S t e n e l l a   c a e r u l e o - a l b u s, the bottlenose dolphin (T u r s i o p s   t r u n c a t u s), and common dolphins. The frontal cavity is homologized with the premaxillary cavity in the white whale, harbor porpoise, S t e n e l l a, bottlenose dolphin, and narwhal, and with the ventral cavity in the pygmy sperm whale (Raven and Gregory, 1933; Kleinenberg and Yablokov, 1958).

The right nasal passage lies inside the upper spermaceti sac. At the very beginning it divides it in two, and then into two unequal parts: a larger upper right part and a smaller lower left part.*

Data obtained indicate that in the early stages of development (at a length of 9 cm) all embryos have two external nares. In one embryo examined which was 9.5 cm long the slits of the nares constituted one wide naris, whereas embryos 12.5 and 19.1 cm long each had two slits (see Figure 5:3). According to Beddard (1919), an embryo 11.4 cm long had two, while an embryo 24.1 cm long had only one slit. According to our materials, all

---

* According to Howell (1930), Raven and Gregory (1933), and Sleptsov (1952), the right nasal passage lies between the upper and lower spermaceti sacs.

FIGURE 67. Inner epithelial lining of frontal sac
of the sperm whale head

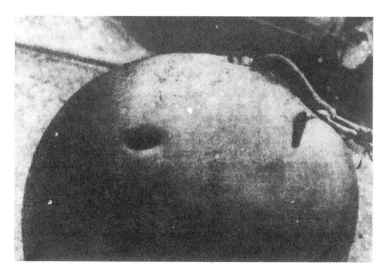

FIGURE 68. One of the two known cases of a second (right) naris being found in the
sperm whale (photo by Veinger)

embryos more than 26 cm long have one narial slit. It can be assumed
that in sperm whale embryos at a stage of development corresponding to
a length of 20—24 cm, one nostril is formed. However, the nostril acquires
the shape and position on the head that it has in the adult animal only when
the embryo is about 50 cm long. Until then the narial slit consists as it
were of two parts: the right part lying in the middle of the forehead and
the left part lying at an angle on the left half of the head. The right part
of the narial slit becomes overgrown, but the subcutaneous passage from
the left naris into the distal cavity, and the right passage remain; the left
naris gradually swivels parallel to the body axis and assumes the typical
"S" shape characteristic for the adult.

107   The shape of the two narial slits of the embryo examined from above
closely resembles that of a half-moon, i.e., like that of the other toothed
cetaceans, but in the sperm whale the narial slit is divided in the middle
by a septum.

That the sperm whale's having a solitary naris on the left side of the
anterior part of the head is a secondary phenomenon is supported by the
arrangement of the bony nasal passages, which in no way differs from that
of the bony nasal openings in the skull in all other representatives of the
Odontoceti. It is of interest that Latyshev reported a catch, in the Antarctic
in 1965, of a sperm whale 15.5 m long, in which on the right half of the
anterior part of the head there was an ellipsoid pigmented opening measuring 6 × 8 cm and 8—10 cm deep, displaced forward from the left naris. It can
be asserted that this was not the completely overgrown slit of the second
right naris. G. M. Veinger has reported two such cases to us: one specimen
was caught in the North Pacific in 1967 (Figure 68), the other in 1969 in the
Antarctic.

Several views have been expressed concerning the functions of the
epicranial nasal passages. Howell (1930) believes that the cavities of the
nasal passages are not the result of evolutionary adaptation but, on the
contrary, are "phylogenetic relicts." This is hardly likely, since no such
structures have apparently existed at any time in land mammals (Yablokov,
1961). Moreover, it is hard to believe that such complex structures would
be without a function (Kleinenberg et al., 1964).

Winge (1921) conjectured that air pressed out of the lungs at great depths
enters the cavities of the nasal passages. A. V. Yablokov (1961) doubted this
108 on the grounds that if air is forced from the lungs into these cavities, exchange will be unable to proceed in the lungs. Later Kleinenberg et al.
(1964) pointed out that the air is not forced out from the lungs, since the
pressure of the surrounding medium acts equally on the lungs and on the
nasal passages.

In the opinion of Raven and Gregory (1933), the complex of the nasal
passages participates in the regulation of pressure in the lungs when the
depth of submersion changes; they consider this to be accomplished by the
passage of part of the air from the lungs into the nasal passages and
cavities as a result of contraction of the muscles of the spermaceti organ.
Further, according to the same data, the frontal sac lightens the posterior
end of the spermaceti organ, i.e., it acts as a hydrostatic apparatus, and
also participates in the overlapping of the bony nasal passages.

Sleptsov (1948, 1952), while not denying the functions of the epicranial
passages of the sperm whale as presented by Raven and Gregory (1933),
believes the main purpose of the right nasal passage — transformed, in

his opinion, into an air sac — and of the frontal cavity to be the creation of an additional reserve of air approximately equal to the amount of air in the lungs (i.e., 7—8 thousand liters), thus giving the sperm whale a doubled supply of air (the lungs and the right passage with frontal sac). The air from the right nasal passage (air sac) can, in his opinion, pass into the lungs as required. According to this hypothesis, filling of the sac must take place as follows. From the ventilated lungs the sperm whale, closing the left naris, exhales air into the right nasal passage and its expansions, where the air is retained by muscular valves; it then reopens the left naris and fills the lungs with air (Sleptsov, 1952). In the author's opinion this also enables the animal to remain under water for very long periods. This view has become fairly widely accepted (Tomilin, 1957; Zemskii, 1962; and others).

Later investigators (Lawrence and Schewill, 1956; Kleinenberg et al., 1964) showed, however, that after submersion, all communication between the epicranial passages and the lungs ceases, since the external openings of the bony nasal passages and of the palato-pharyngeal sphincter are closed, and air cannot travel from the sacs into the lungs or back. Furthermore, even if communication between the epicranial passages and the lungs were not interrupted, owing to the actual construction of the lungs from the functional-anatomical point of view any air other than that which was there on entry into the lungs would not be used for respiration. Thus air from the epicranial passages cannot participate in the gas exchange taking place in the sperm whale's lungs. Moreover, as already mentioned, it cannot be accepted that the right passage, which is essentially a slit, is an air sac and a storage receptacle for large reserves of air.

Kleinenberg and A. V. Yablokov (1958, 1961) consider that the importance of the epicranial passages and cavities lies in the fact that by the pressure of the air in them, which is compressed under the hydrostatic water pressure, they ensure tight closure of the nasal opening and the bony nasal passages. Thus the greater the pressure, the more firmly are the passages sealed. Tomilin (1957) expressed the well-founded view that the air sacs of a toothed whale together with the blowhole constitute a sound-signalling organ. Sounds are probably produced when a portion of air is forced from one sac into the other (Kleinenberg et al., 1964). When the air is squeezed through in this way the various thin partitions between the sacs inevitably vibrate. This hypothesis has been lent weight by direct observations during whaling of sound-producing white whales.

Another sound-producing mechanism is also considered probable (Bel'kovich and Yablokov, 1963a): when the animal dives, owing to the simultaneous closure of both the external valve leading into the nasal passages and of the palato-pharyngeal sphincter into the cavities of the bony nasal passages, the air pressure is kept close to atmospheric pressure, i.e., a pressure which is lower than that in the air-conveying cavities. Adjustable opening of the aperture leading from the epicranial passages into the bony nasal passages must, in the authors' view, lead to the emission of ultrasonic vibrations. The authors see a difficulty in the generation of sounds according to this hypothesis owing to the very small volume of air enclosed in the air-conveying sacs and the limited volume of the cavity of the bony nasal passages. As a result, owing to the establishment of a balance of pressures in the cavities of these sections, sounding may be of very short duration. This hypothesis is even less plausible when applied to the sperm whale due to the relatively even smaller volumes of the cavities of the bony cranial passages in the extremely flattened skull.

Recent investigations apparently also do not exclude the possibility of sound production by discharge of the air present in the sacs through the naris.

Malyshev (1966) indicates that the sperm whale has developed labia vocales (without lateral pockets), at the base of which lies the thyroarytaenoid muscle. We do not believe that these can act as sound generators, but what other function they might have is not clear.

The sound-generating mechanism has been insufficiently studied, not only in the case of sperm whales but also for dolphins, which have been relatively better investigated in this respect. Nevertheless, it is clear that the complex of epicranial nasal passages in the sperm whale is a sound generator.

Once it is denied that the right nasal passage acts as an additional reservoir for pulmonary respiration, the slitlike right passage linking the frontal and distal cavities is seen to be ideally suitable for participation in sound generation; we will discuss this after describing hypotheses concerning the functional significance of the spermaceti organ.

SPERMACETI ORGAN

Obviously the epicranial nasal passages and the cavities which transect the spermaceti sacs or pass around them must be functionally closely connected with the spermaceti organ. Naturally, too, we should take the "spermaceti organ" to denote the entire complex of these structures.

Let us examine the structure of this organ and what is thought to be its role in the life of the animal.

Until now it has been accepted (Sleptsov, 1952; and others) that the spermaceti organ of the sperm whale should be divided into two sacs (we also maintain this). The differences in their structure led Pouchet and Beauregard (1885), Howell (1930), and Raven and Gregory (1933) to regard the upper part of the spermaceti organ as a spermaceti sac [case] (or as the spermaceti organ) and the lower part as a special tissue containing spermaceti (junk). The upper rounded, almost cylindrical spermaceti sac lies under a layer of solid fat with a large amount of connective tissue and
110 is shifted slightly to the right of the midline. It is enclosed in dense fibrous tissue which lines the surface of the lower spermaceti sac and is a kind of continuation of it. In the middle and parietal parts the upper spermaceti sac lies below a strong tendinous-muscular layer; in the middle part there are more tendons, while in the parietal part muscles predominate (see Figures 65:9 and 66:3).

The upper spermaceti sac consists of loose tissue with a high content of spermaceti (see Chapter 18), part of which usually flows out when the head is dissected.

The lower spermaceti sac (or lower part of the spermaceti organ, if the two sacs are regarded as parts of a single whole) consists of more solid spermaceti (with a higher melting point, according to Sleptsov, 1952) than the upper one, and contains a larger amount of connective tissue. The upper part of the lower sac surrounds the upper sac on all sides and, as already mentioned, consists of fibrous tissue. Considering that in fact the one sac (the upper) is as it were enclosed in the other (the lower), the two can be taken to constitute a single formation enclosed under a layer of fat and a tendinous-muscular layer and lying on the widened trough-shaped bed formed by the maxillary bones (see Figure 66).

Raven and Gregory (1933) believed that the spermaceti organ (together with the nasal passages) acts as a hydrostatic apparatus and participates in pressure regulation in the depths.

Sleptsov (1952) considers the above-enumerated functions of the supra-cranial cushion as a whole to be secondary, but names as additional functions only amortization, which counteracts the pressure of the counterflows on the organism during diving, and means of defense and attack. The right (lower) sac, in his opinion, acts as a support for the right nasal passage and at the same time as a regulator of the link between the right nasal passage and the frontal sac.

Even from the standpoint of general evolutionary morphology (Severtsov, 1939; Shmal'gauzen, 1968), it is quite clear that the complex and literally unique apparatus — the spermaceti organ (spermaceti sacs, passages, and cavities) — is multifunctional. In our opinion, sound genera-tion is carried out with the participation of the whole apparatus or a con-siderable part of it — at any rate, structures that at first sight are not associated with this and were formerly examined in isolation.

Furthermore, what were once quite obscure details in the structure of the spermaceti organ and the air passages acquire a definite significance when united in a single functional purpose.

Hypothetically the operation of this complex apparatus of sound generation as a whole can be represented as follows. It is assumed that each or some of the strong tendons with terminal muscular heads comprising a muscular-tendinous layer of the head is joined to a certain section of the upper sperma-ceti sac. It is interesting that the tissue of the sac is not homogeneous in structure. Together with spermaceti which is quite fluid there are denser interlayers with a large amount of connective tissue, which in a way separate the mass of spermaceti into a series of wide disks (see Figures 65, 69).

When the muscle bundles of the muscular-tendinous layer contract, a certain displacement of the upper spermaceti sac and compression of the
111 frontal cavity is possible, as indicated by Raven and Gregory (1933). In this case the air streams into the right nasal passage. Successive (or nonsuccessive) contraction of the muscles and pulling of the tendons neces-sarily leads to a change in the position (or shape) of the individual disks of the spermaceti sac. As a result, a system of slits of various width or even of cavities may be formed in the right passage (enclosed in the sac of loose spermaceti); air passes through this and causes the walls of the passage to vibrate, generating sound. By a slackening of the muscles of the tendinous layer the air can be readmitted to the frontal cavity. The left nasal passage, whose only function is to let air through, is enclosed in very dense tissue and has the definite invariable form of a lumen.

A. V. Yablokov (in litt.) proposed that the distal cavity of the sperm whale, anteriorly bordering the upper spermaceti sac, can, when periodically filled with air, be a distinctive sound-isolating curtain and render the sperm whale completely mute for some moments (the air layer in the cavity is an ideal barrier to sound). Developing these ideas further, it can be surmised that owing to such a structure, the possibility exists in principle of producing short impulse sound messages of any frequency. Existing records of sounds from sperm whales closely match this scheme of sound generation.

In 1962 the hypothesis was advanced that the concave skull, like any bone, is a poor conductor of ultrasound and may be the screen of a reflector which collects and reflects sounds, while a fatty (frontal) protuberance (in the sperm whale the spermaceti organ) containing a certain type of fatty tissue, in which the speed of transmission of sound waves is equal (or 112 nearly equal) to the speed of their transmission in water, acts as a hydroacoustic lens for more precise hydrolocation (Evans and Prescott, 1962; Bel'kovich and Yablokov, 1963a, c).

In the authors' opinion, the ultrasonic waves arising in the epicranial nasal passages are evenly distributed to all sides. A considerable number of them, entering the reflector of the skull, are reflected and concentrated by the "sonic lens," and then a narrow beam of ultrasonic waves travels in a definite direction (hypothesis of an ultrasonic "projector").

The focusing of the sonic beam may change owing to mobility of the epicranial region (judging by the arrangement of the musculature and ligaments), and perhaps due to changes in the shape of the lens itself. We may develop this hypothesis and suggest that the sperm whale's upper spermaceti sac, divided into a number of disks, represents a complex system of such lenses.

Experimental modeling of a dolphin's head in order to study the suggested sound directionality and its formation (the sound source was set up on the skull or in the head of a dead dolphin, and the sounds were picked up by a receiver) above all confirmed that even one skull gives directionality to sound of any frequencies, and the degree of its directionality increases as the sound wave frequencies are increased (Romanenko, Tomilin and Artemenko, 1965). Finally, in experiments with an entire head, with high-frequency sound waves (more than 80 kilohertz), the diagram of directionality was half as wide as in the first variant of the experiment (with a skull). Naturally, the effect of the activity of the sound-producing, reflecting and focusing systems of the animal organism is not to be compared with the model used. Investigators have proved experimentally only the basic correctness of the hypothesis concerning sound directionality.

Bel'kovich and Yablokov (1963 a, c) suggested that focusing of the beam of ultrasonic waves at a certain distance in front of an animal's head results in a fairly strong ultrasonic shock of the order of many watts, which toothed whales, and in particular the sperm whale which has a frontal protuberance of extremely complex structure, can use as an effective instrument for stunning and immobilizing prey far away ("ultrasonic beam" hypothesis).

It may be said that this is the sole hypothesis which explains the sperm whale's ability to defend itself against fast-moving animals at great depths in conditions of perpetual darkness.

If this hypothesis is proven for smaller Cetacea, the study of which (including experimental study) is less problematic, then in the case of the sperm whale it finds sound anatomical, functional, and ecological confirmation. Apparently the best model of an ultrasonic projector to take is the head of a sperm whale, beaked dolphin or freshwater dolphin, in which the spherically concave frontal surface of the skull would be a perfect screen.

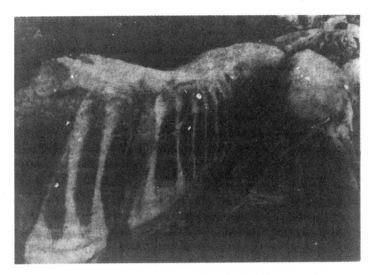

FIGURE 69. Upper spermaceti sac separated from the head (denser interlayers can be seen in the loose spermaceti. Photo by A. Yablokov)

Ol'shevskii and Shashev regard the spermaceti organ as a generator and at the same time as a receiver of new, recently described waves of an electromagnetic type called hydronic. These are transmitted in the water at speeds close to the speed of light and are collected by receivers of electromagnetic and acoustic vibrations (the newspaper "Komsomol'-skaya pravda" of 20 April 1967). The authors consider that sounds formerly recorded for toothed whales are actually traces of hydronic waves and that marine animals are not capable of generating sounds of several 113 thousand kilohertz. It is still too early to speak of the reliability and significance of this hypothesis. We should admit that we do not know enough about the functional significance of the distinctive skull and spermaceti organ of toothed whales.

LARYNX, TRACHEA, BRONCHI

The larynx and pharynx of the sperm whale are basically no different in structure from the larynx of other toothed whales described earlier (Weber, 1928; Kleinenberg and Yablokov, 1958; and others). The principal feature of the pharyngeal structure of toothed whales consists in the constant separation of the esophageal and respiratory tracts. Mention of this separation in the sperm whale was made already by Jackson (1845).

The arytenoid cartilages together with the epiglottis form the distinctive laryngeal tube, which as a pharyngeal protuberance runs through the entire lumen of the pharyngeal passage, enters the bony nasal passages, and is closed here by muscles of the palato-pharyngeal (laryngo-pharyngeal) sphincter, which surrounds and compresses the base of its spear-shaped head (see Figures 58, 70). This sphincter is not located in the soft parts of the palate but is surrounded by the bony walls (bony tube) formed by the pterygoid and the palatine bones (Kleinenberg et al., 1964). Such a structure protects the air passages from the entry of water through the mouth when the animal feeds under water.

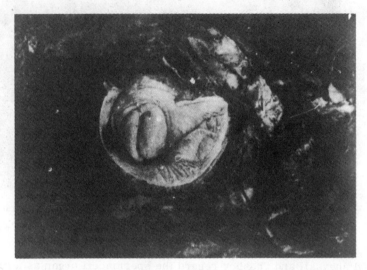

FIGURE 70. Top of laryngeal tube and palato-pharyngeal sphincter of the sperm whale (photo by A. Yablokov)

Thus the structure and arrangement of the musculature in toothed whales ensure that the laryngeal tube be held constantly in the skull, while the musculature of the larynx itself moves the arytenoid cartilages and epi-glottis, opening and closing the passage into the larynx and the air passages 114 to the lungs. It is interesting that the structure of the larynx, and in this case the mutual position of the laryngeal tube and the skull, is different in different species of toothed whales. In deep divers (sperm whale, beaked dolphins, in particular Baird's beaked whale) the prolonged larynx enters farther into the tube formed by the bones of the skull (Yablokov, 1961) than in whales which dive to lesser depths.

In sperm whales the trachea is wide, especially in relation to its length, and short both absolutely and relatively (about 4% of the body length, Table 16) in comparison with the trachea of other mammals (including marine animals); however, it is of the same type as, for example, in the white whale (Kleinenberg et al., 1964).

TABLE 16. Size of trachea in the sperm whale

Length of animal, m	Sex	Trachea		Reference
		length, cm	width, cm	
4.9	Female	20	10	Jackson (1845)
9.0	"	—	14	Sleptsov (1952)
16.0	Male	—	20	Our data

Kleinenberg et al. (1964) consider that the main difference between the trachea of toothed whales (e.g., white whale) and that of many other mammals, particularly of baleen whales, is that the rings of the trachea are closed and form a noncollapsible tube in the white whale. Jackson (1845) counts in the sperm whale trachea, as in that of other Cetacea he investigated, about seven rings of irregular form. According to his description, one of these rings is very wide, whereas the others are narrow and anastomose.

According to our material, the flattened dorsoventral cartilaginous tube of the trachea has a somewhat more complex structure and the seven rings in the trachea can be counted only very arbitrarily. Although the rings are of approximately the same size, they are distinctly separated from each other only in the dorsal part of the trachea; at the sides and on the ventral surface they are joined together for a considerable distance. Thus in the anterior part of the trachea the first four rings are fused, while in different sections in the posterior part the fifth ring is partially fused with the sixth and the sixth with the seventh. The fifth ring is superimposed on the fourth, also on the ventral surface and the sixth ring is partially superimposed on the fifth.

A special feature of the trachea and bronchial tree in the sperm whale (noted already by Jackson in 1845), as also in cattle, the white whale, and the narwhal, is the presence of a prearterial (tracheal) bronchus departing from the trachea up to its bifurcation and passing into the apex of the lung (see Figure 71). The noncollapsible tubes of the bronchi are also formed by cartilaginous rings, which continue in the pulmonary bronchi. The anlage of the respiratory organs is visible in a sperm whale embryo 8.5 mm long as a tube running along the ventral wall of the esophagus and dividing into a right and a left bronchial stem, the ends of which are widened and represent the mesenchymal primordia of the lungs (Golub, Leontyuk, and Novikov, 1968).

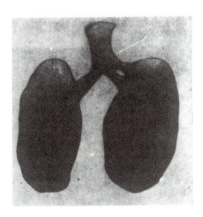

FIGURE 71. Lungs of a prenatal sperm whale embryo (photo by A. Yablokov)

115

The rings of the bronchi differ in width both from ring to ring and within one ring, but in general they are narrower than the rings of the trachea. In the individual sections the rings grow together or converge, and one of the rings forms a butt between two opposite rings.

Owing to such a system of supporting rings of the conduction paths they are not forced to contract under any hydrostatic pressure. This implies that inside the cavity of the trachea and of the large bronchi there should be an area with near-atmospheric pressure. This interesting suggestion put forward by Kleinenberg et al. (1964) requires confirmation by further investigations into functional anatomy.

LUNGS

A general morphological description of the lungs of the sperm whale can be found in Jackson (1845). A fairly detailed account of the histological structure is given by Murata (1951). The sperm whale's lungs do not differ in the main, anatomically and histologically, from those of other Cetacea described in works of a general nature (Zhedenov, 1961, 1965; Slijper, 1962; and others) and specialized works (Haynes and Laurie, 1937; Belanger, 1940; and others).

Each lung of the sperm whale (and of any other toothed cetacean) consists of one long, flattened, oval-triangular lobe (Figure 71). The greater part of the lung tissue in all whales, and in particular the sperm whale, is situated on the dorsal side of the thoracic cavity (Slijper, 1962). According to Zhedenov (1965), the unilobate structure is a secondary phenomenon arising from the reorganization of lobate lungs upon the transition to the aquatic mode of life.

The size of the lungs depends on that of the animal, as indicated by Kleinenberg et al. (1964) and confirmed by Table 17.

(116) TABLE 17. Size of lungs in the sperm whale

Length of animal, m	Sex	First lung		Second lung		Reference
		length, cm	width, cm	length, cm	width, cm	
4.2 (embryo)	Male	63	30	58	29	Our data
4.9	Female	62	35	—	—	Jackson (1845)
14.2	Male	145	—	—	—	Our data
15.0	"	111	43	—	—	" "
15.6	"	145	—	165	—	" "
16.0	"	170	70	170	70	Sleptsov (1952)

In toothed whales the size of the lungs varies greatly depending on the degree to which they are filled with air, which does not always leave the lungs or their parts, due (according to Kleinenberg et al., 1964) to collapse of the alveolar sphincters.

In the histological preparations which we obtained, the respiratory part of the sperm whale lung* showed different variants of combination of the hyaline cartilage and the muscle fibers in the small bronchi and the bronchioli.

The small bronchi have cartilaginous supporting plates of various, mainly irregular form (Figure 72).

The alveolar ducts have numerous muscular ring-sphincters without
116 cartilages, owing to which the air from the alveoli does not enter the conduction paths even under pressure approaching hydrostatic pressure at the time of the respiratory pause when the animal submerges deep in the water.

The terminal bronchioli (short in sperm whales, according to Murata, 1951), which are situated between the two above-described sections of air passages, are intermediate between them regarding their structure; in the

---

* The description of the histological preparations was made in consultation with A. V. Abuladze, senior coworker of IBR AN SSSR.

larger, cartilaginous elements predominate, in the smaller, muscle fibers. Murata (1951) also mentioned that the sperm whale has ringlike cartilages and circular smooth muscles in the walls of the bronchioli of about 1 mm diameter. He believes that the muscular sphincters in the lungs are best developed in deep-diving Cetacea — sperm whales and beaked dolphins.

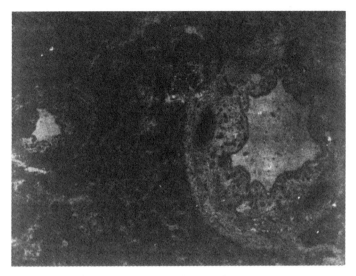

FIGURE 72. Photograph of a histological section of a sperm whale lung

117   The form of the cell nuclei of the interalveolar septa in the lungs of the sperm whale is peculiar to the muscular structures and indicates possible penetration by the muscle fibers of the interalveolar spaces, as occurs also in the lungs of the white whale (Kleinenberg et al., 1964).

The histological picture of a microscopical section of the sperm whale's respiratory region is striking in respect of the abundant blood supply: all the vessels are overfilled. Such a cross section, which is evidently usual for the sperm whale, is observed in other animals only in a case of hyperemia.

The stroma of the lungs shows very clearly expressed capillaries filled with formed elements of the blood arranged in one row. In well developed interalveolar septa with a thickness of up to 60μ (Murata, 1951) in the preparations examined there is not one, as in land mammals, but two capillaries. They envelop and entwine around their alveolar spaces and are directly contiguous with them, becoming their "walls." This can be explained by the need for as close a link as possible between the blood and air and extremely rapid gas exchange. The same structural feature has been noted for other Cetacea (Haynes and Laurie, 1937).

GAS EXCHANGE

The main physiological features of respiration in diving animals were stated by Kleinenberg (1956) to be the large volume of the lungs with an increased number and size of alveoli, the high oxygen capacity of the blood, the insensibility of the respiratory center to the accumulation of carbon dioxide in the organism, the large amount of muscle hemoglobin, the vascular reflexes, and finally, the unusually high degree of development of the rete mirabile.

The sperm whale certainly dives deeper and spends more time under water than any other mammal, and therefore the physiology of its gas exchange obviously must be more specific, or rather more complex, than that of any other cetacean, with maximum utilization of all the reserves and potentials of the organism, highly organized and specialized in this respect.

It is of interest to clarify what permits the animal to remain under the water for up to 1.5 hours at depths of several kilometers. Howell (1930) experimentally checked the absorptivity of the spermaceti oil in relation to carbon dioxide and found that spermaceti cannot absorb carbon dioxide in large quantities. He believes, however, that his original material was unsuitable for such experiments, and he recommends continuing experiments in this direction using fresh spermaceti and a higher pressure.

The morphological structure of the thorax of the sperm whale, like that of other toothed whales, suggests its high compressibility (Tomilin, 1951; Kleinenberg, 1956; Yablokov, 1961), resulting from the small number of sternal ribs (3—5), the segmented sternum, and the position of a considerable part of the lungs outside the thorax, i.e., the absence of conditions and morphological features of structure protecting the lungs from high pressure, as this was formerly expressed (Kandror, 1941; Ognev, 1951; Zenkovich, 1952).

Other evidence that the internal organs of the whale are not protected from pressure consists in the feeding on deepwater animals at considerable
118 depths, the internal pressure in the body cavity of which amounts to many tens of atmospheres, so that such a pressure must evidently exist also in the whale's body cavity (Yablokov, 1961). The gas exchange processes either operate normally under pressure (since the blood pressure in the capillaries rises to the same degree that the pressure of gases in the alveolar air increases, meaning that the relative partial pressure of gases of the air and the tension of gases in the blood does not change), or else under these unusual conditions they may change completely (Kleinenberg et al., 1964).

It has been established that in Cetacea the respiratory center is insensitive to the accumulation of carbon dioxide, this permitting a long delay of respiration and so a fuller use of the oxygen supply. As is known, other mammals utilize less than half their oxygen reserves, since the life activity of the organism is regulated by the carbonic acid content and not by the oxygen consumption. In aquatic animals the regulator of respiratory movements is the oxygen content of the blood, a diminution of which induces these movements (Irving, 1938; Kreps, 1941). From this the conclusion may be reached that one of the factors determining the animal's long stay under water is the need for an increased oxygen reserve and above all an increase in the overall supply of air in the lungs, in other words, enlargement of the lungs themselves. On the other hand, the existence of large air-filled cavities can lead to excessive and dangerous compression of the thorax, so that the solution may lie, on the contrary, in a decrease of the amount of air (Slijper, 1962). Evolution has solved these contradictions.

It is known that energy expenditure in a warm-blooded animal changes in proportion to the body surface area. The size of the lungs and their capacity are proportionate to the body weight. Proceeding from these biological laws, Kreps (1941) concluded that an increase in body size places the animal in more favorable circumstances in relation to the oxygen supply in the lungs; in other words, with the relatively lower expenditure of energy in a larger animal not only the absolute but also the relative oxygen supply is greater.

Krogh (1934), who for a 122-ton Balaenoptera musculus determined a lung volume of 14,000 liters (including 2,800 liters oxygen), calculated that the oxygen supply would here suffice for 50 minutes' swimming time at a speed of 3 miles per hour.

For the sperm whale this conclusion is very interesting, not so much in relation to the physiology of the individual's respiration (although a large body size can explain its capacity for remaining under water longer than other toothed whales) as in the increased diving possibilities of large males as compared with females (which dive to much lesser depths than males and for a shorter time).

Slijper (1962) writes that it is surprising how much blood flows from a sperm whale when it is dressed. This is evidently connected with the large size of the body, since even the maximum weight of the blood of a sperm whale is [only] 3.9% of the weight of the body (Zenkovich, 1937), i.e., less than in the European beaver, seals, and land mammals (about $10-13\%$ of body weight according to Irving, 1938; Kreps, 1941; Korzhuev and Glazova, 1967a). The Black Sea dolphin is intermediate in this respect: according to available data, the amount of blood in the organism constitutes 6.5—8.3%
119 of the body weight (Korzhuev and Balabanova et al., 1965; Korzhuev and Glazova, 1967a). However, the data given on blood weight in sperm whales are to be verified.

The organism's capacity for accumulating and utilizing oxygen depends not only on the overall volume of blood but also on a whole series of morphological and functional adaptations.

According to the material of several authors (Koshtoyants, 1950; and others), one form of the adaptation of the blood to oxygen absorption is a decreased size of the erythrocytes, i.e., enlargement of their surface area (and probably the special structure of their membranes), which facilitates and accelerates binding of the oxygen (and hence determines the binding of a large amount of oxygen in a specific period of time — A. B.).

Irving (1939) and Korzhuev (1952), however, determined that the erythrocytes of toothed Cetacea (dolphins) are almost equal in size to those of man, but are somewhat more numerous.

Slijper (1962), also proceeding from the advantage of an enlarged overall surface of the red blood corpuscles, suggested that the greater size (10.5μ) of the erythrocytes in the sperm whale as compared with other mammals actually denotes a surface that is twice as large as in man. Thus the available data and opinions on this question differ greatly so that there is a need for further specialized comparative investigations of comparable material according to a single method.

It has been established by other authors (Kreps, 1941; Korzhuev, 1949; and others) that the oxygen content in the blood of marine mammals, particularly dolphins, is on average greater than in land mammals and man. According to Korzhuev (1952) and Korzhuev and Bulatova (1952), the oxygen content in the blood of dolphins reaches 30% volume in some specimens; this exceeds the oxygen content in the blood of terrestrial animals. The same authors indicate that the hemoglobin concentration in the blood of dolphins is greater (39–45%) than in man and other land mammals (30–34%). The hemoglobin concentration also reaches 19–20 g per kg body weight, which far exceeds that of many mammals.

The hemoglobin content in the blood of various animals according to Tawara (1950) is (in g/100 cm³):

sperm whale 15.8
sei whale 15.6
cow 12.4

However, we can agree with Kleinenberg (1956a) that merely a greater oxygen content as compared with that of other mammals could evidently not guarantee a longer delay in respiration for the sperm whale. The main part in supplying the organism with oxygen during diving is apparently played by the muscle myoglobin. Thus, according to Kreps (1941), Tawara (1950) and Slijper (1962), the myoglobin content is 8–9 times higher in the sperm whale than in land mammals, and as a result, the mass store of oxygen in the body is about twice as great. For a comparison of the myoglobin content between baleen whales and the sperm whale we may cite the data of Tawara (1950), which show that the muscles of the sperm whale con-
120 tain 3–5 times (depending on type of muscles) as much myoglobin as, for example, the muscles of the sei whale. The coloration of the musculature is darker in aquatic animals than in land animals, this being visual proof of the greater content of myoglobin, which includes dark pigment; in the sperm whale (as in beaked whales) the musculature is virtually black, much darker than in baleen whales (Scholander, 1940, and many others). An interpretation of such a path of evolution from possible variants of adaptation to lengthy submersion is given by the experiments of Millikan (1939) and other investigators, who indicate that the myoglobin combines with oxygen several times more rapidly than the hemoglobin of the blood. Due to the special features of the muscle hemoglobin the deposited oxygen can ensure respiration of the muscle cells with a high frequency of contractions (Koshtoyants, 1950).

Thus the evolution of Cetacea proceeded in the direction of an increase in the amount of oxygen so vital to a deep-diving animal, not on account of an increase in the volume of the blood but on account of a change in the various qualitative characteristics of the blood. This is one of the most conclusive manifestations of the high degree of adaptation of whales, especially the sperm whale, to the aquatic mode of life.

Adaptive specialization undoubtedly proceeded also in other directions, which together led to the formation of many physiological features of the organism providing for prolonged submersion. Some of these physiological features have already been studied. It was noted, for example, that at the time of the respiratory pause an abrupt change takes place in the work of the heart. The heart rate is halved and this is accompanied by an abrupt weakening of the heartbeat, i.e., slowing down of the circulation, which possibly leads to a reduction of the total expenditure of energy and to more economical oxygen consumption (Kreps, 1941).

In the opinion of Irving (1939), and Kreps (1941), even more significant for respiration is the so-called vascular reflex at the time of the interruption in respiration, which leads to compression of the vessels of the muscles and, on the other hand, to an intensification of the circulation with increased blood pressure through the brain; this is natural since the brain is extremely sensitive (by comparison with the muscles) to oxygen deficiency. Lengthy submersion at a considerable depth without any adaptations to maintain the oxygen supply to the brain would lead to asphyxiation. The vascular reflex is distinctly pronounced in the beaver, muskrat, and seal, i.e., in typically aquatic mammals. During diving and the pause in respiration, circulation proceeds in the Cetacea mainly through the rete mirabile, which consists of vascular plexi of arteries and veins distributed from the base of the skull along the thorax. This considerably restricts the sphere of circulation, permitting a more economical consumption of the oxygen reserve in the blood and facilitating the working of the heart, the activity of which is weakened at this moment (Scholander, 1940; Kleinenberg, 1956a; Slijper, 1960). Remarkably, the existence between the ribs of a "Cretan labyrinth of vermicelli-like vessels," inflated with blood, in which the sperm whale "carries a surplus stock of vitality in him" was already indicated by Melville in 1851, who correctly connected this feature of anatomy with the possibility of prolonged submersion.

An interesting suggestion was made (Kleinenberg et al., 1964) that at great pressures all the gas exchange processes taking place in the organism
121 are different in aquatic mammals and land mammals. From this it may be concluded that it is precisely the great depth which ensures the aquatic animal's long underwater stay.

In the 1930s the question was debated in scientific circles of the possibility of caisson disease (embolism) or of diver's disease in whales, resulting in the formation in their tissues under water pressure of an additional quantity of dissolved nitrogen which, when the animals surface rapidly, i.e., with a rapid drop in pressure, is released from the solution (what is called "boiling of the blood") and, forming bubbles, obstructs the vessels. Naturally for sperm whales this problem could be of prime importance but, as was shown by Kandror (1941), this disease has to be ruled out in whales and other marine mammals since they go under water with one volume of air, and thus also with one portion of nitrogen, which cannot supersaturate the organism. Herein lies the radical difference in physiology between the oxygen supply under water of the whale organism and that of a man with an aqualung or in a diving suit, whose organism is constantly supplied with new portions of air containing nitrogen for respiration.

It is therefore clear that the specialization of the organs ensuring the most complete and rapid gas exchange that is characteristic for the marine mammal must be expressed particularly strongly in the sperm whale. In relation to some structures this specialization is of a quantitative nature, but in individual cases new structures and functional adaptations arise. Far from all of them are known. Functional and experimental confirmation is still required for the interesting hypotheses concerning the mechanism for generating ultrasound and its precise and powerful focusing.

Chapter 8

UROGENITAL SYSTEM

The urogenital system of sperm whales as a whole has been little studied. Relatively great attention has been paid to the morphology of the reproductive organs, particularly the ovaries and testes, the function of which is of interest in connection with determination of age, intensity of breeding, and other aspects significant in determining the state and dynamics of the animal's population.

UROPOIETIC ORGANS

A fairly complete description of the uropoietic organs of males and females has been given only for the white whale (Kleinenberg et al., 1964). A fragmentary description of this system in the sperm whale is given by Jackson (1845). The morphology of the cetacean kidneys (with the finback whale as an example) is given by Cave and Aumonier (1962).

The kidneys of the sperm whale are paired. Each kidney is elongate-oval, slightly compressed. The kidneys of the sperm whale, like those of other Cetacea, belong to the multiple type, i.e., they consist of a large
122 number of separate small lobules and constitute a conglomerate of uniform small formations.

The size and weight of the kidneys vary from 50×25 cm and 12 kg (in a very young animal) to 120 cm (length) in a sperm whale 16.6 m long (according to our measurements). In large males the weight of one kidney may reach 20 kg (Sleptsov, 1952).

Each sperm whale kidney consists on the average of 2,000 lobules or renculi which are united mainly in primary groups of three, and these primary groups are in turn concentrated in secondary groups of about 50 lobules (counts were made on the kidneys of prenatal sperm whale embryos in the North Pacific). In the total number of kidney lobules the sperm whale does not differ from other large Cetacea. It is thought that the large number of independent structures is due to the need for stronger uropoiesis in water and also to the size of the body (Yablokov, 1961).

The size and weight of a single lobule can also vary, in large males (16.5 m) reaching a length of 4 or even 5 cm (along the long axis) and a weight of 14—15 g.

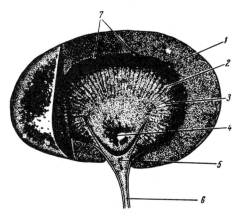

FIGURE 73. Structure of a renculus (lobule) in the sperm whale (section):

1 — uropoietic zone (cortical substance); 2 — boundary zone; 3 — abducent zone (medullary substance); 4 — renal papilla; 5 — renal calyx; 6 — stem of ureter; 7 — blood vessels.

In sperm whale embryos and young, as in the embryos and young of other toothed whales (Kleinenberg, 1956), the kidneys are relatively much larger than in the adult. This is apparently because the kidneys play a greater role in the metabolism of the young organism.

Each lobule has a relatively simple structure (Figure 73), which is essentially no different from that of the typical mammalian kidney, resembling most of all the structure of the furrowed multipapillar lobules of cattle (Klimov and Alaevskii, 1951). Evidently the kidneys of Cetacea are the outcome of the evolution of this type, expressed in the complete division of each lobe into many parts. In each lobule there can be distinguished a uropoietic zone (or cortical substance), a central or abducent zone (medullary substance), a renal papilla, and a renal calyx (Figure 73). Judging from the illustration of a finback whale kidney given by Cave and Aumonier (1962), this kidney differs from that of a sperm whale in that it is much more rounded (nearly spherical), and in that in the sperm whale kidney which we described the papilla and calyx cut into the abducent (medullary) zone; according to the illustration of Klimov and Alaevskii (1951), this is characteristic for the kidney lobes of cattle. In addition, Cave and Aumonier (1962) note as a feature of the renculi of Cetacea a clearly expressed penetration of the calyx walls by muscle and collagen fibers. The fibers are arranged in the form of a basket, surrounding and partially enveloping the medullary pyramid. In our examinations of several kidney lobules of various sperm whales we did not find such good development of the porta or deep penetration of tissue elements at the border of the boundary layer.

The histology of the sperm whale's renculus is also similar to that of other mammals, including man. A histological section of the lobule clearly shows in the cortex a large number of glomerules with glomerular capsules and convoluted tubules (Figure 74), and in the medullary substance mainly straight tubules and bundles of plethoric capillaries.

123

125

FIGURE 74. Photograph of a histological section of a renculus in the sperm whale

From each lobule emerges a separate stem, and the stems join to form large branches which empty into the ureter.

As they leave the kidneys, the ureters bend toward the tail (in males passing from above and under the vasa deferentia) and enter the caudal part of the urinary bladder from the dorsal side. The ureter has thick muscular walls. Its mucosa is gathered in numerous longitudinal folds; the thickness of the walls gradually decreases in the direction of the bladder.

The urinary bladder of the sperm whale is as in any other cetacean oval-oblong and relatively small. Thus in males 14.2 m long it had a length of 70 cm and a maximum width of 19 cm, while in an animal 16.6 m long it was 60 cm long and 20 cm wide. Meanwhile, in a 3-m-long female embryo it was 22 cm long and 11 cm wide, in other words, it can be stated that the urinary bladder (like the kidneys) is relatively more strongly developed in the embryo than in the adult animal. Thus the length of the bladder in a large embryo and suckling constitutes $1/14$–$1/12$ of the body length, in adults only $1/30$–$1/20$ (Jackson, 1845; Beddard, 1900, and our measurements). Moreover, the capacity of the bladder of an adult sperm whale probably does not exceed a few liters. With age the bladder assumes a somewhat more elongate shape.

124   The mucosa of the urinary bladder is gathered in small, mostly longitudinal folds. The muscular walls are 2.5–3 cm thick. In the sperm whale, as in other mammals, particularly ungulates, at about the level of the lower third of the bladder the folds of the mucosa converge at an angle, forming ureteric elevations which rise conspicuously above the

other smaller folds. On these elevations open slitlike, sickle-shaped curved apertures of the ureters which are situated about 5 cm apart and, as in many mammals, at different levels.

The ureteric elevations are united at the corner into a ureteric fold, which along the gradually narrowing neck of the urinary bladder passes into the urethra by a urethral fold (crest) that is higher than all the others.

In males the urethra joins with the vasa deferentia (the latter enter the urethra) in the region of the colliculus seminalis, forming the urogenital canal. In the prenatal specimen which we examined, slitlike openings of gland ducts, apparently of the preputial glands, opened into the urethra in this region. These were also found in the white whale (Kleinenberg et al., 1964).

The urethra passes from the ventral side of the penis and opens by a slitlike aperture at its pointed tip.

In females the urethra passes along the ventral side of the vaginal wall and opens at the base of the clitoris.

GENITALIA

Female genitalia. Matthews (1938) gives a general description of the outward appearance of the external genitalia of sperm whales and individual measurements. Fragmentary descriptions of the internal structure of the genital system can be found in Jackson (1845) and others.

The macro- and microstructure of the ovaries and oogenesis are described in the works of Chuzhakina (1955, 1961, 1965), Berzin (1961, 1963), and Best (1967).

External genitalia. The entrance to the vagina — the genital cleft — is bounded by two ridgelike, thickened large labia (Figure 75). Labia minora, present in several species of Cetacea (Slijper, 1966), are absent in the sperm whale. The caudal margin of the cleft is rounded, the cranial margin narrowed and traced for a long distance in the form of a narrow slit.

The external genitalia are pigmented like the adjacent parts of the body. The genital cleft of an adult female is 50—75 cm long. In its anterior corner is the clitoris up to 12—15 cm high. The clitoris is not always visible from the surface in sexually immature and barren females, but is always conspicuous in females in the later stages of pregnancy and in nursing females. The clitoris is colored like the abdomen or slightly lighter. At the caudal end of the cleft lies the anal aperture, which is located in a single cloacal fold with the genital and urinary aperture. The latter lies at the base of the clitoris on its inside and has a diameter of up to 1.2—1.4 cm.

About 20 cm from the center of the genital cleft on both sides of it are the narrow clefts of the mammillary pouches of the mammary glands, parallel to the genital cleft; the clefts of the mammillary pouches of many other species of Cetacea lie at an angle to the genital cleft. The clefts of the pouches are 18—20 cm long, or, according to Sleptsov (1959), up to 35 cm.
126 In nursing females the nipples of the mammary glands protrude to a height of 9—10 cm, and the color of the nipples is usually very slightly lighter than the general coloration of the abdomen (Figure 75).

FIGURE 75. External genitalia of female sperm whale

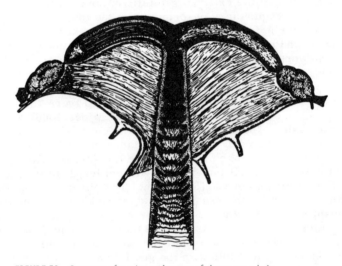

FIGURE 76. Structure of vagina and uterus of the sperm whale

Vagina and uterus. We dissected and examined the genitalia of embryos of various ages and also of several adult females in different physiological states; we also took photographs and made drawings (Figure 76).

The size of the vagina and uterus depends mainly on the physiological state of the animal. Thus the length of the vagina in a newborn female was 80 cm (Jackson, 1845), in sexually immature females up to 120 cm, in barren females up to 160 cm, and in those nursing or pregnant, about 180—200 cm.

The dark pigmentation of the body is observed also in the vagina at a depth of 10—18 cm from the entrance, after which there is an abrupt lightening to whitish pink. In the anterior part of the vagina, at a distance of 15 cm from the entrance in sexually immature and up to 30 cm in mature females, there is a smooth mucosa without folds or with scarcely noticeable plication. There is no mucus in this section.

Deep in the vagina dense transverse folds begin to appear on the surface, each of which does not encompass the entire circumference of the vagina but converges with the other, opposite fold. The folds gradually become higher and thicker. In sexually immature females the folds are denser, with a height of up to 2.2 cm. This section of the mucosa proceeds for about 12 cm. A slight longitudinal folding appears (folds 1—1.5 cm high). In mature females, on the surface of the vagina in addition to the transverse folds there is longitudinal folding. Individual folds among the transverse folds of this section can reach a size of 10—12 cm and may already encompass the entire circumference of the vagina. Thus each transverse fold of this section is intersected by shallow, thin longitudinal folds. In adults the transverse plication extends for about 80 cm from the entrance to the vagina. Toward the top of the vagina the transverse folds gradually become smaller while the size of the longitudinal folds increases to 3—4 cm in adults and up to 1.5 cm in immature animals. The even, soft longitudinal folds pass into the uterus. Jackson (1845) gives a similar general description of the folds of the vaginal mucosa in a female suckling 4.9 m long.

There is relatively little mucus in the vagina of immature animals, and in nursing and barren females there is none in the region of the lower, nonplicate part and the first folds of the vagina. Higher up, thick mucus covers the whole surface of the vagina, closing the folds. The greatest amount of mucus is found in pregnant females.

Meigs (1849, in Kellogg, 1938) and Ommaney (1932) indicated the presence of bony formations in the vagina and cervix that prevents ejection of the embryo from the uterus during deepwater submergence and the corresponding increase in pressure; however, this was not confirmed by our data.

There are reports that in immature Balaenopteridae, especially the finback whale (Wheeler, 1930) and the right whale (Omura, 1958), there is a transverse hymen closing the entrance to the vagina and separating it from the urogenital vestibule. There was no hymen in the large embryos and immature sperm whales which we examined. The opening of the urethra
27 opens in the sperm whale, as in the white whale (Kleinenberg et al., 1964), at the base of the clitoris; it is therefore evident that in no toothed whale is there either a urogenital sinus or a vestibule.

All investigators, whether they give a detailed description of the structure of the reproductive organs or not, indicate the bicornuate uterus inherent in all Cetacea. Often they describe in whales a clearly expressed cervix uteri, typical for all animals with a bicornuate uterus, with a strong muscular sphincter separating the corpus of the uterus from the vagina.

Our material, however, indicates that there is no expressed cervix in sperm whales, nor a corpus uteri* lying between the cervix and the horns of the uterus.

* Kleinenberg et al. (1964) mention a clearly expressed cervix in the majority of white whales examined, which may indicate that it is evidently not distinctly expressed in all animals. The fact that no boundary is noted between vagina and uterus was already mentioned by Jackson (1845) in the case of a sperm whale suckling 4.9 m long.

The right and left horns of the sperm whale uterus open independently into the vagina (see Figure 76), and in accordance with the accepted classification (Klimov and Alaevskii, 1951; and many others), they should be termed right and left uteri, while the entire uterus is referred to the double type. However, confirmation of this requires detailed embryo logical, histological, and morphophysiological analyses.

The size of the uterus varies greatly: in sucklings (Jackson, 1845) and immature animals it is 50 cm long, in barren and lactating animals up to 100—110 cm, in pregnant females up to 400 cm or more.

The mucosa of the uterine wall consists of thick, uniform dark pink folds. The uterine walls of adults are thick (up to 5—6 cm), usually permeated by blood vessels.

The special constrictor of the genital cleft begins at the ventral margin of the caudal half of the pelvis. Its muscular bundles, which are directed downward, somewhat anteriorly and medially, form an irregularly polygonal flat muscle belly of the constrictor. The latter is directed toward the anal-genital cleft and approaches the clitoris. Adjoining the caudodorsal edge of the vulvar constrictor is the anterior end of the mammary gland, into which pass some of the muscular bundles (see Figure 40:16). At the base of the clitoris the muscle fibers of the constrictor of the vulva converge and pass into a tendon which joins the same tendon of the right side. The medial, deeper bundles of the constrictor are located below the mammary gland. They begin at the special cartilage which surrounds the genital cleft dorsally and laterally. From this cartilage muscular bundles depart toward the mammary gland, the lateral surface of the genital labia, and the anal aperture. On contraction the inner muscular bundles cause the genital labia to be pressed toward the clitoris. The outer bundles of the constrictor work to close the genital cleft.

In front of the constrictor of the genital cleft lies a small, narrow muscle which encompasses the ventral half of the vagina and the urethra in a semicircle. The ends of this muscle insert on the lateral wall of the vagina. On contraction it compresses the urethra, preventing urination.

The caudal margins of the right and left uteri and the sides of the vagina pass into the thick and dense mesentery (or the wide uterine ligament — the mesometrium). The mesentery is pierced by blood vessels, some of which proceed to the vagina, while at the base they reach the uteri. The mesentery is unusually strongly developed, because of the need to support the uterus with the large embryo. Evidently owing to these ligaments the abdomen of the female is inconspicuously deformed, the streamlining is little disrupted, and resistance to the water stream is increased negligibly even in the later stages of pregnancy, when the embryo can be half as long as the female.

The mammary glands of the sperm whale consist of two elongate (up to 120 cm long), slightly convex glandular bands from 2 to 15 cm high (Omura, 1950; Tomilin; our material) lying along the sides of and slightly in front of the anal-genital cleft below the dermal-fatty layer in the subcutaneous connective tissue. According to the data of Tomilin (1957), the thickness of the mammary glands in lactating animals becomes almost 2—2.5 times greater (to 12 cm) than in nonlactating females. According to Omura (1950) and our own material, during lactation the size of the mammary glands increases only slightly more than during other physiological periods, and from

128

the surface of the body this increase can be discerned only vaguely. The nipples protrude from the clefts of the pouches only while the animals are nursing.

According to Sleptsov (1952), during the embryonic development of whales four to eight pairs of nipples are often laid down. The same author mentions the occurrence in an adult female sperm whale of additional atavistic nipples and correctly states that this may indicate multiple births in the ancestors of whales.

The sperm whale's mammary glands, like those of other Cetacea (Slijper, 1966), are divided into a large number of lobes and lobules. The small ducts which pass from the small lobules empty into the large duct which in the nipple reaches a considerable size (mammillary sinus — Sleptsov, 1952). Slijper compares this duct with the milk receptacles in the cow's udder. Examination of histological preparations of mammary glands confirms the basic similarity in structure of these glands with those of other mammals.

It is morphologically incorrect to call the mammary glands of Cetacea an udder (Astanin, 1958, and others), since this suggests that the glands of the right and left sides of the animal's body are fused.

The ovaries are situated in the upper lateral part of the abdominal cavity in the immediate vicinity of the kidneys. The external appearance of the sperm whale's ovaries is described by Matthews (1938). They are oblong bodies, flesh-colored with various tinges, circular in young animals and more elongate in adults (Figure 77). Their surface is smooth and even, sometimes covered with shallow grooves, rarely tuberous, always more even than in baleen whales.

(129)

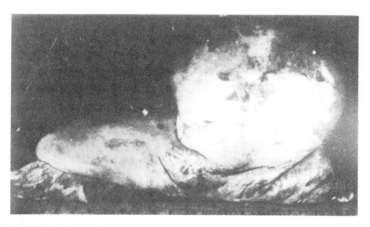

FIGURE 77. Sperm whale ovary with the corpus luteum of pregnancy (CLP)(embryo 360 cm long; at base of the CLP a trace is seen of the CLP of the previous pregnancy with light scars at the top)

The average ovary size in sperm whales in our collections is 19.5 × 9.5 cm in mature females. Maximum dimensions are 27 × 14 cm and 37 × 10 cm; the maximum weight of ovaries of a barren female according to Matthews' data (1938) is 680 g, according to our data 1,000 g, and according to Best's (1967) data 2,200 g. The maximum size of ovaries in mature females is 8 × 4 cm and 8 × 5 cm, and total weight 95 g.

After sexual maturity, some of the follicles, including quite large ones, lie in the body of the ovary, but most of them, unlike those of many other mammals, are located on the surface of the ovary at all stages of development from the smallest — in the form of bluish transparent or semitransparent vesicles — to the largest.

129   One of the follicles (rarely two), on reaching a size of 5—6 cm (Graafian follicles), bursts (Berzin, 1963; Best, 1967), releasing the egg. Best (1967) discovered that the size of the Graafian follicles in the sperm whale shows a tendency (statistically significant) to increase with an increase in the size and age of the female.

After fertilization the corpus luteum of pregnancy develops. It can be situated at various points in the ovary. According to our observations, it is usually located at one of its poles, usually the anterior.

The corpus luteum of pregnancy (CLP) on the sperm whale ovary is a body which rises above the surface of the ovary, separated from it by a more or less clearly expressed constriction (see Figure 77); this is not, however, as sharply expressed as in baleen whales or some toothed whales, especially the black whale (Comrie and Adam, 1938) and the killer whale.

The dimensions of corpora lutea on sperm whale ovaries are given below according to various authors:

Region	Size, cm
North Pacific, after	
Chuzhakina (1961)	16—5.8
Berzin (1963)	$\frac{13-7}{9.7}$
Ohsumi (1965)	$\frac{12}{10.5}$
Southern hemisphere, after	
Best	$\frac{10.2-5.3}{7.5}$

Note. The numerator gives the maximum and minimum sizes, the denominator the average size.

130   Matthews (1938) attempted to trace the decrease in size of the CLP with growth of the embryo, but unsuccessfully. Chuzhakina (1961) also failed to observe changes in the CLP diameter during pregnancy. Nor in our material is any distinct correlation found between the size of the CLP and the embryo, but nonetheless division of the embryos into "small" and "large" with corresponding differences in CLP sizes has shown (Berzin, 1963) that the average size of the CLP in ovaries of small embryos is 9 cm and in ovaries of large embryos 10 cm, i.e., the opposite of what Matthews (1938) expected. Best (1967) found that in sperm whales, as in baleen whales

and especially in the humpback whale, growth of the CLP proceeds in the early stage of pregnancy (up to an embryo length of about 1 m) and then does not change in size subsequently; this defines better the correlation we obtained.

According to Chuzhakina (1961), the CLP is smaller in females which are giving birth for the first time than in those which have given birth repeatedly.

At the top of the CLP there may be a small "crater," scar, or whitish "end-plate," which remains at the bursting point of the follicle and the exit of the egg cell. However, this is not always marked. According to our data, there is a clearly expressed "crater" only in 13% of CLPs, a scar or mark in 64%, and in 23% there are no marks on the surface.

The internal macroscopic structure of the CLP varies. In the center of the CLP in the mass of lutein tissue there is generally a capsule — a cavity with dense walls of connective tissue. In our material there was a central cavity in 63% of the CLPs examined. According to Chuzhakina (1961), on the other hand, in 63.9% of CLPs no such cavities were found. The size of the cavity can vary, sometimes the entire cavity consists of connective tissue, and in some cases, its diameter may be 7 cm but more often 2.5—3.5 cm. Best (1967) links the central cavity with the degree of rupture of the follicle at ovulation.

The microscopic structure (Chuzhakina, 1961) shows that at the very beginning of pregnancy the lutein cells have a polygonal shape and a radial direction. Also radially directed are the connective-tissue fibers and the blood vessels, with a minimal content of fatty inclusions. Subsequently, the radial arrangement of the lutein cells is enhanced, but in the following periods of pregnancy this arrangement of the cellular tissues is disrupted, enlargement of the fatty granules in the lutein cells takes place, and the process of pycnosis and karyolysis of the nuclei is intensified. These changes, which Chuzhakina calls regressive, begin in CLPs of embryos with a size of about 2 m and continue until birth. There is some doubt as to whether this process is regressive, since in contrast to some other mammals in which the hormonal function is taken up in the later months by the placenta (and the CLP undergoes involution), in whales the CLP functions throughout pregnancy, stimulating development of the mammary glands in the last months.

After birth the CLP becomes **the corpus luteum of lactation (CLL);** its size begins to decrease, and it becomes embedded in the stroma of the ovary.

During lactation the size of the resorbing corpus luteum is 30—50 mm, according to Nishiwaki et al. (1958), and at the end of lactation up to 25 mm. According to Ohsumi (1965), the average diameter of the CLL is 33.6 mm (range 20—53 mm). According to our material, the CLP can reach a size of 70 mm and at the end of the period 25—35 mm (Berzin, 1963). Best (1967) gives the same variations in size of the CLL with an average of 4.67 cm, which, according to his data, constitutes 37.7% of the average size of the CLP at birth.

131   In the following years the process of resorption of the marks continues gradually. **The marks* of the corpora lutea (MCL)** of recent pregnancies

---

* The term "mark," proposed by V. A. Zemskii (1956) is in our view better than "scar" in that it covers more fully all the signs characteristic of the resorbing corpus luteum.

are noticeable during macroscopic examination of the ovaries and protrude above the surface as a hemispherical swelling. However, in comparison with the marks on the ovaries of baleen whales, which protrude above the surface in an almost spherical formation with a constriction at the surface, those on sperm whale ovaries protrude far less and are always without a constriction, even in the case of fresh marks of recent pregnancies. If there was a crater or scar on the CLP, the mark bears a resemblance to a scar or crater.

On nonfixed ovaries, owing to the increased amount of connective tissue in the marks, they are hard in comparison with the remaining mass of the ovary and are readily felt. If the corpus luteum has a central cavity the mark bears the same cavity or traces of it. It is understandable that the kind of mark and its size depend on how long ago the pregnancy dates. The mark of a very old pregnancy can sometimes not be felt from the surface and so pass unnoticed.

Most investigators consider that the marks of the corpora lutea of pregnancy on sperm whale ovaries, as on those of baleen whales, are preserved throughout life. We did not find very small and poorly discernible, almost vanishing traces, and this confirms the general opinion.

The marks of the corpora lutea of pregnancy do not have a regular circular shape, and therefore their measurement in cross sections is difficult. Nevertheless, to illustrate the course of regression, we give measurements of marks on the ovaries of a lactating female 10.9 m long. On one ovary marks were found with dimensions of 40 mm (mark corresponding to lactation), 25, 24, and 20 mm, and on the other, marks of 22, 20, 19, 18, and 13 mm. In our material the size of the last mark was smallest (Berzin, 1963). Nishiwaki et al.(1958) discovered 10-mm marks and according to their data the marks reach such a size three to four years after births and still continue to be resorbed.

Best (1967), who divides the marks into three groups ("young," "medium-aged," and "old"), indicates the presence of still smaller old marks (up to 7 mm); when the average size of old marks is 13.5 mm, the minimum size of mark is 3 mm according to Ohsumi (1965), but such measurements of the MCL are doubtful.

It has been established that the possibility of ovulation is uniform and proceeds regularly in each ovary, so that the number of marks of ovulation in the ovaries is also uniform (Ohsumi, 1964; Best, 1967).

But a similar regular distribution in the formation of marks is not observed in each ovary taken separately.

Even without a documented analysis of sperm whale ovaries a definite polarity in the localization of the MCL is discernible, as in some other kinds of baleen and toothed whales. Best (1967) made corresponding measurements and found appreciable asymmetry in the accumulation of marks at different ends of the ovary.

Marks of atretic follicles on sperm whale ovaries are quite clearly distinguished from the MCL, as in other toothed whales (Sleptsov, 1952; Yablokov, 1959; and others). Best (1967) distinguished two types of marks
132 of atretic follicles, the nature and size of which depend on the stage of development of the follicle at the onset of degeneration. The marks of atretic follicles disappear completely after a short time.

In mammals a distinction is generally made between spontaneous ovulation, occurring automatically at definite intervals, and induced ovulation, where rupture of the developed follicle does not occur if mating did not take place. Such ovulation almost invariably ends in pregnancy.

Almost all investigators (Mackintosh and Wheeler, 1929; Wheeler, 1930; etc.) agree on the spontaneous character of ovulation in baleen whales. In this case, marks of ovulation and of pregnancy remain on the ovaries. Zemskii (1953, 1956, 1958) and M. V. Ivashin (1958) discovered a difference in the micro- and macroscopic structure of these two types of mark in baleen whales.

There is no unanimity among investigators concerning the character of ovulation in toothed whales. Sleptsov (1952) considers ovulation to be of the induced type in the whole order Cetacea. A. V. Yablokov (1959), Kleinenberg and Yablokov (1960), and Kleinenberg and G. A. Klevezal' (1962), who studied Black Sea dolphins and the white whale, believe that ovulation is induced in all toothed whales. Comrie and Adam (1938) think ovulation is spontaneous in Pseudorca crassidens, as does Matthews (1938) in the case of the sperm whale, although they do not mention differences in the marks of the two types. Sokolov (1954), in the light of observations on dolphins, concluded that ovulation is induced, and in his 1961 work he put forward this view tentatively. Chuzhakina (1955) reported two types of mark and mentioned their possible distinction (but without indicating the differences between them). According to her initial data, in sperm whales the number of marks of ovulation amounts to up to 2% of the total number of marks. Such a figure could be within the limits of permissible error and still does not prove that ovulation is spontaneous in this kind of whale. In a subsequent work (1961) Chuzhakina reported only on marks of the corpus luteum of pregnancy, and determined age according to their number; this enables us to conclude that there are marks of one type only, i.e., of induced ovulation. Nishiwaki, Ohsumi, and Hibiya (1958), and Ohsumi (1965) reported the existence of two types of mark. but also failed to mention differences between them.

Our macroscopic examination of numerous marks did not demonstrate a regular difference in them such as their different origin would lead one to expect; the small differences noted in the structure of the marks were visible also in the structure of the corpora lutea themselves (the embryo being present in the uterus). Recently Best (1967) claimed to have found differences between the two types of mark. According to his data. the marks of the corpus luteum of pregnancy are larger and more regularly round than the marks of the second type. In the light of the controversies mentioned above, this conclusion should be treated with caution.

In baleen whales under conditions of monogamy, when mating can take place much more often (and the possibility of fertilization increases). the number of marks on the ovaries, for example in the case of the finback whale, is far greater, 33—49 (Zemskii, 1955, 1958; Nishiwaki et al., 1958).

On the ovaries of polygamic sperm whales, however, with a theoretically lesser possibility of fertilization, the number of marks is less than half that on the ovaries of baleen whales, 16—20 (Matthews, 1938; Nishiwaki et al., 1958; Berzin, 1961, 1963; Chuzhakina, 1961).

Thus there is probably a considerable difference in the oogenesis of the ovaries in baleen and toothed whales, particularly in the rate of accumulation of marks of the corpus luteum, depending on whether the animal is mono-, di-, or — for example in the case of the finback and great blue whale

133

(Wheeler, 1930) – polyestral, but also on the type of ovulation. Sperm whales can be classed as monoestral animals (Berzin, 1963; Ohsumi, 1965), mostly with an induced type of ovulation. It should be noted, however, that in several cases it is evidently to be dismissed that all marks of ovulation on sperm whale ovaries correspond to previous pregnancies, since their number apparently exceeds the possible maximum number of births in the light of the animal's age as determined by the dentin layers. Moreover, as already mentioned, in some animals ovulation and copulation do not always end in pregnancy (Densley, 1934, in Matthews, 1938).

It seems that in general induced ovulation is biologically more advantageous, giving a greater chance of conception, the more so in the case of polygamy. With purely spontaneous ovulation only frequent coupling can ensure conception. We can agree with Astanin (1958), who wrote that "induced ovulation seems to be more widespread than is generally thought." Moreover, we are not at all inclined to divide ovulation categorically into two radically different types. It seems that even in the case of spontaneous ovulation a definite reflex effect on ovulation can be caused not only by the act of copulation itself but also, for example, by the prolonged "love-play,"

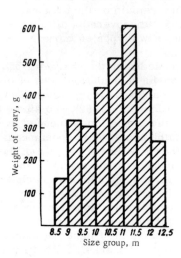

FIGURE 78. Changes in the weight of the ovary (one) in dependence on the body length of female sperm whales

contact of the genitalia, etc., recorded in the case of Cetacea (apparently the observations in question were of dolphins in oceanaria) preceding copulation (Slijper, 1966) and, finally, simply by the appearance of the male. Furthermore, with spontaneous ovulation, conditions and morphophysiological adaptations can and must be created which are optimal for fertilization (odors, habitus of female during estrus, etc.) and which attract the male. In considering human reproduction, Willey (1959) formulated a thesis to the effect that " ... all parts of the reproductive system in both sexes, as also various physiological and psychological sex-linked phenomena, have a single purpose – to ensure successful union of the egg and sperm"; this applies in a uniform if not very high degree to all animals, including whales.

As the female grows and marks of corpora lutea accumulate with age, the weight of the ovaries increases,* attaining a maximum in animals 11–11.5 m long (Figure 78). Best (1967) indicates a rise in weight with an increase in the body length and age of the female. After an average weight of 620 g per ovary is reached, in the subsequent size groups of animals the ovaries begin to decrease in size; this, as already suggested

134

---

* For a comparison of the weight of ovaries of various animals we took the average weight of the two ovaries, and in the case of a pregnant female the weight of the ovaries without the corpus luteum of pregnancy, since this formation changes greatly in time and in different individuals, and furthermore, its weight often exceeds that of the ovary itself.

in the case of the humpback whale (Ivashin, 1959), is connected with the extinction of ovarian activity or in general with the onset of the climacteric period (Chuzhakina, 1961; Berzin, 1963; Best, 1967). In baleen whales Laws (1961) notes only a very slight decrease in fecundity with age and a distinct absence of climacterium (see also Chapter 13).

Male genitalia. Not even a superficial description exists of the entire reproductive system of male sperm whales.

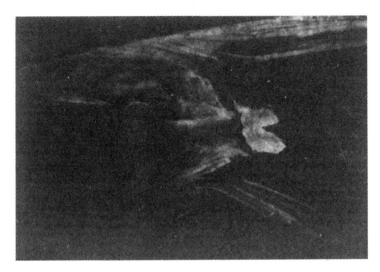

FIGURE 79. External genitalia of a male sperm whale; the anal opening is visible (photo by A. Yablokov)

General descriptions of the penis and testes can be found in Matthews (1938), and a few data are given by Hentschel (1910), Tomilin (1957), and Slijper (1966). Certain structural features of the genitalia of small embryos are given by Beddard (1919). The histological structure of the testes is described by Matthews (1938), Clarke (1956), Berzin (1963, 1965) and others.

In the usual state the penis of the sperm whale, like that of other whales, lies in a deep fold and protrudes only on erection (or shortly after death) (Figure 79). The cleft of the genital fold outwardly resembles that of the female, but in the male the anal opening is separated from the genital fold by a large, distinctly expressed perineum, the length of which is from 40 cm in the prenatal embryo and a newborn to 160 cm in large specimens (it averages 130 cm in mature animals). Attention should be drawn again to this basically well known difference, since it is our firm conviction that its disregard leads to errors involving the classing of some males as females (external examination of a large proportion of males fails to reveal 135 the penis) at whale-processing plants and resulting in the mention of extremely large females in statistical reports (see Chapter 2).

The testes are bean-shaped (Figure 80), round in section, smooth, and flesh-colored. In the sperm whale, as in other Cetacea, there is no scrotum and the testes are located in the abdominal cavity. This is regarded as a secondary phenomenon (Klimov and Akaevskii, 1951).

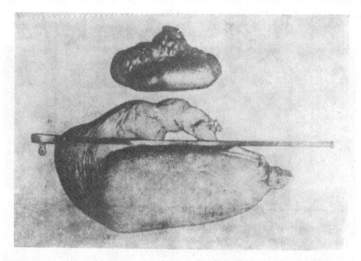

FIGURE 80.   Testes (with epididymides) of the sperm whale:

above — testis of immature male (length 10.0 m);   below — testis of mature male (length 14.2 m).

The testes are situated behind the kidneys and are directed obliquely forward and to the sides.

The size and weight of the testes can vary greatly (Table 18). In baleen whales there is a considerable and abrupt increase in size or weight after sexual maturity is reached (Nishiwaki and Hibiya, 1951; Ivashin, 1959). A similar phenomenon was noted by Matthews (1938) in the sperm whale. However, the data of Nishiwaki and Hibiya (1952) and also our own extensive material do not confirm a rapid change in the weight of sperm whale testes following maturity. Matthew's error may have been statistical.

But of course there must be some increase in the volume and weight of the testes following the attainment of maturity, since the seminal ducts expand, being filled with sexual products. This is not seen on a general graph of the dependence of the testes' weight change on body length (Figure 81), due to the considerable individual variations in body length at the onset of sexual maturity and to the fairly regular maturation of each testis.

After the onset of sexual maturity there is a gradual increase in the weight of testes until the animals reach a length of 15—15.5 m. Their weight then decreases in line with the gradual slackening off of activity of the testes and the decline of sexual activity.

A pair of very heavy testes weighed 13.6 kg according to Nishiwaki, Hibiya, and Kimura (1956) but 13.4 kg according to our data, and one of the testes in a sperm whale 15.8 m long weighed 8.57 kg. With accurate weighing a difference is always found between the right and left testis. In small

138

specimens the two testes generally have a very similar weight. As
the weight of the testes increases there is an increase in the number
of pairs with noneven weight, and the difference also increases, constituting in individual cases 2.5—2.8 kg. According to Nishiwaki and Hibiya
(1951) and our own data, no clear pattern can be established in the difference between the weight of the left and right testis of sperm whales.

TABLE 18. Size and weight of testes of sperm whales inhabiting the North Pacific (our data)

Length of animal, m	Right testis		Left testis		Number of dentin layers in teeth
	weight, g	size, cm	weight, g	size, cm	
9.2	460	18 × 6	500	18 × 7	9
9.4	430	16 × 8	430	16 × 8	8
9.5	500	20 × 8	550	20 × 8	11
10.0	1,300	22 × 11	1,450	25 × 11	12
11.0	950	23 × 8	900	23 × 8	14
11.1	1,000	24 × 11	1,000	24 × 11	19
11.1	800	25 × 9	900	26 × 8	16
11.1	1,150	24 × 11	1,700	28 × 12	14
11.2	950	22 × 11	530	20 × 9	14
11.3	950	23 × 9	1,200	24 × 12	15
11.6	750	20 × 8	800	24 × 8	19
11.8	1,500	31 × 9	1,800	38 × 10	16
12.0	1,400	22 × 14	1,600	28 × 14	17
12.0	2,400	27 × 12	2,400	33 × 14	29
12.3	1,400	25 × 11	1,200	23 × 10	27
12.9	2,450	29 × 13	2,250	31 × 11	21
13.1	1,700	29 × 10	1,700	40 × 11	—
13.5	2,200	32 × 14	2,250	35 × 12	25
13.7	—	36 × 16	6,000	38 × 20	40
14.0	4,050	27 × 15	2,450	26 × 16	30
14.2	6,500	43 × 17	6,500	35 × 18	36
14.7	3,300	42 × 14	4,450	45 × 16	30
14.8	5,100	44 × 16	5,000	44 × 16	54
15.2	5,330	35 × 15	4,000	36 × 14	44
15.6	7,500	49 × 19	5,000	52 × 15	—
16.0	5,300	41 × 17	6,000	39 × 18	38

The epididymis, situated at the cranial end of the testis, passes along
its side and ends at the caudal end, giving rise to the vas deferens.
The testis and epididymis are enclosed in a common tunica and are
attached by a wide mesentery which diverges radially anteriorly, laterally,
and posteriorly, overlapping the kidney.

Each vas deferens is directed toward the cranial end of the testis.
In this section it is strongly convoluted so that it takes the form of
"congested masses," as in Stenella (Fraser, 1950).

From the cranial end of the testis the vas deferens is directed
medially and, now curving less, passes under the ventral side of the
ureter and at the level of the cervix vesicae enters the common tunica
with the convoluted vas deferens of the other testis. The two vasa
deferentia pass together above the dorsal side of the urethra under the

rectum, straightening out gradually. At the colliculus seminalis the vasa deferentia enter the urethra by openings situated close together.

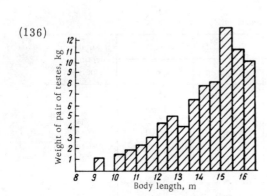

(136)

FIGURE 81. Weight changes in the testes as a function of body length in the sperm whale

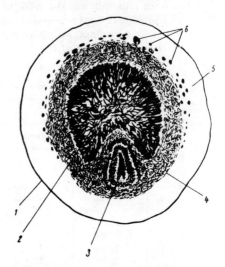

FIGURE 82. Cross section through the penis in the sperm whale (at approximately its middle):

1 — dermal layer; 2 — corpus cavernosum; 3 — urogenital canal with corpus cavernosum; 4 — layer of dense connective tissue; 5 — tunica albuginea; 6 — blood vessels and nerves.

In sperm whales, as in other toothed whales (Kleinenberg et al., 1964), there are no vesicular glands; it is therefore difficult to determine the beginning of the ejaculatory ducts.

The penis is conical, gradually narrowing (see Figure 79), circular in section (Figure 82), with a somewhat obliquely truncated end. It is usually colored like the body or very slightly lighter. Hentschel (1910) considers that the penis is even somewhat darker than the trunk. Such a relationship between the color of the penis and body can apparently exist in very old animals, in which the penis retains its original coloration and seems darker in comparison with the body, which is somewhat lightened by numerous patches, marks and scars. According to Tomilin's data (1957), the penis is dark brown. Matthews (1938) found only partial pigmentation of the penis, especially of its distal part. We noted a large male, caught in the northeastern Pacific, in which the entire penis together with the adjacent part of the abdomen was light-colored.

The externally slitlike dermal fold concealing the penis is also pigmented internally.

All small embryos examined showed the penis or the clitoris, which at this stage of ontogeny is very similar to a penis; however, in males with a body length of up to 6—7 cm the penis was directed backward and then bent forward. In males in the early stages of development (in an embryo 12 cm long) the anal opening was separated from the genital fold by a large

perineum. In females the "penis" (clitoris) is directed backward, and
the opening of the urethra is visible at its base. In female embryos
138 11—12 cm long the "penis" is already beginning to descend into the cloacal
fold; in embryos 15—25 cm long it already lies in the genital fold and is
reduced until it reaches the normal size of the clitoris. In embryos about
50 cm long the size of the clitoris is approximately twice the regular size
(with consideration of the body length).

The difference noted by Beddard (1919) in the position of the external
genitalia of male embryos 11.4 and 21 cm long is erroneous: judging from
the description, the larger embryo was in fact a female.

The maximum length of the penis according to Tomilin's data (1957)
is 150 cm (with a circumference of 50—55 cm), according to Boschma's data
(1938) 190 cm, and according to our material more than 200 cm. A certain
correlation is observed between penis size and body size (Table 19).

TABLE 19. Size of penis in the sperm whale

Length		Diameter of penis	Reference	Length		Diameter of penis	Reference
of animal, m	of penis, cm	at base, cm		of animal, m	of penis, cm	at base, cm	
10.6	93	17		13.0	110	20	
10.6	97	13		13.0	96	15	
11.0	90	—		14.4	145	—	
11.1	93	14		14.7	143	20	
11.2	78	13	Our material (North Pacific)	14.8	120	16	Our material (North Pacific)
11.4	115	18		14.8	203	—	
11.8	112	17		15.0	125	18	
12.0	110	16		15.0	168	—	
12.3	125	15		15.5	127	20	
12.6	170	19		16.0	190	35	Boschma (1938)
13.0	103	17		17.4	122	47	Hentschel (1910)
				18.0	140	43	Boschma (1938)

The penis begins at the pelvic bones, on which its muscles insert.
According to Kleinenberg et al. (1964), the paired retractor muscles serve
to retract the penis after erection, but according to Slijper (1966), the
retractor acts as an inhibitor in regulating the extension of the penis on
straightening. The organ is surrounded by the very thick and dense tunica
albuginea consisting of collagenous fibers of connective tissue (see Figure 82).

In the sperm whale, as in other Cetacea, there is no os penis. Analysis
of the structure of the penis leads to the conclusion that when the penis is
filled with blood its further consolidation is possible only without conspicuous
thickening or extension on straightening, i.e., the penis of the sperm whale,
like that of other whales, is of the fibroelastic type (Slijper, 1966), characteristic for the Artiodactyla.

The organs of urine excretion in the sperm whale, as in other Cetacea,
ensure intensive urine formation and frequent urination.

Extensive material has been collected on the morphology and histology
of sperm whale ovaries, but until now this has not provided a categorical
answer to the complex question of the nature of ovulation in these whales.

CENTRAL NERVOUS SYSTEM AND SENSE ORGANS

"We have in common with animals all kinds of rational
activity .... analysis .... synthesis .... experiment ...."

Engels

In recent years the central nervous system and sense organs of Cetacea have aroused great interest, since it has been established that toothed whales show precise orientation, conditioned reflexes, a high level of training capabilities, and delicate interrelationships between individuals.

Meanwhile the structure of the central nervous system has been studied relatively thoroughly only in the case of small Cetacea, while the sense organs have received little or no study.

BRAIN

In large whales, particularly in the sperm whale, the structure of the brain has been relatively well studied by Kojima (1951) and Ries and Langworthy (1937). Our description is given mainly after these authors with a few of our own data.

Shape and size. The sperm whale is an extremely brachycephalic animal, i.e., its brain is almost spherical (Figure 83). The brain of a sperm whale 15.2 m long weighed 8.2 kg and had the following measurements* (Kojima, 1951): along the vertical axis 17.5 cm, between frontal and occipital margins (sagittal axis) 25.5 cm, along the transverse axis 30.8 cm, with a certain asymmetry (right hemisphere 15.8, left hemisphere 14 cm). Although Kojima (1951) admits a decrease and change in weight (and in shape) after fixation, it is interesting that the weight ratio between the right and left hemispheres is 1:0.9. This suggests a certain asymmetry in the brain structure, but further proof is required.

The weight of the brain according to 22 measurements in mature animals of both sexes varied between 5.46 and 9.23 kg (Table 20).

The weight of the brain is not correlated with the length of the animal according to the state of maturity and, in contrast to most other organs, does not increase as the body becomes larger. Thus the difference in brain weight in various specimens can be assumed to be due only to individual differences. This can be taken as a rule for highly developed mammals.

---

* The dimensions changed somewhat after fixation and storage; in particular the height of the brain decreased.

TABLE 20. Weight of the brain of sperm whales from the North Pacific

Length of body, m	Sex	Weight of brain, kg*	Reference	Length of body, m	Sex	Weight of brain, kg*	Reference
10.6	Male	7.4 }	Our material	15.2	Male	8.0 }	
11.5	"	7.3 }		15.2	"	7.7	
12.0	"	8.3	Data of A.V.Yablokov	15.5	"	7.0 }	Kojima (1951)
				15.5	"	8.0	
14.0	"	8.6 }		15.5	"	9.0 }	
14.9	"	7.0		15.7	"	8.8	Our material
14.9	"	7.0		15.9	"	7.0	Kojima (1951)
14.9	"	7.3 }	Kojima (1951)	16.0	"	6.5	Sleptsov (1952)
14.9	"	8.0		16.5	"	6.4 }	
15.9	"	8.2		16.5	"	8.0 }	Kojima (1951)
14.9	"	9.2 }		16.5	"	8.7 }	
15.0	"	6.7	Data of A. V. Yablokov	10.4	Female	6.5 }	Our material
15.0	"	9.2	Our material	10.9	"	5.5 }	

* In all cases the weight of the brain was determined in the fresh state. For the weighings performed by Sleptsov (1952) no such explanation was given.

139   The average weight of the brain in mature male sperms (according to 20 weighings) is 7.9 kg, in mature females (2 weighings) 6 kg. The brain of sperm whales is heavier than that of baleen whales of the same length.

140

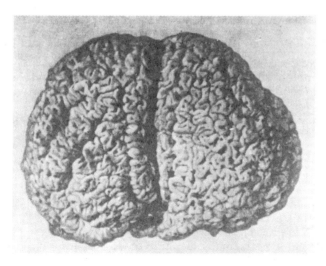

FIGURE 83. Brain of the sperm whale (dorsal view; (photo by Veinger)

Kojima (1951), relying on earlier data and his own, concluded that following fixation the weight of the brain decreases by an average of 0.5 kg. Similar data are reported for other Cetacea, and therefore this should be mentioned when indicating the brain weight.

In the sperm whale, as in other toothed whales, olfactory bulbs are not expressed; all that is visible is a slight trace of a nerve passing along the olfactory sulcus. On the surface of the base of the brain the olfactory zone is relatively large and thickened and lies between the lower surface of the upper lobe and the optic nerve (see Figure 85). The cortex of the prosencephalic hemispheres in Cetacea is gathered in numerous gyri of complex configuration (folds). The number of gyri is greater in sperm whale hemispheres than in those of the most highly organized animals. Their arrangement displays a definite system similar to that in predators or ungulates. Attempts at a detailed homologization of the gyri and sulci must be abandoned for the time being in view of the difficulty of making an exact comparison of the formations mentioned (Kleinenberg et al., 1964).

On the dorsal surface of the brain nearly all the sulci run in a sagittal direction. Here one can distinguish a cruciform sulcus, which is situated very obliquely, and two large, almost straight sulci, the entolateral and lateral (Kojima, 1951). The lateral sulcus passes on each hemisphere quite symmetrically for a considerable distance along the occipital lobe to the lateral temporal lobe.

On the lateral surface there is a symmetrical Sylvian fissure, which is contiguous with the ecto-Sylvian fissure and the supra-Sylvian fissure, beginning in the lateral part of the frontal lobe and extending to the middle of the Sylvian fissure.

The sulci and gyri in the sperm whale (see Figure 83) are on the whole similar to those of other toothed and baleen whales. Investigators have noticed, however, that in the sperm whale brain the uncinate process consists of three compartments.

The cortex (gray matter) in the sperm whale, as in other mammals, consists of six layers (Kojima, 1951), which indicates localization of functions in the cortex (Bets, 1881, in Klimov and Akaevskii, 1951) in this species.

The first molecular* layer, which is 0.24—0.80 mm thick, is sharply distinguished from the subsequent deeper-lying layer. Scattered in it are small, round nerve cells and even more disperse large nerve cells measuring $10/30\mu$ (maximum diameter along the surface of the cortex and maximum diameter vertical to the cortex surface).

The second layer is an outer layer, granular, very narrow, 0.20—0.88 mm thick but clearly discernible; it contains a large number of round or pyramidal nerve cells measuring $5/15—18/20\mu$.

The third, thick (0.4—0.6 mm) layer of small pyramidal cells bears scattered granular cells of various size, $9/15—24/18\mu$, and numerous pyramidal cells (their number increases with depth).

The fourth layer is an inner granular layer, characterized by a small number of granular cells, many of which are located in this layer of the cortex in other mammals.

The fifth layer of large pyramidal cells, 0.2—0.4 mm thick, contains relatively large cells (about $18—24/30\mu$) forming groups which are mainly

---

* The names of layers are given after Klimov and Akaevskii (1951).

polygonal or triangular. In some sections there are giant pyramidal cells forming a conspicuous layer.

The sixth layer of polymorphic cells is 0.8—1.0 mm thick; in it are scattered relatively large, pyramidal, circular, or stellate cells measuring 18—24/30μ and cells of other shapes.

142   The number of nerve cells in the brain is on the whole large. The number, concentration, size, form, and proportion of cells of different shape and their structure vary in different sections of the brain.

It is of considerable interest to study the cytoarchitectonic features of the cortex (taking into account its colossal mass and the complex structure of the sulci and gyri).

On the ventral surface at the point where in other mammals the olfactory lobes are situated, in the sperm whale (as in other whales and especially the white whale), there is the so-called bare Broca's area, which is flattened-oval and is formed by heads of caudate nuclei. Laterally it is contiguous with the optic chiasma. As in other toothed whales, there are no olfactory bulbs. From Figure 84 it can be seen that the corpus callosum attains considerable development (as in the white whale — Kleinenberg et al., 1964).

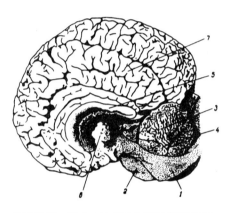

FIGURE 84. Median sagittal section through the brain of the sperm whale (Ries and Langworthy, 1937; our notation):

1 — medulla oblongata; 2 — pons; 3 — cerebellum; 4 — fastigium; 5 — corpus callosum; 6 — massa intermedia; 7 — medial surface of right hemisphere.

The **cranial nerves.** As in other mammals, the origin of the main cranial nerves in the sperm whale can be traced on the ventral surface of the brain (Figure 85).

In the sperm whale and other toothed whales there is no first pair of cranial nerves. A barely visible trace is discernible at the point where they should occur.

The optic nerve (second pair) is well-developed and is flattened-oval. The intricate fibers are enclosed in a firm membrane and reach the optic chiasma at an angle of 45° (in the white whale at an angle of 90°).

The chiasma itself is relatively flattened and thin.

The third pair of nerves (oculomotor) at the base take the form of several small roots which are then collected into one bundle; this pair appears on the ventral surface of the brain stem.

Only Ries and Langworthy (1937) found a trochlear nerve (fourth pair), probably because of its very small size. This is characteristic for several other toothed whales, for example the white whale.

The trigeminal nerve (fifth pair) is single and is one of the three largest cranial nerves. It arises from the lateral surface of the stem of the medulla oblongata between the pons and the upper corner of the cerebellum. Its mandibular and maxillary branches are well developed, but only a remnant of the optic branch is preserved.

The abducens (fifth pair), like the other nerves of the eye muscles, is weakly developed.

The acoustic nerve (eighth pair) and facial nerve (seventh pair) are the largest of the cranial nerves. They also originate on the ventro-
143 lateral surface of the stem of the medulla oblongata. Their strong development is certainly connected with the active work of the echo-locating apparatus (see Chapters 7 and 15).

The glossopharyngeal nerve (ninth pair) and vagus nerve (tenth pair) depart from an eminence on the ventrolateral surface of the medulla oblongata. These nerves originate not in a dense bundle (like the fifth, seventh, and eighth pairs) but in a group of separate nerve roots; in particular the glosso-pharyngeal nerve consists of at least six such radial roots (see Figure 85).

The cranial fibers of the eleventh pair (accessory nerve) form two groups; the cranial part of the fibers originates at the stem of the medulla oblongata as distinct roots at the level of the vagus but closer to the midline.

In the mesencephalon (brain stem) well developed, massive acoustic tubercles are visible, set a consider-able distance apart.

The cerebellum in the sperm whale, as in other mammals, is con-siderably developed; this is connected with the high degree of coordination of movements and, in the Cetacea, moreover with the aquatic mode of life with high swimming abilities. The cerebellum, which is the central organ of automatic (reflex) regulation of motor functions, ensures the change in equilibrium and the position of the body in space; the high level of de-velopment of this organ corresponds to the high mobility of the sperm whale, which is manifested in the skir-mishes among themselves, in the hunt for mobile and evasive squid, in games and leaps which, of course, require a very high degree of coordination.

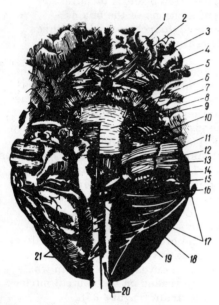

FIGURE 85. Base of the brain in the sperm whale (Ries and Langworthy, 1937):

1 — rudimentary ducts of olfactory nerves; 2 — optic nerve; 3 — tuber cinereum; 4 — mam-millary bodies; 5 — optic tract; 6 — oculomotor nerve; 7 — cerebral process; 8 — trochlear nerve; 9 — pons; 10 — trigeminal nerve; 11 — facial nerve; 12 — acoustic nerve; 13 — abducens; 14 — corticospinal fibers; 15 — glossopharyngeal nerve; 16 — vagus; 17 — cranial and spinal branches (spinal accessory nerve); 18 — lobule of cerebellum; 19 — middle accessory oliva; 20 — first cervical (occipital spinal nerve); 21 — hypoglossal nerve.

The cerebellum can be divided into three parts: the small nerve of the cerebellum and the two large hemispheres. The transverse diameter of the widest part of the cerebellum varies from 15 to 17.5 cm (Ries and Langworthy, 1937; Kohima, 1951).

Morphological material, especially on the structure of the sperm whale brain, indicates that all or nearly all the conclusions reached by investigators

144 on the high degree of development of the central nervous system, on the possibilities of processing complex conditioned reflexes and other manifestations of the superior organization of higher nervous activity in small toothed whales may be applied in full to the sperm whale.

At the same time it is clear that Langworthy's conclusion (1932) that the structure of the cortex in whales is relatively primitive (with numerous nerve cells and weak differentiation into layers) is incorrect, as indicated by Kojima's (1951) studies of the sperm whale. This is undoubtedly an animal with a cortex of complex structure corresponding to complex psychic manifestations. The sperm whale brain must possess an extreme plasticity in the functional respect and practically inexhaustible possibilities for establishing links between stimuli and the form of reaction. Moreover, due to the complex structure of its cortex, for a vast number of nerve cells the sperm whale brain must ensure not only the accumulation of a colossal number of fixed and predetermined reactions to stimulation from the environment elaborated during the course of evolution, but also the accumulation of individual forms of reaction which are arbitrary (volitional or conscious), elaborated and accumulated by the animal during life.

The sperm whale's brain structure is such that this can be said to be a "thinking" animal, capable of displaying high "intellectual abilities."

SENSE ORGANS

Organ of sight. The structure of the eye in the sperm whale was examined by Rochon-Duvigneaud (1940), the eye musculature and innervation by Hosokawa (1951) and also superficially by Bennett (1836) and by several other authors.

In the adult the dimensions of the eye and its parts show no distinct correlation with the dimensions of the body (our measurements on two animals; Hentschel, 1910; and others). For example, according to our data, in males 12—13 m long the diameter of the eyeball is 6.5—7.5 cm. Approximately the same size (5.9 and 6.2 cm) is indicated by Hentschel (1910) for a large male 17.4 m long and by Bennett (1836) for an adult female (Sleptsov, 1952, indicates eyeball measurements of up to 15—17 cm). The eyes of sperm whales are relatively smaller than those of baleen whales (for example, in comparing eye size in a humpback whale and a sperm whale of the same length a difference of about 12 cm).

The eyelids are without lashes and tarsal cartilages; the conjunctiva is strongly vascularized and filled with blood (Bennett, 1836).

A characteristic feature of the eyes of whales (including sperm whales) is the thick sclera (Figure 86). Both absolutely and relatively the sclera of the whale is several times thicker than that of land mammals and Pinnipedia (in particular, Eumetopias stelleri) and constitutes nearly half the diameter of the eyeball. In the specimens examined the thickness of the sclera reached 2.2 cm.

The dense cornea is flat, reminiscent of that of fish; externally it is covered with a firm keratinized epithelium. Due to the presence of a flat cornea in Cetacea the anterior chamber of the eye typical for mammals is virtually absent. In the sperm whale the remains of this chamber, which lies between the pupil and the cornea, take the form of a narrow slit. The diameter of the cornea is 2.5 cm.

145 The black iris (diameter in sperm whales about 3 cm) is pierced by a bean-shaped pupil with a convex margin (Figure 87). The elongate shape of the pupil increases the field of vision (Astanin, 1958). The pupil is without muscles, and its size and shape are therefore constant. In one of the specimens examined, a male 13 m long, the retina was 1.5 mm thick.

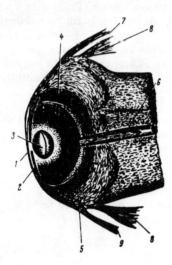

FIGURE 86. Structure of the eye in the sperm whale (sagittal section):

1 — cornea; 2 — iris; 3 — crystalline lens; 4 — sclera; 5 — retina; 6 — optic nerve — fasc. opt.; 7 — m. rectus sup.; 8 — m. retractor; 9 — m. rectus inf.

Vision evidently does not play an important role in the life of whales, particularly of the sperm whale, but the optic nerve is thick both absolutely and relatively (up to 4.5 mm).

The crystalline lens in sperm whales, as in other aquatic animals (Shmal'gauzen, 1947), has the form of a slightly compressed sphere (see Figure 86). Its diameter is 0.9—1.5 cm (Hentschel, 1910; our measurements). Soon after dissection of an eyeball fixed in formalin and extraction from the cavity of the eye cup and the corpus vitreum, the lens darkens and becomes almost black. The surface is weakly united with the corpus vitreum which fills the cavity of the eye cup. The corpus vitreum shows no signs of fibrosity. The inner cavity of the eye cup in the sperm whale is irregular in shape (in man, for example, the eye cup is circular). In the specimens we examined the diameter of the inner cavity of the eye cup was 3.6 cm and its depth 2.4 cm.

The eyeball of whales is virtually immobile and accommodation is impossible (Kellogg, 1928); the muscles of the eyeball are less differentiated than in other mammals, and their innervation is correspondingly weaker.

Because the eyes of the sperm whale are deep-set and are arranged at the sides of the wide head, in front of the head there is an unscannable "dead" area — up to 10° forward and 40—50° backward (Aschley, 1942; Mann Fischer, 1946; Slijper, 1962, Figure 88).

In "Moby Dick" the sperm whale's ability to see the surrounding world with eyes of such a structure evoked astonishment and admiration: ... "True, both his eyes, in themselves, must simultaneously act; but is his brain so much more comprehensive, combining and subtle than man's, that he can at the same moment of time attentively examine two distinct prospects, one on one side of him, and the other in an exactly opposite direction? If he can, then it is as marvellous a thing in him, as if a man were able simultaneously to go through the demonstrations of two distinct problems in Euclid."

FIGURE 87. Iris

146

The sperm whale's organ of sight plays a much smaller receptory role not only in relation to the organs of sight of other mammals owing to their position, but also in relation to the organs of sight of most species of Cetacea due to a primarily deepwater mode of life with a virtual absence of light. In the surface layers of water, where sight could act as one of the main organs of perception (Beale, 1839; Bennett, 1940), the sperm whale generally does no hunting.

FIGURE 88. Field of vision of the sperm whale (Slijper, 1962, after Mann Fischer, 1946)

Factual proof of the unimportant role of the organ of sight in the sperm whale's life can be found in the widely known case of a captured large male with long-standing trauma (or disease) of the eyes which rendered it blind; the stomach was filled with food to the same degree as in the case of sighted animals (Beale, 1835). The receptory function of the eyes is to a large extent (and at depths apparently completely) substituted by perfect ultrasonic echo-location.

Nevertheless, according to observations (see Chapter 15), while the sperm whale is at the surface sight has a definite importance in the system of sense organs.

Chemoreceptors. Long ago investigators were surprised by the presence in whale brains of the remains of a weakly developed olfactory apparatus "the purpose of which is difficult to understand" (Howell, 1930). It was thought that in whales, with the transition to an aquatic mode of life, the very need for a sense of smell disappears. However, in the cortex of toothed whales all the regions without exception are present, including the olfactory (Fillimonov, 1949). Moreover, Kruger (1959) indicated that, firstly, it is not quite correct to link the level of olfactory reception with the disappearance or underdevelopment of individual parts of the brain and, secondly, that the brain structure of Cetacea enables us to speak of a well developed organ of hearing in whales.

Gradually observations accumulated and suggestions were made concerning the possibility that whales obtain information about minimal changes in salinity and the chemical composition of the water in general. In toothed whales (Yablokov, 1957) there are perianal glands, the ducts of which open directly into the water, and preputial glands are found also in the sperm whale (see Chapter 8). All this suggests that certain secretions are discharged into the water, i.e., implies the transmission of signals.

Despite indirect morphophysiological confirmation of the sperm whale's ability to detect changes in the chemical composition of the environment, importance also attaches to the very small volume of the urinary bladder relative to the body weight (in whales in general, including sperm whale), and also the structure of the urogenital canal, throughout the length of which there are no sphincters. These features of the urogenital apparatus indicate
147 that frequent urination and its signalling significance are possible in principle and also necessary. The motionless and dense aquatic medium ensures a prolonged period of olfactory signalling activity and creates exceptionally favorable conditions for it. This suggestion was confirmed experimentally in oceanaria by staining the urine of dolphins (Yablokov, 1959, 1961a).

All this naturally indicated that receivers of such information must exist.

A. V. Yablokov (1957, 1961a) studied six species of toothed Cetacea and concluded that these animals have a special organ similar to the olfactory organ of land mammals which is capable of discerning chemical irritations of the environment.

FIGURE 89. Photograph of a histological section of the base of the sperm whale's tongue. The taste bulbs are visible (1)

Analysis of all sections of the body of toothed whales shows that the only possible place where the chemoreceptors (taste organs) could be located would be the oral cavity, which is constantly washed by water. When the base of the tongue was examined, distinctive fossae were found, lined "not with a multilayered epithelium but with a prismatic epithelium of few layers" with numerous ducts of the mucoprotein glands. The constant presence of these structures in all toothed whales examined implied that these formations may also act as special chemoreceptors (Yablokov, 1961a).

In connection with these interesting theories, special attention was devoted to studying the structure of the base of the sperm whale tongue. Histological examinations of this area established that the structure of the root of the sperm whale tongue is characterized by the presence of connective-tissue papillae, bands ascending through the entire layer of flat multilayered epithelium (Figure 89). In this layer, in places where the connective-tissue papillae with blood vessels are very high and reach the very top, quite specific groups of round, nonkeratinized epithelial cells are visible, distinguished from the other cells of the layer also by their color. It was noted also that the blood vessels enter these formations. The presence of the connective-tissue papillae with the blood vessels is apparently not accidental (the nerve fibers are not revealed when the method of general staining is used, but judging from indirect data they always reach these formations). It is more than likely that these specific groups of cells are analogous to the taste bulbs of other mammals (a similarity is observed also in their external appearance).

148   These histological investigations confirm that toothed whales have organs of chemical reception. These functionally distinctive taste organs can detect "smells" dissolved in the water in the form of admixtures of any composition, announce changes in salinity, etc. The discovery of these organs has broadened our knowledge concerning the high degree of adaptability of sperm whales to life in the water.

Even this relatively brief examination of the brain of the sperm whale shows that the organ is highly developed; this is expressed in the complex structure with laminar differentiation of the cortex, which indicates the possibility of acquiring and accumulating life experiences and realizing associational functions of the highest (psychic) order. The high degree of development of the acoustic (and facial) nerves ensures operation of the precise and powerful ultrasonic locator. The highly developed cerebellum indicates mobility, with excellent coordination of movements. Chemoreception greatly broadens the possibilities for acquisition of information.

DISTRIBUTION

Many researchers have studied the factors involved in the distribution of sperm whales in the World Ocean, since this knowledge is essential for successful whaling of this commercially important species.

Chapter 10

DISTRIBUTION AND MIGRATIONS

The results of observations have shown that the distribution of sperm whales depends primarily on that of their major food — cephalopod mollusks — and on suitable conditions for breeding. Considerable differences have been noted in the character of distribution of the various sex and age groups.

It is also known that most species of Cephalopoda are relatively thermophilic and to a high degree stenohaline animals which prefer tropical and subtropical seas with a salinity above 30 and even 35‰ (Kondakov, 1940; Slijper, 1962; our data). In connection with this, "the Cephalopoda attain their greatest abundance, both in regard to numbers of species and numbers of specimens, in the belt of equatorial and temperate seas, in regions within latitudes 40°N and 40°S" (Kondakov, 1940). The distribution of sperm whales in other regions of the World Ocean are concentrated in the same latitudes.

Extraordinarily good swimmers, squid travel along the warm currents (mainly the deep ones) into higher latitudes of both hemispheres (Kirpichnikov, 1950). The sperm whale follows them and individual large animals reach the waters of Greenland and to the edge of the antarctic ice.

The stenohaline character of the main food of sperm whales seems to explain the rare appearance of the whales in the freshened waters of some of the outlying seas.

The male sperms can be called the cosmopolitans of the World Ocean's pelagial (Slijper, 1962), and in general, the range of the species can be approximately limited by the 300-m isobath.

The range of the females, as well as of immature animals of both sexes, accompanied by a limited number of mature males, is considerably narrower. 150 Usually, the harem animals do not venture beyond 45° latitude in either hemisphere.

Most authors restrict the distribution of female sperm whales to the coordinates 40°N and 40°S (Sleptsov, 1952; Tomilin, 1957; Slijper, 1962; and others) or, which is more or less the same, to the 20° isotherm (Gilmore, 1959).

However, with regard to the range of the females, it is not quite correct to confine them strictly to the warm tropical and subtropical latitudes, since long ago it was noted that females with their 4—6-m long young and shoals of small animals entered the waters of Kamchatka, the Komandorski Islands, and British Columbia (Tomilin, 1936; Scheffer and Slipp, 1948; Sleptsov, 1950, 1952).

The first detailed maps of distribution plotted by G. Bolau (1895) and Townsend (1931) already show that the main mass of sperm whales to the north of the equator (at latitudes from 25° to 40°) stays from April to September and from October to March in the region between 0° and 25°N. In the southern hemisphere the whales keep farther away from the equator from October through March than between April and September. At any rate, the shift of the herds in summer to the north in the northern hemisphere and to the south in the southern hemisphere is quite clearly perceived as presented diagrammatically in Figure 90.

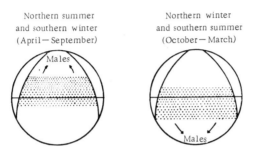

Northern summer
and southern winter
(April — September)

Northern winter
and southern summer
(October — March)

FIGURE 90. General diagram of sperm whale migrations (Mackintosh, 1965)

A most important problem to be clarified in the distribution of both sperm and other whales is the degree of isolation of the herds, the degree of their localness, and, if exchange among them is possible and does occur, then to what extent.

Mackintosh (1965) was convinced that there cannot be any rapid exchange among the herds of the Atlantic, Indian, and Pacific oceans, although mixing is possible at the southern ends of the continents. At the same time, in his opinion, such a clear division into northern and southern herds has not been observed in the sperm whale as in baleen whales. Other authors confirm this stricter localization of herds (Klumov, 1955; Tomilin, 1957; Omura, 1957; Fujino, 1963).

Tomilin (1957) critically examined available data of previous years (Beale, 1835; Melville, 1851; Frederiks, 1853) on finds of harpoons that indicate the possibility of distant journeys by wounded sperms, for example, from Greenland out of the North Atlantic into the North Pacific (moreover, within a few days), from Peru to the Pacific coast of North America and from Japan to Chile and considers them dubious. We must agree with Tomilin that some of the information on very long and extremely strenuous travels of sperm whales belongs to the legends characteristic of the early studies of these giants of the ocean. However, the latest tagging data demonstrated that distant migrations of sperm whales are possible and are carried out. Proof is seen in their passage from the North Atlantic from 21°33'N, 17°55'W to the South Atlantic to 33°20'S. 16°52'E (Ivashin, 1967).

151   The distribution of sperm whales has been most fully presented on the
maps of Townsend (1931, 1935) who plotted them from data of more than
150 years of commercial whaling by American whalers (from 1761 to 1920
about 37,000 were caught).   However, the distribution of the species in the
northern waters was not shown at all in these maps.   The summary by
A. A. Kirpichnikov (1950) is the latest successful study which fully elucidates
the distribution in both hemispheres.   Gilmore (1969) and Mackintosh (1965)
also give distribution maps.

PACIFIC OCEAN

     Up to the present, sperm whales have dominated commercial whaling
over the huge expanse of the Pacific, where they occur in both relatively
and absolutely large numbers due to the many regions with a favorable
ecology (in particular, there are more areas with a warm hydrological
regime, i.e., tropical and subtropical waters in the Pacific, than in the
Indian and the Atlantic oceans together) (Figure 91).
     During the past hundred and fifty years a considerable redistribution
of accumulations has taken place in the North Pacific as a result of whaling
in different regions and of various intensity.   Thus, for example, on the maps
of Murray (1866), Bolau (1895), and Townsend (1935) the major areas of
sperm whale concentrations lay within the boundaries of the tropical and
subtropical waters, and no mention was made of the presence of the species
around the Aleutian Islands or in the Bering Sea.   Obviously, this picture of
distribution reflected not the actual but the conjectured one, according to the
operation of the whaling vessels and by the observations carried out.
Matsuura (1935) states openly that up to 1927 no hunting of sperm whales
had been carried out in the Kurile Islands area, in particular off Iturup
Island, because the sperm whales had been wrongly considered not to inhabit
the cold waters of these latitudes.   The northernmost part of their range
has become known only since the 1930s, i.e., after Soviet vessels began to
operate there.
     Due to the development of Soviet and Japanese whaling and the step-up
of investigations (particularly since tagging was begun in 1949), the distribution in the northwest part of the Pacific has been relatively well studied.
     There are few sperm whales in the Yellow and the East China seas,
apparently in connection with their freshening by the Hwang Ho and Yangtze
rivers (Kirpichnikov, 1950) and their shallow waters.   G. Allen (1938, in
Tomilin, 1957) mentions the only recorded instance of the beaching of a
young animal in 1924 on the shore of Tinghai (26°20') in the East China Sea.
     Matsuura (1935) mentions captures of single specimens in the area of
Taiwan Island, and according to Omura (1950, 1955), the catches of sperms
in this region amounted to 1—4.7% of the total volume of Japanese whaling.
Farther south of Taiwan Island, in particular off the Philippines, there are
relatively more specimens (Matsuura, 1935).   There is no reliable information on the occurrence of sperm whales to the east of these islands, but it
is quite probable that the whales inhabit these waters permanently as
Townsend (1931) mentions the capture of several in the Babuyan channel in
February, and early in July 1967 some groups of 6—30 animals were detected

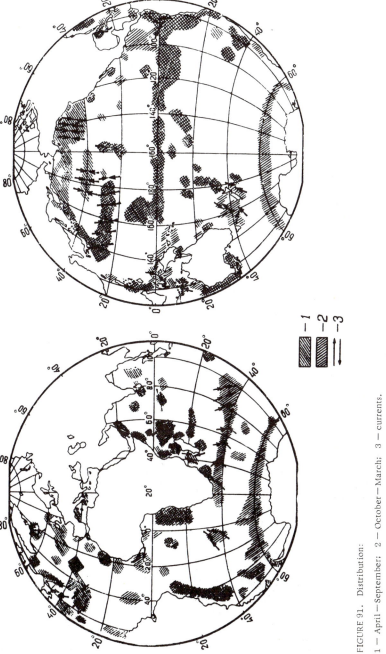

FIGURE 91. Distribution:

1 — April—September; 2 — October—March; 3 — currents.

153 from on board the SRT "Vityaz." In the northwest part of the Philippine Trench relatively few specimens have constantly been caught (from January through July) by the shore whaling stations situated on the islands of Okinawa, Kyushu, and Southern Honshu (Matsuura, 1935; Omura, 1950, 1955; Miyazaki, 1954; Nishiwaki, 1966).

The number of sperm whales has been greatly increasing in the Bonin Islands area. As early as the last century they were commercial items for American whalers and, judging from Townsend's maps (1931, 1935), they were taken in this area from April through September. Until recently the Japanese whalers were operating in the same region (from January to May with peak catches in March) (Omura, 1950; 1955; Miyazaki, 1954; Nishiwaki, 1966), and as can be seen from the maps presented by Miyazaki and Nishiwaki, most sperms were captured on the oceanic side of the islands.

Sperm whales are rarely encountered in the waters of South Korea; Matsuura (1935) notes single cases of capture in individual years (1926). Sleptsov (1961c), using data of Japanese experts, mentions sperm whales off the coast of South Korea and explains their scant presence in this region by the considerable freshening of the waters, so that conditions are unfavorable for cephalopods. A certain number of sperms are captured in May off the western shore of Kyushu Island and also in the area of Senzaki in the Korean Strait, at the entrance to the Sea of Japan (Matsuura, 1935; Omura, 1950; Miyazaki, 1954), evidently during the migration of solitary individuals into this sea. Matsuura, (1935) and Tomilin (1957) also consider this region as a transit area for sperm whales.

The Sea of Japan as a whole presents rather unfavorable conditions for mollusks and whales. Omura's (1950) view is that sperm whales cross to the north through the east side of the sea, keeping to the warm Tsushima Current.

Cases were noted of the occurrence of sperm whales in Peter the Great Bay and their entry into Golden Horn Bay (Zenkovich, 1937a). The last communication (if it is not based on personal observations) may give rise to doubt as the author frequently found that the lesser rorqual and Berardius, that periodically enter this bay, were also called sperm whales.

Sperm whales enter the northern part of the Sea of Japan still less frequently and Far Eastern whalers have not observed any accumulations during all their numerous crossings from Vladivostok to La Pérouse Strait. Tomilin (1957) notes that it was in the Samarga Bay area that in May 1944 sperm whales were observed for the first time. There are data on finds in the northern part of the Sea of Japan, where the whales penetrate apparently through La Pérouse Strait from the Sea of Okhotsk. For example, a large group migrating to the southwest were observed at the beginning of July 1965 from the diesel ship "Chernyakhovskii" in the region 45°12'N and 140°E.

Single appearances of sperm whales in Tatar Strait have been noted. In 1964 on the west shore of Sakhalin, near Khoe village, a 15-meter sperm whale was beached (the "Leninskoe Znamya" newspaper of 28 December 1964 Sleptsov (1952) also mentioned their occurrence in Tatar Strait.

The small numbers of sperm whales in the Sea of Japan are confirmed by observations made from exploratory vessels of TINRO that operate permanently in these waters. Each year between 1961 and 1968, single 154 specimens were found off North Korea in February—April, which suggests that they may stay in this sea the entire year.

Thus, the species is rare all over the Sea of Japan. Until recently this was attributed to the isolation of the sea, and the consequently unsuitable habitat for Cephalopoda (Tomilin, 1957), or to the freshening of its northern waters. Rovnin (in litt.), however, justly considers these arguments to be inconclusive (cf. the still more isolated Mediterranean Sea) and also demonstrates that in regard to salinity, conditions in the Sea of Japan are fairly favorable for cephalopods. In his opinion, the reasons should be sought in the proximity of the Sea of Japan to the freshened and shallow East China Sea, which prevents the entry of sperm whales from the south, and also in the presence of a sharply expressed cyclonic circulation that encompasses a considerable area; these factors, according to our data, are rather disadvantageous for deepwater fauna.

Relatively recently the waters of the oceanic side of Honshu Island and the northern part of Hokkaido were considered major areas of sperm whale habitation. The number of animals in these waters fluctuates by seasons: fewest in April—May, gradually more by July—August, fewer in September, and maximal in October and November. The regions adjacent to the Japanese islands are, at the same time, the wintering grounds for the Asian herds of sperm whales (in the Ogasawara region whaling is carried out in winter, December—March), the maximum number accumulating here in November (Matsuura, 1935). According to the data of Omura (1950), sperm whales occur in the Honshu area throughout the year. The work of Soviet research vessels bears out the year-round occurrence of the whale in these waters.

Large and regular accumulations are formed in the area of the Kurile Islands. As already mentioned, this region was unknown to whalers of the last century, while quite recently this region has come to be one of the leading ones in the world with respect to sperm whale abundance.

Intensive whaling in the current century has made it possible to study the distribution in these waters in detail. According to Matsuura (1935), sperm whales are hunted off the Kuriles from May through September, catches reaching a peak in July—August; later Soviet whaling ships fished for sperm whales in the same region from April to November. According to whaling data up to 1961, abundance along the Kurile Chain was high. The major accumulations were formed from the Pacific side of the islands in waters adjacent to the islands from Boussole Strait to Kruzenshtern Strait, to the east and southeast of Paramushir Island and to a lesser degree to the southeast of Iturup Island. Relatively large numbers accumulated in the straits between the islands.

The animals reached the Sea of Okhotsk through the Kurile straits, where they periodically formed accumulations in the area between Iturup and Paramushir islands but much more numerous ones in the area of Simushir, Matua, and Shiashkotan islands.

In recent years of whaling in these waters in July and early August the number of whales began to decrease, to increase in September and the first third of October owing to their movement to the south.

The number of whales drops in the Sea of Okhotsk with increasing distance from the Kurile Islands. In the southern part of the sea, sperms are constantly noted from the Kuriles to Sakhalin, north of Hokkaido (Sleptsov, 1952, 1961; Tomilin, 1957; Nishiwaki, 1966; and others). Cases have been reported of appearances in La Pérouse Strait and in the Aniva Gulf, where in 1949 one sperm was stranded on the shore in the region of the town of Makarov (Tomilin, 1967).

The whales used to be observed regularly in the area of the Vavilov volcano and the Academy of Sciences elevation; however, in 1967 during an expedition of the "Vityaz" no sperm whales were found there. According to most of the information obtained, sperms rarely occur along the eastern shore of Sakhalin. Sleptsov (1952) observed only solitary individuals in the Terpeniya Cape area and near the northern tip of Sakhalin, and concluded that ventures into these waters are episodic. Tomilin (1957) considers that sperm whales occur frequently off eastern Sakhalin, but he does not support his claim with any concrete data. The exploratory vessels of TINRO that carried out observations on whales in these areas did not discover any sperm whales, and from the same observations it may be assumed that they are rare in the central part of the sea as well.

Rovnin (in litt.) is evidently right in explaining the features of the distribution in the Sea of Okhotsk by the negative temperatures at 200 m and below in the central part of the sea and along eastern Sakhalin and, on the other hand, the positive temperatures in the southern part of the sea, along the Kuriles and Kamchatka. Sperm whales have been permanently noted off Kamchatka. They reached here to the north up to 56°N, forming concentrations periodically off the southern part of the west shore of Kamchatka and, according to our observations, above the TINRO depression. The effect of the anticyclonic circulation causes downwelling (see Chapter 31), and thus, probably favorable conditions for sperm whales over the TINRO depression.

Sleptsov (1952) mentioned that sperms live in the northwestern Sea of Okhotsk, particularly in Tsugaru Strait and off the Shantary Islands and Iony Island.

Scouting carried out in summer 1967 did not disclose any sperm whales in this region, so that apparently conditions are unfavorable in this part of the sea.

Rovnin (in litt.) considers the 300-m isobath as the boundary of distribution in the west and in northwest. He connects occurrence not directly with depth but with the presence of the warm layer of oceanic waters in places where depths exceed 300 meters. This assumption is probably justified.

Off eastern Kamchatka sperm whales have been encountered almost everywhere forming accumulations in the area of Kronotski Gulf, Morzhovoi Bay and Shipunskii Cape; here they were captured by whalers of the Soviet fleet "Aleut" during many years.

The main wintering grounds of sperms living off the shores of Asia are the waters from Hokkaido Island to the southern Japanese islands (Townsend, 1931, 1935; Matsuura, 1935).

The main migration route of the majority of sperm whale herds from the Asian shores in March—April lies between the Philippines and the southern Japanese islands along the oceanic coasts of Japan and the Kuriles to Kamchatka. The whales usually reach the waters of the Northern Kuriles in late April or early May. These dates, however, may shift (Tarasevich, 156 1965). Isolated specimens are the first to arrive; then in May groups begin to appear, and from the second third of the month harems are noted.

The females together with the immature animals of these herds go northward to 51° (Omura, 1950) — 55°N (Sleptsov, 1950, 1952) and even to 59°N, reaching Govena Cape (Berzin and Rovnin, 1966). Throughout the season they may keep to the area of the Northern Kuriles and only in spring approach the northernmost boundaries of their range (approximately in the middle of May) or in late fall.

Our data confirm the opinion of Townsend (1931) and Murray (1935) that the main wintering grounds of sperm whales inhabiting the shores of Asia are those from Hokkaido to the southern Japanese islands. The animals begin to move south by the routes described above at the end of September. Some (both large males and females and immature animals, sometimes also sucklings) remain for wintering in their summer habitat in the waters of the Komandorski Islands, in the Sea of Okhotsk, and off the Kuriles (particularly the central and southern islands). This was the case in 1930, 1932, 1934, and 1947 (Matsuura, 1935; Tomilin, 1936; Sleptsov, 1952). In the Kuriles area sperms of all sex and age groups were encountered in relatively large numbers during a cruise of the whaling vessel "Musson" (Berzin and Rovnin, 1966).

Until recently data on the distribution in the northeastern part of the Pacific were more limited and were confined to information on catches from coastal and pelagial whaling bases (Kellogg, 1931; Pike, 1964; Rosenblum, 1962; Rice, 1963; and others). The waters of the Aleutian Islands (Bering Sea) have been somewhat better studied in this connection, but data on the distribution of whales, in particular of sperm whales, in this region are restricted to general descriptions that merely indicate finds of whales in a particular locality (Tomilin, 1936, 1957; Klumov, 1956; Berzin, 1959; Arsen'ev, 1961; and others). But whereas some idea was gained regarding the distribution of male sperms in these regions, no information at all was available on the distribution of the females and small schooled animals until recently and their occurrence was noted more or less only off Southern California.

The insignificant recent hunting of sperm whales off the Pacific coasts of North America plus the lack of knowledge of the areas of occurrence of the females of this stock induced Tomilin to assume (1957) that there were fewer sperm whales in this part of the ocean than off the shores of Asia.

The increased whaling by pelagic fleets in recent years, the year-round exploratory work carried out by TINRO vessels throughout 1959–1963, and the establishment of regions of concentration of males and females have testified to the great abundance of these stocks, which at a certain stage of current whaling considerably exceeded that of herds inhabiting the waters off the coasts of Asia.

According to recent observations (Berzin and Rovnin, 1966), the northern boundary of the summer range of females and young passes on the average, in the southern part of the Gulf of Alaska, approximately along 50–51°N. Nishiwaki (1967) considers the 10° isotherm, approximately coinciding with 50°N, to be the average northern boundary of the distribution of females and small males in the North Pacific. Within this range harem animals are distributed unevenly, with several places of concentration. The chief mass accumulations are situated on the line which passes from 38°N and 142°W to the northeast up to 45°N and 135°W, then to the northwest from 50°N to 138°W, and further to the west with a little rise to the north up to 52°N and 148°W.

The highest concentration of shoals was observed in the region the center of which lies within coordinates 50°N and 138°W. The other strip extends from 42°N and 140° northwest to 50°N and 154°W. In addition, a large accumulation of females was noted in the area with its center at 41°N.

In early and late spring, females and young move north. Turner (1886, in Tomilin, 1957) mentions the case of a sperm whale suckling 610 cm long beached on the western side of Unalashka Island. The observations of TINRO and whaling vessels also testify to periodic approaches of adult females and young animals to the latitudes of the Aleutian Islands. Larger females penetrate a little further north than younger ones. Remembering the case of a female stranded on Saint Paul Island in 1919 (Tomilin, 1957), it may be assumed that at certain, most favorable periods females move up the coasts of North America to 57° N.

All these data allow us to state that Gilmore (1959), in analyzing the stranding of nine sperm whales (two of them females) in the upper part of the Gulf of California, was wrong to doubt the accuracy of sex definition only because the region is in his opinion remote, from the area of occurrence of harem herds (though in principle such an error is possible, this is a question of females 11.55 m long and longer).

The migration of sperms of harem herds from the wintering grounds begins in March and continues through April and May. In the area of the Aleutian Islands the first specimens were encountered in early March, but it is quite possible that these had wintered in the area. The main arrival of sperm whales into these regions is observed in April. At first the accumulations are formed in the Bering Sea in direct proximity to the islands. In May the number of animals increases and the area of their occurrence expands.

The migration routes in these regions are known to run along the Aleutian Islands Arc westward in the direction of the Komandorski Islands (Sleptsov, 1952; Klumov, 1956; Sleptsov, 1961b), through the Aleutian straits into the Bering Sea and along the continental slope to Cape Navarin (Berzin, 1959; Arsen'ev, 1961). The northernmost points of occurrence here are at 62° N (Tomilin, 1936, 1957; Omura, 1950, 1955; Klumov, 1955; Berzin and Rovnin, 1966). According to Vinogradov (1949) and Arsen'ev (1961), sperm whales are found at still more northern latitudes, at 64 and even at 68° N, but the reliability of these observations is doubtful (particularly the last one). To the north of Cape Navarin, i.e., in the Gulf of Anadyr, Bering Strait, and the Chukchi Sea, the local population does not have any knowledge of the sperm whale (Tomilin, 1957). Nikulin (1947), who investigated the occurrence of whales in the Chukchi Sea, does not mention them either. Nasu (1963) considers that the northern boundary of sperm whale distribution passes along 60° N, while Tomilin (1936, 1957) and Omura (1955) believe it to run along 62° N from Cape Navarin to the Pribilof Islands, and this corresponds to our numerous data. It is shown below that this boundary of distribution is not accidental but strictly determined.

The bulk of males occur from Kodiak Island west along the Aleutian Arc up to the Komandorski Islands. Large permanent accumulations of sperms have been observed to the south of Kodiak Island, south of Unimak Strait, 158 northwest of the Rat Islands, south of the Near Islands, and east, south, and northwest of the Komandorski Islands.

Nasu (1963) reports that sperm whales are most numerous in the region of 180°. Soviet fleets discovered substantial accumulations of large sperms in the fall at 40°N between 175°E and 175°W. This region was named the "Central" one. On Nishiwaki's map (1967) the distribution of sperm whales (of both males and females) in individual regions of the North Pacific contradicts our data of whaling and exploration, especially in the "Central" region.

The regions of sperm whale accumulations naturally change from year to year, but not significantly. Arsen'ev (1961) points out that in 1958–1959 the largest accumulations were observed to the west of the Near Islands, i.e., somewhat north of our proposed middle region of concentration during the period 1958–1964.

In the Bering Sea an abundance of sperms was noted in the area to the north of the Pribilof Islands, where the highest concentration rate was to the north of Atka Island. In the western part of the sea the animals were observed from Karaginski Island to the east more or less along 58° to 180°N, then along the coast southwestward toward the Dezhnev Gulf, and further along the coast to the southwest of Karaginski Island forming a distinct ring with its center roughly at coordinates 59° N and 175° E. In this region there were large accumulations to the east and southeast off Karaginski Island, to the south of the Cape Olyutorski, and southeast of the Dezhnev Gulf. In the Bowers Bank area sperm whales occurred in small numbers. They were evenly distributed over the continental slope, without forming any noticeable accumulations, but nevertheless a relatively large concentration was observed approximately midway between the Pribilof Islands and Cape Navarin. It was in this region that the largest males, 14.1 m long on the average, or with a maximum length of 17.3 m, were noted (Berzin and Rovnin, 1966).

Information on the wintering grounds in these latitudes was very scant until recently. Insignificant numbers of whales were caught along the Californian coast and Lower California (Pike, 1954; Tomilin, 1957; Rice, 1963). According to our data, the area of the wintering grounds is to the south of 35°N and spreads roughly from the Hawaiian Islands to California. Thus, from January to February 1964 sperm whales were detected by exploratory vessels at coordinates 24°30'N and 135° 30'W, 32° N and 137°W, 22°N and 149° 30'W, and 22° N and 112°W. It may be assumed that the majority winter in the area situated closer to the coasts of America than to the Hawaiian Islands coast (Berzin and Rovnin, 1966).

Some of the animals (e.g., off the coasts of Asia) remain in their summer habitat for wintering, according to data obtained from the vessels. It can be assumed that in winter sperm whales usually keep to the same regions as in summer, sometimes forming accumulations of 80–100 individuals, as was observed in January 1964 in the region north of the eastern part of the Aleutian Islands. In the Gulf of Alaska sperm whales are rarely found in winter and then in small numbers. In the waters of Central California the males remain permanently during winter (Rice, 1963).

Certain authors believe that there is only one herd of sperm whales in the North Pacific. Thus, Sleptsov (1952) thinks that a single North Pacific herd inhabits the northern part of the ocean and that during the fall migrations, the whales descend along the coasts of the Kuriles and Japan, move toward Bonin, the Marianas and Caroline islands, and possibly reach the Hawaiian Islands, joining the whales coming from California. He also considers that the whales of the northern part of the Pacific are not isolated from those of the southern part.

However, most authors (Zenkovich, 1934, 1936, 1937; Tomilin, 1939, 1960; Omura, 1955, 1957) point to the fact that the northern half of the Pacific contains two herds of sperm whales: the Asian herd, which migrates along the shores of Asia and the summer range of which covers the waters of

North Japan, the area off the Kurile islands, the Sea of Okhotsk and the waters of Kamchatka, and the American herd, which migrates along the American continent and moves in the direction of the Aleutian Islands.

Finally, some investigators divide the sperm whale populations much more finely, particularly, the North Pacific populations. Thus, Klumov (1955) believes that the sperm whales living off the shores of Asia are subdivided into two local herds which have their own wintering grounds and summer habitat: Northern Kurile and Southern Kurile (according to the summer regions). He assumes the whales of the American population also to have a similar division. However, the results of tagging, particularly of that carried out by Soviet researchers, do not confirm this (see Figure 92) because many of the sperm whales tagged in the region of habitat of the Northern Kurile herd returned from the Hokkaido Island region, i.e., from the area where the other herd ought to have occurred.

Omura (1957) sees a discrepancy between the results of tagging that testify to the possibility of distant migrations of whales from the western and eastern regions of the ocean, and studies of blood types, which indicate the existence of different herds. He concludes that the herds winter in various regions and in summer mingle in the northern waters, to go their own ways to various wintering grounds at the approach of winter.

Fujino (1963), having analyzed the results of Japanese tagging (1949–1962) and the research into blood types (1959–1962),* also assumes that there are two herds in the northwestern part of the ocean, but according to him, one of them winters in the area of the central and southern Kuriles and in summer keeps to the waters of the Aleutian Islands, while the other herd winters off Japan but spends the summer around the Kurile Islands and Kamchatka, and does not move eastward beyond 70°E.

On the basis of observations of the direction of whale movements that were conducted from exploratory and whaling vessels we surmised (Berzin and Rovnin, 1966) that the migration of sperm whales in the northern part of the Pacific follows not one, two, or three routes along the shores of Asia and America but numerous routes that are constant for each group; it may even be that the shift of the animals approaches that of a broad front.

The notion that with the onset of the migration period (which is considerably prolonged), large groups migrate northward, each moving from its wintering grounds, appears much more plausible. This is more or less the picture which emerges upon analysis of our and other data. For instance, in the maps of Townsend (1931, 1935) the whales are shown to be more or less evenly distributed over the entire subtropical zone from the coast of America to the shores of Asia.

According to available schemes of migrations, all these whales must have traveled thousands of miles to reach the shores of the corresponding continents. It is hard to imagine that animals which, for example, had wintered in an area to the west of Hawaii, should with the onset of spring migrate thousands of miles eastward in order later to pursue a route along the American coast to the central part of the Aleutian Islands, for instance.

We tentatively determined several migration routes in the northeastern part of the Pacific: the first route runs along the coast of North America (approximately along 130°W) up to 50°N, from where part of the herd

160

---

* Analyses of blood carried out by Japanese scientists demonstrated that in sperm whales from the coastal waters of Japan, the soluble substance Jn_2 is present in 42.3%, whereas it is absent in animals from the region of the Aleutian Islands (from the northern part).

migrates to the Alexander Archipelago, while the other part turns west toward the region between 50 and 150°W; the second route passes through the open ocean along 145–150°W also to 50°N; the third route runs approximately along 162–167°W, to the eastern Aleutian Islands. From here some of the whales turn toward Kodiak Island and the northern part of the Gulf of Alaska, while the rest move in the western direction and reach the Komandorski Islands. Part of the herd enters the Bering Sea through the straits of the eastern Aleutian Islands and, moving along the continental slope, reaches the shores of Asia. The routes may run into each other in regions with the most favorable conditions for habitat; more whales pass by here than in other areas. Such routes are observed relatively close to the coasts of the continents, the continental slope of the Bering Sea, the island arc of the Hawaiian Submarine Ridge, the meeting points of warm and cold waters and so on.

It has also been assumed that sperm whales are the very whales for which an artificial division into Asian and American, tying them strictly to the shores of the respective continents, could be rejected. This division was based on observations most of which had naturally been made at various times, mainly close to the continents.

The principle of local herds is not refuted in this case but it is interpreted on a somewhat different plane than by Klumov (1955). If we maintain the view that there are very fine divisions of herds into small local groupings which have their own foraging grounds in the summer areas, then in the light of the most recent tagging data it should be assumed that whales which have wintered, for instance, off the southern Japanese islands migrate for the summer to the eastern Aleutian islands or to the Gulf of Alaska.

It would be more correct to consider that sperm whales are local in the sense of the immiscibility of herds and in the absence of a broad interchange of specimens among the herds. Each herd evidently has its strictly defined wintering grounds, but the area of the summer habitat of each herd being vast, the herds cross extensively from one foraging ground to another, for example, from the western part of the Pacific to the eastern and vice versa. With the fall, the herds pursue their routes to the wintering grounds. A similar relationship to the regions of summer and winter habitat has been discovered in animals performing long migrations, birds in particular, in which the existence of numerous independent populations is not excluded.

There is a certain periodicity in the formation of sperm whale accumulations within the boundaries of the summer range. Upon arrival at the summer region, the whales shift regularly, periodically forming accumulations in the most favorable foraging areas (Berzin, 1959a).

In summer 1965–1967 Soviet whaling fleets operated in the 40° latitudes (from 175°W to 175°W), i.e., a little higher than the region defined by Townsend. It was probably at the same longitudes that the Soviet fleets caught the male sperm whales of the same herds that had been taken by whalers in the last century. Almost all the specimens taken were large males, and analysis of the animals' age showed that on the whole they were much older than the animals from herds that already had been fished for many years in the northwestern and northern regions of the North Pacific. This gives grounds for believing that no hunting of sperm whales had been carried out here for many years. It is also known that since the end of the 19th century no whaling vessels had visited the above regions.

161

It may be assumed that this region is the home of an isolated (to some extent) population whose members do not move to higher latitudes, those of the Komandorski and Aleutian islands, for the summer period. The wintering area and area of habitat of the females of this population obviously lie somewhat farther south, somewhere in the region of the Marshall Islands. Only tagging will help to give the final answer to this question.

In recent years Rovnin studied the distribution of whales in the Pacific Ocean; he continued the analysis of data on local nature of sperm whale herds and confirmed that there is a separate herd in these regions which has since been named the Central (or Hawaiian) herd. Thus, it can be considered that three main populations — Asian, Central, and American — can be isolated in the northern part of the Pacific (without excluding a more fractional division into herds). So far the existence of these herds has not been contradicted by any reliable data.

Quite comprehensive information is available on the occurrence of sperm whales in the central regions of the Pacific, dating to the time when sailing vessels of the whaling fleet of the 18—19th centuries were in operation (Beale, 1835; Bennett, 1840; Murray, 1866; Bolau, 1895; Townsend, 1935). These sources, with some modifications and additions, were used by Kirpichnikov (1950), Tomilin (1936, 1957), Gilmore (1959), Mackintosh (1965), Ohsumi (1966) and many others. Though this information refers to the distant past and there are indications as to severe exhaustion of the herds in these regions as a result of overintensive whaling, we do thereby gain an idea of the nature of sperm whale distribution at present.

In the 19th century the major regions of intensive hunting of sperm whales in the Pacific Ocean were situated around the Marshall and Hawaiian islands, mainly in the north and northeast* and over almost the entire near-equatorial belt. The area between Peru and the Marquesas Islands used to be considered one of the best whaling regions in the world. The shore whaling stations of Peru still catch a large number of sperm whales here.

Another important whaling region lies between Borneo and the Philippines (the Sulu and Celebes seas), the waters of the Moluccas, and the coastal waters of the Lesser Sunda Islands. Boschma (1938), with reference to Van Musschenbroek (1877), mentions that sperms come to these waters
162 from the south and migrate through the Banda and Celebes seas toward the Philippines from which they then return.

Many authors (Beale, 1835; Bennett, 1840; Townsend, 1931, 1935) indicate the waters of New Guinea and the islands of Bonin, Fiji, Samoa, Tonga, Society, Tuamotu, Marquesas, Gilbert's, Cook and the Solomons as areas with accumulations. The whales remain all the year round in all these regions. Some details of the distribution, in particular pertaining to areas of concentration, that are found in the literature have already been mentioned above; here, we will deal with the more important data that have emerged in order to have concrete starting points for conducting exploratory investigations, specifically in the central regions of the Pacific. It has been pointed out that tropical waters promising for whaling are those to the north of Morotai Island (Moluccas), off Timor Island, between 12—16°N and 112—120°E, the Gulf of Panama, the region between 5—10°S and 105—125°W, the waters off the New Guinea coast (from 140 to 146°E), those off New Ireland Island

* Recent observations have not confirmed any considerable concentrations of sperm whales off the Hawaiian Islands, particularly to the east of them.

(from St. George Cape to St. Mary Cape), off the eastern coasts of New Britain Island, to the north of the Solomon Islands, along the equator from 168 to 175° E, the southern side of the Ellice Islands, to the north off the Fiji Islands, the waters midway between the South American Continent and the Galápagos Islands, the waters off Peru (from the equator to 16° S), from the Fanning Island (atoll) (159°W and 4°N), and to the southeast as far as Christmas Island.

Clarke (1962) in 1959 made a month-long (October—November) research voyage off the coasts of Peru, Chile, and the Galápagos Islands and reports that most of the 150 sperms recorded stayed in groups of up to 20—25 specimens mainly toward the Galápagos Islands.

In 1965—1968 the research whalers "Vnushitel'nyi" and "Druzhnyi," and the SRTM "Tamango" obtained comprehensive and interesting data on the distribution of sperm whales in the central part of the Pacific throughout the year. Large herds (of 25—30, 50—60, and 250—300 animals) consisting mainly of females, schooling males and juveniles, were encountered early in March off Mexico (Cape Sikatula). In November, to the south of the Gulf of Tehuantepec, two herds were encountered, one consisting of 35 large sperms, the other of 80—100 males and females, and two more herds consisting of young animals (one of 40—50, the other of 20 — 25 specimens). In September 1965 — January 1966 more than ten herds (from 8 to 250—300 animals) were found in the region between 01°30'S and 17° S and from 115°W to 79°20'W.

A particularly large concentration was observed in January in a region the center of which lay at coordinates 14°30'S and 82°W. According to Rovnin's observations, about $1/3$ of the animals recorded were of commercial size. Clarke (1962) emphasizes the absence of sperm whales in the littoral zone, whereas according to the data of the above-mentioned cruise, a large concentration was noted in the area of the 200-mile fishing zone off the coasts of Peru and Chile in December and January (Rovnin, 1966, 1967).

In the western regions of the Central Pacific in the spring—summer period (for the northern hemisphere) large groups and herds of sperm whales were noted off Nauru and Molden islands (up to 200 animals) and herds consisting of 100—200 whales off New Ireland Island, the Solomon Islands, and the New Hebrides. Females with young constituted the bulk of the whales encountered but there were also many large males. If the conclusion of experts as to the exhaustion of sperm whale reserves in the tropical regions of the Pacific due to overintensive whaling was correct at the time, at present their abundance here may be considered to have been restored.

There are fewer sperms off Chile than off the northern coasts of North America, but nevertheless until recent years the shore stations of this country caught over 1,000 animals. According to Townsend (1931), accumulations were noted around the Juan Fernandes Islands (on the Valparaiso latitude). It was here, in May 1958, in the Concepcíon Bay, that several groups of females with offspring, 20—40 animals in each group, were noted (Zenkovich, 1960). Murray (1866) reports on the occurrence of sperm whales from 37°S southward along the Chile coast up to Chiloé Island (43° S). Zenkovich (1960) recorded 7 groups of sperm whales somewhat farther north. The whales live here all the year round.

In late October and early November 1958 Clarke (1962) found some small groups of sperm whales in the littoral zone, to the south of Valparaiso city, and determined that the number of whales detected during the cruise off the coasts of Chile was only one-third the number encountered during the cruise along the Peruvian coast.

There is almost no information on the habitat of the sperm whales in the extreme south of Chile and off the Strait of Magellan, but in the opinion of Kirpichnikov (1950), a certain number of males appears here in summer. Townsend (1931) also mentions catches of solitary animals in January and February.

In the southwestern part of the Pacific sperm whales of various sex and age groups stay more or less throughout the year. They have been noted off the coasts of Australia from 25 to 34°S, between Australia and New Zealand, from East Cape to North Cape to the north of New Zealand, and around the Kermadec Islands (Beale, 1835; Murray, 1866; Townsend, 1931).

Kirpichnikov (1950) thinks that the virtual absence of sperm whales in the catches taken by New Zealand in the 1930s and 1940s did not fully reflect the abundance of the whales in these waters. His assumption has proved to be correct in recent years: after the hunting of humpback whales ceased here, a single coastal whaling station, that had just one whaling vessel, caught 114 whales in 1963 and 134 in 1964.

According to data of Soviet whaling and scouting, mainly herds of sperm whales — females and immature animals — keep to the waters adjacent to the southeastern side of South Island; the southern boundary of their range in summer runs along 46°S. Off the east side of Cook Strait and to the east of New Zealand, off Chatham Island, abundant accumulations of large, solitary males are observed, particularly in fall (April). According to Vladimirov (in litt.), this very region also differs from the others in the variety of forage for the whales.

Recent data show that mainly herds of females and immature animals keep to the southern coasts of Australia, around Tasmania. No sperm whales have been noted in Bass Strait. The larger, mature males that form mixed herds periodically approach, in particular the southwestern coasts of Tasmania. The number of harems is decreasing to the south of Tasmania. The southern border of distribution in summer in this region passes along 49°S (see Figure 91).

164 ATLANTIC OCEAN

Data on the distribution of sperm whales in this ocean are quite numerous, but most of them are based on whaling of previous years (Bennett, 1840; Murray, 1966; Townsend, 1931, 1935).

More recent information is presented by Kirpichnikov (1950), Brown (1958), and Slijper, Van Utrecht, and Naaktgeboren (1964).

In the Atlantic Ocean male sperm whales penetrate much further to the north than in the Pacific due to the North Atlantic Current and its relatively warm branch the West Greenland Current that later passes into the Irminger Current (Wallo, 1948; Kirpichnikov, 1950). These currents extend beyond the limits of the Arctic Circle and reach the latitudes of Greenland, Iceland and the Barents Sea. Here (70—75°N) the males penetrate. Solitary large animals have been noted off Spitsbergen and west of Jan Mayen Island (Beneden, 1888).

According to available information, the sperm whale is an infrequent visitor to the southeastern part of the Barents Sea up to the Kanin Peninsula. Lepekhin (1805) found teeth of a whale that had been stranded on the shore of the peninsula, and in 1932 Biryulya (quoted in Tomilin, 1957) discovered a large male 16 m long on the same shore, on Kanin Nos Cape. In the past there were reports of single specimens reaching the Murman Coast (Tomilin, 1936).

Murray (1866) wrongly rejected the possibility that sperm whales penetrate into Greenland waters, although Zorgdrager long ago (1798, in Boschma, 1938) reported captures off North Cape in 1718 and in 1719, while Fabricius (1870) considered the sperm whale as a representative of the Greenland fauna. Lousier (1812, in Boschma, 1938) mentioned the capture of four sperms in Davis Strait. Brown (1868) noted the scant numbers of sperm whales in these latitudes but also recorded his catch in the region. In 1937 seven whalers captured 181 males in Davis Strait (Tomilin, 1957). Kirpichnikov (1960) states that six sperm whales were caught in 1946 off southeastern Greenland and in Davis Strait. The animals appeared here in July—September.

The east coast of Iceland is usually reached by sperm whales in July (Collett, 1911—1912). In 1968—1969 up to 10 animals a year were captured near Iceland, and in 1949 (Tomilin, 1957) 28 males were taken. The appearance of sperm whales off Northern Iceland, in Denmark Strait and Davis Strait was noted on Gilmore's maps (1959).

It has long been known that sperm whales occur off Norway (Linnaeus, 1746; Collett, 1911—1912). Every year specimens were captured off the western coasts, though in small numbers: in 1926 two animals were taken; in 1939, 14 animals in June, July and September; and in 1946 from May to September, 21; in 1947, 16, including one female (Harmer, 1928; Kirpichnikov, 1950). The warm and saline current passing near the shores of Norway apparently creates favorable conditions for sperm whales.

In summer 1949, mainly in August, 53 male sperms were captured off the Faeroe Islands. The whaling station on the Shetland Islands takes from one to 31 specimens from April through September. There was one female among the 11 whales caught in Hebrides waters in 1927 (Tomilin, 1957).

Sperm whales appear frequently off the coasts of Scotland, England, and Ireland, a fact confirmed by strandings on British beaches (Harmer, 1927), and off the west coast of Ireland the whales used even to be regularly captured, though in small numbers (Kirpichnikov, 1950). Females with their sucklings also entered these latitudes, as they have been found (though extremely rarely) among dead animals on the coasts of Great Britain (Harmer, 1928). According to data of Slijper et al. (1964), in the Atlantic, females as a rule reach no higher than 40°N, some possibly to 50°N, but not farther than 54°N. The discovery of 17 sperm whales stranded near Hamburg in December 1723, eight of which were females (Slijper, 1962), testifies to the possibility of their reaching these latitudes.

Sperm whales are quite often beached on the coasts of Holland. Using the material of Van Deinse (1931), who recorded 41 cases of beaching here (half of them in December, January, and February), A. Tomilin (1957) concluded that these animals occur in the North Sea the year round. There are reports of arrivals (three cases) in the Baltic Sea (Jaffa, 1909, in Tomilin, 1957). Kirpichnikov (1950) considers the above data extremely vague, and the appearance of single animals very rare, as the Baltic Sea is shallow, greatly freshened and, therefore, not suitable for permanent habitation.

Kirpichnikov (1950) mentions a small catch of these whales off the shores of Labrador, where in 1943—1946 one whaling station captured about 22 specimens from July through October, and also Newfoundland, where during the same period the station captured 13 animals in 1939. Tomilin (1957) considers that migrating animals were caught here, descending along the continent to their breeding grounds in the direction of the Gulf of Mexico, the Antilles and Bermuda.

Summing up the data on seasonal fluctuations of distribution in the North Atlantic, Townsend (1931) shows that the major accumulations north of 25°N arrive in April—September, whereas between 25°N and the equator in October—March. The northernmost region of accumulation noted by this author in the North Atlantic is southeast of the British Isles (at 50—52°N and 21—24°W).

Presenting maps of sperm whale catches, Townsend (1931, 1935) distinguishes several whaling regions that existed in the North Atlantic in the 19th century. Some of these have not lost their importance. A more detailed analysis of these maps is given below.

A good region for whaling used to be that east of the Bermuda Islands and around them, encompassing mainly the area of the Sargasso Sea (approximately between 35—57°W and 30—40°N, with its center at 31°N and 50°W).

In these regions, particularly in the Bermuda area, sperm whales have been lately found relatively rarely (Kirpichnikov, 1950). These are considered to be breeding grounds judging from Wheeler's report (1933) of a newborn sperm whale captured in these waters in 1932. Analyzing the data of the maps, it can be stated that the main accumulations can be formed in the northern hemisphere in June—September, less in October and November, and they begin to arrive in April—May. Individuals were noted in December, January and February.

166   All researchers agree that the region around the Azores with its center at 37°N and 22—33°W is the main focus of sperm whale concentration in the North Atlantic. Male sperms inhabit these waters all the year round, but the greatest general abundance occurs in June—October.

Females are almost absent in winter and spring, but plentiful in summer and fall (Mousinho—Figueiredo, 1957). The highest catches are taken in August—September, large numbers in June—July, fewer in October—November, and single individuals in December. Analyzing observations from ships, Slijper and Van Utrecht (1959), call this region a reservoir for the distribution of sperm whales to other regions.

A region can be distinguished off the North American coast to east of Cape Hatteras, along the Gulf Stream with its center at 36°N, 70°W, in which the whales stay mainly in May—July, to a lesser extent in April, and found even in January. Judging from Gilmore's maps (1959), sperms inhabit this region all the year round. At present no whaling is carried out here; however, Kirpichnikov (1950) believes that sperm whales are definitely present here.

Quite an important sperm whaling region (in the past) is seen along 25°W with the center in the waters of the Cape Verde Islands and further south to the equator. Here accumulations are formed in October—March; there are fewer animals in April and September, but they have been observed also in July.

An accumulation is formed in April—May in a rather large region with its center at 40°N and 12°W. Solitary specimens are encountered here throughout the year.

Townsend mentions another region in the Gulf of Mexico which sperm whales inhabit in March—July. Information on stranding here testified to the year-round presence of various sex and age groups.

The waters off Madeira (31—36°N and 22—24°W) and to the west were recently relatively good whaling grounds all year round. For instance, 166 sperm whales were captured here in 1946. Concentrations are also formed off the Canary Islands in August—January, and in June—September off the extreme northeastern coasts of Africa (Morocco).

The Gulf of Guinea, part of which lies in the southern hemisphere, is a locality of year-round habitation (Tomilin, 1957). This has been attested to by observations from transport and other vessels (Brown, 1958). There is a report that at the end of April 1948, the Soviet flotilla "Slava" encountered at 08°37'N and 09°33'E several shoals (of about 50 specimens) of young sperm whales with females (Kirpichnikov, 1950).

In the opinion of Tomilin (1957), only migrating males are captured off Spain and, particularly, Portugal. In the 1930s, off the Spanish coasts (Cape Finisterre) about 30 animals were caught per season, and in the waters of Portugal (station at Setubal) 30—50 sperms were captured in 1947—1949. There are recorded observations of sperm whales inhabiting the Bay of Biscay (Brown, 1958; Slijper and Utrecht, 1959).

The narrow but deep Strait of Gibraltar is crossed by sperm whales
167 mainly in spring. Together with the strong sea current they reach the Mediterranean Sea, with its fauna rich in cephalopod mollusks. Relatively numerous sperm whales arrive in this sea also in December—February (Bolognari, 1957).

Sperm whales have been recorded in the Ligurian and Tyrrhenian seas. In May 1948 vessels of the "Slava" encountered about ten females with young at 40°19'N and 4°57'E (70 miles north of the Balearic Islands) and a group of young sperms off Corsica (Kirpichnikov, 1949). They pass from these regions into the Ionian and Adriatic seas (Pouchet and Beauregard, 1892; also Riggio, 1893 and Monticelli, 1906, quoted in Tomilin, 1957). There are reports that the whales are found far to the east, near Alexandria and even off Palestine (Acaroni, 1944, in Tomilin, 1957; Bolognari, 1957).

Mainly small harem animals have been noted to enter the Mediterranean (Bolognari, 1957). Summing up the features of distribution in the North Atlantic by seasons, Townsend reports that the major accumulations in the region situated north of 25°N occur in April—September, while in the region between 25°N and the equator in October — March.

In the South Atlantic, taking into consideration Townsend's data (1935), the following two regions of concentration can be determined: the large and quite distinctly outlined region near the coasts of Africa (off Angola) between 5—24°S and 4—2°E and its shores (in this region more or less uniform accumulations are formed all the year round) and the region located off Tristan da Cunha and to the northeast (sperm whales stay here in November—March, but solitary animals are encountered in April and September). In these regions Soviet Antarctic whaling fleets noted abundant accumulations (hundreds of specimens) of harem animals in the second half of April 1962.

Off the Atlantic coast of Central and South Africa, in the region from the equator to the latitude of Cape Town, sperm whales are also taken, though in smaller numbers than baleen whales (sperm whale catches constitute about 10% of the total landings of whales). In 1913 there were 14 whaling stations along this coast. In 1925, off the French Congo,* 35 sperms were captured, amounting to 8% of all whale catches, and in 1935—1936 (the last year of whaling) 54 sperm whales. Off the shores of Angola 140 animals were caught in 1927—1928. Farther south, off the Southwest African coast, the station "Whale-Fish" (22°30'S) caught 14 sperm whales in 1926—1927 (the last whaling season). Still fewer sperm whales were delivered to the "Saldan" station situated farther south (34°S), frequently only four or five specimens; only in individual years (1947) their number increased to 48 (46 males and 2 females according to Kirpichnikov, 1950). The whaling season off Southwest Africa is the summer of the southern hemisphere.

Kirpichnikov (1950) writes that the farther south from the equator the whaling areas are situated along the west coasts of Africa, the smaller is the proportion of sperm whales taken in the total catch of whales. The relatively small number of sperms off the coasts of Angola, Southwest Africa and in the adjacent regions is probably the result of the strong influence of the cold Benguela Current which flows along the west coast of Africa toward the Cape of Good Hope until it meets the South Equatorial Current. Comparing the catches of sperm whales off Southwest Africa with those off Southeast Africa, Kirpichnikov attributes the low catches in the 168 former region to the presence of hydrological conditions favorable to plankton development, i.e., favorable for baleen whales, while hydrological conditions off eastern Africa are favorable for Cephalopoda and thus sperm whales.

An area is distinguished off the South American coast from about 40—55°S along the littoral to 6°S, where major sperm whale concentrations are found off the southern shore of Brazil and the coast of Uruguay (33°S and 47°W) in the zone of the warm Brazil Current in any month of the year with a slight increase in midsummer of the southern hemisphere (January—February).

Kirpichnikov (1950) explains the irregular and low catches of sperm whales off the Falkland Islands, Patagonia and Tierra del Fuego by un- favorable hydrological conditions formed by the cold Falkland Current coming from the south. Tomilin (1936) reports on an encounter near Patagonia of enormous shoals of males and females with young. According to our data, in this region, evidently depending on the conditions of the particular year, lies the southern boundary of the range of harem animals, in the southern half of the Atlantic, approximately along 50—54°S. We encountered large accumulations of small shoal animals.

Summing up and comparing the occurrence of sperm whales in the North and South Atlantic it is of interest to present Brown's data (1958) from a number of observations of whales on a stretch of 1,000 miles. Average density over the entire North Atlantic is 0.2, and over the South Atlantic 0.24 specimen per 1,000 miles. In the so-called North European zone of the Atlantic Brown considers the density to be 0.27 specimen, and in the African waters 0.48 per 1,000 miles. He determined that the population density of all whales, including sperm whales, is greater in the South than in the North Atlantic.

* Since August 1956 called the Republic of Congo (Kinshasa and Brazzaville).

INDIAN OCEAN

Published data on the distribution of sperm whales over this expanse
are relatively limited, as until recently whaling was quite insignificant
here.

Besides data from the literature (Beale, 1835; Murray, 1866; Townsend,
1931, 1935; Kirpichnikov, 1949, 1950; Brown, 1957; and others), material
received from Soviet whaling fleets and the shore whaling stations of
Australia were used for the present survey.

Sperm whales stay in the Indian Ocean throughout the year, but their
abundance varies according to seasons. Their distribution is determined
by the distinctive hydrological regime of this ocean.

In the last century the favorite grounds for sperm whaling were off the
coasts of Zanzibar, Mozambique and Mozambique Channel, where whaling
lasted from May through July, off the Comoro Islands and Aldabra,
Madagascar, the Seychelles and Mascarene Islands, on the vast chain of
banks stretching between them, Christmas Island, the Keeling Islands,
and also the Amirantes, in the Arabian Sea (between Socotra Island and the
Arabian Peninsula), in the Persian Gulf and the Red Sea, and off the west
coast of Australia (Beale, 1835; Murray, 1866; Kirpichnikov, 1950; Tomilin,
1957). The waters off Southeast Africa are considered one of the most
important world regions of sperm whaling. The great abundance of the
species in these regions is caused by the very favorable ecological conditions formed by the warm Mozambique Current flowing from the north and
169 mixing with the Agulhas Current (Kirpichnikov, 1950).

In this region (in particular, near Durban) sperm whales stay all the
year round; from September their numbers increase, reaching a peak in
the summer months and falling to a minimum in midwinter. It is noteworthy that here, as for the northern waters of the Pacific, an increase in
the numbers of females and small males is noted in fall and spring
(Gambell, 1967). Most medium-sized and large sperms migrate north
across the Durban area, apparently after the majority of females have
passed there. The animals apparently migrate south after September.
As a rule, concentrations are rarely found on the continental shelf, excluding
the region to the south of Durban, although the shelf there is very narrow
and passes only 15 miles from the shore (Bannister and Gambell, 1965;
Gambell, 1967).

Brown (1957), having analyzed records of vessels (unfortunately very
limited, only 33 observations) from 1952 to 1956 in this ocean, made a
comparative assessment of individual regions which is in good agreement
with the distribution of sperm whales according to Townsend's maps (1935).
The largest number (1.15 animals per 1,000 miles) was recorded in the
Gulf of Aden and adjacent waters. According to these data, the region
situated between South Africa and South Australia occupies second place
by number of whales. A minimum number of whales is found in the central
part of this region (0.07 animal per 1,000 miles). In the Arabian Sea and
Bay of Bengal 0.56 and 0.37 specimen are encountered per 1,000 miles,
respectively.

Examination of ship records of encounters of sperm whales north and
south of the equator shows that in spring (March—May) the whales are most
abundant to the north of the equator, while there are somewhat fewer of them
here in the fall (September—November). Only a tenth as many whales were

recorded in these regions in the other seasons. To the south of the equator sperm whales are observed in large numbers during the southern summer (December—February) and southern winter (July—August), but there are only 2.5—3 times more in comparison with other months, i.e., the seasonal fluctuations are much smaller than to the north of the equator. Townsend (1935) assumes migrations in the southern direction (to the north of the equator) at the beginning of winter in the northern hemisphere and migrations to the north (to the south of the equator) at the beginning of winter in the southern hemisphere.

Data on distribution obtained during recent years by Soviet fleets agree on the whole with those of past years. South of the equator sperm whales predominated at latitudes between South Australia and South Africa during the summer of the southern hemisphere (December—January). Large concentrations were noted here north of Amsterdam and Saint Paul islands; there were relatively large numbers of whales off the southern side of the Hindustan Peninsula, near the exit from the Gulf of Aden, to northeast of Madagascar (off the Amirantes and Providence Island). Many specimens were found in the fall (May) off the southeastern shores of Africa.

Sperm whales inhabit the waters of the western shores of Australia practically all year round, their numbers increasing in the northern regions in winter and in the southern regions in summer (Gilmore, 1959). Beale (1835) had pointed out that sperm whales live off the northwest coasts of Australia. Off the western shores of the continent, according to data obtained by aerial observations, the whales remain farther away from the coast than at the southern shores, where they keep to the edge of the continental shelf (Bannister, 1965—1966). Males migrate for the winter from the subpolar regions into the regions of the southwest coasts of Australia. It has also been suggested that females migrate for the summer period from the tropics to Albany (Sperm Whaling at Albany.— Norsk hvalf. tid., No. 11, 1958).

The general direction of the migrations is determined by the shore line according to Bannister (1965—1966).

All the regions of occurrence in the Indian Ocean lie between the 40 latitudes in the tropical and subtropical zones, and naturally they are occupied almost completely by herds of harem animals which, according to data of recent years, ascend to the south (particularly in the central part of the ocean) as far as 44°S. Soviet fleets noted the approach of a considerable number of adult males to the waters of southwestern Australia in May.

Slijper, Van Utrecht, and Haaktgeboren (1964) studied data over three-years from questionnaires given to Dutch vessels, and noted sharp predominance of sperm whales to the north of the equator in winter. The authors speak of the absence in these waters of the migrations typical in the Pacific and Atlantic oceans. They assume that specific migrations occur here, determined by the direction of the monsoon current, which passes here in winter and summer in exactly opposite directions.

170

ANTARCTIC

There is no mention at all of sperm whales' inhabiting the waters of the Antarctic in the works of Beale (1835), Murray (1866), or Bolau (1895). Murray's map (1866) confines the area of distribution to the tropical and subtropical latitudes. Beddard (1900) and even Townsend (1931) report that only single "vagrants" approach the Antarctic from time to time.

By now no one believes that sperm whales are rare visitors to antarctic waters. The very first voyage of the Soviet flotilla "Slava" to the Antarctic in 1946—1947 showed that sperm whales are frequently encountered not only in the high latitudes of the southern hemisphere but also approach the edge of drift ice and enter the regions of brash ice accumulations. In February in this region, not far from the floes of drift ice at 66°S and 14°W, five sperms were captured. During the following cruise on 21 March six whales were taken 30 miles from Princess Martha Coast (69°S and 0°30'E), higher than the considerable masses of drift ice. Thus, in the southern hemisphere sperm whales ascend to much higher latitudes than in the northern hemisphere.

Stomach fullness of sperm whales captured in the high latitudes was poor (according to Kirpichnikov, 1950), indicating unsatisfactory conditions in these waters. Cephalopods are less numerous in the Antarctic in both species and numbers, than in the warm waters of the low latitudes; sperm whales are therefore distributed here relatively more evenly than in the low latitudes, do not form large and dense accumulations, but move from one region to another in groups (Kirpichnikov, 1950).

Examining the distribution of sperm whales in the latitudinal direction, it should be stressed that in the north, the geographical boundary of antarctic waters is the line of the Antarctic Convergence (line of contact of the northern and southern waters), which in various regions passes at different latitudes with insignificant deflections according to the year and season. In the Indian Ocean it passes on the average along 50°, in the Pacific Ocean along 50—60°, and in the Atlantic along 45—55° (after Ditrikh and Kalle, 1961).

For convenience of fishery statistics it is considered that all regions in all the oceans lying to the south of 40° belong to the Antarctic. Therefore, in using the data of the International Whaling Statistics (IWS) some reservations will be introduced in the appropriate places because it is more correct to consider the distribution of animals in a geographical region with the particular ecological conditions.

It is difficult to speak of the prevalence of sperm whales in relation to a latitude using IWS data, as these reflect mainly the intensity of whaling in a particular region or particular latitude (Table 21). For instance, the whaling data for 1962/1963 suggest a predominance of sperm whales between 50 and 60°S, but in recent years fleets have operated for a considerable time at still lower latitudes hunting sperm whale herds and for example, in the 1963/64 and 1964/65 seasons most sperms captured occurred at latitudes between 40 and 50°S.

During recent seasons (in particular, in 1963—1965 many sperms were caught off the southern coasts of New Zealand, i. e., outside the Antarctic, in temperate latitudes, and it would be incorrect to draw any conclusions on the latitudinal distribution on the basis of these data. Better not to take them into consideration and to assume that (taking the last years as a guide) the latitudinal distribution is typical for antarctic waters.

173

Latitudes of catch regions	Number of specimens				
	1962/63	1963/64	1964/65	1965/66	1966/67
40—50	1317	3379	2620	2019	1921
50—60	1973	1833	1203	1013	442
60—70	1467	1427	379	1500	2385
70—80	—	—	—	—	198

It may be said that in the Indian and Atlantic ocean sectors the sperm whales inhabit on the whole lower latitudes than in the Pacific region of the Antarctic, where the range of males lies almost completely below 60°S. Judging from the absence of sperms in the catches above 70°, the animals apparently do not as a rule occur in such latitudes.

It is known that as antarctic waters have no natural geographical boundaries of meridional direction, they have, for convenience, been divided into six sectors according to longitude. In accordance with this agreement the distribution of catches of sperm whales is given in Table 22 from IWS data.

172 TABLE 22. Catches of sperm whales according to sectors of the Antarctic

Sector	Seasons					
	1931/32 — 1966/67		1963/64		1966/67	
	captured					
	specimens	%	specimens	%	specimens	%
I (120° W — 60° W)	2,373	2.4	6	—	1	—
II (60° W — 0°)	21,432	21.6	1,026	15.5	499	10.1
III (0° — 70° E)	32,524	32.8	1,773	26.7	1,151	23.3
IV (70° E — 130° E)	20,840	21.0	1,400	21.1	777	15.7
V (130° E — 170° E)	19,054	19.2	2,434	36.7	2,091	42.2
VI (170° E — 120° W)	2,984	3.0	—	—	431	8.7

Analysis of multiannual whaling data indicates a circumpolar distribution in the Antarctic. Judging from whaling, fewer sperm whales inhabit the central and eastern Pacific waters of the Antarctic (sectors I and VI). Sperms predominate in sectors III, V, and IV, i.e., in the Atlantic and Indian waters. But here too their abundance is not the same everywhere. Thus, according to Holm and Jonsgård (1959), the fewest sperms were caught (according to data of Norwegian whaling for 1950 — 1956) between 30 and 70°W (Scotia Sea).

According to the same authors, they remain in abundance in summer in the area between 30°W (Atlantic Ocean) and 60°E (Indian Ocean). The greatest concentrations occur in the region of the South Sandwich Trench, north and northwest of Enderby Land (Pacific Ocean), and also in the sector within 120 — 130°E. Large accumulations have been noted in recent years (particularly in 1963—1964) in the sectors 80—90°E and 60—70°S, 40—60°E and 40—50°S, along the entire zone situated between 40—50°S and 140—170°E, and between 50 and 60°S and from 40°W to the zero meridian.

During the 1966/67 whaling season (data of IWS) very few sperm whales were encountered in the central Pacific waters of the Antarctic, and they were virtually absent in East Pacific waters.

Due to lack of information, it is impossible to determine how long the males stay in the south-polar waters, but judging from whaling data, they occur here in the summer months (December—January). In the area of South Georgia Island (54°30'S and 36°30'W) sperms occur from October through April—May, with a peak as a rule in March, sometimes in February, January or even December (Kirpichnikov, 1950; data of IWS).

Kirpichnikov (1950) believes that sperm whales frequently move from region to region in the antarctic waters, rising and descending in the latitudinal direction depending on the shifting of the ice margin and the migrations of Cephalopoda.

Males come into antarctic waters from their wintering habitat, i.e., from the same regions that they had abandoned when they left the harem herd as they became older, each year from then on with the coming of spring migrating south, into cold waters following the cephalopods moving in this direction together with deeper, warmer, and more saline waters.

Matthews (1938) assesses the migrations of sperm whales in these regions according to the results of whaling at South Georgia Island off Southeast Africa (Natal). In comparing the two curves of the monthly catch in these regions the peaks are seen to occupy a successive position in time, i.e., males appear off Natal in the southern fall after their abundance 173 declines off South Georgia Island. The sperms which appear off the island in the first months of the year are on their way in low subtropical latitudes, while the whales that occur around the island at the end of the year are males migrating to higher latitudes. Matthews substantiates his assertions by his observations of a diatom film which is present on whales caught in the first months of the year and absent on animals captured in later months. This film proves that the animal has spent a certain time in the antarctic zone and is possibly returning north. Hart (1935) established that the film of diatoms covers whales in the cold waters of the polar latitudes.

In analyzing Matthews' statements on the migrations in these regions, we may conclude that sperm whales wintering off Natal pass by South Georgia Island and move on farther south. It can be assumed that this coincidence, though not a chance one, is determined by the scarcity of whaling data for the adjacent regions; moreover, male sperms wintering off Southeast Africa migrate for the summer to the south, forming good commercial accumulations (see Table 4) in sector III (for example, to the northeast of Enderby Land) during the same time at which males that were wintering beyond the 40th latitudes to the north of South Georgia Island approach and move on further south.

Females usually do not rise to high latitudes, and only one case of capture is known (a pregnant female) in November 1925 near South Georgia Island (Matthews, 1938). Jonsgård (1960) reports that the minimum dimensions of sperm whales penetrating antarctic waters is 10.7 m. This figure seems to have been taken from statistical data; animals of this size have in fact been captured outside antarctic waters in temperate latitudes, and the minimum size of males reaching antarctic waters is about 12 m or just a little under.

175

TAGGING

Tagging is obviously one of the most important methods for studying various aspects of the biology and stocks of whales. In the first place it helps determine the paths of seasonal migrations and clarifies problems connected with distribution (local nature of herds, extent of interchange, etc.), the life span, and even population abundance of herds. Tagging has become of decisive value in cases when exact determination of age and growth rate is required.

Tagging of whales began in 1924 in the North Atlantic. The first type of tag entered only the superficial layer of fat and was unsuccessful; in 1932 another design was brought out, and this one, with various improvements, is still being used.

At present all whales are tagged with a tag that consists of a thin-walled tube of stainless steel 23 cm long with a diameter of 1.5 cm and a lead or steel tip 3 cm long. The number of the tag and the country and town to which the tag should be returned are engraved on the tube. The tag is placed in a cardboard cartridge case charged with smokeless gunpowder. The tag is shot from a 12 caliber smoothbore gun of special design from a distance of 70 to 100 m. Each shot is recorded in the logbook of the ship, and the results of shooting are indicated. When a whale is tagged, the number of the tag, the date, coordinates, species of whale and other information are recorded. A reward is given for finding the tag and returning it with as

174 detailed information as possible (the species of whale, date, and coordinates must be indicated).

Up to 1938 the majority of whales (98%) were tagged in the Antarctic, and a few in the North Pacific (by Japan). The tagged items were mostly baleen whales, which constituted the bulk of whaling.

After the Second World War Japan began to expand tagging to the northwestern part of the Pacific, where sperm whales have become the object of tagging (and the basis of whaling). Special ships were allocated for conducting the tagging and as a result, tagging operations were performed on a large scale.

TABLE 23. Number of sperm whales tagged in the northern and central parts of the Pacific Ocean

Year	Japan	USSR	Canada	USA	Year	Japan	USSR	Canada	USA
1949	239	—		—	1959	9	88		
1950	195				1960	39	92		
1951	223			—	1961	16	2	From 1955 to	
1952	400			—	1962	18	8	1965 44 specimens	From 1962 to
1953	310	—		—	1963	21	47		1965 102
1954	265	197		—	1964	40	39		specimens
1955	235	—		—	1965	31	31		
1956	14	66	From 1955 to 1965 44 specimens	—	1966	47	270	34	—
1957	29	51		—	1967	90	115		
1958	38	333		—	1968	111	117		

In the USSR, whale tagging has been carried out since 1952, at first in the Antarctic, but since 1954 in the Far East mainly in the Kurile whaling region (Sleptsov, 1955a).

176

Tagging of whales in the northern part of the Pacific Ocean is carried out by the USA and Canada as well as by Japan and the USSR (Table 23).

Up to the 1960s tagging was carried out mainly in the whaling grounds, for the most part in the northwestern regions (off Japan, Kurile Islands and less off Kamchatka). In subsequent years the area of tagging expanded mainly owing to the development of operations from Soviet research and whaling vessels. Recently the region encompassed occupies both the entire northern Pacific and also regions of its central part. All sperm whales tagged in sectors D and E (Figure 92) were tagged from Soviet vessels.

Another distinctive feature of Soviet whale tagging in the Pacific is that it is carried out at a time when whaling operations are not going on in the area, so that tagging is, in essence, performed the year round. These two principal features of present tagging (i.e., its continuousness and its performance in areas where whaling is not being done) yield the most interesting results, permit optimum use of tagging, and are especially valuable for a study of the local nature of herds and their migration routes.

Out of all animals tagged the greatest number of sperm whales were tagged in the Pacific Ocean, mainly in its northern half. Japan has carried out most tagging in these regions, followed by the USSR, which by the end of 1968 had tagged 1,456 sperm whales. The results of tagging in the southern hemisphere (mainly in various antarctic sectors) are presented in Table 24. In addition, in 1965—1966 Australia tagged 92 sperm whales (data of the scientific committee of IWS).

TABLE 24. Number of sperm whales tagged in the southern hemisphere

Period	Antarctic regions, sector							North of 50°S	Total
	I	II	III	IV	V	VI	total		
1932—1939	—	1	28	4	—	—	33	—	33
1945—1957	—	6	5	—	—	—	11	—	11
1957—1960	—	—	1	9	2	—	12	3	15
1960—1965	3	6	5	9	2	1	24	53	77
1965—1966	—	—	—	—	—	—	4	135	139

The rate of recovery of tags from sperm whales is about 5% according to Japanese and Soviet material. The percent of recovery varies from year to year sometimes reaching 11 (for example, from the number of tags successfully shot in 1963). According to Japanese data (Kawakami and Ichihara, 1958), the best recovery is observed within five years from the day of tagging (a year later 9 tags were recovered, but after 8 years — only 3). According to Soviet data, tags were recovered at different intervals: from several hours to 12 years (one tag). This was also the longest interval before recovery recorded in the Japanese material (two tags, Omura and Ohsumi, 1964); the greatest number of tags was recovered in the first three years (50%).

Results of Japanese and Soviet tagging in the Pacific Ocean have been summarized in Figure 92, based on a Japanese map-diagram.

The largest number of tags was recovered in the Kurile-Hokkaido region (Ivashin and Rovnin, 1967), and this is the same region where the largest number of sperm whales was tagged.

177

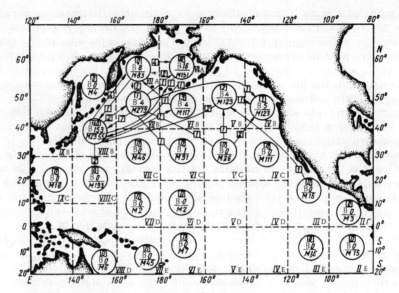

FIGURE 92. Results of Soviet and Japanese tagging of sperm whales in the northern and central parts of the Pacific:

M — number of sperm whales tagged in sector; B — total number of tags found in sperm whales captured in the sector; figure in square in circle — number of tags discovered in sperm whales that had been tagged in the same sector; figure in square with an arrow — number and direction of tagged sperm whales that have moved from óne sector to another.

The main conclusions drawn after analyzing the results of tagging (possibility of distant crossings in the places of summer habitat, change of opinions in regard to the local nature of herds, etc.) have been described above.

The recovery of sperm whale tags in other regions of the World Ocean is very low — just a few tags, including seven Soviet ones found by Japanese fleets and at whaling stations of the Union of South Africa. One of the tags recovered shows that sperm whales can cross the equator. A sperm whale 10.4 m long that was tagged from a Soviet vessel in the North Atlantic, off the Azores, was captured in the South Atlantic, off the shores of South Africa 4.5 years later (Ivashin, 1967). Another sperm whale tagged southwest of the Bay of Bengal was recovered in the same region two and a half years later. The other whales with tags were captured in the regions where they had been tagged or nearby. It would be premature to draw any broad conclusions from such a minimal number of tags recovered from such a gigantic expanse of water.

Chapter 11

PATTERNS OF DISTRIBUTION

If we could clarify the patterns of sperm whale distribution, further study of the biology of sperm whales and whaling would both benefit.

CAUSES OF MIGRATIONS

Clarke (1957) claims that the migrations of sperm whales are determined by the movements of Cephalopoda. At the same time, Clarke (1957) and Tomilin (1962) write that the causes of the seasonal migrations are not quite clear, as the whale finds a ready supply of food throughout the year.

The opinion has become widespread that sperm whales, like all other whales, migrate to the high latitudes of both hemispheres to foraging grounds in order to accumulate energy reserves for the starvation or semistarvation wintering period in the warm breeding areas. The condition factor of these animals increases sharply from spring to fall (Ruud, 1952; Klumov, 1955; Tomilin, 1957).

It has been proved, however, that in many cases the change of the temperature conditions (in particular the lowering of temperatures from summer to fall) and the onset of the breeding period do not influence the start of the fall migration (Berzin, 1963).

Without a many-sided detailed analysis of data two questions were brought up: 1) as to whether the generally accepted concept of a clear division of 177 the areas of occurrence into foraging and breeding areas, and of the existence of foraging in the usual sense of the word, should not be revised, and 2) to what extent the conditions of habitat of this species are the same in the northern and southern regions in various seasons (Berzin, 1963).

In discussing this we shall analyze the following data.

Omura (1950) notes the tendency for the fat to thicken in the sperm whale after August (off Japan). Data presented by Tomilin (1937) and by the author show (Tables 25, 26) that no increase whatsoever in the thickness of the fat, let alone a sharp one, occurs from spring to fall in sperm whales inhabiting either hemisphere.

Moreover, fat thickness in an arbitrary place is frequently even greater at the beginning of the season than at the end, and no greater at the end of the season than in the middle (see Tables 25, 26). Sleptsov (1952) notes that sperm whales have a higher condition factor in spring than in other seasons. This distinguishes them from baleen whales, which are less fat in spring. It is safe to say that the thickness of fat fluctuates very insignificantly during a season, depending upon the average size of the animal* or on the feeding conditions in the particular season in one region or another.

TABLE 25. Changes of fat thickness in male sperm whales of the northern hemisphere (Pacific Ocean), cm

Month	Tomilin (1937)				Our data			
	1933	1934	1935	1936	1956	1958	1959	1960
March	—	—	—	—	—	—	—	9.5
April	—	—	—	—	—	—	—	8.8
May..........	—	12.9	12.1	12.3	11.4	10.7	11.3	8.8
June..........	12.0	12.5	12.4	12.7	9.7	10.6	10.6	9.8
July	12.8	12.7	12.7	12.6	11.0	11.0	11.3	11.6
August	10.5	12.6	—	13.2	10.6	10.8	11.2	11.2
September.......	12.3	11.8	—	—	9.5	10.8	11.7	9.3
October	12.5	—	12.5	11.4	10.7	10.5	10.7	9.9

The absolute thickness of fat in itself is certainly not conclusive proof of the presence or absence of dynamics of accumulation of fat reserves, but this index does show the unjustified use of the term "fattening" for sperm whales in the same sense as it is used for terrestrial animals, in which the thickness of the subcutaneous fat does sharply increase toward winter (sometimes two or three times).

TABLE 26. Changes of fat thickness in male sperm whale of the southern hemisphere (Antarctic, our data), cm

Month	1962/63	1963/64
November	11.9	10.8
December...............	12.4	10.9
January	13.0	11.0
February	12.2	10.7
March	11.7	11.0

Taking into consideration the possible claims to the representativeness of the material on fat thickness, for proving the absence of a "fattening" period 178 in the sperm whale, let us consider the data on the oil content in the blubber of sperm whales (Table 27).

It is seen from Table 27 that according to Kizevetter (1953), there is a slight increase in the oil content in sperm whale blubber toward the fall, whereas (according to our data) in whales from the northern part of the Pacific the oil content fluctuates little during the season over the entire whaling period (and also the thickness of the blubber), and by no means increases toward late fall.

Let us consider the unfortunately very few data (Table 28) on fatness dynamics, obtained after comparing the quantity of oil extracted from sperm that were captured in the North Pacific (according to Tomilin, 1937).

* For a comparative analysis we utilized only males more than 13 m long.

180

TABLE 27. Changes of the oil content in the blubber of sperm whales, %

Month	Our data*		Kizevetter, 1953
	1963	1964	
April	60.3	63.4	—
May	71.5	65.0	43.5
June	—	—	44.5
July	62.6	—	48.5
August	51.4	68.3	46.1
September	61.2	63.2	—
October	52.1	—	—

* The analyses were performed in technological laboratories of the Far East whaling fleets.

These data (Table 28) were presented in order to show (Tomilin, 1935, 1957) the increase in the condition factor of sperm whales toward winter and the existence of a fattening period. In our opinion, such an insignificant fat increment in the organism from spring to fall cannot be used to confirm that a fattening period exists. In fact, in each of the three years a slight but definite decrease of oil output is found toward winter. Tomilin (1957) called this a "fatness leap" in the summer months and was at a loss to understand it. It is noteworthy that a roughly similar picture is observed in the changes of fat thickness and oil content. This cannot be a coincidence, and could not be observed if a fattening period did exist. It is quite incorrect to compare or, even more, to draw a complete analogy between the wintering of whales and hibernation in terrestrial animals (Klumov, 1955) disregarding whether wintering in the regions of winter or summer habitat is meant.

TABLE 28. Dynamics of oil yield from sperm whales, tons, average per animal

Month	1934	1935	1936
May	8.93	9.23	6.63
June	8.68	10.63	9.47
July	9.00	10.54	7.49
August	—	—	11.72
September	10.23	—	—
October	9.77	9.87	8.08
November	—	—	8.08

Hibernation is a deep and total state of torpor of the organism; "among mammals hibernation is inherent in species which have a primitive physiological organization, particularly those that have preserved the capacity to lower the body temperature to the temperature of the environment" (Kalabukhov, 1936, p. 197), with a substantial slowing down of the heart rate and reduction of the number of respiratory movements.

Hibernation is never observed in animals which can perform distant migrations, for example birds (Kalabukhov, 1936). But even if the possibility of a confusion of terminology is admitted and by the wintering of whales the winter sleep is meant (as in bears, badgers, raccoon dogs, etc.), this comparison must still be denied.

Characteristic for both these groups of animals, that possess physiological adaptation to unfavorable conditions, is the so-called accumulation of fat for a foodless and cold winter under strict conditions of immobility in order to cut down on energy consumption. The magnitude of energy reserves stored up for maintenance of vital activity even during torpor can be judged from the amount (or thickness) of the fat (or oil); for instance, as a result of oil accumulation the weight of the suslik is doubled (Kalabukhov, 1936). In bears, which sleep through the winter, fat thickness increases several times toward winter.

In our opinion, the above numerous data on changes in fat accumulation in sperm whales constitute sufficient proof to consider that it is wrong to extend the terminology accepted for some terrestrial animals to them: as the whole life of the whale is continual movement, no amount of fat reserves would be enough for even the shortest period.

The terms "fattening" and "fattening grounds," etc. can be retained for baleen whales, in which, according to available materials, accumulation of oil toward the fall does occur (the yield of oil in the finback whale is doubled as winter approaches (Kizevetter, 1953)). But a priori we may deny outright the concepts of a winter without food and a sleep or hibernation. Data have been accumulated that confirm a supply of food for baleen whales in their wintering grounds (Bogorov, 1960; Vinogradov and Voronina, 1963; and others), and we also have records of direct observations on the feeding of baleen whales in subtropical and tropical regions of the Pacific and Indian oceans (Rovnin, 1966, 1967, and the observations of research staffs of whaling fleets).

Furthermore, acknowledging the sufficiency of food reserves for whales in the warm zones of the oceans, it should be recognized in general that any sort of thickening of the heat-regulating fat covers is physiologically pointless (and even harmful) in that this prevents heat transfer (the need for which becomes imperative during the wintering period).

It has been shown that a drop in the water temperature cannot by itself cause all age groups of sperm whales to retreat from northern waters, because even females with their sucklings were noted repeatedly in winter (Matsuura, 1935; Sleptsov, 1952; Berzin and Rovnin, 1966; our data) in particular, in the Sea of Okhotsk and off the Kurile Islands at water temperatures of below 3—10°C.

Only a progressive diminution of the quantity of the main food with the onset of cold weather can be considered to cause the gradual retreat of most sperm whales, including some females, to the south in the wake of migrating Cephalopoda. In the opinion of most researchers, migrations of harems in which the females are at the late stages of pregnancy are determined by the tendency to seek warm and calmer waters.

This assumption, which is quite justified for baleen whales (and thus apparently came to be applied to the sperm whale) may raise doubts. There are observations that sperm whale pups are encountered in cold waters in late fall off the Kurile Islands and Amsterdam Island and in the Atlantic Ocean off Tristan da Cunha (our data; Zemskii, 1962). In addition, according to some, in the fall the number of nursing females increases on the Kurile Islands. Zemskii (1962) writes that the available facts do not

correspond to the accepted concept of the sperm whale pup in tropical
and subtropical waters, and he even assumes that females move to give birth
180 in colder waters, as the latter are less dangerous than the shark-populated
tropical waters.

These data are probably insufficient for refuting the currently held views
on breeding in warm waters, but they give enough reason to doubt their
absolute justification.

Relatively few sperm whales, obviously depending on the food reserves,
remain for winter in the northern regions. The same is observed in other
migrating animals, for example, birds, which can winter in nonfreezing
waters, i. e., in places where they can find food despite the temperature of
the environment.

At this stage it is difficult to define the factors which induce a considerable proportion of sperm whales to migrate from warm waters abundant in
cephalopods throughout the year (Clarke, 1957; Tomilin, 1962).

Tomilin (1957, 1960, 1962) thinks that all large, "massive" whales are
subject, in tropical waters, to difficulties of thermoregulation, the organs
of which function well only if there is a sharp difference between the body and
environmental temperatures. Where the environmental temperature is
close to that of the animal's body, overheating of the organism can occur.
Thus, waters with minimum temperature are more favorable for thermoregulation. In Tomilin's opinion, sperm whales are an exception in this case
because they dive to great depths and lower water temperatures and therefore do not experience thermoregulatory difficulties in tropical waters. It
is difficult to establish to what extent the change in depth affects the thermoregulation of the sperm whale; at any rate, with our current knowledge,
the possibility of any intensive heat transfer of the organism in deep waters
cannot be theoretically confirmed because it has been shown that during
submersion and the pause in respiration, the so-called vascular reflex
comes into play, drawing the bloodstream away from the body surface
(Irving, 1939; Scholander, 1940; Kreps, 1941; and others). Thus, it is safe
to say that in all deep-diving animals thermoregulation must function mainly
near the surface.

It is known that the smaller the relative surface of a body (i. e., the
larger the animal), the less the heat transfer; moreover, large whales
have more thermoregulating blubber than small whales. It can be assumed
in this connection that the departure of some sperm whales from warm
waters, adult animals being the first to go, is caused by the fact that waters
with a lower temperature contribute to better thermoregulation.

Toward spring in the northern waters of the northern hemisphere (or in
the southern waters of the southern hemisphere), abundant food resources
begin to build up and a favorable temperature regime for whales is created,
factors which determine the migration of sperm whales to high latitudes.

Furthermore, if one agrees with the hypothesis (Rovnin, in litt.) that the
central (tropical) regions of oceans are the focus of settlement of Cetacea,
then one can say that the annual "pulsating" migration to higher latitudes is
a natural tendency of the species to spread and to increase its range.

Investigating sperm whale ecology, we suggest that the composition of
the food in the regions of summer habitat is more or less identical with
that in the winter regions not only in quantity, but also in quality (Berzin,
1963). Let us analyze data on the ecology and seasonal distribution of

Cephalopoda. Some species of tropical and subtropical cephalopods (Alloposus mollis, Amphitretus pelagicus, Architeuthis japonica) are known to migrate over distances of 1,500 — 2,000 km during one or two months (Akimushkin, 1963). In June — July they were found in the stomachs of sperm whales captured off the Kurile Islands. In addition, practically all species of squid, which are the main food item of sperm whales in the northern part of the Pacific Ocean, Gonatus fabricii, Galiteuthis armata, Taonius pavo, Moroteuthis robusta, Onychoteuthis banksii, are cosmopolitan (Akismushkin, 1963). Thus, there is no reason to assume that sperm whales migrating in winter to more southern regions (in the northern hemisphere) find themselves in very different ecological conditions. These data can be added to others to prove the absence of a fattening period or definite fattening grounds with regard to sperm whales.

We cannot claim to have even touched upon all the causes of the seasonal migrations of sperm whales. The above survey and discussion of certain views show that many facts cast doubt on widely accepted theories. The problem is in urgent need of further study.

SOME PATTERNS OF SPERM WHALE DISTRIBUTION

The discovery of patterns in the distribution of marine animals, including whales, is a subject for closer investigations.

In recent years certain patterns have been detected in the formation of accumulations of baleen whales. The essence of these patterns lies in the fact that the feeding grounds (concentrations of plankton, small schooled fish and their consumers) are confined to places of upwelling of deep waters, enriched in biogens (Uda and Nasu, 1956; Nemoto, 1959; Nasu, 1963; Zavernin, 1966; Chernyi, 1966; and others). In regard to sperm whales, only some relationships have been noted, but they have not been explained. Taking into account the obviously inadequate knowledge of the ecology of Cephalopoda, indications that sperm whales are confined to regions of cephalopod concentrations are also evidently unsatisfactory.

Kirpichnikov (1950) brought forward data pointing to the significance of warm currents reaching into colder (northern and southern) waters, and he also explains the concentrations of sperm whales on the banks not far from great depths by a better accessibility of demersal animals in these places for the whales.

Uda and Nasu (1956) confine the formation of sperm whale accumulations (as well as those of baleen whales) to the zones of the warm Kuroshio current and the cold Oyashio current. Holm and Jonsgård (1959) connect the formation of accumulations in the antarctic waters with the periods of full moon and new moon; during the full moon a tendency is noted in the animals to concentrate on the banks, whereas at the new moon they form concentrations near the banks and deep down.

We think that the reason that investigations of this vital problem have been so few is in the predominantly deepwater mode of life of sperm whales and of the animals associated with them by the food chain.

184

There is practically no information on biomasses at depths of several hundred meters according to various ocean regions, or in any case, there 182 is no information that would give us the opportunity to compare these regions according to the biomasses of those animals that are food for the sperm whale.

It has been established (Zenkovich, 1951; Vinogradov, 1955; Manteifel'; 1959, 1961; and others) that deepwater fauna develops in dependence on the foraging conditions of the surface productive layer in the presence of vertical migrations (mainly diurnal), both of surface marine organisms (zooplankton primarily) into deeper layers, and also of deepwater animals toward the surface layers.

If this is accepted without reservation, sperm whales would concentrate in all cases in the places of outflow of deep waters enriched in biogens, in places with a high biological productivity, and in plankton fields, as in the case of baleen whales. However (excluding the waters of, for example, the polar front, as will be explained below) baleen whales do not form concentrations in the same places as toothed whales as a rule.

It is obvious in any case that the number of whales in a particular region is usually directly proportional to the amount of food in the respective waters.

Let us construct a very general hydrodynamic scheme of the movement of waters, formation of food reserves, and feeding relations (see Figure 93). In essence, the scheme is very arbitrary, but from the point of view of comparison it permits us to assess the formation of the food biomass in the deep waters that differ in their dynamics.

From the place of their upwelling, waters saturated with organisms that have developed in them begin to spread, their biomass gradually becoming depleted. However at the point of sinking of these waters, all that is left that is valuable in regard to nutrition begins to descend into the depths so that conditions are formed for the development of large organisms such as deep-sea squid and fish.

Without overestimating the "rain" of dead bodies for the nutrition of deep-sea animals, it is nevertheless clear that it is more effective in the zone of sinking than in the zone of upwelling. And whereas under usual conditions, a considerable part of the organic matter of dead plankton becomes dissolved already in the 100-m layer (Skopintsev, 1947), in the zone of sinking optimum conditions are formed for the transport of organic substances into the deep layers. On the other hand, due to reasons of a purely hydrodynamic character, and also as a result of the inevitable presence in this zone of a layer of density "jump"(and thus a considerable increase of water density and viscosity), in the zone of upwelling the rise of dead plankton remains is delayed and hence the underlying layers of water become impoverished (Manteifel', 1961).

In addition, the thermocline apparently can to a certain extent (depending on the magnitude of the gradients in it) prevent vertical migrations of organisms, in particular, migration of little-mobile forms. In the zone of sinking the influence of the thermocline on migrations must be much weaker.

It is noteworthy that in the depths, in places of upwelling, intensive development of life must be repressed because of oxygen deficiency. On the other hand, in places of sinking, oxygen reaches the deep layers in maximum quantities.

In the regions of meetings of currents, primarily on the lines of
183 convergences, there occurs a kind of summation of two volumes of biomasses, descending deeply, and in these regions still more favorable
conditions are formed for the development of a deep-sea fauna of large
animals (Berzin, 1966).

Thus, it follows that at the same depths in different regions with
sinking, the conditions for development of large fauna will be the better,
the greater the rate of sinking, and the latter depends primarily on the
speed of the converging currents. At depths of some hundreds of meters
(Figure 93) the volume of food biomass for sperm whales per unit water
volume in position 3 will be greater than in positions 2 and 1, i.e., greater
than in any other place at the same depth (Berzin, 1966).

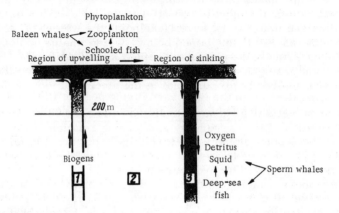

FIGURE 93. Scheme of ecological conditions in regions of upwelling
and sinking (for explanations see text)

The above theoretical assumptions can be confirmed on the example of
the region situated east of Cape Olyutorski in the Bering Sea. The distribution of sperm whales (according to our data), the distribution of squid
(after Akimushkin, 1963), and the currents of this region were mapped in an
attempt to establish the patterns of distribution of the whales. Sinking
along the periphery of the cyclonic current formed in this region coincides
strikingly with the distribution of squid and sperm whales along the periphery of a circle with its center at coordinates 59°N and 179°E (Berzin
and Rovnin, 1966) (Figure 94).

Let us consider the peculiarities of distribution of sperm whale concentrations in other regions of the World Ocean. The occurrence of sperm
whales on the map (see Figure 91), plotted on the basis of all known data,
can be considered to depend not upon commercial zoning, but only upon the
ecological conditions that are formed in a particular region, because the
observations of present day whaling and research-exploratory work together
with data from the operations of 19th century whalers encompass the distribution of sperm whales in all regions and in all seasons.

The coincidence of sperm whale concentrations with the lines of the subtropical and subarctic convergences is a demonstrative example confirming

the relationship between their distribution with areas of sinking. In the eastern part of the Indian Ocean a characteristic northward shift is
184 observed of the sperm whale accumulations and of the line of convergence (Morskoi Atlas (Marine Atlas), 1953; Ditrikh and Kalle, 1961; Figures 91 and 94).

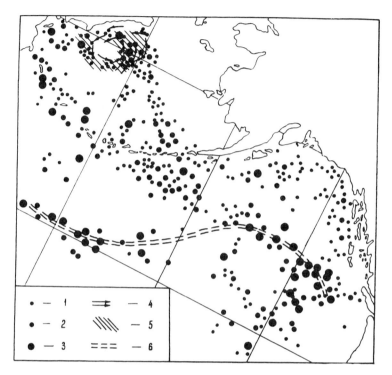

FIGURE 94. Distribution of sperm whales in the northeastern part of the Pacific compared with the ecological conditions:

1 — more than 3 specimens; 2 — more than 15 specimens; 3 — more than 50 specimens; 4 — currents; 5 — regions of squid accumulations (after Akimushkin, 1963); 6 — line of convergence.

Sinking is known to occur also with some degree of intensity in the northern hemisphere along the periphery of cyclonic gyrals, along the right side of currents, as well as at the divergence of the right sides of currents, etc. (in the southern hemisphere the dynamic processes are directly opposite to those in the northern hemisphere).

The formation of permanent concentrations of sperm whales in the regions of sinking is confirmed by data from regions situated in the Mozambique Channel, northeast of Madagascar, off the southwestern tip of Australia, north, northwest, west and east of New Zealand, and elsewhere (Figure 91).

Examining the waters of the polar fronts, we see that in these regions, because of the specific convergence of waters with sharply different hydrological characteristics (Izhevskii, 1958, and others), conditions are formed that are favorable both for vigorous development of plankton and for development of deep-sea fauna owing to sinking (here it occurs relatively more intensively as a result of a concentration of surface 185 waters). Thus, these regions show all the necessary conditions for baleen and sperm whales. The Pacific waters of Japan and the Southern Kuriles (Uda, 1954) where the cold Oyashio Current meets warm waters, can be considered a typical example of a region with similar conditions. Conditions resembling those described above are developed in the Galapagos area in the Pacific, where the cold Peru Current intrudes from the South into warm tropical waters.

It may also be assumed that in places of sinking waters (at depths of 1,000—1,500 m) there are more favorable conditions for the development of benthos and benthos-feeders (and hence broader food reserves for sperm whales).

Outwardly, the above statements contradict the existing views on regions of sinking, particularly the regions of the zone of convergence (excluding the polar fronts) as being the poorest in life (Ditrikh and Kalle, 1961, and others). Usually referred to as similar regions are the waters adjacent to the Hawaiian Islands, the latitudes of the Azores and Madeira, and the Sargasso Sea, the last being defined as a region "with the least mass of living matter."

In these cases, it is obvious that a comparative estimate of the abundance of live organisms is made only of the surface photosynthetic layer of any region. If this is not so, an error is inevitable in the estimation of the food resources of these regions and, in particular, in the assessment of the reserves of the deep waters (because sperm whales would not form accumulations (frequently large ones) in all seasons of the year in places where there is nothing for them to feed on).

Wrong determination of the productivity of waters is likely due to the absence of data on the true biomasses of the deep waters, including chiefly fast-moving forms of squid, deep-sea fishes and other animals (which can be explained by the absence of suitable fishing gear).

The present views have been based on material of many years' standing and on averaged data for vast water areas.

Work on verifying these theories is continuing on the basis of concrete material obtained by exploratory voyages of PINRO vessels followed by more accurate analysis of the hydrology of sperm whale habitats. The data obtained for the Pacific Ocean and Sea of Okhotsk in most cases confirm the relations described above (Rovnin, in litt.), demonstrating the futility of seeking a relationship between the distribution of sperm whales and the food reserves and hydrology of the surface waters. Factors favorable for the formation of life in the depths determine also the regions of habitation where sperm whales live. Of special interest is the connection clearly corroborated by Rovnin (in litt.), between sperm whale distribution and the amount of oxygen dissolved in the water at 500 m (all dependences are naturally considered through the feeding relations).

It cannot be assumed that all the relations discovered encompass all the factors which restrict the distribution and concentrations of sperm whales. It is obvious that certain patterns revealed may not be confirmed in regions of oceanic islands, where a deep-sea fauna can arise as a result of dynamic processes differing from those described above; relations of this kind are necessarily expressed less distinctly on the migration routes.

It is quite evident that the distribution of sperm whales is determined by an intricate complex of factors which future biological and hydrological investigations will help to disclose.

MAIN FEATURES OF BIOLOGY

An all-embracing study of the biology of large whales is a matter of unusual difficulty, since their life goes on out of man's sight, and therefore not all aspects have been investigated in equal detail.

The feeding habits of sperm whales have been described fairly thoroughly though not for all regions of the World Ocean), but their breeding requires closer investigation.

From time immemorial observations and assumptions have accumulated, until finally, special investigations of the mode of life of the species were launched.

Data on age are broadly discussed in this section, because although they do not bear directly on the biology of the animal, they do play an important part in solving many related questions.

Chapter 12

FEEDING

Most of the published information on the feeding habits of sperm whales is based on random observations, analysis of stomach contents of single specimens, or of a general nature (Kolnett, 1798; Beale, 1835, 1839; Monaco, 1888; Bennett, 1840; Bullen, 1899; Hollis, 1939; Millais, 1906; Bartsch, 1916; Hjort, 1933; Zenkovich, 1934, 1936; Smirnov, 1935; Tomilin, 1935, 1940; Gregory, 1937; Matthews, 1938; Kabrera and Gepes, 1940; Kellogg, 1940; Arsen'ev and Zemskii, 1952; Clarke, 1954, 1955, 1957, 1962; Kirpichnikov, 1945, 1950; and many others).

Along with this, in recent decades the feeding of sperm whales in various regions of the World Ocean has been studied and elucidated in more detail (Zenkovich, 1937b, 1945; Tomilin, 1936; Robbins, Oldham, and Geiling, 1937; Omura, 1950; Pike, 1950; Mizue, 1951; Sleptsov, 1952; Akimushkin, 1954, 1955; Betesheva and Akimushkin, 1955; Clarke, 1956; Berzin, 1959; Korabel'nikov, 1959; Betesheva, 1961; Tarasevich, 1963; Okutani and Nemoto, 1964).

Concentrated study of the main food item of sperm whale, the Cephalopoda, was carried out by Kondakov and later by Akimushkin. The keys to the species of Cephalopoda made by Akimushkin according to their rostra greatly facilitate research into the stomach contents and contribute 187 to more accurate results (Figure 95).

METHODS FOR STUDYING FEEDING

Study of sperm whale feeding involves many methodical difficulties, first of all because of the gigantic stomach (even the empty stomach of a whale 11 m long weighs about 100 kg, and that of a 16-m-long specimen weighs 250 kg;

Sleptsov, 1952, 1961). Furthermore, direct observations of feeding are more or less impossible because the animal feeds at great depths.

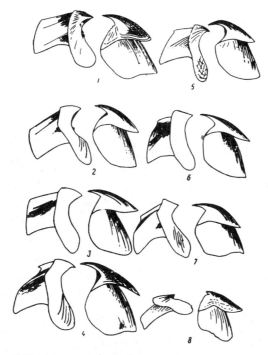

FIGURE 95. Jaws (rostra) of Cephalopoda (after Betesheva, 1961, and Akimushkin, 1963):

1—Gonatus magister; 2—Gonatus fabricii;
3—Galiteuthis armata; 4—Chiroteuthis
veranyl; 5—Gonatus fabricii (var separata):
6—Taonius pavo: 7—Onychoteuthis banksii;
8—Alloposus mollis.

Betesheva and Akimushkin (1955) measured the capacity of the stomach, determined the weight of its contents, and calculated the amount of food remains in it. A sample weighing up to 500 g was taken from the stomach of each animal and fixed in formalin and also well preserved specimens of fish, cephalopods, and large bones that were not part of the sample.

After prolonged towing of sperm whales, particularly to coastal whaling stations, intact or even semidigested organisms are seldom observed in the stomach, and the amount of food is usually small.

The first compartment of the stomach contains the largest amount of undigested food (Figure 96) and therefore as a rule (Mizue, 1951; Tarasevich, 1963; Okutani and Nemoto, 1964) only the contents of this is examined. Tarasevich (1963) collected the entire contents of the first stomach compartment and weighed them in parts, while whole or poorly digested organisms were selected separately; she then determined the number of organisms belonging to the same species, and a sample from the batch was fixed in formalin. In addition, she took 400—500 g of rostra. If there were fish in the batch, she weighed this. She collected otoliths and bones of all fish and determined the species of food items mainly from these (Figure 97 A, B, C).

188   Betesheva (1960) took account of the contents of all three stomach compartments.

To obtain comparative data on the quantitative feeding of sperm whales for various regions, years and months of one season, Tarasevich (1963) divided the stomachs under analysis into 4 categories according to the degree of fullness:

1) quite full (more than 20 kg);
2) average, or moderately full (from 20 to 11 kg);
3) fairly empty (less than 10 kg);
4) empty.

FIGURE 96.   Contents of the first compartment of the stomach of sperm whale, consisting of squid and lancetfish (North Pacific, whaling base "Vladivostok"; photo by Doroshenko)

Betesheva (1963) divided stomachs into the same 4 categories, but according to different degrees of fullness. We also used similar methods for evaluating the quantitative character of feeding in the Bering Sea (Berzin, 1959). Obviously the methods should be unified, which may involve further elaboration.

In the survey of data on sperm whale feeding in the World Ocean the Antarctic is treated separately.

PACIFIC OCEAN

In the Pacific the sperm whale has been and still is the leading commercial species, and therefore we have a maximum amount of information analysis on feeding in this ocean, particularly in the northern part.

189 The first fairly comprehensive data on the feeding of sperm whale in the North Pacific, mainly in the Komandorski-Kamchatka area, were published by Tomilin (1936) and Zenkovich (1937).

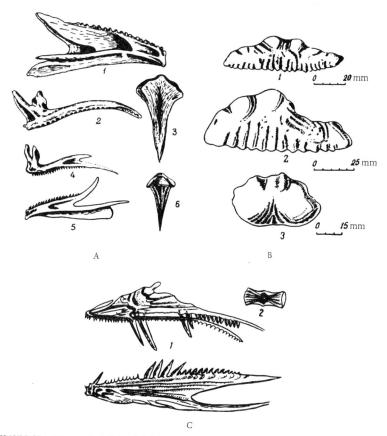

FIGURE 97. Bones and otoliths of fish from sperm whale stomachs (Betesheva, 1961):

A — bones: 1 — mandibular, 2 — maxillary, and 3 — vomer of Coryphenoides pectoralis (macrurid); 4 — maxillary, 5 — mandibular, and 6 — vomer of Hemimacrurus acrolepis; B — otoliths: 1 and 2 — Coryphenoides pectoralis; 3 — Hemimacrurus acrolepis; C — bones: 1 — jaws and 2 — vertebra of lancetfish — Alepisaurus aesculapius.

Only in recent years, owing to the enormous quantity of material collected — 1,141 analyzed stomachs of sperms from the Kuriles waters (Betesheva and Akimushkin, 1955; Betesheva, 1961) and 2,744 stomachs of sperms from around Japan (Mizue, 1951)* has it become possible to state that the North Pacific has been studied in detail as compared with other regions of the World Ocean.

* Unfortunately, Mizue gives only a superficial qualitative analysis of this material.

According to available data, 25 species of Cephalopoda and 37—38 species of fish have been determined for the Pacific (Appendix I).

In the northwestern part of the ocean, in the waters adjacent to the Kurile Islands and Japan, the diet of the sperm whale consists of about 28 species of cephalopods, * including 21 species of squid (Decapoda) and 6 - 7 species of octopus (Octopoda) (Betesheva and Akimushkin, 1955; Betesheva, 1961).

In her study Betesheva (1961) gives only 14 cephalopods determined accurately down to species, 6 mollusks of undetermined species, and in addition a group of "miscellaneous" mollusks. Tarasevich (1963) adds 4 more species of squid and 3 species of Octopoda.

The main food items in this region are squid of the family Gonitidae: Gonatus magister, G. fabricii, Meleagroteuthis separata, and Galiteuthis armata. They were encountered in the stomachs of practically all sperm whales and constituted on the average 50—80% of all Cephalopoda. The first two species may account for up to 65% of the entire volume of food (Akimushkin, 1954; Betesheva, 1961; Tarasevich, 1963). G. magister is found in 99—98% of stomachs. Meleagroteuthis separata and Galiteuthis armata constituted from 4 to 11% in various years. The frequency of occurrence of the latter species fluctuates unusually widely from year to year — from 2 to 97% (Betesheva, 1961). Betesheva notes the increasing importance of the mollusks Taonius pavo and Gonatopsis borealis in 1953 and 1954 in comparison, for instance, with 1959. According to the same data, the length of squid, Gonatopsis borealis, Moroteuthis robusta, Architeuthis japonica, did not exceed 1.5 m and more frequently varied between 40 to 80 cm. In this region, of the Octopoda that constitute the diet, Alloposus mollis is of greatest significance, 38% on the whole, in the Kuriles area, becoming dominant (to 50%) off the southern island, plus Octopus gilbertianus, with a frequency of occurrence to 15% in individual years.

According to Tarasevich (1963), the squid Gonatopsis borealis and Taonius pavo were frequent items in the stomachs of sperm whales in addition to G. magister, G. fabricii, and G. armata. G. borealis was observed most frequently, whereas G. magister comes only fourth in frequency. Altogether 11 species of squid were found, i.e., the species composition of squid is more uniform in the diet of sperm whales in the Sea of Okhotsk.

Betesheva (1961) found more than 24 species of fish (including several undetermined species), among them the macrurids Coryphaenoides pectoralis,** and Hemimacrurus acrolepis, taking first place, found in 33—60% of stomachs (depending on the year), while second and third in importance are sharks and Alepisaurus. The length of the sharks (Squalus acanthias) encountered in stomachs is 16—125 cm, with a maximum of nine specimens in one stomach. Up to 8 specimens of Alepisaurus aesculapius, about 130 cm long, occur per stomach, with a frequency of occurrence of up to 25%. The incidence of redfish (Sebastodes sp.) varies widely from year to year, from 2.7 to 12% in 1955, for example.

---

* Since not all the Cephalopoda were accurately determined to species level, they do not all appear in the list of food items.

** In Appendix I listed as Laemonema longipes.

The following demersal fish are of considerable significance for a sperm whale in this region, according to Betesheva (1961): rays (Raja sp.), up to 100 cm long, large gobies (Myoxocephalus sp. joak) weighing 191about 5 kg, Aptocyclus ventricosus, anglerfish (Oneirodes sp.), Cottidae gen. sp., Gadidae gen. sp., and walleye pollock (Theragra chalcogramma). The same author mentions the presence of Eleginus gracilis navaga, Oncorhynchus gorbusha, Pleurogrammus sp., Gadus morhua macrocephalus, Podomema longipes, * Myoxocephalus verrucosus, Cololabis saira, and Somniosus sp. (208 cm long) in stomachs.

According to the data of Mizue (1951), based on analysis of feeding data from more southern waters (Japan), two species of redfish can be added to the list of food items, Sebastodes flammeus and S. iracundus, 3 species of clupeids, Sardina melanosticta, ** Etrumeus micropus and Engraulis japonicus, mackerel, Scomber japonicus, Sc. tapeinocephalus, † and krill.

According to Betesheva (1961a), the proportion of stomachs filled with fish or with fish and squid varied for the waters of the Kuriles area from 30% (in 1951), 20% (in 1953 — 1954) to 12% (in 1955) of the total number of stomachs examined.

On the other hand, Mizue (1951), found fish in the stomachs of only 93 out of 1,117 sperm whales captured in Japanese waters, or in 8.3% of the total number of stomachs filled with food (or 3.4% of all stomachs examined).

Omura (1950) investigated the contents of 555 stomachs of sperm whales that were taken near Japan (including the Bonin Islands), and presented a detailed analysis of changes in the degree of stomach fullness by months.

Zenkovich (1934, 1937) and Tomilin (1936) mentioned that the stomachs of sperm whales taken in the northernmost Komandorski-Kamchatka region contained 3 species of squid, i.e., Gonatus magister, Gonatus fabricii, Moroteuthis robusta, Octopoda — Octopus vulgaris, Paroctopus gilbertianus, and crab, Hyas coarctatus, Chionocetes sp., Paralithodes camtshatica, and P. brevipes.

It is seen from material collected in 1947 in the region of the Komandorski Islands and of Olyutorski Gulf and analyzed by Sleptsov (1961 c) that Architeuthis japonica and Octopus gilbertianus can be added to the above Cephalopoda that make up the diet of the sperm whale.

Rays were also found in sperm whale stomachs (Raja smirnovi), whereas sperm whales caught off the Komandorski Islands yielded fishes of the family Scorpaenidae (rockfish — Sebastodes ruber) and bottom fish (Aptocyclus ventricosus).

Sleptsov (1952) reports, without differentiating the regions of the Bering Sea and of the Kuriles, that sperm whales in these regions feed on Pacific lamprey (Entosphenus tridentatus), Pacific cod (Gadus morhua macrocephalus), greenling (Pleurogrammus monopterygius), and on Macrurus sp., Plagyodus aesculapius, †† Squalus acanthias, and saury.

* In Appendix I listed as Laemonema longipes.
** In Appendix I listed as Sardinops sagax melanosticta.
† In Appendix I listed as Scomber japonicus tapeinocephalus.
†† In Appendix I listed as Alepisaurus.

Analysis of the stomach contents of 110 sperm whales from the Koman-
dorski area and from the waters of the western part of the Aleutian Islands
resulted in the discovery of five more species of squid of the suborder
Oegopsida: Gonatopsis borealis, Meleagroteuthis separata,
Galiteuthis armata, Onychoteuthis banksii, and
Chiroteuthis veranyi* (Berzin, 1959).

192 According to us, in the Bering Sea and in the adjacent regions of the
Pacific squid of the family Gonatidae predominate, i.e., as in the more southern regions, but with a sharp prevalence of Gonatopsis borealis
(including also large specimens up to 130 cm long) and Moroteuthis
robusta, the frequent presence of which is indicated by the hard to digest
cartilaginous cones of the gladii up to 30 cm long, that belong to large squid
(2.5—3 m long). In the stomach of a 14-meter sperm whale captured off the
Komandorski Islands we found a well preserved Moroteuthis robusta
290 cm long (with the tentacles). Thus, our material contradicts Sleptsov's
statement (1952) that this species of squid is encountered comparatively
rarely to the north of the Kuriles.

The fishes found in sperm whale stomachs in these regions proved to
represent 8 families: Agonidae, Scorpaenidae, Plagyodontidae, ** Rajidae,
Petromyzonidae, Cottidae, Cyclopteridae, and Macruridae. Most abundant
is Aptocyclis ventricosus (Pallas), which was discovered in 32% of
stomachs each containing from 1 to 30 specimens. Second place by frequency
of occurrence and first place by the index of stomach contents is occupied,
according to our data, by the genus Sebastodes, representatives
of which were found in numbers of 25 specimens per stomach. The stomachs
of three sperms yielded up to 10 specimens of Alepisaurus
aesculapius about 120 cm long. Rays (Raja) and eggs of two other
species of ray (up to 25 specimens per stomach) were found in sperm whales
from the Olyutorski area. Fish of the genus Percis (P. japonicus
Pallas) was found in two stomachs, and in two others one Pacific lamprey
(Entosphenus tridentatus Richardson). One stomach revealed
a representative of the family Cottidae — Myoxocephalus verrucosus
sp., while another three contained large crabs, Lithodes aequispina
(determined by Kardakova).

Later, Okutani and Nemoto (1964) investigated the feeding of sperm whales
near the Aleutian Islands, in the Gulf of Alaska, and in the Bering Sea and
added the species Mastigoteuthis sp. and Stigmatoteuthis sp. to
the list of squid discovered here.

Robbins, Oldham, and Geiling (1937), proceeding from investigations
carried out in 1936 — 1937 at whaling stations on the Queen Charlotte Islands,
reported on the frequent occurrence of Acrotus villoughbyi (synonym
Icosteus aenigmaticus) and mentioned the presence of M. robusta
and M. octopi, as well as of small cod and lamprey.

Pike (1950) points out (after analysis of 50 stomachs of sperms which had
been captured in the waters of British Columbia) that the diet of the whale in
these waters includes large amounts of the squid Gonatus fabricii
40 cm long and M. robusta 2.5 m long. In 16 stomachs Icosteus
aenigmaticus 130 cm long were found; this species was considered fairly

* The last two species were determined by their rostra by Akimushkin; one species could not be determined.
** In Appendix I, listed as Alepisauridae.

rare along these coasts; remains of Sebastodes ruberrimus were encountered in the same number of stomachs. Rays (Raja rhina) were found in ten stomachs and lampreys in one. Fish resembling salmons were found in three stomachs. Eggs of squid were also observed.

Analysis of stomachs of sperms caught by Soviet fleets in the open regions of the northeastern Pacific in recent years (Tarasevich, 1968 and our data*) showed that the list of food items can be augmented by adding the squid Taonius pavo, Chiroteuthis veranyi, Meleagroteuthis separata, Galiteuthis armata and Gonatus magister, found in the majority of stomachs investigated, and also Architeuthis japonica, Octopodoteuthis longiptera, Gonatopsis borealis, Stigmatoteuthis dolfeini, Onychoteuthis banksii, Alloposus mollis, and Octopus gilbertianus. In the Bering Sea in the Pribilof area and Bering Sea slope the main food consisted of G. fabricii and G. armata (encountered in almost 100% of stomachs and also G. magister and M. separata (Tarasevich, 1968).

Alepisaurus aesculapius, found in more than half of all stomachs examined in amounts of 5 specimens per stomach, and Pseudopentaceres richardsoni (Smith) (on one day found in the stomachs of twelve sperm whales — up to 8 specimens in each), can be added to the list of fish eaten by sperm whales in these regions of the Pacific, according to recent data (Tarasevich, 1968; our data). Also discovered were Sebastodes alutus, Aptocyclus ventricosus, and Macrurus.

In the stomachs of sperms captured in regions more to the south of the North Pacific coast, particularly in the regions of Central California, squid were noted (in 96% of all stomachs examined): M. robusta, G. borealis, Onychoteuthis sp., and Octopus sp. in 11% of stomachs. Sperms taken here yielded remains of the sharks Apristurus brunneus and Squatina californica, blackcod Anoplopoma fimbria, greenling, Ophiodon elongatus, and Tartletonbeania crenularis (Rice, 1963).

According to Clarke (for the scientific subcommittee of the International Whaling Commission (IWC)), the sperm whales devour enormous quantities of Ommatostrephes gigas** in the southeastern part of the Pacific.

Data collected recently by Soviet fishing fleets (Vladimirov and Yukhov, in litt.) show that the stomachs of sperm whales taken in the southwestern Pacific (regions of New Zealand, Chatham Island, and Tasmania) mention the cephalopods Stenoteuthis bartrami, Histioteuthis bonelliana, and representatives of the genera Onychoteuthis and Architeuthis; Octopoda were discovered in some stomachs. According to material collected by the research group of AKF (Antarctic Whaling Flotilla) on the "Sovetskaya Rossiya" in the waters of New Zealand, squid were found in 84% of stomachs examined in April 1967.

The stomachs of sperm whales taken in these regions (Vladimirov and Yukhov, in litt.) yielded representatives of the family Scorpaenidae (Helicolenus papilosus), Chimaeridae, and rays (Raja sp.) and their eggs; sharks were also noted: in the first stomach fins and jaws were

---

* The determinations of Cephalopoda in our collection from various regions for recent years were made by workers of TINRO (of whole specimens by Shevtsov, of rostra by Panina); fishes were identified by Fedorov.

** In Appendix I listed as Dosidicus gigas.

discovered, in the second and third whole sharks 1.5 and 2 meters long respectively (according to preliminary definition, the larger of them was C e t o r h i n u s   m a x i m u s), and in the fourth stomach a large (100 cm long) embryo (or a newborn? — A, B) of the same species.

In addition, in eight stomachs of sperms from these waters colonial tunicates (P y r o s o m a) and shrimp were noted and in the stomachs of whales captured off the southeast coast of New Zealand Phaeophyceae.

194 OTHER REGIONS OF THE WORLD OCEAN

In all other regions of the northern and southern hemispheres feeding has been studied less; only limited information is available on a few, relatively small regions.

Atlantic Ocean. The northern part of the ocean, particularly the area of the Azores and Madeira, has been relatively well studied (Clarke, 1955, 1962). Clarke mentions that 8 species of squid (the author is doubtful about two of them), which are given in Appendix I, are included in the food of sperm whales in the Azores and Madeira area. H i s t i o t e u t h i s   b o n e l l i a n a (in 59%) and C u c i o t e u t h i s   u n g u i c u l a t u s (in 39% of all stomachs investigated) occur most frequently. Out of the total number of cephalopod rostra (4,000) discovered in the stomach of a sperm whale taken in the region of Madeira, 88.3% belong to H i s t i o t e u t h i s   b o n e l l i a n a . By their mass the remains of mollusks of this species constitute only about 1/3 of the total weight of squid found in the stomach. The proportion of A r c h i t e u t h i s , by number of rostra, is only 1.7%, but according to mass, this species makes up about one half of the total weight of squid found. Octopoda and Cranchiidae constitute in mass respectively about 1.5 and 1% of the total weight of mollusks, L e p i d o t e u t h i s   g r i m a l d i i and C u c i o t e u t h i s   u n g u i c u - l a t u s each about 5% of the total weight of mollusks, and in all less than 2% of the total number of rostra. O n y c h o t e u t h i s   b a n k s i i , not noted previously in the stomachs of sperms from these waters, was included in the diet provisionally according to the remains of one squid, and G a l i t e u t h i s   a r m a t a was also included with reservations.

Clarke (1955) described an undamaged gigantic squid of the genus A r c h i t e u t h i s discovered in the stomach of a male sperm whale 14.3 m long, taken in the Azores area. The overall size of this mollusk was 10.5 m and it weighed 8 kg. The length of the body without the tentacles was 2 meters; width of thickest arm 14 cm, eye diameter 18 cm. Four species of fish were found in the stomachs of sperms captured in the same region: barracuda, yellowfin tuna, and two species of large bathypelagic anglerfish — C e r a t i a s   h o l b o e l i and H i m a n t o l o p h u s   g r o e n l a n d i c u s (Clarke, 1956).

Shmidt (1924, in Tomilin, 1957) mentions the discovery of a large eel (A n g u i l l a sp.) in the stomach of a sperm whale. Backus (1966) reports finds of A l e p i s a u r u s (2 specimens in a stomach) and sharks C e t o r h i n u s 3 m long.

For the southern regions of the Atlantic Ocean there was formerly only an indication by Matthews (1938), who had investigated the stomach contents of two sperm whales taken off the southwest shores of Africa; he mentions Cephalopoda and teleosts.

Akimushkin (1963) determined squid, Octopodeuthis longiptera sp., from the stomach of a sperm taken in the South Atlantic (20°S and 25°W). A specimen captured in the region of Tristan da Cunha yielded squid 70—100 cm long the species of which could not be determined (Korabel'nikov, 1959).

John Millet (1906) reported on remains of the blue shark, Carcharias glaucus, * and invertebrates in the stomach of a sperm whale killed off Iceland.

There are very few data on the feeding of sperm whales in the **Indian** 195 **Ocean.** Matthews (1938) gave information on the quantitative stomach full-ness of 34 sperms caught off southeastern Africa, and a general indication as to the part played in the diet by Cephalopoda and teleosts in this region. According to Chabb (1918, in Tomilin, 1957), "a 3-meter long shark of un-determined species" was extracted from the stomach of a sperm whale captured in the same region. There is a note by Hollis (1939) to the effect that off the Australian coast of the Indian Ocean sperm whales feed on Octopoda (species were not determined because digestion had proceeded too far).

FIGURE 98. Squid of the genus Architeuthis, 19 m long, from the stomach of a sperm whale (Indian Ocean, whaling flotilla "Sovetskaya Ukraina"; photo by Dolgushin)

In the stomachs of sperms taken by Soviet whaling fleets in the Indian Ocean in the region northwest and west of Australia as far as the islands of New Amsterdam and Heard and their vicinity squid were found: Moroteuthis robusta, Histioteuthis bonelliana as well as Stenoteuthis bartrami and one more representative of the family Ommatostrephidae. Representatives of the genus Architeuthis are encountered in the belt from 35° to 45°S, from South Africa to Australia (Yukhov, in litt.), including very large specimens. One of them, 19 m long, was found on the "Sovetskaya Ukraina" (Figure 98).

* In Appendix I listed as Prionace glauca.

199

Recent collections point to the quite frequent occurrence of barracuda, Sphyraena sp., porcupine fish, Duodon sp., and representatives of the family Ceratiidae in the diet of Indian Ocean sperms.

For feeding in **antarctic waters,** Matthews (1938) carried out observations on the quantitative stomach fullness of 42 sperm whales captured in the waters 196 of South Georgia Island. The author did not determine the systematics of the food remains from the stomachs and indicated only the presence of Cephalopoda and teleosts in various stages of digestion.

Korabel'nikov (1959) determined three species of squid in the stomachs of 129 sperm whales captured by the whaling flotilla "Slava" in 1956—1957. Remains of a gigantic Architeuthis sp. reaching, judging from some measurements, a length of about 12 m (eye diameter 16—17 cm, length of head 30 cm), were obtained from the stomach of a 15.8-m sperm killed off the Southern Orkney Islands (Atlantic sector). Here, evidently Onychoteuthis banksii is of prime importance in the diet, remains being present in all dissected stomachs. This species predominates in the stomachs of sperm whales taken in all the whaling areas of the Antarctic. One species of small squid could not be determined even to the genus level. Remains of Architeuthis at least 10 m long were found in the stomach of sperm captured somewhat farther west in the region east of the South Shetland Islands. According to our collection, Moroteuthis robusta (from a region northeast of the Balleny Islands) should be considered part of the nutrition of sperm whales in the Antarctic.

Fishes were found by Korabel'nikov (1959) in only six stomachs (5.2% of those examined) in amounts of 1—7 specimens. A rare but widely distributed bathypelagic species, the large anglerfish (Ceratias holboeli), was discovered in the stomach of a sperm caught south of the Falkland Islands (four fish of the same species up to 49 cm long and weighing up to 2.5 kg were found in the stomach). Clarke (1954) had earlier indicated that sperm whales feed on this species, after he discovered the fish in the stomach of a 15-m sperm taken in 1947 at 61°20' S, and 102°50' E. Another species, mentioned by Korabel'nikov, is Dissostichus eleginoides, found in the stomach of a sperm whale 15 m long taken near Tierra del Fuego (7 specimens 70—90 cm long and weighing up to 10 kg). In 1962 in this region, fish of this species from 45 to 138 cm long and weighing up to 44 kg were found by Solyanik (1963) in the stomachs of 3 sperm whales (up to 20 specimens per stomach). There is also a report by Semskii (1962) on stomachs containing representatives of the same family (Nototheniidae) up to 1.5 m long.

In recent years, the Soviet Antarctic flotillas (Vladimirov and Yukhov, in litt.) have noted the frequent presence of D. mawsoni (Figure 99) up to 170 cm long (as a rule 120—140 cm) and weighing about 74 kg, in stomachs of sperms. Specimens of this species are generally encountered off the Balleny Islands and in adjacent regions up to 140°W.

A third species of fish determined by Korabel'nikov (1959) is the southern poutassou (Micromesistius australis). Two specimens about 40 cm long were taken from the stomach of a 15.7-m sperm whale caught south of the Falkland Islands. Finally, a ray (Raja griseocaudata) 105 cm long, determined by Korabel'nikov, was found in a sperm captured off Tierra del Fuego (the Estados Island area).

This review of available data shows that in the Antarctic, fish is of lesser significance for the sperm whale than in other regions of the World Ocean. Korabel'nikov also mentions finding large Crustacea in the stomach of one sperm whale.

Thus, the basic diet of sperm whales in all regions of the World Ocean is made up of approximately 40 species of Cephalopoda (only 30 have been 197 determined to genus or species), including 2 species of squid and 9 of Octopoda. Squid is of far greater importance than octopus everywhere, amounting to 80% of the entire food bolus (Akimushkin, 1955). They are represented mainly by deep-sea species of various size from small, 5 — 10 cm long, to very large, 10 — 12 m or longer. It is noteworthy that species inhabiting the surface waters, e.g., the very widespread and abundant in the North Pacific Ommatostrephes sloanei pacificus, which serves as food for the most varied pelagic animals (including baleen whales), do not form part of the sperm whales' diet.* However, another, much larger representative of the family Ommatostrephidae — Ommatostrephes, (Dosidicus) gigas — is consumed by sperms off the South American coast of the Pacific. The virtual absence of surface-dwelling Cephalopoda in the stomachs of these whales is readily explained by the fact that the sperm whale feeds in deep waters.

FIGURE 99. Specimen of Dissotichus mawsoni, from the stomach of a sperm whale (Antarctic, Antarctic whaling flotilla "Sovetskaya Ukraina"; a coconut is placed next to the fish for comparison; photo by Tkachenko)

In littoral waters, the significance of Octopoda for sperms is sometimes greater, especially of those that have a pelagic mode of life, e.g. Amphitretus sp. (pelagieus) and Alloposus mollis; they are sometimes found in 50% of the total number of stomachs examined.

Because our knowledge of the feeding of sperm whales in the different oceans is uneven, it is difficult to make a complete analysis from the comparative geographical aspect. Moroteuthis robusta and representatives of the genera Architeuthis and Onychoteuthis are food items in all oceans.

* In an earlier work Akimushkin (1955) states that Ommatostrephes sloanei (determination by Klumov) is eaten by sperm whale, but his monograph of 1963 refutes this.

198   More than 50 species of fish belonging to 35 families have been found in the stomachs of sperm whales inhabiting various regions of the World Ocean, the large majority of these in sperm whales that were captured in the North Pacific. The poor species composition of Cephalopoda and fish eaten by sperms in the Atlantic and Indian oceans and in antarctic waters is apparently explained by the scarcity of knowledge on feeding in these areas.

Five species of deep-sea Gadidae are food for the sperm whale in all regions of the World Ocean. The family Scorpaenidae is represented by 6 species, 5 of which (genus Sebastodes) are noted only in the stomachs of sperm whales from the North Pacific. Two families of sharks, Squalidae and Squatinidae, are also included in the diet of sperm whales in the Pacific Ocean.

Even a cursory analysis of the contents of sperm whale stomachs shows that their food spectrum is quite strictly limited to deep-sea organisms. Discovery of isolated animals (inhabitants of the surface layers) in stomachs does not mean that sperm whales feed in these horizons (even taking into account the possible rise of deep-sea animals toward the surface), since if this were the case, they should certainly constitute at least some noticeable proportion of the diet. Finding such species would rather confirm the possibility that animals usually inhabiting the surface layers penetrate to the depths.

The proportion of various food items can vary greatly in different regions and in the same region according to months, seasons, and years, and also depending on the sex and age (size) of the whales; nevertheless, various species of Cephalopoda predominate almost always and everywhere. At least 95% of the entire mass of food consumed consists of Cephalopoda and about 5% of fish.

According to Mizue (1951), the ratio of empty to full stomachs is the same in males and females, but there is a difference between the sexes in the qualitative composition of the food. The stomach contents of males from Japanese waters are more variegated in stomachs of females, in particular, show less Octopoda, and no sharks. Food items such as deep-sea fishes, crab, etc., are usually encountered only in males (Betesheva, 1960; Tarasevich, 1963).

Tarasevich (1963) asserts that in individual years the diet of males may be more monotonous than that of females (as, for instance, in June—July 1961, in the area of the Kuriles).

Judging from the stomach contents and scars on the body, females hardly ever attack such large squid as adult males do (Matthews, 1938; Betesheva, 1960, 1961). According to Tarasevich, squid from water layers closer to the surface water layers predominate in the stomachs of females from the Kuriles.

The index of stomach fullness varies also by years. For example, the stomachs of whales taken in waters adjacent to the Kurile Islands in 1959—1960 were better filled than the stomachs of specimens taken in 1961 (Tarasevich, 1963). This seems to be due to different ecological conditions, especially better food supplies. Tarasevich (1963) also notes that the frequency of occurrence of certain items varies from month to month in the same region but in different years. Thus, the percentage of the main species of squid was lower in 1961 than in previous years; Octopoda and 199 fish were encountered more frequently (the latter was observed in 50% of stomachs). The composition of the food naturally changes also by regions, mainly in the latitudinal direction. From juxtaposition of data on the nutrition of sperm whales, in particular in the Kurile Islands area, we see that in the southern waters of this area the food is much more varied with regard to the species composition of squid and fish (Akimushkin, 1954; Betesheva, 1960; Tarasevich, 1963). To the north (Bering Sea and adjacent regions of the Pacific) the food of sperm whales is again more monotonous (Berzin, 1959). The diet in Japanese waters is apparently less varied than in the Kuriles area (Betesheva, 1960), but this can be attributed to the much fewer data available for these waters. At the same time, a comparison of degrees of stomach fullness shows that the feeding grounds in the Kuriles are more abundant in food than around Japan. Twice as many sperms with empty stomachs were captured off Japan than near the Kuriles (Betesheva, 1961). Betesheva (1960), comparing her data with Japanese material, notes a change of the species composition of the food depending on the distance of the feeding areas from the shore (i.e., depending on depths). Whereas the stomachs of sperm whales caught in the littoral waters of Japan, in the shallow waters of the Sarychevo, Onekotan, Paramushir, and Shumshu islands (Kuriles), in the region of Cape Olyutorskii, and in the shallow waters of the Komandorski Islands, contained in addition to squid small Octopoda, Scorpaenidae and Gadidae, rays and gobies, the stomachs of sperms captured in the Kuriles area at great depth disclosed mainly pelagic species: squid, sharks, and deep-sea fishes (Macrurus, Alepisaurus, anglerfish, etc.).

Crustacea may be present in the stomachs of sperm whales if they feed in the near-bottom layers, for instance remains were found of five species of crab including such large ones as Paralithodes camtshatica and P.brevipes, Pagurus sp. (Hollis, 1939), and two species of bivalved mollusks. Many researchers point out that demersal organisms — sponges, starfish, sea-cucumbers, and ascidians — find their way into the stomach of sperm whales (Akimushin, 1954; Clarke, 1956; Berzin, 1959; Nemoto and Nazu, 1963; etc.).

Japanese investigators (Mizue, 1951; etc.) have noted krill in the food of two female sperms, Ash (1962) discovered shrimp (also noted by Vladimirov in the stomach of one whale taken in the southwestern part of the Pacific off New Zealand) and Andrews (1916) mentioned lobster to be part of the diet.

There are some reports of sperms feeding on warm-blooded animals: Goldberg (1901) reported on his finding skin and claws of seal (species was not determined) in the stomach of an old male from the waters of Norway, and Murphy (1924) reported on vibrissae.

Of course, apart from the above factors which determine the food spectrum of sperm whales, all other conditions being equal, their diet depends entirely on the composition of food items inhabiting the same horizons where sperm whales feed in a particular region. Thus according to Okutani and Nemoto (1964), the farther away from the Aleutian Islands in the Bering Sea, the more fish begin to prevail in the diet, and on the other hand, in the littoral zone of the Gulf of Alaska fish are predominant, while squid prevail in the middle of the gulf.

The stomach of a sperm is usually filled with remains of bodies of Cephalopoda — heads with crowns of tentacles separated from the trunk (mantle), numerous chitinous jaws (rostra), usually small (from 0.5 — 1.5 cm),

200 that belong to small cephalopods (10 — 30 cm long) (Tomilin, 1957), but
sometimes large (up to 12 cm; our collections from the stomachs of
antarctic sperm whales), belonging to gigantic squid. A large number of
light crystalline lenses of Cephalopoda have been found (from minute ones
to large ones of 3 — 4 cm diameter), gladii (axial supporting lamillae), and
the bones or even intact specimens of fish (Figure 99). Stomach contents
including numerous Ascaridae (A n i s a k i s) usually fall out of the stomach
upon dissection (Figure 96).

In 1966 and 1967 in the New Zealand region, parasites of fish (?)
(Isopoda) of different dimensions, including large ones of up to 5.5 cm
(Figure 100), were discovered in the stomaches of five sperm whales.

FIGURE 100. Parasites of fish — Isopoda — from the
stomach of a sperm whale (Antarctic)

In this connection should be remem-
bered Clarke's suggestion (1962)
that when analyzing feeding according to numbers of rostra, it be taken
into consideration that many squid
devour one another. The same
applies to fish.

It is not quite clear whether the
rostra and the gladii are digested in
the sperm whale stomach.
Sleptsov (1952) found the duodenum
remains of cephalopod rostra that
looked like membranes and on the
basis of this he assumed that the
squid rostra had been digested by
the sperm whale. Other researchers
did not succeed in following the
digestion of rostra. Betesheva (1960)
concluded that the gladii are
digested completely already in the
stomach.

According to the percentage of
empty stomachs indicated by various
authors as well as the proportion
of stomachs with different degrees
of fullness one can on the whole
compare feeding in various seasons (if the analysis is on a large scale) or
in different regions provided that the whalers have a similar work regime,
because in any case the degree of stomach fullness depends greatly on the
time that elapses from the moment the whale is killed to dissection (digestion
can continue also after death). In connection with this we cannot compare the
food reserves of regions in one of which a pelagic flotilla operates while in
another whalers deliver their catches to processing enterprises that have
their base on shore. This obviously explains the very low percentage of
empty stomachs in sperm whales captured in the Bering Sea area (less than
3%; Berzin, 1959), in comparison with the Kurile Islands region, that has
the same abundance of food supply (21% empty stomachs, according to
Betesheva, 1960).

In regard to the total amount of food in a stomach, Betesheva (1961) notes
that it did not exceed 200 kg. According to other data, stomachs contained

201 up to 500 squid (G o n a t u s   f a b r i c i i), which judging from the uniform state of digestion had been swallowed at more or less the same time. It was calculated on this basis that a sperm whale 13 — 14 m long can consume at least 2 — 3 tons of squid in the course of 24 hours (Sleptsov, 1952). Kellogg (1940) gives more modest figures and believes that a sperm whale eats up to about one ton of food a day.

Pokrovskaya (in Akimushkin, 1955) counted up to 28,000 rostra in a stomach of a sperm whale, which corresponds to 14,000 squid. Finds of 5,000 — 7,000 rostra are very frequent (Betesheva, 1960). Thus, stomachs of sperms often contain gigantic numbers of rostra which apparently accumulate after several intakes of food (Betesheva, 1961). According to Sleptsov (1952), the rostra in stomachs are remains of Cephalopoda swallowed as a result of a hunt lasting one, two, or a maximum of three days. All this shows that it is small squid moving in shoals that are mostly eaten (it is hard to believe that these animals, even if such a number of them were caught during several days of continuous hunting, had been located far away from each other). Many published confirmations exist of the extreme abundance of shoals of Cephalopoda (Akimushkin, 1955).

Together with the shoals of squid that are relatively monotonous in regard to species (nevertheless, not fewer than 4 species are usually encountered in stomachs of whales), the stomachs of sperm whales (in particular in the Kuriles region) may contain up to 22 species of Cephalopoda simultaneously (Betesheva and Akimushkin, 1955). These data imply the presence of multispecies shoals (or concentrations) of Cephalopoda in the deep waters.

As already mentioned, sperm whales can also catch huge cephalopods, generally of the genus A r c h i t e u t h i s (found in the stomachs of sperms from the Indian, Pacific, and Atlantic oceans). Of course, whole gigantic mollusks are very rarely found in stomachs. However, the opinion of Clarke that sperm whales are able to swallow still larger squid than the 10.5-meter mollusks described by him from the Azores (see above) was confirmed by the discovery in 1964 of a 12-meter A r c h i t e u t h i s weighing 200 kg in the stomach of a sperm whale captured in the Antarctic (Komsomol'skaya Pravda of 7 January 1965).

But naturally, only remains of these gigantic animals are as a rule found in the stomachs. Korabel'nikov (1959) mentions his find of remains judging from which the size of the mollusk was about 12 m. From the stomach of another sperm whale a tentacle 793 cm long was extracted (Beale, 1839). Barch (1916) mentions a piece of tentacle 17 cm thick (it can be assumed that even if this tentacle were one of the thickest, the length of the cephalopod would be 13 — 15 m).

Clarke (1955) thinks that although very large mollusks are rarely found in sperm whale stomachs, they are swallowed much more frequently than assumed, but during its death throes the whale regurgitates them; Clarke confirmed this with two personal observations. Whalers in the Far East report on similar observations.

As already noted, the marks left by suckers with horny serrate crowns and by the hooks of tentacles and the arms of large cephalopods are frequently 202 found on the body (mainly on the head) of sperm whales. Matthews (1938) describes marks of suckers of up to 10 cm in diameter, and Kondakov (1940) of up to 20 cm in diameter; the latter believes that they might have belonged to Architeuthis 18 m long. Clarke (1955) also speaks of very large sucker marks. Our material revealed rows of old marks (rings) on the thoracic fin, about 5.5 cm in diameter in one sperm whale 14.7 m long. In another old sperm, 14.9 m long, with a head almost white from scratches and scars, there were marks of suckers about 20 cm in diameter. A 13.9-m sperm whale had deep parallel scratches, partly suppurative, with lacerated margins, from 30 to 100 cm long and about 4 cm wide in the middle, widest part (see Figure 12). *

Berill (in Akimushkin, 1963a) writes that judging from imprints of suckers left on the body of the sperm whale, the length of a gigantic cephalopod may be up to 45 m. Akimushkin mentions reports of finds of huge fragments of cephalopod arms (described and measured by skippers), so thick that "one's arms hardly go around them." Others were 14 m long and 75 cm thick. He also thinks that even if raconteurs exaggerated the size of their finds no more than 100%, the squid to which the tentacles belong, "were about 100 m long."

There are many authentic reports of very large Cephalopoda. Some have observed fights between sperm whales and the mollusks (Bullen, 1898; Zenkovich, 1936; etc.). According to Bullen, who saw a gigantic squid struggling with a sperm whale on the surface in tropical waters, the mollusk was the same size as its enemy, whose head was almost completely covered by the body of the squid. The black eyes, not less than 30 cm in diameter, were very conspicuous on the white body of the mollusk. Clarke (1955) writes that he began to be less skeptical of such descriptions after he himself had seen a huge mollusk. Kotovshchikov (1931, in Kondakov, 1940) and Zenkovich (1936) also give eye-witness accounts of fights between sperm whales and gigantic squid.

Kondakov (in Sleptsov, 1940) assumes that the sperm whales always emerge the victors of these battles and ascribes their victory to the fact that in his opinion, deep-sea mollusks lose their strength when they rise to the sea surface together with the whales. This view is probably too categorical because we simply do not know, and are hardly in a position to know, of cases when the outcome can be otherwise.

Eschricht as early as 1849 divided all whales into four groups according to mode of feeding. Tomilin (1954) distinguished several more groups, leaving the sperm whale in the same group of "teuthophages" (the main genus of the order Cephalopoda — Teuthis).

In recent years our knowledge on the feeding of the sperm whale has considerably grown and it might be more correct to transfer the species to the group of "teuthoichthyophages" on the basis of data indicating that the proportion of stomachs containing a certain amount of fish can sometimes reach 35 or even 50% (Tarasevich, 1963).

FOREIGN BODIES IN THE STOMACH

By now quite an impressive number of finds are known of nonfood objects in the stomachs of sperm whales.

* Marks of this kind could also be inflicted by the teeth of other sperm whales (see Chapter 18).

FIGURE 101. Foreign bodies from the stomachs of sperm whales

Similar finds are mentioned by many authors (Turner, 1903; Millais, 1906; Hollis, 1939; Pike, 1950; Sleptsov, 1952; Clarke, 1956a; Berzin, 1959; Zemskii, 1962; etc.); Nemoto and Nazu (1963) devoted a special paper to them. The stomachs of sperms taken by Soviet whaling flotillas in 1958—1966 in the North Pacific yielded the following items: high rubber boots, red gloves of thick rubber, bundles of insulated wire, glass floats of fishing nets, plastic toys such as a revolver, car, handbag, pitcher, small pail, and dark-skinned doll, and various tubes and jars of cosmetics (Figure 101). In the stomachs of scores of sperm whales delivered to the "Skalistyi" processing plants in 1961 sometimes several vinyl chloride bags were found, as well as coconuts which in recent years were discovered in the stomachs of sperm whales from other regions of the World Ocean (Nemoto and Nasu, 1963; our data). A deep-sea sponge, Neptune's goblet, 12 cm in size, was found in the stomach of a sperm taken in Aleutian waters (Berzin, 1959). Nemoto and Nasu (1963) mention finding another species of deep-sea sponge — Hexasterophora. The authors report that judging from the skeleton, the sponge was alive when it was swallowed.

According to the data of the above authors, the list presented of objects
204 swallowed by sperm whales can be supplemented with fishing gear swallowed together with fish, nets with hooks for squid fishing, empty bottles, a wooden box, pieces of the flesh of baleen whales, apples, sand (up to 4.5 liters in one stomach), and a piece of coral. Among objects discovered in the stomachs of sperm whales captured in 1962 in the Antarctic by the research group of the "Yurii Dolgorukii" whaling base are two big hunks of wood, one of irregular shape, average dimensions 64 × 21 × 20 cm, and another in the shape of a beam 60 × 10 × 10 cm, at one end of which 4.5 cm nails protruded.

Nemoto and Nasu (1963) report that the stomachs of many specimens taken in 1954 — 1961 in Aleutian waters of the Bering Sea shelf each contained one stone, while the stomachs of two sperms each had 40 — 50 stones. Almost all these stones were small (weighing less than 300 g), but three of them weighed between 500 and 1,400 grams. Andesite is encountered most frequently among the stones swallowed (60%), and propylites, basalt, liparite, sandstone, etc., are also present. Almost all the stones are of volcanic origin. The authors report that the stones were found in the first compartment of the stomach, but several were also discovered in the second compartment.

Hollis (1939) and Fike (1950) mention finding stones in the stomachs of sperm whales from the northern part of the Pacific Ocean. In 1960 a sperm whale whose stomach yielded a bucket (15 — 17 kg) of stones of various size was delivered to the "Podgornyi" processing plant. Without refuting the assumption that stones in the stomachs of small toothed Cetacea contribute to the grinding of food, Beddard (1900) and Sleptsov (1952) believe that sperm whales swallow stones rarely and by accident while hunting for food at the bottom and that they are not true gastroliths. The sperm whale, like other marine mammals that have stomachs of complex structure, evidently rids itself of stones only by belching or regurgitation (V. S. and A. V. Yablokov, 1961). The view held by Nemoto and Nasu (1963) on the possible passage of stones through the intestine is not borne out by any weighty arguments.

A report was published in a popular journal "Natural History" (April 1947; quoted in Budker, 1959) that in old documents (it was not pointed out precisely which) a description had been discovered of hunting sperm whales from whale boats. In 1891 one of the whale boats of the ship "Star of the East" was destroyed by a huge sperm whale. After the accident it was found that one of the whalers had disappeared. The whale was quickly killed and the next morning opened up. The unconscious man (he regained consciousness only four weeks later) was found in the stomach. Details of the case are described as told by the young man himself. He recovered and went on sailing, as testified by the physician who treated the victim. Only the parts of the body unprotected by clothing such as the hands, neck, and face, that became as white as snow, were evidence of the tragedy that had taken place.

Budker (1959) writes that the same copy of the journal published the opinion of an American scientist from New Bedford, Murphy, who considers that cases of whalers being swallowed during struggles with sperm whales are apparently not so rare but he rejects outright the possibility of an outcome such as the one described above. He also established that the ship "Star of the East" did not figure in any marine register of those years. Evidently looking for sensation, the magazine "Vokrug Sveta" [Around the World], (No. 2, 1959) published an article by Revin, "One Chance in a Million," after the article had been reprinted without any critical comment appearing in many newspapers of the USSR.

Klumov (1959) made a detailed analysis of most of the possible and inevitable factors which should have affected the swallowed whaler, almost all of which rule out the plausibility of the incident. In brief, they are as follows: trauma upon being seized in the whale's jaws, the fluid medium in the stomach, the effect of the abundant and strongly acting gastric juices, suffocation due to lack of oxygen, etc. Incidentally, the wide discrepancies in the descriptions of this case should be noticed. For instance, the article

205 by Revin mentions that the man was in the stomach for two hours (in accordance with which Klumov gives his analysis), while in Budker's article (1959) and apparently in the original it is stated that he was in it just under 24 hours. This makes the "case" absurd altogether. Therefore, supporting Klumov, we did not consider it necessary to examine in detail the morphophysiological proofs of the spuriousness of the tale.

Since not all researchers are unanimous in their evaluation of the events described (Tomilin, 1965) the unrealistic nature of the case can be confirmed by the material of the same magazine "Natural History" (June 1947; quoted in Budker, 1959), which published a piece by E. Davis, who witnessed a similar event in 1893. David felt obliged to write to this magazine after he had read the description of what had happened on board the "Star of the East." The following took place according to him: a young whaler, having fallen from an ice floe, was swallowed up by a huge sperm whale. The animal was fatally wounded by a small gun on board the whaling ship and the next day the whale was found floating with its belly up. When its stomach was opened the whalers discovered their comrade with injuries on the chest which were certainly the cause of his immediate death and the exposed parts of his body were semidigested. It is noteworthy, writes Davis, that lice on the seaman's head were still alive. Thus, according to the length of stay of the human body in the sperm whale's stomach the two cases are analogous but the outcome quite different. This proves once again the implausibility of the sensational story of Jonah.

Chapter 13

BREEDING

The biology of reproduction of large Cetacea has been little investigated, particularly in reference to the females of sperm whales. Breeding of sperm whales in the Pacific Ocean has been examined in recent decades by a large group of researchers: Omura, Ohsumi (Kimura), Nishiwaki, Hibiya (1951—1965), Sleptsov (1952), Chuzhakina (1955, 1961), Pike (1954), Berzin (1961, 1963), Clarke, Aguajo, and Paliza (1964); in the North Atlantic Clarke (1956); in the Antarctic and in subtropical regions of the southern parts of the Indian and Atlantic oceans Matthews (1938), Gambell (1966), Bannister (1965—1966), and Best (1967).

Japanese scientists have conducted most comprehensive investigations of reproduction in sperm whales. A leading recent work on females is that by Ohsumi (1965), based on extensive original material obtained in 1960—1962 at the Japanese shore stations, and also on analysis of published sources and statistical data.

PAIRING AND CALVING

Times of pairing. It was discovered long ago that various physiological periods occur in the same season in both the northern and the southern hemisphere. Furthermore, it has been found that sperm whales can mate in essentially all seasons in both hemispheres (Matthews, 1938; Mizue and Jimbo, 1950; Zenkovich, 1952; Sleptsov, 1952; Berzin, 1963; Clarke et al., 1964; Ohsumi, 1965; and others). However, not all share this opinion. For instance, Gambell (1966) considers that pairing and calving occur at definite times. Dates of pairing and peak periods according to various authors, are presented in Table 29.

206 Ohsumi (1965) presents a detailed picture of dates and rate of intensity of pairing by months in both hemispheres according to numerous measurements of embryo from different regions. For the most part conception occurs in February—June (71%) and August—December (67%) in the northern and southern hemisphere respectively. The peak of pairing, according to the same author, occurs in the northern hemisphere from 11 April to end of the month, and in the southern hemisphere from 11 October to the end of the month.

We plotted the size of embryos from 1941—1962 on graphs constructed separately for the northern and southern hemisphere (Figure 102) characterizing all the major dates and periods of the sexual cycle, according to data of the IWS. Gambell (1966) thinks that there is a difference of several months in the duration of the pairing period and calving in the population from the Pacific Ocean in comparison with similar periods in sperm whales from the North Atlantic and southeastern part of the Indian Ocean.

TABLE 29. Dates of pairing and calving

Region	Pairing		Calving		Reference
	season	peak	season	peak	
Northern hemisphere of the World Ocean	February — July	April	—	August	Ohsumi (1965)
Pacific Ocean	—	June — July	May — September	—	Matsuura (1935)
	January — May	March	July — October	—	Mizue & Jimbo (1950)
	January — June	March — April	May — October	July — August	Chuzhakina (1961)
	January — May	—	May — August	—	Slijper (1962)
	March — July	March — April	June — September	August	Our data
Atlantic Ocean	January — July	April — May	May — November	July — August	Clarke (1956)
Southern hemisphere of the World Ocean	July — December	September	September — April	February	Matthews (1938)
	August — December	—	December — April	—	Slijper (1962)
	July — December	September	November — May	February	Clarke et al. (1964)
	August — December	October	—	February	Ohsumi (1965)
	October — April	December	January — August	April	Gambell (1966)
	August — December	September — October	November — May	December	Our data

Having confirmed and developed the conclusions of Laws (1961) for finback whales that with age of the female the pairing peak occurs at much earlier dates, Ohsumi (1965) calculated the dates of conception for various age groups and found a difference in the rate of conception (an earlier pairing period with older females). In his opinion the gradual rise in the catches of younger animals (from spring to fall) in Japanese coastal whaling testifies to the same. If older females are the first to migrate to the north, leaving the breeding grounds before the young ones, it means they have earlier pairing seasons.

Ohsumi (1965) obtained a certain shift of the average date of conception from year to year. He indicates that from 1946 through 1962 the earliest date (averaged) of conception was 6 April 1947 and the latest one 20 May 1948. Thus, according to him, the range of annual fluctuations of the calving date reaches six weeks. The same fluctuations in dates of calving were discovered earlier in sperm whales from the northwestern part of the Pacific (Berzin, 1963).

207 There have been quite a few observations of the intimate sides of life such as pairing and calving in Cetacea kept in oceanaria, but not so in the case of large whales, in particular sperm whales, observations of which have been casual, isolated, and the descriptions sometimes doubtful. However, there is no special reason to believe that pairing and calving in sperm whales differ in principle from those in small cetaceans.

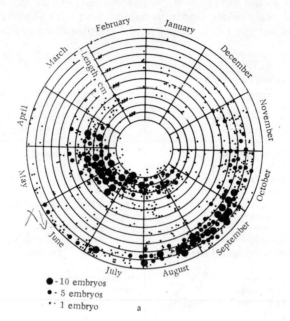

● - 10 embryos
● - 5 embryos
·· 1 embryo   a

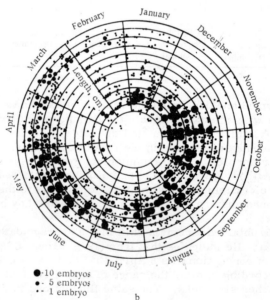

●-10 embryos
● - 5 embryos
·· 1 embryo   b

FIGURE 102. Occurrence of sperm whale embryos of different size according to months:

a — in the northern hemisphere; b — in the southern hemisphere (data of IWS).

In Cetacea that have a penis of the fibroelastic type (which does not change its dimensions upon erection), i.e., such as is present in most Actiodactyla (Slijper, 1966), coitus is brief, measured in seconds. Poses of two kinds have been noted during the pairing of sperm whales: vertical — belly to belly (the animals "stand" in the water, their heads sticking out, and horizontal, lying on the side (Bennett, 1840; observation by Zimin during the research-exploratory cruise of the SRTM "Tamango" in tropical regions of the Pacific in 1968). In the first case the act lasts a few seconds (Slijper, 1966), in the second, from 10 to 30 seconds (Ruspoli, 1955). Another horizontal position on the back has also been described (Dudley, 1725).

Times of calving. According to most researchers, calving can take place during almost the entire year, at any rate the calving period is very drawn out. Nevertheless, there is a period of mass calving. The peak, as well as of the pairing period, occurs in one season in both hemispheres. Information on the dates of calving is given in Table 29.

Ohsumi (1965) specifies precisely the peak dates of calving in sperm whales: the last third of August for the northern hemisphere, the last third of February for the southern hemisphere. He also calculated that in northern whales 71% of calving takes place from June through October, 21% occurs in August, and only 11% in January — April. In the southern hemisphere 67% of calving occurs in December — April and only 9% in July — October.

The duration of pregnancy has been determined differently. Scammon (1874) considers it to be ten months, while according to Harmer (1933), Matsuura (1935), Zenkovich (1952), Sleptsov (1952), Chuzhakina (1955), and Tomilin (1957), it is 11 — 12 months.

209   Matthews (1938) was the first to substantiate a term of 16 — 17 months. The same (or almost the same) length of time is supported by Mizue and Jimbo (1950), Clarke (1956), Nishiwaki et al. (1958), Laws (1959), Berzin (1961 — 1963), Chuzhakina (1961), Slijper (1962), Clarke, Aguajo and Paliza (1964), Bannister (1965 — 1966), Ohsumi (1965), and Gambell (1966).

Ohsumi (1965) gives the precise figure of 16.4 months but rightly says that there must be individual deviations. Clarke et al. (1964) consider the duration of pregnancy in sperm whales from the North Atlantic to be 2 — 4 weeks shorter than in other oceans (the smaller size of embryos in these waters is thereby explained). Ohsumi (1965) did not discover such a difference.

Growth rate of embryos. Having averaged the length of embryos by ten-day periods for both hemispheres, Ohsumi (1965) plotted curves of growth which are taken (his conclusion) as straight lines. According to the average length of embryos as calculated by him, it can be assumed that the growth rate is constant throughout pregnancy (Table 30). But the growth rate of an embryo is not constant (see Figure 102). We thus calculated the average length of embryos of both sexes at the end of each month and obtained several mean lengths that differed from those obtained by Ohsumi (Table 30). These figures show that the embryos have an uneven rate of growth: in the first two months the embryo grows to about 20 cm; in each of the subsequent four months the increment is equal to 20 cm, in the 7th — 9th month 25 — 30 cm, in the 10th and 11th month 45 cm, in the 12th — 15th month 30 cm, and in the 16th month the increment is only 20 cm. This nonuniformity of the growth rate makes it possible to distinguish three periods of development; in the first month the growth rate is relatively slower (1st period), then more intensive (2nd period), and finally in the last month it slows down again (3rd period). As to the last month one has to agree with Ohsumi (1965) that the growth rate calculated is lower than the actual (because the largest embryos could already have been born) and as a result the average length of embryos for that month is diminished.

TABLE 30. Growth of sperm whale embryos (in both hemispheres)

Month of pregnancy	Length of embryo, cm		Month of pregnancy	Length of embryo, cm	
	Ohsumi (1965)	our data (mean length)		Ohsumi (1965)	our data (mean length)
1st	6	10	9th	210	170
2nd	24	20	10th	234	215
3rd	52	30	11th	262	260
4th	76	50	12th	289	290
5th	103	70	13th	314	320
6th	127	90	14th	341	350
7th	155	115	15th	369	380
8th	183	140	16th	393	400

A table of the growth rate of embryos at two-month intervals is presented by Chuzhakina (1961).

Having summed up the length of embryos (data of IWS for 1937—1961), Ohsumi (1965) obtained a different distribution of frequencies of occurrence of monthly lengths in the northern and southern hemispheres, which in his opinion indicates a difference of the respective herds. Clarke, Aguajo, and Paliza (1964) drew attention to the same.

Ohsumi (1965) calculated (data of IWS) the ratio of male to female embryos and found that males amount to 48.1% in the North Pacific, 56.2% in the waters of Chile and Peru, and 45.6% in the waters of South Africa. The average percentage of males is 51.03, i.e., the sex ratio of sperm whale embryos can be considered as 1:1.

Size of the newborn. There is no information on direct measurements of sperm whales at birth, so that the body length of the newborn has to be judged from the size of the largest embryos and the smallest sucklings. The largest embryos, according to data of IWS and our own, are 460—600 cm long. Ohsumi (1965) is probably right to doubt the existence of embryos almost 6 m long. He figured that out of almost 2,700 embryos recorded by IWS only 0.22% were 49—520 cm long. The length of the smallest sucklings is given below:

Length of body, cm	Reference
371	Clarke (1956)
386	"
389	"
404	"
404	Wheeler (1933)
404	Matthews (1938)
430	Bennett (1840)
486	Jackson (1845)
515	Matsuura (1940)
515	"
550	Harmer (1933)
562	Our data*

* Female suckling was caught accidentally by the
"Tamango" in 1968 in the central regions of the
Pacific (Zimin, in litt.)

Besides direct measurements of embryos before parturition and of sucklings (which testify to considerable variations of length at birth), there are
many figures of average lengths of sperms at birth which were determined
by the method of growth curves.

Length of body, cm	Reference
320 — 420	Sleptsov (1952)
392	Clarke (1956)
396	Nishiwaki et al. (1958),
	Slijper (1962)
400	Matthews (1938)
402 — 405	Clarke et al. (1964),
	Ohsumi (1965)
415	Laws (1959)
420 — 450	Matsuura (1940)
425	Bannister (1956 — 1966),
	Gambell (1966)
427 — 457	Mizue & Jimbo (1950)
430	Bennett (1840)
450	Zenkovich (1952, 1954)

There is a definite sexual dimorphism in the newborn, expressed in
different lengths. Matthews (1935) pointed out that males predominate
among the large embryos (lengths of over 3.9 m). Tomilin (1936) also
considers that newborn males are about 4 m long while females are somewhat shorter. Naturally, having only their own material as a basis, the
authors hesitated to assert the existence of sexual dimorphism in size
already in large embryos and in the newborn. Summarizing the data accumulated made it possible to state positively (Berzin, 1963, 1964; Clarke et al.,
1964; Ohsumi, 1965) that there are variations in the size of males and
211 females already in the embryonic period. Clarke et al. (1964) contend that
the growth rate curves of male and female embryos at first run parallel and
then diverge because of the higher growth rate of the males and that at an
equal duration of pregnancy males are 12 cm longer than females at birth.

215

Analysis of the material implies that as in other mammals, the length of sperm whales at birth may very widely fluctuate (by almost 2 m) at average lengths of about 400—420 cm.

Births in sperm whales have been witnessed, particularly by the Far Eastern whalers, relatively often but in all cases these were observations (mainly from a great distance) of the general circumstances, the behavior of females during parturition, and the appearance of the newborn at the water surface. All Cetacea give birth under water, and therefore there is no certainty that details of the process described for small toothed whales after observations in oceanaria will be characteristic also for sperm whales. But it is also evident that there should not be any essential differences. Tail presentation occurs in newborn sperm whales, as in other Cetacea. Our observations of the position of large embryos in the uterus testify to the fact that in individual cases the embryo lies with the head toward its mouth. But evidently, as in other whales (Slijper, 1966), this does not mean that head presentation occurs. This position of the embryo in the uterus is due to the fact that in all Cetacea the anterior part of the body is heavier than the posterior, and as a result the head immersed in the amniotic fluid (the volume of which in Cetacea is absolutely and relatively much greater than in other mammals), has to be directed ventrocranially (Slijper, 1966).

This is how Pervushin (1966) describes his observation on the parturition of sperm whales. "On 26 March 1964, at a point with coordinates 37°01'S and 71°44'E, two groups of sperm whales were spotted, about 20 animals in each. From a distance of about 50 meters, we noticed the unusual position of one whale which, having breached for 1/4 of its trunk, stayed in the vertical position with the head up. Approaching almost up to it, we saw next to the whale a just born calf, about 4 meters long still connected with the umbilical cord. The water around was stained with blood and placenta remains were clearly seen near the calf. The calf kept close to the female, its caudal flukes were rolled into a fist. The newborn performed short spoutings at intervals of 0.5—1.0 minutes. Two more females were together with them and they dived all the time, supporting the newborn. When the ship came close up to the whales with its stern, the mother took up a stand between the vessel and the calf and started to flic it with her tail away from the approaching danger.

During tagging we observed three more females that took vertical positions and after some time bloodstains and one newborn sperm appeared near them. Then in a group of females one more calf was discovered, which had probably been born a few hours earlier because although it kept in the water more confidently, its flukes were not unrolled completely and their ends were down. The caudal peduncle was limp and apparently the calf did not yet have control over it."

212 LACTATION

Bennett (1840) considered that the period of lactation lasts about a year. Matsuura (1935), Matthews (1938), Chuzhakina (1955), and Tomilin (1957) report that lactation in sperm whales lasts for 6—7 months. However, recently most researchers support Bennett. Zenkovich (1952),

Sleptsov (1952), Clarke (1956), Nishiwaki et al. (1958), and Chuzhakina (1961) report one year. Berzin (1963), Clarke et al. (1964) confirm this by describing a pregnant nursing female with an embryo 310 cm long. The embryo of another lactating female was 300 cm long (Ohsumi, 1965).

Matsuura (1935) considers lactation to be over at a length of the newborn of 8—9 m. According to Matthews (1938), the embryo's length at this time is 6.6—6.8 m., according to Sleptsov (1952) 7.5—7.8 m; Clarke (1956) considers that the average length of young sperms finishing suckling is 6.7 m. Two sperm whales 6.7 m long fed on squid, according to Nishiwaki et al. (1958), and in this connection the body length at the end of lactation is considered to be 6.1 m. The last conclusion is probably justified because we examined a sperm 6.2 m long which was completing suckling and a specimen 6.9 m long that was already feeding quite independently. Ohsumi (1965) considers the body length of young animals to be 6—7 m at the end of the lactation period. It would probably be wrong to try to achieve absolute unity and too precise evaluations of lengths because of the considerable individual variability in length already during embryonic development. Moreover, Ohsumi (1965) assumes (on the basis of available observations on the feeding of small toothed whales in the oceanaria), that a few months after birth the sperm whale can feed simultaneously on its mother's milk and on animal food.

The end of lactation coincides with the formation of two age layers on the teeth, i.e., lactation lasts about a year.

Lactation does not prevent pairing and a new pregnancy, as in other species of baleen (Chittleborough, 1958; Ivashin, 1959) and toothed whales (Matsuura, 1935; Sleptsov, 1941; Sokolov, 1964; Tomilin, 1957; Yablokov, 1959; Kleinenberg and Yablokov, 1960; Berzin, 1961; Ohsumi, 1965). Data show that simultaneous lactations and pregnancies in sperm whales are not as rare as previously thought.

Nursing in sperm whales has not been precisely described. It is assumed that the female moves slowly during feeding, the calf approaches the nipple from behind and the female turns on her side to some degree (Bennett, 1840; Bullen, 1898). There is also Dudley's note (1725) that the female lies on her back during nursing, but this is probably wrong. The young whale seizes the erect nipple in the corner of the mouth (Sleptsov, 1952; Slijper, 1966; etc.), and the female (as in other Cetacea) injects milk straight into its mouth by contraction of muscles (Zenkovich, 1938; Sleptsov, 1952; etc.). Sleptsov (1952) notes quite correctly that in contrast 213 to the tongue of adult sperm whales, which is relatively short, the tongue of the newborn is long and reaches the anterior sections of the jaws.

The calf feeds under water, and therefore morphophysiological adaptations follow the line of the creation of conditions for maximum intake of milk in the shortest possible time.

The milk of all whales is very fat (from 30—53% fat), 3—5 times more fat than the milk of terrestrial mammals (Slijper, 1966). The fat content obviously varies depending on the lactation period and other factors (the method of taking samples, etc.), and therefore various conclusions are possible in comparative evaluations. Thus Zenkovich (1938, 1952), who determined the composition of the milk of large species of whales, considers the milk of the sperm whale to be the least fat, while Slijper (1966), on the contrary, considers that it is so fat that it "is like butter." The composition 214 of the milk of sperm whales is shown in Table 31 according to various data.

TABLE 31. Composition of the milk of sperm whale, %

Fat	Water	Dry residue	Reference
37.38	55.35	7.27	Takemura (1927) *
36.53	57.72	5.75	Ibid.
15.12	69.37	15.51	Tomilin and Sak (1934) *
36.32	54.22	9.46	Zenkovich and Andrianov (1936) *
38.2	55.25	6.55	Zenkovich (1938)
36.32	54.22	9.46	Ibid.
40.50	40.50	—	Slijper (1962)
36.3 — 38.2	54.2 — 55.3	6.5 — 9.5	Baev (in Kizevetter, (1953)
37.3	54.7	8	Bodrov and Grigor'ev (1963)
30.4	53	4.7	Our data **

* These data are given after Tomilin (1957).

** The analysis was carried out in the technological laboratory of the whaling base "Vladivostok" in the North Pacific.

Another characteristic feature of the milk of Cetacea is the high content of protein (up to 11—12%, i.e., on the average twice as much as in the milk of terrestrial animals), and of calcium and phosphorus, which is apparently connected with the rapid growth weight (Slijper, 1962, 1966).

(213)

FIGURE 103. Nursing female sperm whale. The swollen nipples and streams of milk are seen (photo by Blokhin)

According to Sleptsov (1952), about 45 liters of milk are present in the mammary glands of sperm whales. Observations at the dressing platforms show that with strong pressure applied to the area of the glands near the nipples, a stream of milk 1.5—2 cm in diameter and up to 2—3 liters in quantity may gush out (Figure 103).

ONSET OF SEXUAL MATURITY IN MALES

Many researchers in various countries have studied the onset of sexual maturity in sperm whales in different whaling regions. Particularly

intensive research in this direction has been done by Japanese scientists —
Nishiwaki, Hibiya, Ohsumi, and others (1951—1958) — on Antarctic and
North Pacific sperm whales. Animals in the southeastern Pacific have
been investigated by Clarke, Aguajo, and Paliza (1964) and sperms of the
North Atlantic by Clarke (1956). Matthews (1938) determined the onset of
maturity in males of the southern hemisphere in the Indian and Atlantic
oceans from limited material that included several animals of small
dimensions (i.e., just such as are needed for this particular problem), and
merely according to the presence of spermatozoa in the seminal ducts he
determined that the length of males at the onset of maturity is about 12 m.

Later, Nishiwaki (1955) determined the length of a sperm whale at
maturity to be 12.5 m using the same method (proceeding from the same
criteria of maturity). Meanwhile even the attempt to determine the time of
maturation of males according to animals coming to antarctic waters for the
summer was pointless as was found later (not to mention the defects of the
method), because with rare exceptions, the whales reach maturity long
before they come to this region.

Nishiwaki, Hibiya, and Kimura (1956), who studied males from the
Aleutian Islands, could only indicate (for the same reasons) that all sperm
whales longer than 11.6 m are sexually mature.

Some authors (Sleptsov, 1952) determined maturity by analysis of a smear
from the epididymis, which is not always reliable. Sounder conclusions were
obtained from investigations by Clarke (1956), Nishiwaki, et al. (1958),
Berzin (1963—1965), Clarke, Aguajo, and Paliza (1964), that were based on
a histological analysis of material obtained from the necessary contingent
of young males.

Until the works by Chittleborough (1955) and Clarke (1956) appeared, the
presence of spermatozoa in the seminal ducts was considered the criterion
of maturity in sperm whales (Nishiwaki and Hibiya, 1951—1952; Nishiwaki,
1955; Nishiwaki, Hibiya, and Kimura, 1956; etc.). Chittleborough (1955)
examined the seminal ducts of humpback whales and established that the
presence of spermatozoa is not the main character for determining the
physiological state of the animal because even in the pairing period there
are very few spermatozoa present in the sperm whale. However, Matthews
215 (1938) noted that there are always many more spermatozoa in the sperm
whale than in baleen whales. He found spermatozoa all the year round and
denies that there is a definite season of sexual activity in male sperms.
He also considers that the presence of spermatozoa (and consequently of
sexual activity) does not depend on the presence of females.

On the basis of histological studies (mainly analysis of the diameters
of seminal ducts), Clarke (1956) concluded (as did Chittleborough for
baleen whales) that the sexual activity of male sperms bears a seasonal
character, and the presence or absence of spermatozoa cannot be a reliable
indicator of the physiological state. Clarke suggested that animals whose
testes have large and open seminal ducts (independently of whether there is
sperm in them) should be considered mature. Guided by this, Clarke (1956)
indicates a smaller body length at the onset of maturity in males than all
the preceding authors.

Nishiwaki, Ohsumi and Hibiya (1958) agreed with Clarke and determined
on the basis of a histological analysis of 54 testes that the length of male
sperm whales in the North Pacific at the onset of maturity is approximately
29.5 m, i.e., the same as determined by Clarke for these waters.

*either 9.5 metres
or, more probably, 29½ feet.*

We were unable to follow the activity of the testes of sperm whales in all seasons (but all summer sperm whales are in a state of sexual activity), and therefore we could not draw any conclusion on the seasonal variations in the activity of males. However, we uphold the view held by Matthews (1938), who investigated males almost all the year round (except in May, September, and December) and who considers that a season of sexual activity in male sperms is absent and breeding is possible throughout the year. * Along with this, the absence or presence of spermatozoa is an unreliable criterion for determining the stage of maturation because even in testes that are in a state of activity sperm cannot be found on all sections in the ducts (Clarke, 1956; Berzin, 1963, 1965).

With microscopical examination of histological sections of testes samples we determined the approximate percentage of open and closed ducts. Using an ocular micrometer we calculated the diameter of the duct and sometimes also that of the lumen. When determining the number of open and closed ducts, one should be guided by the sections of ducts with a more rounded form, because the ducts are very twisted, and some closed, long, and bent ducts visible in the field of the microscope may in fact be only the walls of open ducts. The same should be taken into account when measuring the diameters of the ducts.

The results of our analysis of sections made in different areas of the testis confirmed the data of Matthews (1938) and Nishiwaki, Hibiya, and Kimura (1956), which indicate that the seminal ducts develop nonuniformly 216 in different parts of the testis. For instance, in the sample of a testis of an 11.5-m sperm whale, taken from the middle, 80—90% of the seminal ducts were small and closed. In a sample from a thicker part of the same testis all the ducts were large and more than half of them had a wide lumen. In a sample from the middle of the testis of an 11.8-m whale all the ducts were small and closed, while in the terminal parts 90—95% of the ducts were large, with a wide lumen. Similar findings were obtained with other testes of sperm whales, even though the size of one specimen, for example, was 12 m and the age 9 years.

The investigations show that maturation proceeds faster in the terminal parts of the sperm whale testis than in the middle part (Berzin, 1963, 1965).

Proceeding from these data for comparable material it is essential to analyze samples taken from specific areas of the testis.

The methodology becomes still more complicated due to the fact that maturation of the testis may proceed differently even on a small area and opposite results can be obtained also when investigating sections from different, even closely situated samples. For instance, in a specimen 11.5 m long one half of the section consisted wholly of typically closed ducts, whereas all the ducts of the second half were large and open. The two parts of the section were separated by strands of connective tissue. Thus, if the section passed just a little to the side, in one case 100% maturation could be asserted but in the other case, immaturity of an 11.5-m whale. Matthews long ago (1938) drew attention to this complicated character of the tissue of the testis.

* The presence of sperm in the seminal ducts all the year round is not yet proof of the absence of seasonality in the sexual activity of males. As such (very indirect) proof one may accept only an accurate quantitative analysis of the state of the testes in a large number of males in all seasons. Proceeding from general concepts and analogies, we believe that seasonality in sexual activity must be expressed also in male sperm whales. — Editor

A true picture of the physiological state can be obtained by taking several samples from a testis (in small sperm whales, in addition, by taking samples from different testes). For example, Nishiwaki, Hibiya, and Kimura (1956) noted that in 12 cases out of 106, one testis was mature and the other not. This result might be erroneous due to the mentioned peculiarities of maturation of the seminal ducts.

It is desirable to reinforce conclusions on the physiological state of the animal with an analysis of the presence of spermatozoa in the epididymis. In our material such control made it possible in a number of cases to specify more precisely and even to change the conclusions drawn from results of examination of sections; this will be discussed below.

More details are appropriate on the histological characteristics of the seminal ducts of sperm whales that are at various degrees of maturity.

Examination of histological sections of testes of immature whales reveals seminal ducts without pronounced lumina (Figure 104). All the ducts are small — from 65 to 105μ, the average diameter being 70μ.

Animals which show single, well expressed open ducts up to 200μ in diameter are considered as being at the stage of sexual maturation. The diameter of closed ducts sometimes begins to increase too, attaining 180μ. Sperms with spermatozoa already appear in the epididymis of such animals.

Chittleborough (1955) and Ivashin (1959) assume that testes with most ducts open are found in animals attaining maturity, whereas in mature animals all the ducts are open. There may be some variation in the course 217 of spermatogenesis in sperm whales and baleen whales (particularly, in the humpback whale); if not, it would be more correct to call mature those whales in whose testis at least half the ducts are open, while whales where sections showed only single open ducts are still maturing. At the same time, the very definitions "attaining sexual maturity," "on the verge of sexual maturity," as well as the groupings, should be considered arbitrary because of the above methodical procedures, and also the nonuniformity in the maturation of the tissues of each testis. According to our material, when sections showed about 50% of open ducts, there was much ripe sperm in the epididymis. Moreover, the presence of closed seminal ducts is possible even in large animals (14 m long) with a large quantity of ripe spermatozoa because of uneven testis maturation.

Thus, sperm whales showing 50% or more open ducts on sections should be considered mature.

Wide and open ducts (Figure 105) from 80 to 220μ in diameter are seen on sections of the testis in fully mature sperm whales. The average diameter is 130μ, and that of the lumen 56μ. Only in individual cases does the entire section show open, large ducts in which, however, no lumen is seen. The diameter of such ducts reaches 200μ; they usually lie in small "islands," among ducts with lumina.

Analysis of material showed that male sperms up to 9.0 m long are all immature. Active sexual maturation begins in animals 9.1—9.5 m long, and some of this length are fully mature. In the size group of 9.6—10.0 m 5 out of 6 specimens proved mature. All sperms more than 11.7 m long were mature. Most sperm whales become mature when attaining the length of 10.0 m although we found animals that were mature (according to both the ducts and 218 the presence of spermatozoa) in the northwestern part of the Pacific at a length of 9.2 m.

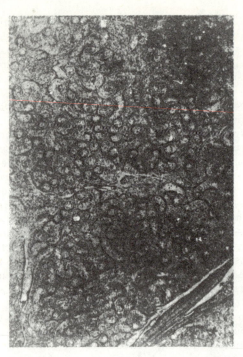

FIGURE 104. Photo of a histological section of the testis
of an immature sperm whale 9.5 m long, aged 3.5 years
(x 50; North Pacific)

Thus the process of sexual maturation in male sperm whales is to be considered much extended and maturity to be reached at various dimensions of the body. The length of 9.5 m can be taken as the average for the northwestern part of the Pacific (Berzin, 1966).

According to Pike (1954), males from the northeastern Pacific mature at a length of 10.9 m. When the Soviet flotillas started commercial whaling in the northwestern regions, histological studies were conducted (using the above criteria) of 35 testes, specially selected from extensive material of animals with lengths close to that at which maturity is reached. It emerged that maturation in these regions is also very drawn out and occurs at various sizes. An animal of 9.0 m may be mature but most of this length are just starting to mature (the diameter of the seminal ducts begins to increase, and single open ducts appear). The majority of animals 10.0 — 10.3 m long from this region were already mature, but about 30% in the group 10.5 — 11.0 m long were still immature. All the whales over 11.0 m long were in fact mature, according to these data, and only one specimen of 11.8 m (judging from the state of the seminal ducts) was only just approaching full maturity.

On the whole, our material showed that 9.5 — 10.0 m can be considered the average length at the onset of maturity in male sperm whales of the northeastern part of the Pacific Ocean.

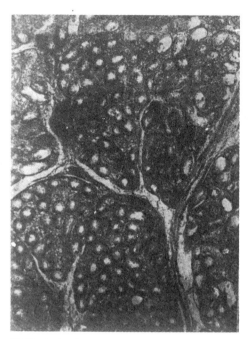

FIGURE 105. Photo of a histological section of the
testis of a mature sperm whale 11.8 m long aged 7.5
years (x 50; North Pacific)

Nishiwaki and others (1958) determined on the basis of limited material
that male sperms inhabiting the waters of Japan mature at around the age of
5 years.

The same time for the onset of sexual maturity (Berzin, 1963, 1965) was
219 established on very extensive material (male sperms from a more northern
region — the Kurile Islands) according to the minimum number of layers of
dentin in already mature animals and the maximum number of layers in
immature sperm whales. Thus, the average age at which maturity is
reached in males from the northwestern Pacific can be considered to be 5
years.

The onset of maturity in male sperm whales of the northern part of the
Atlantic (the Azores area) was determined by Clarke (1966). According to
his histological investigation, the length of animals at this stage of
physiological development is 9.6 m, i.e., approximately equal to the length
of Pacific sperm whales at the same stage of development.

The problem of maturation of sperm whales in the tropical and subtropical regions of the Pacific (the coast of Chile and Peru) was clarified
by Clarke, Aguajo, and Paliza (1964) on the basis of a histological investigation of 162 males taken by shore whaling stations of these countries.
The group of whales with length 9.6 — 9.8 m contained 50% mature and 50%
immature animals. This length was therefore accepted as the average at
which maturity is reached.

According to Bannister (1965—1966), the average length of male sperms from the west coast of Australia is 9.7 m at the onset of maturity.

In recent years Soviet fleets have carried out selective sperm whaling in the lower latitudes of the southern hemisphere with the aim of investigating small males captured at random and of using the present criteria to obtain original data. In this region, as in others of the World Ocean, sexual maturity in sperm whales occurs at various lengths: some were mature at 9.5 m, but most animals of such a length were still immature. The majority reach maturity at a length 10.5—11.0 m, though individual specimens 11.5 m long are still completing maturation. Investigation of smears from the epididymis of single, small specimens in the subtropical and tropical regions of the Indian Ocean (material of research groups of the whaling flotillas) showed that most testes of animals 9.5—10.5 m long contained ripe spermatozoa. These data are not sufficient to indicate the precise average length of animals at the onset of maturity, but in any case the true figure is much smaller (by about 1.5—2 m) than that indicated by Matthews for the animals of these regions. Thus, all recent data show that the size of male sperm whales in the two hemispheres is more or less the same at the onset of maturity.

The length of whales, in particular blue whales — B a l a e n o p t e r a m u s c u l u s (Nishiwaki and Hibiya, 1951) and in the humpback (Ivashin, 1959) — at the time of maturity can be determined by the considerable increase in the weight of the testes which occurs at the corresponding stage of development of the animal. According to Matthews (1938), a similar phenomenon is observed in sperm whales. However, data given by Nishiwaki and Hibiya (1951) as well as our material (see Figure 81) do not indicate the existence of an abrupt increment in the weight of testes of sperm whales after attainment of maturity, and it is impossible to know the moment of onset of maturity from the character of a curve of testes weight and body length. Matthews' error (1938) can be ascribed to lack of accurate statistics. Nevertheless, after the onset of maturity in sperm whales some increase in the volume and weight of the testes does of course take place. This is not seen in a general graph because of the considerable individual variations in body length at which maturity is reached (this conceals any possible abrupt increment) and also because of the fairly uniform maturation of the testes.

According to Clarke (1956), the weight of the testes of sperm whales from the Azores area is approximately 1,500 g at the onset of maturity. In our material a sperm whale 9.2 m long with testes weighing 960 g was already mature, while a specimen 9.4 m long with testes weighing 860 g was still immature and an animal 9.5 m long with testes weighing 1,050 g also turned out to be immature. On the basis of data obtained it was determined (Berzin, 1963—1965) that the weight of the testes at the onset of maturity in sperm whales averages 1,000 g, which is in good agreement with the data of Nishiwaki et al. (1958).

ONSET OF SEXUAL MATURITY IN FEMALES

The question as to when maturity is reached in female sperm whales is naturally of still greater interest. Although the answer is in principle simpler than for males, there are, nevertheless, fewer data. This can be explained by the fact that the females mature early, at any rate at a length much smaller than that at which the vessels operating both in the pelagic flotillas (11.6 m) and also those based at coastal enterprises (10.7 m) are permitted to catch them.

Matsuura (1935) points out that pregnant females 9.1 m long are found in the waters of the northern part of the Pacific. Matthews (1938), guided by his find in the southern hemisphere of a pregnant female 9.5 m long thinks that maturity is reached at a length of 9.0 — 9.5 m. Omura (1950) reports with some reservation that the length is 9.1 m or a little less. Data of Nishiwaki and Hibiya (1951) confirmed Matthew's conclusions. Zenkovich (1952) points out that the minimum size of a pregnant female is 9 m and considers that females are mature at 8.5 m. Sleptsov (1952) examined two pregnant females 7.3 and 7.9 m long.

According to the data of IWS, Tomilin (1957), out of 130 embryos of females from Japanese waters, found 12 in females 9 m long. Reports of the discovery of two pregnant females 6.4 m long (according to the same data) from Peruvian waters are of interest.

Clarke (1956) reports that the length of a female sperm whale in the North Atlantic was 8.8 m at the onset of maturity. According to Nishiwaki et al. (1958) females from the North Pacific are also of this length when maturity is reached.

It seems to be correct that not only females in the ovaries of which there are traces of a former or a present pregnancy but also those whose ovaries contain ripe follicles (even if they have not burst) should be considered mature. On the basis of relatively little material from the Kuriles area it was determined that the body length of females at the onset of sexual 221 maturity is about 9 m (Berzin, 1961). Further data obtained in subsequent years made it possible to specify the dates of attainment of maturity more precisely in female sperm whales of the northwestern Pacific: the average length of females at maturity was determined as 8.3 m (Berzin, 1963).

Clarke, Aguajo, and Paliza (1964) consider 8.4 — 8.6 m to be the average length for female sperm whales of the southern hemisphere (for the Pacific Ocean) at which maturity is reached (in their opinion this applies to 50% of females), while Bannister (1965 — 1966) considers the average length for females from western Australia to be 8.8 m.

Thus, at present researchers consider that the onset of maturity in female sperm whales from any region of the World Ocean occurs at an average length of 8.3 — 8.8 m.

The age at which female sperm whales reach maturity was determined as about 1.5 years by individual scientists (Matthews, 1938; Sleptsov, 1952; Chuzhakina, 1955) before age determination methods were worked out. Only after the dentin method had been elaborated (Nishiwaki et al., 1958; Berzin, 1959 — 1961) did it become possible to define the age of maturity. It was found that in females it is 4 — 5 years (8 — 10 layers of dentin). Data accumulated subsequently led to more accurate determination: according to Berzin (1963), the age is 3.5 years on the average. Japanese researchers (Ohsumi et al., 1963) soon revised their view on the periods of formation of the dentin layers, and as a result their figure for the duration of immaturity in females was doubled. However, Gambell and Grzegorzewska (1967) proved that two layers of dentin are formed each year. Considering the practical importance of solving this problem, more data and more work on the matter are required.

As the above shows, the first pregnancy may occur either later or earlier than the mean dates indicated. Ohsumi (1965) for instance, pointing to the long-drawn-out character of the onset of sexual maturity in females of the North Pacific, reports that a female may conceive for the first time when the teeth have either 6 or 18 layers of dentin (age from 3—9 years).

SEXUAL CYCLE OF FEMALES

Matthews (1938) determines the duration of the sexual cycle of female sperm whales to be equal to two years (or a little less). Clarke (1956) considers the cycle to last 3 years (16 months of pregnancy plus 13 months of lactation and 7 months of rest).

Taking into account that lactation does not prevent a new pregnancy, the duration of the sexual cycle can be considered to average 2 years (Berzin, 1963), although it may be somewhat longer or shorter depending on the interval between parturition and repeated pregnancy.

222 In determining the duration of the sexual cycle it is of great importance to clarify the relationship between the number of ovulations and age and also the total number of ovulations a year. Marks of the former pregnancy are readily identified on ovaries (see Chapter 8). According to our determinations (proceeding from the formation of two light layers of dentin on the teeth annually), it can be considered that one mark of ovulation (pregnancy) is formed on the average every two years (Berzin, 1963). Later, Ohsumi (1965) investigated the relationship between age and number of ovulations in 892 females from the waters of Japan. He showed that there are individual variations in the ovulation cycle and that this, with the extended attainment of maturity, determines variation in the relationship between age and number of ovulations.

Ohsumi's results (particularly the curve of the relation of the number of ovulations to the number of dentin layers, the average age at a certain number of ovulations, the considerable variations in the number of ovulations in females of the same age, etc.) are similar to our own. Furthermore, Ohsumi (1965) confirms an increased interval between ovulations with age (Berzin, 1963), i.e., a gradual attenuation of ovarian activity.

However, on the basis of an analysis of much more extensive material than ours, Ohsumi concluded that the mean duration of the sexual (ovulation) cycle is equal to the time taken for 3.7 dentin layers to be formed.

Proceeding from the fact that the proportion of pregnant females is 26—29%, Ohsumi determined that the breeding cycle is 3.4—3.8 years (1 year 0.26—0.29), while proceeding from the number of ovulations a year, the duration of the breeding cycle was determined as 3—4 years (average 3.7).

Several types of breeding cycle can be isolated, making allowance for age-dependent variations in the physiology of females (Ohsumi, 1965). The 4-year cycle (type B), which ends with ovulation after an eight-month rest, is considered as the most frequent and typical cycle (for females from the coastal waters of Japan). In the 3-year cycle (type E) conception occurs at the end of lactation. The 2-year cycle (type F) takes place when females become pregnant in the same breeding season and the subsequent parturition occurs with the cessation of the lactation period. To confirm this type of sexual cycle Ohsumi reports a case of a lactating female with an embryo 300 cm long. The two last types of cycle are observed more frequently in females. There are also 16—17-month breeding cycles (type G), when females become pregnant again immediately after parturition. The longest cycle (type A) extends over 7.2 years. This cycle becomes more frequent with age. Ohsumi justly considers that sperm whales show a complex of types of breeding cycles. For instance, a combination of cycles with a certain prevalence of type B is typical for sperms inhabiting the waters of Japan. With age the longer cycles become more frequent to a greater or lesser degree.

Let us analyze the rate of accumulation of marks of ovulations in various size groups of females from the northern part of the Pacific. It was pointed out above that females 8.6—9 m long are, usually, completing maturation (100% of females whose length exceeds 9 m are generally mature). Half of the females of this size examined by us had calved once (or were pregnant 223 for the first time), but on the other hand, one female with five marks of ovulation (traces of pregnancy) was noted. In a size group of animals 10.1—10.5 m long 57% of the females had 5—8 marks of corpora lutea and only one female displayed one pregnancy. A slowing down of the growth rate is characteristic for females of this size group. As a result, numerous marks of corpora lutea accumulate in this interval, which is attested to by the wide range of the number of marks (from 1 to 20).

The next size group is as numerous as the preceding, but it does not include young females that have less than four marks of pregnancies. Females, the ovaries of which have 6—9 marks of pregnancies, are encountered more frequently in this group (50%).

The majority of females are 10.1—11.0 m long (two size groups). They are still capable of bearing young, since the average number of marks of pregnancies is 5—9.

There are relatively few females 11.1—11.5 m long: it is difficult to isolate among them specimens with the highest rate of occurrence of marks of corpora lutea. The females of this size group as well as those of the next (11.6—12.0 m) have almost lost their childbearing capacity. The maximum number of pregnancy marks was noted in females of these size groups. For instance, females 11.2 and 11.6 m long had 19 and 20 marks of corpora lutea, respectively.

In our material the size group of 12.1—12.5 m long was represented by only one barren female, 12.4 m long, with 18 marks of corpora lutea.

The increase of the number of marks of corpora lutea can be followed in the graph (Figure 106).

According to Ohsumi, females may be encountered (though very few among the many examined) in which 24, 25, 30, and even 37 marks of corpora lutea can be counted on the ovaries.

The percentage of pregnant females naturally sharply increases after maturity is reached and reaches its maximum by the age of 7 — 10 years, after which it begins to diminish gradually with age of the animals (Figure 107). The number of annual ovulations also drops with age, and this should be taken into account when working out the breeding cycle.

There are reports on changes in the percentage of pregnant females*
depending on the season and the region. For instance, Ohsumi (1965)
notes about 50% pregnant in May, 42% in September, and 30% in October and
November. The slackening off of pregnant females toward the fall is
explained by the intensification of parturitions in this season in the northern
hemisphere. The proportion of pregnant females may vary by regions as
follows (naturally, in each region the proportion will change also by months):
according to Matsuura, the number of pregnant females off Japan is 33—34%,
in the waters of South Africa 86% (Matthews, 1938), and in the Azores area
only 27%, according to Clarke's calculations (1956). We determined the
proportion of pregnant females in the Kuriles area to be 63%. In this
connection a comparison of percentages in different regions of the World
224 Ocean, which is of definite interest for a comparative analysis of variations
in the state of the breeding part of herds (for example, under the influence
of whaling), must be carried out carefully and only provided that there is
seasonal comparability of the available material.

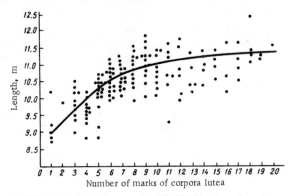

FIGURE 106. Relation between length of body and number of
marks of corpora lutea

Ohsumi (1965) introduced substantial corrections in the determination of
the percentage of pregnant females by his analysis of the essence of the process in time. He showed that it is wrong to calculate the total percentage
of pregnant females under the condition of a 16-month pregnancy (not for
commercial characteristics, but, for instance, for calculating the duration
of the sexual cycle, etc.) in certain, separately taken periods of the season
for the northern hemisphere from May to August, because the figure obtained will include pregnant animals that had conceived already in the
preceding sexual cycle and this leads to erroneous conclusions. Having
made recalculations and having determined the percentage of pregnant sperms
that conceived in the current year (he evidently means in the current
sexual cycle), Ohsumi convincingly showed that in this case the percentage
of pregnant animals, for instance, in the waters of Japan, will be on the
average only 26—29%.

* The percentage of pregnant females was determined from the total number of mature animals. Females
which even in the absence of an embryo show corpus luteum of pregnancy are considered pregnant.

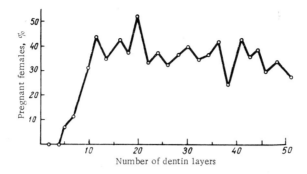

FIGURE 107. Variation in the percentage of pregnant sperm whales with age (Ohsumi, 1965)

225 **Multiple pregnancies.** The presence of more than one corpus luteum on ovaries testifies to more than one ovulation in one period of estrus. Ohsumi calculated that the frequency of occurrence of 2 corpora lutea (determinations in 446 females) is equal to 0.67% (three specimens), and 3 corpora lutea were found in only one sperm whale (0.22%).

Multiple pregnancies are rarely observed in sperm whales, although the number of corpora lutea of pregnancy may not correspond to the number of embryos. In the case of single-ovum twins there may be more embryos and fewer in the case of resorption of one of the embryos in the early stages. Thus Chuzhakina (1955) notes that out of two sets of twin embryos in her material one set was from a single ovum, while in the other set one of the embryos was resorbed (when the length of the second was 95 cm). As early as 1840 Bennett, and also Beneden and Gervais (1880) reported on the birth of twin sperm whales. Matsuura (1935) and Matthews (1938) record that the proportion of females with twin embryos was 0.60% of all pregnant females investigated by them. According to multiannual data of Ohsumi (1965), twin embryos constitute 0.45%. The view has been expressed (Tomilin, 1957) that one of the embryos is resorbed because the female cannot nurse two large calves. However, in our material and in that of IWS twins without any traces of resorption were noted, and frequently not small or medium size, but also large, almost of prenatal dimensions. Thus in the North Pacific in 1965 we found twins, a male and a female 348 and 334 cm long respectively, and in 1968 two male twins 347 and 266 cm long; IWS data give twin embryos 274 and 279 cm long (males), 244 and 152 cm (male and female), and 271 and 340 cm (females). This also indicates that there must be cases of birth of twins. So far it is not known whether the female is capable of nursing two newborn.

According to a report from British Columbia (Canada), on 20 May 1962 a female of 11.6 m with three embryos 270, 183, and 147 cm long (sex not determined) was captured. Still, multiple pregnancies are obviously less common in sperm whales than in baleens, in which, for instance, embryo triplets are encountered quite frequently. Even 7 large embryos, 97–135 cm long, have been recorded in a finback whale (Tomilin, 1957).

The discrepancy between the number of cases of finding two corpora lutea of pregnancy (0.67%) and the number of cases of encountering twins (0.45%) is striking. It can be explained, firstly, by the difficulty of detecting embryos at the very early stages of development, and, secondly, by the possibility of losing large prenatal embryos in the killing and towing of females, particularly if the belly of the whale is opened while still at sea (which is done to cool the carcass by Japanese whalers who are based at shore enterprises (Ohsumi, 1965)).

Not all aspects of the biology of reproduction of sperm whales have been sufficiently studied. This applies primarily to determination of the duration of the sexual cycle, which may last from 2—7 years, depending on age. The periods of pairing and calving in sperm whales are greatly extended, with a peak of pairing in spring and of calving in fall in both hemispheres. After a 16—17 month pregnancy, the newborn has a length of 400—420 cm, with already marked sexual dimorphism in size. Lactation, lasting a year or a year and a half, does not prevent pairing and new pregnancy. Sexual maturity in males is attained at an average length of 9.5—10 m, in females at 8.3—8.6 m in all regions of the World Ocean (at the average age of 5 years in males and 3.5 years in females).

226

Chapter 14

AGE AND METHODS OF ITS DETERMINATION

The material of the present chapter does not strictly belong in this section, but due to the importance of age determination for understanding the biology of the animals, as well as for establishing the effect of whaling on the abundance of herds, a broad discussion of this topic is most necessary. Growth is also considered in this chapter.

The age of many animals can be determined by direct observations of growth and development from birth to old age and death. But there are a number of animals which are either very difficult or almost impossible to keep in captivity, particularly for many years; in addition, continuous observations are ruled out because of their concealed mode of life. All this results in serious difficulties of finding accurate morphological age criteria. The large Cetacea are prime examples of such animals.

The abundance of all herds of commercial species of whales in the World Ocean, particularly of sperm whales, became so drastically reduced a few years ago due to intensive whaling that an immediate assessment of the reserves was called for and determination of their conformity with the level of whaling.

The most reliable concept of abundance and its changes under the influence of whaling would be yielded by a comparison of figures of absolute abundance of whales for a number of years, obtained from direct recordings of whales at sea. However, so far there are no such perfect methods of recording, and therefore no figures for the absolute abundance of the main commercial species.

Study of the age composition of whale herds thus has been and is the only reliable way in which to evaluate the comparative state of their abundance.

METHODS OF DETERMINING AGE

For a long time there was no reliable method for determining the age of sperm whales.

Dewhurst (1834) made the first attempt to determine the age, or rather the growth period, of whales. From the plates of whalebone he established that growth in baleen whales continues for 20 — 25 years.

There was no published data on the age of toothed whales up to the middle of the 1950's except for a communication by Vasil'ev (1891) on the discovery of a harpoon in the body of a not particularly old sperm whale, killed 40 years after it had been wounded (Tomilin, 1957).

The work of a Russian scientist, V. O. Kler (1927), giving methods of 227 finding precise criteria of the age of animals by the so-called isodynamic planes of growth in the compact bone tissues, was of considerable interest in this regard. He was the first to assume that age layers can be found in bones of marine mammals. However this work was not taken up until the 1940's.

For a long time the length of the body was the only criterion used for comparison of individual specimens and groups of whales. Wheeler (1930) asserted that length cannot be an indicator of age and that the use of average lengths can disorientate the researcher. Subsequently many investigators began to compare captured baleen whales according to the number of traces of corpora lutea on the ovaries and the extent of ossification of the vertebral column, using these characters to distinguish various age groups.

The first data on the age of sperm whales and a division into age groups, the time of onset of sexual (according to ovaries and testes) and physical (according to synostosis of epiphyses with bodies of vertebrae) maturity on the basis of graphic relationships by body length were given in a monograph on the biology of sperm whales by Matthews (1938). Even the most perfect methods of age determination by traces of corpora lutea on ovaries can give only the relative and incomplete age (and then also only of females where mainly males are caught commercially). In connection with this, scientists are seeking organs in which age characters could be directly fixed (for either sex). Methods of age determination from plates on the whalebone have been worked out for baleen whales (Tomilin, 1939; Ruud, 1940). Sheffer (1950) calculated the age of fur seals by the thickenings on the roots of their canines, while Laws (1952, 1953) determined the age of the northern elephant seal by counting the number of rings on transverse filings of their teeth, and also mentions the existence of layers in the teeth of the sperm whale. A similar indication can be found in Tomilin (1957).

It has long been known that layers are periodically formed in the teeth of marine mammals. According to Sergeant (1959), Lancaster as early as in 1867 noted layers in the cement in beaked whales. In Beneden's atlas (1868—1879) the lamination is distinctly seen in a figure showing a filing of a sperm whale's tooth.

However, only the investigations by Sheffer and Laws on determination of the age of pinnipeds gave impetus to similar research on Cetacea. Thus, Nishiwaki and Jagi (1953) investigated the growth of spectacled dolphin's teeth. Laws and Purves (1956) suggest a method of determining the age of baleen whales by lamination of the core of an ear plug discovered in the auditory meatus and described by Lillie in 1910. Subsequently this method was improved by many Soviet and other researchers. It is not applicable to toothed whales (including the sperm whale) because of the absence of ear plugs in them and the different structure of their auditory meatus, but the principle is very similar to that of the method of age determination by teeth.

Systematic work on methods for age determination of sperm whale age according to hard bony structures were begun in the Soviet Union in 1957 at the "Aleut" whaling base and in later years continued at processing combines of the Kurile Islands, where it was possible to collect material from females and young animals. Taking into consideration that it is best to 228compare results obtained with different methods, data obtained from an analysis of teeth were compared with results of an analysis of ovaries (Berzin, 1961, 1961a). In addition, since lamination was revealed only in teeth, taking into account the data of Kler (1927) and Chapskii (1952), who examined the possibility of determining the age of pinnipeds according to the compact sections of skeletal bones, we made an attempt to find in the skeleton of toothed whales (including sperm whale) compact bones or at least separate sections of them with growth layers.

Calculation of these layers would have yielded additional material which could be used for comparison with that obtained during the investigation of teeth. We thus made filings of diaphyses of flipper phalanges (which in pinnipeds show age layers) of pelvic bones, sections of upper and lower jaws, and filings of different bones of the fornix cerebri.

The studies showed that the phalanges of the thoracic flippers, remains of pelvic bones, as well as the large majority of other bones of the skeleton of sperm whales have a porous structure without evident lamination. In some compact sections of bones of the fornix no lamination was found on first examination either. Yet it is the bones of the skull that are used for studying the growth periods of other mammals (Kler, 1927). The surface of the sawed section becomes heavily covered with fat during butchering and therefore the structure of the bone frequently cannot be investigated.

A certain uneven lamination was found in filings of the upper jaw and was relatively noticeable on transverse filings of the lower jaw, particularly if performed immediately behind the toothrow, where the bone is still quite thick and at the same time the structure of the bone tissue is not disturbed by the tooth sockets. During 1957—1958 filings of lower jaws from over 200 sperm whales were made (Berzin, 1959, in litt.; Berzin, 1963). A preliminary analysis of this material showed that the layers are usually not sufficiently clear to be able to establish a direct relationship between the increase of their numbers and the dimensions of the body (not to mention that preparation of the filings is very tedious so that this method, even if successful, could not be recommended for large-scale application). Laws (1960) also reports finding layers on the lower jaw of a sperm whale. This work was continued by Nishiwaki, Ohsumi, and Kasuya (1961) for determination of sperm whale age, and by Kleinenberg and Klevezal' (1962, 1968) for determination of the age of dolphins.

Determining age by the teeth. Process of dentin lamination. The so-called prenatal dentin layer is readily seen on a filing of an embryonic tooth; the dentin is quite homogeneous in structure, without any signs of lamination. With the transition from embryonic to postembryonic development as a result of changes in feeding, a line of neonatal dentin is formed (Nishiwaki and Jagi, 1953). After the birth and formation of the neo-natal line in the teeth of sperm whales there occurs a regular formation of dentin layers and a gradual filling of the pulp cavity and deposition of cement from its surface along the entire toothrow. Thus the number of dentin layers in unerupted teeth or, more precisely, in teeth with preserved dentin are equal over the entire toothrow. There are definite differences in the growth and lamination of dentin in various marine mammals. In pinnipeds, and also in most representatives of the family Delphinidae, the layers of dentin are deposited more or less parallel to the outer walls of the tooth, or rather, at a small angle to the axis of the tooth, whereas in the killer whale, for instance, each successive layer goes from the apex to the base of the tooth. With age the pulp cavity gradually narrows and when the tooth ceases to grow, the canal remains, later probably also disappearing.

In the teeth of sperm whales the layers of dentin are laid down at an angle of 15—30° to the axis of the tooth in early and adult age (Figure 108),

229

with a gradual increase of the angle to a right angle by the time the pulp
cavity closes (Figure 109) (Berzin, 1961, 1963).

FIGURE 108. Longitudinal filing
of the first tooth of a male sperm
whale 14.5 m long, aged 15 years
(North Pacific, method of Bow
and Purday (1966) using graphite)

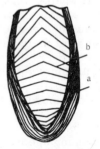

FIGURE 109. Diagram
of the structure of a
sperm whale tooth with
the pulp cavity filled
with dentin (the apex of
the tooth is not shown):

a — layer of cement;
b — layer of dentin.

Selecting teeth for age determination. The differences
mentioned above in the scheme of dentin layers proved to be very significant
for determining the age of sperm whales. For animals in which the process
of dentin deposition is the same as in pinnipeds and dolphins (except beluga)
transverse filings of teeth can be made. This will cross all the age layers.
A transverse filing of a sperm whale's tooth made at any point will not intersect all the layers, and therefore the more laborious longitudinal filing has
to be done. Moreover it is necessary to take only teeth that are not worn
down, i.e., those with intact dentin. Thus, examination of most teeth taken in
1958 (when the method was being perfected) from the middle of the toothrow

230 of the lower jaw (as the largest teeth) yielded interesting data on the growth and wearing of the layers depending on age, but did not show the total number of age layers and so the method was found unsuitable for determining age. This mainly applies to large sperm whales, in which some of the apical layers of the middle teeth, sometimes a very considerable proportion of them, always prove to be worn down (see Chapter 6 and Figures 45, 51). The teeth of the first and last pairs erupt much later than the middle ones, and consequently become worn later. The first pairs of teeth are straight and therefore more convenient for filing than the last pairs of curved teeth of the lower jaw (Berzin, 1961).

The teeth of the upper jaw, recommended by Japanese investigators (Nishiwaki, Ohsumi, and Hibiya, 1958) to be used for analyzing the age of sperm whales, did not satisfy us because they do not erupt in all specimens and, in contrast to teeth of the lower jaw, unerupted maxillary teeth are not seen from the surface. Furthermore the growth of upper jaw teeth terminates early, so that the full age of old sperms is not reflected by them (admitted by the authors themselves). Thus the first (or the second) pair of mandibular teeth proved to be the most suitable for determining age (Berzin, 1961, 1963). In 1967 Gambell and Grzegorzewska came to the same conclusion.

Methods of counting the layers. The teeth were extracted from the jaw with special chisels (with blades in the form of a groove) or narrow knives. They were then boiled to separate the dense connective tissue and then filed so that one surface passed precisely along the longitudinal axis of the tooth. In AtlantNIRO (Kaliningrad) this operation is carried out with two thin milling cutters attached to one roller, which makes it possible to saw off a plate of any thickness from the middle of the tooth. These plates are convenient for work and storage.

The surface of the sawn-off portions was ground with files and on an emery wheel. Gambell and Grzegorzewska (1967) recommend using river sand. One should outright reject polishing the surface because the visibility of the layers is not thereby improved and counting of them is hampered at different angles to the light.

The filed surface of the axial sawing shows a row of layers and stripes of different width and various shades (from light, almost white, to dark yellow, almost brown). The layers are situated at various angles to the axis of the tooth and form a "little spruce tree" (see Figure 108). On the transverse filing concentric layers can be seen, resembling a section of a tree trunk. Close examination reveals an alternation of relatively wide, light layers separated by sharp, dark bands. One or two or sometimes even 5 bands, less intensively stained and narrower than the layers, are seen inside each layer.

This relationship of tones is preserved only in reflected light. With transmitted light the picture becomes just the opposite: the wide and light layers are seen dark and opaque, whereas the narrow bands appear light and transparent. Thus, the color density of the layers of dentin does not correspond to their optical density. The coloration of the layers in reflected light will be discussed below.

The width of layers of dentin can change somewhat both in different animals and within one tooth. Usually the width of layers of the upper and middle part of the tooth is the same (0.66 mm on the average). As a rule, nearer to the pulp cavity in old animals (i.e., filled with dentin) the

231width of the layer decreases to 0.4—0.3 mm. In females the layers are on the average somewhat narrower than in males (Berzin, 1963).

To avoid confusion we shall from now on call layers only the wide, light bands of dentin, whereas the narrow, dark dentin separating the layers will be termed bands, and the dark, hardly noticeable narrow layers of dentin inside the light layers will be called stripes.

Only the layers are counted when determining age because only they are distributed along the entire length of the tooth with a definite regularity and almost always have more or less definite width. The ridges on the teeth and the layers of cement correspond to them too. All the stripes within the layers are distributed without any evident pattern; their number within a layer may vary and sometimes they are absent altogether (or are not visible). The visibility of the layers is not uniform, in the different sections of a tooth, and therefore the best position to the light should be chosen for each section.

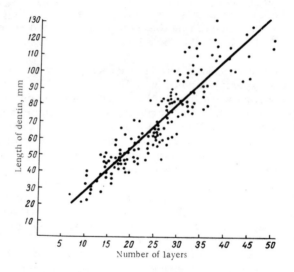

FIGURE 110. Correlation between the length of dentin and the number of dentin layers (age)

Bow and Purday (1966), processed the tooth surface with nitric, hydrochloric, and formic acids and found that a 5% solution of the last produced the best results in improving the visibility of the layers on filings of sperm whale teeth. After the tooth has been kept in formic acid for 30 hours at room temperature and then washed in water, the light and dark layers and the bands look like ridges and grooves. The results of processing carried out by us with this method show its great effectiveness: the layers become well marked and can be counted even in teeth in which they were almost invisible before processing.

The formation of dentin layers proceeds continuously during the life-span of the sperm whale and quite uniformly until the pulp cavity is comple-232tely filled up, and therefore the size of tooth is naturally directly proportional to the number of dentin layers (Figure 110). Thus, knowing the average thickness of the layers (different for females and males) the number of layers, i.e., the age of the animal, can be determined with a relatively small error according to the length of dentin. Of course, it is better to determine age by a direct counting of layers and to use the ratio between number of layers and length of dentin only in determining the age of old sperm whales, in which an insignificant number of the apical layers of teeth are worn down; this ratio can be utilized when the need arises to determine age by the teeth present. In such cases, having determined the approximate thickness of the dentin layers and their angle of inclination, one can as if reproduce the worn part of the tooth and add the number of worn layers to the number counted (Figure 111). This method of age determination has an advantage over that which uses the relief of the whale-bone plates (in whales up to 4 years old, maximum up to 6 years), since here the investigator cannot find out which part of the plate had been already worn down or become broken off (Tomilin, 1945, etc.).

FIGURE 111. Diagram of the possible reconstruction of the worn-down part of a middle tooth of a sperm whale

FIGURE 112. Diagram showing dentin layers united (a) with layers of cement, (b) at the base of the tooth

The systematic lamination of cement, noticeable upon longitudinal and transverse filing, occurs on the surface of the tooth. At the base of the tooth each layer of cement unites with the next layer of dentin at an angle so that the number of cement and dentin layers is equal (Figure 112). As a rule the cement layers are thinner.

After the pulp cavity has closed, the deposition of dentin ceases and determination of age by the dentin layers becomes practically impossible, whereas on the cement surrounding the base of the tooth a certain number of layers can still be counted.

Owing to the curves of the cement layers on the surface, ridges resembling those on the teeth of pinnipeds are formed at the point of junction with the dentin layers. Sometimes ridges are seen over the entire surface of the tooth (Figure 113), but they are usually noticeable only at the very base. Both the cement layers and the ridges are indicators of age, but they are not distinctly noticeable in all teeth (particularly the ridges) and are incomparably less reliable indicators than the dentin layers (Berzin, 1961, 1963).

Etiology and periodicity of dentin deposition. Different coloration or optical density of the dentin layers and bands of the teeth of marine mammals is explained by the different degree of dentin calcination. For a long time there was no unanimous opinion as to which layer is more calcinated, the light, nontransparent or the dark, transparent.

Investigations using various methods of processing the surface of filings have shown that the dark (transparent) bands and strips of dentin are to be 233 considered hypercalcinated (Klevezal', 1963, 1966; Kleinenberg and Klevezal', 1968; our data).

The cause of cyclic variations in the rate of dentin formation in the teeth of marine mammals and the various degree of its calcination undoubtedly lies in the periodic change of the total metabolism (changes in the content of vitamin D, activity of endocrine glands, particularly of the parathyroid, etc.). But these are factors of a physiological nature, directly affecting the activity of the dentin forming cells (odontoblasts), and they do not reveal the main biological reasons for the formation of dentin layers. In order to assert the periods of the formation of dentin layers we must know the main ecological factors which act on the organism and determine endocrine activity, eliciting the formation of additional amounts of vitamin D, etc.

Scientists disagree as to what causes the formation of dentin of different degrees of calcination. For instance, Laws (1953), studying the layers of

FIGURE 113. Age ridges on a sperm whale tooth (male 12.1 m long aged 7 years)

dentin of various structure and the patterns of their formation in the elephant seal (M i r o u n g a l e o n i n a), reports that the light (nontransparent) dentin is formed while the animal is on land, and he conjectures that solar rays (ultraviolet) play the decisive role in the formation of light dentin. Under UV action vitamin D is produced in the organism and this, in conjunction with the parathyroid glands, determines the deposition of calcium in the tissues, here in the tooth tissue.

Fisher (1954) studied the development of teeth and the age of harp seal (P a g o p h i l u s g r o e n l a n d i c u s) and he, on the other hand, connects the intensity of activity of the odonto-blasts with the nutrition of animals in general and with the assimilation of vitamin D with the food in particular. In his opinion this results in the appearance of a wider light (nontransparent) dentin layer in the period of intensive feeding, i.e., during the marine period of the animal. Similar conclusions were drawn by Rasmussen (1957) after studying material on the harp seal, McLaren (1958), using extensive material on the ringed seal (P u s a h i s p i d a) in the Canadian sector of the Arctic, and by Popov (1960), examining the hooded seal (C y s t o p a o r a c r i s t a t a).

In developing this hypothesis, Klevezal' (1963) came to an interesting conclusion; she considers that "the main reasons for different calcination of dentin are not seasonal fluctuations in calcination rate, but regular changes of the growth rate of the organic matter of the tooth in the presence of an equal rate of calcination."

In any case the periodicity of formation of the bands in the teeth of pinnipeds can be considered proved: one layer, consisting of bands of light and dark dentin, is formed per year.

234   No wide, dark layers that would indicate periods of prolonged starvation (as is observed in pinnipeds) are seen in the teeth of sperm whales. Solar rays cannot influence the formation of layers in the teeth of this species, which remains all the time in water; nor does the sperm whale molt, a process which obviously disrupts the calcium metabolism in pinnipeds and

leads, according to most authors, to the appearance of a dark ring of loose dentin.

Researchers who have studied the problems of determining the age of large whales do not give the etiology of the transverse striation of whalebone plates (Tomilin, 1939, 1945; Ruud, 1940, 1945; Nishiwaki, 1950, 1952) or of layer formation in the ear plug (Laws and Purves, 1966; Nishiwaki, 1957a; Nishiwaki, Isihara, and Ohsumi, 1958) or finally of lamination of teeth in the sperm whale (Nishiwaki, et al., 1958); they confine themsleves to mentioning the presence of regular annual migrations in whales.

Nishiwaki, et al. (1958) proceeded from an analysis of the number of layers in the teeth of 91 sperms (and by analogy with the finback whale) and calculated that two layers of light dentin are formed annually in the teeth of sperm whales. The same conclusion was drawn from Soviet data (Berzin, 1959—1961).

In 1963 Ohsumi, Kasuya, and Nishiwaki revised their opinion on the periodicity of layer formation and suggested (by analogy with the bottle nose dolphin — Tursiops truncatus) that in the sperm whale less than two layers are formed annually, possibly only one, two-colored dentin layer.

We also renewed our efforts to clarify the rate of dentin deposition in sperm whale teeth. It was decided to trace the course of lamination, i.e., the process of thickening of the growth layer contiguous with the pulp cavity and the seasonality of appearance of layers of various density. For this a large series of teeth from specimens captured between March and October of the same year was divided into groups; teeth received within 15 days of each month were grouped together. From each group 10 − 30 teeth were analyzed. Naturally attention was paid mainly to the teeth of whales which were taken in spring and fall, because the character (color and density) of the summer layer of dentin is unambiguous.

As already pointed out, the thickness of the layers of each tooth is a fairly constant magnitude (it diminishes insignificantly with age). Therefore in analyzing a tooth one can proceed from the fact that the thickness of a light layer that has completed growth (from one dark band to another) must be equal to the thickness of the preceding light layer.

The analysis showed the following. In the first half of March the formation of light dentin in teeth is mostly coming to an end; its thickness is equal to 3/4 of the total thickness of a dentin layer. In the second half of the month the development of light dentin is completed in 41% of the teeth investigated, in 40% of teeth dark bands of various thickness appear, while in 19% of teeth a dark band has already formed and the deposition of light dentin has begun.

In April, in 54% of teeth the deposition of new light dentin had begun (up to a third as thick as that of a complete layer), in 38% the formation of a dark band was ending, and in 80% the dark band had not begun to form yet and a wide light layer was seen. In the first half of the month the number of teeth with a wide light layer increased to 20% and this served as one more proof of the periodicity of formation of layers (see further).

In May, 80% of the teeth examined had a light layer of dentin, the thickness of which reached 1/5—1/3 of that of a complete layer; more than 30% had a complete or almost complete layer of light dentin. Less than 12% of teeth (in the first half of the month) were with a dark band.

235

In June and July 100% of teeth had a light layer of dentin of various thickness; in June, in 66% of teeth the thickness of the layer was about 3/4 (or a bit more) of the thickness of a complete layer, 25% had a light layer of dentin half as thick as a normal layer, and in two teeth the formation of the light layer had just begun.

In August the formation of the light layer of dentin was completed in the majority of teeth examined.

In September there was a layer of dark dentin in 27% of teeth (almost all such teeth were collected in the second half of the month); in the other teeth the light layer was still forming, its thickness hardly exceeding half that of a complete layer in some teeth.

The teeth of whales killed in October are of great interest. In many of the teeth examined that month, formation of the light dentin layer was still being completed; in 57% of teeth a dark band was seen but in 40% (of the total number examined) the light dentin had already begun to appear (its thickness on the average attaining 1/4 of that of a complete layer). Undoubtedly, this was a new light layer which formed after the typical dark band of the fall dentin, since in June, July, and August the thickness of the light layer already considerably surpassed that of the newly formed light October layer of dentin.

Analyzing the material according to the formation of the growth layer in sperm whale teeth by months on the basis of limited knowledge of the ecology of sperm whales, we can state that:

1) beginning approximately from the second half of April a wide layer of light dentin begins to form in the teeth of sperms of the North Pacific. Food is usually abundant at this time and consists mainly of highly nutritious Cephalopoda rich in vitamins including vitamin D (Laws, 1953). It is possibly this that determines the intensive growth of dentin;

2) in the second half of September — first half of October a narrow, sharp band of dark dentin is formed and then another wide light layer which develops intensively on the average up to the second half of March, when it is replaced again with a narrow band of dark dentin;

3) the light layer of dentin of the winter period is similar in character and thickness to that of the summer period. In connection with this we may assume (see Chapter 11) that there is no winter starvation in sperm whales and that calcium metabolism goes on in winter in the same way as in summer. It also seems that the species composition and the quantitative proportion of food items are more or less the same winter and summer. Due to this the question was raised of revising the earlier views on "foraging grounds" of sperm whales, etc. (Berzin, 1963).

Analysis of our data on growth layers confirmed the formation of two light layers per year.

Ohsumi et al. (1963) consider that the dark bands are formed from October to the end of April. However, the authors investigated the teeth of sperm whales taken from April to October, that is precisely in the period of formation of a light layer of dentin and the beginning of formation of a dark band (October). We had data obtained in March—October; analysis showed that all the teeth of animals captured in the first half of March had a light layer of dentin of various width. In specimens taken in the second 236 half of the month 40% of teeth similarly had a light growth layer and even in the first half of April 20% still did not have the dark band. In many teeth of whales taken in the second half of March and the first half of April the dark band had only just begun to be formed and was hardly discernible. All this ought not to have been so in the case of the formation of dark dentin layer in October — April. As has been shown, light dentin began to emerge after the formation of the dark fall band in 40% of sperm whales taken in October. This was no doubt a new light layer being formed after the typical dark band, since in June, July and August a gradual growth of the light layer took place but its thickness already in these months considerably surpassed that of the light (October) layer forming anew.

Japanese researchers, who discovered a dark band of dentin in sperm whale teeth early in October and in November, apparently believe that it is formed in the winter period, and they omit the formation of the light winter layer.

It is important to bear in mind that the teeth of sperm whales differ in form, character of growth, and filling of the pulp cavity as well as in structure of dentin lamination from the teeth of seals and bottlenose dolphins, in which researchers claim one two-color layer of dentin is formed each year. This is not a chance phenomenon and is confirmed by the different ecology of these animals. All large Cetacea perform fairly regular migrations covering considerable distances, while, according to the numerous observations of Essapian (1962), the same bottlenose dolphins are encountered in the same waters during the entire year and no signs of any long seasonal migrations are noted, if we do not count the foraging movements in pursuit of shoals of fish within a range of several miles.

While considering the formation of one two-color layer of dentin a year in the sperm whale tooth, we have to acknowledge that the lactation period, for instance, lasts about two or more years, which contradicts all biological observations. Finally one of the factors negating the possibility of the formation of two layers of dentin a year in sperm whales is, according to Japanese researchers, the good state of sperm whale herds in the coastal waters of Japan, which could not have occurred in the case of two layers of dentin a year. This argument is very doubtful because it is known that some Japanese shore stations (as well as Soviet ones on the Kuriles) have been closed and quotas on sperm whale catches were introduced in 1959. The data of the Japanese themselves show that a shifting of whaling regions farther from the shores of Japan has occurred, resulting from excessive coastal whaling.

It may be assumed that if the suggested periodicity of layer formation suggested by the Japanese were indeed true, i.e., as twice as low a growth rate, with a doubly later beginning of the reproductive activity of females, sperm whales off the shores of Japan would have been completely destroyed long ago.

In concluding that in the teeth of sperm whales less than two layers of dentin are formed a year, the Japanese utilized material from eight tagged specimens the age of which was determined by the teeth of the upper jaw (the accuracy of such determination should be doubted because of the difficulty of counting the layers and the early filling of the pulp cavity). Let us examine the published results which, so Japanese experts believe, confirm 237 the deposition of less than two layers, and possibly of one layer a year.

Firstly, in three sperms the ratio of the number of counted layers exceeded four times the number of years elapsed since the day of tagging. Secondly, the number of dentin layers in the teeth of one specimen was double the number of years elapsed since tagging. Thirdly, the age of four animals was just a little under the number of years determined by the number of dentin layers (accepting the formation of two layers a year), which may be within the limits of the error caused by determining age by the upper teeth. Moreover, in the drawings made by Ohsumi et al. (1963), two or more typical layers were in our opinion unjustifiably fixed in some cases as one layer (according to our counting methods). We think that these authors are wrong to refer to the work by Omura and Kawahami (1956) on whale tagging in order to prove their arguments and to assert that these authors demonstrate a slower growth rate of sperm whales than is generally accepted. Omura and Kawahami (1956) doubted only the concepts (that existed until the age determination method by lamination dentin was worked out) that the whales attain adult size within barely half a year of lactation. Furthermore, Nishiwaki et al. (1958) themselves quite correctly had already utilized the work by Omura and Kawahami for confirmation of the formation of two layers of dentin a year.

In 1967 Gambell and Grzegorzewska, having processed 659 mandibular teeth of sperm whales from the waters of South Africa (Durban) and the Antarctic captured during the entire year, demonstrate very convincingly the formation of two layers annually (2 two-color ones). Dividing the teeth into three groups, they conducted an analysis of formation of the layers similar in principle to the analysis described above; in particular, they traced the formation of the dark layer with respect to the pulp cavity. According to the results of these analyses, a dark band in most teeth (incidentally, the authors do not deny appreciable individual variation) occurs twice during 12 months, at first at the margin of the cavity, then at a certain distance, and finally at a maximum distance (equal, obviously, to the width of the light layer — A. B.) from it. Thus, according to their data, the light bands also increase twice a year.

It cannot be asserted that the etiology of dentin lamination has been fully clarified and the periodicity of deposition irrefutably proved. Possibly, the steady rhythm of lamination (two layers a year) may be disturbed by some factor. This important problem requires thorough investigation.

The appearance of dark stripes inside the light layers of dentin can be explained by the presence of brief periods of reduced feeding, by a disturbance of calcium metabolism with moving from one foraging ground to another, or by other ecological factors affecting the rate of dentin formation and the degree of calcination.

In females no variations were found in the degree of calcination or in the rate of dentin deposition due to pregnancy and lactation. Only after the onset of sexual maturity are there more intensive and frequent disturbances of metabolism (reflected in the dentin in the form of numerous, closely situated, thin, dark stripes). In the first years of life (10 — 12 layers) calcination of dentin in males and females proceeds approximately uniformly, and the difference in calcination of layers in the apical part of each tooth 238 is insignificant (lamination is weakly marked), apparently because the animals are not yet sexually active, and also because in the first years of life, sperm whales for the most part do not perform distant migrations.*

* In many laboratories of the world intensive work on interpreting these stripes is being carried out at present. We may eventually be able to trace by them the manifestation of various biological rhythms in the life of animals. — Editor

Determining age by the lower jaw. Nishiwaki, Ohsumi, and Kasuya (1961) investigated layer formation in the lower jaw of sperm whales and established that the number of layers can be different over various sections: fewer in the anterior and posterior parts of the jaw than in the middle part. They also confirmed the conclusion (Berzin, 1959, in litt.; Berzin, 1963) that the mandibular layers are not pronounced sufficiently clearly everywhere. According to their data, they are most distinct in the area behind the last teeth, in the upper lateral part of the section.

Nishiwaki et al. (1961) perceived a fairly distinct correlation between the dentin layers and the layers of bone tissue of the lower jaw up to the formation of 13 layers on the latter. After this the number of layers in females remains constant (about 14) and does not correlate with the number of layers in the teeth. Judging from one specimen of an antarctic male sperm, somewhat more layers (up to 18) may be formed in males. Thus, these researchers conclude that determination of age according to tissue layers can be carried out only up to a certain age, and in this respect the above-described method is much less suitable (and much more laborious as well) than the method using the dentin.

Determining the age of females by the ovaries. In use for a relatively long time is the method of age determination of females by the number of marks of corpora lutea remaining on the ovaries evidently throughout life and corresponding to the number of ovulations of pregnancies.

In principle the method is simple; the total number of marks of corpora lutea is calculated and, knowing the number of ovulations for a sexual cycle (in the case of induced ovulation, this number corresponds to the number of pregnancies that have taken place), the number of such cycles can be determined. Knowing the duration of the cycle it is possible to determine the number of years during which the female bore offspring since the onset of maturity (or rather, since the moment of first fertilization) until death.

But despite its apparent simplicity, there are very many disputable and unsolved aspects to this method, firstly, because there are various views on the character of ovulation and, in the case of spontaneity, the number of ovulations per sexual cycle has to be determined, and, secondly, the duration of the sexual cycle is considered variously. Taking all this into consideration, one can say that for obtaining accurate results the interval between the appearance of each mark of a corpus luteum must be known

The shortcoming of this method in any case is that it is impossible to determine the exact age of the animal, firstly, because we cannot know how
239 much time elapsed up to the first pregnancy and secondly, because it is impossible to determine how long ago the activity of the ovaries ceased. Moreover, it is impossible to account for a regularity of calving, as periods of calving and the duration of individual cycles are complex and vary during the life-span.

This method of age determination can be utilized as an additional means in comparing the relative age of females from various regions (populations and herds) and by years in the same commercial regions. At the same time, a precise determination of the number of pregnancies and of their periodicity is a prerequisite for establishing the potential and actual breeding abilities of a herd.

DETERMINATION OF THE ONSET OF PHYSICAL MATURITY

In general, an animal becomes physically mature when the organism has completed its growth. Growth comes to an end when ankylosis (ossification) of the greater part of the vertebral column ceases.

The presence of a layer of cartilage between vertebrae serves as a sign that the epiphyses have not completely grown together with the bodies of the vertebrae and ossification has not yet occurred. Toward the onset of physical maturity the layer of cartilage is very thin. After ankylosis, a whitish line passes at the site of union of the epiphysis with the body of the vertebra, but sometimes it disappears without trace.

Flower in 1864 (quoted in McIntosh and Wheeler, 1929) showed that ossification of the epiphyses begins from the neck and tail sections and proceeds from both ends to the middle of the vertebral column. McIntosh and Wheeler (1929) carried out experiments to determine physical maturity in the finback whale and blue whale. Following Flower, they examined only the dorsal and lumbar pelvic vertebrae. Wheeler (1930) continued his work on the definition of the onset of physical maturity in finback whales according to ossification of epiphyses, connecting it with an analysis of traces of ovulation on the ovaries. Emphasizing the difficulty of conducting these investigations (mainly because of the speed of processing the body — even at that time!), he was able to study only three or four vertebrae taken from different sections. He usually examined one vertebra from the posterior end and one from the middle of the lumbar section, one in the thoracic region, and one or two as close to the head as possible. He demonstrated that in some specimens the vertebrae would be united with the epiphysis but the thoracic vertebrae could not as yet.

Having analyzed about 200 finback whales, Wheeler (1930) asserted that the fusion of epiphyses with bodies of vertebrae proceeds at an uneven rate and is completed in the region of the anterior thoracic vertebrae. When the epiphyses of these vertebrae ossify, physical maturity is attained and growth of the animal ceases.

Ohsumi, Nishiwaki and Hibiya (1958) devoted considerable effort to determine physical maturity in finback whales in the northern part of the Pacific Ocean. They analyzed 20 vertebrae (2 — 8 from various sections) and according to their material, no ossification is observed until the onset of sexual maturity. Ossification of the anterior end of the vertebral column begins at the time when the ossification which began from the posterior end of the spine reaches the end of the lumbar vertebrae. The cartilages of the epiphyses of the 3rd — 6th thoracic vertebrae are the last to ossify.

Among the studies on physical maturity of antarctic sperm whales, that of Matthews (1939) deserves mention. Without discussing his unsubstantiated figures of the age of onset of physical maturity (about 8 — 10 years) let us look at the factual data. In female sperms 10.6 m long, the caudal and posterior lumbar epiphyses are anklyosed, while the epiphyses of the anterior lumbar and thoracic vertebrae are still separated from their bodies by thick layers of cartilage. In females 11.5 m long all the vertebrae were ankylosed. Matthews believes that growth of the female ceases at a body length of 11.0 — 11.5 m.

Out of 25 males examined by him, ankylosis was at the initial stage in only two. In one male 15.3 m long the posterior lumbar vertebrae were fully ankylosed, and in the anterior thoracic vertebrae there was still a layer of cartilage, though thin; in a male of 16.7 m the lumbar and the posterior thoracic vertebrae were completely ankylosed, whereas in a specimen 16.6 m long (i.e., very slightly smaller), the posterior thoracic vertebrae were separated by a thick layer of cartilage. Matthews concluded that male sperms continue to grow until they reach the length of 16.5 — 17.5 m (or a little less).

Work in this direction but on sperm whales of the northern part of the Pacific was carried out by Kimura (1957), who determined the length of males at the onset of physical maturity to be equal to 15.8 m and of females 10.9 m. Nishiwaki, Ohsumi, and Hibiya (1958) did not conduct any investigations of their own but, using the data of Kimura on the length of sperm whales at physical maturity, connected length and age data and came to the conclusion that sperm whales attain physical maturity at the age of "over 18 years."

In the Soviet literature, information on the ossification of the sperm whale skeleton is found in Zenkovich (1952). This author classes whales into four age groups by the degree of skeleton ossification. The characters that he states are specific for the various age groups cannot, in our opinion, be established with modern techniques of whale dressing.

Material collected in the North Pacific (Kuriles region) from 20 sperm whales of which 12 were males and 8 females (most of the material concerning physical maturity was examined by Borisov) shows that males 8.4, 9.8, 11.2, 11.3, and 14.0 m long (age 13.5 years), 14.8 m (age 14 years), and 15.9 m (16 years) were physically still immature.* In a sperm whale 15.2 m long (age 22 years) the 4th and 5th thoracic vertebrae still had sutures. This specimen was close to attaining physical maturity. Only one animal 16.4 m long (age 23 years) was physically mature. Such a result was quite natural; with a minimum number of old males in the whaling region off the Kuriles where these investigations were carried out in 1960 and 1961, the proportion of physically mature whales was also minimal.

Results of investigations of physical maturity of sperm females in the same region are the following: females 9.8 m long (age 8 years), 10.3 m long (age 9 years), 10.1 m long (age 10 years), and 10.2 m long (age 6 years) 241 were physically immature. In a female of 10.1 m (age over 16 years) the posterior cordal vertebra had grown together with the epiphyses, and the last thoracic vertebrae still had a very thin strip of cartilage. Thus, this female was close to maturity. In females 11.1 m (age 15 years), 11.3 m (age 15 years), and 10.9 m long (age 25 years) all epiphyses had grown together with the bodies of vertebrae without the light traces of sutures, i.e. they were physically mature. One female 11.3 m long (age 23 years) was also physically mature although the 3rd — 6th thoracic vertebrae showed scarcely discernible whitish traces of sutures (no suture was seen in the 10th thoracic vertebra).

Analysis of our data suggests that physical maturity in male sperm whales of the northern part of the Pacific is attained at the age of about 23 years. These figures are in good agreement with the material on the cessation of growth of the body, according to which physical maturity is attained at a length of 15.9 m on the average, i.e., at the age of 23 — 25 years (see Figure 115).

* To find out the degree of ossification, parts of some vertebrae were cut off with an axe in various sections of the vertebral column (after the meat was removed from the backbone) and the degree of ankylosis was determined.

245

According to our data, physical maturity in females is attained at the age of about 15 — 16 years, much earlier than in males (Berzin, 1963). The age indicated is somewhat less (by 2 — 3 years) than that of attainment of maturity determined by cessation of body growth (Nishiwaki et al., 1958; our data). This can be apparently explained by the scarcity of data, though such an insignificant discrepancy is of no importance. Introducing some correction into the figures obtained, physical maturity in female sperm whales of the Northern Pacific can be considered to be reached at the age of about 17 years.

These data agree well with the earlier sexual maturation of females in comparison with males.

Some information on the variations in time of onset of physical maturity and the relation between sexual and physical maturity will be dealt with below.

GROWTH

Using data on age determination in sperm whales, let us determine the relation between age and length (Figure 113). Two curves (one for males, the other for females) characterize the growth of sperm whales. It is worthwhile to note that there is a fairly wide range of length variations within each age and the range increases with increasing age.

After birth, males and females grow intensively and in a year reach an average length of 6 m. Thus, the increment for the first year is 170 — 200 cm (Nishiwaki, Ohsumi, and Hibiya, 1958; Berzin, 1963 — 1964). Matsuura (1935) determined the average annual increment for the first year of life to be approximately 120 cm. The figures for increment presented by Sleptsov (1952) differ sharply from these data. In his opinion, sperm whales reach a length of 7.5 — 7.8 m already in the first six months. In the light of recent data this is much exaggerated.

In the second and third year the growth rate decreases and the annual increment is 1 m. The whales attain a length of 8 m at the age of 3 years. After this the growth rates of males and females begin to differ noticeably (see Figure 115). The increment of the female body in the 4th year of life is reduced to 50 cm a year. The main causes of the lower growth rate of females are probably the earlier sexual maturation of females (maturity is attained at the average age of 3.5 years at a length of 8.3 m) and the beginning of breeding. Some females begin to reproduce by the end of the second year and their growth rate immediately slows down. Probably animals that start to breed early do not reach the general average length, whereas the size of females which begin to breed later (in the 4th or 5th year or still later) surpasses the mean.

After females reach 11 m (at the age of about 17 years) growth in length ceases (physical maturity has been attained). The difference in length at the onset of sexual maturity probably also determines the considerable variations in the size of females by the time growth comes to an end.

Laws (1956) asserts that the ratio of the length of the female whale at the onset of sexual maturity to the length after cessation of growth is a constant magnitude. Consequently, the earlier the female starts to reproduce, the earlier growth ceases, and the reverse. This statement fully coincides with our data.

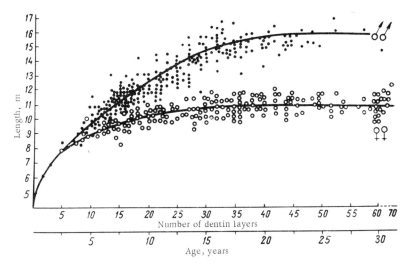

FIGURE 114. Relationship between length of body and age of male and female sperm whales (North Pacific, data of 1957—1960, Berzin, 1963)

If proceeding from this we derive a value for the ratio of the average length at the onset of sexual maturity to the length of the body at the onset of physical maturity in females, the magnitude received will be equal to 72.7%, i.e., smaller than the magnitude presented by Laws (85.1%) and much smaller than the magnitude presented for finback whales (92.4%, after Ohsumi et al., 1958).

The oldest females determined by us were of the following ages (according to layers of dentin): 30 years (specimen 10.9 m long); 33.4 years (specimen 11.4 m long); over 30 years (four specimens 10.9—11.7 m long); over 35 years (two specimens 11.1 and 12.4 m long). The oldest female according to Nishiwaki et al. (1958) was 24.5 years old, and by Ohsumi's data (1965)* 243 32 years old (64 growth layers).

Growth of males proceeds as follows. On attaining 8 m, by which time they have already surpassed females in growth, their own growth rate hardly slows down (about 80 cm a year). After they reach sexual maturity (on the average, at the age of 5 years at a length of 9.5 m) males in contrast to females continue to grow intensively. Having reached an average length 15.9 m at the age of 23—25 years, growth ceases (physical maturity has been attained) (Figure 115), and the length of the body practically no longer correlates with age.

It is known that after physical maturity is attained in animals (the age of which is well established) even a certain decrease in the size of the body is noted. It is of interest that we observed a similar phenomenon in sperm whales. Characteristically, the largest males, 16.8—17 m long, are on the whole somewhat younger than whales 15.5—16 m long; the teeth of the latter also more frequently looked older. A similar peculiarity is apparently inherent also in females.

* Age was calculated in 100 females.

The oldest male sperm whales from Japanese material (Nishiwaki et al., 1958) was 32 years old, i.e., the age limit determined by various authors for sperm whales of the northern part of the Pacific Ocean is approximately the same.

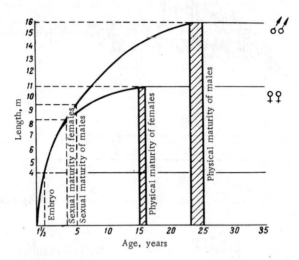

FIGURE 115. Growth of male and female sperm whales, onset of sexual and physical maturity

Analysis of data, particularly comparison of teeth from the oldest animals, shows that 35 years, maximum 40 years, will evidently be the maximum age which can be determined according to teeth because of the closure of the pulp cavity and due to the wearing of the upper layers of dentin. In general, age cannot be determined by very old teeth, or at least only very approximately.

However, the age of sperm whales as determined by us is far from being the limit for these animals, as our observations over many years did not reveal a single male with teeth that were lost or worn down to the gum. Yet such specimens were still caught relatively recently (Sleptsov, 1952). The current absence of sperm whales of an age approaching the natural lifespan can be explained by the intensive rate of whaling in the North Pacific.

244

Chapter 15

MODE OF LIFE

In the present brief survey we will discuss the structure of various groupings of sperm whales of different sex and age and the relations within them, particularly those of behavior connected with prolonged submergence at great depths; the modes of foraging and the causes of stranding will also be examined.

Some aspects of the mode of life have already been touched upon in the chapters dealing with the sense organs, respiration, etc.

Observations on the life of these animals have built up over decades thanks to seafarers, whalers, and naturalists. The works by Scoresby (1820), Beale (1835), Bennett (1840) and Melville (1851) provided a solid basis on which to expand our knowledge on the life of this animal.

STRUCTURE AND SIZE OF GROUPINGS

The structure of a sperm whale herd is determined primarily by the sharp sexual dimorphism in size and by the harem mode of life of the major breeding part of the herd.

Harems usually consist of 10 — 15 (Tomilin, 1957), 20 — 50 (Bennett, 1840), 30-40 (Zenkovich, 1938a) sexually mature females and include at least one male. Up to 50 — 100 females can make up large harems (Matsuura, 1935). Sleptsov (1952) also indicates harems of several scores of females. However, D. Caldwell, M. Caldwell and D. Rice (1966), having critically analyzed all available reports and observations on the composition of harems, doubt that the ratio of males to females in a harem can be larger than 1 — 12. Sometimes several harems are united into a large herd of over 100 animals (Tomilin, 1957), according to Beale (1835), even up to 400 — 500 lat. At the beginning of the century in the waters of Patagonia at 42 — 50°S a herd of 3,000 — 4,000 sperms of both sexes with their young was encountered (Tomilin, 1936).

Naturally, the observer can judge the number of animals in a herd only approximately because in a large herd not all the whales are present at the surface at the moment of observation (Bennett, 1840). Sometimes shoals of 245 females mingle with herds of young males 9 — 12 m long. Frequently there are large males in the mixed shoals but shoals are also encountered consisting only of the males with sucklings (Sleptsov, 1952).

Rice (1963) describes groupings of sperm whales off the coast of California as follows:

1) large herds consisting of 20—50 sexually immature females, pregnant females, lactating females with calves, immature and mature males up to 11 m long;

2) groups including up to 12—15 young adult males (10.5—14 m long), which keep together within an area of 5—10 km³ and migrate together from one region to another;

3) solitary old males 12—17 m long.

Clarke (1956) notes two types of groups off the Azores:

1) herds consisting mostly of pregnant females;

2) mixed herds which include very young but no longer suckling females and males.

According to Matsuura (1935), during hunting in herds, very often four sperms (one adult female and animals of about 4, 7.5—8, and about 9 m) isolate themselves from the main group. This is presumably one family which constitutes the main unit in the herd. Interestingly, similar phenomena probably exist in herds of the white whale (Bel'kovich and Yablokov, 1965).

During whaling in the region of the Kuriles (communication by Skipper Tashcheev) it was noted that sometimes the leader of a normal harem does not stay amongst the females but follows at a certain distance (sometimes up to a mile away from them). In large harems (40—50 females) very frequently 3—4 adult males stay, either leading the females or flanking the herd or else, more rarely, bringing up the herd in the rear, probably as a defense (Beneden, 1889).

It used to be widely believed that large adult males at least 15 m long are the leaders of harems (Matsuura, 1935; Zenkovich, 1938a; Sleptsov, 1952; etc.). However, recently, on the basis of a histological analysis and data of large-scale weighing of testes, it was shown (Berzin, 1963, 1965) that such males show a decrease of testes weight and partial closure of the seminal ducts. Consequently sexual activity declines and these animals cannot possess a large harem herd. The leaders of harems could in this case be males 13—14.5 m long or even shorter but the question arises, how it happens that large and physically stronger animals yield to younger and weaker ones? Rosenblum (1962) assumes that not only younger males but also females expel the old males from the herd. He thinks that the parallel scars on the head of large males are inflincted by the front teeth of females or young and active males. Rosenblum does not exclude either a possible loss of "sexual desire" on the part of large old males.

Beale (1835) presents observations of an experienced whaler, Skipper Newton, who had hunted sperm whales for many years in the region between Peru and California. According to these observations, in the tropical breeding regions no males over 11 m long have ever been seen with females. Groups of larger "bachelors" were seen at a distance of 2—8 miles from groups consisting of females, calves, and small bulls.

246   Caldwell, etc. (1966) also conclude from observations by whalers that old males keep more or less apart from the herd of females, and that the main role in breeding is assumed by young males. These authors doubt the correctness of applying the concept of "harem" to the mode of life of sperm whales, as in a group with females there can be besides large males also somewhat smaller but sexually mature males. Our data of observations and recent whaling confirmed that in mixed groups of the harem type there are frequently no large males at all. This implies that males which have

recently attained sexual maturity participate in breeding. However, it is for the time being difficult to define the structure of sperm whale groupings precisely.

It has not been clarified whether the adult males that leave the harem herds in spring return. Matthews (1938) believes that they do return to the parental herds, but Jonsgard (1960) gives data that refute this.

According to observations, there is a tendency for the number of solitary males to increase farther away from the equator toward the Antarctic. Thus Clarke (1962) calculated that near the equator only 4% of all males remained alone, whereas off Chile and Peru the number of solitary males increased to 56% of all males encountered.

It is known that most males upon reaching a length of about 12 m leave the parental herd and migrate to the colder waters of high latitudes (see also Chapter 10).

Male sperms form groups of a definite size (and age) composition, as already pointed out by Beale (1835); Zenkovich (1934) noted that specimens assemble into groups of one size during migration, which was explained by the need for uniform conditions of swimming during prolonged migrations.

It is thought that one of the main reasons for this grouping together of males of the same size is the nonuniform ability to dive and catch animals of various dimensions (Tomilin, 1957; Tarasevich, 1967), and consequently there are differences in the optimal hunting grounds, which in turn depend on the ecological conditions obtaining in them. For example, in June 1958, during whaling in the region northeast of Cape Olyutorski (in the Bering Sea), the "Aleut" flotilla caught about 80 almost single-sized animals in two days, which constituted the entire catch for this time.

In one-size groupings of relatively small, mature males the animals prove to be close in age, whereas in groupings of large whales (that are of various ages at a uniform length) the animals are sometimes of approximately the same age or of different ages.

In addition, specimens not only of close sizes but also of the same biological rhythm are found in groups as a result of the extended breeding period and the gradual isolation of males of various physiological condition (Tarasevich, 1967).

Observations during hunting in harem herds are of interest. Data presented by one whaler show that females from one region and caught from one herd are mostly in a uniform physiological state, for instance, at the same or a very similar stage of pregnancy.

Recent material (Veinger, in litt.) confirms that the groupings of sperm whales show closely allied relations similar to those noted earlier in the white whale (Bel'kovich and Yablokov, 1965).

247 RESPIRATORY RHYTHM

In the opinion of Tomilin (1957) the most characteristic feature in the behavior of sperm whales in comparison with other large whales is their prolonged respiratory pause during submersion and the numerous spoutings between dives. The duration and depth of diving, all other conditions being equal, evidently depend on the size of the animal (see Chapter 7). As a rule, after a longer submersion there follows a longer stay on the surface, a large number of intermittent dives and spoutings (the exhalations and inhalations necessary for ventilation of the lungs).

Gaskin (1964) considers that the sperm whale plunges to the depths after an interval of at least 10 minutes, during which it lies immobile on the surface as if in a "state of shock." This peculiarity is often exploited by whalers for approaching to shooting distance.

Tomilin (1957) reports that after 50 — 70 minutes' submergence, 45 spoutings were observed in one specimen, and 35 — 40 in another. The same duration of submergence was fixed by Scammon (1874) and Hopkins (1922). There are also communications on an 80-minute submergence (Beale, 1839; A.H. Clark, 1887). We find information in Bennet (1840) and also in Tomilin (1957), based on observations of whalers, on a 90 — 100-minute maximum submergence of isolated specimens. All these figures are established only for large (16 — 18 m) males.

The spoutings (exhalation-inhalation) follow each other at average intervals of 10 — 15 seconds (Tomilin, 1957). Gaskin (1964) reports that undisturbed sperms spout every 25 — 30 seconds. Ashley (1942) mentions a rule noticed by whalers (which is in our opinion unfounded) according to which the number of inhalations and exhalations is equal to the number of minutes spent under water. Scammon (1874) presents the example of a whale which had been under water for 55 minutes and later exhaled 55 times. Davis (1926) believes that after prolonged submergence, a sperm usually inhales 50 — 70 times within approximately 10 — 12 minutes (Beale, 1839; Scammon, 1874).

Tomilin (1957) writes that in different places and at different times the duration of a certain stage of the respiratory rhythm varies in the same animals, apparently depending on the depth of the dive, which is determined by the vertical distribution of food items. On the other hand, for a given place and time the number of spoutings, the intervals between them, and the duration of submergence are sometimes very regular. A more constant respiratory rhythm is characteristic for large animals; they stay longer under water, dive to greater depths, and perform a larger number of spoutings than small whales.

According to Vasil'ev (1891), one sperm whale was not once under water for less than 50 or more than 52 minutes during one day and, having surfaced, breathed not less than 46 and not more than 48 times.

According to Scammon (1869), a large whale taken off the Galapagos breathed in and out 55 times while on the surface for 10 minutes; when diving, it showed its tail, which projected 1.5 m out of the water and the animal disappeared for 45 minutes, producing 55 spoutings afterwards. Thus it continued for five hours, during which the whale moved in a straight 248 course. Another specimen after each dive remained on the surface for 57 minutes (Scholander, 1940).

Small sperms stay under water for less time (about 20 min), and their respiratory rhythm is less regular. Females remain under water approximately the same length of time as males of their size. All animals of one group dive and surface almost simultaneously, staying under water on the average for 20 minutes and, then surfacing to breathe in and out 35 or 40 times within about 4 minutes, Beale (1835) and Scammon (1869) report that females spend more time ventilating their lungs than males. In frightened animals the regularity of the respiratory rhythm is disturbed. Beale (1835) gives an example of a male which was breathing 60 times but on being alarmed, cut the number by half and plunged into the depths. In such cases the animal cannot stay under water as long as usual.

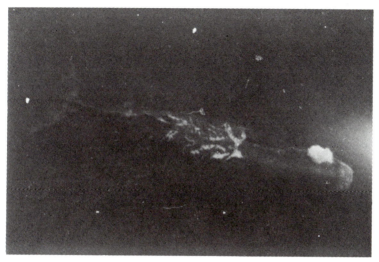

FIGURE 116. A sperm whale which has surfaced. Before the head appears above the water the air can be seen emerging (photographed by Veinger from a helicopter)

According to Beale (1835), with intermediate submersions a ten-second pause between spoutings is divided into 3 seconds for exhalation and 1 second for inhalation.

According to Scammon (1874) and Ashley (1942), sperm whales surface in the horizontal position but in such a way that the highest point of the head (the area of the blowhole) appears above water before the rest of the body. As soon as the blowhole emerges, exhalation takes place.

As a result of observations and experiments with dolphins Tomilin (1947, 1955) came to the conclusion that the act of respiration in Cetacea is an unconditioned reflex which comes into play at the change of the medium from water to air, and he introduced the concept "surfacing reflex." Owing to this, whales can effect exchange of air in the lungs even in the unconscious state (during sleep, badly wounded, etc.). However, Caldwell et al. (1966), referring to available observations on sperm whales, "that deliberately" close their blowhole (Hopkins, 1922; Davis, 1926), particularly during skirmishes, report that sperms can consciously control the respiratory act.

Subsequent observations showed that the animals can actively intervene also at the beginning of the respiratory act. Thus in photos of sperms in the water taken by Veinger from a helicopter (Figure 116), it is clearly seen that in individual cases exhalation begins before the appearance of the head above the surface. Without denying the advantage of such physiological

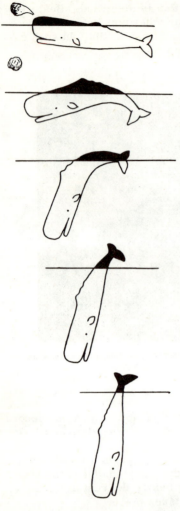

adaptations as the respiratory reflex, we may conclude that the mechanism of respiration in Cetacea, particularly in sperm whales, is still better perfected than has been assumed.

The first exhalation after deep submergence resembles, according to Clarke (1954), the "sound of an explosion" and is heard 250 m away; the following exhalations are not so loud. In our opinion Clarke overestimates the sound effect of the first exhalation, although sounding is like steam ejected from a narrow spout and it can be heard at such a distance (250 m).

The diffuse spouting of the sperm whale is inclined somewhat to the left and forward at an angle of 45°. The height of the jet of air is, according to Bennett (1840), from 180 to 240 cm, according to Hazen (1854), not more than 270—300 cm, according to Ashley (1942) from 300 to 360 cm, and according to Tomilin (1957), from 2 to 5 m. Slijper (1962) points out that the height of spouting depends on the size of the animal but in determining this height an error is usually admitted because of the optical illusion created by the angle of the fall of the jet and by the angle of vision of the observer, but in fact it is higher (up to 5—7.5 m). The spouting of young animals is, according to Tripp (1938), thin and about 30 cm high. A cloud of mist remains for about one second (depending on the weather) after the head of the animal has disappeared under water.

FIGURE 117. Successive stages of submersion of sperm whales (Gaskin, 1964, supplemented by Rovnin)

In all their variety of form and magnitude, the spoutings of whales bear the same physiological character. Their basis is a condensate of air exhaled from the lungs.

According to Bennett (1840), Melville (1851) and Ashley (1942), the air exhaled by sperm whales is "moist and evil-smelling" and irritates the human skin. However, this was not confirmed by our observations and the above reports are probably erroneous.

Before diving into the depths, the body of the animal bends and projects from the water to a much greater height than during intermediate descents (Figure 117); a "hump" is seen on the surface, then the upper part of the caudal peduncle, and finally, as a rule almost straight up (to height of 1.5—2 m) the caudal flukes ("butterfly") are thrust up and the animal plunges steeply (Beale, 1835; Davis. 1926; and many others).

DEPTH OF SUBMERGENCE

The depth to which sperm whales descend has not been fixed by direct observations, so that a discussion can be based only on various indirect data. Finds in stomachs of stones (sometimes many), large, heavy sponges, bottom crabs, and demersal Octopoda, the case of capture by the "Aleut" of a sperm whale on whose lower jaw a pairing of an airplane wheel was tightly clamped (our material), and so on attest to the fact that the animal reaches the very bottom. This assumption is confirmed by the discovery in stomachs of Cephalopoda which inhabit depths of 300 — 400 m (Betesheva and Akimushkin, 1955). However, the most convincing proof of deep submersion are the breaks and damage caused to telegraph cables lying on the seabed.

Heezen (1957) analyzed reports of American telegraph companies in which all cases of disruptions to communication were registered. Damage caused by sperm whales was recorded 16 times on underwater cables 150,000 km long (Yablokov, 1962). Heezen noted six cases of damage to cables at a depth of about 900 m. The maximum depth at which a sperm whale was found entangled in a damaged cable was 1,135 m. A case is known of damage to a cable linking up Lisbon and Malaga 2,200 m down. In this case there was no intact corpse in the cable, but from the character of the damage and the remains of the body it was assumed that here too the culprit was a sperm whale. The animal is assumed to be able to reach still greater depths (Yablokov, 1962). *

SPEED OF MOVEMENT

The character and speed of movement of sperm whales are determined by different factors (feeding, resting, migrating or being pursued). Un-251disturbed, the animal moves at a speed of 2.5 — 3 knots (Beale, 1835; Scammon, 1874; Clarke, 1887; Davis, 1926), calmly and regularly working its flukes. Going at full speed, the whale moves at a speed of 5 — 7 knots. At these and lesser speeds the hump sticks up slightly above the surface and eddies are formed around it. According to the force of these eddies, experienced whalers of the last century determined precisely the speed of the whale's movement even from a distance of 4 — 5 miles (Beale, 1835).

Frightened, pursued, or lightly wounded sperms can develop a speed of up to 7 — 12 knots (Beale, 1839; Bennett, 1840; Andrews, 1916; and others). Upon being discovered, it proceeds in one direction, moves along the surface for a longer time, performs stronger thrusts with the tail, and sticks its head high out of the water (it plays the same role as the prow of a ship), thereby reducing drag and increasing the speed of movement. A speed of 12 knots is maximal (Beale, 1835). Slijper (1962) considers the average speed of movement to be equal to 10 knots and reports that a speed of 20 knots has been observed. We may agree with Gaskin (1964) that an average speed of 10 knots is an overestimate and that a speed of 20 knots can be developed by a sperm only when it is seriously frightened or wounded and only for a short

---

* According to a report by Norris (in litt.), using the method of triangulating location clicks in 1970, American scientists determined the maximum depth of submersion of the sperm whale as 2,500 m. — Editor

time. Bennett (1840), Brown (1887), Davis (1926), and Clarke (1954) also pointed to a maximum speed of 20 knots.

Sperm whales can keep a constant speed and a straight course for a very long time (days on end) (Scammon, 1874).

Foraging sperms generally move slowly, and at random, remaining under water for a long time (Tomilin 1957).

GREGARIOUSNESS

It is known that in the herds of females and young animals (harem type) the herd instinct, or rather the feeling of "comradeship," is strong and the relations of females to young display unusually developed maternal devotion up to self-sacrifice (Dudley, 1725; Colnett, 1798; Beale, 1835; Melville, 1851; Scammon, 1874; and others).

In December 1955, in the area of the central Kuriles, from on board the whaling vessel "Musson" we had the opportunity of observing a group of animals (mainly females) that, disregarding the danger, again and again came up to a fatally wounded member of their group. Nishiwaki (1962) describes a case (and gives a photograph) of how immediately after the largest animal was hurt, a few of its group took up a position with their head toward the injured one, forming, as it were, a gigantic petal. They did not break their ranks despite the fact that the hunt went on. Far Eastern whalers (Kuz'min, in litt.) were witnesses to a similar defense line in 1968 in the northern part of the Pacific, when an obviously aggressive group of whale killers approached the herd (which included young animals). The young were inside a large circle formed by the adults. It is remarkable that terrestrial mammals, particularly hoofed species, act in exactly the same way in similar circumstances. Since time immemorial whalers have utilized this remarkable devotion of sperm whales to one another and, as Beale (1835) writes, have craftily destroyed whole herds by surrounding them with several vessels. Similar indications of this exploitation of the protective instict among the members of a group can be found in Bennett (1840), Olmstead (1841), Jones (1861), Scammon (1874), and Jenkins (1921).

Cases have been described of more active intervention by sperm whales in the fate of "comrade in distress"; for instance, sperms have dived under the ship in order to reach a wounded animal and pull it away from the dangerous spot; in several cases they have broken harpoons, bitten through harpoon lines to free their "comrade", or even attacked boats and destroyed them (Colnett, 1798; Bennett, 1840; Whitecar, 1860; Chatterton, 1926; Murphy, 1947; I. Johnson and E. Johnson, 1959). However, not all such instances can be interpreted as a manifestation of "comradeship." Evidently in a number of cases, sperms, frightened, startled or simply alarmed by the cry of the wounded and the general commotion, may accidentally smash boats.

The maternal instinct is still more strongly developed in sperm whales. There are descriptions of how a female protects or saves her calves. Purrington (1955) presents a drawing (Figure 118) in which a female is shown with her suckling in her teeth, the latter having been pierced by a harpoon, and he quotes the famous whaler Scoresby: "In 1811 one of my harpooners attacked a suckling in the hope that the female would come closer for him to get her. And, in fact, she came up to the boat, seized her calf and dragged

it away from the ship with surprising force and speed for about 600 feet."*
Tomilin (1962) expresses his doubts as to the reliability of this description.
Nordhoff (1895) also describes the behavior of a female protecting her calf.
Canadian whalers knew well (Purrington, 1955) that a female would never try
to escape while her calf is alive and they often used this, taking into
consideration however that at this time she is a dangerous adversary and is
to be treated with caution. Still firmer confirmation of strong maternal
253 devotion in sperm whales is the case of a female following the boat to which
her calf was tied (Robbins, 1899). Scammon (1874) observed how a female
helped her calf to escape by holding it up with her thoracic fins.

(252)

FIGURE 118. Female sperm saves her wounded calf (Purrington, 1955)

On the other hand, there are reports that contradict this self-sacrificing
behavior (M. Caldwell and D. Caldwell, 1966). Cases are known when a
female has abandoned offspring at a critical moment (Bullen, 1899; Whipple,
1955). It is assumed, however, that such is induced by the death of the
calf. In the case of death the female, and the entire herd, abandon the calf
immediately (Davis, 1874; Brown, 1887).

Naturally small calves are confused and remain for a long time in one spot
or near the ship where the mothers are killed (Beale, 1839; Bennett, 1840;
and our observations).

The attitude of females to males in the group also proves to vary. A case
is described where a female did not leave a harpooned male and was also shot
(Pullen, 1899); in all other cases the females did not go near the wounded
males. Yet most observers testify to the fact that if a female is wounded the
males do not leave her despite the presence of a vessel (Davis, 1874).

Young but already sexually mature sperm whales that have left the harem
herds also keep together in large groups but their behavior differs from that
of sperms from family groups. If one of the young is wounded, the rest
display total indifference or move aside. Beale (1835) writes that only once
did he see young sperm whales help each other and only very briefly.

* [Retranslated from the Russian.]

257

Finally, so far it is difficult to explain other than by the herd instinct and the sense of devotion cases when whales have accompanied ships of various classes during actual whaling (the word "pursued" used sometimes has a nuance of aggressiveness and seems less suitable to us). Tomilin (1957) describes a case when the floating base "Aleut" was followed by two males at a distance of 20—30 m during 30 minutes, while before that a large sperm whale moved for some time alongside the cutter "Zyuid."

The simultaneous action of animals of one herd or of one group is characteristic and was noted by whalers long ago (Bennett, 1840). Animals in a group as if at a signal dive in, come up to the surface, and inhale almost all at the same time. Millet (1924) considers that in mixed herds all the animals adapt to the smaller, weaker members of their group and he gives examples of where all the animals of a large mixed herd dived down for only 10—15 minutes whereas individuals could have stayed under for an hour. Synchronized action is especially characteristic during an emergency (Caldwell et al., 1966).

BELLIGERENCY

There have been numerous descriptions and mentions of fierce fights among large males for females. The major weapon of defense and attack in sperm whales is the hammerlike head (Sleptsov, 1952). According to Sleptsov, who described "battles" between males (based on accounts of whalers that hunted off Kurile Islands), during the encounter sperms inflict heavy blows on each other with their forehead (like rams), often leaping out of the water at this time. An accurate and detailed scientific description of 254 this kind is so far not available. Hopkins (1922) describes a case where a male and a female with her calf which were pursued by whalers started moving in the direction of a large herd (about 100 females). As soon as the male approached the herd, another large male left it and rushed toward the intruder "menacingly thrusting his jaws out of the water." They fought jaw to jaw, then drew apart, and again rushed to the attack; the water around them was so turbulent that it was difficult to see anything. Big chunks of flesh and fat torn from their heads were allegedly seen in the water. Both animals flagged; the smaller one (the newcomer) swam slowly away from the herd, and the victor did not pursue it. The larger whale was taken: it had a broken jaw which "was hanging out of its flesh," many teeth were broken, and there were deep wounds in the head.

Two cases of fights between males were observed in the Atlantic by Zenkovich (1962).

COLLISIONS WITH VESSELS AND ATTACKS ON VESSELS

The literature contains many reports on accidental collisions of vessels of different classes with sperm whales (mainly sleeping). We find accounts on similar incidents in Slijper and Utrecht (1959). In 1955, the "Amerskerk," which was moving at a speed of 17 knots, collided with a sleeping sperm whale and cut into it; the animal was killed. The passenger ship "Constitution" in 1956 and the "Prince Alexander" suffered similar collisions with sperm whales. The tug steamer "Zarya" on her way to Evensk also ran into a sperm whale that was lying quietly on the surface, the bow of the tug boat was raised half a meter and the ship listed at 15° (the newspaper "Magadanskaya pravda," July 1956).

According to some observations (Gaskin, 1964), sperm whales apparently out of curiosity come so close to vessels that they are almost pressed to the hull and hence are struck by the propeller. This happened to two sperms that came close up to the "Muiderkerk." A similar incident is presented in Jacques Cousteau's film "The Silent World."

It is hard to say whether the acts of wounded sperms which, having dived with harpoons in their body and coming up under the bottom of the whaling boat, cause damage to the latter, are random or deliberate. We are inclined to believe these collisions as fortuitous, particularly if one remembers that after shooting, the whaling ship proceeds forward and is almost straight over the spot where the sperm whale has dived. Thus, in 1947, off the Komandorski Islands a 17-m sperm whale inflicted a blow on the stern of the "Entuziast" of the "Aleut" whaling flotilla, broke the propeller shaft and damaged the steering. A similar incident occurred in the Antarctic, where as a result of collision with a sperm whale, the "Slava 10" of the "Slava" flotilla was so damaged that it was out of operation for several weeks. Naturally the lighter the ship the more dangerous is collision with a sperm.

In popular literature, or science fiction, particularly in former years, numerous indications, descriptions or drawings can be found of premeditated attacks of furious sperm whales, not only on whaling boats, but also on large vessels. For example, a sperm called "Timor Jack," the hero of innumerable tales, was said to smash every whaling boat sent against him. Sperm whales "New Zealander Jack," "Paita Tom," "Morkan," and "Don Miguel" have also been claimed to have broken many whaling boats.

255 Melville (1851) asserts that a sperm whale sometimes possesses sufficient knowhow and malicious intent to ram, smash, and sink a large ship deliberately, and moreover this was not uncommon practice. Haley (1948), Stackpole (1953), and Zenkovich (1962) support this opinion. Beale (1835), presenting many cases of attacks of sperm whales, nevertheless believes them to be exaggerated. Perhaps Tomilin (1957) is justified when he considers that in the majority of such cases (including also those where the acts of sperm whales seem deliberate) it is just a question of casual buttings by deafened and disoriented animals. In any case, some attacks can be considered to be reliably documented. Thus, for example, the destruction of an American ship, the "Essex," in the Pacific Ocean in 1820. An enormous sperm whale, which happened to collide with the ship's hull and to break her keel, emerged in close proximity and, rushing with "great malice" toward the ship, inflicted a mighty blow with its head. The ship immediately filled with water and capsized. The whale hunters survived and jumped into boats, but only one of these with three men reached the shores of Peru and lived to tell the tale (Beale, 1835; Melville, 1851). A sperm whale twice rammed a large whaling vessel, the "Parker Cook" (Starbuck, 1878). Metal parts and pieces of wood marked with the name the "Ann Alexander," sunk two months earlier, were discovered in the head of a sperm whale caught in 1851 (Zenkovich, 1962; Sawtell, 1962).

In addition, many authors have quite convincingly shown that the sperm whale is the first to attack the approaching whaling boats, ramming them with its head (at this time the jaw with its sharp teeth can be opened so wide that it forms a right angle with the trunk) and thrusting with its tail. The animal comes up to the boat, its head high above the water, or it turns over with its belly up, or lies on its side with its mouth open (Bennett, 1840; Melville, 1851; Hazen, 1854; Scammon, 1874; Hammond, 1901; Beane, 1905; Hopkins, 1922; Ferguson, 1936; Ashley 1942; Haley, 1948; Stackpole, 1963).

If the whaling boat happens to be seized in the jaws in a case of attack from below, the boat can be cut in two. Furthermore, the whale may bite at the debris of the boat it has destroyed (Whitecar, 1860; Scammon, 1874; Brown, 1887; Beane, 1905; Hopkins, 1922; Cook, 1926). Sperms may vary their method of attack. Hopkins (1922) reports that one attacked the boat by biting it with the teeth, but directly after that it attacked another one by ramming it with its head.

CHARACTERISTIC POSES

Sperm whales in nature frequently assume various characteristic poses. According to Beale (1835), an extraordinary sight is a sperm in a vertical position, when its head rises above the water like a "black rock jutting out of the ocean." Near Bering Island Tomilin (1957) also observed for 15—20 seconds the head of a sperm whale stretching out for 2/3 of its length perpendicular to the water surface. And two days later in the same region he spotted a sperm standing vertically with its head down and its tail sticking out of the water. According to Beale, the first pose is assumed when the whale is frightened by something and wants to get a better and a quicker all-round view. Ashley (1942) considers that such a pose is taken up "in anger."
256 Having taken a vertical position, the sperm whale slowly makes a full revolution around its axis. But usually, writes Beale (1835), whales turn on their sides when looking at a vessel. The same was indicated by Gaskin (1964) (Figure 119).

FIGURE 119. Some poses assumed by sperm whales (Gaskin, 1964):

1—vertical; 2—horizontal.

In a state of fright the sperm whale can change its behavior abruptly. Beale describes "sweeping," when the badly scared animal moves its tail from side to side, and if taken on the line, it can coil many meters of it over its body by "rolling over" on the surface.

Though older sperms are not so cautious as young ones (Beale, 1839), in all cases a successful catch* depends not so much on the vessel's speed as on a noiseless and careful approach. Whalers have tried to approach the animals either head on or from the rear as far as possible, even though these are the most dangerous positions; but the men are thus concealed from the eyes of the whale. Haley (1948) writes that the sound of an oar against the boat could put the entire herd to flight and a click of the shutter of an underwater camera could make the animals change their course. Sperm whales are frightened by the noise made by dolphins leaping out of the water (Bennett, 1840). As a matter of fact, the sperm whale has no enemies in the ocean (besides man), and therefore, it can hardly be said that it is the existence of foes that has made these powerful animals so easily frightened in a number of cases.

A scared sperm whale as a rule escapes danger by fleeing from the spot, diving straight down or quickly submerging while remaining horizontal (Caldwell et al., 1966). The latter way is the rarer, as most frequently the whale plunges down. Sometimes it may go halfway to meet the danger, as has already been described, in order "to cross swords with the enemy," or according to reports by Bennett (1840), Bullen (1899), and Kinsley (1884), it may lie immobile "with bated breath" as if paralyzed, sometimes not even reacting to contact.

There are some accounts (with illustrations) about the games played by sperm whales with objects floating on the surface such as boards and logs (Slijper and Utrecht, 1959; Nishiwaki, 1962; Slijper, 1962).

In some cases a sperm whale lying on the surface starts making furious splashes with strong and rapid movements of the tail, and these splashes are seen several miles away; sometimes it will lie immobile, stretching its 257 head out of the water and raising now one and then another flipper. Rovnin observed peculiar behavior of sperm whales in the tropical waters of the Pacific; one threw its tail high and almost straight; however, it did not dive but fell on the water with noise and splashing.

BREACHING

The most striking poses are assumed by sperm whales during leaps especially when they are breaching (Beale, 1839; Bennett, 1840; Hopkins, 1922; Davis, 1926; Gaskin, 1964). Beale (1835) considers that the sperm whale is capable of jumping out of the water only after having descended to a certain depth and gathered momentum by powerful and frequent thrusts of the tail. Probably this opinion is justified in the main, if one remembers that the greater the depth of submergence of the body, the density of which is less than that of water, the greater is the force with which it breaks the

---

* The abundance of references to very old works dealing with the behavior of sperm whales should not surprise a reader familiar with the characteristics of whaling. A long time ago excellent possibilities really existed for observing the whales from sailing boats and row boats in immediate proximity. In addition, one should bear in mind that before the invention of the harpoon gun, whalers were forced to study the peculiarities of the whales' behavior in more detail and more scrupulously not only for the success of whaling but also for their own safety. — Editor

surface. The angle of inclination of the sperm whale's body to the water surface at the point of breaking the latter is about 45°, in which case the tail flukes are parallel to the surface. While falling the animal turns slightly to the side (Figure 120) or onto the belly (Darwin, 1882; Ashley, 1942), or, according to an observation of Rovnin (oral communication), off the Galapagos, onto its tail.

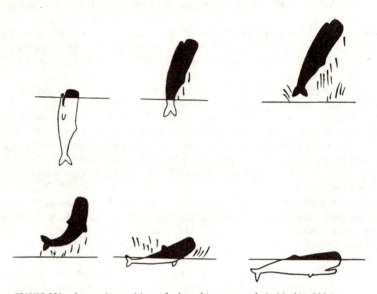

FIGURE 120. Successive positions of a breaching sperm whale (Gaskin, 1964)

A whale can leap out of the water two or three times, and according to Beddard (1900), even four times in succession. Gaskin (1964) believes that the sperm breaches after a particularly prolonged and deep submersion. Most authors consider that the animal does not emerge completely from the water. The splashes are heard up to a distance of 2 miles (Gaskin, 1964) when it is falling into the water and they are seen up to 15 miles away 258 (Scammon, 1869; Beddard, 1900). Darwin, who observed the leaps of sperm whales off Tierra del Fuego, compared the sound to a distant salvo. Beale (1839) assumes that sperm whales free themselves of ectoparasites in this manner, and Tomilin (1957) agrees with this. But it is quite possible that the breachings of whales are (as in many mammals) just an expression of "high spirits" and playfulness.

SLEEP

There have been no direct observations of sleeping sperms. There exists a view (Kleinenberg et al. 1964; Tomilin, 1965), that all Cetacea, including sperm whales, can rest (sleep) at any time of the day or night, remaining for a long time on one spot (the body of a whale, particularly when the lungs are filled with air, has a positive buoyancy and is maintained automatically at the surface). Evidently also, the blowhole, in sperm whales as in dolphins, appears periodically above the surface as a result of feeble movements of the sleeping animal's tail (more rare than during wakefulness). The duration of sleep seems to depend on many factors.

SOUNDS

The behavior of sperm whales indicates that intercommunication is possible (Beale, 1835), moreover in the briefest space of time and at long distance. An alarm signal is transmitted 6—7 miles (Bennett, 1840; Hopkins, 1922; Davis, 1926; Ashley, 1942; Gilmore, 1961). Whales were known to emit sounds even in ancient times, although the sperm whale remained "mute," as far as man was concerned, longer than other animals.

Whalers know well the sperm whale's ability to be very sensitive to sound. For instance, a sperm does not react to the shooting of a tag but at the same time it may become frightened by a sudden splash if a wrongly aimed tag falls into the water; or sperms that do not react to the regularly mounting roar of a motor may be frightened by a sudden change in the intensity of its sound (Beale, 1839; Caldwell, 1966; our observations). The possible reaction of sperm whales to the sound of an oar touching a boat, to the click of the shutter of an underwater movie camera has already been described.

It is also known that stranded animals can emit sounds which, judging from descriptions, vary quite considerably. A herd of 30 females beached on the coast of France gave out a roar that was heard for more than 4 km around (Beddard, 1900). According to Slijper (1955), sperm whales stranded on the Azores uttered loud cracking sounds. Whalers have told that such sounds are distinctly heard in the air under the most varied circumstances (Bennett, 1840), but mainly in cases where animals suffered pain (communications by Latyshev, Zimin, "Aleut" whalers, etc.). Not knowing the source of these sounds, whalers until recently considered that the animals were gritting their teeth.

Worthington and Schevill (1957) described three types of underwater sound emitted by five sperms which were approached by a boat off North Carolina. The first type of sound heard in the hydrophone before the whales became visible resembled low roars at 0.5-second intervals, increasing in intensity toward the end of a series. The second type was like 259 a sharp groan similar to the dry grating of a rusty hinge. Each sound lasted 5 seconds. The most common sounds were like fairly loud, sharp clicks and were produced at intervals of 0.5—0.2 seconds. Researchers have counted up to 73 clicks in succession but usually in series of 20 or about 20. The authors mention that sounds of this type were recorded twice. The famous underwater investigator Haas heard a loud croak when he was taking pictures of the mouth of a harpooned and dying sperm whale in the Azores area. The sound was very strong and clear and was not accompanied by movement of the lower jaw, (Slijper, 1962).

The signals of a wounded sperm whale in Cousteau's film "The Silent World" match Haas' observations. The film shows how other animals approach the wounded in response to its prolonged croaking. But Schevill and Watkins (1962), having made a recording of sounds, consider clicks to be the only type of sound emitted by sperm whales. This was confirmed by the acoustic studies of Backus and Schevill (1966), during which clicks were recorded and analyzed in more than 200 encounters with sperms. The authors give a physical characterization of this type of sound. The clicks are complex in their frequency structure but the predominant frequency of sounds is about 5 kHz with an upper threshold of about 32 kHz. The average interval between clicks varies between 0.025 and 1.25 sec. This means that the degree of repetition of clicks varied from 1 to 40—50 clicks a second (but as a rule not more than 7 per second). The frequency of clicks in series is much lower in sperm whales than in other toothed cetaceans (for instance, in the bottlenose dolphin the frequency of this type of sound reaches 400— 800 per second).

Each click in the sperm whale consists of a series of very short sound pulses. The series studied showed that the number of pulses per click (from 1—9) may vary slightly, as also the duration of the pulses (from 2 to 0.1 ml/sec), the intervals between them (2—4 ml/sec) and the relative amplitude of pulses. The range of duration of each click is 2—4 ml/sec (Figure 121). This multi-pulse clicking has been called by researchers explosive pulse. In cases when one click consisted of a single pulse the number of clicks per second was maximal (up to 50).

Oscillograms have shown that series of clicks differ from specimen to specimen, in other words, a definite individuality is noted. Moreover, although pulses within one click differ, the first pulse of one click resembles the first of the following click, the second resembles the second pulse of another click, and so on.

The high speeds of the sound (1,200—1,500 m/sec) make it an operative source of information which can be coded in length, frequency and periodicity of signals (Kleinenberg, et al., 1964). Vision is less important to sperm whales than to other marine mammals (along with the river dolphins that live in turbid water). A case is known when a blind sperm whale was captured (Beale, 1835); the animal became blind long before its death, but even so it was in as good condition as other whales of its size. This example shows that in this whale, sight does not play the main role in providing the animal with information about its surroundings. On the contrary, it can be considered that sperms utilize sound on a much wider scale and much more sensitively than other marine mammals.

260   Undoubtedly, sperm whales as well as their small relatives the dolphins utilize various types of sound for general orientation (navigation). By means of echo signals sperms obtain the information on the distance of the shore, depths, and bottom relief necessary for guiding them to the goal, as well as information on the appearance of food items.

Experiments and observations on dolphins have shown that the accuracy of such information is unusually high and diverse. Backus and Schevill (1966) consider that the explosive character of the impulses noted by them is the most suitable for echolocation.

Deciphering the significance of the physical characteristics of a particular signal is of great interest. Considerable success has already been achieved in deciphering signals uttered by small whales in captivity. In analogy with dolphins some authors (Kleinenberg et al., 1964; Backus and Schevill, 1966) consider the clicking and crackling sounds in sperm whales to serve for the precise hydrolocation necessary when feeding, particularly in deep waters. From an analysis of various acoustic properties of the sound produced by sperm whales Backus and Schevill (1966) conclude that a sperm can locate squid at a distance of up to 400 m. These authors were the first to note also that oscillograms of consecutive clicks are similar in one animal but vary in different specimens. The authors suggest that the individual variations noted in clicking, as well as the recorded short, irregular transmissions repeated several times during some tens of seconds in a corresponding set of circumstances (the boat is surrounded by 20 sperms), imply that this type of sound is utilized by the whales not only for echo sounding but also for diverse communcation among the members of a herd.

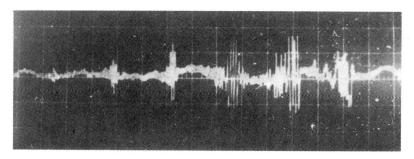

FIGURE 121. Oscillogram (phonogram) of the click of the sperm whale (after Backus and Schevill, 1966)

We can be confident that many types of sound produced by sperm whales which, as in dolphins, serve as SOS, feeding, nuptial, and other signals, will be discovered, recorded and deciphered.

Tomilin (1965) assumes that the underwater acoustic channels, in which particularly favorable conditions are created for the passage of sounds (minimum absorption) that have been discovered in oceans, can serve for the long-range orientation necessary during migrations. Sounds can pass more or less fully intact through these channels for up to several thousand kilometers.

It has been suggested that ultrasound be used not only as a means of location and information but also as a type of fishing gear.

FEEDING HABITS

The hunting tactics of the sperm whale have long been discussed. Beale (1835) thought that on reaching a definite depth the animal stops, opens its mouth so that its lower jaw can make a right angle with the upper jaw, and stays put in this position. Squid, fish and miscellaneous items are attracted by the light-colored palate, the tongue, and particularly by the glistening teeth. Strange though it may sound, this fantastic hypothesis found many supporters.

Tomilin (1936) considered that the sense of touch is of great significance for sperm whales when catching food. Sleptsov (1952) suggested that the whale "listens in" to its prey and then follows it with its eyes. These and numerous other similar theories are on the whole attempts to explain some-how or other the methods the sperm uses to obtain food in the depths. For instance, it is quite obvious that in the eternal darkness of the deeps (according to Matsushita, 1955, feeding goes on more intensively precisely at night) only objects that emit light can be noticed (and this cannot be said about the organs of the oral cavity of the sperm whale). But even if the conditions of illumination were more favorable, the position of the whale's eyes is such that they do not meet the elementary requirements for the detection of food items. The sperm's eyes are situated practically flush with the body and along its sides, so that there is a dead area in front of the head exactly near the mouth (Ashley, 1942; Mann Fischer, 1946; Slijper, 1962; see Figure 88).

Thus, with this situation, at a depth of some 100 m both prey and hunter probably are invisible to each other. Moreover, squid are known to be much more mobile than sperm whales. For instance, even small squid can develop speeds of up to 40 km an hour (Zuev, 1964) and larger specimens still higher speeds, far outdistancing sperms.

But the mystery of how this whale feeds deepened in view of the following circumstances. To support his hypothesis described above, Beale (1835) gives an example of a capture of sperm whales in normal condition, one of which was blind while two others had deformed jaws. Bullen (1899) also has similar descriptions. Up to 10 sperms with badly deformed jaws were recorded in our materials. These were in the same condition as all the other animals and had well filled stomachs, the contents of which did not differ qualitatively from those of other sperm whales caught the same day.

All who have witnessed considerable deformation of the lower jaw never noted any effects of these injuries on the condition of the animal.

The observations testify also to the fact that old sperms which have lost teeth or have teeth worn down to the gums, as well as young immature specimens with unerupted teeth, feed normally (Scammon, 1874; Gelett, 1917; David, 1926; Sleptsov, 1952; our data). Caldwell et al. (1966) and the authors of the present monograph also confirm that even the bodies of large squid and fish as a rule display no traces of a sperm whale's teeth (see Chapter 6).

All the above suggests that neither the teeth nor the lower jaw need to participate in obtaining food and in the digestive process.

Obviously, we do not know enough of the ecology of sperm whale feeding. We can agree with Caldwell et al. (1966), because they ascribe the main importance in the process of swallowing to "sucking" movements of the tongue. But this naturally does not provide a solution to the main aspects of feeding as a whole.

When ultrasound of echo-sounding frequencies was discovered in small toothed whales, numerous experimental confirmations and subsequent proof of the directional focusing of the sound beam made it clear that the sperm whale can find food even in complete darkness. This provided a clue to solving the mystery of the blind specimen described by Beale.

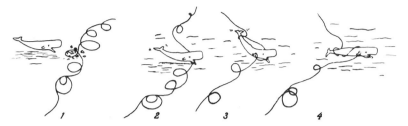

FIGURE 122. Hypothetical scheme of how a sperm whale comes to be entangled in a telegraph cable lying on the bottom:

1 — the animal is swimming above the bottom; 2 — the lower part of the body enters a loop of the freely lying cable; 3 — it attempts to get free, and flipper and tail are caught by the neighboring loops; 4 — completely entangled, the whale dies on the bottom (Heezen, 1957).

In 1963 Bel'kovich and Yablokov suggested a calculation according to which at superhigh frequencies, for instance, 186,000 kHz emitted by dolphins, acoustic pressure must be created on account of considerable intensity of the ultrasonic beam. It has been calculated that an intensity of sound of $10\,\mathrm{W/cm^2}$ in water corresponds to an ultrasonic pressure of 6.5×10^6 dyne/cm^2 (about 6.5 atm). Concentrating a sound of this intensity on a selected object, the animal can create short-term pressure which must act as an ultrasonic blow capable even if briefly, of halving stunning, and paralyzing the object. So far there have been no such calculations of the intensity of ultrasound emission by sperm whales, but if theoretical calculations are confirmed (i.e., if the hypothesis of an "ultrasonic beam" is justified), it will be proved that due to the structural peculiarities of its head, the sperm whale is characterized by very powerful and exact ultrasonic emission.

FIGURE 123. Two variants of entanglement in underwater telegraph cables:

1 — a sperm which became entangled in 1940 off Peru at 830 m; 2 — a sperm which became entangled in 1931 off Ecuador at about 900 m (Heezen, 1957).

With the confirmation of ultrasonic attack on mobile prey, the process of acquiring food will become clear (particularly in a case of food capture by a sperm with a badly injured, inoperative lower jaw). So far the hypothesis of the "ultrasonic beam" has not been refuted; it even explains much from the point of view of the quite specific ecology of the species.

Thus, in the light of available data and hypotheses, food capture by sperm whale is visualized as follows. Having dived, the animal covers several hundred meters, investigating the surrounding waters by echo sounding with ultrasound of varying frequency (for dolphins it will be from 12 to 170 kHz) and intensity. Analyzing the returning signals, it receives the most detailed information on the objects around it. If the animal dives to the bottom, it swims with wide-open mouth (underwater cables damaged by sperms were usually coiled round the lower jaw (Figures 122, 123)). When mobile squid and fish are discovered, the ultrasonic beam narrows and focuses on them, its frequency sharply increases, and the prey is stunned and then seized.

APPROACH TO SHORES AND BEACHING

The steeper the coastal slope, the closer to shore the sperm whale comes. Though possessing perfect orientation in water, sperm whales nevertheless, like many other toothed whales, find themselves periodically stranded on the shore in groups or singly.

The literature is full of descriptions, enumerations or mentions of isolated and mass beachings of sperm whales on the shores of almost all continents (Lillie, 1915; Tomilin, 1937, 1957; Gilmore, 1957, 1959; Caldwell, Inglis, and Siebenaler, 1960). The British Museum of Natural History even issued periodically special surveys on whales, including sperms, stranded on the coast of Great Britain (Harmer, 1927). Detailed accounts are presented by Beddard (1900) and Boschma (1938). Sometimes such occurrences have enabled the boundaries of distribution to be more accurately defined, especially in the case of females with young (for instance, the stranding of one female on the shore of St. Paul Island).

Magnus (1651) gives the first reliable report of a stranded sperm in the 13th century.

Among the first cases recorded is that of a sperm whale beached in November 1577 on the shores of Holland in the lower reaches of the River Schelot near Antwerp. Sperms came aground on the coast of England in 1606, 1626, and 1646. Strandings on the coast of Norway were observed in 1713, 1780, and 1849. *

In 1723, 17 specimens, males and females, became stranded in the mouth of the Elbe. Mention of this is made by Beddard (1900) and many others.

Up to 1938, 44 cases of beaching were recorded (after Boschma) only on the coast of Denmark. Six cases of stranded sperms were reported on the North Sea coast of Germany in 1575, 1604, 1721, and 1762.

In 1788 twelve males were stranded in shallow waters in the Thames estuary. In 1863, five sperm whales entered the mouth of the Loire and after three days got stranded on a sandy strip. On the coast of France sperm whales were stranded in shallows in 1741, 1761, and 1769. In March 1784, 32 animals, most of them females, came up on the sand in a harbor in Brittany during a strong southwesterly wind.

In Ireland three times sperm whales were stranded (one each time) on the shallows on the eastern coast; no exact dates were indicated for the first two, the third was in 1961. In 1695 three strandings in shallows were observed in Ireland and one each in 1750, 1766, and 1889.

---

* All information on beachings without reference to a source is quoted after Boschma (1938).

Harmer (1927) tells of three cases of beaching, in 1913, 1916, and 1917 on the English coast.

In 1890 a young male came aground near La Rochelle (Bay of Biscay). In July 1937 two males got stranded near Dunkirk. Other cases were noted on the Provence coast in 1856 and 1862.

In 1555 near Trieste, strandings of sperm whales were recorded; some years before this a sperm was stranded in Etruria (in Traviska); its skeleton was exhibited in Florence. In the same years a sperm whale came aground near the River Arno in Tuscany and in 1601 another one on the eastern coast (Ancona). There were fourteen cases of beaching on the coast of Italy between 1715 and 1874. In 1903 the body of a female was discovered on Lipari Island (Tyrrhenian Sea, off northern Sicily).

Twice sperm whales were stranded on Tenos Island; the latter case was recorded in 1840. One case was noted near Alexandria in 1838.

Beaching of young sperms in the 1830's was observed in Bermuda and near New York. In 1842 a female got stranded on the shore in Vineyard Sound. At the end of the 18th and beginning of the 19th century sperms came aground off Madras (Bay of Bengal) and three got stranded on the coast of Ceylon.

Lillie (1915) describes the beaching of 36 males and one female on the vast sandy beach of Perkins Island off Tasmania in February 1911.

On the northwestern part of North Island (New Zealand) 27 females and young were stranded in 1895 and 25 sperms 6.7—13.7-m long in March 1918.

In January 1954 an 11-m specimen was found stranded in shallow water at the entry into a swampy reach of the Fasna River near the village 265 of Malaya Bodiena "on the small shore." In November 1955 a sperm whale 12 m long was moving with great difficulty in the direction of the village Zhoal toward a large sandy shallow area above a depth of about 3.5 m. It was killed by fishermen in canoes by means of hand harpoons after a three-hour battle; the whale could not "effectively defend himself" because the struggle was going on in very shallow waters (Cadenat, 1956).

In the northeastern part of the Pacific on the eastern side of the Gulf of California, nine sperm whales 10.6—13.7 m long, including seven males, in April 1953 found themsleves stranded on the shore (see Figure 125); in December 1954, one male 13.1 m long, was beached on the western side of the same part of the gulf. In January 1954, 22 males from 10.7 to 12.2 m long were stranded on the western side of the lower part of the gulf (Gilmore 1957, 1959).

In the Gulf of Mexico a case of stranding of a large male was noted in the middle of March 1910 in Port Arthur (State of Texas).

Sixteen sperms were stranded in early February 1888 in the northwestern Atlantic on Cape Canaveral, Florida (Gilmore, 1959). Later 3 specimens were beached on the coast of Florida; and another male, also here, in August 1939, and another one 14.6 m long in the winter of 1955, as well as a suckling about 5.4—5.8 m long in December 1957 (Caldwell, Inglis, and Siebenaler, 1960).

In 1919 a male came aground on Saint Pierre Island, and in 1914 one on St. George Island; it was here that in May 1923 three males were beached (Dallas Hanna, 1924).

In mid-July 1881, one suckling 610 cm long was beached on the western shore of Unalaska Island (Turner, 1886, quoted in Tomilin, 1957).

Cases of stranding are known on the coasts of the Soviet Union. In October 1928, a sperm was beached not far from the mouth of the Zhupanov liman on an underwater sandbar (Tomilin, 1957). In September 1932 a sperm whale was reported to have been stranded on the shore of the Kanin Peninsula.

In 1955 a female about 8 m long was found on the shore in the region of Bobrovye Stolby on Mednyi Island (Komandorski Islands).

In summer 1957 on Iturup Island (Kuriles) a large sperm entered Kosatka Bay. A group of scientific workers of TINRO (Belkin, in litt.) watched the animal come in close to the shallow coastal waters, and despite the still decreasing depth, move nearer and nearer to the shore, where the whale processing plant "Kosatka" is situated, until it could get no farther (Figure 124). The whale was killed in the shallows and taken to the plant.

In the late fall of 1964 a large specimen was discovered in the northern part of Tatar Strait in the shallow waters of Sakhalin. The animal was pulled onto the shore with a tractor.

As evident from the above, stranding and beaching of sperm whales are fairly frequent phenomena, and many researchers even consider them usual (Gilmore, 1959).

Since sperm whaling is not carried out in all regions of habitat or in all seasons, whereas of the animals can be stranded anywhere at any time, such cases expand our knowledge on the boundaries of distribution in general and in different seasons, and also enables us to assess the age- and sex-dependent features of distribution, etc. In view of this, such cases should be described in as much detail as possible.

The elucidation of the reasons for stranding (sometimes en masse) of these highly organized animals, which have a perfect echolocation apparatus that permits them to orientate themselves well in the water, is of greatest importance.

266 Various explanations have been given. Gilmore (1959) assumes that strandings are determined by the following:

1) the strong herd instinct and the presence of group leaders;

2) the sensitive nervous system (panic overtakes the animals as an unconscious, blind reaction to some unknown cause);

3) inability to live in shallow waters.

Stranding is assumed to result mainly from the first and third factor.

Frazer attributes the phenomenon to the shifting of food items driven to the shore under the action of strong winds; the pursuing whales thus also enter the danger zone.

The essence of beaching was understood and experimentally confirmed by Van Heel (1962), who showed that almost all the strandings of whales occur on coasts with a very gentle slope or on muddy shores, in which cases the direction-finding echo either comes from all sides or is absent. It is this that causes total loss of orientation. The author also points out that the wind and waves contribute to disorientation by roiling the sandy or muddy bottom; suspended particles interfere with obtaining a clear echo. A ship's sonar, utilized by Van Heel especially for these purposes, helped to arrive at these conclusions.

Tomilin (1965) considers that the main reason that entire herds of whales are beached is that they receive distress signals from one or several whales that are already stranded and rush to their aid. Tomilin in this case demonstrates this blind mutual assistance on the example of Black Sea dolphins,

267

FIGURE 124. Moment of stranding of a large male sperm in Kosatka Bay (Iturup Island, Kuriles; photo by Belkin)

pilot whales, and small killer whales. One can see that essentially his hypothesis, analyzed and supplemented by the latest data, represents the first of the reasons indicated by Gilmore in 1959.

Bel'kovich et al. (1967) also state that a whale, on finding itself on the shore, gets into a panic and sends a distress signal to its "comrades," which then rush into the same trap.

Supporting Van Heel (1962), we also analyzed all the cases of strandings, most of which (those pertaining to sperm whales) are described above.

Upon examining descriptions of places of strandings, it becomes clear that in all cases without exception they have occurred in various kinds of shallow water-sandy bars or shoals, lowland and swampy river estuaries, flat, sand or pebble beaches (Figure 125). In fact Van Heel only confirmed the effect, well known to navigators and radar operators, of a weak acoustic or electromagnetic echo from a very gently sloping shore. Even with the most perfect direction-finding devices in these cases accidents cannot be excluded. It is true in this respect that the devices have an essential advantage in that the point of pulse emission is higher, and therefore the angle with the reflecting plane is larger.

Some suggestions may be given to explain on the surface incomprehensible behavior of animals that go aground. Apparently, when the sperm whale touches the bottom with its belly (and probably even before) it will already be too late to avoid complete stranding because in order to turn round it needs a considerable depth under it to be able to curve its body in the vertical plane. Thus, the whale will continue to move toward the shore and the amplitude of flexures of the caudal peduncle will now decrease. The animal will proceed all the while the water level gives the possibility of forward movement with the locomotor organ of such a principle of action. It is this inexplicable striving to get out of the water as far as possible on the shore that surprised witnesses of the death of whales: observation of the entry of a sperm into Kosatka Bay on the Kuriles (personal communication of Belkin) and another case on the coast of Africa (Cadenat, 1956).

Bel'kovich et al. (1965, 1967) note that oceanic species of Cetacea living far from the shore are more frequent victims and explains this by the fact that the dive of the coastal species is steeper (and the locator in this case operates like an echo sounder). In our opinion this is not correct, because sperm whales dive no less steeply. No doubt, species inhabiting coastal waters have developed perfect adaptations which enable them to live near the land that is so dangerous for them which naturally could not be developed in the oceanic species, particularly in sperm whales. For instance, Van Heel (1962) determined that in the turbid waters of shallows it is better to utilize 268 sounds of lesser intensity for orientation and that (Belkovich et al., 1965) the bottlenose dolphin, which is not afraid of shallows, acts accordingly in turbid water, namely, emits signals of lesser intensity in comparison with those produced in clear water. Naturally, a sperm whale lacks such adaptation. (Is this not why sperms, while hunting at the bottom, sometimes snatch inedible objects?)

FIGURE 125. Beached male sperm whales on the shore of the Gulf of California in 1953 (Gilmore, 1957)

As to mass strandings of sperm whales, it may be assumed that animals that have rushed to aid their fellow in distress in answer to its call fail to get the warning signal (echo) and find themselves in an invisible trap without reaching the original victim. Thus, the cases of beaching confirm once again the presence of direction-finding devices in toothed whales but they do not testify to disruption of their function as has been thought by some specialists.

Despite the information gathered over the centuries, the mode of life of sperm whales is little known. "The living whale. . . . is only to be seen at sea in unfathomable waters" (Moby Dick). Man is still forced merely to construct theories of what goes on under the water. Nevertheless, what we do know confirms the presence of a high level of mental and adaptive organization.

Chapter 16

ENEMIES, DISEASES, PARASITES

ENEMIES

Discussing possible enemies of sperm whales, one could say that the killer whale might be a real foe. Yet so far there has been no mention of remnants of sperm whales having been found in the stomachs of killer whales (Tomilin, 1957), and the latest Japanese and Soviet findings also do not indicate this. The few cases of attack of killer whales on newborn sperms (in spite of the active defense reflex of the herd) reported by scientific workers (Kuz'min, in litt.) and whalers operating off the Kuriles are too rare for us to brand killer whales as serious enemies of the sperm whale. Large individual male sperms are too strong for killer whales and thus immune to attack while a herd possesses a sufficiently strong instinct of mutual aid to give them protection. Beale (1835) does consider the killer whale as an enemy and also swordfish.

Gigantic squid could be considered hypothetical enemies of sperm whales. Guided by mollusks already measured (18 m long) one could presume that in confrontations between small sperms whales and such Cephalopoda, the chances would be equal for both. Still, it will be a long time before this question can be settled.

DISEASES

The diseases of the sperm whale, as of other large whales, have not been studied in detail.

Cases of periostosis with strong curvature of the lower jaw have been
269 described (Slijper, 1936; etc.). In our material we twice found (in 1958 and 1965) sperm whales with a shortened lower jaw (Figure 126) and bony tumors on the vertebral column. Curvature of the spine was noted in 1965.

In 1957 a subdermal tumor, 130 cm in diameter and 70 cm high, was found in the region of the caudal peduncle in a large specimen. Upon dissection, a large amount of serous fluid exuded and necrotized muscles and vertebrae were exposed. However, it is possible that the tumor was formed as a result of a trauma caused by a harpoon because there was a scarred wound about one meter from the tumor (in the direction of the head).

In 1961, in a female 11 m long taken in the area of the Kuriles, a tumor of about 40 cm was noted in the middle of the vagina, completely closing

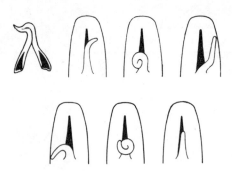

FIGURE 126. Forms of lower jaw injuries in sperm whales (data of various authors and our own)

the lumen. In 1966, in the histological laboratory of the territorial hospital, a tumor on the surface of a mammary gland was examined; it was found to be benign. The tumor covered the nipple with large, hard swellings of dense connective tissue with horny epithelium.

Cockrill (1960) writes that histological examinations of various tumors in sperm whales did not show metastasis, and the encapsulation of tumors is the general trend in whales. The same author noted hemangioma of the liver and chronic tonsillitis in the sperm whale.

In 1966 in a section containing around 10 renculi taken for radiological analysis from a sperm whale captured by the whaling flotilla "Vladivostok" in the northeastern part of the Pacific, one calculus was discovered in each of three renculi; the calculi resembled peas in size and form and were dark gray (oral communication by Doroshenko). Kleinenberg (1956) gives similar indications of urinary calculus in dolphins.

In 1968 on the mother ship "Dal'nii Vostok" a large (up to 70 cm) round swelling with osseous walls was discovered in a sperm whale (Figure 127).

27

FIGURE 127. A cyst isolated from the kidney of a sperm whale (North Pacific, 1968; photo by Blokhin)

It contained a greenish fluid. A renal cyst had presumably developed.

One old male specimen showed traces (scars) of myocardial infarction, in the region of the interventricular septum, and in all whales investigated (sperm, gray, sei) phenomena resembling arteriosclerosis were discovered (Truex, Nolan et al., 1961).

Dental caries have often been described in sperm whales (Pouchet and Beauregard, 1899; Mackintosh, 1919; Keil, 1935; Yablokov and Berzin, 1961). We examined and analyzed ten teeth of sperms at various stages of the progressive decay of dense tissues (Figure 128). According to tentative calculations, one or two carious teeth are found in one out of 8—10 specimens. They are not observed in such numbers (or not at all) in an examination of the oral cavity because caries and cavities develop mainly beneath the gum.

Carious teeth are encountered more frequently in old or, at any rate, fully adult animals. All such teeth were noted only in the lower jaw and as a rule in the middle or in the posterior part of the toothrow. Carious processes go on more intensively in dentin. Analysis of the material and comparison with various theories of the origin of caries in animals made it possible to draw a number of conclusions on the origin of the disease. It is still not clear whether caries are an endogenous or exogenous disease. In sperm whales they are probably of endogenous origin (Yablokov and Berzin, 1961). A chemical-bacteriological origin in the sperm whale is hardly likely, 271as carious cavities usually occur deep under the gum. Furthermore, caries hardly occur in the zone of the possible over-growth of teeth, where naturally the best conditions exist for the development of microorganisms. The marked cleanliness of the oral cavity, which is continuously being washed, and the practical impossibility of food being retained, let alone decaying, in the teeth also speak against a chemical-bacteriological origin of the disease.

(270)

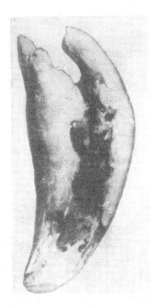

FIGURE 128. A carious tooth of a
male sperm whale (North Pacific)

FIGURE 129. An anomalous tooth with
spreading base filled with osteodentin
(North Pacific)

We noted a case of overgrowth of osteodentin (osteodentin is very often present in a certain amount both in the dentin and in the dental papilla), resulting in deformation of the base of the tooth (Figure 129).

We should also mention again here the well-known find of a sperm whale with a spongy mass instead of eyes (Beale, 1835) (see Chapters 9 and 15).

According to Peele (1932), small skin ulcers are found on sperms which have ambergris in the intestine; however, this has not been confirmed by numerous recent observations.

In large specimens the entire surface of the body (without any definite localization) displays deep pustules, which are usually small (average size 1 — 1.5 cm); sometimes their margins are turned outside.

PARASITES*

Ectoparasites are represented in sperm whales by whale lice, Copepoda and Cirripedia, and by microscopic unicellular algae (Tomilin, 1957).

The lice that are parasitic in sperm whales include the genus C y a m u s, with three species, C . b o o p i s, C . c a t a o d o n t i, C . b e h a m o n d e i,

(272)

FIGURE 130. P e n a l l a on the skin of a sperm whale (North Pacific; photo by Veinger)

(272)

FIGURE 131. Cirriped C o n c h o d e r m a on the teeth of a sperm whale (North Pacific; photo by Veinger)

---

* In this part of the chapter organisms that settle on the body of the whale without using it as food are also described.

and also N e o c y a m u s   p h y s e t e r i s   Buzeta.   Matthews (1938) discovered representatives of C y a m u s in more than half of the animals he
examined in the waters of the southern hemisphere.   According to latest data,
whale lice occur in sperm whales inhabiting all the oceans of both hemispheres
(Buzeta, 1963).   These ectoparasites are generally localized in the region of
the genital and anal openings, more rarely on the remaining surface of the
body.   The areas favored by C y a m u s are open skin lesions, scars,
etc. (Matthews, 1938).

   P e n e l l a   b a l a e n o p t e r a is one of the copepod ectoparasites.
According to published data, it is rarely found on sperms in the southern
hemisphere.   Matthews (1938) observed P e n e l l a on the head and flanks of
one male from the Durban area.   In the northern hemisphere P e n e l l a was
found on a sperm whale from the Adriatic (Pouchet and Beauregard, 1889).
In tropical waters about 20 specimens of P e n e l l a   s p . were taken from one
sperm whale.   In the North Pacific, P e n e l l a (Figure 130) has been discovered on sperm whales repeatedly and in large numbers.   Omura (1950)
considers that this species is more abundant around the Bonin Islands than
in other regions.   He reported that usually not more than a dozen or so are
found but in the region indicated there were up to 50 specimens of P e n e l l a
on individual sperm whales.

   Among the Cirripedia, species of C o n c h o d e r m a occur most frequently
in sperm whales; some are almost always found on the teeth of jaws;
sometimes large specimens are encountered (Figure 131).

273   Freund (1932) mentions two species of C o n c h o d e r m a :   C . v i r g a t u m
and C . c u v i e r .

   In 1958 we took from the body and head of a sperm whale 14.2 m long,
captured in the area of the Komandorski Islands, some ectoparasites which
had not been noted before that were similar in principle to P e n e l l a but
showed some differences.   As Tomilin reported (1962, see Figure 130),
they proved in fact to be P e n e l l a , but densely overgrown in the upper
part with different-aged (different-sized) Cirripedia (C o n c h o d e r m a
v i r g a t u m).

   Clarke (1966) later noted that C . v i r g a t u m can attach itself also to its
relative C . a u r i t u m but prefers P e n e l l a .   According to Clarke (1966),
C . a u r i t u m parasitizes on the average in 2.5% of sperm whales from
various regions (2.2% in the Antarctic, 1.8% in the subtropical and tropical
waters, of Peru, Chile, and South Africa; females from these waters show
4.1% infestation).   The typical site of infestation with C . a u r i t u m are the
teeth of deformed jaws as well as teeth that do not enter the recess of the
upper jaw.   In several cases the lower jaw was the site of attachment and in
one case the penis.

External overgrowths

   Diatoms thickly cover the skin of whales.   On the skin of sperm whales
there are a greater number of forms in summer in cold waters than on the
skin of rorquals; Nemoto (1956) attributes this to the rough skin and to the
great depths to which this whale dives.   Almost all sperms examined by
Matthews (1938) that had been captured in waters of high latitudes

(South Georgia Island) showed diatom film. On the other hand, this author emphasizes that such film is absent on animals from South Africa waters. All investigators note the almost regular presence of a certain amount of diatom overgrowth on sperm whales from cold waters of the northern hemisphere. Nevertheless, the sperm whales are on the whole encrusted with diatoms much less than baleen whales.

The overgrowth usually takes the form of yellow, gray, green and brown spots 2—5 cm in diameter. Small spots are sometimes fused into irregular patches. The spots are situated on various parts of the body without covering large areas. The frontal part, the lower jaw, the neck folds, the anal region, and the dorsal fin are covered most frequently. The back, sides, and flukes are rarely affected (Klyashtorin, 1962).

Coceoneis ceticola, f. costricta predominates among the diatoms; it was encountered in 22 out of 47 animals examined. It is often found with Stauroneis aleutica and C. ceticola var. arctica (Nemoto, 1956; Klyashtorin, 1962). Among the less common species are Nitzschia closterium and Navicola sp. (Matthews, 1938). The latter occurs also on sperm whales from the northern hemisphere (Tomilin, 1962) in which Sinedra sp., Licompofora sp., and Plimosigma sp. are also found (Klyashtorin, 1962).

Other parasites are lamprey, which attach themselves to sperm whales but quickly leave (according to our observations) the bodies of dead animals, and also shark suckers (North Pacific).

274 Helminths*

It is not clear who was the first to record parasitic worms in the sperm whale but it is known that during the 19th century five species of helminths were discovered: Phyllobothrium delphini (Bosc, 1802), Anisakis dussumierii (V. Beneden, 1870), A. simplex (Rudolphi, 1809), Bolbosoma brevicolle (Malm, 1867), and B. capitatum (Linstow, 1880), parasitizing in whales including the sperm whale.

In the 1930's Baylis (1923, 1922) described two species of nematodes: Anisakis physeteris Baylis, 1923 and Anisakis catodontis Baylis, 1929, which are specific parasites of the sperm whale. Of course, these were random finds and naturally did not give an idea on the specific composition of the helminth fauna of this whale.

The development of whaling, improved dissection methods, and the special investigations undertaken in recent decades have certainly contributed to a more comprehensive study. During the last 20—30 years most of the species of worms parasitizing in this animal have been found with the participation of Soviet helminthologists, who have specially investigated marine mammals in both hemispheres and determined 19 species of helminths out of the 29 listed in current descriptions of parasites of the sperm whale. Soviet scientists were also the first to describe 12 species

---

* This part was written by Doctor of Biological Sciences Prof. S. L. Delyamure and Candidate of Biological Sciences A. S. Skryabin.

out of 19 (Gubanov, 1951; Gubanov in the monograph by Delyamure, 1955; Mozgovoi, 1949, 1953; A. Skryabin, 1959, 1961, 1966).

In 1946, on the initiative of Academician K. I. Skrjabin, the Helminthological Laboratory of the Academy of Sciences of the USSR organized the 260th All-Union Helminthological Expedition (CGE) to the Pacific to study the parasitic worms of commercial marine mammals. Participants P. G. Oshmarin and N. A. Shigin dissected sperm whales among other Cetacea (Oshmarin, 1951). According to CGE data, Mozgovoi (1949) described two new species of Anisakis from sperm whales: A. s k r j a b i n i Mosgovoy, 1949 and A. i v a n i z k i i Mosgovoy, 1949. The same author also published (1951) results of studies on Ascaridina collected by the 260th expedition.

In 1951 Gubanov investigated the helminths of whales from the Kuriles and dissected 76 sperms. While processing the collections, he made an extremely interesting discovery by disclosing in the placenta of a sperm whale the largest of all known nematodes, which he described as a representative of a new species and a new genus, P l a c e n t o n e m a g i g a n t i s s i m a Gubanov, 1951. Having investigated all the material, Gubanov established five more new species of parasites for the sperm whale, and the original descriptions were published with the author's agreement in the monograph by Delyamure (1955). This book is the first summary on helminths of Pinnipedia and Cetacea in the world literature. Descriptions and drawings of 18 species parasitic in sperm whales are presented, including Z a l o p h o t r e m a c u r i - l e n s i s Gubanov in Delyamure, 1955 (Trematoda); T e t r a b o t h r i u s c u r i l e n s i s Gubanov in Delyamure, 1955, T r i g o n o c o t y l e sp., P h y l l o - b o t h r i u m d e l p h i n i (Bosc., 1802), D i p l o g o n o p o r u s sp., H e x a g o n o - p o r u s p h y s e t e r i s Gubanov in Delyamure, 1955 (Cestoda); A n i s a k i s c a t o d o n t i s Baylis, 1929, A. d u s s u m i e r i i (Beneden, 1870) Baylis, 1920, A. i v a n i z k i i Mosgovoy, 1949, A. p h y s e t e r i s Baylis, 1923, A.
275 s i m p l e x (Rud., 1809) Baylis, 1920, A. s k r j a b i n i Mosgovoy, 1940, Anisakidae g. sp. (Figure 132), P l a c e n t o n e m a g i g a n t i s s i m a Gubanov, 1951 (Nematoda), B o l b o s o m a b r e v i c o l l e (Malm, 1867) Porta, 1908, B. c a p i t a t u m (Linstow, 1880) Porta, 1908, B. p h y s e t e r i s Gubanov in Delyamure, 1955 (Acanthocephala).

Analyzing his own and published data, Delyamure presented a faunistic and zoogeographical survey of the helminth fauna of the sperm whale.

In 1955, A. Skryabin investigated 140 sperm whales taken in the Kuriles area. In addition to already known species he found two new ones: the cestode T e t r a g o n o p o r u s c a l y p t o c e p h a l u s Skrjabin, 1961, which proved to be a representative of a new genus, T e t r a g o n o p o r u s A. Skriabin, 1961, and the nematode A n i s a k i s p a c i f i c u s A. Skriabin, 1959. It was also he who was the first to find the Acanthocephala B o l b o s o m a t u r b i n e l l a (Diesing, 1851) Porta, 1908 and C o r y n o s o m a s t r u m o s u m (Rud., 1802) in the sperm whale, as well as the larvae of cestodes Tripanorhyncha g. sp. and Tetraphyllidea g. sp. Skrjabin gave a survey of helminths of sperm whales inhabiting Pacific and Far Eastern waters.

Studying the helminthological collections from sperm whales in the southern hemisphere, Markowski (1955) recorded the cestodes T e t r a b o t h r i u s a f f i n i s (Lönnberg, 1891) and P r i a p o c e p h a l u s g r a n d i s Nybelin, 1922 and larvae of Tetraphyllidae g. sp.; Clarke (1962) recorded the cestode-diphyllobotriid M u l t i d u c t u s p h y s e t e r i s Clarke, 1962.

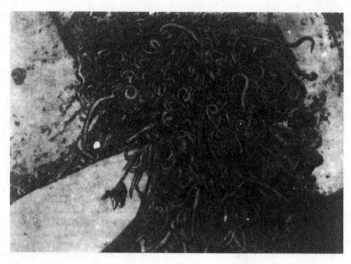

FIGURE 132. Anisakidae in the stomach of a sperm whale (photo by Skryabin)

During the 1963—1964 and 1965—1966 whaling seasons Skryabin investigated the helminth fauna of marine mammals from the Antarctic on the whaling base "Sovetskaya Ukraina." Among other commercial species of whales he studied 681 sperms. The extensive helminthological material collected by Skryabin in the southern hemisphere is still being processed but two new species of parasitic worms of the sperm whale have already been described, the cestode Polygonoporus giganticus Skrjabin, 1967 (new genus 276 Polygonoporus Skriabin, 1967) and the acanthocephid Corynosoma mirabilis Skriabin, 1966. Skryabin was the first to find in the southern hemisphere the acanthocephalid Bolbosoma physeteris Gubanov, in Delyamure, 1955.

Thus by 1967 Soviet and other researchers had recorded Trematoda, Cestoda, Nematoda, and Acanthocephala in the sperm whales of the World Ocean, altogether 29 species, including larval forms. Their descriptions are given below.

Trematoda

Order **Fasciolata** Skrjabin et Schulz, 1937
Family **Campulidae** Odhner, 1926
Zalophotrema curilensis Gubanov in Delyamure, 1955 (Figure 133:1)

Host: Physeter macrocephalus L. — sperm whale.
Localization: bile ducts.
Distribution: Sea of Okhotsk (Kuriles).
Description of species (after Gubanov from Delyamure, 1955. Abridged).
Elongate, leaflike. The cuticle is covered in the anterior half of the body with small spinules which become fewer toward the posterior end. Body

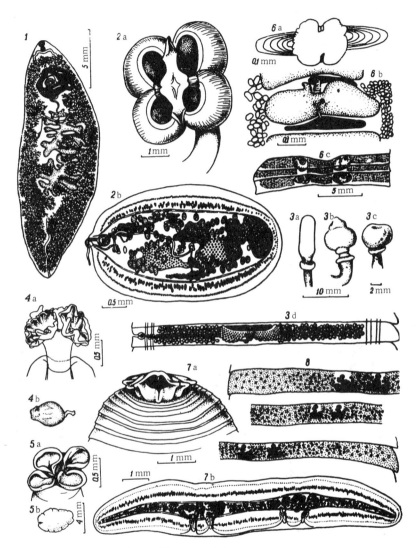

FIGURE 133. Helminth fauna of the sperm whale

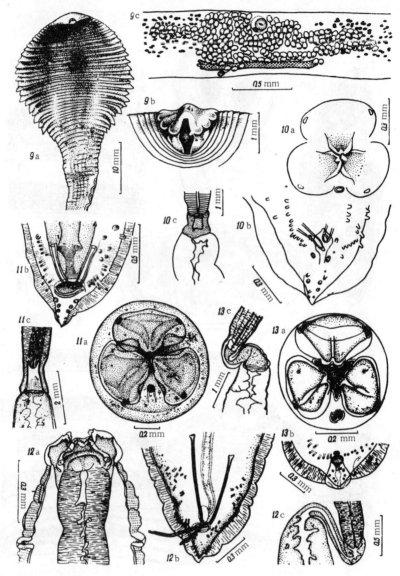

FIGURE 133. (Cont.)

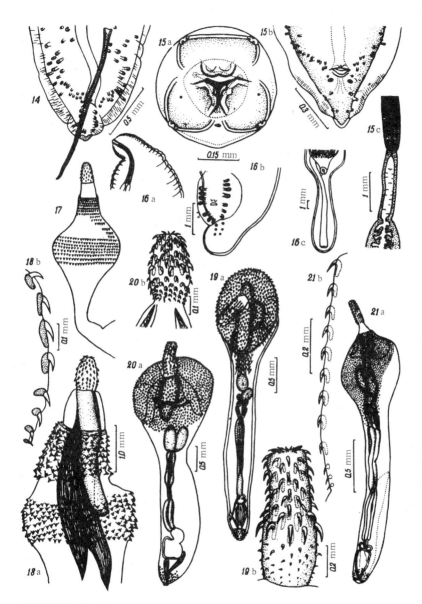

FIGURE 133. (Cont.)

18.0—22.5 mm long, maximum width 5—7 mm. Oral sucker terminal, 0.2 mm long and 0.60—0.64 mm wide; abdominal sucker with a diameter of 0.8—0.9 mm, situated in the first third of the body. Prepharynx absent. Pharynx 0.54—0.56 mm long, 0.40—0.44 mm wide. Esophagus absent. Two branches of the intestine originate directly at the pharynx and extend to the posterior end of the body. Median and lateral diverticula branch off from the intestine.

The genital opening is situated medially, 0.40—0.58 mm in front of the abdominal sucker. Bursa 1.2 mm long and 0.3 mm wide, situated to the right of the abdominal sucker. Testes deeply lobate, situated in the second third of the body on the midline. Anterior testes 2.5 mm long, and 2.5—4.1 mm wide, posterior testis 2.4—6.0 mm long and 2.6—3.6 mm wide. Ovary lobate, 0.5—1.2 mm long and 1.5—1.9 mm wide, lying in front of the anterior testis. Mehlis' gland 0.4 mm in diameter, situated at the posterior margin of the ovary. Vitellaria consisting of individual groups of follicles. They are fused in the anterior part of the body between the pharynx and the anterior loops of the uterus. The posterior boundary of the vitellaria is situated at a distance of 0.3—0.6 mm from the posterior end. The uterus lies between the abdominal sucker and the ovary. Eggs 0.080—0.090 mm long and 0.050—0.060 mm wide, oval in cross section.

Cestoda

Order **Cyczophyzzidae** Beneden, in Braun, 1900
Family **Tetrabothriidae** Linton, 1891
Tetrabothrius affinis (Lönnberg, 1891) Lönnberg, 1892 (Figure 133: 2 a, 2b)

Hosts: Balaenoptera borealis Less. — sei whale; B. musculus — blue whale; B. physalis (L.) — finback whale; Physeter macrocephalis L. — sperm whale.
Localization: intestine.
Distribution: Europe (off Norway), South Africa (Capetown), New Zealand, Antarctic.

280   **Description of species (after Delyamure, 1955. Abridged).** Length 20—39 cm. In some specimens the body is almost cylindrical, in others dorsoventrally compressed. Maximum width of the body of compressed specimens 6.0—6.2 mm at a thickness of 2.0—2.6 mm; contracted specimens are 3.1 and even 3.6 mm thick. Scolex with four muscular, deep, cup-shaped suckers. The length of the scolex is 1.88—2.0 mm, its width 3.2—3.8 mm. At the apex it is rectangular, 2.2—2.8 × 3.1—3.8 mm. The apical organ is situated on its upper surface. A neck is not expressed. Length of segments in middle third of body 0.140—0.157 mm at a width of 4.298—4.375 mm. In the posterior third of the body the segments increase greatly in length and at the same time become narrower: length 0.787—875 mm, width 1.750—2.350 mm. The strobila of sexually mature forms consists of several hundred segments. Musculature well developed (particularly the inner longitudinal layer).

Testes numerous, oval, 0.086—0.105 × 0.157—0.192 mm. Bursa almost spherical; when the cirrus is evaginated, it is 0.210 mm long and 0.175 mm wide. Cirrus without armature.

Female genital system in the hermaphroditic segment consisting of ovary, vitellarium, Mehlis' gland, uterus, vagina, and tubular uterine organ. The ovary is drawn out along the width of the segment and is situated ventrally. Vitellarium compact, located in front of the ovary, directly at the layer of circular musculature. Vagina beginning near the Mehlis' gland and extending to the side of the segment. Near the bursa it expands, describes several loops, and enters the genital cloaca. Uterus laid down in the form of a transverse tube; as it is filled with eggs, it acquires a saclike form, widens, and eventually occupies almost the entire segment. Eggs 0.021 — 0.030 mm long and 0.013 — 0.016 mm wide.

Tetrabothrius curilensis Gubanov in Delyamure, 1955

Hosts: P h y s e t e r   m a c r o c e p h a l u s L.
Localization: small intestine.
Distribution: Sea of Okhotsk, Pacific Ocean (region of the Kuriles).
Description of species (after Gubanov, in Delyamure, 1955). Length 1.02 — 1.97 mm. Scolex with four deep cup-shaped suckers. Laterally its length is 1.113 mm; apically it has the form of a rectangle 3.67 × 3.27 mm (in this case the suckers are 1.78 mm long and 1.47 mm wide). Scolex arranged on the thin, dorsoventrally compressed neck, which is 0.58 mm wide. Hermaphroditic segments 0.71 mm long and 3.10 — 4.51 mm wide, ripe segments 0.73 long and 5.77 mm wide.

About 80 — 89 testes are scattered on both sides of the segment. Bursa oval, 0.126 — 0.147 mm long and 0.105 mm wide, almost spherical in ripe segments. Cirrus smooth. Genital cloaca long and muscular; bursa emptying into its bottom.

Ovary 1.05 — 1.32 mm long, with a maximum width of 0.315 mm, with small lobes departing in various directions. Vitellarium lobate, situated ventral to the ovary, 0.630 — 0.672 mm long and 0.168 — 0.210 mm wide. Mehlis' gland oval, 0.105 × 0.097 mm. Vagina emptying into genital cloaca, ventral to the bursa. Uterus laid down in the form of a transverse sac, eventually forming diverticula. Eggs 0.012 mm long and 0.010 mm wide.

281 **Priapocephalus grandis** Nybelin, 1922 (Figure 133: 3a, 3b, 3c, 3d)

Hosts: P h y s e t e r   m a c r o c e p h a l u s L. — sperm whale: B a l a e n o p-
t e r a   b o r e a l i s Less. — sei whale; B . m u s c u l u s — blue whale; B.
p h y s a l u s — finback whale; E u b a l a e n a   g l a c i a l i s   a u s t r a l i s
Desm. — right whale.
Localization: intestine.
Distribution: South Africa, Southern Scotland, Southern Georgia, Azores.
Description of species (after Nybelin, 1922. Abridged and supplemented). Strobila markedly dorsoventrally flattened, ribbonlike, comparatively weakly velate. The largest of available fragments with a scolex reached a length of 85 cm, with maximum width 12 mm and thickness 2 mm. Ripe segments are usually 0.4 — 0.5 mm long and 5 — 6 mm wide. Scolex strongly widened anteriorly, conical, acorn-shaped or flattened-spherical. The following part tapers stalklike and is surrounded by a circular expansion resembling a

285

collar. Length of scolex (including the ringlike ridge) 6.5 mm, maximum
diameter of widened anterior part 3.7—4.0 mm, that of the collar 3 mm. The
anterior end of the scolex up to the ridge is embedded in the intestinal wall
of the host, in which case the ridge may act as a sucker; the scolex is very
difficult to separate from the host tissue. Longitudinal muscle fibers
arranged in numerous bundles and singly.

Testes, 0.1 mm in diameter, packed close together in two fields, number-
ing up to 300—400. The bursa cirri is pear-shaped, sometimes even retort-
shaped, 0.23 — 0.26 mm long and 0.10—0.11 mm wide. The cirrus is scattered
with short spines. The vagina opens ventral to it.

Ovary 1.48—1.65 mm wide, slightly displaced porally. Vitellarium 1 mm
wide, situated in the anterior part of the segment. In young ripe segments
the uterus is in the form of a tube drawn out along the width of the segment;
it later widens, more or less displacing all the other organs. Eggs
(Markowski, 1955) 0.083—0.099 × 0.066 mm, with oncospheres of 0.050—
0.033 mm.

Trigonocotyle sp.

Gubanov (1952) found cestodes which he determined as Trigonocotyle
sp. in the small intestine of a sperm whale and Baird's beaked whale that
were captured in the Kuriles region.

Order **Tetraphyllidea** Carus, 1863
Family **Phyllobothriidae** Braun, 1900
Phyllobothrium delphini (Bosc, 1802) larvae (Figure 133: 4a, 4b)

Definitive, intermediate and accessory hosts unknown.
Reservoir hosts: Balaena mysticetus L. — bowhead whale;
Mesoplodom bidens (Sow.) — Sowerby's whale; Physeter macro-
cephalus L. — sperm whale; Kogia breviceps Bl. — pygmy sperm
whale; Grampus griseus (Cuv.) — Risso's dolphin; Delphinus
delphis L. — common dolphin; Tursiops truncatus (Montagu) —
bottlenose dolphin; Globicephalis melas (Traill) — pilot whale;
Leptonychotes weddelli Gill. — Weddell's seal.
Localization: skin, subcutaneous adipose cellular tissue, liver.
Distribution: Atlantic Ocean (Azores, Cape Finisterre, and other points),
Mediterranean (Gibraltar, Corsica), Pacific Ocean (Komandorski and Kurile
Islands), waters of Australia, Antarctic.
Description of species (after Delyamure, 1955. Abridged). Whitish
yellow, irregularly shaped cysticerci, 9—15 mm long, 5—8 mm wide, and
3—5 mm thick. Walls of sac compact and comparatively thick. Inside the
fluid-filled sac the scolex is invaginated; it has four cross-wise diverging
short processes each of which bears one very plicate bothridium 0.678—
0.700 × 0.867—0.886 mm; a round, small sucker of 0.207—0.792 mm
diameter is situated at the base of the bothridia.

Apical accessory sucker is present. Cervix clearly marked in specimens
with extended scolex.

Tetraphyllidae sp. larvae (Figure 133: 5a, 5b)

Definitive, intermediate, and accessory hosts unknown.
Reservoir host: Physeter macrocephalus L.
Localization: subcutaneous adipose cellular tissue.
Distribution: Southern Georgia, Pacific Ocean (Kuriles region).
Description of species (after Skrjabin, 1965). Comparatively small, elongate, white larvae, 4.5 — 5.0 mm long and 3 mm wide. Externally they differ from Ph. delphini in the smaller sac and in the presence of a dense connective-tissue sheath with walls 2.0 — 3.5. mm thick which is formed from the tissues of the host. The scolex is invaginated inside the sac for 2.1 mm. Walls of sac very thick. Scolex with 4 bothridia, 0.50 — 0.58 mm long and 0.45 — 0.55 mm wide, distributed on short peduncles.

No other organs of attachment were discovered on either the bothridia or the scolex.

Order **Trypanorhyncha** Diesing, 1863
Trypanorhyncha sp. larvae

A. S. Skrjabin (1965) found larvae of helminths belonging to this order attached to the stomach wall in sea lion, sperm whale, sei whale and lesser rorqual taken near the Kuriles.

Marine mammals probably become infested with these parasites while feeding on cephalopods and teleosts, which are frequently invaded by larvae of Trypanorhyncha.

283 Order **Pseudophyllidea** Beneden, 1850
Family **Diphyllobothriidae** Luhe, 1910
Diplogonoporus sp.

In the bile ducts of a sperm captured near the Kurile Islands (Sea of Okhotsk), Gubanov (1952) found fragments of a diplogonad cestode without scolex, and of course could not determine it accurately.

Multiductus physeteris Clarke, 1962 (Figure 133: 6a, 6b, 6c)

Host: Physeter macrocephalus L.
Localization: bile ducts.
Distribution: Antarctic.
Description of species (after Clarke, 1962. Abridged). A specimen with scolex was examined the strobila of which consisted of three fragments with a total length of 18 m without the terminal segments. Segments velate. Behind the scolex they are 3.5 mm wide (maximum width 3 cm). Ripe segments about 8 mm wide. The spherical scolex is 1.5 mm wide and 1.2 mm thick; it bears on the ventral and dorsal surfaces deep bothria, the margins of which are brought close together at the base of the scolex. The scolex overhangs the first segments.

Longitudinal musculature very powerful, its fibers gathered into two layers lying in the cortical parenchyma; the ventral layer is better developed. In a fully developed segment there are about 185 muscular bundles constituting the inner layer of the dorsal cortex and a small number of them in the ventral cortex. In ripe segments the inner and outer layers of muscles are separated by the vitellaria. The transverse musculature is not gathered into bundles and is less developed. Dorsoventral fibers are situated between the longitudinal muscles.

The excretory system, situated in the medullary parenchyma, consists of numerous thin-walled longitudinal canals, 0.021 mm in diameter united by irregular transverse anastomoses. There are from 40 to 70 canals in cross sections through ripe segments.

The nervous system is represented by two longitudinal cords situated midway between the genital complex and the lateral margin of the segment.

Each ripe segment has two genital complexes. The numerous testes lie in the medullary parenchyma, usually in more than one row. About 10 testes per segment are seen in a longitudinal section, and about 70 in a cross section; they measure 0.015×0.032 mm. Ejaculatory duct entering the very muscular seminal vesicle, which is 0.063 mm long; its configuration depends on the degree of contraction. The muscular bursa, 0.092 mm long and 0.134 mm wide, adjoins the seminal vesicle ventrally. Its walls consist of longitudinal and circular muscle fibers.

The opening of the vagina is situated somewhat behind the bursa cirri on the midline of the genital complex. It lies behind the pouch in which the uterine pore opens with the cirrus; the uterine pore may open in the common, shallow, and papilla-free genital atrium. The walls of the middle part of the vagina have villi directed into the lumen, and the terminal part has a powerful sphincter. The ovary is situated ventrally in the posterior part of the segment. Its width is 2.94 mm and its thickness in the median part, without constriction is 0.059 mm. A short duct extends from spermatheca 284 to oviduct. The oviduct comes close to the shell gland, but before joining it enters the canal of the vitellarium. The uterus is at first thin-walled; it then widens, forming the uterine sac, which is noticeable as a bulge on the surface of ripe segments. It is connected with the uterine pore by a thin-walled canal. The vitellarium, situated behind the Mehlis' gland, is united with the duct that runs from central part of the medullary parenchyma. Smaller ducts extending from the vitellaria and lying between two layers of longitudinal musculature empty into the main vitelline duct. The lateral vitelline fields in front of the bursa do not unite. Eggs are 0.063 mm long and 0.047 mm wide; they have a thick membrane and are operculate.

Tetragonoporus calyptocephalus A. Scriabin, 1961
(Figure 133: 7a, 7b)

Host: **Physeter macrocephalus** L.
Localization: bile ducts.
Distribution: Pacific Ocean (Kuriles).
Description of species: (after Skryabin, 1961. Abridged). Two fragments were investigated: one large, 5 m 98 cm long, with scolex, and the other

11 cm long. The scolex is 0.8 mm long, 1.96 mm wide, and 1.5 mm thick, bilobate, with a flattened apical organ in the form of a corolla with deep incisions above the bothria. The upper part of the bothria is greatly widened and forms two cup-shaped depressions 0.42 mm long and 0.6 mm wide; the margins of the lower part of the bothria come close together and overhang the first segments. A cervix is absent.

Strobila consisting of more than 45,000 very short and wide segments. Maximum width of segments 16 mm. The segments are velate and are of various size. Usually groups of segments of three different sizes — small, medium, and large — alternate along the strobila. The folds of the larger segments often cover the small segments following them. In most cases the segments are tetragonads, but there are also segments with three or two genital complexes. No patterns could be established in the distribution of segments with different numbers of genital complexes.

The genital openings open under the folds of the segments lying in front: anteriorly there is the male opening, behind this the opening of the vagina, and the opening of the uterus is situated either to the right or to the left of the opening of the vagina. The internal longitudinal muscles are very powerful; thickness of their layer 0.23 — 0.29 mm, thickness of transverse muscles 0.040 — 0.057 mm. Dorsoventral muscles relatively weakly developed. Longitudinal canals of excretory system lying in medullary parenchyma, their diameter varying from 0.019 — 0.17 mm. Large and small transverse canals reach them. Some of the longitudinal canals are fused into larger ones, while others branch into smaller canals; therefore, the number of longitudinal canals in different segments usually varies from 30 to 40.

Testes oval, extending dorsoventrally, antero-posteriorly compressed, 0.075 — 0.095 × 0.055 — 0.060 mm, and 0.015 — 0.025 mm thick. Seminal vesicle with thick walls, rounded, with a diameter of 0.095 — 0.14 mm, situated dorsal to the cigarlike bursa, which runs dorsoventrally. The bursa is 0.33 — 0.42 mm long and 0.9 — 0.12 mm wide.

285 The uterus describes 6 — 7 loops drawn out dorsoventrally. Eggs 0.057 — 0.061 mm long and 0.046 — 0.049 mm wide; they have a distinct operculum of 0.021 mm diameter. The thickness of the membrane is 0.0037 mm.

Hexagonoporus physeteris Gubanov in Delyamure, 1955
(Figure 133: 8)

Host: Physeter macrocephalus L.
Localization: small intestine.
Distribution: Sea of Okhotsk (Kuriles).
Description of species (after Gubanov in Delyamure, 1955. Abridged).
Two fragments (hermaphroditic and mature) without scolices were examined. The transverse muscles of the body are represented by numerous bundles of fibers. Two clearly marked lateral excretory canals have a diameter of 0.08 — 0.10 mm.

Each hermaphroditic segment, which reaches a length of 0.50 — 0.55 mm, contains six complexes of gonads distributed in pairs, although each opens independently on the ventral surface in the anterior part of the segment. The male and female pores of each complex are situated side by side, the opening of vagina being at the posterior margin of the male opening. The numerous testes are dispersed almost over the entire segment. Bursa cirri rounded, with a diameter of 0.08—0.10 mm. Cirrus not armed. Ovary bilobate, 0.1 mm long and 0.3 mm wide. Numerous vitelline follicles are present in the cortical parenchyma. Uterus forming 4—7 loops on each side of the midline. Eggs oval, 0.068—0.072 mm long and 0.052—0.056 mm wide, brownish, or with a thick membrane.

Polygonoporus giganticus A.Skriabin, 1967 (Figure 133: 9a, 9b, 9c)

Host: Physeter macrocephalus L.
Localization: intestine.
Distribution: fifth whaling sector of the Antarctic.
Description of species (after Skryabin, 1967. Abridged). Very large cestodes. Individual fragments of the strobila were up to 5 m long. Total length of body about 30 m, maximum width 45 mm. Scolex 1.0 mm long and 1.55 mm wide, bilobate, with a flattened apical organ in the form of a corolla with deep incisions above the bothria. Bothria in the form of longitudinal slits, widest in their median part. Cervix absent. Anterior part of strobila forming a rounded, spoon-shaped expansion 24 mm long and 24.5 mm wide, with strongly serrate lateral margins that are slightly depressed on the ventral side. The anterior, expanded portion of the strobila apparently serves as an additional holdfast in the intestine of the host. Ribbonlike strobila, markedly dorsoventrally compressed, following the rounded expansion. Segments short and wide, slightly velate. Their length along the entire strobila (apart from its anterior end) varies from 0.2 to 1.0 mm.

The number of genital complexes varies greatly in segments from different sections of the strobila. Examination of a fragment with scolex showed that the anlage and development of five genital systems, arranged in five 286 longitudinal rows approximately equally spaced, occur in each segment. Two or even three median rows of genital complexes can become doubled, so that segments with 7 and 8 complexes are formed. In rare cases their number in individual segments increases to 9 owing to the single complexes that are formed between the rows. The lateral margins of the segments have fairly deep tranverse folds which sometimes continue to the middle of the segment, crossing one, two or even three extreme rows of genital systems. At these intersections the genital systems become doubled, arranged one in front of the other. In such segments divided in half the number of genital systems increases to 10, 12 or even 14.

The genital openings open on the ventral side of the anterior boundary of the segment — the male opening anteriorly, then the vaginal opening, while the uterine pore is shifted somewhat back and to the side (right or left) of the vagina. Internal longitudinal muscles very powerful. Transverse muscles comparatively well developed. Dorsoventral muscles represented by numerous bundles. The numerous longitudinal canals of the excretory system lie in the well developed medullary parenchyma. In some places two adjacent canals fuse into one larger one, or else large canals branch into one larger one, or else large canals branch into two small ones. About 80—85 longitudinal canals were counted on cross sections of large segments

Testes rounded or slightly oval, 0.11—0.12 × 0.08—0.11 mm, with a thickness of 0.02—0.04 mm; thick-walled seminal vesicle 0.13—0.15 × × 0.19—0.20 mm, dorsal to the cigarlike bursa and clearly separated from it. Bursa 0.30—0.38 mm long and 0.11—0.12 mm wide.

In ripe segments the ovary is bilobate, greatly drawn out in width, particularly in the marginal rows of the genital complexes. Mehlis' gland present. Vitelline follicles 0.022—0.030 × 0.050—0.070 mm. Uterus in hermaphroditic segments forming 2—3 loops on each side of the midline. Eggs 0.071—0.076 mm long and 0.052—0.057 wide, with a distinct operculum 0.021—0.022 mm in diameter. Thickness of egg membrane 0.003—0.004 mm.

Order **Ascaridida** Skrjabin et Schulz, 1940
Family **Anisakidae** Skrjabin et Karochin, 1945
Anisakis physeteris Baylis, 1923 (Figure 33: 10a, 10b, 10c)

Host: Physeter macrocephalus L.
Localization: stomach.
Distribution: Atlantic Ocean (Saldanha Bay, South Georgia Island), Indian Ocean (Durban), Pacific Ocean (waters of Japan), Antarctic (Ross Sea).
Description of species (after Baylis, 1923; from Mozgovoi, 1953. Abridged). Large parasites. Cuticle with fine transverse striation. Lips relatively small. Dorsal lip bearing two double lozenge-shaped papillae, each latero-ventral lip one such papilla and one a very small, simple papilla. Cervical papillae situated 1.0 mm from the cephalic end. Esophagus long. Ventricle short and straight, 1.0 mm long, maximum width 1.1 mm. Excretory opening situated between base of the lateroventral lips.
Male. Length 70.0—90.0 mm, maximum width 3.0 mm. Esophagus 287 6.0 mm long. Caudal papillae numerous. There is no distinct boundary between the postanal and preanal papillae. Spicules not of equal size, very short and slightly curved. Length of right spicule 0.35 mm, of left spicule 0.4 mm.
Female. Length 80.0—112.0 mm, maximum width 4.0—4.5 mm. Esophagus 7.0 mm long. In specimens 88.0 mm long the vulva is situated 19.0 mm from the cephalic end. Eggs round, 0.06 mm in diameter, with a thick membrane.

Anisakis skrjabini Mosgovoy, 1949 (Figure 133: 11a, 11b, 11c)

Hosts: Physeter macrocephalus L.—sperm whale; Hyperoo-don ampullatus (Forst.)—bottlenose whale.
Localization: stomach, small intestine.
Distribution: Pacific Ocean (Komandorski and Kurile Islands), Sea of Okhotsk, Antarctic.
Description of species (after Mozgovoi, 1953. Abridged). Large parasites, white. The body is thick. Cuticle transversely striated. Lips widening at the base and tapering anteriorly. Papillae situated on their outer surface; two double papillae on the dorsal and one double and one small, single

papilla on each lateroventral lip. Cervical papillae convex. Esophagus is cylindrical. Ventricle straight. Excretory opening situated between lateroventral lips.

Male. Length 90.0—130.0 mm, maximum width 2.1—2.9 mm. Esophagus 6.0—6.9 mm long, maximum width 0.90—1.15 mm. Length of ventricle 0.89—1.0 mm, width 0.92—1.05 mm. Cervical papillae situated 0.80—1.05 mm from cephalic end. Caudal papillae numerous (86—94 pairs). There are 6 pairs of postanal papillae and 80—88 pairs of preanal papillae, situated on both sides of the body in irregular rows. The ornamentation of the postanal area with numerous denticles is striking. Spicules short, subequal. Length of right spicule 0.320—0.340 mm, of left 0.352—0.380 mm, with a width of 0.040—0.060 mm.

Female. Length 98.0—158.0 mm, maximum width 3.5—4.6 mm. Length of esophagus 6.45—7.91 mm, maximum width 1.10—1.31 mm, ventricle respectively 0.95—0.10 mm and 0.93—1.15 mm. Cervical papillae situated 0.881—1.170 mm and vulva 21.5—40.0 mm from the cephalic end, i.e., approximately at the boundary between the first and second quarter of the body. Eggs round or almost round, with a diameter of 0.043—0.056 mm, with a thin membrane.

Anisakis catodontis Baylis, 1929

Host: Physeter macrocephalus L.
Localization: stomach.
Distribution: Atlantic Ocean (Saldanha Bay).
Description of species (after Baylis, 1929; from Mozgovoi, 1953).
Male. Length 80 mm, maximum width 1.3 mm. Cuticle transversely striated. The lips have a wide base and a narrow anterior part with a deep incision in the middle and a projecting serrate margin consisting of coarse, irregular teeth. Esophagus 4.5 mm long and 0.39 mm wide. Ventricle straight, 1.7 mm long and 0.4 mm wide. Nerve ring 0.6 mm and cervical papillae 0.75 mm from the cephalic end. Tail 288 blunt, conical, 0.25 mm long. One pair of postanal papillae. Preanal papillae numerous. Spicules tubular, without alae. Length of left spicule 2.25 mm, of right spicule 1.45 mm, width 0.03 mm.

Anisakis dussumieri (Beneden, 1870) Baylis 1920
(Figure 133: 12a, 12b, 12c)

Hosts: Physeter macrocephalus L.; Poadelphinus longirostris Gray.
Localization: stomach, large intestine.
Distribution: Pacific Ocean (Japan), Bering Sea (Komandorski Islands).
Description of species (after Mozgovoi, 1953. Abridged). Parasites of medium size. Cuticle transversely striated. Cephalic end with one dorsal and two lateroventral lips. Dorsal lip with two large papillae. Each lateroventral lip has one large and one small papilla. The excretory opening is situated between the lateroventral lips. Cervical papillae very large,

nerve ring in front of them. Esophagus almost the same width throughout.
Ventricle S-shaped.

Male. Length 35—39 mm, maximum width 1.0—1.03 mm. Esophagus
3.8—4.0 mm long and 0.27—0.32 mm wide, ventricle 1.45 and 0.267 mm
respectively. Cervical papillae 0.534—0.621 mm and nerve ring 0.45 mm
from cephalic end. Caudal papillae numerous. There are 69—75 pairs of
preanal papillae, 2—3 pairs of adanal papillae, and 7 pairs of postanal
papillae. The other papillae are situated in the second half of the tail.
Spicules of nonuniform size. Length of left spicule 1.85 mm, that of the
right spicule 1.23 mm. Width of spicules at proximal end 0.026 mm.

Female. Length 45.0—64.6 mm, maximum width 1.35 mm. Esophagus
4.1—4.3 mm long and 0.29—0.39 mm wide, ventricle 1.92 mm and 0.27 mm
respectively. Cervical papillae 0.57—0.66 mm and nerve ring 0.48 mm
from cephalic end. Vulva in the middle of the body or somewhat nearer to
cephalic end. Eggs round or almost round, 0.044—0.052 mm in diameter.

Anisakis ivanizkii Mosgovoy, 1949 (Figure 133: 13a, 13b, 13c)

Host: Physeter macrocephalus L.
Localization: stomach.
Distribution: Pacific Ocean (Komandorski area).
Description of species (after Mozgovoi, 1953. Abridged). Nematodes of
average size. Cuticle transversely striated. Dorsal lip bearing two double
papillae, each lateroventral lip with one double and one small, single
papillae. Esophagus slightly curved at first, then widening gradually
posteriorly. Ventricle S-shaped. Cervical papillae very large. Excretory
opening situated between lateroventral lips.

Male. Length 56—85 mm, maximum width 1.73—2.50 mm. Length of
esophagus 5.99—6.50 mm, its maximum width 0.50—0.53 mm; length of
ventricle 2.033—2.198 mm, width 0.410—0.453 mm. Cervical papillae
0.75—0.83 mm and nerve ring 0.51—0.73 mm from cephalic end. Four
289 pairs of postanal papillae. Preanal papillae numerous (more than 80 pairs
on each side). No adanal papillae. Spicules of nonuniform size, large.
Length of right spicule 3.166—3.725 mm, of left spicule 2.2—2.5 mm, width
0.128—0.169 mm.

Female. Length 80.5—97.0 mm, maximum width 2.2—3.0 mm. Esophagus 6.8—7.3 mm long, maximum width 0.57—0.60 mm, ventricle
2.11—2.24 mm long and 0.45—0.52 mm wide. Cervical papillae 1.0—1.3 mm,
and nerve ring 0.74—0.85 mm from cephalic end. Vulva 46.0—52.5 mm
from anterior end in specimens 80.5 and 94.0 mm long. Eggs round, diameter 0.042—0.048 mm.

Anisakis simplex (Rudolphi, 1809) Baylis, 1920 (Figure 133: 14)

Hosts: Eumetopias jubata (Schr.) — sea lion; Mesoplodon
bidens (Sow.) — Sowerby's whale; Hyperoodon ampullatus
(Forst.) — bottlenose whale; Delphinapterus leucas (Pallas) —

white whale; Monodon monoceros L. — narwhal; Delphinus delphi L. — common dolphin; Lagenorhynchus albirostris Gray — white-beaked dolphin; L. cruciger Quoy and Gaimard; Orcinus orca (L.) — killer whale; Pseudorca crassidens (Owen) — False killer whale; Phocaena phocaena (L.) — harbor porpoise; Physeter macrocephalus L. — sperm whale; Berardius bairdii Stein. — Baird's beaked whale; Balaenoptera musculus L. — blue whale; B. acutorostrata Lac. — lesser rorqual; B. borsalis Less. — sei whale.

Localization: esophagus, stomach, intestine.

Distribution: North Sea, Pacific Ocean (Morzhevaya Bay, Kronotski Olyutorski gulfs, waters of Japan), New Zealand.

Description of species (Mozgovoi, 1953. Abridged). Nematodes of average size. Cuticle transversely striated. Mouth surrounded by three lips, one dorsal and two lateroventral. Dorsal lip with two double papillae. Each lateroventral lip with one double and one very small single papilla. Excretory opening situated between lateroventral lips, nerve ring in front of cervical papillae. Esophagus straight. Ventricle S-shaped.

Male. Length 47.0 — 65.5 mm, maximum width 1.3 — 1.7 mm. Length of esophagus 4.6 — 5.2 mm, width 0.314 — 0.401 mm; ventricle 1.95 — 2.20 and 0.276 — 0.352 mm, respectively. Cervical papillae 0.613 — 0.707 mm and nerve ring 0.516 mm from cephalic end. Caudal papillae numerous (6 post-anal pairs, 60 — 70 preanal pairs and one unpaired, 1 — 2 adanal pairs). Spicules nonuniform, left 2.027 — 2.454 mm, right 1.75 — 1.81 mm long.

Female. Length 58.0 — 73.6 mm maximum width 1.8 — 2.3 mm. Esophagus 4.95 — 5.79 mm long and 0.401 — 0.486 mm wide; ventricle 2.05 — 2.35 mm and 0.407 — 0.431 mm, respectively. Cervical papillae 0.642 — 0.791 mm and nerve ring 0.530 — 0.610 mm from cephalic end. Vulva situated at midbody. Eggs round or almost round, 0.047 — 0.053 mm in diameter.

Anisakis pacificus A. Skriabin, 1959 (Figure 133: 15a, 15b, 15c)

Hosts: Physeter macrocephalus L. — sperm whale; Orcinus orca (A.) — killer whale; Balaenoptera physalus (L). — finback whale; B. acutorostrata Lac. — lesser rorqual; Callorhinus ursinus L. — fur seal.

Localization: stomach.

Distribution: Pacific Ocean (Kuriles), Bering Sea (Komandorski Islands).

Description of species (after Skryabin, 1959. Abridged). Relatively large nematodes. Cephalic end with three lips (one dorsal and 2 lateroventral). There are two double papillae on the external surface of the dorsal lip. Each lateroventral lip has one double and one small single papillae. Cervical papillae convex, 0.05 mm in diameter. Excretory opening situated between the lateroventral lips. Esophagus straight. Ventricle straight, rarely S-shaped.

Male. Length 80 — 91 mm, maximum width 1.6 — 1.7 mm. Cervical papillae situated 0.75 — 0.80 mm from cephalic end. Esophagus 5.5 — 6.6 mm long and 0.42 — 0.54 mm wide; ventricle 1.70 — 1.75 and 0.37 — 0.43 mm, respectively. Caudal papillae numerous, including 7 pairs of preanal papillae. Spicules unequal, length of left spicule 2.2 — 3.5 mm, of right spicule 2.2 mm.

Female. Length 88—121 mm, maximum width 2.0—2.7 mm. Cervical papillae situated 0.81—1.25 mm from anterior end. Length of esophagus 6.3—7.5 mm, width 0.5—0.7 mm; length of ventricle 1.8—2.0 mm, width 0.40—0.45 mm. The position of the vulva varies. Generally it is situated in the posterior half, more rarely in the middle of the body, and sometimes in the anterior half. Eggs of irregular oval or rounded form, 0.057—0.049 × 0.047—0.042 mm.

Anisakidae g. sp.

Small sexually immature specimens were recorded by some authors in sperm whales inhabiting the Pacific Ocean.

Order **Spirurida** Chitwood, 1933
Family Crassicaudidae Skrjabin et Andreeva, 1934
Placentonema gigantissima Gubanov, 1951 (Figure 133: 16a, 16b, 16c)

Host: Physeter macrocephalus L.
Localization: placenta.
Distribution: Pacific Ocean (Kuriles), Antarctic.
Description of species (after Gubanov, 1951. Abridged). Very large nematodes covered with a thin, translucent cuticle which has no transverse striation except at the cephalic end. Buccal opening oval, with two simple lateral lips, at the base of which are two pairs of papillae and one amphid. Pharynx cylindrical; esophagus distinctly divided into muscular and glandular sections.

Male. Length 2.04—3.75 m, width 8—9 m. Buccal opening 0.048 × 0.016 mm. Pharynx 0.14 mm long, 0.008 mm wide. The anterior muscular section of the esophagus is 2.18—4.0 mm long and 0.10—0.14 mm wide; glandular section 67.7 mm long and 0.6 mm wide. Caudal end blunt, curved ventrally. Cloacal opening 1.4—1.6 mm from posterior end. Thin cuticular alae 1.26—1.4 mm long, with maximum width 0.6—0.7 mm, situated at sides of cloaca. Four pairs of preanal and 3 pairs of postanal stalklike papillae at the base of the alae. In addition there are 2 adanal papillae. Width of caudal end 1.4—1.9 mm at level of cloaca.

Female. Length 6.75—8.4 m, width 1.5—2.5 cm. Pharynx 0.12 mm long, 0.008 mm wide. Length of muscular section of esophagus 2.7—2.8 mm, width 0.20—0.26 mm; glandular section 63.6, 0.56—0.60 mm, respectively. The caudal end is rounded, drawn out into a pear, divided by a constriction 11.3 mm from the end of the tail. Anus 0.8—1 mm from caudal end. Vulva 12.4—14.8 mm in front of the anus. Uterus multiple (32 uteri). Ovipositor short. Ripe eggs oval, 0.049 mm long and 0.030 mm wide, containing already fully formed larvae.

In view of the fact that mature forms differ sharply from sexually mature forms and occur more frequently, we decided to give a brief description of them.

Immature P. **gigantissima** (after A. Skryabin, 1965)

The body is thin, threadlike, elastic. The oval buccal opening 0.023 mm long is bordered by two simple lateral lips at the base of which 2 lateral and 4 submedian papillae are situated. The pharynx is laterally compressed, 0.12 — 0.14 mm long and 0.023 mm wide (dorsoventral diameter). Esophagus divided into muscular and glandular sections. Cervical papillae in the form of small spinules 0.005 mm high, slightly recurved, situated 0.475 — 0.484 mm from the anterior end. The nerve ring lies 0.11 — 0.12 mm in front of the cervical papillae. The cuticle is 0.011 — 0.019 mm thick and has no transverse striation. The anterior part of the body in very small and young nematodes is gathered into folds (possibly due to fixation).

Male. Length 57 — 86 mm, thickness 0.61 — 0.68 mm. The anterior muscular section of the esophagus is 1.38 — 1.40 mm long and 0.076 mm wide, and the glandular section 42.5, 0.37 — 0.40 mm, respectively. Caudal end blunt, without papillae. Opening of cloaca 0.19 mm from tip of tail.

Female. Length 66 — 103 mm, thickness 0.66 — 0.90 mm. Anterior muscular section of esophagus 1.60 — 1.71 mm long and 0.39 — 0.40 mm wide. Caudal end blunt. Opening of cloaca 0.18 — 0.19 mm from tip of tail. The developing genital system is clearly seen. Vulva 1.33 — 1.40 mm from posterior end, giving rise to 28 — 32 uteri.

Features of the life cycle of P. gigantissima. The life cycle of P. gigantissima, as established by A.Skryabin (1960), is limited by the term of a pregnancy of the sperm whale and must end before the embryo leaves the uterus. Due to this the growth and development of these nematodes coincide to some extent with the growth and development of the sperm whale embryo. .

It is not clear how the nematode enters the uterus of the sperm whale but it certainly does so during the early stages of pregnancy. A. Skryabin discovered these parasites (5.7 — 6.5 mm long) in the uterus, when the embryo 292 of the whale was still very small or not detectable at all and pregnancy was determined according to the corpus luteum on the ovary. When the embryo was 16 cm long, all the specimens of Placentonema were still in the uterus. By the time the embryo reached a length of 18 cm, one third of the nematodes (5 out of 15) had already penetrated into the placenta. When the length of the embryo was 23.0 — 24.5 cm, nematodes were still found by Skryabin in both uterus and placenta. At an embryo length of 36 — 70 cm, all the worms were in the placenta, though externally they differed little from the uterine forms. In this period their length did not exceed 10 cm and their width 0.9 mm. In the placenta of an embryo 122 cm long there were already comparatively large nematodes, the males of which had well developed caudal alae and caudal papillae. Finally gigantic adult specimens were found in the placenta of an embryo 340 — 410 cm long; the females of P.gigantissima had reached a length of 7 — 8 m or more and were 20 — 25 mm wide, while the males were 3 — 4 m long and 8 — 9 mm wide.

In the placenta of the largest embryos, Skryabin found remnants of adult Placentonema and a multitude of ripe eggs containing fully formed larvae.

It is clear from the above that Placentonema passes through at least two stages in its development. At first the nematodes settle in the uterus, and then actively move to the placenta. Those in the uterus are comparatively small, threadlike and mobile, while those in the placenta are huge and immobile. Growth proceeds extremely nonuniformly. In the uterine forms it is almost imperceptible, but after their invasion of the placenta of an already comparatively large embryo, the growth rate is greatly accelerated. Thus the parasite manifests very fine adaptation to the relatively even growth and development of the embryo of the host. Intensive growth of the parasite together with early penetration of the placenta would cause the death of the still weak embryo and consequently, the death of the parasite itself, and a steadily slowed-down growth rate would not allow it to complete its life cycle in the strictly limited amount of time.

Investigating the anatomicomorphological features of young Placento-nema from the uterus, A. Skryabin (1960) attempted to discover the reason for such a large difference in the growth rate. The digestive system in the uterine nematodes was found to be better developed than in the same nematodes from the placenta. But the young parasites feed only orally. Having a thick cuticle and a well developed musculature, they cannot utilize the entire surface of the body for feeding. Adult specimens have a very thin cuticle and almost no musculature. These forms, like many other helminths, feed with the entire surface of their enormous body. Upon growing into the tissue of the placenta, the nematodes begin to feed osmotically, and this coincides with the onset of intensive growth. Favorable conditions of the medium, i.e., abundant food and the enormous placenta, allow them to reach gigantic dimensions in a relatively short period and to complete their life cycle by the time the embryo leaves the uterus.

Acanthocephala

Order **Palaeacanthocephala** Meyer, 1931
Family Polymorphydae Meyer, 1931
Bolbosoma turbinella (Diesing, 1851)

Hosts: Balaenoptera borealis Less.— sei whale; B. musculus — blue whale; B. physalus L.— finback whale; Eubalaena glacialis sieboldi Grey — northern right whale: Megaptera nodosa Bonn.— humpback whale: physeter macrocephalus L.— sperm whale; Hyperoodon ampullatus (Forst.) — bottlenose whale.
Localization: intestine.
Distribution: Atlantic and Pacific oceans (northern and southern hemispheres), Sea of Okhotsk, waters of Japan, New Zealand.
Description of species (after Meyer, 1933, with additions by Harada, 1931). Body thickened, with a well expressed bulb. In life orange, fixed specimens white.
Length of male about 24 mm, of female 26—30 mm. Width of body 3—4 mm. Proboscis is slightly conical, about 0.8 mm long, 0.45 mm wide, with 19 — 20 longitudinal rows of hooks, each row containing 6—7 hooks. Harada (1931) states that there may be 22 longitudinal rows (8 hooks in each row). The most strongly curved hooks are situated in the middle of the proboscis. The length of the mucro of the hook is 0.05—0.07 mm and the length of the root 0.06—0.07 mm. The surface of the bulb is covered with large spines,

situated in tubercles of the cuticle. Proboscis sheath with strong, two-layered walls. Nerve ganglion in middle of proboscis sheath. Lemnisci about 25.0 mm. Testes ovate, about 1.0 mm long, situated in the middle of the body. Cement glands about 10 mm long, tubular, forming three pairs. Eggs 0.155 — 0.170 mm long and 0.028 — 0.036 mm wide.

Bolbosoma brevicolle (Malm, 1867)

Hosts: Balaenoptera acutorostrata Lac. — lesser rorqual: B. borealis Less. — finback whale: B. musculus — blue whale: B. physalus (L.) — finback whale: Physeter macrocephalus L. — sperm whale.
Localization: intestine.
Distribution: northern part of the Atlantic Ocean, South African coast, area of South Georgia Island.
Description of species (after Meyer, 1933; in Petrochenko, 1958). Body comparatively small, the constriction behind the bulb slightly expressed. Length of female 28 mm, of male 26 mm. Proboscis cylindrical, 0.4 — 0.5 mm long. There are 16 — 18 longitudinal rows of hooks on the proboscis (8 hooks in each row, after Porta, 1906). According to Borgstrem, there are 24 — 25 longitudinal rows of hooks on the proboscis (5 hooks in each row). Porta possibly counted hooks in two adjacent rows and in this case ignored the quinuncial arrangement, so that he might have obtained twice as many hooks per row. Length of neck about 0.3 — 0.4 mm. Bulb as long as wide (2.0 — 2.5 mm), covered with spines in its anterior part; 17 anterior transverse rows represented by small spines, and three transverse rows in the median part of the bulbus with large spines. The posterior part of the body is cylindrical and separated from the bulb only by a weak constriction. Baylis (1929) notes that these Acanthocephala showed a red coloration in the small intestine and white in the large intestine. The eggs are ellipsoidal, with three membranes.

Bolbosoma capitatum (Linstow, 1880) (Figure 133, 17)

Hosts: Physeter macrocephalus L. — sperm whale; Steno bredanensis Less., Pseudorca crassidens (Owen) — false killer whale; Globicephalus melas (Traill) — pilot whale.
Localization: intestine.
Distribution: Atlantic Ocean, Mediterranean Sea.
Description of species (from Meyer, 1933). Male 50 — 55 mm long, female 60 — 100 mm long, with a width of 2.0 — 3.5 mm. Proboscis 0.5 — 0.7 mm long, almost cylindrical, rounded at the anterior end. It bears 18 — 20 longitudinal and 12 — 18 transverse rows of hooks of three types, of which the median hooks are the largest. Neck 0.3 — 0.5 mm long. Total length of bulb 4.5 mm, width 3.5 mm; in the anterior and median parts the bulb is covered with spines which are united ventrally. Bulb followed by a narrow area (constriction) 2.0 — 2.5 mm long. Lemnisci relatively short, 3.0 — 4.5 mm long,

situated in the region of the bulb, with numerous nuclei. Uterine bell, uterus, and vagina occupying 5.0—5.7 mm. Eggs 0.12—0.20 mm long.

Bolbosoma physeteris Gubanov in Delyamure, 1955
(Figure 133: 18a, 18b)

Hosts: P h y s e t e r m a c r o c e p h a l u s — sperm whale; O r c i n u s
o r c a (L.) — killer whale.
Localization: small intestine.
Distribution: Sea of Okhotsk, Pacific Ocean (Kuriles area), Antarctic.
Description of species (after Gubanov, from Delyamure, 1955). Large Acanthocephala, in life mostly yellow.

M a l e s reach a length of 30—51 mm at a width of 1.5—2 mm. The body is separated from the bulb by a short and comparatively wide neck. Bulb armed with spinules, divided by a zone without spines into a prebulb, covered with spines, 0.4—1.2 mm long and 0.9—1.0 wide, and the bulb proper, 0.8 — 1.0 mm long and 2.0—2.4 mm wide, also covered with spines. The spines of the bulb and prebulb are large and wide, attaining a length of 0.032—0.040 mm. Proboscis 0.6—0.7 mm long and 0.44—0.56 mm wide, situated on the conical neck, 0.4—1.0 mm long. It is armed with 18—20 longitudinal rows of hooks (6—8 in each row). The blades of the anterior hooks attain a length of 0.078—0.1 mm and a thickness (at the base) of 0.03 mm. The posterior hooks are considerably smaller and thinner, 0.05—0.06 mm long and 0.009 mm thick (at the base).

Cone-shaped proboscis sheath with double walls. Length 1.1—2.6 mm, width 0.4—0.5 mm; nerve bundle situated in the middle of the vagina. The flagelliform lemnisci 2.88—4.0 mm long extend beyond the posterior margin of the proboscis sheath.

Testes oval, lying in the anterior cylindrical part of the body on the midline, one behind the other. Anterior testis 1.3—2.0 mm long and 0.6—1.64 mm wide, posterior 1.4—2.2 mm long and 0.76—1.2 mm wide. Four long, ribbonlike cement glands originate at the posterior margin of the posterior testis and extend almost to the end of the body. The genital opening opens terminally at the posterior end. Genital bursa without finger-shaped processes.

F e m a l e considerably larger than male, reaching a length of 43—87 mm and a width of 1.6—3.2 mm. Prebulb 0.9—1.0 mm long and 1.2—1.6 mm wide; bulb 1.0—1.1 mm long and 2.4—2.8 mm wide. Conical neck 3—5 mm long, with an armed proboscis 0.44—0.6 mm long and 0.46—0.5 mm wide. It bears 18—20 longitudinal rows of hooks (6—7, 7—8 in each row). Size of hooks same in females as in males. Eggs large, elongate oval, with three membranes, the median of which forms protrusions at the poles. Size of eggs 0.167—0.182 × 0.026—0.038 mm.

Corynosoma strumosum (Rud, 1802) Lühe, 1904
(Figure 133: 19a, 19b)

Definitive hosts: marine mammals: E u m e t o p i a s j u b a t a Schr. —
sea lion; O d o b a e n u s r o s m a r u s L. — walrus; C y s t o p h o r a c r i s t a t a

299

(Erxl.) — hooded seal; Halichoerus grypus Fabr. — gray seal; Phoca vitulina L. — common seal; Ph. vitulina largha Pall. — largha; Ph. vitulina rishardii Gray — Richard's seal; Phoca caspica Gmelin — Caspian seal; Pusa hispida Schr. — ringed seal; P. hispida ochotensis Pall. — Okhotsk ringed seal; Pagophoca groenlandica Erxl. — harp seal; Erignathus barbatus Erxl. — bearded seal; Physeter macrocephalus L. — sperm whale; Phocaena phocaena L.; Delphinapterus leucas Pall. — white whale. In addition the parasites have been recorded in birds (cormorants, goosanders, grebes, ducks, gulls, pelicans).

Intermediate hosts: Amphipoda.

Reservoir hosts: many species of marine and freshwater fishes.

Localization: in definitive hosts in the intestine. In intermediate and reservoir hosts in the body cavity, muscles, and internal organs.

Distribution (in marine mammals): Europe, coast of the Atlantic, Greenland Sea, off the shore of the Baltic Sea, Lake Ladoga, White, Barents, and Kara seas, Chukchi and Bering seas, Pacific Ocean and Sea of Okhotsk, Caspian.

Description of species (after Lühe, 1911, with additions by Petrochenko, 1958). Males and females of same size (length about 5 — 6, maximum 9 mm). Body elongate, greatly expanded in the anterior part, armed with spines. Spines on the ventral side extending posteriorly farther than on the dorsal side, but without reaching the posterior end. Spines near the genital opening in the male. Proboscis protruding from the widened anterior section, curved ventrally, more or less cylindrical, slightly widened in the lower third and then narrowing toward the base. Hooks arranged in 18 longitudinal rows (10 — 12 hooks in each row) The 6th or the 5th and 6th, or the 6th and 7th hooks are markedly larger than the preceding hooks; the other hooks, though thick, are much smaller than the above and decrease in size toward the base of the proboscis. Neck conical. Proboscis sheath saclike, with two walls; it extends not farther than the boundary of the widened part of the body. Testes rounded, situated in the narrower part of the body, contiguous. Six cement glands, pear-shaped anteriorly, posteriorly drawn out into tubes. Lemnisci slightly shorter than proboscis sheath. Eggs 0.10 mm long and 0.03 mm wide.

Corynosoma curilensis Gubanov in Delyamure, 1955
(Figure 133: 20a, 20b)

Host: Physeter macrocephalus L.

Localization: small intestine.

Distribution: Sea of Okhotsk (Kuriles area).

Description of species (after Gubanov, from Delyamure, 1955). Small Acanthocephala of a milk-white color. Body club-shaped. Anterior part 296 of body covered with spines, swollen, posterior part cylindrical.

Male 4.1 — 6.8 mm long. Width in anterior part of body 1.1 — 1.3 mm, at posterior end 0.5 — 0.7 mm. Proboscis 0.4 — 0.54 mm long, 0.16 — 0.30 mm wide. It bears 18 longitudinal rows of hooks (8 in each row). The largest hooks occur on the median, expanded part of the proboscis. The blades of these hooks reach a length of 0.60 — 0.65 mm and a width of 0.2 mm (at the base). Hooks at base of proboscis smallest, half the size of the median hooks. Proboscis sheath two-layered, 0.9–1.4 mm long and 0.2—0.4 mm deep. The flagelliform lemnisci are a little longer than the proboscis sheath; nerve bundle situated at the beginning of second half of proboscis sheath. Testes oval, situated at the boundary between the widened and the cylindrical parts of the body. They reach a length of 0.40—0.64 mm and a width of 0.20—0.24 mm. Six cement glands, arranged in two groups of three. The first group is near the testes, the second near the bursa copulatrix. The size of the cement glands varies depending on the size of the parasite (length from 0.5 to 1.4 mm, width from 0.08 to 0.16 mm). Bursa copulatrix without finger-shaped processes. Genital opening opens terminally, surrounded with spines.

Female 6.2 mm long and 1.4 mm wide. Proboscis 0.54 mm long and 0.3 mm wide, bearing 18 longitudinal rows of hooks (8 in each row). The proboscis sheath is 1.0 mm long and 0.36 mm wide. Eggs oval, with three distinct membranes. Polar formations weakly expressed. Length of eggs 0.12 mm, width 0.07 mm.

Corynosoma mirabilis A. Skrjabin, 1966 (Figure 133: 21a, 21b)

Host: Physeter macrocephalus L.
Localization: intestine.
Distribution: whaling sectors III, IV and V of the Antarctic (40°—60° S).
Description of species (after Skryabin, 1966. Abridged). Small, milk-white Acanthocephala. Anterior part of body swollen in the form of a bulb, densely covered with spines; posterior part narrow, its ventral surface is covered with sparse spines approximately for one quarter of its length. There are spines also on the posterior end around the genital opening, males having more than 100, and females usually not more than 12. The neck has the form of a truncated cone. Proboscis almost cylindrical. Hooks distributed on the proboscis in 16 longitudinal rows (11—12, rarely 13 hooks in each row). The longest hooks are situated near the apex of the proboscis, and their length somewhat decreases toward the posterior end, the last 2—3 hooks being smaller than the others and without roots. The 6th, 7th, and 8th hooks are the thickest. However, there are no sharp differences in the size of hooks on the proboscis. Lemnisci wide, flat, rounded.

Male. Length 6.0—11.1 mm. Dimensions for a male 10.5 mm long are as follows: width of anterior part of body 2.2 mm, of posterior part 0.9 mm. Length of proboscis 1.1 mm, maximum width 0.34 mm. Lemnisci about 1.1 mm long. The oval or slightly bean-shaped testes are 1.1 mm long and 0.34—0.45 mm wide. The six extended cement glands lie in the anterior half of the narrowed part of the body.

297   Female. Length 6.4—14.0 mm. In a specimen 9.2 mm long the width in the anterior part of the body is 1.9 mm and in the posterior part 0.7 mm. Proboscis 1.1 mm long and 0.34 mm wide. Lemnisci 1.0—1.1 mm long Length of uterine bell 0.41 mm, maximum width 0.17 mm. Length of uterus is 2.17 mm, maximum width is 0.08 mm. No eggs were discovered in any of the females examined.

Interestingly, C. mirabilis was encountered only in large male sperm whales taken in the Antarctic south of 40° S (Skryabin, 1966).

Brief ecological-geographical survey of the helminths of the sperm whale

Delyamure (1955) was the first to study the zoogeographical peculiarities of the helminth fauna of sperm whales. A. Skryabin continued investigations in this field (1958, 1960). Soviet and other researchers have recently accumulated extensive material.

As seen from the systematic part, 29 species of helminths, including larval and undetermined forms, have been recorded in the sperm whale. Three forms (Diplogonoporus sp., Trigonocotyle sp., and Anisakidae g.sp.) were disregarded by us as being unsuitable for zoo-geographical analysis. The remaining 26 species can be divided into 2 groups: specific and nonspecific helminths for P.macrocephalus.

The first group comprises 13 species of helminths, that have been recorded only in the sperm whale; the second group includes 13 species which have been recorded in the sperm whale and in other animals. The specific helminths are: Zalophotrema curilensis, Tetrabothrius curilensis, Tetragonoporus calyptocephalus, Multiductus physeteris, Hexagonoporus physeteris, Polygonoporus giganticus, Tetraphyllidae g.sp., larvae, Anisakis catodontis, A.physeteris, A.ivanizkii, Placentonema gigantissima, Corynosoma curilensis, C.mirabilis. These belong to 9 genera, five of which have been recorded only in the sperm whale (Multiductus, Tetragonoporus, Hexagonoporus, Polygonoporus, and Placentonema). These genera, as well as the species indicated adequately define the specific nature of the helminth fauna of P.macrocephalus.

Unfortunately, the intermediate hosts of the helminths parasitic in sperm whales (including the specific parasites) are still not known, but they are probably animals that make up the whale's food.

The second group, that of the nonspecific helminths, represented by 13 species, includes 9 species recorded in the sperm whale and other toothed whales: Phyllobothrium delphini, Anisakis skrjabini, A.dussumierii, A.simplex, A.pacificus, Bolbosoma capitatum, B.physeteris, B.turbinella, and Corynosoma strumosum. Some of these species and some others (7) infest the sperm whale and baleen whales (Tetrabothrius affinis, Priapocephalus grandis, Phyllobothrium delphini, Anisakis simplex, A.pacificus, Bolbosoma brevicolle, B.turbinella).

Four species of helminths are common not only to the helminth fauna of toothed or baleen whales but also to that of Pinnipedia (Phyllobothrium delphini, Trypanorhyncha g.sp. larvae, Anisakis simplex, A.pacificus, Corynosoma strumosum); just a few of these helminths are also encountered in fish (Trypanorhyncha g.sp.) and in birds (Corynosoma strumosum).

The above data testify to a wide exchange of helminths among the inhabitants of the sea that arises owing to common ranges, feeding on the same animals which are intermediate hosts of parasitic worms, contacts, and other ecological reasons.

302

At the same time, it is striking that there are fewer species common to both the sperm whale and other animals the lesser the ecological (phylo-genetic) affinity between the groups of hosts compared. For instance, whereas there are 9 species common to the sperm and other toothed whales, the helminth fauna of the former is linked with the baleen whales by 8 species, with Pinnipedia by 5 species, and with other invertebrates by only 2 species.

The distinctive ecology and biology of the sperm whale has led to a helminth fauna which differs both from that of other toothed whales and from that of the baleens.

Because the sperm whale is a widely distributed animal, performing long and distant migrations, the composition of the helminth fauna of sperm whales taken in various geographical zones and in different hemispheres is of much interest. There are 19 species of helminths known in sperm whales of the northern hemisphere and 14 species in sperms of the southern hemisphere. The smaller number of species recorded in the southern hemisphere cannot be considered only as a result of inadequate study in the southern areas, because in recent years quite a large number of sperm whales have been dissected there. Further investigations will undoubtedly introduce corrections into the assumed ratio of species; but it is probably not fortuitous. In 1955 Delyamure established that the helminth fauna of Cetacea of the northern hemisphere is richer than in the southern hemisphere; this agrees with the general biological structure of the World Ocean.

Analysis shows that 7 out of 26 species of helminths (Phyllobothrium delphini, Tetraphyllidea g. sp., Anisakis skrjabini, A. simplex, Placentonema gigantissima, Bolbosoma brevicolle, and B. physeteris) were recorded in both northern and southern sperms. It is hardly likely that infestation with these species occurs in the tropical region, which is reached by sperms of the northern and southern hemispheres at different times. In any case, not one of these helminths has been recorded here so far. Meanwhile, all of them are known as bipolar species, recorded in the temperate zones of both hemispheres. Thus, helminthological data indicate that sperm whales do not cross from one hemisphere to the other. *

Helminths sharply differing both quantitatively and qualitatively have been recorded in sperm whales inhabiting the northern parts of the Pacific and Atlantic oceans. For instance, in sperms of the Northern Atlantic only 4 species of helminths are known (Phyllobothrium delphini, Anisakis simplex, Bolbosoma brevicolle, and B. capitatum), of which, as noted, the first 3 are known in sperm whales of the southern hemisphere. Thus, only one species, B. capitatum, is characteristic for P. macrocephalus inhabiting the northern part of the Atlantic Ocean.

In the Northern Pacific, 17 species of helminths have been recorded in sperm whales, of which only 2 species (Phyllobothrium delphini and Anisakis simplex) have been discovered in sperms of the Atlantic Ocean and 6 have been recorded in sperm whales of the southern hemisphere 299(Phyllobothrium delphini, Tetraphyllidea g. sp., Anisakis skrjabini, A. simplex, Placentonema gigantissima, Bolbosoma physeteris). All the other species of helminths (11)

* For more details on migrations see Chapter 10.

303

have so far been found only in sperm whales from the northern part of the
Pacific (Zalophotrema curilensis, Tetrabothrius curilensis,
Tetragonoporus calyptocephalus, Hexagonoporus
physeteris, Tripanorhyncha g.sp., Anisakis dussumierii,
A.ivanizkii, A.pacificus, Bolbosoma turbinella, Corynosoma curilensis, C.strumosum). It is characteristic that of the
5 genera of helminths parasitic only in the sperm whale, two genera
(Tetragonoporus, Hexagonoporus) are recorded only in animals
from the northern part of the Pacific.

All this characterizes the helminth fauna of sperm whales inhabiting the
northern half of the Pacific, and moreover confirms once again the
distinctiveness of the fauna of the Boreal-Pacific region, where the large
majority of helminths of the sperm whale have been recorded (Delyamure,
1952, 1955, 1956; Delyamure and Skryabin, 1958; Skryabin, 1958, 1960).

WHALING

"No dignity in whaling? The dignity of our calling
the very heavens attest."

"Moby Dick"

Sperm whaling has a two-and-a-half-century history of ups and downs, which should be examined, even if briefly if our picture of this whale is to be complete.

The second part of the section deals with the products of whaling.

Chapter 17

HISTORY OF WHALING (18TH—20TH CENTURIES)

Sperm whaling dates back to 1712 off the coast of America, when a specimen was taken by an American vessel that had been driven into the open sea by a storm (Harmer, 1928).

By 1770 the American fleet that conducted sperm whaling in various regions of the Atlantic, from Newfoundland to the Falkland Islands, consisted of 125 vessels. England joined this profitable enterprise in 1785, and in 1789 a London ship, after sailing round Cape Horn, began to operate in the Pacific Ocean and returned with a splendid booty of whale oil. At about this time the French and the Portuguese also began sperm whaling. In 1789 whaling started to spread also in the Indian Ocean.

Pacific whaling developed rapidly and the coasts of Chile, Peru, and the Galapagos, abundant in sperms, became favorite hunting grounds (Harmer, 1928). According to Harmer's data, whaling of sperms began in New Zealand waters in 1802. In 1820 the British discovered enormous accumulations of sperm whales in Japanese waters; these regions also became favorite whaling areas (Townsend, 1931), and by 1835 almost 100 vessels were operating there. In the Indian Ocean whaling had by now been organized on a large scale, and the year 1837 is considered to mark the peak of its development.

1820—1850 was a period of flourishment. The total number of whaling vessels in 1842 reached 824, of which 594 belong to America. In subsequent years the size of the American fleet grew to 729 vessels, but, in the opinion of Harmer (1928), it is difficult to determine how many were used for sperm whaling. The Hawaiian Islands had become an important whaling center. For instance, in 1846 over 600 vessels entered Honolulu (Slijper, 1962). In 1837 the American fleet alone brought in 127,000 barrels of sperm whale oil; according to calculations made by Zenkovich (1952), this quantity of oil can be obtained from 2,100 sperm whales. According to Scammon (1874), during this successful period of whaling up to 3,800 sperms were captured annually, while Slijper's data (1962) indicate that up to 10,000 sperm whales were taken only in 1842.

From 1846 the American whaling fleet was reduced mainly (Harmer's conclusion) due to the decrease in number of sperms as a result of intensive whaling that exceeded the rate of breeding. Boschma (1938) and Tomilin (1957) believe that the reserves of whales were undermined as a result of plunder in the breeding grounds which were the chief whaling areas.

Having no grounds to doubt the conclusions of these authors, we should nevertheless verify the fact that depletion of the reserves of sperm whales in these years could occur only in whaling regions of previous years, because large areas of the whale's habitat in the northern and southern hemispheres, including the regions with females, were not visited by whalers. Perhaps Slijper (1962) is right in considering that it was the rapid development of the American cotton industry that attracted capital and manpower.

Beginning in 1849, hundreds of San Franciscan seamen tried their luck in the "gold rush." In addition, a large number of ships were lost during the Civil War, and finally in 1859 mineral oils were discovered in Pennsylvania, after which kerosene began to oust sperm whale oil and spermaceti candles from the market.

Harmer (1928) gives data characterizing the yield of spermaceti oil brought in by American vessels between 1810 and 1880:

Period	Yield of spermaceti oil, thousand tons	Period	Yield of spermaceti oil, thousand tons
1810 — 1820	788	1850 — 1860	4,464
1820 — 1830	3,884	1860 — 1870	2,772
1830 — 1840	7,011	1870 — 1880	2,179
1840 — 1850	6,655		

Harmer reports that during subsequent years whaling continued to slacken; in particular sperm whaling by the American fleet almost came to a halt. In 1858, 68 American vessels suffered a loss of a total of 1,000,000 dollars (Zenkovich, 1952).

In these years (maps of Townsend, 1931, 1935), the waters from Peru to the Marquesas Islands were the leading whaling regions in the Pacific Ocean; in the Atlantic-Sargasso Sea, the area between 30° and 40°S off the shores of South America and off Angola (Africa). Townsend singled out some more regions (the islands of Cape Verde, Azores, and Seychelles, as well as the waters of Japan and some other regions).

The sharp reduction everywhere, and in several regions even cessation, of sperm whaling probably led to a certain increase in abundance by the beginning of the 20th century. But at this time whaling was resumed and became mechanized. Beginning in 1910, sperm whaling increased fivefold in the course of five years, yielding more than a thousand specimens a year.

In the 1920's the main whaling regions, according to Harmer (1928), were the waters off the coast of Southeast Africa (Natal), where 511 sperms were taken in 1925, and the waters of Korea and Japan (314 sperm whales in 1925 — 1926). Markedly fewer specimens were caught in the Antarctic, off the coast of Spain and Portugal, and in the southern part of the Pacific
302 Ocean. Still fewer were taken off Kamchatka, the Republic of the Congo, and Angola. In other regions such as the waters of Peru, Norway, Denmark, and the Azores, isolated specimens were captured.

In the thirties sperm whaling was considerably stepped up in the Pacific off the shores of South America, where in Peru (mainly) and Chile by 1937 over 4,000 sperm whales a year were taken. Catches in the waters of Japan,

Korea, and the Kuriles increased (from 360 in 1930—1931 to 1,000 in 1934—1935 and over 1,300 specimens in 1939—1940).

In the northwestern Pacific off Kamchatka and the Komandorski Islands the first Soviet whaling flotilla "Aleut" begins operations; by the end of the decade this flotilla was taking up to 200 sperm whales a year.

Up to the 1932—1933 season maximum catches of sperms in antarctic waters did not exceed a hundred specimens (73 in 1929—1930), more than half of which were taken by shore stations; gradually, however, catches rose: by 1933—1934 they had increased more than sixfold, and in 1938—1939 over 2,500 sperm whales were captured, almost all being taken by deep-sea flotillas.

In the early forties, the war led to a drastic reduction in whaling, and in 1941—1945 deep-sea flotillas did not catch any sperm whales in the Antarctic. Sperm whaling was carried out mainly by the shore stations in the southern hemisphere, which in the first half of the forties caught about 4,000 sperms annually. In 1941—1943 a Norwegian flotilla that was operating off the coast of Peru captured 8,500 sperm whales. In the second half of the decade some countries, for instance Japan, resumed whaling on a large scale; as a result, catches notably increased and by 1950 world sperm whaling achieved an annual catch of almost 10,000 specimens (in 1947—1948, 9,850), of which a little less than 50% were taken in the Antarctic.

In the 1950's the largest numbers of sperms were captured in the waters of Peru (up to 6,300 specimens) and in the Antarctic (up to 5,500).

In these years, despite large catches of these whales, the species constituted a very insignificant proportion (on the average, from 8—10 to 16%) of the total catches of whales in the Antarctic. According to calculations by Zenkovich (in litt.) 18,805 sperms were taken here from 1950 to 1954, while from 1955 to 1959, 34,658. The other regions that were of commercial importance were in the Pacific Ocean, the waters of Kamchatka (up to 1,500 sperm whales a year by the end of the period), Japan (up to 1,400 specimens a year) and the Kurile Islands (up to 2,000 a year by the end of the period), the waters of Natal (up to 900 a year) in the Indian Ocean, and in the Atlantic Ocean, the area of the Azores (catches of 600—700 specimens a year) and the Cape Province (200—300 specimens a year).

Until 1954 deep-sea whaling, mainly of sperm whales in the northern part of the Pacific, was carried out only by one Soviet flotilla, the "Aleut," which caught about 700—800 specimens annually.

In 1954 a Japanese flotilla began sperm whaling, and in 1955 a second one. One of the flotillas concentrated on sperm whaling exclusively, while the other captured a certain number of sperm whales in addition to baleen whales.

Coastal sperm whaling was carried out by very many countries (not counting Japan) and in many regions, but the number of animals taken was insignificant: from single specimens (Brazil, New Zealand, Scotland) to several dozen (Iceland, Norway, Spain, Morocco); at the end of the decade up to 300 animals were caught by Australia. Having captured 41 sperm whales in 1954, the shore station in Spanish Morocco ceased operation. The shore station in Gabon operated during two years (1951 and in 1959) and caught 146 and 14 sperm whales, respectively. Many stations stopped operating in these years: thus, in 1951 after catching 11 sperm whales, Portugal ceased sperm whaling, and in 1958 a station in Greenland closed up after catching 26 sperms.

In the second half of the 50's and in the early 60's appreciable changes occurred in the location of whaling regions in the North Pacific under the effect of intensive deep-sea and coastal whaling. The waters of the Southern and then also of the Northern Kuriles gradually lost their commercial importance, and one after another the processing combines on shore closed down. The waters of Kamchatka, the Komandorski Islands, and of the Western Aleutians, once rich in all species of whales including the sperm, are becoming waste. In these regions the areas occupied by sperm accumulations diminished, the duration of existence of these accumulations gradually decreased, the number of animals in the accumulations declined, and the size of the whales themselves decreased.

In recent years sperm whaling has been carried out mainly by pelagic flotillas in the northern part of the Pacific, around the Aleutian Islands and to the south, in the Gulf of Alaska and south of Alaska. The Soviet flotillas "Aleut," "Dal'nii Vostok," "Vladivostok," and "Sovetskaya Rossiya" operate in these waters. In 1966 the Soviet flotilla "Slava" (that previously operated in the Antarctic) started whaling in the North Pacific. But the "Sovetskaya Rossiya" and "Aleut" stopped whaling. * Two Japanese flotillas have been engaged in sperm whaling. **

The number of sperm whales taken in recent years in the northern Pacific continues to increase; in 1964 a large number of sperms had already been taken (10,314) while by 1967 catches had reached the 15,469 mark. Most of the animals were captured by pelagic whaling fleets, in the main Soviet. In 1967 Soviet whaling flotillas took 3 times as many sperm whales as the Japanese pelagic flotillas (data of IWS).

Sperm whales are taken in abundance off the shores of Japan, mainly in the areas of Sanriku and Hokkaido. Catches in other regions are very low and rarely exceed 50 specimens a year. Recently (1966—1967) sperm whaling has been carried out by nine shore stations with 17—18 whalers who are accustomed to taking 2,100—2,600 sperms annually. Females constitute over 50% of the catches here. According to data of the Japanese Whaling Institute, catches of sperm whales per operation in this region rose only up to 1957—1958, after which they steadily declined. The number of whales migrating along the Asian shores has greatly decreased.

Catches of sperms off the Pacific shores of North America are low. In 1966 ten whalers from 3 stations carried out sperm whaling, and in 1967, 8 whalers from two stations of California and British Columbia, caught during these years 300—400 sperms.

304   In the North Pacific 86,000 sperm whales were taken within 14 years (from 1950), constituting over 73% of total catches from the start of whaling in these waters (Zenkovich, in litt.). In recent years this region of the World Ocean takes first place in sperm whale catches.

In the early 1960's sperm whaling in these regions advanced eastward, yielding first place to baleen whaling, but then again it acquired predominance (it is true that) by this time the mean standard length of animals in the catches had been reduced, and females appeared in the catches throughout the whaling period).

---

* The International Whaling Statistics, obviously following tradition, incorrectly refers the whales taken by the Soviet deep-sea fleets in the northern part of the Pacific to the Kamchatka region, whereas in recent years it is just here that Soviet whalers have hardly operated at all.

** One of the three Japanese flotillas operating in the North Pacific hunts only baleen whales.

The state of the reserves is deteriorating in all indexes in the northeastern regions of the Pacific Ocean as a result of intensive whaling.

According to data of Japanese researchers, the catches obtained by Japanese pelagic flotillas per operation increased from 3.17 animals in 1954 to 3.81 in 1958, and then decreased in 1959 to 3.17. During three seasons the catches remained at approximately the same level and then again sharply dropped to 2.32 specimens in 1962.

The present authors determined the age composition of sperm whales (according to number of layers of dentin) taken in the North Pacific. Sampling was at random, and, consequently the sample reflected the age composition of the captured animals; moreover, since whaling in high latitudes does not have a selective character during the greater part of the season (as it has in the waters of the Kuriles area, for instance), the age composition obtained should show the age structure of the stocks inhabiting these waters in the summer period.

Since 1963 determination of the age composition of sperm whales taken by Soviet flotillas is carried on a wide scale and over a vast expanse. The age composition of over 8,000 sperms was determined by TINRO workers (with the author's participation) in the North Pacific between 1959 and 1968.

The diagram (Figure 134) shows the changes in the age composition determined by a number of layers of dentin in the teeth of male sperm whales that were captured in the northern part of the Pacific from 1959 to 1968.

A certain deterioration of the age composition, discovered at the end of 1961 (Berzin, 1963, 1964a), was noted also in subsequent seasons. In comparing the age composition of sperm whales taken in recent years with that in 1959, it is seen that the number of sperms of the youngest age group was almost trebled in individual years (1966), whereas the number of animals in the older groups decreased more than five times. A shift of the main whaling regions within the limits of the northern part of the Pacific Ocean affected the age composition of whales taken. For instance, the catches of a substantial number of large males in 1966 in the so-called central Pacific region resulted in a considerable increase of the percentage of animals of the oldest age group in comparison with the percentage of these animals taken in all recent years. In subsequent years, as was to be expected, the number of animals of this group began to decrease sharply, as seen in the diagram.

By the end of 1963 it had become clear (Berzin, 1964a) that there was an urgent need of protective measures for the sperm whales that come to the subarctic latitudes for the summer. Absence of stringent international restrictions may prove to be fatal for the North Pacific sperm whales.

In the southern half of the Pacific (outside the Antarctic) sperm whales are captured mainly by shore stations of Peru. Catches here have steadily dropped in recent years: in 1961, 3,600 specimens, 2,023 in 1964, and in 1966 only 862. In 1967 Peru did not take any whales at all. Eight whaling vessels were operating off the coast of Chile and captured 533 sperm whales. In these whaling regions, moreover, besides the reduced total volume of catches (from 2,300 in 1958) the mean standard length of animals has fallen from 12.1 to 10.5 m.

In the southeastern Pacific the single, small station of New Zealand, that has one whaler and which has stopped humpback whaling, is increasing its catches of sperms. For example, whereas up to 1963 this station had taken practically no sperm whales, in 1963 and in 1964, 114 and 134 animals, respectively, were caught. In subsequent years the station did not work.

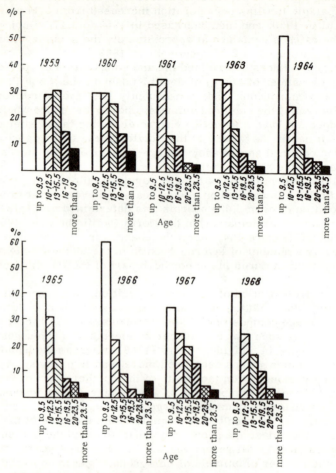

FIGURE 134. Age composition of male sperm whales taken in the North Pacific in 1959—1968

In the Atlantic Ocean a larger number of countries than in other oceans and various latitudes carry out sperm whaling, but the stations are not as well established and have small fleets. The largest number of sperm whales is taken by the shore station of Saldanha (Cape Province) in Southeast Africa. In 1967, 5 whalers from this station captured 630 sperm whales.

The whalers of the Azores (who still hunt and process on the 19th century level) carry out relatively intensive and steady sperm whaling. Statistics record a decrease of sperm catches in these regions as well: 478 animals were taken here in 1964, 379 in 1965, and 310 in 1967. On Madeira, not far from this region, 151 sperm whales were taken in 1965, 113 in 1966, and 85 in 1967. Three shore stations of Spain with 3 whalers took 207 sperm whales in 1967; 4 whalers of a station on the west shore of Iceland took 119 sperm whales. The station of the Faeroes gradually reduced its catches from 141 sperms in 1957 to one specimen in 1966; in 1967 it had already stopped working. Brazil captured 20 sperm whales in 1967.

In the Indian Ocean the shore station in Natal continuously increased its catches of sperm whales up to 1965, when 2,814 were taken by 12 whalers. In the following years catches began to drop, and in 1967 only 1,626 sperms were taken. In the southeastern part of the Indian Ocean a shore station with 3 whalers operates on the shore of the Great Australian Bight at Albany.

After the reserves of baleen whales in the Antarctic, and particularly those of humpback whales that wintered off these shores, had been exhausted, Australia began to go over to sperm whaling and by 1964 had taken up to 710 animals (only 7 sperms were captured in 1955). In 1967 the station took 506 sperm whales (see Appendix II).

We must mention the sperm whaling that is as intensive as it is harmful (the breeding part of the population being involved in the catches) that has developed in recent years due to the drop in the reserves of baleen whales in the Antarctic. We are referring to the sperm whaling going on north of 40° S in all three oceans.

Thus, in 1964 nine flotillas (4 Soviet and 5 Japanese) that operated in different latitudes of the southern part of the Indian Ocean captured 2,095 sperm whales. In 1964 two Japanese flotillas took 1,779 sperms in the southern part of the Pacific. In the Indian Ocean to the north of 40°S one Soviet and four Norwegian flotillas captured 442 sperm whales in 1964.

Statistical data testify to an almost ubiquitous reduction of 1) the number of shore bases, 2) the whaling fleet, and consequently, 3) the catches of sperm whales (and obviously also of the numerical abundance of these animals) in almost all the coastal whaling areas of the World Ocean.

Sperm whaling in the Antarctic continues to be of considerable importance, and catches in this region are never below 4,000 specimens per season. The composition of the whaling fleet that has operated in recent years in the Antarctic is shown in Table 32.

TABLE 32. Composition of the whaling fleet in the Antarctic in 1961 — 1968

Country	1961/62 number		1962/63 number		1963/64 number		1964/65 number		1965/66 number		1966/67 number		1967/68 number	
	floating base	whaling vessels	floating base	whaling vessels	floating base	whaling vessels	floating base	whaling vessels	floating base	whaling vessels	floating base	whaling vessels	floating base	whaling vessels
Japan	7	85	7	79	7	78	7*	71	5	52	4	44	4	43
Norway.	7	71	4	32	4	33	4	36	2	21	2	21	1	5
USSR	4	67	4	70	4	68	4	65	3	55	3	55	3	49
Great Britain	2	22	1	9	—	—	—	—	—	—	—	—	—	—
Netherlands	1	15	1	11	1	11	—	—	—	—	—	—	—	—
Total	21	260	17	201	16	190	15	172	10	128	9	120	8	97

* One Japanese flotilla was not engaged in sperm whaling in antarctic waters.

A maximum number of sperm whales in the waters of the Antarctic were taken by deep-sea flotillas in the 1963—1964 season and constituted 6,651 animals, of which more than 50% was taken by the Soviet flotillas. In subsequent years the catches decreased and in the 1966—1967 season they amounted to 4,960 animals (only three countries operating). The number of sperms taken in the Antarctic by the Soviet Union is increasing each year and constitutes 80% of world catches in these waters. Up to 1966—1967 in the same high latitudes one or two shore stations operated on South Georgia Island; they captured 17 sperm whales in the 1965—1966 season (in the following seasons the station abandoned sperm whaling).

Sperm whaling in the Antarctic (Appendix II) has expanded due to the decreased numbers of baleen whales that used to be the main items. The gradual reduction in the number of flotillas sent to the Antarctic as well as the cessation of whaling by Great Britain and then by the Netherlands is explained by the decrease in the numbers of baleen whales.

With increased catches of sperm whales, the dimensions of the animals have decreased. Average sizes of sperm whales taken in the Antarctic are given below (Jonsgard, 1960; IWS).

Season	Size, m	Season	Size, m
1937/38	16.2	1957/58	14.5
1938/39	16.1	1958/59	14.4
1946/47	15.3	1959/60	14.4
1947/48	15.5	1960/61	14.3
1951/52	15.2	1961/62	14.1
1952/53	15.2	1962/63	14.2
1953/54	15.0	1963/64	13.8
1954/55	14.9	1964/65	13.9
1955/56	14.7	1965/66	13.8
1956/57	14.8		

Jonsgard (1960), analyzing the effect of whaling on the state of sperm whale herds in the Antarctic, points out that the percentage of large (15 m and longer) sperm whales is steadily decreasing and the percentage of small ones (less than 15 m) rising; whereas, for example, in 1948—1949 the proportion of large males was 64%, by 1958—1959 it constituted only 16.5%. The same author reports that according to data of Norwegian whaling, there is no relationship between the average size of animals, months of catches, and geographical location of the catch region. But according to Kirpichnikov (1950), such a relationship can be perceived.

The results of age determinations in male sperms taken by the "Sovetskaya Rossiya" in 1962—1967, which are presented in the diagram (Figure 135), do not show so far a notable deterioration in the state of the stocks. The average age of antarctic male sperm whales was 13—15 years in 1966—1967. Nevertheless, one inevitably notes a regular increase in the catches of the number of younger animals and the $3^1/_2$ times decrease of older sperms. Comparison of the age structure of animals taken in the North Pacific and in the Antarctic testifies to a better composition of the herds in the southern latitudes. It should be mentioned that the decrease in the average length of the animals taken could have (and should have) occurred due to the intensification of whaling in the more northern waters, where the smaller, herd animals inhabit. This refers in equal measure to the age composition as well.

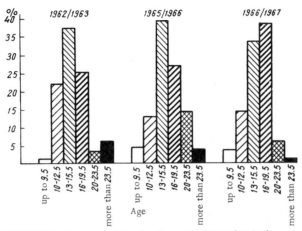

FIGURE 135. Age composition of male sperm whales taken in the Antarctic

In the 1966—1967 season in the Antarctic and in the calendar year 1967 in other regions of the World Ocean, 12 countries (16 flotillas, 26 shore stations, and 250 whaling vessels) captured 25,921 sperm whales, more than 50% (14,775 specimens) being taken by Soviet whalers (IWS). For the other countries the catches were distributed as follows:

Country	Number of sperms	Country	Number of sperms
Japan	6,007	Portugal	395
South African Republic	2,256	Canada	306
Norway.	617	Spain	207
Australia.	586	United States	100
Chile	533	Brazil	20

Rational, economically viable whaling of male sperm whales in the northern and southern waters (above 50°) can be carried out on a large scale. In case of excessive catches in these waters the average length (and age) of the animals will reach that at which the male sperms leave the harems (about 12 m), and it will fluctuate around this size, whereas a deterioration in the state of the reserves can be expressed only in a decrease in the number of adults taken. As a result of intensive whaling the number of male sperm whales in the high latitudes may decrease to a certain fairly high limit depending on the numerical strength of the herds taking part in breeding and equal approximately to the number of annual progeny; it will not decrease subsequently independently of the intensity of whaling. In view of this it will be possible, without any damage to the major breeding part of the population (and thus to the stocks as a whole) to have quite a high annual catch of adult sperms.

But this will be only on condition that whaling be stopped in both hemispheres at latitudes below 40°.

SPERM WHALING

With current techniques, whaling is considered simpler in the case of sperms than where the majority of baleen whales are concerned. The sperm whale is less mobile, less swift and less agile, and stays longer on the surface, particularly after prolonged submersion, than other whales. If a whaler manages to "catch up with" the whale soon after it breaks the surface, the animal may not even react to the approach of the vessel. In view of this, experienced harpooners (Golovlev, 1960) at first approach the whale as closely as possible at full speed and then at a distance of about 300 m switch to minimum speed in order not to frighten it; they frequently turn off the engine and proceed under the vessel's own momentum, but they must do so on the right side of the tail, leaving the animal on the left at an angle of 45°. The whale is shot at a point in front of the dorsal fin (at a distance of about 1.5 m) at the line of the water surface. In this case the harpoon with grenade penetrates the trunk from right to left and enters the heart.

FIGURE 136. Shot from a harpoon gun from a whaling vessel (photo by Veinger)

310

The vessel must move slowly in the wake of the sperm, which makes several turns under the water; its behavior must be patiently studied in order to note characteristic features during several dives and to act accordingly. There is no difference in principle in the search, hunt, and shooting of sperm whales and rorquals (Figure 136). After the animal has been shot and dragged to the bows, all sperm whales, without exception, as well as other whales have air pumped into them by compressors for better bouyancy. In the 18th and 19th centuries whalers took sperm whales (and not rorquals) because these whales and also right whales were thought not to sink after death. At present sperm whales are considered to sink after death, and in fact, some of them do, primarily young animals, that have a smaller amount of fat.

FIGURE 137. Present-day hunting of sperm whales off the Azores. A harpooner casts his harpoon into a 16-m male (Clarke, 1953)

If the hunt continues, the whale that has been pumped with air is usually left "afloat," leaving in it a flag and a radio buoy, and often also a passive reflector for locating the animal by ship's radar. At dusk or after whaling ceases, the whaler collects the whales killed and tows them to the base.

Under conditions of modern whaling, with fast and powerful vessels, only a very prolonged dive and surfacing at a considerable distance from the place of diving may give the sperm a chance to escape pursuit; whalers abandon the hunt in such cases.

The Azores and Madeira are areas where sperm whaling is still carried out with equipment and methods that have scarcely changed for a hundred years. This interesting yet inexplicable practice deserves more detailed description.

Observations on whales in these regions are performed all the year round from dawn to dusk from coastal observation points high up in cliffs. A white flag and a rocket announce the detection of spoutings. Boats, 10.5 — 11.5 m long, which have six pairs of oars and a crew of seven, are lowered into the water. Such a boat carries sailing equipment (jib). Motor boats tow the men into the immediate vicinity (within a mile) of the whales. This is the main purpose of the motor boats, unless we count the fairly frequent need to rescue whalers following accidents during operations (Clarke, 1953).

When the sperm whale is quite near, the harpooner kneels in the bow, and if the boat managed to come up to within several meters of the whale (sometimes the bow even touches the animal), the harpooner raises his arm and throws a 3-m harpoon made of forged iron on a wooden pole (Figure 137). The wounded sperm is then finished off with spears 3.5 m long with a tip of 1.5 m, petal-shaped at the end, attached to a 2-m pole.

The processing of the whales is carried out with methods that are no more modern than the hunting itself. At some stations, flensing is done by rolling the whale along the shore; the blubber is boiled in kettles.

The motor boats and radio and telephone communication between some observation points are actually the only elements that distinguish present-day whaling in the Azores from whaling in the days of Herman Melville and Captain Scoresby.

Chapter 18

COMMERCIAL WHALING

In writing the present section we drew on material of I.I. Khar'kov (1940), I.V, Kizevetter (1953), V.A. Bodrov, S.N. Grigor'ev, and V.A. Tver'yanovich (1958), Bodrov and Grigor'ev (1963), and some other authors as well as our scant data and material of scientific groups of Soviet whaling bases.

WEIGHT AND CHEMICAL COMPOSITION OF THE SPERM
WHALE'S BODY

Naturally, the weight of the body depends primarily on the length of the animal, as is shown in Table 33, based on mean monthly (December — March) tables of determination of the weight of raw material brought in by Soviet Antarctic flotillas (the weighings were recently carried out at Soviet whaling bases under the guidance of scientific workers).

The weight of the animals varies also in the course of the year.

Zenkovich (1937) suggests the following formula for determination of the weight of a sperm whale:

$$\frac{LD^2}{3},$$

whcre L is the zoological length of the body; D is the maximum height of the body.

The error using this formula, according to the author, is from 1.03 — 4.2%.

Omura (1950) suggests the following formulas for determining the weight of a sperm and its parts:

for determining the total weight of the body $P = 0.000137^{3.18}$

flesh — $P = 0.0000367\ L^{3.24}$

fat — $P = 0.0000452\ L^{3.18}$

bones — $P = 0.000041\ L^{2.88}$

viscera — $P = 0.0038\ L^{1.64}$,

312 (where L is the length of the body).

The relative weight of organs and parts is given below.

Part of body	Weight, percentage of body weight	Part of body	Weight, percentage of body weight
Fat	22.8	Lower jaw.................	1.5
Spermaceti fluid	6.7	Ribs	4.1
Spermaceti sac	14.8	Thoracic fins with scapulae	2.0
Tendons	3.6	Pelvic bones	0.5
Meat	19.7	Sternum	0.7
Skull	9.7	Caudal flukes	1.4
Vertebrae	7.6	Viscera	4.9

The blubber is of a dirty or grayish white color, and on the whole has a more compact consistency than that of baleen whales.

Denser fat with a large amount of connective tissue and correspondingly a higher content of adipocere* is situated on the head (particularly around the eyes) and on the lower jaw (4—5% adipocere); the last has in essence very little in common with fat. Of lowest density (smallest number of connective tissue fibers) and greatest adiposity is the fat situated on the ventral side near the thoracic fins and in the dorsal fin (56—64% adipocere). The fat of the head contains on the average 24—27% and that of the trunk 50—60% adipocere. On the whole, the fat on the dorsal side is more fatty (40—64% adipocere), than on the sides of the trunk and on the belly (31—58% adipocere). An average 44—47% adipocere is contained in the blubber. The content of adipocere changes substantially even in one area depending on the position of the layer; the fat content is highest, 65—80%, in the middle layers, while closer to the epidermis or muscle tissue it decreases to 15—20%. The thickness of the fat naturally differs also in different parts of the body. Whereas the thickest layer, situated on the ventral side near the thoracid fins is 30 cm thick, the layer on the head and in the caudal part is only 4—6 cm thick.

TABLE 33. Dependence of the body weight of the sperm whale (in tons) on the body length

Length of body, m	Tenths of a meter									
	0	1	2	3	4	5	6	7	8	9
11	—	—	—	—	—	—	19.5	20.0	20.5	21.0
12	21.6	22.1	22.6	23.2	23.8	24.4	25.0	25.6	26.2	26.8
13	27.4	28.0	28.7	29.4	30.0	30.7	31.4	32.1	32.8	33.5
14	34.3	35.0	35.8	36.5	37.2	38.3	38.9	39.6	40.5	41.2
15	42.1	43.0	43.9	44.7	45.6	46.5	47.4	48.3	49.2	50.1
16	51.1	52.1	53.1	54.1	55.1	56.1	57.1	58.1	59.2	60.2
17	61.3	62.4	63.5	64.6	65.7	66.8	68.0	69.2	70.4	71.6

It is usual to measure fat thickness in a selected area — at the side of the body at the level of the dorsal fin. The chemical composition of the

* It has been suggested that the fatty substances of toothed whales in distinction from the pure fat of baleen whales be called adipocere.

subcutaneous fat of two sperms is shown in Table 34. Of course, the composition is different in various parts of the body of one animal and in the same section in various animals (in particular, variations in adipocere content in the selected area place can amount to 10%).

The density of the fat is $0.87-0.9 \, g/cm^3$ (at 20°C), i.e., the fat of toothed whales is on the whole lighter than that of baleen whales (density $0.91-0.93 \, g/cm^3$).

TABLE 34. Chemical composition of the subcutaneous fat of sperm whales, %

Moisture	Adipocere	Dry and fat-free matter
37.01	43.91	18.67
33.11	47.60	19.29

Spermaceti contains 97—98% adipocere. The amount of spermaceti varies greatly and depends mainly on the size of the body, increasing from 2.7% in the young animal to 10.8% in a large male 18 m long.

The **bones** of the sperm whale differ in their chemical composition. The content of adipocere in the vertebral column varies from 13 to 53%; it increases from the caudal part (47—54% adipocere) toward the head and then becomes almost constant. The amount of moisture in the vertebral column varies from 10.6 to 38%. The content of adipocere in the upper jaw in the same animal is from 33.5 to 50.6% and in the ribs from 14.5 to 35% (average 26%).

The **flesh** is coarse-fibered, dark, almost black; its chemical composition hardly changes according to season. The leanest flesh is along the vertebral column (1.2—3% adipocere). The chemical composition of the flesh is given in Table 35.

TABLE 35. Chemical composition of sperm whale flesh, %

Flesh	Moisture	Adipocere	Protein
From the back	72.9 — 73.9	1.8 — 2.8	22.1 — 23.4
From under the vertebral column	73.2 — 75.7	1.2 — 2.8	21.7 — 23.9
From the belly	71.5	5.7	21.4
From the ribs	69.2	8.5	21.0

The **viscera** are lean; only the intestines, as seen from results of chemical analysis presented in Table 36, have about 15% adipocere.

TABLE 36. Chemical composition of sperm whale viscera, %

Organ	Moisture	Adipocere	Protein
Lungs	77.9	2.8	17.4
Liver	74.1	4.1*	19.46
Heart	78.4	7.1	—
Stomach	80.4	1.9	—
Intestines	68.7	15.2	—

* Averaged data of K. A. Mrochkov (1951) and N. M. Gavrilenko (1951).

318

According to data of various authors the liver of all whales is rich in vitamin A; the average content in the liver of North Pacific sperm whales varies from 5,200 — 79,500 (average 14,000 — 26,000) IU per gram. Such fluctuations are explained by individual variations of animals, different methods of preparation, and also by the different content of vitamin A in animals of different length (and age); as a rule the larger the animal, the greater the vitamin A content in the liver.

According to Mrochkov (1951), in sexually mature sperm whales from the Antarctic the content of vitamin A in one gram of liver is from 4,320 — 15,280 IU. The vitamin A content in two females (same data) was more than 2,400 and 11,570 IU per gram. The liver of an immature male contained still less vitamin A (1,850 IU per gram).

One gram of adipocere of the liver in the sperm whale contains up to 720,000 IU vitamin A, on the average about 328,000 IU (Bodrov and Grigor'ev, 1963), much more than in baleen whales. The sperm whale liver also contains vitamins of the B complex (B_1, B_2, B_{12}) and folic acid.

PROCESSING AND UTILIZATION OF THE RAW MATERIAL

The procedure for processing sperm whales differs somewhat from that in the case of baleen whales. The whale delivered to the base is raised on a slipway to the flensing deck (or platform), a transverse vertical cut is made with a flensing knife on the head about 15 — 20 cm from the end of the upper jaw and a horizontal cut, and as a result a segmental incision is formed which is connected with the longitudinal cut through the blubber from tail to head. The fat on the head having been trimmed from the segmentary incision, a cleaver is introduced which is connected to the hooks of pennants of 5-ton winches and the blubber is removed (Figure 138); the animal is turned over (for removal of the fat from the other side of the carcass) with the aid of two winches: a 10-ton winch connected with a strap running under the carcass and placed on the thoracic fin and a 5-ton winch connected with the strap fixed to the lower jaw. The ribs are separated from the vertebral column by means of a winch and hook-shaped knife.

The head is opened (Figure 139) for removal of the spermaceti sac, which is divided up and the parts placed in kettles (Figure 140). The skull and other bones are sawn into pieces and sent for fat extraction together with other flesh and bone scraps.

The fat and flesh and bone scaps are preliminarily cut into equal pieces (approximately 40×80×60 cm) before being placed in the kettles. The liver is extracted, cut into pieces, and sent to be frozen or salted.

The stomach, heart, kidneys, and other viscera are as a rule boiled with other raw fats. The layers of flesh removed (usually from the back, more rarely from the belly) are cut into pieces weighing 10 — 15 kg and placed in a meat cutter. Fat flesh is boiled.

The teeth are extracted after the lower jaw has been kept for 1 — 2 hours in hot water in open kettles (at a temperature above 100°C exfoliation of tissues occurs, and the teeth lose their value as a material for handicrafts) or longitudinal cuts are made at both sides of the tooth line and the toothrow is pulled together with the connective tissue between the teeth. Large teeth (over 8 cm long) without fractures, chips, or fissures are considered the most valuable. The total weight of a sperm whale's teeth is in the range of 5 — 14 kg.

When the tendons from the so-called tendon corpus are processed at the base, after removal of the frontal blubber, the first layer of tendinous tissue is cut out with a flensing knife before the head is severed; the second layer is cut off already after removal of the spermaceti corpus and opening of the head. Tendons extracted from the layer (by means of hooks manually or with electrical block and tackle, and clamping device) are washed in water and preserved by salting (dry salt in casks) or drying. Up to 170 kg raw salted tendons can be obtained from one sperm whale.

FIGURE 138. Removing the blubber from a sperm whale (whaling base "Aleut")

When butchering the sperm whale the intestine must be carefully examined, particularly the large and small intestines, which may contain ambergris (see below). It may fall out from the anus already upon removal of the blubber.

The fat from the raw materials is obtained by various means but the one most commonly used at modern processing enterprises is rendering in kettles with direct steam while the rotors mix and mechanically break it up.

The stock, consisting of fat, water and fat-containing small protein and bone particles, is formed after 2 — 3 hours' boiling at a temperature not above 150°C at 4 atm.

The mass is continuously charged into a fat separator. The fat is freed of impurities in fat separators, settling tanks or decanters. The purified fat is poured into tanks and the dense bone-protein residue obtained during boiling and separation of the fat is used for the production of feed meal.

Cut into pieces or usually in the form of a pasty mass, the spermaceti fat is boiled in similar kettles separately from the other raw material. The fat products obtained from sperm whales contain 42 — 46% blubber-adipocere, 22 — 26% spermaceti and jaw adipocere, and 24 — 30% bone and meat fat.

The usual yield from one sperm is 11—14 tons of adipocere and up to 2 tons of spermaceti.

The fat or oil yield depends mainly on the size of the animal, its physiological state, age, etc.; these factors substantially affect the fatness of the animal. For instance, the total fat yield from one male 15.3 — 15.9 m long with an average 10.5-cm-thick fat layer amounts to 8.5 tons, with a 11.6-cm layer it is 8.7 tons, and with a 13.2-cm layer it is 9.6 tons. The fat yield from whales (11.6 — 12.0-cm fat layer) is shown below:

Length, m	Fat yield from one animal, tons
7.6 — 10.6	— (2.1)*
11.6	2.4 — 6.3 (3.6)
13.4 — 13.7	5.8 — 6.9 (6.0)
14.2 — 14.9	6.2 — 8.5 (7.6)
15.0 — 15.9	8.2 — 10.7 (9.6)
16.1 — 16.5	9.2 — 11.7 (10.0)

* Figures in parentheses denote the average yield of fat.

The fatty substances of sperm whales are characterized by the considerable content of unsaponifiable substances represented mainly by high molecule aliphatic alcohols (mainly oleic, 70%, and cetyl alcohols) and ethers, fatty acids and also hydrocarbons. The color of adipoceres varies from light yellow to dark yellow. The odor is little perceptible, specific, resembling that of fish.

(316)

FIGURE 139.   Dressing the head of a sperm whale (whaling base "Aleut")

The adipocere of sperm whales contains much more unsaponifiable substances, particularly the adipocere of the fat of cephalic spermaceti cells (30 — 40%) and has iodine numbers much lower than the oil from the fat of baleen whales. The adipocere of the blubber of sperm whales contains 31.8% glycerides and 34.2% fatty acids. The saturated fatty acids in them are mainly palmitic and myristic acids, while the unsaturated ones are physetoleic, oleic, and gadoleic acids. The adipocere of the flesh contains 55% glycerides, while the level of unsaponifiable substances is lower than in the adipocere of the blubber. The fatty substances isolated from the bones are intermediate in their physicochemical indexes between subcutaneous and cephalic adipoceres.

321

FIGURE 140. Removal of the upper spermaceti sac from the head of a sperm whale (whaling base "Aleut")

According to the analytical results obtained by TINRO technologists, the industrial sperm whale adipocere has the following chemical and physical indexes: acidity 1.5; iodine number 75.2; density (at 15°C) 0.8694 g/cm³; content of unsaponifiable substances 34.3%.

The adipocere obtained from raw spermaceti consists of solid (spermaceti) and fluid (spermaceti oil) parts which are a mixture of glycerides of unsaturated acids and higher unsaturated alcohols. The cephalic adipocere of sperm whales becomes solid at 7.8—15°C; it contains up to 63% fatty acids (lauric, myristic, capric, palmitic, tetradecenoic, zoomaric and others) and about 39% aliphatic alcohols.

The spermaceti isolated from cephalic adipocere by repeated crystallization and purification is a light, bright, coarse-crystalline mass, without taste or odor, readily soluble in ethyl ether, chloroform, carbon disulfide, and essential oils. The spermaceti consists of fatty acids (about 50%) the main components being palmitic acid, cetyl palmitate, cetyl stearate, and other esters. The density of spermaceti (at 15°C) is 0.085—0.095 g/cm³, the iodine number is 3.0—9.3, and the melting point is 41—46°C.

Spermaceti oil is a mixture of the low molecule fractions of spermaceti adipocere and the low molecular fractions of crystalline spermaceti dissolved in them. It contains up to 44% unsaponifiable substances and glycerides in a larger quantity than the natural adipocere.

The liver to be processed in vitamin plants, can be salted in casks, barrels or tanks, or frozen in blocks. The last method is used in the modern whaling bases.

The best method of extracting oil and vitamin A from the liver is hydrolysis cum extraction; the yield of vitamin A may be as large as 90—95%. The protein part of the liver in the form of meal enriched by B vitamins is better preserved using this method.

According to various authors the vitamin A level in the liver adipocere (and in the liver itself) varies greatly; it may be as high as 720,000 IU per gram of liver adipocere, but the average amount is 400,000 IU per gram. The corium of a sperm whale, consisting of the most densely intertwined collagenous tissue, can be classified as raw leather or hide. In principle it is also possible to use the dermal layer of the sperm whale, which is fat-saturated (just like the dermal layer of baleen whales). But this would be too complicated. Therefore only the 12—28-mm-thick corium of sperm whales is used as hides in the leather industry. A layer of up to 50-mm thickness can be removed from the head, where the corium is particularly compact and contains a large amount of connective tissue; this layer can be removed as two cuts up to 25 mm thick.

When preparing hides, cuts are made on the body of the sperm whale using definite procedures for obtaining two or three layers of hides (depending on the size of the animal).

The yield of the raw hides, depending on the size of the animal (surface hide and weight), is characterized by the figures in Table 37.

TABLE 37. Yield of raw leather hides from a sperm whale

Length, m	Surface of hides, m²	Weight of hides, kg
11.0	40.0	530
12.0	48.0	635
13.0	55.0	725
14.0	63.0	830
15.0	70.0	925
16.0	78.0	1,030

The hides are cut into sheets of 70—120 × 50—80 cm. The prepared sheets are trimmed on so-called splitting-belt machines. The whale hides are preserved by salting (wet salting in revolving drums or dry salting in stacks).

The defects in the corium of sperm whales arising during life as a result of parasites, sores or warts make it impossible to produce large sheets of hide. If there are large numbers of larvae of cestodes of the species Phyllobothrium delphini the hides of sperms cannot be used in the leather industry (Sokolov, 1955a), because the capsules leave holes right through the hide.

The hides of whales are processed by vegetable or chrome tanning. Then they can be used for manufacturing soles, gauntlets, and other items.

Since special equipment and large production areas are required for the preparation of whale hides, it is difficult to carry out the process on the floating bases and thus it is preferably done out on the shore. For this reason, industrial utilization of the sperm whale corium as hides began in the USSR in 1949 after the Kurile shore bases had been put into operation.

Below are statistical data on the production of hides in Soviet shore bases (Kurile Islands).

Year	Weight, tons	Year	Weight, tons
1950	677	1954	333
1951	676	1955	591
1952	601	1956	980
1953	519	1957	918

At present since the shore whale-processing enterprises have shut down in the USSR, no sperm whale raw hides are taken off.

Utilization of raw material. The fatty substances obtained in sperm whale processing are unsuitable for human consumption because of the high content of unsaponifiable substances; they are being used as technical oils. The adipocere of sperm whales finds wide application in industry.

The fatty acids are used in the soap industry and the unsaponifiable substances in manufacturing fine detergents (such as "Novost'"); the high molecular aliphatic alcohols in the leather and rubber industries in the manufacture of cosmetics, in greasing of wool, and flotation of ores; the stock after fat extraction is used for preparation of gelatin. Low molecular fatty acids (capric and lauric) can be used for obtaining aromatic substances. Kizevetter (1953) considers that separation of adipoceres into individual components is desirable for more efficient utilization of fats of the sperm whale.

Spermaceti oil is used as lubricants for fine mechanisms. Solid spermaceti is used as carriers in manufacturing many medical and cosmetic products, mainly various face creams and ointments, and for the production of lithographic ink, and for degreasing of wool.

The best kind of candles that burn without soot were made of spermaceti before the appearance of gas.

The therapeutic properties of spermaceti have been known for a long time; for instance, it is very good for treatment of burns.

The meat of sperm whales is inedible because it contains adipocere, but it is rich in proteins and is therefore valuable for the production of feed meal. Addition of feed meal to animal fodder contributes to growth, weight increment, improvement of general state, and fattening. Boiled sperm whale flesh can be used for feeding fur-bearing animals and in the preparation of dry protein.

The liver of whales, particularly of the sperm, is the most valuable raw material for the vitamin industry. Edible and medicinal oils are enriched with vitamin A obtained from whale liver. According to Bukin and Skorobogatova (1951), the liver of one sperm is equivalent to 3.3 kg carotene (5.5 billions IU). Such an amount of carotene is obtained when processing over 50 tons of carrots. The vitamin A level in the liver of one sperm whale is equal to the amount of vitamin A in 100 tons of the best butter; this amount of the vitamin is also sufficient for enriching 100 tons of margarine with vitamin A.

The liver of whales, and particularly that of sperm whales, can be used in the manufacture of kampolon MZh,* an antianemic preparation, containing the B vitamins and used for intramuscular injections in the treatment of malignant anemia.

---

* [Soviet trade mark.]

320   The semifinished product for kampolon MZh is usually prepared at the
whale processing bases; it is obtained by boiling the fresh liver with
subsequent pressing of an aqueous extract which then is concentrated by
evaporating up to a certain density. The compact residue of the liver after
the boiling is hydrolyzed to make the extraction of vitamin A possible. The
yield of kampolon MZh constitutes on the average 5% of the weight of the
liver. The liver can be also used for the production of feed meal.

The tendons of the sperm whale's head can be utilized (and have been
utilized in the Soviet Union) for manufacturing glue.

The teeth are good material for handicrafts. They are readily processed
and beautiful when polished. A pattern of alternating parallel, ringed,
(depending on the position of the plane of the cut), white yellowish, light
brown streaks of dentin is seen on the yellowish surface of the cross section
of the tooth.

Ever since whaling started, the skilled hands of bone carvers have carved
out of sperm whale teeth canes, chess pieces, cigarette holders, pipes,
wine cups, knife handles, whips, umbrellas, napkin rings, studs,
buttons, etc., as well as figures of animals (whales, penguins, etc.), and
even minute sailing and whaling boats. Many objects can be made out of
pieces of bone, particularly of the lower jaw. At the present time there
are large workshops using raw material from the Antarctic.

In Japan and Norway small centers are organized for bone carving
and their products are sold to many countries. Painting on polished teeth,
by searing, dyes, ashes or India ink after making notches with needles
or knives is very popular.

The whalers of the 18th and 19th centuries were great masters in
carving. When the whaling fleet still consisted of sailing ships, turning
items from sperm whale teeth brightened up the long foggy periods and
the months spent in hunting for whales. The teeth were distributed according
to the rank of the crew members (Melville, 1851; Caldwell, 1961).

Ambergris can be found in one (Boylsten, 1724), or even in 3 — 4 sperm
whales (Ivashin, 1963) out of a hundred.

This substance has long been known to man; the ancient Greeks and
Romans were very familiar with it and ascribed healing properties to it. In
those days ambergris was considered either bitumen discharged by underwater springs, or a biological product of some insect similar to honey and
silk, or a resin secretion from tree roots (some even suggested increasing
the quantity of ambergris by planting trees along seashores), or the
droppings of a mysterious bird, or beehives treated by salty seawater. In
those days this substance was found floating in the sea or lying on the sandy
coastal beaches, mainly in the tropical and subtropical regions of oceans.

In a number of regions of the Middle East and Asia ambergris has been
considered (and is still considered) as an antispasmatic drug; the Turks
used it as an aphrodisiac. In Mecca it was used as incense for fumigation.
In the Orient, ambergris was used as a spice. For a long time it was applied
in the treatment of epilepsy, typhoid, asthma, and other diseases. Ambergris was incorporated into creams, candles, face powder, lipstick, etc.
Seamen used it as a laxative.

Boylsten (1724) was the first to point out that ambergris originates from
sperm whales and that it is located near the whale's genitals. Dudley
(1725) also considers ambergris to be a biological product of the sperm
whale. He reports (from communications of whalers) that the substance

is found in a special oval pouch more than one meter long situated at the root of the penis and is encountered only in old males.

Schwediawer (1783) thought that ambergris was the excrement of sperm whales mixed with fragments of cephalopod rostra and he gives a comprehensive description of it.

Ambergris is a solid, opaque substance found as irregularly shaped lumps, although sometimes some lamination is found (Schwediawer, 1783; Tomilin, 1957); it is fairly fragile, with a pungent, unpleasant, specific and stable odor (Figure 141). The smell, however, becomes pleasant with time, similar to musk, ladanum, jasmine, etc. With increasing age of the ambergris, the odor intensifies.

FIGURE 141. A piece of ambergris weighing 420 kg found in a sperm whale in the Antarctic in 1953 (Clarke, 1954)

Beneden and Gervais (1880) consider that ambergris has the odor of musk due to Cephalopoda and in particular to E l e d o n e s (cuttlefish E l e d o n e s m o s h a t a, according to Ivashin, 1963), distinguished by a characteristic smell of musk.

The color of ambergris is from light to almost black, sometimes with an inclusion of purple pigment (Tomilin, 1957). The quality of the light ambergris is considered the best. When extracted from sperm whales, the ambergris is covered with a layer of dark, sticky, mazutlike substance.

Schwediawer (1783) writes that when chewed, ambergris has an earthy taste and sticks to the teeth, as well as to cold steel when it is crushed.

The major feature in the determination of ambergris is the presence of small, dark inclusions of remnants of chitinous rostra of Cephalopoda on the fracture (Schwediawer writes that at one time these were mistaken for the claws of birds and for shells). Carter and Elsey (1954) report that fish bones, and diamtomaceous algae, etc., can be encountered in ambergris. According to Tomilin (1957), inclusions and other foreign bodies constitute 25% of the weight of ambergris. Examination of material by Ivashin (1963) and the present author does not confirm such a proportion of inclusions.

Ambergris has a density (at 15°C) of 0.73—0.95 g/cm³ (Kizevetter, 1953; Ivashin, 1963; Ivashin, 1968), depending partially on the degree of ripeness. Because of this density it is found both in the sea and on the shore. However in our collection one of the pieces found on the whaling base "Sovetskaya Rossiya" in the season of 1961—1962, was so dense that it sank both in salt and in fresh water. According to the data of Ivashin (1968), ambergris has the following chemical composition (in %):

Pristane $(C_{18}H_{38})$*	2—4	Coprosterol	1—5
Ambrein	25—45	Betone	3—4
Cholesterol	0.1	Coprostanone	3—4
Epicholesterol	30—40	Free acids	5—8
		Residue insoluble in ether	10—16

* [The formula of pristane is $C_{19}H_{40}$ or $C_{20}H_{42}$.]

Thus, the bulk of commercial ambergris consists of nonvolatile, high molecular alcohols. It dissolves in ether, warmed alcohols, and oil. It melts at 60—65°C. It evaporates at 100°C, and softens from the warmth of the hands, according to most authors (Tomilin, 1957; and others) and according to our data. Ivashin (1963), however, does not confirm this physical characteristic. Placed on heated metal, ambergris burns up with abundant smoke and disappears without trace. When brought to fire it enflames and is combusted giving a pure, bright bluish flame until it is completely burnt up. A needle heated to red heat (Schwediawer, 1783) passes through ambergris, and at the place where it passes produces a blackish fat; the substance does not stick to the needle. As a rule, ambergris occurs in small pieces (from some 100 g to 1,000 g) and usually only one piece in an animal. However, there are many cases where much larger lumps of ambergris have been extracted from sperm whales and sometimes several pieces were found. In the Arctic whaling fleet "Sovetskaya Ukraina" (Ivashin, 1963) in 1961, 63 pieces of ambergris were found in a sperm whale 14.4 m long; the largest lumps weighed 11,080, 5,950, 1,100, 900 and 725 g, and the weight of the other pieces was between 1—2 and 50 g. Total weight was 20.5 kg and there were also several small pieces, each of which weighed up to 900 g. According to Carter and Elsey (1954), some thousand pieces of ambergris with a total weight of 163 kg were extracted from a male sperm whale on the shore station of Vancouver Island in British Columbia in 1952. At present, ambergris is frequently found in even larger amounts and in even larger pieces. Thus, according to Clarke (1954), in 1947, on the whaling base "The Southern Harvester" a piece of ambergris weighing 154 kg (340 lb) and 66 cm in cross sectional diameter was discovered in a sperm whale; off the coast of Australia a sperm was killed and a piece of ambergris weighing 419 kg (924 lb) was discovered in it, and finally, on the English whaling base mentioned above a piece of ambergris weighing 420 kg (926 lb) with the maximum diameter of 165 cm (Figure 141) was extracted from a 14.9 m sperm whale caught in the Antarctic in 1953. Clarke considers this find to 323 be the second heaviest amount of ambergris in a single lump. He considers the piece of ambergris that belonged to a Dutch company and weighed 491 kg as the largest in the world (Beneden and Gervais, 1868—1880). But Clarke reports that this piece weighed only 445 kg. However, Beneden, Gervais, and Clarke express their doubts that this piece was extracted from a single sperm whale.

Clarke (1954) reports that a Brazilian vessel "Arax" collided at sea with a "smelly gray mass" of ambergris weighing 10 tons and he is sure that (if the weight of the mass was not exaggerated) it was an unusual floating accumulation of a large number of ambergris pieces closely adhering to one another.

Among the pieces of ambergris found on shore we would mention a 60-kg piece found in 1929 on the shore of the Zhupanovo esturary in Kronotskoi Gulf on Kamchatka (Zenkovich, 1952); this find is interesting as an example of ambergris collected in northern latitudes.

One of the ships of the "Aleut" (Zemskii and Berzin, 1959) was the first whaling base in the USSR to discover a lump of ambergris (weighing 351 g) in 1958; this late date can be explained by the lack of knowledge of Soviet whalers about the external form of this material. The whalers of the Ukraine (Odessa) were informed of this find, and on the next cruise, in 1958—1959 on the Arctic whaling flotilla "Slava" an 850-g piece of ambergris was extracted from a sperm whale. During the next cruise, in 1960—1961, ambergris was found in eight sperms (total weight of the pieces 177 kg); in the 1961—1962 season the Soviet flotillas in the Antarctic collected 120 kg of ambergris. From then on Soviet whalers have collected such amounts of ambergris that there is no longer any need to import it. In 1964—1965 the Arctic whaling flotilla "Slava" found 465 kg of ambergris, while the "Yurii Dolgorukii" collected 900 kg of this material. Among the large pieces of ambergris found by the Soviet whaling bases let us mention the 102-kg piece, the 130-kg lump found by the whaling base "Yurii Dolgorukii" in 1964—1965, and a 270-kg piece extracted from a 15.5 m sperm whale by the sailors of the "Sovetskaya Rossiya" in 1967 (Ivashin, 1968).

Ambergris is freed of admixtures, dried and left to "ripen." During the storage of raw ambergris the material is dried to a large extent in small pieces (weighing up to 1 kg); the weight loss is 35—37% of the original weight, while in large pieces it may be as high as $1/7—1/8$ of the total weight. Thus, the weight of a 48.5-kg piece decreased by 7.5 kg during 45-day storage, a 102-kg piece lost water at a rate of 455 g/day during a month of storage (Ivashin, 1963, 1968).

The quality of commercial ambergris is determined mainly by color and odor. Black ambergris is considered the least valuable, the brown variety is valued somewhat higher. Light and dark gray ambergris is widely used in the cosmetics industry. The value of golden and white ambergris is very high; this material is very fragile evidently because of its long-term stay in the sea and may disintegrate when touched by hand (Ivashin, 1968).

There were conflicting theories as to the origin of ambergris in the late 19th and early 20th century. Pouchet and Beauregard (1892) assumed that ambergris is a gallstone. Others thought that the substance consists of the whale's feces acted on by the seawater under certain conditions. The investigators who consider that ambergris is formed in the intestine also

differ in their opinion about its origin. Some of them consider it a product of normal secretion of the rectum, others as the chitinous jaws of Cephalopoda, digested under specific conditions, while still others believe that it is the result of the reaction of the sperm whale's organism to
324 irritation by small parasites whose habitat is the small intestine (Tomilin, 1957).

The conclusion drawn by Schwediawer back in 1783 is more reliable and finds more protagonists (Clarke, 1954a and others), viz. that ambergris consists of hardened excrements of the sperm whale mixed with particles of Cephalopoda Rostra. Ivashin (1968) proposed the following theory. A sticky, dark tarlike mass is formed during the digestive process. This is the parent material of ambergris. The mass has a very viscous consistency. It advances gradually along the intestine and, if conditions are favorable, forms a lump and envelops the small, hard formations (undigested food remains) encountered en route. Gradually, foreign inclusions are accumulated in the new, small lump and pieces of the mass stick to it.

Schwediawer (1783) writes that pieces of ambergris may cause swelling in the lower part of the belly and constipate the intestine, and as a result the sperm whale becomes thin, sluggish and "apathetic"; it may even be fatal. He also points out that ambergris has frequently been found in dead whales floating on the surface. Atwood, 1869, had a similar opinion; he pointed out that ambergris was found in two lean sperm whales, while Peale (1932) gave further evidence of the harmful effect of ambergris on the whale body; he pointed out the simultaneous presence of ambergris in the animal and sores on its body. However, all later observations (Clarke 1954a, Ivashin, 1963, and our observations) do not lead to the conclusion that there are any noticeable differences between sperm whales with and without ambergris.

The site of ambergris in the body of sperm whales, which until quite recently was disputed, seems to be quite certain today. The substance is formed in the intestines and is retained mainly in the colon and rectum. Ivashin (1968) calculated the average annual increment to be between 8 and 14 kg.

It had been considered until quite recently by experts that ambergris is encountered only in males, although contrary evidence was provided as early as 1783 by Schwediawer; this author noted that ambergris is found also in female sperm whales, though its occurrence is much less frequent and the pieces are smaller. Moreover, the author reports that ambergris of females is cheaper not only because the smaller pieces weigh less, but because large pieces of ambergris are older and possess to a greater degree the properties valued in the material.

Clarke (1954a) considers that it is possible to obtain ambergris in the laboratory by cultivating the feces of sperm whales under favorable conditions.

At present the expensive ambergris finds its application mainly in cosmetics, where its property to adsorb, intensify, and stabilize for years the volatile and delicate fragrances is utilized. Substitutes of ambergris produced in recent years are of much poorer quality than the genuine article. The Soviet perfumes "Moskva Belokamennaya," "Kometa," "Yaroslavna," and others are manufactured with natural ambergris.

At the present stage of commercial whaling, when the reserves of whales (including sperms) are being exhausted, efficient utilization of the whales caught (including the raw material) is a very urgent problem. All the

technical and scientific prerequisites for a rapid solution are available;
first the catching of such items as sperm whales, which are the most important species, and secondly, the modern whaling bases. The latter make
it possible to obtain from the whale a rich assortment of valuable products
which will certainly be in great demand on the world market.

APPENDIX I

Species recorded as food items for sperm whales in the World Ocean*

Item	Ocean				Remark
	Pacific	Atlantic	Indian	Antarc- tic	
CEPHALOPODA					
Decapoda					
Lepidoteuthidae					
Lepidoteuthis grimaldii		+			
Cucioteuthis unguiculatus		+			
Octopodoteuthidae					
Octopodoteuthis longiptera	+	+			
Onychoteuthidae			+		
Onychoteuthis banksii	+	+?		+	Type species
Moroteuthis robusta	+		+	+	in the
Tetronychoteuthis dussumierü		+			Antarctic
Gonatidae					
Gonatus magister	+				
G. fabricii	+				
Gonatopsis borealis	+				
Architeuthidae					
Architeuthis sp. (japonica)	+	+	+	+	
Histioteuthidae					
Meleagroteuthis separata	+	+	+	+	
Histioteuthis bonelliana	+				
Stigmatoteuthis dolfeini	+				
Ommatostrephidae					
Dosidicus gigas	+				
Illex ilecebrosus	+				
Sthenoteuthis bartrami	+		+		
Chiroteuthidae					
Mastigoteuthis sp.	+				
Chiroteuthis veranyi	+				
Cranchiidae					
Crystalloteuthis behringiana	+				
Galiteuthis armata	+	+?			
Taonius pavo	+				
Octopoda					
Octopodidae					
Eledone moschata	+				
Octopus vulgaris	+				
O. gilbertianus	+				
Paroctopus conispadiceus	+				
P. gilbertianus	+				
Alloposidae					
Alloposus mollis	+				

*   The list has been drawn up on the basis of data taken from works by Akimushin, Berzin, Betesheva, Clarke, Korabel'nikov, Mitsue, Sleptsova, Okutani, and Nemoto, Tarasevich, Tomilin, Zenkovich, and others.

Item	Ocean				Remark
	Pacific	Atlantic	Indian	Antarc-tic	
Bolitaenidae					
Japetella heathi	+				
Amphitretidae					After Akimushkin
Amphitretus sp.	+				(1963); evidently
Stauroteuthidae					pelagicus
Grimpoteuthis albatrossi	+				
PISCES					
Petromyzonidae					
Entosphenus tridentatus	+				
Lamnidae					
Cetorhinus maximus	+?	+			
Carcharinidae					
Prionace glauca		+			
Scyliorhinidae					
Apristurus brunneus	+				
Squalidae					
Squalus acanthias	+				
Dalatiidae					
Somniosus sp.?(pacificus?)	+				
Squatinidae					
Squatina californica	+				
Chimaeridae					
Rajidae					
Raja rhina	+				
R. griseocaudata		+			
Clupeidae					
Sardinops sagax melanosticta	+				
Etrumeus micropus	+				
Engraulidae					
Engraulis japonicus	+				
Salmonidae					
Oncorhynchus gorbuscha	+				
Oncorhynchus sp.	+				
Alepisauridae					
Alepisaurus aesculapius	+				
Myctophidae					
Tarletonbeania crenularis	+				
Anguillidae					
Anguilla sp.	+				
Moridae					
Laemonema longipes	+				
Scomberesocidae					
Cololabis saira	+				
Gadidae					
Gadus morhua macrocephalus	+				
Eleginus gracilis	+				
Theragra chalcogramma	+				
Micromesistius australis	+	+		+	
Gadidae gen. sp.	+				

Item	Ocean				Remark
	Pacific	Atlantic	Indian	Antarc-tic	
Macruridae					
Hemimacrurus acrolepis	+				
Nematonurus pectoralis	+				
Sphyraenidae					
Sphyraena sp.	±	+	+		
Nototheniidae					
Dissostichus eleginoides		+		+	
D. mawsoni					
Scombridae					
Scomber japonicus japonicus	+				
S. japonicus tapeinocephalus	+				
Scorpaenidae					
Sebastodes ruberrimus	+				
S. ruber	+				
S. flammeus	+				
S. fracundus	+				
S. alutas	+				
Helicolenus papilosus	+				
Histiopteridae					
Pseudopentaceros richardsoni	+				
Hexagrammidae					
Ophiodon elongatus	+				
Pleurogrammus monopterygius	+				
Anoplopomidae					
Anoplopoma fimbria	+				
Cottidae					
Myoxocephalus sp. (joak)	+				
M. verrucosus	+				
Cottidae gen. sp.					
Cyclopteridae					
Aptocyclus ventricosus	+				
Agonidae					
Percis japonicus	+				
Thunnidae					
Thunnus alalunga			+	+	Oralbacore
Icosteidae					
Icosteus aenigmaticus	+				
Diodontidae					
Diodon sp.				+	
Himantolophidae					
Himatolophus groenlandicus	+	+			
Oneirodidae					
Oneirodes sp.	+				
Ceratiidae					
Ceratias holböeli	+			+	
CRUSTACEA					
Euphausiacea					
Decapoda					
Hippolytidae	+				
Paguridae					
Pagurus sp.	+				

Item	Ocean				Remark
	Pacific	Atlantic	Indian	Antarctic	
Lithodidae					
Paralithodes camtshatica	+				
Paralithodes brevipes	+				
Lithodes aeguispina	+				
Majidae					
Chionoecetes	+				
Hyas coarctatus	+				
Incalcarea					
Scyphozoa					
Bivalvia					
Pectinidae					
Chlamys islandicus					
Cardidae					
Limopsis vaginatus					
Holothurioidea					
Ascidiae	+				
Pyrosoma sp.	+				
Chaetognatha					
Parasagitta (?) sp.					
Phaeophyta					
Laminariales					
Lessoniaceae					
Nereocystis	+				

APPENDIX II

Statistics of sperm whaling[*]

Region	Year	Number of specimens	Region	Year	Number of specimens
North Atlantic and the Arctic as a whole	1937	289	Norway	1937	20
	1938	86		1938	9
	1939	40		1939	14
	1940	6		1940	—
	1941	5		1941	5
	1942	2		1942	2
	1943	10		1943	6
	1944	21		1944	4
	1945	26		1945	4
	1946	52		1946	21
	1947	55		1947	16
	1948	112		1948	47
	1949	157		1949	20
	1950	170		1950	79
	1951	178		1951	76

[*] Data of International Whaling Statistics.

Region	Year	Number of specimens	Region	Year	Number of specimens
	1952	59		1952	51
	1953	148		1953	44
	1954	168		1954	94
	1955	142		1955	44
	1956	277		1956	58
	1957	210		1957	30
	1958	288		1958	92
	1959	152		1959	31
	1960	262		1960	84
	1961	238		1961	88
	1962	234		1962	91
	1963	252		1963	107
	1964	196		1964	49
	1956	103		1965	27
	1966	125		1966	36
				1967	22
Scotland	1950	—			
	1951	1	West Greenland	1937	—
				1938	—
Faeroes	1937	11		1939	—
	1938	7		—	—
	1939	9		1946	6
	—	—			
	1946	14	West Greenland	1947	6
	1947	15		1948	6
	1948	30		1949	3
	1949	53		1950	5
	1950	46		1951	6
	1951	70		1952	5
	1952	1		1953	4
	1953	52		1954	9
	1954	11		1955	9
	1955	69		1956	14
	1956	97		1957	28
	1957	57		1958	26
	1958	40		1960	—
	—	—		1961	—
	1962	7			
	1963	8	Portugal	1947	50
	1964	5		1948	35
	1965	6		1949	23
	1966	1		1950	10
				1951	11
Iceland	1937	21			
	1938	20	Madeira	1951	182
	1939	4		1952	156
	—	—		1953	107
	1948	15		1954	122
	1949	28		1955	175
	1950	11		1956	168
	1951	13		1957	168
	1952	2		1958	174

Region	Year	Number of specimens	Region	Year	Number of specimens
Newfoundland and Labrador	1937	19		1959	86
	1938	—		1960	168
	1939	13		1961	129
	1940	6		1962	171
	1941	—		1963	186
	1942	—		1964	133
	1943	4		1965	15
	1944	17		1966	113
	1945	22		1967	85
	1946	11			
	1947	18	Azores	1947	565
	1948	14		1948	698
	1949	53		1949	484
	1950	29		1950	423
	1951	12		1951	741
	1952	—		1952	623
	1953	—		1953	528
	1954	—		1954	683
	1955	—		1955	664
	1956	13		1956	536
	1957	14		1957	671
	1958	7		1958	527
	1959	1		1959	485
	1960	1		1960	438
	1961	—		1961	374
	1963	1		1962	412
	1964	4		1963	472
	1965	—		1964	478
	1966	2		1965	379
	1967	—		1966	297
				1967	310
Spain	1950	3	Africa as a whole	1965	3,606
	1951	35		1966	3,119
	1952	94			
	1953	38	Natal	1937	508
	1954	105		1938	425
	1955	158		1939	615
	1956	234		1940	482
	1957	241		1941	476
	1958	149		1942	123
	1959	182		1943	299
	1960	122		1944	448
	1961	98		1945	414
	1962	167		1946	659
	1963	113		1947	502
	1964	182		1948	846
	1965	164		1949	694
	1966	203		1950	391
	1967	207		1951	910
				1952	356
South Atlantic (north of 40°N)	1955	39		1953	353
	1956	121		1954	400
	1957	53		1955	602

Region	Year	Number of specimens	Region	Year	Number of specimens
				1956	474
Operations en route to antarc-	1958	16		1957	763
tic regions and on the way	1959	16		1958	738
back from the Antarctic	1960	34		1959	824
	1961	121		1960	1,024
	1962	358		1961	1,004
	1963	435		1962	1,640
	1964	442		1963	1,771
	1965	51		1964	2,113
	1966	334		1965	2,814
	1967	420		1966	2,435
Africa as a whole	1937	710		1967	1,626
	1938	473	Madagascar	1937	—
	1939	676		1938	48
	1940	482		1939	61
	1941	476		—	—
	1942	123		1949	1
	1943	299		1950	64
	1944	448			
	1945	414	Gabon	1949	—
	1946	659		1950	—
	1947	550		1951	146
	1948	1,015		1952	—
	1949	965		—	—
	1950	693		1959	14
	1951	1,319			
	1952	796	Morocco	1948	64
	1953	618		1949	61
	1954	441		1950	77
	1955	602		1951	52
	1956	474		1952	39
	1957	1,232		1953	13
	1958	1,432		1954	41
	1959	1,489			
	1960	1,793	Cape Province	1937	207
	1961	1,769		—	—
	1962	2,581		1947	48
	1963	2,462		1948	105
	1964	2,841		1949	209
Cape Province	1950	161	North Pacific as a whole	1961	113
	1951	211		1962	232
	1952	331		1963	225
	1953	252		1964	169
	—	—		1965	248
	1956	469		1966	294
	1958	694	U.S.A. (Oregon)	1961	3
	1959	651		1962	—
	1960	769		1963	—
	1961	765		1964	1
	1962	941			
	1963	691	Columbia	1937	265
	1964	728		1938	252

Region	Year	Number of specimens	Region	Year	Number of specimens
	1965	792		1939	—
	1966	684		1940	126
	1967	630		1941	233
U.S.A. (California)	1937	—		1942	130
	1938	—		1943	69
	1939	—		—	—
	1940	4		1948	28
	1941	1		1949	69
	1942	3		1950	40
	1943	3		1951	153
	1944	1		1952	128
	—	—		1953	275
	1947	5		1954	226
	1948	32		1955	320
	1949	28		1956	127
	1950	—		1957	190
	1951	26		1958	112
	—	—		1959	260
				1962	172
Alaska (pelagic whaling)	1937	56		1963	147
	1938	63		1964	105
	1939	49		1965	151
	1940	177		1966	229
	1941	156	Japan	1948	823
North Pacific (in general)	1937	321		1949	501
(excluding waters of Japan,	1938	315		1950	1,429
North Korea, Bering Sea,	1939	49		1951	1,283
Kamchatka, Kuriles)	1940	307		1952	1,071
	1941	390		1953	1,186
	1942	133		1954	1,487
	1943	72		1955	1,506
	1944	1		1956	2,125
North Pacific as a whole	1945	—		1957	2,361
	1946	72		1958	2,588
	1947	206		1959	2,104
	1948	198		1960	2,107
	1949	182		1961	2,101
	1950	103		1962	1,685
	1951	239		1963	1,714
	1952	144		1964	1,800
	1953	275		1965	1,800
	1954	226		1966	2,101
	1955	320		1967	2,635
	1956	136	Bonin Island (pelagic	1946	72
	1957	204	zone)	1947	201
	1958	120		1948	131
	1959	284		1949	85
	1960	30			

Region	Year	Number of specimens	Region	Year	Number of specimens
Bonin Island (pelagic zone)	1950	63	Brazil	1966	24
	1951	60			
	1952	18	Peru	1941	1,914
Ryukyu Island (Okinawa)	1957	—		1942	3,346
	1958	—		1943	3,299
	1959	7		—	—
	1960	14		1947	2,887
	1961	9		1948	2,498
	1962	—		1951	6,365
	1963	1		1952	37
				1953	1,260
Japan, North and South	1937	640		1954	4,134
Korea (as a whole)	1938	785		1955	1,869
	1939	1,266		1956	2,019
	1940	1,306		1957	2,381
	1941	1,298		1958	2,554
	1942	427		1959	3,399
	1943	727		1960	3,451
	1944	990		1961	3,602
	1945	266		1962	3,301
				1963	3,241
				1964	2,023
North Pacific and Bering	1952	—		1965	922
Sea	1953	—		1966	862
	1954	491	Chile	1937	254
	1955	1,084		1938	203
	1956	1,598		1939	341
	1957	1,700		1940	78
	1958	1,500		1941	59
	1959	1,800		1942	54
	1960	1,800		1943	60
	1961	1,800		1944	367
	1962	3		1945	373
	1963	114		1946	343
	1964	134		1947	720
	1962	2,549		1948	731
	1963	2,700		1949	731
	1964	2,461		1950	769
	1965	2,460		1951	733
	1966	3,000		1952	790
	1967	3,000		1953	698
Brazil	1947	—		1954	798
	1948	—		1955	746
	1949	—		1956	1,171
	1950	—		1957	2,299
	1951	—		1958	2,062
	1952	1		1959	2,062
	1953	1		1960	1,886
	1954	1		1961	2,160
	1955	1		1962	2,280
	1956	3		1963	1,494
	1957	2		1964	1,213
	1958	4		1965	267

Region	Year	Number of specimens	Region	Year	Number of specimens
	1959	11		1966	669
	1960	29		1967	533
	1961	102	Kamchatka	1937	198
	1962	85		1938	64
	1963	42		1939	154
	1964	4		1940	—
	1965	13		1941	—
New Zealand	1937	—		1942	215
	1938	1		1943	216
	1939	—		---	—
	1940	2		1946	316
	1941	—		1947	—
	1942	—		1948	574
	1943	—		1949	774
	1944	—		1950	587
	1945	—		1951	765
	1946	—		1952	731
	1947	9		1953	865
	1948	—		1954	816
	1949	—		1955	996
	1950	—		1956	998
	1951	—		1957	1,174
	1952	—		1958	1,430
	1953	—		1959	1,560
	1954	—		1960	2,228
	1955	—		1961	1,868
	1956	—		1962	1,955
	1957	2		1963	5,125
	1958	—		1964	5,432
	1959	—		1965	8,196
	1960	—		1966	9,476
	1961	—		1967	9,430
Kuriles	1949	986	Australia	1937	3
	1950	1,471		1938	—
	1951	1,462		—	—
	1952	1,641		1947	—
	1953	1,521		1948	—
	1954	1,192		1949	—
	1955	1,494		1950	—
	1956	1,693		1951	—
	1957	1,821		1952	—
	1958	2,184		1953	—
	1959	1,878		1954	—
	1960	1,487		1955	7
	1961	1,401		1956	61
	1962	1,347		1957	139
	1963	659		1958	283
	1964	452		1959	138
South Pacific (north of 40°N).	1957	48		1960	282
Operations en route to	—	—		1961	454
the Antarctic	1962	164		1962	592
	1963	1,219		1963	629

Region	Year	Number of specimens	Region	Year	Number of specimens
	1964	1,779		1964	710
	1965	400		1965	668
	1966	160		1966	606
Indian Ocean (north of 40°N).	1957	23		1967	586
Operations en route to	—	—			
the Antarctic	1962	371			
	1963	2,005			
	1964	2,095			
	1965	1,768			
	1966	1,440			
	1967	896			

APPENDIX III

Sperm whaling in the Antarctic and other regions

Season	Number of specimens			
	in the Antarctic		in other regions	total
	pelagic whaling	total		
1919/20	8	—	—	—
1920/21	31	—	—	—
1921/22	3	—	—	—
1922/23	23	4	—	—
1923/24	66	17	—	—
1924/25	59	35	—	—
1925/26	37	25	—	—
1926/27	39	22	—	—
1927/28	72	12	—	—
1928/29	62	31	—	—
1929/30	73	34	—	—
1930/31	51	27	—	—
1931/32	13	3	—	—
1932/33	107	107	—	—
1933/34	666	659	—	—
1934/35	577	556	—	—
1935/36	399	396	—	—
1936/37	926	856	—	7,197
1937/38	867	824	2,896	3,734
1938/39	2,585	2,468	2,926	5,511
1939/40	1,938	1,853	2,733	4,671
1940/41	804	778	4,837	5,565
1941/42	109	—	4,848	— 4,992
1942/43	24	—	5,479	5,344

Season	Number of specimens			
	in the Antarctic		in other regions	total
	pelagic whaling	total		
1943/44	101	—	2,513	2,614
1944/45	45	—	1,624	1,669
1945/46	273	216	3,188	2,461
1946/47	1,431	1,298	6,115	7,546
1947/48	2,622	2,494	7,228	9,850
1948/49	4,078	3,865	4,938	9,016
1949/50	2,727	2,570	5,492	8,219
1950/51	4,968	4,742	13,313	18,281
1951/52	5,485	5,344	6,073	11,558
1952/53	2,332	2,185	7,245	9,577
1953/54	2,879	2,700	10,664	13,543
1954/55	5,790	5,708	9,803	15,593
1955/56	6,974	6,881	11,616	18,590
1956/57	4,429	4,345	14,727	19,156
1957/58	6,535	6,310	15,311	21,846
1958/59	5,652	5,437	15,646	21,298
1959/60	4,227	4,138	16,117	20,344
1960/61	4,800	4,666	16,330	21,130
1961/62	4,829	4,743	1,847*	23,316
1962/63	4,771	4,771	23,087	27,858
1963/64	6,711	6,651	22,544	29,255
1964/65	4,352	4,211	21,196	25,548
1965/66	4,555	4,538	22,828	27,378
1966/67	—	4,960	—	—

* Various official sources give different numbers of whales caught in this year.

Bibliography

Publications in Russian

Akimushkin, A.A. Golovonogie mollyuski v pitanii kashalota (Cephalopoda in the Diet of the Sperm Whale). — DAN SSSR, Vol. 96, No. 3. 1954.

Akimushkin, I.I. O kharaktere pitaniya kashalota (On the Nature of Sperm Whale Feeding). — DAN SSSR, Vol. 101, No. 6. 1955.

Akimushkin, I.I. Golovonogie mollyuski morei SSSR (Cephalopoda in the Seas of the USSR). — Izdatel'stvo AN SSSR. 1963.

Akimushkin, I.I. Primaty morya (Primates of the Sea). Geografgiz. 1963a.

Aleev, Yu. G. Telo del'fina kak nesushchaya ploskost' (The Dolphin's Body as a Bearing Surface). — Zoologicheskii Zhurnal, Vol. 44, No. 4. 1944.

Aleev, Yu.G. O sozdanii telom nektonnykh zhivotnykh vertikal'nykh poperechnykh sil (Creation of Vertical Transverse Forces by the Body of Nektonic Animals). — In Sbornik: "Issledovaniya po bionike." Kiev. 1965.

Aleev, Yu.G. Statodinamicheskie tipy nektonnykh zhivotnykh (Stock-Dynamic Types of Nektonic Animals). — In Sbornik: "Ekologicheskie issledovaniya nektonnykh zhivotnykh." Kiev. 1966.

Arsen'ev, V.A. Rasprostranenie kitov v Beringovom more i vozmozhnosti razvitiya kitoboinogo promysla (Distribution of Whales in the Bering Sea and the Potential Development of Whaling). — Trudy Soveshchanii Ikhtiologicheskoi Komissii AN SSSR, No. 12. 1961.

Arsen'ev, V.A. Mechenie kitov na Dal'nem Vostoke (Tagging Whales in the Far East). — Rybnoe Khozyaistvo, No. 4. 1965.

Arsen'ev, V.A. Mechenie kitov (Tagging Whales). — In Sbornik: "Migratsii zhivotnykh," No. 1. Izdatel'stvo AN SSSR. 1969.

Arsen'ev, V.A. and V.A. Zemskii. V strane kitov i pingvinov (In the Land of Whales and Penguins). Izdatel'stvo MOIP. 1951.

Arsen'ev, V.A. and B.A. Zenkovich. Nauchno-issledovatel'skie raboty (Scientific Research Work). — In Sbornik: "Kitoboinyi promysel Sovetskogo Soyuza." Chapter II. Moskva. 1955.

Astanin, L.P. Organy tela mlekopitayushchikh i ikh rabota (The Organs of the Mammalian Body and Their Function). Moskva, Izdatel'stvo "Sovetskaya Nauka." 1958.

Baturin, A.D. Promysel kitoobraznykh i lastonogikh Dal'nevostochnogo kraya (Whaling and Sealing in the Far East). — Proizvoditel'nye Sily Dal'nego Vostoka, No. 4. "Zhivotnyi Mir." Khabarovsk — Vladivostok. 1927.

Bel'kovich, V.M. Nekotorye osobennosti krovosnabzheniya i teplootdachi kozhi belukhi (Some Characteristics of Blood Supply and Heat Exchange in the Skin of the White Whale). — Tezisy dokladov III nauchnoi molodezhnoi konferentsii. Trudy IMZh AN SSSR. Moskva. 1959.

Bel'kovich, V.M. O fizicheskoi termoregulyatsii belugi (Delphinapterus leucas Pall.) (Physical Thermoregulation in the White Whale (Delphinapterus leucas Pall.)). — Trudy Soveshchanii Ikhtiologicheskoi Komissii AN SSSR, No. 12. 1961.

Bel'kovich, V.M., S.E. Kleinenberg, and A.V. Yablokov. Zagadka okeana (The Riddle of the Ocean). Moskva, Izdatel'stvo "Molodaya gvardiya." 1965.

Bel'kovich, V.M., S.E. Kleinenberg, and A.V. Yablokov. Nash drug del'fin (Our Friend the Dolphin). Moskva, Izdatel'stvo "Molodaya gvardiya." 1967.

Bel'kovich, V.M. and A.V. Yablokov. Sravnitel'no-anatomicheskie dannye k modelirovaniyu priemno-peredayushchikh ustroistv gidrolokatora kitoobraznykh i lastonogikh (Comparative-Anatomical Data for Simulating the Reception-Transmission Sonar Devices in Cetacea and Pinnipedia). — Tezisy konferentsii po bionike. Moskva. 1963.

Bel'kovich, V.M. and A.V. Yablokov. Molodost' drevnei nauki (The Youth of Ancient Science). — Priroda, No. 8. 1963 a.

Bel'kovich, V.M. and A.V. Yablokov. Obitateli morya "delyatsya opytom" s konstruktorami (Dwellers of the Sea "Share Their Experience" with Constructors). — Nauka i Zhizn', No. 5. 1963 b.

Bel'kovich, V.M. and A.V. Yablokov. Kit — ul'trazvukovoi prozhektor (The Whale as an Ultrasonic Projector). — Yuzhnyi Tekhnik, No. 3. 1963 c.

Bel'kovich, V.M. and A.V. Yablokov. O strukture stada zubatykh kitoobraznykh (Odontoceti) (On the Structure of a Stock of Toothed Whales (Odontoceti)). — In Sbornik: "Morskie mlekopitayushchie." Moskva, Izdatel'stvo "Nauka." 1965.

Bereznikov, V. Norvezhskie morskie zverinye i kitovye promysly v 1893, 1895 gg. (Hunting Whales and Marine Animals in Norway in 1893, 1895). — Vestnik Promyshlennosti, Vol. 11. Sankt-Peterburg. 1896.

Berzin, A.A. O pitanii kashalota v Beringovom more (Feeding of the Sperm Whale in the Bering Sea). — Izvestiya TINRO, Vol. 47. 1959.

Berzin, A.A. Razvedka i mechenie kitov (Scouting and Tagging of Whales). — Promyshlennost' Primor'ya, No. 9. 1959 a.

Berzin, A.A. Materialy po razvitiyu zubov i opredeleniyu vozrasta kashalotov (Data on the Development of Teeth and Age Determination in the Sperm Whale). — Trudy Soveshchanii Ikhtiologicheskoi Komissii AN SSSR. I Vsesoyuznoe Soveshchanie po Ekologii i Promyslu Morskikh Mlekopitayushchikh 1959 g., No. 12. 1961.

Berzin, A.A. O metodikakh opredeleniya vozrasta samok kashalota (Physeter catodon) (Methods of Determining the Age of Sperm Whale Females (Physeter catodon)). — DAN SSSR, Vol. 139, No. 2. 1961 a.

Berzin, A.A. Metody opredeleniya vozrasta i vozrastnoi sostav stad kashalotov Tikhogo okeana (Methods of Determining the Age and Age Composition of Sperm Whale Herds in the Pacific). Vladivostok. 1963.

Berzin, A.A. Rost kashalotov severnoi chasti Tikhogo okeana (Growth of Sperm Whales in the North Pacific). — Trudy VNIRO, Vol. 53; Izvestiya TINRO, Vol. 52. 1964.

Berzin, A.A. Opredelenie vozrastnogo sostava stada kashalotov Beringova morya i prilezhashchikh chastei Tikhogo okeana (Determination of the Age Composition of Sperm Whale Stocks in the Bering Sea and Adjacent Areas of the Pacific). — Trudy VNIRO, Vol. 53; Izvestiya TINRO, Vol. 52. 1964 a.

B e r z i n, A. A. Opredelenie vozrasta nastupleniya polovoi zrelosti samtsov kashalota severnoi chasti Tikhogo okeana (Determination of the Onset of Sexual Maturity of Sperm Whale Males in the North Pacific). — In Sbornik: "Morskie mlekopitayushchie." Moskva, Izdatel'stvo "Nauka." 1965.

B e r z i n, A. A. Nastuplenie polovoi zrelosti i tempy vosproizvodstva samok kashalotov severnoi chasti Tikhogo okeana (The Onset of Sexual Maturity and Rates of Breeding of Sperm Whale Females in the North Pacific). — Annotatsii nauchnykh rabot po issledovaniyu syr'evoi bazy rybnoi promyshlennosti Dal'nego Vostoka v 1959 — 1962 gg. Vladivostok. 1965 a.

B e r z i n, A. A. Voprosy ekologii kashalota (Problems of Sperm Whale Ecology). — Tezisy dokladov III Vsesoyuznogo soveshchaniya po izucheniyu morskikh mlekopitayushchikh. Vladivostok. 1966.

B e r z i n, A. A. and A. A. R o v n i n. Raspredelenie i migratsii kitov v severo-vostochnoi chasti Tikhogo okeana, v Beringovom i Chukotskom moryakh (Distribution and Migration of Whales in the Northeastern Part of the Pacific and in the Bering and Chukchi Seas). — Izvestiya TINRO, Vol. 58. 1966.

B e t e s h e v a, E. I. Pitanie kashalota (P h y s e t e r c a t o d o n) i berardiusa (B e r a r d i u s b a i r d i i Steineger) v raione Kuril'skoi gryady (Feeding of the Sperm Whale (P h y s e t e r c a t o d o n) and of B e r a r d i u s b a i r d i i Steineger in the Kurile Waters). — Trudy Vsesoyuznogo Gidrobiologicheskogo Obshchestva, Vol. 10. 1960.

B e t e s h e v a, E. I. Pitanie promyslovykh kitov prikuril'skogo raiona (Feeding of Commercial Species of Whale in the Kuriles Region). — Trudy IMZh AN SSSR, No. 34. 1961.

B e t e s h e v a, E. I. Pitanie promyslovykh kitov prikuril'skogo raiona (Feeding of Commercial Species of Whale in the Kuriles Region). — Trudy Soveshchanii Ikhtiologicheskoi Komissii AN SSSR, No. 12. 1961 a.

B e t e s h e v a, E. I. O stroenii zheludka i kishechnika usatykh kitov (Structure of the Stomach and Intestine of Baleen Whales). — In Sbornik: "Morskie mlekopitayushchie." Moskva, Izdatel'stvo "Nauka." 1965.

B e t e s h e v a, E. I. and I. I. A k i m u s h k i n. Pitanie kashalota (P h y s e t e r c a t o d o n) v raione vod kuril'skoi gryady (Feeding of the Sperm Whale (P h y s e t e r c a t o d o n) in the Kurile Waters). — Trudy IO AN SSSR, Vol. 18. 1955.

B e t e s h e v a, E. I. and N. I. S e r g i e n k o, O morfologii zheludka i kishechnika zubatykh kitov (Morphology of the Stomach and Intestine of Toothed Whales). — Zoologicheskii Zhurnal, Vol. 43, No. 6. 1964.

B o b r i n s k i i, N. A. et al. Opredelitel' mlekopitayushchikh SSSR (Key to the Mammals of the USSR). Moskva, Izdatel'stvo "Sovetskaya Nauka." 1944.

B o d r o v, V. A. and S. N. G r i g o r' e v. Pererabotka kitovogo syr'ya na kitobazakh (Processing of Raw Whale Material at Whaling Bases). Pishchepromizdat. 1963.

B o d r o v, V. A., S. N. G r i g o r' e v, and V. A. T v e r' y a n o v i c h. Tekhnika i tekhnologiya obrabotki morskikh mlekopitayushchikh (Techniques and Technology in the Processing of Marine Mammals). Pishchepromizdat. 1958.

Bogorov, V.G. Geograficheskie zony v pelagiali tsentral'noi chasti Tikhogo okeana (Geographic Zones in the Pelagial of the Central Pacific). — Trudy IO AN SSSR, Vol. 41. 1960.

Brem, A. Zhizn' zhivotnykh (Life of Animals). — "Mlekopitayushchie," Vol. 1, Sankt-Peterburg. 1904.

Bukin, V.N. and E.P. Skorobogatova. Pechen' kitov kak syr'e dlya polucheniya vitamina A (The Liver of Whales as Raw Material for Obtaining Vitamin A). First Collection. — Vitaminnye resursy rybnoi promyshlennosti. 1951.

Chapskii, K.K. Morskie zveri Sovetskoi Arktiki (Marine Animals of the Arctic). Izdatel'stvo Glavsevmorputi. 1941.

Chapskii, K.K. Opredelenie vozrasta nekotorykh mlekopitayushchikh po mikrostrukture kosti (Age Determination of Some Mammals According to the Bone Microstructure). — Izvestiya Estestvenno-Nauchnogo Instituta im. Lesgafta, Vol. 25. 1952.

Chepurnov, A.V. Skorosti dvizheniya kitov i nekotorye osobennosti ikh vneshnego stroeniya (Speeds of Movement of Whales and Some Features of Gross Morphology). — In Sbornik: "Issledovaniya po bionike." Kiev, Izdatel'stvo "Naukova dumka." 1965.

Chepurnov, A.V. Stroenie i gidrodinamicheskie kachestva khvostovogo plavnika nekotorykh kitoobraznykh (Structure and Hydrodynamic Properties of the Caudal Fin of Some Whales). — In Sbornik: "Ekologo-morfologicheskie issledovaniya nektonnykh zhivotnykh." Kiev, Izdatel'stvo "Naukova dumka." 1966.

Chernyi, E.I. Raspredelenie usatykh kitov v zavisimosti ot gidrologicheskikh uslovii (Distribution of Baleen Whales in Relation to Hydrological Conditions). — Izvestiya TINRO, Vol. 58. 1966.

Chuzhakina, E.S. K voprosu o tsikle razmnozheniya kashalotov (The Breeding Cycle of Sperm Whales). — Trudy IO AN SSSR, Vol. 18. 1955.

Chuzhakina, E.S. Morfologicheskaya kharakteristika yaichnikov samok kashalota (Physeter catodon L., 1758) v svyazi s opredeleniem vozrasta (Morphological Characteristics of the Ovaries of the Sperm Whale (Physeter catodon L., 1785) in Connection with Age Determination). — Trudy IMZh AN SSSR, No. 34. 1961.

Chuzhakina, E.S. Sozrevanie i atreziya follikulov v yaichnikakh kashalota (Maturation and Atresia of Follicles in Sperm Whale Ovaries). — In Sbornik: "Morskie mlekopitayushchie." Moskva, Izdatel'stvo "Nauka." 1965.

Delyamure, S.L. Zoogeograficheskaya kharakteristika gel'mintofauny lastonogikh i kitoobraznykh (Zoogeographical Description of the Helminth Fauna of Pinnipedia and Cetacea). — Trudy Gel'mintologicheskoi Laboratorii AN SSSR, Vol. 6. 1952.

Delyamure, S.L. Gel'mintofauna morskikh mlekopitayushchikh v svete ikh ekologii i filogenii (Helminth Fauna of Marine Mammals in the Light of Their Ecology and Phylogeny). Izdatel'stvo AN SSSR. 1955.

Delyamure, S.L. Ob amfiboreal'nom i bipolyarnom rasprostranenii gel'mintov morskikh mlekopitayushchikh (Amphiboreal and Bipolar Distribution of Helminths of Marine Mammals). — DAN SSSR, Vol. 107, No. 4. 1956.

Delyamure, S.L. and A.S. Skryabin. Naibolee obshchie zakonomer-
    nosti geograficheskogo rasprostraneniya gel'mintov morskikh
    mlekopitayushchikh (The Most Usual Patterns of Geographical
    Distribution of Helminths of Marine Mammals). — Izvestiya
    Krymskogo Otdela Geograficheskogo Obshchestva Soyuza SSR,
    No. 5. Simferopol'. 1958.

Ditrikh, G. and K. Kalle. Obshchee morevedenie (General Marine
    Science). Leningrad, Gidrometeoizdat. 1961.

Druzhinin, A.N. K voprosu o stroenii, funktsii i genezise perednego
    poyasa konechnostei u Delphinus delphis (Structure,
    Function, and Genesis of the Pectoral Girdle in the Dolphin
    Delphinus delphis). — Zoologicheskii Zhurnal, Vol. 4,
    Nos. 3 and 4. 1924.

Dvigubskii, I.A. Opyt estestvennoi istorii vsekh zhivotnykh Rossiiskoi
    imperii. Ch. 1. "Zhivotnye mlekopitayushchie" (Attempt at a
    Natural History of All Animals of the Russian Empire. Part 1.
    "Mammals."). 1829.

Efremov, P.G. Iz praktiki raboty kitoboev (Reports of Whalers). —
    Izvestiya TINRO, Vol. 35. 1951.

Filimonov, N.I. Sravnitel'naya anatomiya kory bol'shogo mozga mleko-
    pitayushchikh (Comparative Anatomy of the Mammalian Cortex).
    Izdatel'stvo AN SSSR. 1949.

Frederiks, N. Merkatorskaya karta pyati chastei sveta, izobrazhayushch-
    aya khod, vremennoe i postoyannoe mestoprebyvanie kitov
    razlichnogo roda s pokazaniem udobneishego vremeni lova ikh
    (Mercator Map of the Five Parts of the World, Depicting the Move-
    ment, Temporary and Permanent Occurrence of Whales of Different
    Genera and Indicating the Best Time for Catching Them). — Vestnik
    Imperatorskogo Russkogo Geograficheskogo Obshchestva, Part. 7.
    Sankt-Peterburg. 1853.

Fujina Kadzio. Opredelenie razmnozhayushchikhsya subpopulyatsii
    kashalotov v vodakh Yaponii i Aleutskikh ostrovov metodom
    issledovaniya tipov krovi (Determination of Reproducing Subpopula-
    tions of Sperm Whales in the Waters of Japan and the Aleutian
    Islands Using the Method of Investigating Blood Types).
    (Russian Translation from Japanese 1963.)

Gapponovich, A. Kitoobraznye i lastonogie Dal'nego Vostoka
    (Cetacea and Pinnipedia of the Far East). — Rybnye i pushnye
    bogatstva Dal'nego Vostoka. Vladivostok. 1923.

Golovlev, I.F. Tekhnika kitoboinogo promysla (Whaling Techniques).
    Kaliningrad. 1960.

Golub, D.M., A.S. Leontyuk, and I.I. Novikov. Materialy po
    embriologii kitoobraznykh. Zarodysh kashalota (Physeter
    catodon) 8.5 mm dliny (Data on Whale Embryology. The Embryo
    of the Sperm Whale (Physeter catodon) at 8.5 mm). — Zoo-
    logicheskii Zhurnal, Vol. 47, No. 5. 1968.

Grebnitskii, N.A. Komandorskie ostrova (The Komandorski Islands).
    Sankt-Peterburg. 1902.

Gubanov, N.M. Gigantskaya nematoda iz platsenty kashalota Placento-
    nema gigantissima nov. gen. nov. sp. (A Giant Nematode
    from the Placenta of the Sperm Whale, Placentonema

gigantissima nov. gen. nov. sp.).— DAN SSSR, Vol. 77, No. 6. 1951.

Gubanov, N.M. Gel'mintofauna promyslovykh zhivotnykh Okhotskogo morya i Tikhogo okeana (Helminths of Commercial Animals of the Sea of Okhotsk and the Pacific). Author's Summary of Candidate Thesis. Moskva. 1952.

Gudkov, V.M. Ob osobennostyakh okraski kashalotov vod Dal'nego Vostoka (Features of Coloration of Sperm Whales from Far Eastern Waters).— Trudy IO AN SSSR, Vol. 71. 1963.

Ivanova, E.I. Kharakteristika proportsii tela kashalota (Physeter catodon) (Description of the Proportions of the Body of the Sperm Whale (Physeter catodon)).— Trudy IO AN SSSR, Vol. 18. 1955.

Ivanova, E.I. Morfologicheskaya kharakteristika kashalota (Physeter catodon) raiona Kuril'skikh ostrovov (Morphological Description of the Sperm Whale (Physeter catodon) of the Kurile Islands Region).— Trudy IMZh AN SSSR, No. 34. 1961.

Ivanova, E.I. Proportsii tela i kharakter rosta kitov Dal'nego Vostoka (Body Proportions and Growth Characteristics of Whales of the Far East).— Trudy Soveshchanii Ikhtiologicheskoi Komissii AN SSSR, No. 12. 1961 a.

Ivashin, M.V. Metodika opredeleniya sledov zheltykh tel beremennosti i ovulyatsii u gorbatogo kita (Methods of Determining Marks of the Corpora Lutea of Pregnancy and Ovulation in the Humpback Whale).— Trudy VNIRO, Vol. 33. 1958.

Ivashin, M.V. O razmnozhenii gorbatogo kita (Megaptera nodosa) v yuzhnoi chasti Atlanticheskogo okeana (Breeding of the Humpback Whale in the Southern Atlantic). — Informatsionnyi sbornik VNIRO, No. 7. 1959.

Ivashin, M.V. Ambra (Ambergris). — Zoologicheskii Zhurnal, No. 7. 1963.

Ivashin, M.V. Ambra i promysel kashalotov (Ambergris and Sperm Whaling). — Priroda, No. 7. 1966.

Ivashin, M.V. Kashalot perekhodit ekvator (The Sperm Whale Crosses the Equator). — Rybnoe Khozyaistvo, No. 1. 1967.

Ivashin, M.V. Laboratoriya v kashalote (A Laboratory in the Sperm Whale).— Khimiya i Zhizn', No. 2. 1968.

Izhevskii, G.K. Vody polyarnogo fronta i raspredelenie atlanticheskikh sel'dei (The Waters of the Polar Front and the Distribution of Atlantic Herring). Moskva, Izdatel'stvo VNIRO. 1958.

Izhevskii, G.K. Okeanologicheskie osnovy formirovaniya promyslovoi produktivnosti morei (Oceanological Principles Governing the Commercial Productivity of Seas). Pishchepromizdat. 1961.

Kalabukhov, N.I. Spyachka zhivotnykh (The Hibernation of Animals). 1st edition. 1936. 2nd edition. 1946. Khar'kov. 1956.

Kandor, I.S. O vozmozhnosti "kessonnoi bolezni" u zhivotnykh v usloviyakh estestvennoi sredy (The Possibility of Animals' Contracting "Caisson Disease" in the Conditions of Their Natural Environment).— Priroda, No. 5. 1941.

Khar'kov, I.I. Materialy k vesovomu i khimicheskomu sostavu kitov (Data on the Weight and Chemical Composition of Whales). — Trudy VNIRO, Vol. 15. 1940.

Khar'kov, I.I. Ispol'zovanie podkozhnogo sala kashalotov dlya poluch-
eniya zhira i kozhevennogo syr'ya (Utilization of the Blubber of
Sperm Whales to Obtain Fat and Raw Hide). — Rybnoe Khozyaistvo,
No. 7. 1952.

Kirpichnikov, A.A. Kashalot v vodakh Antarktiki (The Sperm Whale
in the Waters of the Antarctic). — Rybnoe Khozyaistvo, No. 4. 1949.

Kirpichnikov, A.A. Krupnye kitoobraznye v Sredizemnom more (Giant
Whales in the Mediterranean). — Priroda, No. 8. 1949 a.

Kirpichnikov, A.A. O sovremennom rasprostranenii kashalotov v
mirovom okeane po promyslovym dannym (Present-Day Distribution of Sperm Whales in the World Ocean According to Commercial
Data). — Byulleten' MOIP. Otdel biologicheskii, Vol. 55, No. 5.
1950.

Kirpichnikov, A.A. Nablyudeniya nad raspredeleniem krupnykh kitoobraznykh v Atlanticheskom okeane (Observations on the Distribution of Giant Whales in the Atlantic). — Priroda, No. 10. 1950 a.

Kizevetter, I.V. Zhiry morskikh mlekopitayushchikh (Fats of Marine
Mammals). Vladivostok. 1953.

Kleinenberg, S.E. Mlekopitayushchie Chernogo i Azovskogo morei
(Mammals of the Black Sea and Sea of Azov). Izdatel'stvo AN SSSR.
1956.

Kleinenberg, S.E. Osobennosti dykhaniya kitoobraznykh (Features of
the Respiration of Whales). — Uspekhi Sovremennoi Biologii, Vol. 41,
No. 3. 1956 a.

Kleinenberg, S.E. K voprosu o proiskhozhdenii kitoobraznykh (On the
Origin of Whales). — DAN SSSR, Vol. 122, No. 5. 1958.

Kleinenberg, S.E., V.M. Bel'kovich, A.V. Yablokov, and
M.N. Tarasevich. Belukha (Beluga). Moskva, Izdatel'stvo
"Nauka." 1964. *

Kleinenberg, S.E., V.M. Bel'kovich, and A.V. Yablokov. O
vyrabotke edinoi metodiki izucheniya morskikh mlekopitayushchikh
(Development of a Unified Methodology of Studying Marine
Mammals). — In Sbornik: "Morskie mlekopitayushchie." Moskva,
Izdatel'stvo "Nauka." 1965.

Kleinenberg, S.E. and G.A. Klevezal'. K metodike opredeleniya
vozrasta zubatykh kitoobraznykh (Methods of Age Determination
in Toothed Whales). — DAN SSSR, Vol. 145, No. 2. 1962.

Kleinenberg, S.E. and G.A. Klevezal'. Opredelenie vozrasta
mlekopitayushchikh po sloistym strukturam zubov i kosti (Age
Determination of Mammals from the Laminar Structures of the
Teeth and Bones). Izdatel'stvo "Nauka." 1967.

Kleinenberg, S.E. and A.V. Yablokov. K morfologii verkhnikh
dykhatel'nykh putei kitoobraznykh (The Morphology of the Upper
Respiratory Tract of Whales). — Zoologicheskii Zhurnal, Vol. 37,
No. 7. 1958.

Kleinenberg, S.E. and A.V. Yablokov. Materialy po biologii
razmnozheniya belukhi severnykh morei SSSR (Data on the Biology
of Reproduction of the White Whale in the Northern Seas of the
USSR). — Trudy PINRO, No. 12. 1960.

* [English translation by IPST Cat. No. 1923. TT 67-51345.]

K l e r, V. O. K metodike issledovaniya periodiki rosta. Metod izodina-
    micheskikh ploskostei (Methods of Investigating Growth Periodicity.
    The Method of Isodynamic Surfaces). — Zoologicheskii Zhurnal,
    Vol. 7, No. 5. 1927.

K l e v e z a l'. G. A. O prichinakh sloistosti dentina zubov morskikh
    mlekopitayushchikh (On the Causes of Lamination of Dentin in the
    Teeth of Marine Mammals). — Tezisy dokladov II Vsesoyuznogo
    soveshchaniya po izucheniyu morskikh mlekopitayushchikh.
    Izdatel'stvo AN SSSR. 1963.

K l e v e z a l', G. A. Vozrastnye izmeneniya v strukture dentina, tsementa
    i periostal'noi zony kosti mlekopitayushchikh (Age-Dependent
    Variations in the Structure of Dentin and Cement and the Periosteal
    Zone of Mammalian Bones). Thesis. Moskva. 1966.

K l e v e z a l'. G. A. and S. E. K l e i n e n b e r g. Opredelenie vozrasta
    mlekopitayushchikh (Determination of the Age of Mammals). Moskva,
    Izdatel'stvo "Nauka." 1967.

K l i m o v, A. F. Anatomiya domashnikh zhivotnykh (Anatomy of Domestic
    Animals). Vol. 1. Sel'khozgiz. 1950.

K l i m o v, A. F. and A. I. A k a e v s k i i. Anatomiya domashnikh zhivotnykh
    (Anatomy of Domestic Animals). Vol. 2. Sel'khozgiz. 1951.

K l u m o v, S. K. O lokal'nosti kitovykh stad (On the Local Character of
    Whale Herds). — Trudy IO AN SSSR, Vol. 18. 1955.

K l u m o v, S. K. Nekotorye itogi ekspeditsii v Beringovo more i na
    Kuril'skie ostrova (Some Results of an Expedition to the Bering
    Sea and Kurile Islands). — Vestnik AN SSSR, No. 5. 1956.

K l u m o v, S. K. Uchast' kitov (The Fate of Whales). — Priroda, No. 3. 1958.

K l u m o v, S. K. Vozmozhen li etot "shans iz milliona"? (Is This "Chance in
    a Million" Possible ?). — Priroda, No. 11. 1959.

K l u m o v, S. K. Sovremennoe sostoyanie zapasov kitov v Mirovom okeane
    i meropriyatiya po ikh okhrane. Okhrana poleznykh zverei (Current
    State of Whale Stocks in the World Ocean and Measures for Their
    Conservation. Protection of Useful Animals). — Okhrana Prirody i
    Ozelenenie, No. 3. 1960.

K l y a s h t o r i n, L. B. Diatomovye obrastaniya kitov dal'nevostochnykh
    morei (Diatom Films on Whales of Far Eastern Seas). —
    Trudy IO AN SSSR, Vol. 58. 1962.

K o c h e v, V. V. and Z. V. M a r i e v a. Tekhnokhimicheskii sostav sala
    kashalota i izmeneniya ego pri obezzhirivanii (Technological and
    Chemical Composition of Sperm Whale and Its Changes upon
    Scouring). — Trudy VNIRO, Vol. 25. 1953.

K o n d a k o v, N. N. Klass golovonogikh mollyuskov (Class Cephalopoda). —
    Rukovodstvo po Zoologii, Vol. 2. Izdatel'stvo AN SSSR.

K o n d a k o v, N. N. Golovonogie mollyuski (Cephalopoda) dal'nevostochnykh
    morei SSSR (Cephalopoda of the Far Eastern Seas of the USSR).
    Izdatel'stvo AN SSSR. 1940.

K o r a b e l' n i k o v, L. V. O pitanii kashalotov v antarkticheskikh moryakh
    (Feeding of Sperm Whales in the Antarctic Seas). — Priroda, No. 3.
    1959.

K o r z h u e v, P. A. Evolyutsiya dykhatel'noi funktsii krovi (Evolution of the
    Respiratory Function of the Blood). Izdatel'stvo AN SSSR. 1949.

Korzhuev, P.A. O formakh lokalizatsii i kolichestve gemoglobina v krovi razlichnykh zhivotnykh (Forms of Localization and the Amount of Hemoglobin in the Blood of Different Animals). — Uspekhi Sovremennoi Biologii, Vol. 33, No. 3. 1952.

Korzhuev, P.A., L.P. Balabanova, S.P. Evtronova, and Z.M. Moderatova. Opyt kolichestvennogo opredeleniya gemoglobina i kostnogo mozga u obyknovennogo chernomorskogo del'fina (Attempt at a Quantitative Estimation of Hemoglobin and Bone Marrow in the Common Black Sea Dolphin). — In Sbornik: "Morskie mlekopitayushchie." Izdatel'stvo "Nauka." 1965.

Korzhuev, P.A. and N.N. Bulatova, Dykhatel'naya funktsiya krovi del'finov (Respiratory Function of the Blood of Dolphins). — Trudy IMZh AN SSSR, No. 6. 1952.

Korzhuev, P.A. and T.N. Glazova. Kontsentratsiya myshechnogo gemoglobina v myshtsakh vodnykh mlekopitayushchikh (Concentration of Myoglobin in the Muscles of Aquatic Mammals). — Biokhimiya, Vol. 32, No. 3. Izdatel'stvo AN SSSR. 1967.

Korzhuev, P.A. and T.N. Glazova. O kolichestvennoi kharakteristike krovi i krovetvornykh organov chernomorskikh del'finov (Quantitative Description of the Blood and Hematopoietic Organs of Black Sea Dolphins). — Evolyutsiya Biokhimii i Fiziologii, Vol. 3, No. 2. 1967a.

Koshtoyants, Kh.S. Osnovy sravnitel'noi fiziologii (Fundamentals of Comparative Physiology). Vol. 1. Izdatel'stvo AN SSSR. 1950.

Krasheninnikov, S.P. Opisanie zemli Kamchatki (A Description of Kamchatka). 1st edition 1775. Izdatel'stvo Glavsevmorputi. 1949.

Kreps, E.M. Osobennosti fiziologii nyryayushchikh zhivotnykh (Physiological Properties of Diving Animals). — Uspekhi Sovremennoi Biologii, Vol. 14, No. 3. 1941.

Kreps, E.M. Ocherk po evolyutsii dykhatel'noi funktsii krovi (Summary on the Evolution of the Respiratory Function of the Blood). — Zhurnal Obshchei Biologii, No. 4. 1943.

Kudryashev, V.A. Vitaminy, ikh fiziologicheskoe i biokhimicheskoe znachenie (Vitamins and Their Physiological and Biochemical Importance). Moskva. 1953.

Kulagin, N.M. Vodnye promyslovye mlekopitayushchie SSSR (Commercial Aquatic Mammals of the USSR). Moskva. 1929.

Kushing, D.G. Mirovoi promysel ryby (World Fishing). — Priroda, No. 12. 1966.

Lagovskaya, E.A. Pechen' kitov kak syr'e dlya polucheniya vitamina A (Whale Liver as Raw Material for Obtaining Vitamin A). — Izvestiya TINRO, Vol. 23. 1947.

Lepekhin, I.I. Dnevnye zapiski puteshestviya po raznym provintsiyam Rossiiskogo gosudarstva (Diary of a Journey through Different Provinces of the Russian State). Sankt-Peterburg. 1805.

Levashova, E.P. Mikrostruktura shkury kita-kashalota (Microstructure of the Hide of the Sperm Whale). — Legkaya Promyshlennost', No. 10. 1954.

Levina, M.Ya. Ob odnoi iz form prisposobitel'noi izmenchivosti amnioticheskogo epiteliya nekotorykh mlekopitayushchikh (v chastnosti, u kashalota) (On one Form of Adaptive Variation of the Epithelium of Some Animals (in Particular, in the Sperm Whale)). — DAN SSSR, Vol. 129, No. 2. 1959.

Lillie, J.   Kak ya nauchilsya govorit' s moimi delfinami (How I Learnt to Speak with My Dolphins). — Nauka i Zhizn', No. 12. 1962.

Lobashov, M. E.   Genetika (Genetics).   Izdatel'stvo LGU.   1967.

Luk'yanova, V. S.   Kolichestvennye kharakteristiki asimmetrii cherepa nekotorykh zubatykh kitov (Quantitative Characteristics of the Asymmetry of the Skull of Some Toothed Whales). — Izvestiya AN SSSR, Seriya Biologicheskaya, No. 3.   1941.

L'vov, V.   Velikany okeana.   Kity i kitoboinyi promysel (The Giants of the Ocean.   Whales and Whaling).   Gosizdat.   1928.

Malyshev, V. M.   Anatomo-gistologicheskie osobennosti stroeniya i innervatsii glotki i gortani kashalota (Anatomical and Histological Properties of the Structure and Innervation of the Pharynx and Larynx of the Sperm Whale).   Synopses of Reports. — III Vsesoyuznoe soveshchanie po izucheniyu morskikh mlekopitayuschikh.   1966.

Manteifel', B. P.   Vertikal'nye migratsii morskikh organizmov.   I. Vertikal'nye migratsii kormovogo zooplanktona (Vertical Migrations of Marine Organisms, I.   Vertical Migrations of Forage Zooplankton). — Trudy IMZh AN SSSR, No. 13.   1959.

Manteifel'. B. P.   Vertikal'nye migratsii morskikh organizmov.   Ob adaptivnom znachenii vertikal'nykh migratsii ryb-planktofagov (Vertical Migrations of Marine Organisms.   The Adaptive Significance of Vertical Migrations of Plankton-Feeding Fish). — Trudy IMZh AN SSSR, No. 39.   1961.

Manteifel', B. P., N. P. Naumov, and V. E. Yakobi.   Orientatsiya i navigatsiya v mire zhivotnykh (Orientation and Navigation in the Animal World). — In Sbornik: "Bionika," Moskva, Izdatel'stvo "Nauka."   1965.

Morskoi atlas (Marine Atlas).   Vol. 2.   Izdatel'stvo Glavnogo shtaba Voenno-Morskikh Sil.   1953.

Mozgovoi, A. A.   Askaridaty mlekopitayushchikh SSSR (Ascaridina of Mammals of the USSR). — Trudy Gel'mintologicheskoi Laboratorii AN SSSR, Vol. 5.   1951.

Mozgovoi, A. A.   Askaridaty zhivotnykh i cheloveka (Ascaridina of Animals and Man).   No. 2.   Izdatel'stvo AN SSSR.   1953.

Mrochkov, K. A.   Soderzhanie vitamina A v pecheni kitov Antarktiki (Vitamin A Content in the Liver of Antarctic Whales). — Rybnoe Khozyaistvo, No. 3.   1951.

Narkhov, A. S.   Morfologiya muskulatury khvostovoi oblasti Delphinus delphis i Tursiops tursio (Morphology of the Musculature of the Caudal Region in Delphinus delphis and Tursiops tursio). — Zoologicheskii Zhurnal, Vol. 16, No. 4.   1937.

Narkhov, A. S.   O prisposoblenii u kitoobraznykh k kormleniyu detenyshei molokom v vode (Adaptation in Whales to Nursing in the Water). — Uchebnye Zapiski Moskovskogo Gosudarstvennogo Pedagogicheskogo Instituta im. V. I. Lenina, No. 186.   1962.

Natarov, V. V. and E. I. Chernyi.   O formirovanii zon povyshennoi biologicheskoi produktivnosti v Tikhom okeane (Formation of Zones of Increased Biological Productivity in the Pacific). — Trudy VNIRO, Vol. 60.   1966.

Nikulin, P. G.   O rasprostranenii kitoobraznykh v moryakh, omyvayushchikh Chukotskii poluostrov (Distribution of Whales in the Seas Around Chukchi Peninsula). — Izvestiya TINRO, Vol. 22.   1947.

O g n e v, S.I. Zoologiya pozvonochnykh (Zoology of Vertebrates). Moskva,
    Izdatel'stvo "Nauka." 1945.
O g n e v, S.I. Ekologiya mlekopitayushchikh. Gl.5. "Prisposoblenie k
    vodnomu obrazu zhizni" (Ecology of Mammals. Chapter 5.
    "Adaptation to the Aquatic Mode of Life"). Izdatel'stvo MOIP. 1951.
O g n e v, S.I. Ocherki ekologii mlekopitayushchikh (Outlines of the Ecology
    of Mammals). — Materialy k Poznaniyu Fauny i Flory SSSR, Novaya
    Seriya, No.26 (11). 1951 a.
O m u r a, H. Migratsii kitov (Migrations of Whales). — Sbornik Materialov
    o Mezhdunarodnom Rybolovstve, No.7. Biblioteka TINRO, No.944.
    (Russian translation from Japanese. 1957.)
O s h m a r i n, P.G. Rabota 260-i Soyuznoi gel'mintologicheskoi ekspeditsii
    (Study of the 260th All-Union Helminthological Expedition). — Trudy
    Gel'mintologicheskoi Laboratorii AN SSSR, Vol.5. 1951.
P e r v u s h i n, A.S. Nablyudeniya za rodami u kashalota (Observations on
    Birth in the Sperm Whale). — Zoologicheskii Zhurnal, Vol.45,
    No.12. 1966.
P e t r o c h e n k o, V.I. Akantotsefaly domashnikh i dikikh zhivotnykh
    (Acanthocephala of Domestic and Wild Animals). No.2. Moskva,
    Izdatel'stvo AN SSSR. 1958.
P o p o v, L.A. Khokhlach Grenlandskogo morya (C y s t o p h o r a c r i s t a t a),
    novyi ob"ekt sovetskogo zveroboinogo promysla (The Hooded Seal
    (C y s t o p h o r a c r i s t a t a) of the Greenland Sea — a New Com-
    mercial Item for the USSR). Thesis. Moskva. 1960.
R e d f i l' d, A.Ts. Evolyutsiya dykhatel'noi funktsii krovi (Evolution of the
    Respiratory Function of the Blood). — Uspekhi Sovremennoi Biologii,
    No.3. 1934.
R e v i n, A. Odin shans iz milliona (A Chance in a Million). — Vokrug Sveta,
    No.2. 1959.
R o m a n e n k o, E.V., A.G. T o m i l i n, and B.A. A r t e m e n k o. K
    voprosu o zvukoobrazovanii i napravlennosti zvukov u del'finov
    (The Problem of Sound Production and Directionality in Dolphins). —
    In Sbornik: "Bionika." Moskva, Izdatel'stvo "Nauka." 1965.
R o v n i n, A.A. K poznaniyu voprosov raspredeleniya kitoobraznykh v
    tropicheskoi zone Tikhogo okeana (Distribution of Whales in the
    Tropical Zone of the Pacific). Synopses of Reports. — III Vseso-
    yuznoe soveshchanie po izucheniyu morskikh mlekopitayushchikh.
    Vladivostok. 1966.
R o v n i n, A.A. Voprosy raspredeleniya krupnykh kitoobraznykh v tropi-
    cheskoi zone Tikhogo okeana (The Distribution of Giant Whales in
    the Tropical Zone of the Pacific). — Sbornik annotatsii nauchnykh
    rabot, vypolnennykh v 1965 g. 1967.
R y b c h i n s k a y a, A.V. Mechenie kitov v Antarktike (Tagging Whales in
    the Antarctic). — Priroda, No.9. 1953.
S e r g i e n k o, M.I. Nekotorye cherty gistologicheskogo stroeniya zheludka
    usatykh i zubatykh kitov (Some Histological Features of the Stomach
    of Baleen and Toothed Whales). — In Sbornik: "Morskie mlekopi-
    tayushchie." Moskva, Izdatel'stvo "Nauka." 1965.
S e v e r t s o v, A.N. Morfologicheskie zakonomernosti evolyutsii (Morpho-
    logical Principles of Evolution). Izdatel'stvo AN SSSR. 1939.

Shmal'gauzen, I.I. Osnovy sravnitel'noi anatomii pozvonochnykh zhivotnykh (Fundamentals of the Comparative Anatomy of Vertebrates). Moskva, Izdatel'stvo "Sovetskaya Nauka." 1947.

Shmal'gauzen, I.I. Faktory evolyutsii (Factors of Evolution). Moskva, Izdatel'stvo "Nauka." 1968.

Shuleikin, V.V. Fizika morya (Marine Physics). Izdatel'stvo AN SSSR. 1953.

Simashko, Yu. Opisanie vsekh zverei, vodyashchikhsya v Imperii Rossiiskoi (A Description of All Animals Found in the Russian Empire). Sankt Peterburg. 1851.

Skopintsev, B.A. O skorosti razrusheniya organicheskogo veshchestva otmershego planktona (On the Rate of Destruction of the Organic Matter of Dead Plankton). — DAN SSSR, Vol. 58, No. 8. 1947.

Skryabin, A.S. Zoogeograficheskaya kharakteristika gel'mintofauny morskikh mlekopitayushchikh Boreo-Patsificheskoi podoblasti (Zoogeographical Description of the Helminth Fauna of Marine Mammals of the Boreal-Pacific Subregion). — Izvestiya Krymskogo Pedagogicheskogo Instituta, Vol. 31. Simferopol'. 1958.

Skryabin, A.S. Novye vidy gel'mintov ot morskikh mlekopitayushchikh Tikhogo okeana i dal'nevostochnykh morei (New Species of Helminths from Marine Mammals of the Pacific and Far East). — Izvestiya Krymskogo Pedagogicheskogo Instituta, Vol. 34, Simferopol'. 1959.

Skryabin, A.S. Gel'mintofauna morskikh mlekopitayushchikh Tikhogo okeana i dal'nevostochnykh morei (The Helminth Fauna of Marine Mammals of the Pacific and Far East). Author's Summary of Candidate Thesis, Simferopol'. 1960.

Skryabin, A.S. Novaya difillobotriida — parazit kashalota Tetragonoporus calyptocephalus n.g.n.sp. (A New Species of Diphyllobothriidae Tetragonoporus calyptocephalus n.g. n.sp.). — Helminthologia, Vol. 3 (1 — 4). 1961.

Skryabin, A.S. Lichinochnye formy gel'mintov ot morskikh mlekopitayushchikh dal'nevostochnykh morei (Larval Forms of Helminths from Marine Mammals of the Far East). — In Sbornik: "Morskie mlekopitayushchie." Moskva, Izdatel'stvo "Nauka." 1965.

Skryabin, A.S. K izucheniyu gel'mintofauny promyslovykh morskikh mlekopitayushchikh Antarktiki (Helminth Fauna of Commercial Marine Mammals of the Antarctic). — Tezisy dokladov itogovoi nauchnoi konferentsii professorsko-prepodavatel'skogo sostava Krymskogo pedagogicheskogo instituta. Simferopol'. 1965 a.

Skryabin, A.S. Novaya korinozoma Corynosoma mirabilis n.sp. — parazit kashalota (A New Species of Corynosoma mirabilis n.sp. — a Parasite of the Sperm Whale). — In: Gel'mintofauna zhivotnykh yuzhnykh morei. Respublikanskii mezhvedomstvennyi sbornik. Seriya Problemy parazitologii. 1966.

Sleptsov, M.M. K voprosu ob asimmetrii cherepa u Odontoceti (On the Asymmetry of the Skull of Odontoceti). — Zoologicheskii Zhurnal, Vol. 18, No. 3. 1939.

Sleptsov, M.M. Razvitie kostnogo cherepa Odontoceti v ontogeneze i filogeneze (Development of the Skull Bones of Odontoceti in Ontogeny and Phylogeny). — DAN SSSR, Vol. 28, No. 4. 1940.

S l e p t s o v, M. M. O biologii razmnozheniya chernomorskogo del'fina (D e l p h i n u s d e l p h i s) (On the Biology of Reproduction of the Black Sea Dolphin (D e l p h i n u s d e l p h i s)). — Zoologicheskii Zhurnal, Vol. 20, Nos. 4 — 5. 1941.

S l e p t s o v, M. M. Giganty okeanov (The Giants of the Oceans). Vladivostok. 1948.

S l e p t s o v, M. M. Novye dannye o raspredelenii samok kashalotov (New Data on the Distribution of Female Sperm Whales). — Izvestiya TINRO, Vol. 32. 1950.

S l e p t s o v, M. M. Kitoobraznye dal'nevostochnykh morei (Whales of the Far East). — Izvestiya TINRO, Vol. 38. 1952.

S l e p t s o v, M. M. Kitoobraznye dal'nevostochnykh morei (Whales of the Far East). Vladivostok. 1955.

S l e p t s o v, M. M. Biologiya i promysel kitov dal'nevostochnykh morei (Biology of Whales and Whaling in the Far East). Pishchepromizdat. 1955 a.

S l e p t s o v, M. M. Kitoobraznye. Geograficheskoe rasprostranenie ryb i drugikh promyslovykh zhivotnykh Okhotskogo i Beringova morei (Cetacea. Geographical Distribution of Fish and Other Commercial Animals of the Sea of Okhotsk and Bering Sea). — Trudy IO AN SSSR, Vol. 14. 1955 b.

S l e p t s o v, M. M. Mechenie kitov v prikuril'skikh vodakh v 1954 g. (Tagging of Whales in the Kurile Waters in 1954). — Trudy IO AN SSSR, Vol. 18. 1955 c.

S l e p t s o v, M. M. Rasprostranenie kitoobraznykh v severo-zapadnoi chasti Tikhogo okeana (Distribution of Whales in the Northwestern Pacific). — Trudy Okeanograficheskoi Komissii AN SSSR, Vol. 3. 1958.

S l e p t s o v, M. M. Raspredelenie kormovykh polei i kitoobraznykh v Okhotskom more (Distribution of Foraging Areas and of Whales in the Sea of Okhotsk). — Trudy IMZh AN SSSR, No. 34. 1961.

S l e p t s o v, M. M. Usloviya sushchestvovaniya kitoobraznykh v zonakh smesheniya kholodnogo (Kurilo-Kamchatskogo) i teplogo (Kurosio) techenii (Life Conditions of Whales in the Zones of Mixing of the Cold (Kurile-Kamchatka) Current with the Warm (Kuroshio) Current). — Trudy IMZh AN SSSR, No. 34. 1961 a.

S l e p t s o v, M. M. Raiony nagula kitov v Beringovom more (Foraging Regions of Whales in the Bering Sea). — Trudy IMZh AN SSSR, No. 34. 1961 b.

S l e p t s o v, M. M. Rasprostranenie kitoobraznykh v Yaponskom more (Distribution of Whales in the Sea of Japan). — Trudy IMZh AN SSSR, No. 34. 1961 c.

S l e p t s o v, M. M. Rezul'taty vzveshivaniya krupnykh i melkikh kitoobraznykh, dobyvaemykh na Dal'nem Vostoke (Results of Weighing Large and small Cetacea Caught in the Far East). — Trudy IMZh AN SSSR, No. 34. 1961 d.

S l y u n i n, N. Promyslovye bogatstva Kamchatki, Sakhalina Komandorskikh ostrovov. Otchet za 1892 — 1893 gg (Commercial Resources of Kamchatka, Sakhalin and the Komandorski Islands. Report for the Years 1892 — 1893). Sankt-Peterburg. 1895.

S m i r n o v, N. A. Uchast' kitov (The Fate of Whales). — Priroda, No. 11. 1928.

Smirnov, N.A.   Morskie zveri arkticheskikh morei (Marine Animals of the Arctic Seas), — Zveri Arktiki. Izdatel'stvo Glavsevmorputi. 1935.

Sokolov, V.E.   Materialy po biologii razmnozheniya chernomorskogo del'fina (Data on the Biology of Reproduction of the Black Sea Dolphin). — Byulleten' MOIP. Otdel biologicheskii, Vol. 59, No. 1. 1954.

Sokolov, V.E.   Shkury kitoobraznykh kak kozhevennoe syr'e (Skin of Whales as Raw Hide). — Trudy MPMI, Vol. 5. 1954 a.

Sokolov, V.E.   Struktura kozhnogo pokrova nekotorykh kitoobraznykh (Structure of the Skin of Some Whales). — Byulleten' MOIP. Otdel biologicheskii, Vol. 6, No. 6. 1955.

Sokolov, V.E.   Raspredelenie lichinok tsestody — Phyllobothrium delphini Bosc. v kozhnom pokrove kashalotov v zavisimosti ot struktury kozhi (Distribution of Larvae of the Cestode Phyllobothrium delphini Bosc. in the Skin of the Sperm Whale in Relation to the Skin Structure). — DAN SSSR, Vol. 133, No. 6. 1955 a.

Sokolov, V.E.   Mekhanizm teplootdachi u morskikh mlekopitayushchikh (The Mechanism of Heat Transfer in Marine Mammals). — Byulleten' MOIP. Otdel biologicheskii, Vol. 63, No. 4. 1958.

Sokolov, V.E.   Opredelenie stadii polovogo tsikla samok del'fina-belobochki Delphinus delphis L. metodom vlagalishchnykh mazkov (Determination of the Stage of the Sexual Cycle in Females of the Common Dolphin Delphinus delphis L. Using the Method of Vaginal Smears). — Trudy Soveshchanii Ikhtiologicheskoi Komissii AN SSSR, No. 12. 1961.

Sokolov, V.E.   Struktura kozhnogo pokrova nekotorykh kitoobraznykh. Soobshchenie II (Structure of the Skin of Some Whales. Communication II). — Nauchnye Doklady Vysshei Shkoly, Seriya "Biologicheskie Nauki," No. 3. 1962.

Sokolov, V.E.   Gistogenez kozhi kashalota i finvala (Histogenesis of the Skin of the Sperm Whale and Finback Whale). — Vestnik Moskovskogo Universiteta, Biologiya, Pochvovedenie, No. 5. 1963.

Sokolov, V.E.   Prisposobitel'nye osobennosti kozhnogo pokrova vodnykh mlekopitayushchikh (Adaptive Features of the Skin of Aquatic Mammals). — In Sbornik: "Morskie mlekopitayushchie." Moskva, Izdatel'stvo "Nauka." 1965.

Solyanik, G.A.   Interesnaya ikhtiologicheskaya nakhodka (An Interesting Ichthyological Find). — Informatsionnyi Byulleten' Sovetskoi Antarkticheskoi Ekspeditsii, No. 42. 1963.

Sushkina, N.N.   Na puti vulkany, kity, l'dy (On the Way Volcanoes, Whales, Ice). Geografgiz. 1962.

Suvorov, E.K.   Proizvoditel'nye sily Rossii. VI. Kitoobraznye (Productive Forces of Russia. VI. Whales). 1919.

Tarasevich, M.N.   Vozrastno-polovaya struktura kosyakov del'fina-belobochki (Age-Sex Structure of Herds of the Common Dolphin). — Trudy Vsesoyuznogo Gidrobiologicheskogo Obshchestva, Vol. 3. 1951.

Tarasevich, M.N.   Materialy po pitaniyu kashalotov severnoi chasti kuril'skikh vod (raion Paramushira, Onekotana, Shiashkotana) (Data on the Feeding of Sperm Whales in the Northern Kurile Waters (Region of Paramushir, Onekotan and Shiashkotan)). — Trudy IO AN SSSR, Vol. 71. 1963.

T a r a s e v i c h, M. N. Promysel kashalotov v severnoi chasti kuril'skikh vod (Sperm Whaling in the Northern Kurile Waters). — Sbornik Referatov, No. 3. 1963 a.

T a r a s e v i c h, M. N. Raspredelenie kashalotov v severnoi chasti kuril'-skikh vod v 1959 — 1961 gg. (Distribution of Sperm Whales in the Northern Kurile Waters in 1959 — 1961). — In Sbornik: "Morskie mlekopitayushchie." Moskva, Izdatel'stvo "Nauka." 1965.

T a r a s e v i c h, M. N. O strukture gruppirovok kitoobraznykh. I. Struktura gruppirovok samtsov kashalotov (Physeter catodon) (On the Makeup of Groupings of Whales. I. The Structure of Groups of Male Sperm Whales (Physeter catodon)). — Zoologicheskii Zhurnal, Vol. 46, No. 1. 1967.

T a r a s e v i c h, M. N. Pishchevye svyazi kashalotov v severnoi chasti Tikhogo okeana (Feeding Relations of Sperm Whales in the North Pacific). — Zoologicheskii Zhurnal, Vol. 47, No. 4. 1968.

T a r a s o v, N. I. O glubine nyryaniya kashalotov (The Depths to Which Sperm Whales Dive). — Priroda, No. 5. 1938.

T a r a s o v, N. I. More zhivet (The Sea Lives). Moskva, Voenizdat. 1949.

T a r a s o v, N. I. Zhivye zvuki morya (Living Sounds of the Sea). — Izvestiya AN SSSR. No. 7. 1960.

T o m i l i n, A. G. Kitoboinyi promysel v SSSR (Whaling in the USSR). — Rybnoe Khozyaistvo, No. 10. 1935.

T o m i l i n, A. G. Kashalot Kamchatskogo morya (The Sperm Whale in the Sea of Kamchatka). — Zoologicheskii Zhurnal, Vol. 15, No. 3. 1936.

T o m i l i n, A. G. Ambra i ee proiskhozdenie (Ambergris and Its Origin). — Priroda, No. 5. 1936 a.

T o m i l i n, A. G. Pryzhki i "instinkt presledovaniya" u kitoobraznykh (Breaching and "Following Instinct" in Whales). — Priroda, No. 1. 1937.

T o m i l i n, A. G. Nekotorye osobennosti v povedenii kitov. Podkhod k beregam i "obmelenie" (Some Characteristics of the Behavior of Whales. Approach to the Shore and "Stranding"). — Byulleten' MOIP. Otdel biologicheskii, Vol. 46, No. 4. 1937 a.

T o m i l i n, A. G. O vzryvakh kitov (On the Breaching of Whales). — Priroda, No. 1. 1937 b.

T o m i l i n, A. G. Nablyudeniya nad dal'nevostochnymi kitoobraznymi (Observations on Far Eastern Whales). — DAN SSSR, Vol. 14, No. 6. 1937 c.

T o m i l i n, A. G. Sezonnoe kolebanie upitannosti kitov (Seasonal Fluctuations of Whale Fatness). — Rybnoe Khozyaistvo, No. 5, 1937 d.

T o m i l i n, A. G. Nekotorye zamechaniya k sistematike, anatomii, biologii i rasprostraneniyu kitoobraznykh severnoi chasti Tikhogo okeana (Some Observations on the Systematics, Anatomy, Biology, and Distribution of Cetacea in the Northern Pacific). — Trudy Rostovskogo Oblastnogo Biologicheskogo Obshchestva, No. 3. 1939.

T o m i l i n, A. G. Nekotorye voprosy iz ekologii kitoobraznykh (adaptatsiya i temperatura vody) (Some Problems Related to the Ecology of Whales (Adaptation and Water Temperature)). — Byulleten' MOIP, Vol. 49, Nos. 5 — 6. 1940.

T o m i l i n, A. G. Opredelenie vozrasta kitov po usovomu apparatu (Determination of the Age of Whales by the Whalebone Apparatus). — DAN SSSR, Vol. 49, No. 6. 1945.

T o m i l i n, A. G.   Novyi vzglyad na fontany kitoobraznykh (A New Look at the Spouting of Whales). — DAN SSSR, Vol. 55, No. 2.   1947.

T o m i l i n, A. G.   Dykhatel'nyi akt i son kitoobraznykh (The Respiratory Act and Sleep among Cetacea). — Priroda, No. 2.   1950.

T o m i l i n, A. G.   O termoregulyatsii u kitoobraznykh (Thermoregulation in Cetacea). — Priroda, No. 6.   1951.

T o m i l i n, A. G.   Opredelitel' kitoobraznykh po povedeniyu i vneshnim priznakam (Key to Cetacea Based on Behavior and External Characters).   Izdatel'stvo MOIP.   1951 a.

T o m i l i n, A. G.   Prisposobitel'nye tipy otryada kitoobraznykh (Adaptive Types of the Order Cetacea). — Zoologicheskii Zhurnal, Vol. 33, No. 3.   1954.

T o m i l i n, A. G.   O golose kitoobraznykh i vozmozhnosti ego ispol'zovaniya dlya ratsionalizatsii promysla morskikh mlekopitayushchikh (On the Voice of Whales and the Possibilities of Using It to Step up the Efficiency of Hunting Marine Mammals). — Rybnoe Khozyaistvo, No. 5.   1954 a.

T o m i l i n, A. G.   O povedenii i zvukovoi signalizatsii kitoobraznykh (Behavior and Signalling of Whales). — Trudy IO AN SSSR, Vol. 18. 1955.

T o m i l i n, A. G.   Zveri SSSR i prilezhashchikh stran.   T. IX. Kitoobraznye (Animals of the USSR and Adjacent Countries. Vol. 9. Cetacea).   Izdatel'stvo AN SSSR.   1957.

T o m i l i n, A. G.   O migratsiyakh, geograficheskikh rasakh, termoregulya- tsii i vliyanii temperatury sredy na rasprostranenie kitoobraz- nykh (Migrations, Geographical Races, Thermoregulation, and the Influence of the Environmental Temperature on the Distribution of Whales). — In Sbornik: "Migratsii zhivotnykh," No. 2.   Izdatel'stvo AN SSSR.   1960.

T o m i l i n, A. G.   Nekotorye sovremennye problemy izucheniya biologii kitoobraznykh (Some Current Problems of Cetacean Biology). — Trudy Soveshchaniya Ikhtiologicheskoi Komissii AN SSSR, No. 12. 1961.

T o m i l i n, A. G.   Kitoobraznye fauny morei SSSR.   Opredeliteli po faune SSSR (Cetacea of the Seas of the USSR.   Keys to the Fauna of the SSSR).   No. 79.   1962.

T o m i l i n, A. G.   Bionika i kitoobraznye (Bionics and Whales). — Priroda, No. 10.   1962 a.

T o m i l i n, A. G.   O prisposobleniyakh kitoobraznykh k bystromu plavaniyu i o vozmozhnosti ispol'zovaniya etikh adaptatsii v sudostroenii (Adaptations of Whales to Fast Swimming and the Possibilities for Utilizing These Adaptations in Shipbuilding). — Byulleten' MOIP. Otdel biologicheskii, Vol. 67, No. 5.   1962 b.

T o m i l i n, A. G.   Intelligenty morskikh putin.   Sekrety povedeniya del'finov i kitov (The Intelligentsia of the Marine Fishing Seasons.   Secrets of the Behavior of Dolphins and Whales). — Priroda, No. 7.   1963.

T o m i l i n, A. G.   O refleksakh Cetacea, svyazannykh s razdrazheniem retseptorov kozhi (On the Reflexes of Cetacea, in Connection with Irritation of the Skin Receptors). — Trudy Vsesoyuznogo Sel'skokhozyaistvennogo Instituta Zaochnogo Obrazovaniya, No. 15. 1963 a.

T o m i l i n, A. G. Istoriya slepogo kashalota (Story of a Blind Sperm
    Whale). Moskva, Izdatel'stvo "Nauka." 1965.

T o m i l i n, A. G. and V. I. P l a v s k i i. Khimicheskii sostav moloka i ego
    kaloriinost' u raznykh grupp mlekopitayushchikh (The Chemical
    Composition of Milk and Its Caloric Content in Various Groups of
    Mammals). — Trudy Vsesoyuznogo Sel'skokhozyaistvennogo
    Instituta Zaochnogo Obrazovaniya, No. 10. 1962.

T r e s k o v s k i i. Kitolovnye karty leitenenta Mori (Whaling Maps of
    Lieutenant Maury). — Morskoi Sbornik, Vol. 18, No. 10. 1855.

U s a c h e v, P. I. Obrastanie kitov diatomovymi vodoroslyami (Diatom
    Films on Whales). — Zoologicheskii Zhurnal, Vol. 19, No. 2.
    1940.

U s o v, P. Zhivopisnaya Rossiya (Picturesque Russia). Edited by
    P. P. Semenov. Vol. 12, Part 2. 1895.

V a d i v a s o v, M. P. Kitoboinyi promysel SSSR na Dal'nem Vostoke v
    1941 — 1944 gg (Soviet Whaling in the Far East in 1941 — 1944). —
    Izvestiya TINRO, Vol. 22, 1946.

V a l l o, K. Obshchaya geografiya morei (General Marine Geography).
    Uchpedgiz. 1948.

V a s i l' e v, M. O shchenke kashalotov (The Sperm Whale Calf). — Morskoi
    Sbornik, No. 5. 1891 a.

V e b e r m a n, E. Kitoboinyi promysel v Rossii (Whaling in Russia). —
    Izvestiya Moskovskogo Kommercheskogo Instituta, No. 2. Moskva.
    1914.

V i n o g r a d o v, M. E. Rol' vertikal'nykh migratsii zooplanktona v pitanii
    glubokovodnykh vidov (The Importance of Vertical Migrations of
    Zooplankton in the Feeding of Deepwater Species). — Priroda, No. 6.
    1953.

V i n o g r a d o v, M. E. Vertikal'nye migratsii zooplanktona i ikh rol' v
    pitanii glubokovodnoi pelagicheskoi fauny (Vertical Migrations of
    Zooplankton and Their Role in the Feeding of the Deepwater Pelagic
    Fauna). — Trudy IO AN SSSR, Vol. 13. 1955.

V i n o g r a d o v, M. P. Morskie mlekopitayushchie Arktiki (Marine Mammals
    of the Arctic). — Trudy Arkticheskogo Nauchno-Issledovatel'skogo
    Instituta, Vol. 202. 1949.

V i n o g r a d o v, M. E. and N. M. V o r o n i n a. Raspredelenie planktona v
    vodakh ekvatorial'nykh techenii Tikhogo okeana (Distribution of
    Plankton in the Waters of the Pacific Equatorial Currents). —
    Trudy IO AN SSSR, Vol. 71. 1963.

V i n o g r a d o v a, N. G. Nekotorye osobennosti rasprostraneniya morskoi
    glubokovodnoi fauny (Some Features of Distribution of the Deep-
    water Marine Fauna). — Trudy IO AN SSSR, Vol. 13. 1955.

V v e d e n s k i i. O neobkhodimosti okhrany kitovogo i drugikh morskikh
    promyslov v nashikh severo-vostochnykh vodakh (The Need to
    Protect Whaling and Other Marine Fisheries in Northeastern
    Soviet Waters). — Priamurskie Vedomosti, No. 11. 1894.

Y a b l o k o v, A. V. Ob organakh khimicheskogo vospriyatiya i zhelezakh
    spetsial'nogo naznacheniya u nekotorykh zubatykh kitov (Organs of
    Chemoreception and Glands with Special Functions in Toothed
    Whales). — Sbornik nauchnykh studencheskikh rabot. MGU. 1957.

Yablokov, A.V. O stroenii zubnoi sistemy i tipakh zubov u kitoobraznykh
    (Dentition and Types of Teeth in Whales). — Byulleten' MOIP. Otdel
    biologicheskii, No. 2. 1958.

Yablokov, A.V. K morfologii pishchevaritel'nogo trakta zubatykh kito-
    obraznykh (Morphology of the Intestine of Toothed Whales). —
    Zoologicheski Zhurnal, No. 4. 1958 a.

Yablokov, A.V. Osobennosti razmnozheniya belukhi kak predstavitelya
    zubatykh kitoobraznykh (Characteristics of the Reproduction of the
    White Whale as a Representative of the Odontoceti). — Tezisy
    dokladov III Nauchnoi molodezhnoi konferentsii. IMZh AN SSSR.
    1959.

Yablokov, A.V. Funktsional'naya morfologiya organov dykhaniya zubatykh
    kitoobraznykh (Functional Morphology of the Respiratory Organs
    of Toothed Whales). — Trudy Soveshchanii Ikhtiologicheskoi
    Komissii AN SSSR, No. 12. 1961.

Yablokov, A.V. Ob "obonyanii" morskikh mlekopitayushchikh (On the
    "Sense of Smell" in Marine Mammals). — Trudy Soveshchanii
    Ikhtiologicheskoi Komissii AN SSSR, No. 12. 1961 a.

Yablokov, A.V. Nekotorye osobennosti mochepolovoi sistemy kitoobraz-
    nykh (Some Characteristics of the Urogenital System of Whales). —
    Byulleten' MOIP. Otdel biologicheskii, Vol. 66, No. 2. 1961 b.

Yablokov, A.V. Osobennosti stroeniya populyatsii kitoobraznykh kak
    evolyutsionnyi faktor (Structural Features of a Whale Population
    as an Evolutionary Factor). Tezisy dokladov I Vsesoyuznogo
    soveshchaniya po izucheniyu mlekopitayushchikh, Vol. 2. Moskva.
    1961 c.

Yablokov, A.V. Klyuch k biologicheskoi zagadke. (Kit na glubine dvukh
    tysyach metrov) (Clue to a Biological Riddle. (The Whale at a
    Depth of 2,000 m.)). — Priroda, No. 4. 1962.

Yablokov, A.V. O tipakh okraski kitoobraznykh (Types of Coloration in
    Cetacea). — Byulleten' MOIP. Otdel biologicheskii, Vol. 68, No. 6.
    1963.

Yablokov, A.V. O probleme rudimentarnykh organov (na primere
    izucheniya morskikh mlekopitayushchikh) (Problem of Rudimentary
    Organs (as Exemplified by Studies of Marine Mammals)). —
    Zoologicheskii Zhurnal, Vol. 42, No. 3. 1963 a.

Yablokov, A.V. Konvergentsiya ili parallelizm v razvitii kitoobraznykh ?
    (Convergence or Parallelism in the Development of Whales ?). —
    Paleontologicheskii Zhurnal, No. 1. 1964.

Yablokov, A.V. Nekotorye aspekty problemy glubokovodnogo avtonom-
    nogo pogruzheniya cheloveka v svete issledovanii biologii
    nyryayushchikh mlekopitayushchikh (Some Aspects of the Problem
    of Deep Autonomous Submersion of Man in the Light of Research
    into the Biology of Diving Mammals). — In Sbornik: "Bionika."
    Moskva, Izdatel'stvo "Nauka," 1965.

Yablokov, A.V. Izmenchivost' mlekopitayushchikh (Variation in
    Mammals). Moskva, Izdatel'stvo "Nauka." 1966.

Yablokov, A.V. and A.A. Berzin. O kariese zubov u kashalota,
    morzha i drugikh mlekopitayushchikh (Dental Caries in the Sperm
    Whale, Walrus and Other Mammals). — Tezisy dokladov I Vsesoyuz-
    nogo soveshchaniya po izucheniyu mlekopitayushchikh, Vol. 1.
    Moskva. 1961.

Yablokov, V.S. and A.V. Yablokov. Kak pronikli valuny i gal'ki v ugol'nye plasty? (How Have Rubble and Pebble Penetrated Coal Beds?). — Priroda, No.3. 1961.

Zaikin, V.V. Razrabotka sposoba obezzhirivaniya sala kashalota s sokhraneniem kozhevennogo syr'ya (Development of a Method of Scouring the Fat of Sperm Whale with Preservation of the Raw Hide). — Trudy VNIRO, Vol.25. 1953.

Zaitsev, V.P., I.V. Kizevetter, L.L. Lagunov, T.I. Makarova, L.P. Minder, and V.N. Podsevalov. Tekhnologiya rybnykh produktov (Technology of Fish Products). — Izdatel'stvo "Pishchevaya promyshlennost'." 1965.

Zavernin, Yu.P. O vliyanii gidrometeorologicheskoi obstanovki na promyslovye kontsentratsii kitov (Influence of the Hydrological Environment on Commercial Concentrations of Whales). — Izvestiya TINRO, Vol.58. 1966.

Zemskii, V.A. Voprosy biologii razmnozheniya finvala Antarktiki (Biology of Reproduction of the Finback Whale in the Antarctic). Author's Summary of Thesis. Moskva. 1953.

Zemskii, V.A. O metodike opredeleniya sledov zheltykh tel beremennosti i ovulyatsii na yaichnikakh samok finvala (Methods of Determining Marks of the Corpora Lutea of Pregnancy and Ovulation of the Finback Whale). — Byulleten' MOIP. Otdel biologicheskii, Vol.61, No.6. 1956.

Zemskii, V.A. Opredelenie sledov zheltykh tel u finvala Antarktiki (Determination of Marks of Corpora Lutea in the Finback Whale in the Antarctic). — Trudy VNIRO, Vol.33. 1958.

Zemskii, V.A. Kity Antarktiki (Whales of the Antarctic). Kaliningrad. 1962.

Zemskii, V.A. and A.A. Berzin. Ambra (Ambergris). — Priroda, No.3. 1959.

Zemskii, V.A. and A.A. Berzin. O redkom yavlenii atavizma u kashalota (On the Rare Phenomenon of Atavism in the Sperm Whale). — Nauchnye Doklady Vysshei Shkoly. Seriya "Biologicheskie Nauki." 1961.

Zenkevich, L.A. Fauna i biologicheskaya produktivnost' morya (Fauna and Biological Productivity of the Sea). Moskva, Izdatel'stvo "Sovetskaya Nauka." 1951.

Zenkovich, B.A. Nekotorye nablyudeniya za kitami Dal'nego Vostoka (Some Observations on the Whales of the Far East). — Rybnoe Khozyaistvo Dal'nego Vostoka, Nos.1 — 2. 1934.

Zenkovich, B.A. Nablyudeniya za kitami dal'nevostochnykg morei (Observations on the Whales of Far Eastern Seas). — Trudy DV FAN SSSR, Vol.1. Seriya Zoologicheskaya. 1936.

Zenkovich, B.A. Vzveshivanie kitov (Weighing Whales). — DAN SSSR, Vol.16, No.3. 1937.

Zenkovich, B.A. O migratsii kitov v severnoi chasti Tikhogo okeana (Migration of Whales in the North Pacific). — Izvestiya TINRO, Vol.10. 1937a.

Zenkovich, B.A. Pishcha dal'nevostochnykh kitov (The Food of Far Eastern Whales). — DAN SSSR, Vol.16, No.4. 1937b.

Zenkovich, B.A. Moloko krupnykh kitoobraznykh (The Milk of Large Whales). — DAN SSSR, Vol.20, Nos.2 — 3. 1938.

Z e n k o v i c h, B. A.   Kitoboinyi promysel v DVK (sezon 1936 g.) (Whaling in
the Far East (Season 1936)). — Priroda, No. 6. 1938 a.

Z e n k o v i c h, B. A.   Temperatura tela kitov (The Temperature of the
Whale's Body). — DAN SSSR, Vol. 18, No. 9. 1938 b.

Z e n k o v i c h, B. A.   Pishcha dal'nevostochnykh kitov (The Food of Far
Eastern Whales). — Referat biologicheskogo otdeleniya AN SSSR
za 1941 — 1943 gg. Izdatel'stvo AN SSSR. 1945.

Z e n k o v i c h, B. A.   Kitoboinyi promysel SSSR i perspektivy ego razvitiya
(Whaling in the USSR and Its Prospects). — Rybnoe Khozyaistvo,
Nos. 10 and 12. 1947.

Z e n k o v i c h, B. A.   Mlekopitayushchie Beringova morya (Spravochnik
dal'nevostochnykh morei) (Mammals of the Bering Sea (Handbook
of the Far Eastern Seas)). — Gidrologiya Morei SSSR, Vol. 10, No. 2.
Beringovo More. Gidrometizdat. 1950.

Z e n k o v i c h, B. A.   Kity i kitoboinyi promysel (Whales and Whaling).
Pishchepromizdat. 1952.

Z e n k o v i c h, B. A.   Estestvennaya istoriya kitov. Prilozhenie I k knige
"Vokrug sveta za kitami" (Natural History of Whales. Supplement I
to "Around the World in Search of Whales"). Geografgiz. 1954 a.

Z e n k o v i c h, B. A.   Kratkaya kharakteristika kitoobraznykh. Prilozhenie II
k knige "Vokrug sveta za kitami" (A Short Description of Whales.
Supplement II to "Around the World in Search of Whales").
Geografgiz. 1954.

Z e n k o v i c h, B. A.   Puteshestvie v yuzhnyi okean i vokrug sveta (A Voyage
to the Southern Ocean and Around the World). Geografgiz. 1960.

Z e n k o v i c h, B. A.   Posleslovie k knige G. Melvilla "Mobi Dik ili belyi kit"
(Epilogue to the Book by H. Melville "Moby Dick, or the White
Whale"). Geografgiz. 1962.

Z e n k o v i c h, B. A.   Kity, ikh promysel v Mirovom okeane i napravlenie
issledovanii (Whales, Whaling in the World Ocean and the Trend of
Investigations). — In Sbornik: "Morskie mlekopitayushchie."
Izdatel'stvo "Nauka." 1965.

Z e n k o v i c h, B. A.   Kity i ikh promysel v vodakh Antarktiki i severnoi
chasti Tikhogo okeana i soobrazheniya o sostoyanii zapasov
(Whales and Whaling in the Waters of the Antarctic and North
Pacific and Concepts on the State of the Stocks). Synopses of
Reports. — III Vsesoyuznoe soveshchanie po izucheniyu morskikh
mlekopitayushchikh. Vladivostok. 1966.

Z h e d e n o v, V. N.   Legkie i serdtse zhivotnykh i cheloveka (The Lungs and
Heart of Animals and Man). Moskva, Izdatel'stvo "Vysshaya
shkola." 1961.

Z h e d e n o v, V. N.   Anatomiya domashnikh zhivotnykh (Anatomy of Domestic
Animals). Moskva, Izdatel'stvo "Vysshaya shkola." 1965.

Z h e m k o v a, Z. P.   O proiskhozhdenii kitoobraznykh (On the Origin of
Whales). — Zoologicheskii Zhurnal, Vol. 44, No. 10. 1965.

Z h u i k o v, D. F.   Yaponskii beregovoi kitoboinyi promysel (Japanese
Coastal Whaling). — Rybnoe Khozyaistvo, No. 7. 1947.

Z u e v, G. V.   Skorost' dvizheniya kal'marov (Speed of Movement of Squids). —
Priroda, No. 9. 1964.

Publications in Other Languages

Abel, O. Die Stammesgeschichte der Meeressäugetiere. — Meereskunde, Jhrg. I. Berlin. 1907.

Abel, O. Die Morphologie der Hüftbeinrudimente der Cetaceen. — Denkschr. Math. Naturw. Klasse Kaiserl. Akad. Wiss. Vol. 81. Wien. 1908.

Abel, O. Die Stämme der Wirbeltiere. Berlin and Leipzig. 1919.

Aflalo, F. G. A Sketch of the Natural History of Australia. London. 1896.

Aguajo, L. A. Observaciones sobre la madurez sexual del cachalote macho (Physeter catodon), capturado en aquas chilenas. Montemar, II (3). 1963.

Alderson, J. An Account of a Whale of the Spermaceti Tribe, Cast on Shore on the Yorkshire Coast, on the 28th of April, 1825. — Trans. Cambridge Philos. Soc., Vol. 2. 1827.

Allen, J. A. Preliminary List of Works and Papers Relating to the Mammalian Orders Cete and Sirenia. — Bull. U. S. Geol. and Geog. Survey of the Terr., Vol. 6. 1881.

Andrée, E. and T. François. Contribution à l'étude des huiles d'animaux marins. Recherches sur l'huile de cachalot et le blanc de baleine. — C. R. Congress Soc. Sav. Paris for 1926 — 1927.

Anderson, J. Nachrichten von Island, Grönland und der Strasse Davis. Frankfurt und Leipzig. 1747.

Anderson, R. J. The Whales and Dolphins (A Zoological Mnemonic). Part II, Belfast. 1896.

Andrews, R. C. Monographs of the Pacific Cetacea. — Mem. Amer. Mus. Natur. History. 1916.

Andrews, R. C. Whale Hunting with Gun and Camera. New York. D. Appleton. 1916 a.

Andrews, R. C. A Remarkable Case of External Hind Limbs in a Humpback Whale. — Amer. Mus. Novitates, No. 9. 1821.

Anon. Baleine — Encyclopédie ou Dict. raisonné des connaissances humaines, mis en ordre par M. de Félice, Vol. 4, Cachalot. Vol. 6, Yverdon. 1771.

Artedi, P. Ichtyologia sive Opera omnia de Piscibus (Pars III, Genera Piscium, Pars IV, Synonymia Nominum Piscum fere omnium). Lugduni Batavorum. 1738.

Ash, C. E. The Body Weight of Whales. —Norsk Hvalf.—tid., No. 41. 1952.

Ash, C. E. Whaler's Eye. New York, Macmillan. 1962.

Ashley, C. W. The Yankee Whaler. Garden City, N. Y. Haleyon House. 1942.

Atwood, N. Ambergris. — Amer. Naturalist, No. 2. 1869.

Backus, R. H. A Large Shark in the Stomach of a Sperm Whale. — J. Mammol., Vol. 47, No. 1. 1966.

Backus, R. H. and W. E. Schevill. Physeter Clicks. — "Whales, Dolphins and Porpoises." Univ. Calif. Press. Berkeley — Los Angeles. 1966.

Bannister, J. L. Sperm Whales. — Annual Rept. Div. Fish and Oceanogr. Commonwealth Scient. and Industr. Res. Organiz. Cronulla. 1965 — 1966.

Barcelo. Note on a Sperm Whale. — An. Soc. Esp. Hist. Nat., Vol. 8. 1879.

Barret-Hamilton, G. E. H. Sperm Whale in Mayo. — Zoologist (Series 3), Vol. 14. 1890.

Bartsch, P. Pirates of the Deep. Stories of the Squid and Octopus. — Smiths, Report. 1916.

Baylis, H. A. An Ascarid from the Sperm Whale. — Ann. a. Mag. Nat. Hist. Ser. 9, Vol. 11. 1923.

Baylis, H. A. Parasitic Nematoda and Acanthocephala Collected in 1925 — 1927. — Discovery Rep., Cambridge, Vol. 1. 1929.

Beale, T. A Few Observations on the Natural History of the Sperm Whale. London. 1835.

Beale, T. The Natural History of the Sperm Whale. London. 1839.

Beane, J. F. From Forecastle to Cabin. New York, Editor Publishing. 1905.

Beddard, F. E. A Book of Whales. London. 1900.

Beddard, F. E. Contributions to the Knowledge of the Sperm Whale, Based upon the Examinations of a Young Foetus. — Durban. Ann. Mus. I. 1915.

Beddard, F. E. Further Contribution to the Anatomy of the Sperm Whale (Physeter macrocephalus) Based upon an Examination of Two Additional Foetuses. — Ann. Durban. Mus., Vol. 2. 1919.

Beddard, F. E. Some Observations upon the Development of the Teeth of Physeter macrocephalus. — Quart. J. Micr. Sci., Vol. 67. 1923.

Belanger, L. F. A Study of the Histological Structure of the Respiratory Portion of the Lungs of Aquatic Mammals. — Amer. J. Anat., Vol. 67. 1940.

Beneden, P. J. Ostéographie des Cétacés vivants et fossiles, comprenant la description et l'iconographie. Atlas VIII. Paris. 1868 — 1879.

Beneden, P. J. and P. Gervais. Ostéographie des Cétacés, vivants et fossiles. Paris. 1868 — 1880.

Beneden, V. Les Ziphoïdes en mers d'Europe. — Mém. couronnes et autres mémoires. October. Bruxelles. 1888.

Bennett, A. G. Whaling in the Antarctic. New York. Henry Holt. 1932.

Bennett, F. D. Narrative of a Whaling Voyage around the Globe, from the Year 1833 to 1836, London: Richard Bentley. 1840.

Best, P. The Sperm Whale (Physeter catodon) off the West Coast of South Africa. 1) Ovarian Changes and their Significance. — Division of Sea Fisheries Investigational Report, No. 61. 1967.

Best, P. The Polarity of Sperm Whale Ovaries. — Norsk Hvalf. -tid., No. 2. 1968.

Birkeland, K. B. The Whales of Akutan. New Haven. Yale University Press. 1926.

Birula, A. A. Über die Seesäugetiere des Weissen Meers. — Zool. Anz. Vol. 107, No. 1/2. 1934.

Blanford, W. T. Mammalia. The Fauna of British India, Including Ceylon and Burma. London, Calcutta, Bombay, Berlin. 1888 — 1891.

Blyth, E. Catalogue of Mammalia in the Museum Asiatic Society. Calcutta. 1863.

Boice, R. C., M. L. Swift, and J. C. Roberts. Cross-Sectional Anatomy of the Dolphin. — Norsk Hvalf. -tid., No. 7. 1964.

Bolau, H. Die geographische Verbreitung der Wale des Stillen Ozeans. — Abhandlungen aus dem Gebiete der Wissenschaft, Hamburg. 1895.

Bolognari, A. A proposito della recente cattura di alcuni asemplari di capodoglio (Physeter macrocephalus) del Mediteranio. — Bull. de l'Inst. océanogr., No. 949, Monaco. 1949.

Bolognari, A. Sulla biologia del capodoglio. — Atti. Soc. Peloritana, Vol. 3, Fasc. II. 1957.

Bonnaterre, J. H. Cétologie. Tableau encyclopédique et méthodique des trois règnes de la nature. Paris. 1789.

Bonnot, P. The Whales of California. — California Fish and Game., Vol. 15, No. 3. 1929.

Boschma, H. On the Teeth and Some Other Particulars of the Sperm Whale (Physeter macrocephalus L.). — Temminckia Leiden, Vol. 3. 1938.

Boschma, H. Double Teeth in the Sperm Whale (Ph. macrocephalus). — Zool. Medeel, D. XX Alf. 3—4. 1938 a.

Boschma, H. Remarques sur les Cétacés à dents, et en particulier sur le cachalot. — Bull. de l'Inst. océanogr., No. 991, Monaco. 1951.

Bow, J. M. and C. A. Purday. A Method of Preparing Sperm Whale Teeth for Age Determination. — Nature, Vol. 210, No. 5034. 1966.

Boylsten. Ambergris Found in Whale. — Phil. trans. Roy. Soc. London, Vol. 33. 1724.

Breathnach, A. S. The Cetacean Central Nervous System. — Biol. Rev. Cambridge Philos. Soc., Vol. 35. 1960.

Brisson, M. J. Regnum Animal in Classes IX distributum. — Le Règne Animal divisé en IX Classes. Paris. 1756.

Brown, J. T. The Whale Fishery, Whalemen, Vessels, Apparatus and Methods of the Fishery. — In G. B. Goode, ed., The fisheries and fishery industries of the United States. II. History and methods of the fisheries. U. S. Comm. Fish. and Fisheries. 1887.

Brown, R. Notes on the History and Geographical Relations of the Cetacea Frequenting Davis Strait and Baffin's Bay. — Proc. Zool. Soc. London. 1868.

Brown, S. G. Whale Marks Recently Recovered. — Norsk Hvalf.-tid., No. 12. 1956.

Brown, S. G. Whales Observed in the Indian Ocean. Notes on their Distribution.— The Marine Observer. London. Vol. 27, No. 177. 1957.

Brown, S. G. Whales Observed in the Atlantic Ocean. Notes on their Distribution, Parts I and II. — The Marine Observer. Vol. 28, No. 181—182. 1958.

Brown, S. G. Whale Marks Recovered during Antarctic Season 1957/58. — Norsk Hvalf.-tid., No. 10. 1958 a.

Brown, S. G. Whale Marks Recovered in the Antarctic Season 1955/56, Africa 1958 and 1959. — Norsk Hvalf.-tid., No. 12. 1959.

Brown, S. G. Whale Marks Recovered in the Antarctic Whaling Season 1959/60. — Norsk Hvalf.-tid., No. 10. 1960.

Brown, S. G. International Cooperation in Antarctic Whale Marking 1957 to 1960 and a Review of the Distribution of Marked Whales in the Antarctic. — Norsk Hvalf.-tid., No. 3. 1962.

Brown, S. G. Whale Marks Recovered during Antarctic Seasons 1960/61, 1961/62 and in South Africa. — Norsk Hvalf.-tid., No. 11. 1962 a.

B r o w n, S. G. International Cooperation in Antarctic Whale Marking 1960
     to 1965. — Norsk Hvalf.-tid., No. 5. 1966.
B r o w n e, J. R. Etching of a Whaling Cruise. New York. Harper. 1846.
B u c h a n a n, J. Y. The Sperm Whale and its Food. — Nature, No. 53. 1896.
B u d k e r, P. Whales and Whaling. New York. 1959.
B u d k e r, P. Les migrations des grands Cétacés. — Compt. rend. Soc.
     Biogéogr., No. 329 — 331. 1961.
B u l l e n, F. T. The Cruise of the "Cachalot" round the World after Sperm
     Whales. London. Smith, Elder. 1898. (Republished in 1905
     and 1958).
B u z e t a, R. B. Cyamidae (Crustacea: Amphipoda) en P h y s e t e r
     c a t o d o n L. capturados en Chile con descripcion de una nueva
     especie C y a m u s b e h a m o n d e i. — Montemar, No. 3. 1963.
C a d e n a t. A propos du cachalot. — Notes afric. LXXI. 1956.
C a l d w e l l, D. K. Scrimshaw: Folk Art of Yankee Whalemen, Los Angeles
     Country Mus., Vol. 17, No. 12. 1961.
C a l d w e l l, D. K., M. C. C a l d w e l l, and D. W. R i c e. Behavior of the
     Sperm Whale, P h y s e t e r c a t o d o n L. — "Whales, Dolphins and
     Porpoises," Univ. Calif. Press, Berkeley — Los Angeles. 1966.
C a l d w e l l, D. K., A. I n g l i s, and I. B. S i e b e n a l e r. Sperm and Pigmy
     Sperm Whales Stranded in the Gulf of Mexico. — J. Mammol.,
     Vol. 41, No. 1. 1960.
C a l d w e l l, M. C. and D. K. C a l d w e l l. Epimeletic (Care-Giving)
     Behavior in Cetacea. — "Whales, Dolphins and Porpoises." Univ.
     Calif. Press, Berkeley — Los Angeles. 1966.
C a l d w e l l, M. C., R. M. H a u g e n, and D. K. C a l d w e l l. High-Energy
     Sound Associated with Fright in the Dolphins. — Science, No. 138. 1962.
C a m p e r, P. Observations anatomiques sur la structure et le squelette de
     plusieurs espèces de Cétacés. Paris. 1820.
C a r t e, A. and A. M c A l l i s t e r. On the Anatomy of B a l a e n o p t e r a
     r o s t r a t a. — Phil. Trans. Roy. Soc. London, Vol. 158. 1869.
C a r t e r, N. Ambergris. — Prog. Rept. Pacif. Biol. St., No. 25. 1935.
C a r t e r, N. and C. E l s e y. Ambergris Found in a British Columbia
     Sperm Whale. — Progr. Rept. Pacif. Coast. St., No. 99. 1954.
C a v e, A. J. E. and F. J. A u m o n i e r. Morphology of the Cetacean
     Reniculus. — Nature, Vol. 193, No. 4817. 1962.
C h a n o t, V. L'ambre gris. — Pêche Maritime, No. 870. 1950.
C h a r l e s w o r t h, F. On the Occurrence of the Genus P h y s e t e r (or
     Sperm Whale) in the Red Crag of Felixstow. — The Quarterly Tour
     of the Geol. Soc. London, Vol. 1. 1845.
C h a s e, O. Shipwreck of the Whaleship Essex. New York. Corinth Books.
     1963.
C h a t t e r t o n, E. K. Whalers and Whaling. New York. William Farquer
     Payson. 1926.
C h e e v e r, H. T. The Whale and his Captors. New York. Harper. 1850.
C h i t t l e b o r o u g h, R. G. Aspects of Reproduction in the Male Humpback
     Whale, M e g a p t e r a n o d o s a (Bonnaterre), — Australian J.
     Marine Freshw. Res., Vol. 6, No. 1. 1955.
C h i t t l e b o r o u g h, R. G. Aerial Observations on the Humpback Whale,
     M e g a p t e r a n o d o s a (Bonnaterre) with Notes on Other Species. —
     Aust. J. Mar. Freshw. Res., 9. 1958.

C l a r k, A. H. The Whale Fishery. History and Present Condition of the
    Fishery.— In: G. B. Goode, ed. The fisheries and fishery industries
    of the United States. II. History and methods of the fisheries.
    U. S. Comm. Fish and Fisheries. 1887.
C l a r k e, M. R. M u l t i d u c t u s p h i s e t e r i s gen. et sp. nov. A New
    Diphyllobothriid Cestode from a Sperm Whale. — J. of Helmintho-
    logy, Vol. 36, No. 1/2. 1962.
C l a r k e, R. Hearing in Cetacea. — Nature, No. 161. 1948.
C l a r k e, R. Ambergris, Soap Perfumery and Cosmetics. — Nat. Inst. of
    Ocean. Collected Reprints. 1949.
C l a r k e, R. Open Boat Whaling in the Azores. — Discovery Repts. 26. 1954.
C l a r k e, R. A Great Haul of Ambergris. — Nature, Vol. 174; Norsk Hvalf.-
    tid., No. 8. 1954 a.
C l a r k e, R. Whales and Seals as Resources of the Sea. — Norsk Hvalf.-tid.,
    No. 9. 1954 b.
C l a r k e, R. A Giant Squid Swallowed by a Sperm Whale. — Norsk Hvalf.-tid.,
    No. 10. 1955.
C l a r k e, R. Sperm Whaling Open Boats in the Azores. — Zoo. Life,
    Vol. 10, No. 2. 1955 a.
C l a r k e, R. The Biology of Sperm Whales Captured in the Azores. —
    Norsk Hvalf.-tid., No. 8. 1956.
C l a r k e, R. Sperm Whales of the Azores. — Discovery Rep., 28. 1956 a.
C l a r k e, R. Migrations of Marine Mammals. — Norsk Hvalf.-tid., No. 11.
    1957.
C l a r k e, R. Whale Observations and Whale Marking off the Coast of Chile
    in 1958 and from Ecuador towards and beyond the Galapagos
    Islands in 1959. — Norsk Hvalf.-tid., No. 7. 1962.
C l a r k e, R. Stomach Contents of a Sperm Whale Caught off Madeira in
    1959. — Norsk Hvalf.-tid., No. 5. 1962 a.
C l a r k e, R. The Stalked Barnacle, C o n c h o d e r m a, Ectoparasitic on
    Whales. — Norsk Hvalf.-tid., No. 8. 1966.
C l a r k e, R., A. A g u a j o, and O. P a l i z a. Progress Report on Sperm
    Whale Research in the Southeast Pacific Ocean. — Norsk Hvalf.-tid.,
    No. 11. 1964.
C l a r k e, R. and S. G. B r o w n. International Cooperation in Antarctic
    Whale Marking from 1945 to 1957. — Norsk Hvalf.-tid., No. 9. 1957 a.
C o c k r i l l, R. The Great Whales of the Antarctic. — Nat. Hist., 67. 1958.
C o c k r i l l, R. Pathology of the Cetacea. A Veterinary Study on Whales.
    Part I. — "Brit. Veterin. J." 116, No. 4. 1960.
C o c k r u m, E. L. Sperm Whales Stranded on the Beaches of the Gulf of
    California. — J. of Mammol., Vol. 37, No. 2. 1956.
C o l l e t t, R. Norges Pattedyr. Kristiania. 1911 — 1912.
C o l n e t t, J. A. Voyage to the South Atlantic and round Cape Horn into the
    Pacific Ocean, for the Purpose of Extending the Spermaceti Whale
    Fisheries. London. 1798.
C o m r i e, L. C. and A. B. A d a m. The Female Reproductive System and
    Corpora Lutea of the False Killer Whale P s e u d o r c a c r a s s i -
    d e n s. — Trans. Roy. Soc. Edinburgh, Vol. 59. 1938.
C o m r o e, J. H. and C. F. S c h m i d t. The Part Played by Reflexes from
    the Carotid Body in the Chemical Regulation of Respiration in the
    Dog. — Amer. J. of Physiol., Vol. 121, No. 1. 1938.
C o o k, G. A. Pursuing the Whale. New York. Houghton Mifflin. 1926.

Cope, E.D. The Cetacea. — Amer. Naturalist, Vol. 24. 1890.

Cornon, R. Les Odeurs Ambrées. — Industries de la Parfumerie, Vol. 10, Nos. 8, 9. 1955.

Cousteau, I.J. The Living Sea. New York. Harper and Row. 1963.

Cousteau, I.J. and F. Dumas. Silent World. Harper. 1953.

Crisp, D.T. The Tonnages of Whales Taken by Antarctic Pelagic Operations during Twenty Seasons and an Examination of the Blue Whale Unit. — Norsk Hvalf.-tid., No. 10. 1962.

Cushing, J.E., N. Calaprice, and K. Fijino. The Ju Blood Typing System of the Sperm Whales and Specific Soluble Substances. — Sci. Rep. Whales Res. Inst., No. 17. 1963.

Cuvier, F. Cetacea. The Cyclopaedia of Anatomy and Physiology, ed. by Robert B. Todd, London, Vol. 1. 1835 — 1836.

Cuvier, F. De l'histoire naturelle des Cétacés. Paris. 1836.

Cuvier, G. Rapport fait à la classe des Sciences mathématiques et physiques sur divers Cétacés pris sur les côtes de France, principalement, sur ceux qui sont échoués près de Paimpol, le 7 janvier 1812. — Ann. Mus. Hist. Nat., Vol. 19. 1812.

Cuvier, G. — Recherches sur les Ossemens fossiles, nouv. éd., Vol. 5. Paris and Amsterdam. 1823.

Dakin, W.J. Whalemen Adventurers. Sydney. Angus and Robertson. 1934.

Dallas, G. Hanna. Sperm Whales at St. Georgia Island, Bering Sea.— J. of Mammol., Vol. 5, No. 1. 1924.

Darling, F.F. Social Life in Ungulates.—In: Structure et Physiologie des Sociétés Animales. Colloques Internationaux du Centre National de la Recherche Scientifique. Paris. 1952.

Darwin, C. A Naturalist's Voyage. London. John Murray. 1882.

Daubenton, L.J.M. Cachalot. Encyclopédie ou Dict. raisonné des Sciences, des Arts et des Métiers. Vol. 2. Paris (The "Recueil des Planches," Vol. 6, containing a figure on a Sperm Whale, is from 1768). 1751.

Davies, J.L. The Antitropical Factor in Cetacean Specification. — Reprinted from Evolution, Vol. 17, No. 1. 1963.

Davis, W.M. Nimrod of the Sea, or the American Whalemen. Boston. Charles E. Lauriat Co., 1926 (1st ed. 1874, New York. Harper).

Dawbin, W.H. New Zealand and South Pacific Whale Marking and Recoveries to the End of 1958. — Norsk Hvalf.-tid., No. 5. 1959.

Dawbin, W.H. The Seasonal Migratory Cycle of Humpback Whales. — "Whales, Dolphins and Porpoises." Univ. Calif. Press, Berkeley— Los Angeles. 1966.

Deinse, A.B. van. Zur Flossenversteifung der Cetaceen. — Anat. Anz., Vol. 49. 1916.

Deinse, A.B. van. Over de Potvisschen in Nederland gestrand tusschen.— Zool. — Meded., Vol. 4. 1918.

Deinse, A.B. van. De Fossiele en recente Cetacea van Nederland. — Diss. Utrecht. 1931.

Denker, A. Zur Anatomie des Gehörorgans der Cetacea. — Anat. Hefte, No. 19. 1902.

Denmead, T. and E.E. Dodd. Whaling on the West Coast of North America. 1911 — 1938. — Proc. 6th Pacific Sci. Congr., Vol. 3. 1940.

Deraniyagala, R. E. P. Some Southern Temperate Zone Fishes, a Bird and Whales that Enter the Ceylon Area (II). — Fac. Arts. Vidyodaya Univ. Colombo, Ceylon. Soplia Leylanica biol. ab. 4081, Vol. 45, No. 1. 1961.

Desmoulins, A. Cachalot. — Dict. class. d'Hist. Nat., Vol. 2, Paris. 1822.

Despelette. Cachalot échoué près de Bayonne. — Hist. de l'Acad. Roy. des Sciences, année 1741. Paris. 1744.

Dewhurst, H. W. The Natural History of the Order Cetacea and the Oceanic Inhabitants of the Arctic Regions. London. 1834.

Döbereiner. Physeter oder Pottwal. — Allg. Enzykl. d. Wiss. u. Künste., ed. by J. S. Ersch and J. G. Gruber, Section 3, Vol. 25, Leipzig. 1850.

Drapiez. Cachalot. — Dict. class. des Sciences. Nat., Vol. 2. Bruxelles. 1853 (1 ed. 1837).

Dudley. An Essay on the Natural History of Whales, with a Particular Account of the Ambergris Found in the Spermaceti Whale. — Phil. Trans. Roy. Soc. London, Vol. 33. 1725.

Dufresne, F. Alaska's Animals and Fishes, N. G. 1946.

Dulles. Lowered Boats. New York: Harcourt, Brace. 1933.

Du Monde Artur. Voyage fait par ordre du Roi sur les corvettes de L'Uranie de la Physicienne 1817—1820. — Histoire naturelle Zoologie. Paris, Pl. 12. 1824.

Edmundson, A. B. and W. Hirs. On the Structure of Sperm Whale Myoglobin. II. The Trypic Hydrolysts of the Denatured Protein. — J. Molec. Biol., Vol. 5, No. 6. 1962.

Edwards, A. J. The Presence of Functional Teeth in the Upper Jaw of [Whales in] the Davis Strait. Delft. 1912.

Engel, S. Respiratory Tissue of the Large Whales. — Nature, Vol. 173, No. 4394. 1954.

Engel, S. Lung Structure. — Charles C. Thomas Publish. Springfield, Ill. 1962.

Eschrict, D. F. Zoologisch—anatomisch—physiologische Untersuchungen über die nordischen Walthiere. — Leipzig, Voss, Vol. 1. 1849.

Essapian, F. S. An Albino Bottlenosed Dolphin Tursiops truncatus. Captured in the United States. — Norsk Hvalf.-tid., No. 9. 1962.

Evans, W. E. and J. H. Prescott. Observation on the Sound Production Capabilities of the Bottlenose Porpoise: a Study of Whistles and Clicks. — Zoologica (U. S. A.), Vol. 47, Pt. 3. 1962.

Fabricius, O. Fauna Groenlandica — Hafniae et Lipsiae. 1780.

Ferguson, R. Harpooner: a Four-Year Voyage on the Barque Kathleen, 1880—1884. Ed. L. D. Stair. Philadelphia: Univ. of Pennsylvania Press. 1936.

Fish, M. P. Marine Mammals of the Pacific with Particular Reference to the Production of Underwater Sound. — Woods Hole Oceanogr. Repts. Tech. Repts., ONR, 8. 1949.

Fisher, H. D. Rapid Preparation of Tooth Sections for Age Determination. — J. Wildl. Managa, 18. 1954.

Fisher, P. Journal de l'Anatomie et la Physiologie, Note sur une déformation pathologique de la mâchoire inférieure du cachalot, 4-me année. 1867.

Fisher, P. Note sur les cachalots échoués sur les côtes océaniques de France. — J. de Zool., Vol. 1. 1872.

Fleming, J. The Philosophy of Zoology. Edinburgh, Vol. 2. 1822.

Flower, W. H. Whale. – Encycl. Brit. 9th ed., Vol. 24, Edinburgh. 1888.

Flower, W. H. and R. Lydekker. An Introduction to the Study of Mammals Living and Extinct. London. 1891.

Fraser, F. C. Report on the Cetacea Stranded on the British Coasts from 1927 to 1932. – Bull. British Mus., Nat. Hist., No. 11. 1934.

Fraser, F. C. Description of a Dolphin Stenella frontalis (Cuvier) from the Coast of French Equatorial Africa. – Atlantic Rept., No. 1. 1950.

Fraser, F. C. Some Aquatic Adaptation of Whales and Dolphins. 1959.

Fraser, F. C. Hearing in Cetaceans. – Bull. Brit. Mus. Nat. Hist., Vol. 7, No. 1. 1960.

Fraser, F. C. Guide for the Identification and Reporting of Stranded Whales, Dolphins and Porpoises on the British Coasts. – British Museum (Natural History). London. 1966.

Fraser, F. C. and P. E Purves. Hearing in Cetaceans. – Bull. Brit. Mus. Nat. History and Zool., Vol. 2, No. 5. 1953.

Fraser, F. C. and P. E. Purves. The Blow of Whales. – No. 176. 1955.

Fraser, F. C. and P. E. Purves. Hearing in Whales. – Endeavour, Vol. 18, No. 70. 1959.

Fraser, F. C. and P. E. Purves. Anatomy and Function of the Cetacean Ear. – Proceedings of the Royal Soc. B., Vol. 152. 1960.

Freund, L. Die Tierwelt der Nord- und Ostsee – Cetacea. XXVII, 12. Leipzig. 1932.

Fujino, K. On the Body Weight of the Sei Whale Located in the Adjacent Waters of Japan. – Sci. Rep. Whale Inst., No. 10. 1955.

Fujino, K. On the Body Proportions of the Sperm Whales (Physeter catodon). – Sci. Rep. Whales Res. Inst., No. 11. 1956.

Fujino, K. Identification of Breeding Subpopulations of the Sperm Whales in the Waters Adjacent to Japan and around Aleutian Islands by Means of Blood Typing Investigations. – Bull. Japan. Soc. Sci. Fish., Vol. 29, No. 12. 1963.

Gambell, R. Seasonal Movement of Sperm Whales. – Aspects Marine Zool. London–New York, Acad. Press. 1967.

Gambell, R. and C. Grzegorzewska. The Rate of Lamina Formation in Sperm Whale Teeth. – Norsk Hvalf.-tid., No. 6. 1967.

Gaskin, D. E. Recent Observations in New Zealand Waters on Some Aspects of Behavior of the Sperm Whale (Physeter macrocephalus). – Tuatara, Vol. 12, No. 2. 1964.

Gaskin, D. E. Whale Marking Cruises in New Zealand Waters Made between August and December 1963. – Norsk Hvalf.-tid., No. 2. 1964a.

Gaskin, D. E. New Zealand Whaling and Whale Research. 1962–4. – N. Z. Sci. Rev. 23 (2). 1965.

Gates, D. G. Sperm Whaling at Albany. – Norsk Hvalf.-tid., No. 11. 1958.

Gawn, R. W. L. Aspects of the Locomotion of Whales. — Nature, Vol. 161, No. 4080. 1948.

Geiling, E. M. K., L. N. Tarr, and A. de L. Tarr. The Hypophysis Cerebri of the Finback (Balaenoptera physalus) and Sperm Whale (Physeter megalocephalus). — Johns Hopkins Hosp. Bull., No. 57. 1935.

Gelett, C. W. A. Life on the Ocean. — Honolulu, Hawaiian Gazette. 1917.

Gerardin, S. Cachalot. — Dict. des Sc. Nat. par plusieurs professeurs du Jardin du Roi, et des principales écoles de Paris, Vol. 6. Strasbourg and Paris. 1817.

Gesner, C. Historiae Animalium liber IIII qui est de Piscium Aquatilium animantium Natura. — Tiguri. 1558..

Gill, T. The Sperm Whale Giant and Pigmy. — Amer. Nature, Vol. 4. 1871.

Gilmore, R. M. Whales Aground in Cortes Sea. — Pacif. Disk., Vol. 10, No. 1. 1957.

Gilmore, R. M. On the Mass Strandings of Sperm Whales. — Pacific Naturalist, Vol. 1, No. 10. 1959.

Gilmore, R. M. Whales, Porpoises and the U. S. Navy. — Norsk Hvalf.-tid., No. 3. 1961.

Goode, G. B. Mammals. A. The Whales and Porpoises. I. The Sperm Whale. The Fisheries and Fishery Industries of the United States. — U. S. Comm. of Fish and Fisheries. Washington. 1884.

Gray, J. E. The Zoology of the Voyage of H. M. S. Erebus and Terror. London. 1846.

Gray, J. E. On the Cetacea Which Have Been Observed in the Seas Surrounding the British Islands. — Proc. Zool. Soc. London. 1864.

Gray, J. E. On the Whales on the Cape with Descriptions of 2 New Species. — Proc. Zool. Soc. London. 1865.

Gray, J. E. Notice of New Species of Australian Sperm Whale (Catodon Krefftii) in the Sydney Museum. — Proc. Zool. Soc. London. 1865a.

Gray, R. W. The Sleep of Whales. — Nature, Vol. 121, No. 3000. 1927.

Gray, R. W. The Blubber of Whales. — Nature, Vol. 121, No. 3055. 1928.

Gray, R. W. Do Whales Descend to Great Depths? — Nature, Vol. 135, No. 3417. 1935.

Gregory, N. Sperm Whale and Squid. — Discovery Rep. 16 (October). 1937.

Grynfeltt, B. Les fibres de Herxheimer et leur changement d'aspects, les modifications de la forme des cellules basilaires dans l'épithélium malpighieus. — C. R. Assoc. Anat. 25 réunion. Amsterdam. 1930.

Guldberg, G. Cetologische Mittheilungen. I. Bemerkungen über das Auftreten und den Fang von Pottwalen (Physeter macrocephalus L.) an den nordeuropäischen Küsten im letzten Decennium. — Nat. Magar. F. Nature, Vol. 39. 1901.

Haas, H. We Came from the Sea. — Garden City, New York. Doubleday. 1959.

Haley, N. C. Whale Hunt. New York. Ives Washburn. 1948.

Hamilton, G. E. Effects of Present-Day Whaling on the Stocks of Whales. — Nature, No. 161. 1948.

Hamilton, G. E. Cetacea of the Falkland Islands. — Commun. Zool. Mus. Nat. Hist. Montevideo, 4 (66). 1962.

Hamilton, R. Mammalia. Whales, etc. Edinburgh–London (The Naturalists Library, Vol. 26). 1852.

Hammond, G. W. On Board a Whaler. New York. Putnam. 1901.

Harada, J. Das Nervensystem von Bolbosoma turbinella. – Japan Journ. Zool., Tokyo, 3. 1931.

Hardy, E. The Sperm Whale. – The Perfume and Essent. Oil Record, Vol. 40, No. 9. 1949.

Harmer, S. F. Report on Cetacea Stranded on the British Coasts from 1913 to 1926. – Bull. Brit. Mus. (Natural History), No. 10, London. 1927.

Harmer, S. F. The History of Whaling. – Proc. Linn. Soc. Sess., 140, 1927–1928. 1929.

Harmer, S. F. Supplement to Willer's Article "Notes on a Young Sperm Whale from the Bermuda Islands." – Proc. Zool. Soc. London, No. 8. 1933.

Harrison, R. J. and J. E. King. Marine Mammals. London, Hutchinson. 1965.

Hart, T. On the Diatoms of the Skin Film of Whales and their Possible Bearing on Problems of Whale Movements. – Discovery Rep. Cambridge, Vol. 10. 1935.

Hartles, R. L. and A. G. Leaver. The Indentifications of Pyrimidines in the Fluorescing Fractions of the Teeth of Sperm Whale. – J. Dental. Res., Vol. 34, No. 6. 1965.

Haynes, M. A. and A. H. Laurie. On Some Histological Structures of Cetacean Lungs. – Discovery Rep. Cambridge, Vol. 17. 1937.

Hazen, J. A. Five Years before the Mast. Philadelphia. Willis, P. Hazard. 1854.

Heck, L. Whales (Cetacea). Brehms Tierleben, 4th ed., Vol. 12. Leipzig and Wien. 1915.

Heel, W. H. D. van. Sound and Cetacea. – Netherl. J. Sea Res., Vol. 1, No. 4. 1962.

Heel, W. H. D. van. Navigation in Cetacea. – "Whales, Dolphins and Porpoises," – Univ. Calif. Press. Berkeley–Los Angeles. 1966.

Heezen, B. C. Whales Entangled in Deep Sea Cable. – Deep Sea Res., Vol. 4, No. 2. 1957.

Hentschel, E. Über einen bei Neufundland gefangenen Pottwal (Physeter macrocephalus L.). – Zool. Anz., Vol. 36. 1910.

Hershkovitz, Ph. Catalog of Living Whales. Washington. 1966.

Hilzheimer, M. Die Wanderungen der Säugetiere. Ergebnis der Biologie, Vol. 5. 1929.

Hjort, J. Whales and Whaling. – Hvalrädets scr., No. 7. 1933.

Hollis, H. Biological Report of the United States Bureau of Fisheries. – Norsk Hvalf.-tid., No. 1. 1939.

Holm, J. and A. Johnsgard. Occurrence of the Sperm Whale in the Antarctic and the Possible Influence of the Moon. – Norsk Hvalf.-tid., No. 4. 1959.

Hopkins, W. J. She Blows! And Sparm at that! New York. Houghton Mifflin. 1922.

Hosokawa, H. On the Cetacean Larynx with Special Remarks on the Laryngeal Sac of the Sei Whale and the Aryteno-Epiglottideal Tube of the Sperm Whale. — Sci. Rep. Whales Res. Inst., No. 3. 1950.

Hosokawa, H. On the Extrinsic Eye Muscles of the Whale with Special Remarks upon the Innervation and Function of the Musculus Retractor Bulbi. — Sci. Rep. Whales Res. Inst., No. 6. 1951.

Howell, A. B. Contribution to the Anatomy of the Chinese Finless Porpoise Neomeris phocanoides. No. 2662. — Proc. U. S. Nat. Mus., Vol. 70, Art. 13. 1927.

Howell, A. B. Aquatic Mammals. Baltimore. 1930.

Howell, A. B. Myology of the Narwhal (M. monoceros). —Amer. J. Anat., Vol. 46, No. 1. 1930a.

Howland. Thar She Blows. New York. Wilfred Funk. 1951.

Huber, E. Anatomical Notes on Pinnipedia and Cetacea. — Publ. Carnegie Inst. Washington, No. 447. 1934.

Huggett, A. St. G. and W. F. Widdas. The Relationship between Mammalian Foetal Weight and Conception Age. — J. Physiol., Vol. 114(3). 1951.

Hunter, J. Observations on the Structure and Economy of Whales. — Phil. Trans. R. Soc. London, Vol. 77. 1787.

Hunter, P. A. Male Spermaceti Whale Physeter Catodon (kato below, odous, a tooth, teeth in lower jaw only). — Lin. Mag. Nat. Hist., Vol. 2. 1829.

Irving, L. Control of Respirations in Diving Animals. — Amer. J. of Physiol., Vol. 123. 1938.

Irving, L. Respirations in Diving Mammals. — Physiol. Reviews, Vol. 19, No. 1. 1939.

Irving, L. and J. S. Hart. The Metabolism Insulation of Seal as Bare-Skinned Mammals in Cold Water. — Canad. J. Zool., Vol. 35. 1957.

Ishikawa, S., Y. Omote, and H. Kanno. Molecular Distillations of Sperm Whale Blubber Oil. — Sci. Rep. Whales Res. Inst., No. 2. 1948.

Ishikawa, Y. Protein Digestive Power of Sperm Whale Pancreatic Enzyme II. — Sci. Rep. Whales Res. Inst., No. 3. 1950.

Ivashin, M. W. and A. A. Rovnin. Some Results of the Soviet Whale Marking in the Waters of the North Pacific. — Norsk Hvalf.-tid., No. 6. 1967.

Iverson, B. Whaling Activity in Iceland. — Norsk Hvalf.-tid., No. 10. 1955.

Jackson, J. B. S. Dissections of a Spermaceti Whale and Three Other Cetaceans. — Boston J. Nat. Hist., Vol. 5. 1845.

Jansen, J. Studies on the Cetacean Brain. — Hvalrädets Skr., No. 37. 1953.

Jenkins, I. T. A History of Whale Fisheries. London. 1921.

Johnson, I. and E. Johnson. Lost World of the Galapagos. — Natl. Geogr. Mag., 115. 1959.

Jones, C. D. Life and Adventure in the South Pacific. New York. Harper. 1861.

Jonsgård, A. On the Stock of Sperm Whales in the Antarctic. — Norsk Hvalf.-tid., No. 7. 1960.

Jonsson, J. Whale Marking in Icelandic Waters in 1965. — Norsk Hvalf.-tid., No. 11. 1965.

Jonsson, J.   Whales and Whaling in the Icelandic Waters. – Norsk
        Hvalf.-tid., No. 11.   1965a.
Joyeux, C. and J. G. Baer.   Cestodes.   Fauna de France. – Fed. Frans.
        Soc. Sc. Nat. (30).   1936.
Kabrera, A, and G. Gepes.   Mammiferos Sud-Americanos Buenos-
        Aires.   1940.
Kalcher, F. H.   Über den Algenbewuchs auf südlichen Walen. – Z. Fisch.
        Hilfwiss. Beihefte.   1940.
Kanwisher, J. and H. Leivestad.   Thermal Regulations in Whales. –
        Norsk, Hvalf.-tid., No. 1.   1957.
Kanwisher, J. and G. Sundnes.   Thermal Regulations in Cetaceans. –
        "Whales, Dolphins and Porpoises." – Univ. Calif. Press.
        Berkeley-Los Angeles.   1966.
Kasuya, T. and S. Ohsumi.   A Secondary Sexual Character of the
        Sperm Whale. – Sci. Rep. Whales Res. Inst., No. 20.   1966.
Kawakami, T. and T. Ichihara.   Japanese Whale Marking in the
        North Pacific in 1956 and 1957. – Norsk Hvalf.-tid., No. 6.   1958.
Keil, A.   Gibt es Zahnfäule bei freilebenden Tieren ? – Kosmos (Stuttgart),
        51, No. 8.   1955.
Kellogg, R.   Whales, Giants of the Sea. – Nat. Geogr. Mag., Vol. 67,
        No. 1.   1910.
Kellogg, R.   The History of Whales, their Adaptations to Life in the
        Water. – Quart. Rev. Biol. Baltimore, Vol. 3.   1928.
Kellogg, R.   What is Known of the Migrations of Some Whalebone
        Whales. – Ann. Rep. Smithson Inst.   1928a.
Kellogg, R.   Whaling Statistics for the Pacific Coast of North America. –
        J. Mammal., Vol. 12.   1931.
Kellogg, R.   Adaptation of Structure to Function in Whales. – Cooperat.
        in Research. Carneg. Inst. of Washington Publ., No. 501.   1938.
Kellogg, R.   Whales, Giants of the Sea. – Nat. Geogr. Mag., Vol. 67,
        No. 1.   1940.
Kellogg, W. N.   Echo Ranging in the Porpoise. – Science, Vol. 128,
        No. 330.   1958.
Kerr, R.   The Animal Kingdom of the Zoological System of the Celebrated
        Sir Charles Linnaeus.   Class I.   Mammalia.   London.   1792.
Kimura, S.   Report on Biological Investigations of the Whales Caught
        in the Northern Pacific in 1956. – Jap. Whaling Assoc.
        (In Japanese).   1957.
Kingsley, J. S.   The Standard Natural History.   Boston: SE Cassino,
        Vol. 5.   1884.
Kojima, T.   On the Brain of the Sperm Whale (Physeter
        catodon L.). – Sci. Rep. Whales Res. Inst., No. 6.   1951.
Kostritsky, L. and A. Piazza.   El cachalote.   Su caza y aprove-
        chamiento en el Peru. Pesca y Caza Lima, No. 5.   1952.
Krogh, A.   Physiology of the Blue Whale. – Nature, Vol. 133.   1934.
Kruger, L.   The Thalamus of the Dolphin (Tursiops truncatus)
        and Comparison with Other Mammals. – J. Compar. Neurol.,
        Vol. 3.   1959.
Kükenthal, W.   Die Hand der Cetacen. – Denkschr. d. med. naturwiss.
        Gesell. Jena, Vol. 3, Pt. 2.   1889.

Kükenthal, W. On the Adaptation of Mammals to Aquatic Life. — Ann. Mag. Nat. Hist., Ser. 6, Vol. 7. 1891.

Kükenthal, W. Untersuchungen an Walen (Zweiter Teil). — Jenaische Zeitschr. f. Naturw., Vol. 51. 1914.

Lacépède, M. de. Histoire naturelle des cétacés. Paris. 1804.

Lang, T. Hydrodynamic Analysis of Cetacean Performance. — Whales, Dolphins and Porpoises. Univ. Calif. Press, Berkeley—Los Angeles. 1966.

Langworthy, O. R. A Description of the Central Nervous System of the Porpoise (Tursiops truncatus). — J. Compar. Neurol., Vol. 54. 1932.

Lawrence, B. and W. E. Schevill. The Functional Anatomy of the Delphinid Nose. — Bull. Mus. Compar. Zool., Vol. 114, No. 4. 1956.

Laws, R. M. A New Method of Age Determination for Mammals. — Nature, Vol. 169. 1952.

Laws, R. M. A New Method of Age Determination in Mammalia with Special Reference to the Elephant Seal (Mirounga leonina L.). — Sci. Rep. Falkland Is. Dependencies Survey, No. 2. 1953.

Laws, R. M. Natural History of the Larger Whales. — Zoo. Life, Vol. 10, No. 2. 1955.

Laws, R. M. Growth and Sexual Maturity in Aquatic Mammals. — Nature, 178. 1956.

Laws, R. M. The Foetal Growth Rate of Whales with Special Reference to the Fin Whale, Balaenoptera physalus Linn. — Discovery Rep., Vol. 29. 1959.

Laws, R. M. Laminated Structure of Bones from Some Marine Mammals. — Nature, No. 187. 1960.

Laws, R. M. Reproduction, Growth and Age of Southern Fin Whales. — Discovery Rep., Vol. 21. 1961.

Laws, R. M. Age Determination of Pinnipeds with Special Reference to Growth Layers in the Teeth. — "Säugetierkunde," 27, No. 3. 1962.

Laws, R. M. and P. E. Purve. The Ear Plug of the Mysticeti as an Indicator to the Age with Special Reference to the North Atlantic Fin Whale. — Norsk Hvalf.-tid., No. 8. 1956.

Leslie, J. Narrative of Discovery and Adventure in the Polar Seas and Regions; with Illustrations of their Climate, Geology and Natural History: and an Account of the Whale Fishery, Edinburgh. Oliver and Boyd. 1850.

Lillie, D. G. Observations of the Anatomy and General Biology of Some Members of the Larger Cetacea. — Proc. Zool. Soc. London. 1910.

Lillie, D. G. Cetacea British Antarctic ("Terra Nova") Expedition. — Nat. Hist. Rep. Zoology, Vol. 1, No. 3. 1915.

Lillie, H. R. The Path through Penguin City. London. Ernest Benn. 1955.

Linne, C. Fauna Suecica, 2nd ed., Stockholminae. 1746.

Linne, C. Systema Naturae, 10th ed., Vol. 1, Holmire. 1758.

Lühe, M. Acanthocephalen. — Die Süsswasserfauna Deutschlands, No. 16. 1911.

Lydekker, R. Cetacea. — Encycl. Brit. II ed., Vol. 5. Cambridge. 1910.

Mackintosh, N. A. The Marking of Whales. — Nature, Vol. 169, No. 4298. 1952.

Mackintosh, N. A. The Marking of Whales. — Norsk Hvalf.-tid., No. 5. 1952a.

Mackintosh, N. A. Observations on Whales from Ships. Report on the First Year's Observations. — The Marine Observer, Vol. 23. 1953.

Mackintosh, N. A. Whale Marks Recently Recovered. — Norsk Hvalf.-tid., No. 12, 1955.

Mackintosh, N. A. The Stocks of Whales. 1965.

Mackintosh, N. A. and J. F. Wheeler. Southern Blue and Fin Whales. — Discovery Rep. 1. 1929.

Macy, W. H. Thar She Blows! or, the Log of the Arethusa. Boston. — Lee and Shephard. 1877.

Magnus, A. De Animalibus, Lib. XXVI, Lugbini. 1651.

Magnus, O. De Gentium Septentrionalium Varüs conditionibus statibusque. Basileae. 1567.

Mann Fischer, G. Ojo y Vision de las Ballenas. — Biologica 4. 1946.

Markowski, S. Cestodes of Whales and Dolphins from the Discovery Reports. Cambridge, Vol. 27. 1955.

Matsushita, T. Daily Rhythmic Activity of Sperm Whales in the Antarctic Ocean. — Bull. Jap. Soc. Sci. Fish., Vol. 20(9). 1955.

Matsuura, Y. On the Sperm Whale Found in the Adjacent Waters of Japan. — Bull. Jap. Soc. Sci. Fish., Vol. 4, No. 2, 1935.

Matsuura, Y. Statistical Study on Whale Foetuses—III. Sperm Whales in the Adjacent Waters of Japan. — Bull. Jap. Soc. Sci. Fish., 9(4). 1940.

Matsuura, J. and K. Maeda. Biological Investigations on Whales Found in the Northern Pacific Ocean (In Japanese). — Hogei Shiryo (Whaling Materials), Shiryo Nihon Hogeiguo Suisan Kumiai (Japan Fisheries Whale Association), Tokyo, Japan. 1942.

Matthews, H. L. The Sperm Whale. — Discovery Rep. Cambridge, Vol. 17, Pl. III—XI. 1938.

Mazák, V. Několik zajímovostí o vorvaních. — Živa, Vol. II, No. 5. 1963.

McIntosh, W. C. On Abnormal Teeth in Certain Mammals, Especially in the Rabbit. — Trans. Roy. Soc., Edinburgh, Vol. 6, Pt. 2, No. 8. 1929.

McKenzie, D. (Letter from Capt. McKenzie to Lieut. Maury, June 8, 1849). — In: Maury. 1854.

McLaren, J. A. The Biology of the Ringed Seal, Phoca hispida (Schreber) in the Eastern Canadian Arctic. — Bull. Fish. Res. Board Canada, No. 118. 1958.

Meek, A. The Reproductive Organs of Cetacea. — J. Anat. Physiol., Vol. 52. 1918.

Melville, H. Moby Dick, or the White Whale. 1851.

Meyer, A. Acanthocephalia. — In Brons "Klassen und Ordnungen des Tierreichs," Vol. 4, Sect. 2, No. 2. 1932—1933. 582 pp.

Mielche, H. Thar She Blows. London. William Hodge. 1952.

Millais, J. C. The Mammals of Great Britain and Ireland. London, Vol. 3. 1906.

Miller, G. S. Jr. The Telescoping of the Cetacean Skull. — Smithson. Misc. Coll., Vol. 76, No. 5. 1923.

Millet, S. A Whaling Voyage in the York Willis, 1849—1850 — Boston, privately printed. 1924.

Millikan, G. Muscle Hemoglobin. – Physiol Rev., Vol. 19. 1939.

Mitchell, E. D. Fisheries Council of Canada. – Annual Review. 1968.

Miyazaki, I. Marking of Whales in Japanese Waters. 1953.

Miyazaki, I. Survey of Whaling Operations from Land Stations in Waters Adjacent to Japan in 1953. – Norsk Hvalf.-tid., No. 4. 1954.

Mizue, K. Factory Ship Whaling around Bonin Islands in 1948. – Sci. Rep. Whales Res. Inst., No. 3. 1950.

Mizue, K. Food of Whales (In Adjacent Waters of Japan). – Sci. Rep. Whales Res. Inst., No. 5. 1951.

Mizue, K. and H. Jimbo. Statistic Study of Foetuses of Whales. – Sci. Rep. Whales Res. Inst., No. 3. 1950.

Mohr, E. Spermacetiöl. Walrat und Döglingöl—Rohstoffe des Tierreichs. 4 Edit. 1930.

Mojsisovics, A. van. Catodontida. Handwörterbuch der Zoologie. – Anthropologie und Ethnologie, herausg. V. G. Jäger, Vol. 2, Breslau. 1883.

Moller, Ch. J. Hvorfor strander hvaler ? – "Vor viden," No. 6. 1963—64.

Monaco, A. Sur un cachalot des Azores. – Comptes Rendus. 1888.

Mori, T. and M. Saiki. Properties of Fats and Oils Contained in Various Parts of a Sperm Whale Body. – Sci. Rep. Whales Res. Inst., No. 3. 1950.

Mousinho-Figueiredo, J. Biologia e pesca dos cachalotes em S. Miguel, Acores. – Bol. pesca., II, No. 55. 1957.

Murata, T. Histological Studies on the Lungs of Cetacea. – Sci. Rep. Whales Res. Inst., No. 6. 1951.

Murdoch, W. G. B. Modern Whaling and Bear Hunting, London. 1917.

Murie, J. On Deformity of the Lower Jaw in the Cachalot. – Proc. Zool. Soc. London. 1865.

Murie, J. On the Organization of the Caaing Whale (Globicephalus melas). – Trans. Zool. Soc. London, Vol. 8. 1874.

Murie, J. Cetacea. – Cassell's Natural History, ed. by P. Martin Duncan, Vol. 2, London, Paris and Melbourne. 1892.

Murphy, R. C. Seals as Sperm Whale Food. – J. Mammal., 5. 1924.

Murphy, R. C. Floating Gold. The Romance of Ambergris. – Nat. Hist., 33. 1933.

Murphy, R. C. Longbook for Grace. New York: Macmillan. 1947.

Murray, A. The Geographical Distribution of Mammals. London. 1866.

Musschenbroek, S. C. J. W. van. Cachelot – Visscherij in den Nederlansch Indischen Archipel. – Tijdschr. Bev. Nijverheid., Vol. 18. 1877.

Nazu, K. Deformed Lower Jaw of the Sperm Whale. – Sci. Rep. Whales Res. Inst., No. 13. 1958.

Nazu, K. Surface Water Condition in the Antarctic Whaling Pacific Area in 1956—57. – Sci. Rep. Whales Res. Inst., No. 14. 1959.

Nazu, K. Oceanography and Whaling Ground in the Subarctic Region of the Pacific Ocean. – Sci. Rep. Whales Res. Inst., No. 17. 1963.

Nelson, E. W. Wild Animals of North America. Washington. 1930.

Nemoto, T. On the Diatoms of the Skin Films of Whales in the Northern Pacific. – Sci. Rep. Whales Res. Inst., No. 11. 1956.

Nemoto, T.   Food of Baleens with Reference to Whale Movements. —
        Sci. Rep. Whales Res. Inst., No. 14.   1959.
Nemoto, T.   New Records of Sperm Whales with Protruded Rudimentary
        Hind Limbs. — Sci. Rep. Whales Res. Inst., No. 17.   1963.
Nemoto, T. and K. Nazu.   Stones and Other Aliens in the Stomachs
        of the Sperm Whales in the Bering Sea. — Sci. Rep. Whales
        Res. Inst., No. 17.   1863.
Neuville, H.   Note sur une anomalie dentaire chez le cachalot. —
        Bull. Mus. Nat. Hist. Paris (2), Vol. 1.   1929.
Neuville, H.   Recherches comparatives sur la dentition des
        cétodontes.   Etude de Morphologie et d'Ethologie. — Ann. sc.
        Nat. (10), Zool., Vol. 15.   1932.
Neuville, H.   Remarques à propos du développement des dents du
        cachalot (Physeter macrocephalus). — Ann. Sc. Nat. (10)
        Zool., Vol. 18.   1935.
New Theory on the Whale. — Norsk Hvalf.-tid., No. 2.
Newman, H. H.   A Large Sperm Whale Captured in Texas Waters. —
        Science N. S., Vol. 31.   1910.
Nishiwaki, M.   Age Characteristics in Baleen Plates. — Sci. Rep.
        Whales Res. Inst., No. 4.   1950.
Nishiwaki, M.   On the Periodic Mark on the Baleen Plates as the
        Sign of Annual Growth. — Sci. Rep. Whales Res. Inst., No. 6. 1951.
Nishiwaki, M.   On the Age Determination of Mystacoceti, Chiefly Blue
        and Fin Whales. — Sci. Rep. Whales Res. Inst., No. 7.   1952.
Nishiwaki, M.   On the Sexual Maturity of the Antarctic Male Sperm
        Whale Physeter catodon L. — Sci. Rep. Whales Res. Inst.,
        No. 19.   1955.
Nishiwaki, M.   Very Small Embryo of Cetacea. — Sci. Rep. Whales
        Res. Inst., No. 12.   1957.
Nishiwaki, M.   Age Characteristics of the Ear Plug of Whales. —
        Sci. Rep. Whales Res. Inst., No. 12.   1957a.
Nishiwaki, M.   Aerial Photographs Show Sperm Whales' Interesting
        Habits. — Norsk Hvalf.-tid., No. 10.   1962.
Nishiwaki, M.   Distributions and Migrations of the Larger Cetaceans
        in the North Pacific as Shown by Japanese Whaling Results. —
        "Whales, Dolphins and Porpoises," Univ. Calif. Press.
        Berkeley—Los Angeles.   1966.
Nishiwaki, M.   Distribution and Migration of Marine Mammals in the
        North Pacific Area. — Bulletin of the Ocean. Res. Inst. Univ.
        of Tokyo, No. 1.   December.   1967.
Nishiwaki, M. and T. Hibiya.   On the Sexual Maturity of the Sperm
        Whale (Physeter catodon) Found in the Adjacent Waters
        of Japan (1). — Sci. Rep. Whales Res. Inst., No. 6.   1951.
Nishiwaki, M. and T. Hibiya.   On the Sexual Maturity of the Sperm
        Whale (Physeter catodon) Found in the Adjacent Waters
        of Japan (II). — Sci. Rep. Whales Res. Inst., No. 7.   1952.
Nishiwaki, M., T. Hibiya, and S. Kimura.   On the Sexual Maturity
        of the Sperm Whale (Physeter catodon) Found in the North
        Pacific. — Sci. Rep. Whales Res. Inst., No. 11.   1956.
Nishiwaki, M., T. Isihara, and S. Ohsumi.   Age Studies of Fin
        Whale Based on Ear Plug. — Sci. Rep. Whales Res. Inst., No. 13.
        1958.

Nishiwaki, M. and M. Jagi. On the Age and the Growth of Teeth in a Dolphin (Prodelphinus caerulaeoalbus). – Sci. Rep. Whales Res. Inst., No. 8. 1953.

Nishiwaki, M., S. Ohsumi, and T. Hibiya. Age Study of Sperm Whale Based on Reading of Tooth Laminations. – Sci. Rep. Whales Res. Inst., No. 13. 1958.

Nishiwaki, M., S. Ohsumi, and Kasuya. Age Characteristics in the Sperm Whale Mandible. – Norsk Hvalf.-tid., No. 12. 1961.

Nishiwaki, M., S. Ohsumi, and J. Maeda. Change of Form in the Sperm Whale Accompanied with Growth. – Sci. Rep. Whales Res., No. 17. 1963.

Nordhoff, C. Whaling and Fishing. New York. Dold, Mead. 1895.

Norman, J. R. and F. C. Fraser. Giant Fishes, Whales and Dolphins. London. 1948. (1st ed. 1937)

Norris, K. S. Some Problems of Echolocations in Cetaceans. – "Marine Bio-Acoust.", Oxford–London–New York–Paris, Pergamon Press. 1964.

Nybelin, O. Anatomisch-systematische Studien über Pseudophyllideen. – Göteborg Vet. Hande 4, 1, följden 26. 1922.

Ogawa, T. and S. Arifuku. On the Acoustic System in the Cetacean Brain. – Sci. Rep. Whales. Res. Inst., No. 2. 1948.

Ogawa, R. and T. A. Kamiya. Case of the Cachalot with Protruded Rudimentary Hind Limbs. – Sci. Rep. Whales Res. Inst., No. 12. 1957.

Ohno, M. and K. Fujino. Biological Investigations on the Whales Caught by the Japanese Antarctic Whaling Fleet, Season 1950/51. – Sci. Rep. Whales Res. Inst., No. 7. 1952.

Ohsumi, S. A Descendant of Moby Dick, or a White Sperm Whale. – Sci. Rep. Whales Res. Inst., No. 13. 1958.

Ohsumi, S. Comparison of Maturity and Accumulation Rate of Corpora Albicantia between the Left and Right Ovaries in Cetacea. – Sci. Rep. Whales Res. Inst., No. 18. 1964.

Ohsumi, S. Reproduction of the Sperm Whale in the North West Pacific. – Sci. Rep. Whales Res. Inst., No. 19. 1965.

Ohsumi, S. Sexual Segregation of the Sperm Whale in the North Pacific. – Sci. Rep. Whales Res. Inst., No. 20. 1966.

Ohsumi, S., T. Kasuya, and M. Nishiwaki. Accumulation Rate of Dentinal Growth Layers in the Maxillary Tooth of the Sperm Whale. – Sci. Rep. Whales Res. Inst., No. 17. 1963.

Ohsumi, S., M. Nishiwaki, and T. Hibiya. Growth of Fin Whale in the Northern Pacific. – Sci. Rep. Whales Res. Inst., No. 13. 1958.

Okutani, T. and T. Nemoto. Squids as the Food of Sperm Whales in the Bering Sea and Alaskan Gulf. – Sci. Rep. Whales Res. Inst., No. 18. 1964.

Oliver, W. R. B. A Review of the Cetacea of the New Zealand Seas. – Proc. Zool. Soc. London. 1922.

Olmstead, F. A. Incidents of a Whaling Voyage. New York. D. Appleton. 1841.

Ommaney, F. D. The Vascular Networks (Retia mirabilia) of the Fin Whale. – Discovery Rep., Vol. 5., Cambridge. 1932.

Omura, H. On the Body Weight of Sperm and Sei Whales Located in the Adjacent Waters of Japan. – Sci. Rep. Whales Res. Inst., No. 4. 1950.

Omura,H. Whales in the Adjacent Waters of Japan. — Sci. Rep. Whales
      Res. Inst., No.4. 1950a.
Omura,H. Whales in the Northern Part of the North Pacific. — Norsk
      Hvalf.-tid., No.6. 1955.
Omura,H. North Pacific Right Whale. — Sci. Res. Whales Res. Inst.,
      No.13. 1958.
Omura,H. and I.Kawahami. Japanese Whale Marking in the North
      Pacific. — Norsk Hvalf.-tid., No.10. 1956.
Omura,H., M.Nishiwaki, T.Ishihara, and T.Kasuya. Osteo-
      logical Note on a Sperm Whale. — Sci. Rep. Whales Res. Inst.,
      No.16. 1962.
Omura,H. and S.Ohsumi. A Review of Japanese Whale Marking in
      the North Pacific to the End of 1962, with Some Information of
      Marking in the Antarctic. — Norsk Hvalf.-tid., No.4. 1964.
Paiva,M.P. and Grangeiro. Biological Investigations on the Whaling
      Seasons 1960—1963 off Northeastern Coast of Brazil. — Arg. Est.
      Mar. Univ. Cear, 5, No.1, Brazil. (Engl.). 1965.
Palmer,T.S. Index Generum Mammalium: A List of the Genera and
      Families of Mammals. — North American Fauna, No.23. 1904.
Pander, C.E.d'Aeton. Die Skelete der Cetaceen, abgebildet und
      beschrieben. Bonn. 1827.
Parry,D.A. The Swimming of Whales and a Discussion of Gray's
      Paradox. — J. Exptl. Biol., 26. 1949.
Parry,D.A. The Anatomical Basis of Swimming in Whales. — Proc. Zool.
      Soc. London, 119. 1949a.
Peach,C.W. On the Occurrence of the Sperm Whale (Physeter
      macrocephalus) near Wick N.B.— Rep. 33rd Meet. Brit. Ass.
      Adv. Sci. 1864.
Pedersen,T. The Milk Fat of Sperm Whale. — Norsk Hvalf.-tid.,
      No.6. 1952.
Peelle,M. Whaling in Northeastern Japanese Waters. — Science, June.
      Vol.75. 1932.
Perkins,P.J., M.P.Fish, and W.H.Mowbray. Underwater
      Communication Sounds of the Sperm Whale (Physeter
      catodon). — Norsk Hvalf.-tid., No.12. 1966.
Peters,N. Ueber eine Darstellung des Pottwales (Physeter macro-
      cephalus L.). — Zool. Anz., Vol.87. 1930.
Pike, G. Stomach Contents of Whales Caught off the Coast of British
      Columbia. — Progr. Repts. Pacific Coast Stat. Fish. Res. Board
      Canada, No.83. 1950.
Pike, G. What Do Whales Eat? — Canad. Fisherm. Septem., Vol.37,
      No.9. 1950a.
Pike, G. Lamprey Marks on Whales. — J. Fish. Res. Board Canada.,
      Vol.8, No.4. 1951.
Pike, G. Whaling on the Coast of British Columbia. — Norsk Hvalf.-tid.,
      No.3. 1954.
Pike, G. Guide to the Whales, Porpoises and Dolphins of the North East
      Pacific and Arctic Waters of Canada and Alaska. — Fish. Res.
      Bd. Canada, Biol. Stat, Circ., 32. 1956.
Pilleri, G. Die Zentralnervöse Rangordnung der Cetacea (Mammalia). —
      Acta anat., No.3. 1962.

Porta, A. Gli Acanthocephali dei Mammiferi. Nota preventiva. — Arch. Parasit. Paris, Vol. 12(2). 1908.

Portier. Physiologie des animaux marins. Paris. 1938.

Post, F. History of the Spermaceti Whale. — In: Murray. 1854.

Pouchet, G. Le cachalot. — Revue des deux mondes, Vol. 90. 1888.

Pouchet, G. Note sur l'évolution des dents du cachalot. — Comptes Rendus, Soc. Biol., No. 11. 1885.

Pouchet, G. and H. Beauregard. Traité d'ostéologie comparée. Paris. 1889.

Pouchet, G. and H. Beauregard. Recherches sur le cachalot. — Nouv. Arch., Mus. Nat. Hist. (3), Vols. 1 and 4. 1889a.

Pouchet, G. and H. Beauregard. Sur un échouement de cachalot à l'Ile de Ré. — C. R. Ac. Sc. Paris, Vol. 110. 1890.

Pouchet, G. and H. Beauregard. Sur un cachalot échoué à l'Ile de Ré. — J. de l'Anat. et de Physiol., 27-me année. 1891.

Pouchet, G. and H. Beauregard. Recherches sur le Cachalot (suite). — Nouv. Arch. du Mus. (3), Vol. 4. 1892.

Pouchet, G. and F. A. Chaves. Des formes extérieures du cachalot. — J. de l'Anat. et de la Physiol., 26-me année. 1890.

Purrington, P. A. A Whale and her Calf. — Nat. Hist., No. 65. 1955.

Purves, P. E. Anatomy and Physiology of the Outer and Middle Ear in Cetaceans. — "Whales, Dolphins and Porpoises," Univ. Calif. Press, Berkeley—Los Angeles. 1966.

Quatrefages, A. Cachalot. — Dict. Univ. d'Hist. Nat. dir. par. M. Ch. d'Orbigny, 2nd ed., Vol. 3, Paris. 1867 (1st ed. 1844).

Quiring, D. P. Weight Data on Five Whales. — J. Mammal, 24. 1943.

Race, G. J., W. L. J. Edwards, E. R. Halden, H. E. Wilson, and F. J. Luibel. A Large Whale Heart. — Circulation, 19. 1959.

Racovitza, E. G. Cétacés. Résultats du voyage du S. J. Belgica en 1897—99. 1903.

Rancurel, P. Note sur la plongée profonde de Tursiops truncatus. — "Cahiers O. R. S. T. O. M., Océanographie," No. 4. 1964.

Rapp, W. van. Die Cetaceen, zoologisch-anatomisch dargestellt. Stuttgart und Tübingen. 1837.

Rasmussen, B. Exploitation and Protection of the East Greenland Seal Herds. — Norsk Hvalf.-tid., No. 2. 1957.

Raven, H. Some Morphological Adaptations of Cetacea for Life in the Water. — Trans. N. J. Acad. Sci., Ser. 2, Vol. 5, No. 2. 1942.

Raven, H. and W. Gregory. The Spermaceti Organ and Nasal Passages of the Sperm Whale (Physeter catodon) and Other Odontocetes. — Amer. Museum Novitates. New York, No. 677. 1933.

Ravenrel, P. Note sur la plongée profonde de Tursiops truncatus. — "Cahiers O. R. S. T. O. M., Océanographie," 2, No. 4. 1964.

Ray, J. Synopsis Methodica Piscium. London. 1713.

Reichenbach, H. G. L. Die Cetaceen oder Walthiere. Dresden und Leipzig, pl. 4—5. 1846.

Reysenbach de Haan, F. W. Listening Underwater: Thoughts on Sound and Cetacean Hearing. — "Whales, Dolphins and Porpoises." Univ. Calif. Press, Berkeley—Los Angeles. 1966.

Rhithie, J. and A. J. Edwards. On the Occurrence of Functional
   Teeth in the Upper Jaw of the Sperm Whale. — Proc. Roy.
   Soc. Edinburgh., Vol. 33. 1913.
Rice, D. W. Progress Report on Biological Studies of the Larger
   Cetacea in the Waters off California. — Norsk Hvalf.-tid.,
   No. 7. 1963.
Rice, D. W. Pacific Coast Whaling and Whale Research. Washington.
   1963a.
Rice, D. W. The Whale Marking Cruise of the Sioux City off California
   and Baja California. — Norsk Hvalf.-tid., No. 6. 1963b.
Ries, F. A. and O. R. Langworthy. A Study of the Surface Structure
   of the Brain of the Whale (Balaenoptera physalis and
   Physeter catodon). — J. Compar. Neurol., Vol. 68. 1937.
Risting, S. Av hvalfangstens historie, Kristiania. Publ. No. 2.
   Fra kommandör Chr. Christensens Hvalfangst Museum
   Sandefjord. 1922.
Robbins, C. H. The Gam. Boston. A. J. Ochs. 1899.
Robbins, L. L., F. K. Oldham, and E. M. Geiling. The Stomach
   Contents of Sperm Whales Caught off the West Coast of British
   Columbia. — Rep. British Columbia Museum, I pl. 1937.
Rochon-Duvigneaud, A. L'oeil des cétacés. — Arch. du Mus. Natl.
   d'Hist. Naturelle, 6th ser., 16. 1940.
Rode, P. La collection de cétacés du Musée Océanographique de
   Monaco. Notes ostéométriques. — Bull. de l'Inst. Océanogr.
   No. 780, Monaco. 1939.
Roest, A. J. Physeter and Mesoplodon Strandings on the Central
   California Coast. Biol. Sci. Depart. Calif. State Polytechnic. —
   J. Mamm., Vol. 45, No. 1. 1964.
Rosenblum, E. E. Distribution of Sperm Whales. — J. Mammals, No. 1.
   1962.
Ruspoli, M. A la recherche du cachalot. Paris. 1955.
Ruud, J. T. The Surface Structure of the Baleen Plates as a Possible
   Clue to Age in Whales. — Hvalradets Scr., No. 23. 1940.
Ruud, J. T. Further Studies on the Structure of the Baleen Plates and
   their Application to Age Determination. — Hvalradets Skr.,
   No. 29. 1945.
Ruud, J. T. Modern Whaling and its Prospects. — FAO Fish Bull.,
   Vol. 5, No. 5. 1952.
Sakiura, H. and K. Nosawa Ozaki. Study on Maturity and Blubber
   Thickness of the Whales Caught in the Adjacent Waters of
   Japan. — Fish. Agency of Jap. Tokyo Government. 1953.
Salvesen, T. E. The Whale Fisheries of the Falkland Islands and
   Dependencies. — Scottish National Antarctic Expedition Rept.
   Sci. Res. Voyage S. J. "Scotia," 4. 1915.
Sanctis, L. de. Monografia zootomico-zoologica me Cepidoglio
   arenato a Porto S. Giorgio. — Atti R. Acc. dei Lincei (3)
   Mem. Cl. Sc. fis., matem. e nat., Vol. 9. 1881.
Sawtell, C. C. The Ship Ann Alexander of New Bedford, 1805—1851. —
   Mystic, conn.: Marine Hist. Ass. 1962.

Scammon, C. On the Cetaceans of the Western Coast of North America. San Francisco. 1874.

Schaler, N. S. Notes on the Right and Sperm Whales. – American Natural., Vol. 7. 1873.

Scheffer, V. B. Growth Layers in the Teeth of Pinnipedia as an Indication of Age. – Science, 112, (2907). 1950.

Scheffer, V. B. and J. Slipp. The Whales and Dolphins of Washington State with a Key to the Cetaceans of the West Coast of North America. – The American Midland Natural., Vol. 39, No. 2. 1948.

Schevill, W. E. Cetacea. – In: P. Gray, ed., The Encyclopedia of the Biological Sciences. New York, Reinhold Publishing Co. 1961.

Schevill, W. E. Underwater Sounds of Cetaceans. – "Marine Bio-Acoust." Oxford–London–New York–Paris, Pergamon Press. 1964.

Schevill, W. E. and A. F. McBride. Evidence for Echolocations by Cetaceans. – Deep-Sea Res., Vol. 3, No. 2. 1958.

Schevill, W. E. and W. A. Watkins. Whale and Porpoise Voices. A Phonograph Record. 24 pp. and a Phonograph Disk. – Mass: Woods Hole Oceanographic Institution. 1962.

Scholander, P. F. Experimental Investigations of the Respiratory Functions in Diving Mammals and Birds. – Hvaltadets Skr., No. 22, Oslo. 1940.

Scholander, P. F. Evolution of Climatic Adaptation in Homeotherms. – Evolution, Vol. 9, No. 1. 1955.

Scholander, P. E. and W. E. Schevill. Counter-current Vascular Heat Exchange in the Fins of Whales. – J. Appl. Physiol., Vol. 8, No. 3. 1955.

Schubert, K. Das Pottwalvorkommen an der Perükuste. – Fischereiwelt, 3. 1951.

Schubert, K. Der Walfang der Gegenwart. Stuttgart. 1955.

Schulte, H. van W. Anatomy of a Foetus of Balaenoptera borealis (In the Sei Whale Balaenoptera borealis Lesson) by R. S. Andrews. – Mems. Amer. Mus. Nat. Hist., New Ser., Vol. 1, Pt. 6. 1916.

Schulte, H. van W. and M. de F. Smith. The External Characters, Skeletal Muscles and Peripheral Nerves of Kogia breviceps (Blainville). – Bull. Amer. Mus. Nat. Hist., Vol. 38, Art. II. 1918.

Schwediawer. An Account of Ambergris. – Phil. Trans., Vol. 73. 1783.

Scoresby, W. An Account of the Arctic Regions. Edinburgh. 1820.

Scoresby, W. Journal of a Voyage to the Northern Whale Fishery. Edinburgh. 1823.

Scott, L. P. Animal Behavior, Chicago: University of Chicago Press. 1958.

Sergeant, D. E. Age Determination in Odontoceti Whale from Dentinal Growth Layers. – Norsk Hvalf.-tid., No. 6. 1959.

Sergeant, D. E. Whales and Dolphins of the Canadian East Coast. Arctic Unit. – Fish. Res. Bd. Canada circ., No. 2. 1961.

Sergeant, D. E. The Biology of the Pilot or Pothead Whale (Globicephala melaena) in Newfoundland Waters. – Bull. Fish. Res. Board Canada, No. 132. 1962.

Sibbald, R. Balaenologia, sive observationes de rarioribus. – Quibusdam Baleanis in Scotia Littus nuper ejectus. Cum., 3 tab. Edinburgh. 1773.

Slijper, E. J.   Die Cetaceen. — Capita Zool., Vol. 7.   1936.

Slijper, F. J.   Cetacea des Mus. R. Hist. Nat. — Bull. Mus. R. Hist. Nat. Belg., 14, No. 10.   1938.

Slijper, E. J.   Comparative Biologic-Anatomical Investigations on the Vertebral Column and Spinal Musculature of Mammals. — Verhandel. Kon. Ned. Akad. Wet. Afd., Natuurk, Sectie, 2, 42, No. 5.   1946.

Slijper, E. J.   Geluiden van walvissen en dolphijnen. — Vakbl. biol., Vol. 35, No. 12.   1955.

Slijper, E. J.   De academhaling van de walvisachtigen. — Vakbl. biol., Vol. 38, No. 7.   1958.

Slijper, E. J.   On the Vascular System of Cetacea. — 15th Inter. Congr. of Zool., Sect. III.   1958a.

Slijper, E. J.   Die Geburt der Säugetiere. — Handbuch der Zoologie, Vol. 8, Ziel. 25, Part 9(9).   Berlin, Walter der Gruyter and Co. 1960.

Slijper, E. J.   Locomotion and Locomotory Organs in Whales and Dolphins (Cetacea). — Symposia Zool. Soc. London, No. 5.   1960.

Slijper, E. J.   Foramen Ovale and Ductus Arteriosus Botalli in Aquatic Mammals. — Extr. de Mammalia, Vol. 25, No. 4.   1961.

Slijper, E. J.   The Still Unexplained Mystery of the Whales. — Norsk. Hvalf.-tid., No. 2.   1961a.

Slijper, E. J.   Whales. Transl. from the Dutch. 1958. London, Hutchinson and Co. Ltd.   1962.

Slijper, E. J.   Functional Morphology of the Reproductive System in Cetacea. — "Whales, Dolphins and Porpoises," Univ. Calif. Press, Berkeley—Los Angeles.   1966.

Slijper, E. J. and W. L. van Utrecht.   Observing Whales. — Norsk Hvalf.-tid., No. 3.   1959.

Slijper, F. J., W. L. van Utrecht, and C. Naaktgeboren. Remarks on the Distribution and Migrations of Whales Based on Observations from Netherlands Ships. — Bijdr. Dierkunde., No. 34.   1964.

Sokolov, W.   Some Similarities and Dissimilarities in the Structure of the Skin among the Members of the Suborders Odontoceti and Mystacoceti (Cetacea). — Nature (Engl.), No. 4715.   1960.

Sonnini, C. S.   Histoire naturelle générale et particulière des Cétacés. — An. 12, Paris.   1804.

Sonntag, C. F.   The Comparative Anatomy of the Tongue of the Mammalia. — Proc. Zool. Soc. London.   1922.

Spaul, E. A.   Deformity in the Lower Jaw of the Sperm Whale (Physeter catodon). — Proc. Zool. Soc. London, Vol. 142, Part 3.   1964.

Spears, I. R.   The Story of the New England Whalers. New York. Macmillan.   1908.

Sperm Whaling at Albany. — Norsk Hvalf.-tid., No. 11.   1958.

Stackpole, E. A.   The Sea Hunters. Philadelphia. J. B. Lippincott.   1953.

Starbuck, A.   History of the American Whale Fishery from its Earliest Inception to the Year 1876. — U. S. Comm. Fish. and Fisheries, Pt. 4, Rept., 1875—1876, Appendix A.   1878.

Stead, D. G.   The Great Whales of Australia and Antarctica. — Austral. Mus. Magaz., Vol. 4.   1930.

Tawara, T. On the Respiratory Pigments of Whales. — Sci. Rep. Whales Res. Inst., No. 3. 1950.

Thiele, J. Handbuch der systematischen Weichtierkunde. Jena. 1935.

Thomas, H. Ambra. — Dragoco Berichte, No. 5. 1955.

Thomas, O. The Mammals of the Tenth Edition of Linnaeus: an Attempt to Fix the Types of the Genera and the Exact Bases and Localities of the Species. — Proc. Zool. Soc. London. 1911.

Thompson, T. Physeter catodon. — Mag. Nat. Hist. London, Vol. 2. 1829.

Thomson, J. H. Letter Relating to the Occasional Deformity of the Lower Jaw of the Sperm Whale. — Proc. Zool. Soc. London. 1868.

Tower, D. B. Structural and Functional Organization of Mammalian Cerebral Cortex: the Correlation of Neuron Density with Brain Size. — J. Compar. Neurol., Vol. 101. 1954.

Tower, W. S. A History of the American Whale Fishery. — Publ. Univ. of Pennsylvania. 1907.

Townsend, C. H. Twentieth Century Whaling. — Bull. New York Zool. Soc., Vol. 33. 1930.

Townsend, C. H. Where the Nineteenth Century Whaler Made his Catch. — Bull. New York Zool. Soc., Vol. 34, No. 6. 1931.

Townsend, C. H. The Distribution of Certain Whales as Shown by Logbook Records of American Whaleships. — Zoologica, No. 1. 1935.

Tressler, D. W. and J. Lemon. Marine Products of Commerce. New York. 1951.

Tripp, W. H. There Go Flukes. New Bedford, Mass. Reynolds Printing Co. 1938.

Trouessart, E. L. Cachalot. — La grande encycl. inventaire raisonnée des sciences, des lettres et des arts, Vol. 8, Paris. 1890.

Trouessart, E. L. Catalogus mammalium tam viventium quam fossilium, nova ed., Vol. 2. Berolini. 1898—1899.

True, F. W. On the Classification of the Cetacea. — Proc. Amer. Philos. Soc., Vol. 47. 1908.

Truex, R. C., F. G. Nolan, R. C. Truex Jr., H. P. Schneider, and H. J. Perlmutter. Anatomy and Pathology of the Whale Heart with Special Reference to the Coronary Circulation. — Anat., No. 4. 1961.

Turner, W. Further Observations on the Stomach of the Cetacea. — J. Anat. Physiol., Vol. 3. 1868.

Turner, W.. On the Capture of a Sperm Whale on the Coast of Argyleshire, with a Notice of Other Specimens Caught on the Coast of Scotland. — Proc. Roy. Soc. Edinburgh, Vol. 7. 1871.

Turner, W. Additional Notes on the Occurrence of the Sperm Whale in the Scottish Seas. — Proc. Roy. Soc. Edinburgh, Vol. 7. 1872.

Turner, W. Notes on Some Rare Prints of Stranded Sperm Whales. — J. of Anat. and Physiol., Vol. 12. 1878.

Turner, W. The Occurrence of the Sperm Whale or Cachalot in the Shetland Seas, with Notes on the Tympanopetrous Bones of Physeter, Kogia and Other Odontoceti. — Proc. Roy. Soc. Edinburgh, Vol. 24, 1903.

Turner, W. The Occurrence of the Sperm Whale or Cachalot in the Shetland Seas. — Ann. Scott. Nat. Hist. 1904.

Turner, W. The Marine Mammals in the Anatomical Museum of the University of Edinburgh. London. 1912.

Uda, M. Studies of the Relation between the Whaling Grounds and the Hydrographical Conditions (I). — Sci. Rep. Whales Res. Inst., No. 9. 1954.

Uda, M. and A. Dairokuno. Studies of the Relation between the Whaling Grounds and the Hydrographical Conditions (II). A Study of the Relation between the Whaling Grounds of Kinkazan and Boundary of Water Masses. — Sci. Rep. Whales Res. Inst., No. 12. 1957.

Uda, M. and K. Nazu. Studies of the Whaling Grounds in the Northern Sea Region of the Pacific Ocean in Relation to the Meteorogical and Oceanographic Conditions. (Part I). — Sci. Rep. Whales Res. Inst., No. 11. 1956.

Uda, M. and N. Suzuki. The Averaged Conditions of the Whaling Grounds and their Trends of Variation during 1946—1955. — Sci. Rep. Whales Res. Inst., No. 13. 1958.

Utrecht, W. L. van. Temperaturregulierende Gefässysteme in der Haut und anderen epidermalen Strukturen bei Cetaceen. — Zool. Anz., Vol. 161, Nos. 3—4. 1958.

Valen, L. van. On the Biphyletic Origin of Cetacea. — Evolution, No. 4. 1967.

Verill, A. H. The Cephalopods of the North-Eastern Coast of America. — Transact. of the Connect. Acad. 1880.

Verill, A. H. The Real Story of the Whaler. New York and London. 1916.

Virey and Desmaret. Cachalot. — Nouv. Dict. d'Hist. Nat. appliquée aux Arts, etc., Paris, Vol. 4. 1816.

Walker, R. On the Cachalot or Sperm Whale (Physeter macrocephalus) of the North East of Scotland. — Scott. Nat., Vol. 1. 1871—1872.

Wall, W. S. History and Description of the Skeleton of a New Sperm Whale Lately Set Up in the Australian Museum, Together with Some Account of a New Genus of Sperm Whales called Euphyseter. Sydney. 1887 (first ed. 1851).

Watson, A. C. The Long Harpoon. New Bedford, Mass: George H. Reynoldes. 1929.

Weber, M. Studien über Säugetiere. Ein Beitrag zur Frage nach dem Ursprung der Cetaceen. Jena. 1886.

Weber, M. Anatomisches über Cetaceen. — Morphol. Jahrbuch., Vol. 13. 1888.

Weber, M. Die Säugetiere. 2. Aufl. Jena. 1928.

Wheeler, J. The Age of Fin Whales at Physical Maturity with a Note on Multiple Ovulations. — Discovery Rep., Vol. 2. 1930.

Wheeler, J. Notes on a Young Sperm Whale from the Bermuda Islands. — Proc. Zool. Soc. London, No. 8. 1933.

Wheeler, J. On the Stock of Whales at South Georgia. — Discovery Rep., 9. 1934.

Whipple, A. B. C. Yankee Whales in the South Seas. Garden City, N. Y. Doubleday. 1955.

White, J. C. Note on a Lower Jaw and a Tooth of a Sperm Whale. — Proc. Boston. Soc. Nat. Hist., Vol. 7. 1861.

Whitecar, W. B. Jr.   Four Years Aboard the Whaleship.   Philadelphia.
        J. B. Lippincott.   1860.

Winge, H.   Grönlands pattedur.   Conspectus Faunae Groenlandicae. —
        Medd. om Grön.   Kjöbenhavn.   1902.

Winge, H.   Udsidt over Hvalernes indbyrdes Sl gtskab. — Vidensk.
        Medd. Dansk naturk. Foren., Vol. 70.   1918.

Winge, H.   Pattedyr — Sl gter III.   Ungulata, Cetacea.   Kjöbenhavn.   1924.

Winge, H.   A Review of the Interrelationships of the Cetacea. — Smithson
        Misc. Coll., Vol. 72, No. 2650.   1921.

Wisloki, G. B.   The Lungs of the Cetacea. — Anat. Res., Vol. 84.   1942.

Worthington, L. V. and W. E. Schevill.   Underwater Sound Heard
        From Sperm Whales. — Nat., Vol. 180, No. 4580.   1957.

Yamada, M.   Contribution to the Anatomy of the Organ of Hearing in
        Whales. — Sci. Rep. Whales Res. Inst., No. 8.   1953.

Yamada, M. and F. Yoshizaki.   Osseous Labyrinth of Cetacea. —
        Sci. Rep. Whales Res. Inst., No. 14.   1959.

Yoshida, M.   Female Sperm Whale Caught in the Aleutian Waters.
        (In Japanese.) Guken—Trushin, 122.   1961.

Zencovich, B. A.   Sea Mammals as Observed by Round the World
        Expedition of the Academy of Sciences of the USSR in 1957—1958. —
        Norsk Hvalf.-tid., No. 5.   1962.

SUBJECT INDEX*

---

* [Page numbers refer to those of the Russian original, which appear in the left-hand margin of the text.]

LIST OF ABBREVIATIONS APPEARING
IN THE TEXT

AKF	Antarkticheskii kitoboinyi flot	Antarctic Whaling Fleet
AN SSSR	Akademiya Nauk SSSR	Academy of Sciences of the USSR
DV FAN SSSR	Dal'nii Vostok Filial Akademii Nauk SSSR	Far Eastern Branch of the Academy of Sciences of the USSR
IMZh	Institut Morfologii Zhivotnykh imeni A. N. Severtsova	Severtsov Institute of Animal Morphology
IOAN	Institut Okeanologii Akademii Nauk SSSR	Institute of Oceanology of the Academy of Sciences of the USSR
LGU	Leningradskii Gosudarstvennyi Universitet	Leningrad State University
MGU	Moskovskii Gosudarstvennyi Universitet	Moscow State University
MPMI	Moskovskii Pushno-mekhovoi Institut	Moscow Fur and Hides Institute
SRT	Srednii Rybolovnyi Trauler	Medium Side Trawler
SRTM	Srednii Rybolovnyi Trauler Morozil'shchik	Medium Side Trawler-Refrigerator
TINRO	Tikhookeanskii Nauchno-Issledovatel'skii Institut Morskogo Rybnogo Khozyaistva i Okeanografii	Pacific Research Institute of Marine Fisheries and Oceanography
VNIRO	Vsesoyuznyi Nauchno-issledovatel'skii Institut Morskogo Rybnogo Khozyaistva i Okeanografii	All-Union Research Institute of Marine Fisheries and Oceanography
ZM	Zoologicheskii Muzei	Zoological Museum